A Guide to Greater Cleveland's Sacred Landmarks

The Sacred Landmarks Series

Laura Wertheimer, Editor   Michael J. Tevesz, Founding Editor

Revelations: Photographs of Cleveland's African American Churches
MICHAEL STEPHEN LEVY

Resplendent Faith: Liturgical Treasuries of the Middle Ages
STEPHEN N. FLIEGEL

Seeking the Sacred in Contemporary Religious Architecture
DOUGLAS R. HOFFMAN

Eric Mendelsohn's Park Synagogue: Architecture and Community
WALTER C. LEEDY JR.   EDITED BY SARA JANE PEARMAN

A Higher Contemplation: Sacred Meaning in the Christian Art
of the Middle Ages
STEPHEN N. FLIEGEL

Dedication: The Work of William P. Ginther, Ecclesiastical Architect
ANTHONY J. VALLERIANO

A Guide to Greater Cleveland's Sacred Landmarks
LLOYD H. ELLIS JR.

The Sacred Landmarks Series includes both works of scholarship and general-interest titles that preserve the history and increase understanding of religious sites, structures, and organizations in northeast Ohio, the United States, and around the world.

A Guide to Greater Cleveland's Sacred Landmarks

Lloyd H. Ellis Jr.

Photography by Eva M. Ellis

The Kent State University Press ▣ Kent, Ohio

Published in cooperation with Cleveland State University's College of Liberal Arts and Social Sciences

Published in cooperation with Cleveland State University's College of Liberal Arts and Social Sciences.

Cataloging information for this title is available at the Library of Congress.

16 15 14 13 12   5 4 3 2 1

This book is dedicated to the builders—those who had the dream. They chose the architect; they supervised the contractor; they raised the money.

Edmund Ahern, Samuel Aiken, Richard Andrews, Juozas Angelaitis, Ahmad Ansari, Hu Auburn, George Babutiu, Everett Moore Baker, H. W. Bartels, John Becka, Alistair Begg, Samuel Benjamin, John Blackburn, Gordon Blasius, Barnett Brickner, Roy Bourgeois, Joseph Boznar, Walter Russell Breed, Frederick Brooks, Howard Brown, Emil Burik, James Butler, Stephen Callos, John Caroll, Peter Cerveny, Armond Cohen, Ira Collins, James Conlon, Vincent Conlon, Oliver Cowles, Robert Dean, Steven Denker, Maxfield Dowell, Wolodymyr Dowhowycz, Sigmund Drechsler, Francis Dubosh, H. P. Eckhardt, Nicholas Elko, W. C. Endley, Floyd Ewalt, Francis Faflik, David Fallon, John Farrell, Frank Halliday Ferris, Stephen Furdek, Joseph Gallagher, James Garfield, William Gaston, Halsey Gates, Sante Gattuso, John Geranios, Ignatius Ghattas, Antonio Gibelli, Joseph Gomez, Daniel Goodwin, Roger Gries, Aaron Hahn, Leo Hammer, Thomas Hanrahan, J. C. Hansen, Joseph Hartel, Vasile Hategan, Hiram Haydn, Joseph Herczegh, Dormer Hickok, Ward Hines, Edward Hoban, J. Mark Hobson, Joseph Hoerstmann, Odie Millard Hoover, Philip Horowitz, Ramez Al Islambouli, Daniel Ivancho, Donald Jacobs, Albert Jeandheur, Nersess Jebejian, John Jones, Virgil Jump, Robert Killam, Edmund Kirby, Edward Kirby, August Kitterer, Ernest Knautz, Joseph Kocinski, Linus Koenemund, Anton Kolaszewski, Joseph Koudelka, Sebastian Kremer, Joseph Kresina, John Krispinski, Henry Ladd, George Landis, Michael Leahy, Andor Leffler, William Leonard, Vasili Lisenkovsky, Epaminonda Lucaciu, Walter Luecke, John Luhr, Henry Lyman, Darshan Mahajan, Timothy Mahoney, Gordon Majors, John Malecha, Francis Malloy, Carl Manthey-Zorn, Flora Stone Mather, Jeffares McCombe, Elias Meena, Peter Metallinos, Charles Haven Meyers, Joseph Militello, Barb Miller, Charles Mills, Charles Mitchell, James Molony, John Nottingham, Abraham Nowak, John O'Brien, Eugene O'Callahan, Patrick O'Connell, John Legare O'Hear, James O'Leary, John Jerome Oman, Wenceslas Panuska, Henry Payne, B. W. Paxton, Joseph Perkins, Harold Cooke Phillips, George Pickard, Bartholomew Ponikvar, John Mary Powers, Amadeus Rappe, Luke Rath, Leonard Ratner, Leo Rehak, Casimir Reichlin, Edward Reilly, Hurbert Robinson, Umberto Rocchi, Rudolph Rosenthal, John Ruffing, Otto Rusch, Carl Ruszkowski, Charles Schneider, Joseph Schrembs, Darrell and Belinda Scott, Lawrie Sharp, Abba Hillel Silver, Daniel Jeremy Silver, Joshua Hoffer Skoff, Arthur Smith, Graham Smith, H. L. Smith, John Solinski, John Spirk, Oliver Stafford, Wilson Stearly, Ner Stroup, Milan Sutlic, Stephen Szabo, Julius Szepessy, Thomas Thorpe, Mircea Toderich, John Townsend, Louis Trivison, the Ukranian Orthodox Community, Jeptha Wade, Jeptha Wade II, Frank Walker, Eugene Ward, Edward Warner, Henry Weseloh, Nicholson White, H. R. Whiting, Alanson Wilcox, Louis Wolsey, Alfred Wright, L. C. Wright, Charles Yoost, and others forgotten by us and remembered by God.

Contents

Illustrations

Preface

Sister Annette was on a tear. Leaning back in her chair beside her spacious desk in her spacious pastor's office in her spacious rectory, she let fly at the purpose of her greater community. Sister was a figure one could imagine as a princess of the church in any other denomination—articulate, vigorous, experienced, and magnetic. Instead of a diocese, however, she had, in desperation, been thrown a crumb. St. Procop, once the largest Czech church in the United States, had been designed poorly. Well before Sister was given responsibility for this decidedly moldy crumb, the parish—financially unable to maintain its building—had been forced to take down its threatening, unstable dome and then, as a further humiliation, had been forced to remove both of its towers. In a cruelly impoverished and unsafe neighborhood, St. Procop School was a distant memory, its convent long abandoned, and the parish unable to pay its yearly diocesan assessment. Sister had rallied her moribund responsibility—a state-supported program for troubled children took over and paid to clean up most of the school, and well-meaning suburban Lutherans and Presbyterians took over the rest of the building for their inner-city missions. The convent became a decidedly low-rent but decent home for men struggling to maintain and improve themselves. The parish paid off its debt and embarked on an energetic feeding program for its neighbors.

However, Sister described how the bishop would decide in three days which fifty-two inner-city parishes would have to close. For more than a year, he had been assisted in this painful process by discussions within "clusters" of congregations. St. Procop was clustered with four other parishes; the bishop asked the cluster to recommend closing two parishes. Two of the five parishes seemed untouchable: La Sagrada Familia had been built by the diocese as a new Hispanic parish, and Our Lady of Mount Carmel had a vigorous school— the only Roman Catholic educational presence in its area. That left St. Colman, St. Stephen, and St. Procop. Irish St. Colman was a marble extravaganza. German St. Stephen, with its complete ensemble of Mayer Munich windows and acclaimed carved wood accoutrements and statuary, was generally acknowledged to be the most beautifully decorated church in Cleveland—the Roman Catholic equivalent, as a landmark, of Eric Mendelsohn's Park Synagogue on the east side of town. From a fine arts and preservationist point of view, Sister Annette clearly held the short straw. In Sister's favor, however, was her stewardship and her parish's missions to the otherwise marginalized. Now, Sister directed her wrath and frustration at other members of her cluster committee. "They dismiss me," she said, "when I talk about hunger and poverty and despair. All they want to talk about is stained glass."

This is a book about stained glass and the buildings that glass illuminates. It is a paean of praise for those who imagined and worked and argued and schemed to put up religious buildings all over Greater Cleveland. Largely unmentioned are the women and men who sacrificed to pay for these dreams. Herein, only fleeting notice is paid to the mission of congregations for any purpose other than for the erection of buildings. Nonetheless, although I only want to talk about the stained glass, this does not mean that there are no other stories.

Twenty years ago, Kent State University Press, in association with the Sacred Landmarks Research Group at Cleveland State University, published *A Guide to Cleveland's Sacred Landmarks*. The authors, Foster and Cara Armstrong, Richard Klein, and their photographer Thomas Lewis, have generously acknowledged that their first edition was very much a group effort involving many others.[1] Nevertheless, the presence of the late Foster Armstrong is everywhere in the original guide, beginning with his decision of which 124 churches (all but one were churches then) to feature, which to only mention, and which to set aside.

Armstrong's taste, architectural sensibility, and interest grace every page of *Cleveland's Sacred Landmarks*. Particularly striking is his interest in—and lucid description of—the various revival styles of the nineteenth and twentieth centuries.[2] Armstrong clearly enjoyed explaining how Cleveland architects responded to revival styles. He relished the enthusiasm with which these architects stirred the pot of revivalism in the buildings they designed. His excitement and his scholarship are so apparent in *Cleveland's Sacred Landmarks* that no attempt has been made to duplicate it here. Armstrong's descriptions of these buildings have been largely rewritten. The reader will note a greater emphasis on the people and process of building and on the buildings' interiors.

There are more than 1,600 religious listings in the Cleveland telephone book. One hundred and fifty-four of them are featured in this guide. How were the buildings in this book selected? Entries were chosen on the basis of architectural and cultural importance, but one may wonder what that means. Aside from Eric Mendelsohn's Park Synagogue, Cleveland is not known for the high quality of its religious architecture. Nevertheless, many local buildings have become indelibly rooted in our visual consciousness. In addition, some very undistinguished buildings have acquired great cultural importance because they form the center of an important Cleveland religious community.

Armstrong's list of 124 landmarks was a logical place to start. His list, and a comparable list of suburban institutions, was initially reviewed by Michael Tevesz, director of the Center for Sacred Landmarks of the Maxine Goodman Levin College of Urban Affairs of Cleveland State University. Michael lives on the West Side and is a Roman Catholic. The list of Catholic churches was then reviewed by Christine Krosel, then director of archival research for the Catholic Diocese of Cleveland. Chris lived in Tremont. Both lists were reviewed with Steve Litt, architectural critic of the *Plain Dealer*. In addition, sources were sometimes asked during interviews: "If you had to identify an institution that should be in this book, other than your own, what would you pick?" Last, the author, who lives in Solon and is an Episcopalian, incorporated some of these suggestions, ignored others, and added some of his own. He, of course, bears sole responsibility for having left undone those things which he ought to have done and having done those things which he ought not to have done.

Many will be gratified that some religious institutions appear in this book, and many will be disappointed that some do not. Every institution enumerated in this book was visited, and the interior of the building, except for one, inspected. A particular effort was made to visit buildings previously identified by Armstrong as sacred landmarks, whatever their redeeming value, because it was thought important that the subsequent history of these buildings be available in an accessible form. One of the buildings Armstrong identified, St. Joseph Franciscan Church, was destroyed before this revision was begun. Another, Euclid Avenue Congregational Church, burned down after the narrative manuscript was completed. Several other buildings are now unoccupied.

The remaining thirteen institutions that Armstrong identified and that are not featured in this book could not be contacted. In some sad cases, the telephone had been disconnected. In other cases, no one answered. Sometimes no one answered repeated messages on the answering machine. Although this probably and unhappily represents a struggling or nonexistent congregation, in at least one case, it certainly represents a lack of interest in the past. Congregations are sometimes obsessively interested in their past, particularly when it is patently better than the present, but some communities are indifferent to their beginnings or distrustful of inquiries. Most institutions were wonderfully cordial, particularly if they were familiar with Armstrong's book. One discouraged pastor refused to have anything to do with this project, probably because he thought his church would be closed. (It wasn't.) Sometimes it was a struggle, by letter and on the telephone, to differentiate the author from those sales representatives who besiege pastors with suggestions for commemorative booklets and parish directories.

Many Christian churches used to be oriented to the east. Most people came in through an entrance on the west end of the building and worshiped facing east. To the left, the north, or dean's side, things were gloomy. To the right, the south, or bishop's side, things were bright and cheery. Some historians observe an academic tradition that churches should continue to be described in this way, irrespective of their actual geographic orientation: front is east, back is west, left is north, and right is south. Many Cleveland churches, however, are not oriented toward the east so that following this convention became hopelessly confusing and directions in this book are geographically correct.[3]

If Armstrong's vivid descriptions of these buildings were so compelling, why publish another book? Three things justify this effort. The bad news first. The last twenty years have not been kind to Armstrong's buildings. Although only two have completely disappeared, many are struggling to stay upright, their original purpose a distant memory. For every First Church of Christ, Scientist—the poster child of restoration—many more are struggling to stay open. Twenty years after the first edition of *Sacred Landmarks,* how many are still ticking?

Second, the original guide only described buildings in the city of Cleveland. This book also considers structures outside of Cleveland in Cuyahoga County. In some cases, particularly in the inner-ring suburbs, the suburban news is as grim as that in the inner city. Once flourishing institutions are on life support or worse. Something needs to be said about these landmarks before they, too, perish. However, much is going on that is inspiring. In some cases structures have new and vibrant life with, or without, their original congregations. New institutions and institutions (how do we say this graciously) "expanding" into the suburbs, continue to build inspirational buildings in Cuyahoga County. In the next edition of this book (2030?) someone else may find that restricting our view to Cuyahoga County was too limited.[4] Third, scholarly fashions, like architectural fashions, change. While I have retained some of Armstrong's judgments concerning religious structures in the city of Cleveland, and have added my own concerning those in the suburbs, I have, in accord with current scholarly fashion, added more material than his group originally included concerning patronage. It is difficult, and dangerous, to discuss the religious practices of others. A good rule is that the less said the better. Every reader, however, understands that writers find it impossible to keep what they think is interesting to themselves. Each of these buildings has a story, and it is a story I love to tell. Why were these wonderful buildings built, and who was responsible?

A great deal of fun is commonly made of the "edifice complexes" of the pastors, priests, and rabbis who dream and plan and plead and argue and supervise the construction of religious buildings. Physically ambitious clergy have been criticized since, and undoubtedly before, the early ninth century when the monks of Fulda complained to Charlemagne of their exhaustion from the relentless building campaigns of their abbot.[5] Without builders, the religious buildings in our area would not exist. These builders are partially recognized in the dedication.

Photographer's Preface

Eva M. Ellis

As Father Hladni walked me to my car, he gestured with irritation at the telephone poles and utility lines in front of St. Paul's Croatian Church. As much as he appreciated the opportunity to serve his people in America, he said, this would never have happened in Croatia. In Croatia the utility lines were all underground.

The telephone poles and the utility lines, the cars and the buses, the street signs and the stoplights, the baby carriages and the bicycles are not underground in the pictures in this book. We have photographed what you will see when you drive around our religious Cleveland.

Acknowledgments

I told Michael Tevesz one too many times over lunch at the Rowfant Club how much I enjoyed Armstrong's guide to religious Cleveland until, exasperated, he told me to go work on a second edition. Over the last year and a half, as I listened to clergy, staff, and devoted members of all kinds of congregations and then transcribed what they said, Michael has been unfailingly encouraging, wise, and helpful. He has been pivotal in seeing this project from idea to manuscript to publication.

Almost half of the institutions in this guide are Roman Catholic. Wherever I turned in their great religious community, people mentioned with awe their diocesan archivist. There was a reason why Christine Krosel was acknowledged as having a hand in every historical project touching the Church in Cleveland: she was its memory. Not only was she renowned for her knowledge of the history of her faith, but she was responsible for the efficient and meticulous physical preservation of its memory. It was Chris who recommended that we widen our list to include suburban Eastern Catholic and Orthodox churches in consultation with Tom Cousineau of Henninger's. I must emphasize, that while I have been welcomed by Chris's community with enthusiasm, I am an outsider. What you read here are my observations and in no way are endorsed by or represent the ideas of the Diocese of Cleveland. Chris died before this book was printed. Her Funeral Mass filled mighty St. Michael Church with four bishops, clouds of other clergy, and hundreds of her friends and admirers. It was a tribute of her Church to scholarship, learning, and history.

Another sustaining influence has been my colleague Father David Novak. His good cheer and unfailing generosity, particularly in opening to me his comprehensive library, has been vital at every turn. My understanding of Lakewood was greatly enriched by the counsel of Shirley Henderson. My wife, in addition to taking the photographs, has played the greatest role in supporting this project. It was she who originally encouraged me to undertake this revision. As with my other professional undertakings, my children cheered me on.

The maps and tour guides were prepared by the Northern Ohio Data and Information Service (NODIS) of the Levin College of Urban Affairs of Cleveland State University. NODIS is directed by Mark Salling. The maps were drawn by Jim Wyles, and the project was coordinated by Sharon Bliss. These three proved to be exceptionally helpful and easy to work with in what initially appeared to be a very simple project. They are recommended to readers who may be challenged by some similar undertakings.

This revision of Foster Armstrong's book was encouraged by its original designer, Will Underwood, who is now director of the Kent State Press. His approval of the project, and its implied promise of publication, opened the doors of most rectories, offices, and rabbis' studies. Christine Brooks, design and production manager of the Press, has a reputation as an exacting editor. She could not have been more helpful and supportive.

This study began with a letter to the person I thought was the leader of each congregation, usually, but not always, a member of the clergy. In response to my outreach, the following individuals were particularly helpful in explaining their institutions and showing me their buildings: Annette Amendolia, Ahmad Ansari, Andras Antal, Michael Arkins, Wayne Arnason, Nathan Arnold, Greg Becker, Daniel Begin, Robert Begin, Kelvin Berry, Wayne Bifano, Russ Bowen, Mike Bowerman, Joseph Boznar, Ted Brogan, George Buchanan, Patricia Burgess, Karen Burt, James Butler, Leonora Butler, Pamela Buzalka, Stephen Callos, John Carlin, Anthony Cassese, Kenneth Chalker, John Chlebo, Gary Chmura, Karen Cohen, Yvonne Conner, Michael Contardi, Dicey Crain, John Cregan, Cyril Crume, Brenda Daniels, Marilyn Demeter, Steven Denker, Lambert DePompei, Dean Dimon, Mark DiNardo, Norma Dolezal, Benjamin Douglass, Jim Doukas, Jerome Duke, Lynn Dycko, Andrew Edwards, David Ernat, Edward Estok Jr., David Fallon, Dan Feeney, Linda Ferro, Laura Fiffick, Miguel Figueroa, Michael Franz, Beverly Gaffney, Rudolph Garfield, Alan Gates, Ann Gilbert, Thomas Gilmore, Mark Giuliano, Frank Godic, Carol Goldsmith, Remus Grama, Jefferson Gray, Merritt Greenwood, Melinda Grohol, Martha Gubernath, Thomas Hagedorn, Michael Hageman, Charles Hall, Kevin Hannah, Andrew Hanovsky, Mirko Hladni, Mark Hobson, Paul Hoffman, Kay Hogg, Kate Hollingsworth, Denise Horstman, Larry Howard, Otmous Howard, Horst Hoyer, Julie Hritz, Charles Hurst, Ramez Islambouli, Robert Kelly, Artak Khachikyan, Naim Khalil, Gediminas Kijauskas, Susan Koletsky, Dave Konarski, Steve Koplinka, R. J. Landgraf, Tom MacMillan, Jerry Madasz, Darshan Mahajan, Walther Marcis, Jose Marrero, Robert Marrone, Chris Martin, John Martin, Martin Massaglia, Andre Matthews, James McCreight, Kathleen McEntee, Joseph McNulty, Laura Medvec, Ernest Mihaly, Barb Miller, Gary Mitchner, Christina Monreal, Shawnthea Monroe, LeRoy Moreeuw, John Nakonachny, Kathy Nikokirakis, Jim Noga, John Nottingham, Hiawatha Nowden, Thomas O'Donnell, Michael O'Grady, John Ojaimi, Keith Owen, Eleni Papouras-Jenks, Peter Parry, F. E. Perry Jr., Padmanatha Pillai, Dianne Piunno, Kenneth Pleiman, Helen Pointer, Bradford Purdom, Philip Racco, Ralph Rosenthal, Anthony Schuerger, Christopher Schwartz, Conrad Selnick, Valerie Shaffer, Haleema Siddiqui, Sándor Siklódi, James Singler, Joshua Skoff, DeWayne Smith, Michael Surufka, Rose Sustersic, Joe Sutowski, Leo Telesz, Gregory Thomas, Taylor Thompson, Rodney Turner, Bella Waller, Anita Weaver, Mark Webster, Terry White, William Wiethorn, Tyree Williams, Bertrice Wood, Meryl Work, Charles Yoost, Terri Young, and John Zdinak.

Like all authors, I am indebted to books as well as people. Several books, in addition to Armstrong's *A Guide to Cleveland's Sacred Landmarks,* were particularly helpful. Most useful was David Van Tassel and John Grabowski's wonderful *The Encyclopedia of Cleveland History.*[1] A close runner-up was Eric Johannesen's *Cleveland Architecture, 1876–1976*[2] More specialized, but a treasure, is the Catholic Diocese of Cleveland's *People of Faith*[3]…if only every religious organization had a comparable handbook.[4]

Several books of a more specialized nature have been helpful or inspiring. These include Michael Levy's *Revelations—Photographs of Cleveland's African American Churches*[5] and Johannesen's *A Cleveland Legacy: The Architecture of Walker and Weeks*.[6] Taylor Moore, formerly rector of St. Christopher's in Gates Mills, famously said that parishes have two kinds of history: those that are printed and those that are told in the church kitchen. A few congregations are fortunate in having written histories that include some of the stories told in the kitchen. These include F. Washington Jarvis's *St. Paul's Cleveland, 1846–1968;*[7] John Bellamy's *Angels on the Heights: A History of St. Ann's Parish, Cleveland Heights;*[8] Walter Leedy's *Eric Mendelsohn's Park Synagogue;*[9] Tom Hagedorn's articles in *St. Patrick, West Park, 150th Anniversary;*[10] Ruth Dancyger's *The Temple-Tifereth Israel;*[11] and John Boyle's *From Ark to Art: The 20-Year Journey of the Civic, Cleveland Heights, Ohio from Jewish Temple to Multi-Purpose Community Facility.*[12] If Cleveland awarded a prize for the best congregation history, three Reformed books would be on the list—Jeannette Tuve's *Old Stone Church*[13] and two works by the accomplished Carol Poh Miller, her Presbyterian prize-winning *Church with a Conscience: History of Cleveland's Church of the Covenant*[14] and her outstanding *This Far By Faith: The Story of Cleveland's Euclid Avenue Congregational Church.*[15] Every church has an interesting story; religious communities only differ in the expressive ability of their storytellers. One of the best storytellers was Alan Davis.[16]

Arcadia, the local history press outside of Charleston, South Carolina, has recently published three books concerning Greater Cleveland congregations: Marian Morton's *Cleveland Heights Congregations;* Barry Herman and Walter Grossman's *Cleveland's Vanishing Sacred Architecture;* and John Sabol's *Cleveland's Buckeye Neighorhood.*[17] Debra First's poignant pictures of the closed Roman Catholic churches are in her *Founded in Faith: Cleveland's Lost Catholic Legacy.*[18]

Introduction

As you drive through small towns in New England, you don't need to look at signs to identify the churches: the imposing white frame one with the spire on the green is Congregational; the little stone one is Episcopalian; the big stone one is Roman Catholic. What makes a building look religious? What do members of a religious institution expect to see when they attend services? For the first 150 years of American history, all churches looked pretty much the same.[1] When the Pilgrims and Puritans came to New England in the early seventeenth century, the practice of their faith in England was against the law. That's why they came. In England, they had initially met more or less secretly in people's houses. As the authorities became more tolerant, the Puritans began to meet in larger buildings, designed for religious purposes. The government of England required them to be reasonably discrete and they developed a style of religious building called the "House Church." House Churches in England looked vaguely like houses but were bigger. When they came to America they were free to build whatever they wanted, but they continued to build and worship in buildings that looked like houses. House Churches became so established as the appropriate style for a religious building that when the Puritans' Anglican and Jewish neighbors began to put up religious structures, it was obvious to them that they should be in the House Church style. St. Paul's Church in Wickford, Rhode Island, built in 1707 and the oldest Episcopal church in New England, is a House Church complete with side entrance. (The little masonry churches came later.) Touro Synagogue, built in Newport, Rhode Island, in 1759, the oldest place of Jewish worship in the Western Hemisphere, was designed to look, from the outside, like an imposing residence.

When memorable churches began to be built in Cleveland, the discontinuity between what the building looked like and what went on inside continued but the outside changed. An Irish priest built a life-size replica of a Saracen-influenced Sicilian church. Another Irishman built an over-life-size replica of an Early Christian Roman basilica. Methodist, Presbyterian, and Baptist congregations met improbably in copies of the great French and British cathedrals of the twelfth and thirteenth centuries. Episcopalians met in something, remodeled of course, that looked like it had been transported from a revolutionary Connecticut town green. Drivers and pedestrians may recognize a building as religious, but the style of the building gives little clue now to the style of worship.[2] Some of us may cling to the faith of our fathers, but not to their architectural sensibility.

Heterodoxy, however, is much more apparent outside than inside. The inside of a religious building is, at least partly, governed by religious practice. This is most obvious when a new congregation takes over a religious building from someone else. The new congregation will rarely change anything on the

1

outside other than the sign. Some immediate changes, however, may be necessary on the inside. Baptist congregations, for example, need some kind of large public baptistery in the front of their new church.

Liturgical churches generally require a processional center aisle and frown on balconies because balconies make it difficult for congregants to make their way from there to the altar. Reformed congregations, in contrast, are most comfortable when they can stay in their seats in a semicircle, often accessible through several radial aisles. The interior design of churches is greatly affected by education requirements. Traditional Roman Catholic churches generally didn't have any. They provided religious education for their children during the week in the separate buildings of their parochial schools. Sunday was for church. Protestants, in contrast, incorporated elaborate Sunday schools into their churches. These Sunday schools developed, in the nineteenth century, into large and complex "Akron Plan" churches, the purpose of which a Roman Catholic would find difficult to understand. Some things on the inside are obvious: the gorgeous furnishings and decoration of the liturgical churches versus the plainness of the Reformed churches, built to focus the mind on the sermon. Some things are subtle: within the United Churches of Christ (the UCC), the pulpit is generally on the right and the lectern is on the left in a formerly Congregational church, while in a UCC church, which was Evangelical and Reformed before the 1957 merger, the pulpit is generally on the left and the lectern is on the right.

Although fashions in religious practice and the space that supports it change, change has been, since the end of the Second Vatican Council in 1965 (hereafter called Vatican II), most obvious in the Roman Catholic Church. There are only two Roman Catholic churches in this book, Resurrection in Solon and La Sagrada Familia on Detroit Avenue in Cleveland, which were built after 1965 and whose original design incorporated the precepts of the Council. Almost all the other Roman Catholic churches have been modified.[3] Although the changes cannot compare with those following the Council of Trent in the sixteenth century when the rood screens came down and the worship space was expanded and rearranged to accommodate a larger and more unified congregation, the Vatican II changes are obvious: (1) the private enclosed baptisteries at the left rear of the churches are no longer used for that purpose, and the baptismal fonts are moved out into the worship space; (2) the altar rails separating the nave from the sanctuary are taken down; and (3) the altar is either moved out from the front wall or a new altar constructed so that the priest faces the congregation.

While it is sometimes difficult to tell them apart from the outside, this does not mean that denominations do not have some common characteristics. Older Roman Catholic parishes occupy a campus: church, school, gym, rectory, and convent. Some of the largest worship spaces in Cleveland are Roman Catholic, although they were built to seat only a fraction of their congregation at one time.[4] Roman Catholic churches usually seat about one thousand. Parishes were very large because the Bishops tried to control where parishes were established so that each parish could support a school. Although most of the Protestant landmarks in this book are good sized,[5] Protestant congregations tend to be much smaller than Roman Catholic. Many Protestant church buildings, however, are actually larger than Roman Catholic churches because the Protestant buildings incorporate the educational, administrative, and social areas that Roman Catholic parishes house outside the church building in the school, gym, or rectory.

The principal Jewish worship spaces built before 1950, which needed to seat all adult males at one time during the High Holy Days, rivaled or exceeded the size of the Catholic Churches. More recently, following the design of Mendelsohn's Park Synagogue, Jewish worship spaces have become expandable to accommodate the varying needs of weekly Shabbat and annual High Holy Days. Jewish educational facilities are extremely ambitious, rivaling those of the Roman Catholic parochial schools.

On July 25, 1924, then the Feast of St. Christopher,[6] Father Richard Patterson stood in front of his parish in Rocky River all day and blessed a long line of cars, trucks, and motorcycles. Each driver received a St. Christopher medal, a written prayer, and a warning that St. Christopher would appear at speeds over 60 mph. In subsequent years Patterson would hand out as many as 1,200 medals every July 25. Many Cleveland religious communities have not adapted as easily to the coming of the automobile. Most of the congregations in this book were built without parking lots.[7] What happens when their immediate neighborhood disappears and their congregants no longer walk to services? Different denominations handle this problem in different ways.

Protestant communities, often uninhibited by hierarchal or historical discipline, have frequently been small and transient. The Protestant landmarks illustrated here are exceptional. They are surrounded by a sea of small religious communities worshiping in storefronts and little churches. There is a great deal of coming and going. Churches are built and abandoned, bought and sold. Church histories often suggest a complicated and confusing free-for-all with respect to doctrine as well who met where and what they built. This is less true of many of the Protestant landmarks in this guide. They tend to have settled into substantial buildings and are trying to hold on with dwindling endowments. Nevertheless there is a feature of Protestant communities which is best described as freshness and spontaneity. Things happen. Congregations move or they battle to stay on.

There are very few Jews now living in the city of Cleveland. This guide documents the orderly progression which has kept their great Cleveland congregations intact over more than 150 years as they moved through a succession of buildings. This progression has the Abrahamic character of a nomadic desert people. When the community moves, their place of worship moves. When the grass gives out, they load up their scrolls and, led by their rabbis and elders, move on. It is the law of the desert, the law of community survival.

This means, in Cleveland, that there are active temples and synagogues where there are Jewish people. They have left traces where they were, but they are no longer there. The result is a remarkable series of building campaigns and a remarkable series of buildings. The building of outstanding, large, contemporary Jewish houses of worship continues.

In contrast to Jewish and Protestant congregations, Roman Catholic parish history is relatively simple: Monsignor O'Somebody came, preached, and built. Amadeus Rappe, the first Bishop of Cleveland, struggled to control this growth and was defeated by his Irish and German clergy.[8] They developed the very American system of nationality churches, which gave this great community so much of its wonderful character. Now Rappe's nightmare has become a reality. After the Second World War the housing stock and environment of Cleveland could no longer support the lifestyle that young Americanized families expected. The automobile allowed them to escape and they were replaced by an ethnic group so devoutly wedded to Protestantism that no effort, no matter how Herculean or imaginative, could involve them in the Roman Catholic Church. Roman Catholic parishes, with few exceptions, do not move. So, on March 15, 2009, the Diocese of Cleveland had to close twenty-nine parishes and merge eighteen. Almost everyone, to paraphrase Mark Twain, agreed with some of the Bishop's decisions (when he closed someone else's church) and almost no one agreed with all of his decisions (when he closed theirs). Of the forty-six Roman Catholic churches that Foster Armstrong identified as Cleveland landmarks, nineteen (41 percent) are closed or closing.

Most of the buildings in this *Guide* were built before 1930 when Cleveland was the sixth largest city in the United States. Today, in the first decade of the twenty-first century, Cleveland flirts with being the poorest city in the country. What happens to our religious buildings, and whether any more are built, depends less on our clergy and people and more on what happens to our city.

To encourage visits to these landmarks, all but one located within Cuyahoga County,[9] fifteen driving tours have been organized. These tours are organized as follows:

Cleveland

1. The Dual Hub Corridor: Downtown; the Euclid Corridor; and University Circle
2. North Central Cleveland: Goodrich-Kirtland; Hough; and St. Clair-Superior
3. Northeast Cleveland: Glenville-Forest Hill; East Cleveland; Collinwood; and Euclid Green
4. South Central Cleveland: Central; Fairfax; and Kinsman
5. Southeast Cleveland: Buckeye-Woodland; Shaker; Mt. Pleasant; Lee-Miles; Corlett; and Union
6. The Broadway Corridor: Broadway and Miles Park

7. The Near West Side: Ohio City and Tremont
8. West Side South: Old Brooklyn; Archwood-Denison; and Fulton Clark
9. West Central Cleveland: West Boulevard-Lorain; Edgewater-Cudell; and Detroit Shoreway
10. West Park: Jefferson; Kamms Corners; Riverside; and Puritas-Longmead

Suburban Cuyahoga County

11. Lakewood; Rocky River; Westlake; Bay Village; and North Olmsted
12. Brooklyn; Parma; and Middleburg Heights
13. Cleveland Heights
14. Shaker Heights; Beachwood; Pepper Pike; and Lyndhurst
15. Orange; Solon; Chagrin Falls; Gates Mills; Highland Heights; and Richmond Heights

Directions for the tour are given at the beginning of each chapter. Each tour description is accompanied by a map that locates each religious building mentioned in the text.

Sacred landmarks in each tour that are identified by number are elaborated on in a historical and architectural description. The current name of the landmark is listed first; the founding congregation, if different from the current congregation, is listed next. Although most landmarks were several years in the making, an attempt has been made to attach a year to each landmark. This is a historical convention and required a judgment by the author. Was it when the cornerstone was laid, when construction began, when construction was mostly finished, when the congregation moved in, when the church was dedicated, or when the mortgage was paid off? If there is a date that the congregation accepts, it is used. Otherwise, the date is usually, but not always, the date of dedication. Thus, these dates are not very accurate (or very consistent). The building address is also provided. The name of the architect, if known, is listed. An attempt has been made to list (see Dedication) those whose idea it was to build the landmark and who saw the project through to completion. (These leaders are identified as "Builders," for want of a better term, and should not be confused with the contractors who bid and supervised each project.)

It should be obvious, but frequently isn't, what religious institutions are called. Many of the major institutions in this book have had a historical continuity which encouraged the use of a generally accepted identification for many years. As communities compete for membership, however, fashions in name, like fashions in architecture and decoration, change.[10] Further, as religious communities appear and disappear, the name of their buildings change. Religious institutions, like people, have the right to be called what they want to be called, but what does that mean? An attempt has been made here to identify buildings by a name on stationary or a web site. This is supplemented by names on signs and in the yellow pages. In a few unfortunate cases, even though the building is clearly abandoned or now used for some unidentified nonreligious purpose, the name of a previous congregation is retained for want of anything better.

With very few exceptions, houses of worship are not public buildings. They are not secret, but they are private. Changing standards of public decorum, civility, and respect for things religious have forced most of the institutions in this book to lock their doors. They are no longer public places of refuge and quiet, open to the public for prayer and meditation. Religious institutions can no longer welcome whoever wants to walk in. Nor are these buildings museums, despite the beauty of their architecture, the richness of their decoration, and the interest, as an exotic culture, which they may provoke. Security in sacred landmarks is further complicated by the fact that many are associated with schools that are now, of necessity, suspicious of strangers. Christian and Islamic institutions are evangelistic, they encourage visitors, but they cannot be counted on to welcome sightseers.

Only a handful of the institutions in this book are open to an unannounced public: Old Stone Church, the Cathedrals of St. John the Evangelist and Trinity, St. Paul Shrine, Holy Rosary, Garfield Memorial, and the Wade Chapel. Volunteers keep some of these open at designated times. Some can afford private security. One sees it as its mission to remain open, whatever the risk of desecration. One is in a neighborhood where desecration would be not only unthinkable but dangerous. The Cathedral of St. John is at the apex of a social pyramid which generally provides a uniformed Cleveland police officer in one of the pews whenever it is open.

Institutions recognized as architectural, decorative, or cultural landmarks are usually proud of what they have and are used to gawkers. They naturally prefer to deal with groups rather than individual walk-ins. Their offices should be consulted to join or arrange a tour. The perceptive reader will also identify other landmarks that have proved impenetrable.

CHAPTER ONE

Sacred Landmarks in the Dual Hub Corridor

The Dual Hub Corridor is defined on the west by Public Square—Cleveland's office, retail, and government center—and on the east by University Circle—Cleveland's cultural, educational, and institutional center. The Euclid Corridor, consisting of Euclid Avenue and the area between Chester Avenue on the north and Carnegie Avenue on the south, connects these two centers. Containing Cleveland's two most important centers and its most important street, one would not be surprised to learn that this district contains many of the city's most significant sacred landmarks.

Tour

Begin this tour at Public Square on Superior Avenue traveling east. To the north is the First Presbyterian Church, the "Old Stone" Church (1). Located on the northwest quadrant of the Square, in the middle of skyscrapers, Old Stone perseveres as one of the oldest buildings in downtown Cleveland. Continuing east, on the northeast corner of Superior at East Ninth Street is the Cathedral of St. John the Evangelist (2), a nineteenth-century building completely rebuilt after World War II. Continue driving east. At the corner of Superior and East 17th Street, turn right (south). On the northwest corner of the intersection is located the headquarters of the Cleveland Fire Department. Historic Saint Peter Church (3) occupies the southeast corner. It is the oldest standing Roman Catholic parish church in Cleveland.

From East 17th, turn left onto Euclid Avenue. This street—called Buffalo Road until 1825 because it was a major route to Buffalo—follows what used to be the Native American Lake Shore Trail. In the nineteenth century, many of Cleveland's richest citizens built their mansions along Euclid, earning it the nickname "Millionaire's Row." The growth of Cleveland's commercial district along this street, however, combined with the construction of the railroad at East 55th Street, led to its abandonment as a residential street. Continue east on Euclid Avenue. You will pass Cleveland State University on the left (north). Trinity Episcopal Cathedral (4) lies on the right at East 22nd Street. Designed by Charles Schweinfurth, Trinity remains one of Cleveland's finest sacred monuments.

Continue east on Euclid, over the Innerbelt, to East 30th Street. Zion Evangelical Lutheran Church (5) is to the south, on the southwest corner of the intersection of East 30th and Prospect Avenue. First Church, Cleveland, originally the First United Methodist Church (6), occupies the southeast corner of East 30th at Euclid, across the street from television station WEWS. J. Milton Dyer designed First Church. Travel east on Euclid, past the Masonic Temple on the left, for two blocks to the ornate St. Paul Shrine (7) located on the southeast corner of the East 40th Street intersection. Originally built as St.

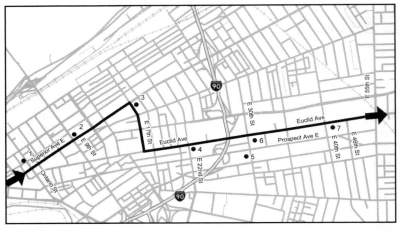

DOWNTOWN
1. First Presbyterian Church (Old Stone Church)
2. Cathedral of St. John the Evangelist
3. Historic Saint Peter Church
4. Trinity Episcopal Cathedral
5. Zion Evangelical Lutheran Church
6. First Church, Cleveland (First United Methodist Church)
7. Conversion of St. Paul Shrine

Paul's Episcopal Church, this building was renamed the Conversion of St. Paul when it was bought by the Roman Catholic Diocese of Cleveland.

Continue east along the new Euclid Corridor, going under the railroad at East 55th Street, and then, farther east, past the Dunham Tavern Museum—the oldest building still on its original foundation in Cuyahoga County. At East 71st Street turn right (south). St. Timothy Missionary Baptist Church (8) is located on the northeastern corner of East 71st at Carnegie Avenue. Scots immigrants built this church as the First United Presbyterian Church. Turn left (east) onto Carnegie.

Turn left onto East 77th Street and travel north. On the southwest corner of the intersection with Euclid is a Church of Jesus Christ of Latter-day Saints. On the southeast corner stands the True Holiness Temple, built as the Second Church of Christ, Scientist. It later served as the Cleveland Playhouse. Turn right (east) onto Euclid. At East 79th Street sits Calvary Presbyterian Church (9), with its great open tower, designed by Charles Schweinfurth as a mission of the Old Stone Church. Continue east on Euclid Avenue. On the southwest corner of Euclid at East 81st Street stand the remains of St. Agnes Roman Catholic Church. The tower is the only thing left standing from this now demolished but once magnificent French Romanesque-style church designed by John T. Comes.

Farther east, on the south side of Euclid, you will find—standing in quick succession—Liberty Hill Baptist Church, formerly the Euclid Avenue Temple/

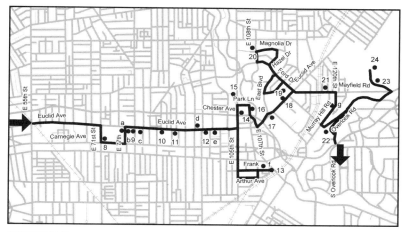

UNIVERSITY

8. St. Timothy Missionary Baptist Church
  a. Church of Jesus Christ of Latter-day Saints
  b. True Holiness Temple
9. Calvary Presbyterian Church
  c. St. Agnes Roman Catholic Church tower
10. Liberty Hill Baptist Church
11. Anglican Church of the Transfiguration
  d. The Euclid Avenue Church of God
12. Euclid Avenue Congregational Church
  e. East Mt. Zion Baptist Church
  f. Second Bethlehem Baptist Church
13. Uqbah Mosque Foundation

14. Pentacostal Church of Christ
15. Temple Tifereth Israel (The Temple)
16. University Circle United Methodist Church
17. Amasa Stone Chapel
18. The Church of the Covenant
19. Florence Harkness Chapel
20. Mt. Zion Congregational Church
21. Holy Rosary Roman Catholic Church
  g. The Lyceum
22. Nottingham Spirk Design Associates
23. Garfield Memorial Monument
24. Wade Memorial Chapel

Anshe Chesed (10), the former Cleveland Playhouse, and the Anglican Church of the Transfiguration, formerly Emmanuel Episcopal Church (11). Gothic-revival architects Ralph Adams Cram and Bertram Goodhue designed Transfiguration, yet it was never completed. The many great modern buildings of the Cleveland Clinic stand behind and between these churches. On the left (north) of Euclid at East 93rd Street sits the Euclid Avenue Church of God (built in 1887 as the Euclid Avenue Methodist Episcopal Church and that subsequently served as the First Church of Christ, Scientist). The building is now vacant. The congregation is suing the Cleveland Landmarks Commission for permission to take down this Badgley-designed building and sell the site, as a parking lot, to the Cleveland Clinic. Stay on Euclid. On the right was the site of the Euclid Avenue Congregational Church (12), which burned down in 2010. East Mt. Zion Baptist Church (originally the Euclid Avenue Christian Church) is on the southwest corner of East 100th Street at Euclid.

Stay on Euclid to East 105th Street. At East 105th, turn right (south). Travel over Carnegie on East 105th and then, south of Cedar Avenue, to Arthur Avenue. Turn left (east) onto Arthur and then left again onto East 108th Street. Turn right onto Frank Avenue. To the left of Frank Avenue's intersection with

Petrarca Road is the Second Bethlehem Baptist Church, built as St. Marian Roman Catholic Church. Private First Class Frank Petrarca, posthumously awarded the first Ohio Congressional Medal of Honor during the Second World War, was brought up at St. Marian. On the right side of Petrarca Road is the minaret of the Uqbah Mosque Foundation (13) with its stylized crescent. Return on Frank Avenue to East 105th and turn right (north). Travel back to Euclid and then continue north on East 105th. On the northeast corner of the East 105th intersection with Chester Avenue is the Pentecostal Church of Christ, formerly the Fourth Church of Christ, Scientist (14). Stay on East 105th for one more block. Temple Tifereth Israel (15) occupies the northwest corner.

Turn right (east) onto Park Lane Avenue entering the University Circle district. Along Park Lane are two great 1923 apartment hotels, one well maintained and the other recently renovated. University Circle, home to many of Cleveland's cultural, educational, religious, and social service institutions, is the only parklike cluster of its kind in the world.[1] Travel east on Park Lane for one block and then turn right (south) onto East 107th Street. On the left, facing east, away from East 107th toward the University Circle Fine Arts Garden, is the University Circle United Methodist Church, formerly the Epworth-Euclid United Methodist Church (16). Bertram Goodhue's masterpiece is known, from the shape of its *flèche,* as the Church of the Holy Oil Can. Turn left on Chester then bear right to get over to Euclid.

Turn left (northeast) onto Euclid. Opposite Severance Hall stands the Amasa Stone Chapel (17), designed by Boston architect Henry Vaughn and located on the Case Western Reserve University (CWRU) campus. On the right, farther east on Euclid, are University Hospitals of Cleveland and the CWRU Medical School. Continue northeast on Euclid. On the left is the large late-English Gothic-revival Church of the Covenant (18), designed by Ralph Adams Cram.

After passing the Church of the Covenant, turn left (northwest) onto Ford Drive. Stay on Ford, named for one of University Circle's most distinguished families, for one block and then turn left (southwest) onto Bellflower Road. On the northwest corner stands Frank Gehry's dramatic Peter B. Lewis Building for the CWRU Business School. Follow the gentle curve of Bellflower Road and note the fortresslike building of the Florence Harkness Chapel (19) located immediately behind the Church of the Covenant. At Bellflower's intersection with East Boulevard, turn right (north). On the left sits Rafael Viñoly's expansion of the Cleveland Museum of Art. Farther north on East Boulevard, also on the left, sits the crystal palace of the Cleveland Botanical Garden. Follow the curve of East Boulevard. On the right lies the recent reconstruction of the Cleveland Institute of Music. Farther on East Boulevard—across Hazel Drive—are the buildings of the Western Reserve Historical Society.

At East 108th Street, turn right (north) just before reaching the Louis Stokes Cleveland VA Medical Center and travel on East 108th to Magnolia Drive. Mt. Zion Congregational Church (20) occupies the northwest corner. This simple contemporary structure serves as a transition from the large institutions of University Circle to the smaller residential mansions of the Wade Park neighborhood. Turn right (east) onto Magnolia Drive and travel on it for one block between residences now converted into fraternity and sorority houses and University Circle institutions. Turn right (south) onto Hazel.

At the end of Hazel, turn left (southeast) back onto East Boulevard. Where East Boulevard forks, take the left (eastern) branch, which is Ford Drive. Travel southeast on Ford to Euclid. Cross Euclid, where Ford becomes Mayfield Road, and continue east. Pass underneath the Rapid Transit tracks and enter Little Italy. At the northwest corner of the intersection of Mayfield and East 120th Street is Holy Rosary Roman Catholic Church (21), an important neighborhood institution. At the Mayfield intersection with Murray Hill Road, turn right (south) onto Murray Hill. On the northeast corner of Murray Hill at Paul Avenue is the former St. John's Beckwith Memorial (Presbyterian) Church. More recently the building became the Lyceum, a conservative private Roman Catholic school. Now it is a craft shop. Travel through the Italian neighborhood along Murray Hill to where Edgehill Road intersects Murray Hill from the left and Cornell Road from the right. Turn left (east) onto Edgehill, climb the hill, and then turn a sharp right (south; almost a "U" turn) onto Overlook Road. Follow Overlook until you see Nottingham Spirk Design Associates (22), the magnificently restored former First Church of Christ, Scientist. Here, you may want to stop and look back down to the part of the city through which you have just traveled.

Although this ends the tour of the Dual Hub Corridor, you may also wish to visit the Garfield Memorial Monument (23) and the Wade Memorial Chapel (24) in nearby Lake View Cemetery. To reach Lake View Cemetery, backtrack (northeast) on Overlook until it intersects with Kenilworth Road. Turn left and travel one block northeast on Kenilworth to its intersection with Mayfield. The main cemetery gate is directly in front of you on the north side of Mayfield. From the cemetery entrance, follow the signs to the memorial and to the chapel.

1. First Presbyterian Church, also known as Old Stone Church (1853 and 1884)
Architects: Charles Heard and Simeon Porter (1853); Charles Schweinfurth (1884)
Builder: Samuel Aiken
Location: 91 Public Square

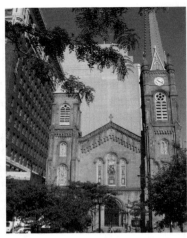

In the first half of the nineteenth century, Cleveland was a small town. From the Old Stone Church's beginning, when Rebecca Carter helped organize it,[2] the history of the church has been the history of Cleveland.[3] Ten Cleveland mayors, including the first, were members. The Connecticut Yankees who established Cleveland were, almost by definition, members of this church. Its fifteen original members—10 percent of the population—made up the Cleveland establishment.[4] In 1819 they founded the church as a Union Sunday school on the second floor of Cleveland's first log courthouse, located on Public Square.

The first Presbyterian church in the Cleveland area, the first church of any kind in the Cleveland area, was the First Presbyterian Church of East Cleveland (see p. 107). The "Old First" was organized in 1807 as a Sunday school in a log cabin at what has become 16200 Euclid Avenue. Many other Protestant churches in Cleveland also began as a Sunday school. This identified a congregation as one served by itinerant clergy (the Roman Catholic equivalent of a Sunday school was a mission). Old First—like the later Old Stone Church, Euclid Avenue Congregational (see p. 38), and Archwood UCC (see p. 226)—was originally a Plan of Union church. In 1801 the Presbyterian and Congregational Churches—separated, as Marilynne Robinson describes them, by a "doctrinal and demographic inch"[5]—agreed to jointly evangelize the frontier in a series of Plan of Union churches. The Plan of Union would fall apart over slavery in 1837.

Incorporated in 1827 as the First Presbyterian Society, the Old Stone Church is the only institution on Public Square that has remained in the same location since its inception there. In 1834, a year before the arrival of Samuel Aiken—their first permanent pastor—the Yankees dedicated the first masonry religious building in Cleveland. This substantial affair had an imposingly high flight of stairs leading up to the main entrance and eighty-four lockable pews. The suspension of the gallery by iron rods is said to be the first use of iron in a public building in Cleveland. In typical Presbyterian fashion, the Yankees built first of stone. They never built a wooden church. Their gray, rough-hammered sandstone "Georgian style" building became known as the "stone church," as would its successor, to distinguish it from "the Brick Church" (St. Paul's Episcopal, 1851) and the "wood church" (First Baptist, 1834). As others built subsequent masonry churches, First Presbyterian earned the nickname the "Old Stone Church."

Old Stone played a major role in Cleveland education and social services. When the congregation could not establish a Sunday school in 1833 because none of the children could read, Old Stone started a free school that then became the first public school. Case Western Reserve School of Medicine was organized in Old Stone parlors in 1843 as the Cleveland Medical College and held its first classes there.[6] In 1863 Old Stone established a "Home for Friendless Strangers" to provide medical care for Civil War refugees from the South. The house rented for this purpose on Lakeside evolved into Lakeside Hospital, which, in turn, evolved into University Hospitals. The Visiting Nurse Association was also organized at Old Stone. In 1865 Lincoln's funeral train stopped in Cleveland. His body was brought down Euclid Avenue to Public Square and placed on a low catafalque.[7] One hundred thousand filed past. The local memorial service with the Lincoln family was, of course, in Old Stone Church. On a lighter note, Samuel Aiken also served as the first chairman for horticulture of the Cuyahoga County Fair, which was held on Public Square.

As the establishment church, Old Stone played an active role in issues, many now thankfully forgotten, that roiled Cleveland in the nineteenth century—Millerism,[8] perfectionism,[9] dancing, speculation, the theater, doing business on the Sabbath,[10] and, of course, all manner of controversies concerning sexual indiscretion. The church was also active in many areas we continue to think of as important—temperance, education, and upright conduct at home and work. It is impossible to identify all the members of this church who have been active in Cleveland philanthropy over the years but two require mention. First, Flora Stone Mather, "philanthropist, benefactress, and humanitarian whose dedication to the religious, educational, and social-reform activities of the city touched the lives of many Clevelanders and Cleveland institutions,"[11] was an active member of Old Stone from childhood. Her most important philanthropy, directly related to the church, was the establishment of Goodrich House, honoring Old Stone's second pastor.[12] Goodrich House, now on East 55th Street—in addition to its social programs for successive waves of needy immigrants from Appalachia, Germany, Ireland, eastern Europe, and northward-migrating African Americans—is the predecessor of not only the Consumer League of Ohio (an important organization promoting women and children's interests and industrial justice) but also the Legal Aid Society, the Cleveland Music School Settlement, and the Society for the Blind. Second, Sarah Elizabeth Fitch, long time superintendent of the Old Stone Sunday school, founded and directed the Women's Christian Association, which became the YWCA.

In the nineteenth century, however, the issue of slavery—above all—preoccupied Old Stone.[13] Differences concerning slavery before the Civil War, together with a growing congregation and the limitations of the first stone church, led to a proliferation of other Presbyterian institutions with leaders coming from the Old Stone community—Second Presbyterian (1837), which became the Church of the Covenant (see p. 52); Free Presbyterian, which became Plymouth Church of Shaker Heights (see p. 335); First Presbyterian of Ohio City;

and Euclid Avenue Presbyterian (1853). To slow the exodus, Samuel Aiken built the present sandstone Romanesque Revival building designed by Charles Heard. At that time, Johannsen comments, "Charles Heard could go in every direction from the Public Square and find buildings of his design."[14] Now only Old Stone, Saint Peter Roman Catholic Church on Superior Avenue at East 17th Street (see p. 18), and the Rowfant Club at East 30th Street at Prospect Avenue remain. The massive rounded hoodmolds over the window and door openings, medieval-style moldings above the base floor, and the squared-off towers of differing height and shape identify Old Stone as Romanesque Revival. Heard designed a remarkably sound building. His stone walls remain protected from heat damage by an inner lining of brick, and these walls have, almost miraculously, survived two disastrous fires. The first fire struck only four years after the building was completed. The one-hundred-foot stream of water from the hand-pumped fire apparatus available at the time could not reach the 250-foot steeple. "Like a flaming torch, it swayed and crashed onto Ontario Street."[15] Heard and Porter rebuilt the interior within a year, and the congregation replaced the spire ten years later.

Heard's plans for the 1853 building included an adjacent building to the north for a chapel, "parlors," and Sunday-school rooms. This structure was removed forty years later and replaced with a new chapel. In 1920, a desk factory on Ontario behind the church was purchased for a parish house. This building and the chapel were removed in 1960 and replaced with a new building with two chapels, a lounge, auditorium, dining hall, kitchen, and many educational and meeting rooms. One of the new chapels, the light and airy Griffiths Chapel, with its organ and wonderful modern front window, is used for small weddings and services.

In 1884, fire struck a second time, spreading from an adjacent theater, built despite the strong moral objections of its owner's father, who was a pillar of Old Stone. Again, Heard's walls withstood the fire. Although the rebuilt blackened spire appeared to have survived, it had to be taken down in 1896 because of structural uncertainties. Again, the interior was completely destroyed. Only some of the chancel furniture and the first row pew where the Lincoln family sat during the memorial service were saved. Nine years earlier, the Episcopalians had moved out to East 40th Street at Euclid Avenue. Could the equally socially prominent Presbyterians be far behind?[16] After vigorous debate, they answered "No." Old Stone would stay on Public Square and stand up to its public duty. Flora Stone Mather's ten thousand dollar donation softened the disappointment of the less stalwart. Charles Schweinfurth, brought to Cleveland to design the gigantic Everett house on Euclid Avenue,[17] went to work on his first public commission. Schweinfurth would go on to design fifteen houses on Euclid Avenue, Trinity Episcopal Cathedral (see p. 21), Calvary Presbyterian (see p. 32), the Union Club, and several buildings for Western Reserve College.

Schweinfurth reinforced the sturdy but damaged exterior walls and totally redesigned the interior of the church into something called "Victorian Romanesque," making it much more elaborate than the original. The six-hundred-seat sanctuary is almost square with a shallow apse. The most interesting features of the golden oak and mahogany remodeled interior required worshipers to look up—graceful carvings, a spacious balcony, and an impressive trussed wood, barrel-vaulted ceiling. Shipbuilders crafted the ceiling timbers; when Old Stone was built, Cleveland was one of the largest shipbuilding centers in the United States. The church's roof rests on two longitudinal trusses that are partially supported by a series of arched braces springing from the side walls. The trusses are treated as false clerestories and admit no natural light; they are artificially lit from behind. The model for the new interior seems to have been the nave of Trinity Church in Boston, designed by Henry Hobson Richardson in 1873. Richardson used a similar semicircular arch with wooden tie beams at the base.

A magnificent John La Farge triple window, with portraits of Amasa Stone's children, overlooks Public Square. Four windows are Tiffany. Chancel walls were painted with religious symbols and inscriptions by Charles's brother, Julius Schweinfurth, in a gold mosaic pattern. The 1977 Holtkamp organ is installed behind the original casework of an 1895 Johnson instrument.

By the beginning of the twentieth century, the area north and east of the church had become one of the worst districts in Cleveland. Adults came to the church from the suburbs; children came to the Sunday school from the neighborhood. Daniel Burnham's famous Group Plan radically changed this situation by replacing the squalor north and east of Public Square with a collection of elegant federal, county, and city buildings around the mall. This purging, which depopulated its immediate neighborhood, forced Old Stone's traditional missions to begin operating at a distance from the church.

Until the 1920s Old Stone had dominated, or at least held its own, among the buildings around Public Square. Then everything changed. Fourteen hundred buildings were razed to build the Terminal Tower complex. The church began to be dwarfed by the other large buildings in its vicinity as its neighborhood changed from one of little, old, deteriorated shops and rundown houses to a neighborhood of impressive skyscrapers and public buildings. Then for fifty years, in the middle of the twentieth century, there was no building on Public Square. The area began to reacquire an atmosphere of destitution and decay. This was dramatically changed in the 1980s when BP America built a new forty-five story tower and Society Bank built a fifty-five story center on the square. In the early nineties, the Terminal Tower complex underwent massive reconstruction. These buildings now dwarf Old Stone's great east spire.

Old Stone is a big institution. In 1977 the Cleveland *Press* reported that more than 150 groups—from Alcoholics Anonymous to Big Brothers—met at the church. Seventeen hundred people attended Old Stone's 150th anniversary dinner in 1970, including Olympic gold-medalist Jesse Owens (the main speaker), Bishop Clarence Issenmann, and fifty-year member Frances Payne Bolton. Weddings have always been an important celebration at Old Stone; almost five hundred couples were married there in 1929, and approximately 250 weddings took place there per year in the 1950s. More than twelve thousand couples have been married in this church, including such luminaries as Bob Feller, Sheila and Gordon MacRae, and Michael Stanley.

As a Reformed church, Old Stone has always been known as a "pulpit church" in which the centerpiece of the liturgy every Sunday is the sermon. The church has also had, because of its resources and its position in the community, a reputation for great music, now centered on its Holtkamp organ. Its musical reputation was cultivated for many years by the director of the Conservatory at Baldwin Wallace and cofounder of the Ohio Chamber Orchestra, Warren Scharf. He directed the choir and Margaret Scharf, dean of the Cleveland Chapter of the American Guild of Organists and professor of organ at Cleveland State, played the Holtkamp.

Old Stone, because of its location, encounters many challenges its founders did not anticipate almost two hundred years ago—the time of its main Sunday service has had to be moved from 11:00 A.M. to 10:00 A.M. because of parking problems associated with Browns and Indians games. In 1998 a giant crane was sneaked into downtown in the middle of the night and then, as all Cleveland watched, replaced the steeple taken down 102 years before. In typical Presbyterian fashion, the new stainless steel steeple was given by an anonymous donor.

2. Cathedral of St. John the Evangelist (1848 and 1946)
Architects: Patrick Keely (1848) and George W. Stickle (1946–48)
Builders: Amadeus Rappe (1848) and Edward Hoban (1946–48)
Location: 1007 Superior

The Cathedral of St. John the Evangelist, although drastically changed in 1946, was Cleveland's second building for Roman Catholic worship and is the oldest still standing.[18] The first Roman Catholic church in Cleveland, almost always identified as St. Mary-on-the-Flats, was dedicated as Our Lady of the Lake in 1840. St. Mary-on-the-Flats was located at a distance from where the first Roman Catholics were living.[19] Recognizing this, its third pastor, Peter McLaughlin, purchased land in 1845 in what was known as the May Woods, a flat marshy tract where the cathedral now stands. In 1847, Pius IX created the Diocese of Cleveland out of the northern half of the Diocese of Cincinnati. While Amadeus Rappe, as first bishop, inherited little more in Cleveland than St. Mary-on-the-Flats and the marsh, his diocese outside Cleveland was substantial—forty-two churches, twenty-one priests, and two convents. On arriving in Cleveland, Bishop Rappe immediately purchased five additional lots in the May Woods and started building.

The Cathedral of St. John was not only one of Patrick Charles Keely's first buildings but also the first cathedral this prolific Roman Catholic architect would complete. In the course of a long career, Keely went on to construct fifteen other cathedrals including those in Boston, Hartford, Chicago, Albany, and Charleston. Keely's cathedral in Cleveland was a substantial nine-hundred-seat, relatively plain, brick building with enough historic touches so that it could be described as ornamental Gothic. The interior of the original cathedral can still be seen from inside the present building. It features the soaring plastered neo-Gothic vaulting that became a feature of so many nineteenth-century Cleveland churches. The original 170-foot-long building extended approximately to the crossing of the present building so that the pre-Vatican II high altar of the original cathedral was in essentially the same place where the post-Vatican II altar is now. The building was originally glazed by the Morgan Firm of Buffalo, New York. In 1902 the Mayer family of Munich reglazed the cathedral, and these splendid windows have been preserved in their original position so that the view of the nave from the crossing is not unlike what it was one hundred years ago. During construction the congregation, drawn from St. Mary-on-the-Flats, worshiped in a small adjoining frame chapel that was eventually hauled thirty blocks east up Superior Avenue to become the first church of Immaculate Conception Parish (see p. 78).

Despite a succession of campaigns to maintain the cathedral and improve its ability to serve its function, there were problems. In 1928 the magnificent tall steeple was condemned. A stubby affair that dramatically changed the profile of the building replaced it. In another realm of controversy, there had been several proposals to move the seat of the bishop. In the early twentieth century, Bishop Ignatius Horstmann purchased property adjacent to St. Agnes with the intention of building a new cathedral at East 79th Street at Euclid Avenue. Horstmann's successor, John Patrick Farrelly, purchased a home in Cleveland Heights and there was thought of moving to the Heights. Bishop Farrelly then purchased the site of Severance Hall and commissioned plans for a great Romanesque church there. The bishop established a boy's high school in University Circle (Cathedral Latin) in anticipation of the new cathedral. Bishop Joseph Schrembs actually put the present cathedral property up for sale in 1924; however, it proved more advantageous to sell the University Circle property, and Schrembs subsequently announced that the cathedral would stay where it was.[20]

Immediately after the Second World War, the new bishop, Edward Hoban, decided to enlarge the cathedral and reface the hundred-year-old building with Tennessee Crab Orchard Stone. The stubby tower came down, replaced with a stone tower in the angle between the new south transept and the nave of the renovated building. Ceremonies were moved to St. Agnes. When work was completed in 1948, the width and height of the building was unchanged. New were north and south transepts and a 38-foot choir. They completely renovated the interior furnishings, including the main altar and altar screen, and created a mortuary chapel for all of the former bishops. The cathedral has two Holtkamp organs. Renovation of the cathedral is a continuing process and new statuary and accoutrements continue to be installed.

Cleveland has been a training ground for senior members of the Roman Catholic Church in the United States. Auxiliary Cleveland bishops have gone on to become archbishops of Philadelphia and Atlanta and the cardinal archbishop of Washington, D.C.

3. Historic Saint Peter Church
(1859)
Architects: Heard and Porter
Builder: John Luhr
Location: 1533 East 17th Street

Saint Peter was the oldest existing Roman Catholic parish in Cleveland and its building, a familiar religious landmark occupying the southeast corner of Superior Avenue at East 17th Street, is the oldest existing parish church in the diocese.[21] Established as a church for German immigrants more than a century and a half ago, Saint Peter Church outlived most of its daughter parishes and was reborn in the 1980s in a spectacularly restored space, as an "intentional community" drawn from five of the seven counties in the Diocese of Cleveland.

These daughter parishes played an important role in the growth of the diocese. Amadeus Rappe, who was French and the first Roman Catholic bishop of Cleveland, established what is now Saint Peter in 1853 to minister to his growing German community. After worshiping in St. Mary-on-the-Flats for a year, the parish moved into a basement chapel in the cathedral as they began building their first combination church-and-school at Saint Peter's present location. The West Side Germans had refused to move and remained behind in St. Mary-on-the-Flats. Reconstituted as St. Mary's of the Assumption in 1854, the West Siders stayed at St. Mary-on-the-Flats for ten years until they finally completed their church on Carroll Avenue.[22] Meanwhile, in 1855 the pastor of Saint Peter rented a room for a school for children living too far south to attend Saint Peter School. Two years later a proper school was built, and an assistant from Saint Peter began saying Sunday Mass in a classroom. By 1862 this had evolved into what became the parish of St. Joseph Franciscan.[23] Saint Peter Parish established a second German outpost in 1887—St. Francis of Assisi on the corner of East 71st Street at Superior.

Back at East 17th Street, the present church was dedicated in 1859. Its beautifully kept wood-paneled brick rectory was the oldest continually occupied residence in the city of Cleveland until its doors were closed in 2010.

A 250-foot bell tower with spire was built in 1865. Lightning destroyed the steeple in 1918, and it was replaced with a shorter, square tower. The bells were removed and the tower further shortened and capped in 1984, only to be rebuilt in 2005 complete with Gothic finials and reinstallation of the bells in an attempt to restore the structure to something of its nineteenth-century appearance.[24] The interior was revised in 1885, 1929, 1943, 1965, and 1989–91.

In 1874 the parish completed a magnificent High Victorian school immediately to the east of the current church. The school was taken down in 2009.[25] In anticipation that the cathedral would be moving to the present site of Severence Hall, the Brothers of Mary, who had staffed the Saint Peter School since 1863, left in 1922 to establish Cathedral Latin High School in University Circle. Two years later, this parish established Saint Peter High School. With the construction of a new high school building in 1966, this evolved into Erieview Catholic High School, a joint endeavor with St. Stephen High School and the Academy of Our Lady of Lourdes. The new high school hoped to capitalize on I. M. Pei's ambitious Erieview Project that sought to revitalize the aging district northeast of the downtown Cleveland core. The high school closed when the Erieview Project became a victim of the regional suburban shopping center. Its building was extensively renovated in 1995 to become the Bishop Cosgrove Center, a shelter for the needy.

In the 1980s, as pieces of the deteriorating building rained down on passersby, Saint Peter defiantly refused to succumb to the age of its building and the ills of its surroundings. It developed a chaplaincy for Roman Catholic students at neighboring Cleveland State and, as the students helped to revitalize the parish, Saint Peter began to draw the spiritual, personal, and material resources of the suburbs into a parish built on a pastoral team led by particularly dynamic clergy.

Saint Peter shares a challenging corner with a major county welfare office to the west across 17th Street, and the headquarters of the Cleveland Fire Department, complete with responding fire apparatus, diagonally northwest across Superior. The surface of the building is faced with a composite cement product, mimicking masonry. The basic structure of the building is flavored with neo-Gothic stone pointed arches above window and door openings and occasional side wall buttresses. During the early Gothic Revival period (1820–60), the use of one or two Gothic elements was thought sufficient to indicate that the architect was attempting to create a Gothic impression. The usual church form was a simple basilica with a steeple over the entrance. Saint Peter on the east side and Episcopalian St. John's on the west side represent typical churches of this era. In contrast, the exuberant details on the old school to the east of the church and the rectory to the south showed how Gothic Revival gained traction during the High Victorian period (1860–90).

Over the years most of Saint Peter's church furnishings, of modest value to begin with, were many times replaced. When the church was last renovated in 1989–91, almost everything was taken out, the walls and slender wooden neo-Gothic columns whitewashed, and furnishing begun all over again. Only spared was some statuary, the stations, and the tall Munich-style lancet-shaped 1904 Von Gerichten windows, originally installed to celebrate the fiftieth anniversary of the parish. What made these beautifully restored windows so special in the sophisticated high-art environment in which they found themselves was their commonness—memorials in German were dedicated by foremen, seamstresses, a blind-maker, a gardener, a mortician, and a tailor. These were not Mayer Munich windows. Saint Peter's windows were manufactured by a Columbus company that made windows for more than 850 churches in the United States. Three whitewashed statues, one from Munich and two by Ohio artisans, looked like they had survived 150 rough and tumble years.

Local craftsmen also created the rest of the contemporary and high-art furnishings. The Fletcher-Lively organ was enlarged with four additional ranks by Holtkamp. A particularly rich collection of work by Cleveland sculptor Norbert Koehn included the carved limestone altar in the center of the apse. Its Gothic arches echoed the architecture of the church. Koehn's corner carvings of David, Moses, Isaiah, and Mary Magdalene linked the old and new covenants. He also carved the cross and tabernacle door in the chapel and, in the sanctuary, a statue of the Good Shepherd, a nativity triptych, and a crucifix. To complete his contributions, Koehn reinstalled the nineteenth-century painted-on-copper Belgian stations of the cross into an innovative movable triptych. This triptych, usually in the narthex, was moved into the sanctuary during Lent.

Radical reorientation of the nave replaced the old pews. Congregants sat facing each other instead of all facing the same direction. This, together with the simplification of the decoration, preserved the architectural integrity of the nineteenth-century structure while opening up the space of this modified *hallenkirche* into an organic whole.[26] This emphasized the unity of the congregation as it moved from the body of the nave, where the Word was proclaimed, and gathered around the altar in the apse, where the Eucharist was celebrated. The acoustics of the worship space were enhanced by the plain furnishings, slate floor, and plaster walls.

On March 15, 2009, Bishop Richard Lennon announced the closing of Historic Saint Peter Church. The parish celebrated its final Mass on Easter Sunday 2010 and closed its doors itself. The parish had negotiated an agreement with the diocese to cancel the bishop's scheduled final Mass, the following Sunday, to canonically close the church. Members of the parish organized a Community of Saint Peter in a building on the corner of East 71st Street at Euclid Avenue to continue Saint Peter's social, educational, and prayer ministries. On March 1, 2012, the Vatican Congregation for the Clergy ruled that Bishop Lennon had failed to follow church law and procedure in closing Saint Peter.

4. Trinity Episcopal Cathedral

(1901)
Architect: Charles
Schweinfurth
Builder: William Leonard
Location: East 22nd Street at
Euclid Avenue

Trinity Parish, established in 1816, is the oldest organized religious body in Cleveland.[27] Although first meetings of the parish were in a home across the Cuyahoga River in what was then known as the Village of Brooklyn,[28] from 1816 to 1820 the congregation typically met in the Village of Cleaveland (the original name for Cleveland). The parish then decided to move permanently to Brooklyn. Five years later, the congregation again changed its mind and relocated to Cleveland. There it shared with the Presbyterians (but at different hours) the second floor of the log courthouse and jail on Public Square. In 1829 Trinity moved into an up-to-date frame carpenter's Gothic-style church on the corner of St. Clair Avenue at Seneca (now West Third Street). This was the first church building in Cleveland. In 1834 the West Side parishioners left to establish St. John's Episcopal Church in Ohio City (see p. 185). The East Side members remained at St. Clair. The growth of the East Side congregation during the 1840s and 1850s, and a disastrous fire in 1853, led, in 1855, to construction of a Gothic-style church two blocks east of Public Square on Superior Avenue. A brick chapel was erected south of this church in 1865.

The pyrotechnic and unusually named Philander Chase had established the Diocese of Ohio in 1818 as the first American Episcopal diocese outside the original thirteen colonies. Before he left Ohio to serve as a missionary in southern Michigan (going on to become bishop of Illinois), Chase established the seat of his diocese in the relatively central location of Gambier, Ohio. He also established an Episcopal college (Kenyon) and seminary (Bexley Hall) there. By 1867, Cleveland Episcopalians were agitating for a diocese of their own. In 1875, they were rewarded with the Diocese of Ohio. Forty-one southern Ohio counties became the Diocese of Southern Ohio at Cincinnati. Bishop Leonard's 1890 decision to establish an Episcopal cathedral in Cleveland more or less coincided with Trinity's decision to move out of downtown to Millionaire's Row on Euclid Avenue. Trinity acquired a large property east of 22nd Street between Prospect Avenue and Euclid. The parish offered its new upscale location and the prospect of a large new religious building to the bishop, and he took it. The Episcopalians, as was their custom, began to build slowly.

Over the last hundred years, the Trinity neighborhood has gone from great elegance, when the cathedral was built, to decrepitude and decadence in the middle of the twentieth century, to the present safety of being almost completely embraced by a growing, prosperous, upright, and secure Cleveland

State University. While Trinity may not always agree with all of the plans of its rapidly growing neighbor, it is now in an incomparably preferable situation to when it was the only economically viable institution of unquestioned probity in the neighborhood. For one hundred years, until the construction of its educational and administrative Trinity Commons in 2002, the cathedral was the newest building on the Episcopalians' lot. Mather House, Cathedral Hall, and the now destroyed ancillary building beside the cathedral were all built before the cathedral. This was much more obvious before the construction of Trinity Commons allowed the other structures to be either removed or refurbished. This center of Episcopalianism in northern Ohio has four elements—the 1901 cathedral in front of its Cathedral Hall built in 1895; the 2002 prize winning Trinity Commons that houses educational and administrative elements of the cathedral and the diocese; Mather House, formerly a retirement home for Episcopalians; and a large parking lot under which 114 environmental-award-winning four-hundred-foot-deep geothermal wells provide heat and cooling for the complex. Trinity Commons houses three cathedral-related shops on Euclid. Its Gallery at Trinity is in the restored Rorimer Brooks Company decorative arts studio. The Rorimer Brooks studio was important in the arts and crafts movement, and the ceiling and woodwork of the gallery are outstanding.

Cleveland architect Charles Schweinfurth, who designed the interior of the Old Stone Church and many of the mansions on Millionaire's Row, was commissioned to design the new cathedral. Although late Gothic Revival architects carefully studied European medieval architecture and attempted to give their buildings a more or less convincing medieval flavor, no one could (because of the expense, to say nothing of the building code), or really would want to, replicate a Gothic cathedral in downtown Cleveland. Nevertheless, a hundred years ago people strongly believed that some styles were more religious than others. Johannesen has described the belief of early twentieth-century architects that "a permanent expressive value had been embodied in the styles and forms of certain ages."[29] Trinity Cathedral was one of the first American late Gothic Revival buildings.[30] This style is different from early Gothic Revival buildings such as Patrick Keely's 1848 Cathedral of St. John the Evangelist (see p. 16) and its seemingly endless nineteenth-century Cleveland Roman Catholic successors. American late Gothic Revival made at least a gesture in the direction of archaeological authenticity. In the case of Trinity this was toward the English perpendicular style. Ralph Adams Cram, the tireless oracle of American Gothic Revival, thought English perpendicular was a particularly appropriate source of archaeologically correct revival church architecture (see also Cram's Church of the Transfiguration, p. 36, and Church of the Covenant, p. 52). Schweinfurth submitted plans for both a Romanesque and a Gothic structure. After much discussion, the leaders of the congregation selected the English Gothic-style alternative. Construction began in 1901, with the finished cathedral consecrated in 1907. Sixteen bishops attended Trinity's consecration and the service took so long that only the bishops, other clergy, and the cathedral chapter were offered Communion.

The exterior of the building is constructed of Indiana limestone laid in courses. Windows, doors, capitals, and gargoyles are Gothic. The clerestory, gable, baptistry, and tower windows are filled with cut-and-molded limestone tracery. The main entrance, from Euclid Avenue, is through three deeply recessed, molded, and carved arched openings. The plan is cruciform, with the Lady Chapel on the right and the original parish buildings on the left. The clergy room, sacristy, dean's room, chapter room, parish house, choir room, and Cathedral Hall, all older than the cathedral, connect to the newer structure along an aisle east of the choir. Although Charles Brush (inventor of the Brush arc lamp and a founder of General Electric) supervised the installation of the cathedral's electrical system in 1905, gaslight originally lit the building.

Trinity's great bell tower, supported in the interior by four cruciform pillars with ornately carved capitals, rises from the crossing of the nave and transepts. Inside the cathedral, this tower, forty-feet square, rising up 108 feet from the floor of the crossing, proves one of the most inspiring religious spaces in Cleveland. The large choir is as deep as the nave. The recent decision to replace the pews in the nave and transepts with movable chairs has made the relatively small worship area much more usable. With half of its sanctuary occupied by its large choir, together with the new altar at the crossing, this cathedral has only about half the seating that would be anticipated in such a large building, making it more of a shrine (to nineteenth-century northern Ohio affluence?) than a diocesan cathedral. With pews, the seating capacity was approximately eight hundred. With chairs, Trinity can seat only five hundred comfortably—seven hundred in a pinch.[31] When the pews were taken out, holes in the marble floor were filled with marble from the same quarry in Italy as the original.

One of the most sumptuously decorated religious buildings in Cleveland, Trinity serves as the Reformation's answer to St. Stephen (see p. 256). As Johannesen wrote, "All of the interior furnishings were executed in conformity with the design of the building. The altar and reredos, choir stalls, pulpit and lectern, executed in marble and wood, create a unity that gives a genuinely exalted character to the church, considered by many to be Schweinfurth's masterpiece."[32] The interior facings of the walls are of russet-colored, vitrified brick, perhaps a holdover from the original Romanesque design, with cut-and-molded limestone pillars, arches, and chiaroscuro carved trimmings. The spandrels of the arches of the nave and sanctuary are of heavily molded stone with panels formed by tracery moldings. The ceilings of the nave and transepts are plain, early Gothic barrel vaulting in English oak supported by heavily molded principal ribs springing from above each pillar and intersecting with the molded and carved ridge rib.

The church has more than 619 angels in its interior decorations, including one staring down at the bishop from the cover of his chair to ensure good behavior. The sanctuary ceiling is more elaborate in design than the ceiling in the nave.

At the south wall, the choir meets a rich, perpendicular, eighteen-foot-high altar screen based on that of Winchester Cathedral. With Christ at the center, the screen includes fifty-eight other carved figures—including Moses, David, Polycarp, and King Arthur. The freestanding altar beneath it was part of the original design. The elaborate choir stalls were carved in Oberammergau.

The splendid Pavonzano marble pulpit was carved in place and is so heavy that it immediately began to sink into the floor and is now supported on a foundation of its own, extending down through the undercroft. An immense eagle lectionary commands that side of the choir. Trinity has two Dutch tracker organs: a 1976 Flentrop choir organ and a 1977 Flentrop great organ, accessible by a marvelous, public curvilinear iron stair.[33] The cathedral is glazed with a sumptuous ensemble of glass by Willet, Connick, Tiffany, Heaton, Hardman, Burnham, and others.[34] Particularly notable are Burnham's fifteen nave and transept aisle windows of the life of Christ and of Mary and the west transept Hardman Nativity window. The Tiffany angel window in the sacristy was brought from the brick church on Superior. Trinity has a wonderful baptismal font with a carved canopy representing the cathedral tower in miniature.

The windows and altar of the Lady Chapel beside the choir are from the predecessor Trinity parish. The altarpiece is by Puccio di Simone, a fourteenth-century Florentine student of Bernardo Daddi. The comfortable and gracious wood-paneled chapter room is lined with portraits of the bishops of Ohio. The large Cathedral Hall houses a variety of competing activities, including many of the most ambitious cultural, social, educational, and administrative activities of the cathedral and the diocese. This is also the site of the cathedral's famous labyrinth for prayerful meditation and the cathedral's large feeding program for the needy who live beyond its Cleveland State buffer. A Chapel of Peace is located in the undercroft with a columbarium for ashes.

5. Zion Evangelical Lutheran Church (1902)
Architect: Frank Walker
Builder: Carl Manthey-Zorn
Location: 2062 East 30th Street

The Lutheran church in the United States is characterized by a good deal of coming and going and, in Cleveland, Zion Evangelical has frequently been in the lead of these movements.[35] The first Lutheran church in Cleveland is usually considered to have been Schifflein Christi, founded in 1834.[36] Nine years later, the more Lutheran, as different from the more reformed, Germans in

Schifflein Christi split off as Zion Lutheran. It was Zion Lutheran that would become known in Cleveland as the mother of Lutheran churches. Zion Lutheran was responsible for founding five other Missouri Synod churches in northeast Ohio. First it rented the Concert Hall on the third floor of a business building in what is now the Warehouse District. Then it built a frame church where Public Hall now stands on the mall. Later, it moved that church to lots across East Ninth Street from Progressive Field. There Zion Lutheran settled into a new school and church before moving out to East 30th Street at Prospect Avenue in 1902.

All this was part of the German invasion and fluorescence in Cleveland, which faded after 1914 (see Christ United Methodist Church [p. 263], Fellowship Missionary Baptist Church [originally Grace Lutheran Church; p. 82], Greater Friendship Baptist Church [originally First Evangelical and Reformed Church; p. 101], Immanuel Evangelical Lutheran Church [p. 234], St. John Nottingham Lutheran Church [p. 112], Liberty Hill Baptist Church [originally Euclid Avenue Temple; p. 34], St. Luke's United Church of Christ [p. 224], St. Michael Church [p. 231], Historic Saint Peter Roman Catholic Church [p. 18], St. Stephen Roman Catholic Church [p. 256], Temple Tifereth Israel [the Temple; p. 44], Trinity Evangelical Lutheran Church [p. 192], and Iglesia Emmanuel [originally Trinity United Church of Christ; p. 230]).

Zion Lutheran is important for two reasons in addition to its participation in the high tide and low ebb of *Germania* in Cleveland. First, on December 24, 1851, Heinrich Christian Schwan, the new pastor of Zion Lutheran, when it was where Public Hall now stands across the street from City Hall, walked into the nearby forest and chopped down a small evergreen. That afternoon, he and his wife decorated their tree with cookies, ribbons, nuts, candles, and a silver star he had brought over from Germany. After he read the Christmas story that night beside the blazing tree, he was almost run out of Cleveland for idolatry. However, the *Tannenbaum* tradition caught on and Zion Lutheran's was to be the first Christmas tree in a church in the United States.

Second, when the congregation was still in the Concert Hall, they held the first of a series of meetings that would ultimately lead to the organization, in Chicago in 1846, of the Lutheran Church-Missouri Synod. The Missouri Synod is the largest conservative Lutheran organization in the United States. In the nineteenth century its conservatism was associated with a dislike for the use of English that was creeping into the traditional Lutheran German liturgy. In terms of theology, the Missouri Synod opposes the union of Lutherans with Reformed (as in the union of the Schifflein Christi with the United Church of Christ). Heinrich Schwan moved on from his interest in Christmas trees to high office in the Missouri Synod, serving as synodical president for more than twenty years.

Zion Evangelical stands on the corner of Prospect Avenue at East 30th Street among the few remaining mansions and apartments that harken back to its neighborhood's more prosperous era. The neighborhood has been greatly improved by the destruction of the rowdy and disreputable Sterling Hotel across the street. This hotel served as the headquarters of the Cleveland mob during much of the twentieth century.

The church is a large brick building with clever pseudo-Gothic brick trim. It manages to be substantial without being overpowering. Masonry trim about the windows is handsome and discrete. An attractive, stylistically consistent rectory attaches to the southern part of the church. A handsome, if weathered, parochial school stands across a small lot farther to the south. The basic proportions of the front facade, although slightly more vertical, are similar to those of the Old Stone Church. Details such as rounded arches above some of the windows, corbel tables below the roofline on the west tower and below the belfry on the east tower, and the squared-off bell towers with pyramidal roofs are Romanesque. However, the main perpendicular-style windows with their tracery, the dormers at the top of the higher bell tower, and the pointed arches above the door are Gothic.

The 1,200-seat semicircular interior, with its spacious balcony, unexpectedly faces west (the entrance off Prospect is from the north). Worshipers thus face away from the large east window behind them on East 30th and toward an elaborate carved dark wood altar with four life-sized statues of Matthew, Mark, Luke, and John flanking Christ. The statues are white in contrast to the dark wood of the altar. It is said that the statues were originally polychromed but a previous pastor returned from his vacation to find them whitewashed. The statues and altar were brought from the second church, across from Progressive Field. Four columns, plain except for gilded Corinthian capitals, soar dramatically up to the plastered arches of the usual Victorian Revival Gothic vaulting. From the center vault hangs an immense French chandelier. This auditorium enjoys good sightlines and excellent acoustics, much better than the more traditional axial Missouri Synod church. An attractive moderately large rose on the south wall balances the large perpendicular windows on the north and east.

6. First Church, Cleveland,
(First United Methodist Church) (1904)
Architect: J. Milton Dyer
Builder: Charles Mitchell
Location: Euclid Avenue at East 30th Street

The great crossing of the First United Methodist Church, fifty-feet square and soaring one hundred feet into its tower, proves one of the most inspiring spaces in Cleveland.[37] It is a completely open space, without pillars or support other than the walls. The breathtaking grandeur of this huge vertical space, with its gilded decoration, is magnified by the seemingly endless sheets of glass in its twelve great lancet windows. Lower down, the sensation of almost incredible richness is amplified by both large figured windows in the shallow transepts and the great traceried north window. A strong curved dark wood balcony that hangs rather close to the floor enhances the power of the seemingly short nave before the crossing. The sense of width of the 1,200-seat space is intensified by the absence of a center aisle (two aisles divide the curved auditorium seating) and the sloped floor. The shallow apse is completely occupied by the choir, the pulpit, seating for the clergy, and a five thousand-pipe Casavant organ, the largest between New York and Chicago. The exterior of this building is almost exactly described by its interior. Once the interior is understood, it is found to be telegraphed by each of the carefully articulated masses of the Indiana limestone exterior. It is impossible to imagine a more straightforward building. What you see is what you get—there are no surprises. There is no religious hocus-pocus in this Methodist structure.

The detailing, consistent with its period, is perpendicular Gothic. Johannesen wrote, "It is difficult to avoid the suspicion that the new church was designed specifically to rival the Trinity Episcopal Cathedral that was rising just two blocks away. It is more than coincidence that the external profile of Dyer's church is almost a duplicate of Schweinfurth's cathedral, although the interior was planned as a preaching auditorium in contrast to a Eucharistic sanctuary. The exterior features the two buildings have in common are too obvious to ignore—the great square crossing tower with three lancets and corner pinnacles, the gabled facade with pinnacles, a traceried window, and a vestibule with three entrances, the transepts repeating the facade composition."[38] The church now seems out of place in the commercial district that surrounds it. The few remaining mansions and apartment buildings one block south along Prospect Avenue are more consistent with the character of this religious landmark.

Johannesen described J. Milton Dyer as "one of the most versatile and original architects in Cleveland" history.[39] After studying for five years at the École des Beaux-Arts, twice as long as the average American architect, Dyer only practiced actively for about ten years before World War I. In a burst of creativity, Dyer designed the protomodern Brown Hoisting Machinery Company (1902), the highly individual Brooklyn Savings and Loan Association (1904), the Northern Renaissance Tavern Club (1905), First Church (1905), the Wrightian Peerless Motor Car Company (1906) and the Sterling and Welch Company (1909), the exotic Cleveland Industrial Exposition Building (1909), the English manor Edmund Burke house (1910; now the Music School Settlement), the advanced Cleveland Athletic Club (1911), and the Beaux-Arts Cleveland City Hall (1916). Frank R. Walker and Harry E. Weeks worked in Dyer's office until personality problems appeared to end Dyer's career. Then, in 1940, Dyer unexpectedly returned at age seventy to give Cleveland its Coast Guard station, "the finest and 'most beautiful' in the nation."[40]

Early in the nineteenth century, a Bostonian who owned a piece of property on Public Square across the street from Old Stone Church, decided to give it to anyone willing to build a Methodist Church on his plot. The packet containing the deed was returned (apparently people knew what was in the envelope) because no one was interested enough to pay the twenty-five cents postage due.[41] By 1827, however, Methodist circuit riders had organized a society. There was finally enough enthusiasm to justify construction of a church in 1835 at East Third Street at St. Clair Avenue (in the middle of the present mall). The Methodist community sold this in the late 1860s and built again on the corner of East Ninth Street at Euclid Avenue. This was replaced in 1874 with a substantial neo-Gothic building, which, in turn, was sold to what has become the Ameritrust bank. The community moved out to East 30th Street at Euclid. The *Encyclopedia of Cleveland History* states, "Methodists in Cleveland have had neither the numbers nor the prominence they have enjoyed in other areas of the country."[42] Whether this is true or not, they have put up or purchased a remarkable number of religious landmarks in Cleveland.[43] The fifteen Methodist churches featured in this book are twice as many as those of any other Protestant denomination.

On November 8, 2009, the congregation of First Church voted to merge with Epworth-Euclid Methodist Church, at Epworth-Euclid, and name their newly combined congregation the University Circle United Methodist Church (see p. 47).

This building was then leased to Cleveland State University (CSU). CSU used the church's administrative spaces and classrooms to establish, in company with the Cleveland School District (the Cleveland public schools), the Campus International School. The Campus International School opened early primary grades in the fall of 2010. The sanctuary, with its magnificent organ, became the temporary home of the Euclid Avenue Congregational Church after fire destroyed that church in March 2010.

7. Conversion of St. Paul Shrine, originally St. Paul's Episcopal Church, see p. 329 (1875)
Architect: Gordon W. Lloyd
Builder: Frederick Brooks
Location: 4120 Euclid Avenue

As the government pours millions into the resuscitation of Euclid Avenue, it is tempting to pass by the last half of the biphasic history of this building and concentrate on the first half when, as St. Paul's Episcopal Church, it stood in the center of Millionaire's Row, the "most beautiful street in the world" and was the site of two weddings attended by presidents of the United States.[44] St. Paul, however, was an Episcopal parish for fewer than fifty-five years. It has been a Roman

Catholic institution for more than eighty years. When Episcopal Bishop William Leonard signed over the property to Catholic Bishop Joseph Schrembs in 1930, he is reported to have said, "All Gaul is divided into three parts and Schrembs has all three."[45]

Roman Catholic occupation of the building, so unlike what the Episcopalians were doing, has been important for three reasons. First, it established a community of cloistered nuns to perpetually adore the Blessed Sacrament. Second, it established a community of friars to minister to the part of Cleveland most people were fleeing. Third, it beautifully maintained this historic building. The principal mission of the Franciscan Poor Clares of Perpetual Adoration is to pray before the exposed Sacrament twenty-four hours a day. At least one of them has been doing this, behind a screen at the front of the church, since 1931. Ten years before, Bishop Schrembs had invited two sisters to establish themselves in a small house in University Circle. The bishop purchased St. Paul to accommodate the growing community. More recently, in 1978, Archbishop James Hickey asked the Capuchin Friars of Pittsburgh to help with the shrine. From their friary in the old rectory beside the church, the brothers tend to the spiritual needs of the shrine, including—in addition to those of the nuns—the needs of lay members of the parish established at St. Paul together with a large ministry of Reconciliation. (The Capuchin friars hear confessions from downtown and inner-city walk-ins.) Over the years, the brothers have also provided pastoral assistance to inner-city institutions such as the cathedral, St. Thomas Aquinas, St. Philip Neri, and Holy Trinity-St. Edward. As they have meticulously maintained their Victorian Gothic extravaganza, the communities have made relatively few changes to the building. A large but unobtrusive convent for the nuns attaches to the south side of the building, away from Euclid Avenue. A screened area to the left of the altar, surmounted by more than fifty praying angels, allows the cloistered community to participate in public ceremonies and a matching screen at the altar allows nuns behind the altar to pray before the Sacrament in privacy. The dark wood screens and confessionals are consistent with the original church furnishings. Two large windows on either side of the sanctuary have been replaced with Zettler glass illustrating the mission of the shrine. The other windows date from 1875. The Sacred Host is exposed in an elaborate monstrance on the Altar of Repose. This altar is under a gold canopy decorated with cherubim. All this manages to remain consistent with the original dark church furnishings. In the back of the nave are modern paintings by Sister Mary Thomas, one of the cloistered nuns.

This Berea sandstone, rock-finished, inventive Victorian Gothic structure was "the largest and most imposing in the city" when it opened in 1876.[46] The stone base of the church is coursed, and upper areas are randomly coursed. Designed to hold nearly one thousand worshipers, St. Paul Shrine follows the then fashionable asymmetrical style of Victorian English country Gothic architecture. The architect, Gordon W. Lloyd of Detroit, was popular with vestries of Episcopal churches and cathedrals in Michigan, Ohio, and Pennsylvania. The church is cruciform in plan. The "unique" 120-foot octagonal louvered tower is supported by four slender and exaggerated turrets with crocketed pinnacles.[47] Carved porches project over west- and north-facing stoops.

The squarish proportions of the aisled nave in front of the generous balcony appear low. The open, decorated wood trusses create the general effect of an overgrown English parish church. The hammerhead, mahogany-beamed ceiling rises above the nave supported by a series of columns and gothic arches decorated in gold leaf and period colors. The chancel, with its low-church centralized "holy table," was at first only distinguished from the nave by a pointed arch and the fact that it was elevated a foot above the nave floor. A "high church" renovation in 1909 elevated the chancel another two feet and installed a marble altar.[48] The beam and panel ceiling is complemented by the walnut pews. The floor is white and light-colored limestone terrazzo with orange and dark gray to black limestone terrazzo trim.

St. Paul's Episcopal Church, established by the second bishop of Ohio in 1846, became part of the "smells and bells" controversy that preoccupied the Episcopal Church in the nineteenth century. The Oxford movement, which promoted a more "Roman" sacramental style of worship, had swept up Trinity, Cleveland's first Episcopal parish. The bishop, "obsessed with the dangers of ritualism," established St. Paul's as a low-church antidote despite the strident protests of the Trinity people, who viewed the new parish as intruding on their territory and poaching their parishioners.[49] With the bishop's support, the little congregation built a small frame church that was torched ten days before completion, probably by people from Trinity. Bad feelings between the two parishes would continue until Trinity ultimately prevailed with its designation as the cathedral (see p. 21) and St. Paul's retreated to Cleveland Heights (see p. 329). After the fire, St. Paul's regrouped, with Presbyterian and Baptist support, and constructed a splendid brick building with a 161-foot spire that became a Cleveland landmark. Led by the dynamic Frederick Brooks, brother of Episcopal saint and Massachusetts Bishop Phillips Brooks, St. Paul's marched out to Millionaire's Row, leaving Trinity far behind in membership and resources. At that time Cleveland was so prosperous that the vestry sold the lot under the old church downtown for enough to construct all of this building. When Elizabeth Sherman, niece of both William Tecumseh Sherman and Senator John Sherman ("the Ohio icicle"), married Senator Donald Cameron of Pennsylvania at St. Paul's, there were so many military and naval officers in attendance that the government had to anchor a cruiser off Cleveland to put them up because the hotels were full. A changing neighborhood and a bad rector, however, ended this success. The parish was lucky that there was enough to pick up and take on the move out to Cleveland Heights.

On March 15, 2009, Bishop Richard Lennon announced the closing of the parish associated with the Conversion of St. Paul Shrine. The monastery of the Poor Clares and the friary of the Capuchins will continue at St. Paul Shrine.

The bishop hopes that the lay parishioners will transfer their allegiance to the cathedral. The Capuchins will continue saying Mass and hearing confessions although they will no longer marry or bury parishioners or otherwise conduct the Shrine as an organized parish.

8. St. Timothy Missionary Baptist Church, originally First United Presbyterian Church (1891)
Architect: Sidney R. Badgley
Builder: Unknown
Location: 7101 Carnegie Avenue

St. Timothy Missionary Baptist Church was organized at a "musical tea" in 1940 by former members of the Messiah Baptist Church.[50] Calling Henry Lyons as Pastor, the congregation met in homes, in the Sardis Baptist Church, in the Cedar YMCA, and on the third floor of Friendship Baptist Church (Temple Tifereth Israel; see p. 130) before purchasing their present building in 1943. Following Lyons's death, the rapidly growing community called upon John Weeden from Indianapolis, and he served forty-one years until his death in 1988. For twenty years, Tyree Williams led this remarkably stable and energetic congregation until his death in 2011.

The First United Presbyterian Church (as distinct from the First Presbyterian, or the Old Stone Church; see p. 12) was founded by the Rev. J. W. Logue in 1843 as part of the Northfield Association of Presbyterian Churches. These Presbyterians, known as "the UPs,"[51] were theologically and socially conservative, of unquestioned Scots heritage, and most common in western Pennsylvania and eastern Ohio. The congregation built two churches downtown: Michigan Avenue at Seneca Street (the site is now buried under Tower City Center) and then on Prospect Avenue at East Ninth Street. They built this third church on Carnegie Avenue in 1891. After selling this building, the congregation moved to a location across the street from Cleveland Heights High School. This fourth building was acquired by the Heights Youth Club in the first decade of the twenty-first century as the "UPs" faded into the greater world of Presbyterianism.

This landmark, so well known to Clevelanders driving downtown from the East Side, is much larger than it appears from a hurried glance driving down Carnegie. The large stone building extends north of the main thoroughfare. Tower, chimneys, and gables are of solid masonry. A commercial building to the north is attached to the church with a second story clear-glazed walkway designed to allow the north rose of the church to continue to be seen from the street. The resulting religious complex is surrounded by large parking lots, the former site of the parsonage to the east and, across East 71st Street to the west, the former site of Horn Auto Body, another Cleveland landmark before its destruction in a spectacular fire in 2004. Although not as robust as Badgley's Pilgrim Congregational Church (see p. 202), the coarsed ashlar stonework, broad roof planes and gables, and deep-set window and door openings were obviously influenced by Boston architect Henry Hobson Richardson's Romanesque.

St. Timothy is another church like North Presbyterian (see p. 74) and Holy Rosary (see p. 59) where the main worship space is elevated high above the street, allowing generous natural lighting to the ground floor. As at North Presbyterian, the stairs inside the street entrance are divided left and right and rise to two small anterooms that open into a large rectangular auditorium. Badgley designed semicircular seating. St. Timothy's growing congregation required that seating be reorganized in an axial pattern with narrow central and side aisles and long pews. It has a beautiful dark wood, timbered ceiling. An arch with two Corinthian columns rises at the front. The elevated stage is brought out laterally on both sides to accommodate the music program. The quite unusual, early twentieth-century glass is well maintained. The glazing is nonfigurative. Relatively large, palm-sized pieces of colorful glass are leaded into simple floral patterns in the side windows and the large north and south roses.

9. Calvary Presbyterian Church (1887)
Architect: Charles Schweinfurth
Builder: Hiram Haydn
Location: Euclid Avenue at East 79th Street

Calvary Church, established to keep up with Presbyterian flight from the inner city, has itself been struggling for almost one hundred years with Presbyterian flight from it.[52] Hiram Haydn, pastor of the Old Stone Church, founded the Calvary Mission and Sunday school in an abandoned chapel at East 75th Street in the late 1870s. For the next twenty years Calvary was staffed by clergy from Old Stone. Referred to as the Calvary Chapel of the Old Stone Church, the frame building was moved in the middle of the night by horse-drawn wagon to this East 79th Street site in 1880. The move coincided with Haydn's departure from Old Stone for four years to become secretary of the American Board of Commissioners for Foreign Missions of the Congregational Church. In his absence,

Calvary built and dedicated the imposing Gothic Revival stone chapel that is now located south of the present church. The original wooden building was used as a Sunday school until an annex was added to the stone chapel. In 1884, Old Stone was gutted by fire. Haydn returned to Cleveland to rebuild somewhere. Old Stone debated whether to stay on Public Square or follow its congregation eastward up Euclid Avenue. In the end, a decision was made to rebuild on Public Square. Three years later Charles Schweinfurth, the architect who rebuilt the Old Stone Church after the fire, began construction of the equally imposing Calvary building, still a "chapel" of Old Stone.[53] After the present church was built, the congregation remained part of Old Stone Church with clergy commuting from Public Square until 1892, when Calvary was finally organized as an independent Presbyterian church.

By the turn of the century, Calvary had grown to more than six hundred members, many deeply committed to foreign missionary work. Then, before the First World War, the neighborhood began to change. The large comfortable homes of the nineteenth century gave way to a population living in working-class apartment houses. The church adapted from serving an upper-class community to serving a community where people worked with their hands. The 1923 merger with the Bolton Avenue Presbyterian Church on East 89th Street at Cedar Avenue expedited this transition (see Antioch Baptist Church, p. 138). Calvary also continued to serve a substantial suburban population. Congregants came from places as distant as Lakewood until well after the Second World War. The creation of a strong working-class congregation focused Calvary, during the 1930s and 1940s, on serving its immediate community. Calvary would be involved again, in the 1970s and 1980s, in efforts to improve its Euclid Avenue neighborhood.

The immensity of this massive neo-Romanesque presence in the newly refurbished Euclid Corridor is more obvious from off the main street, to the east or west, than from Euclid. A significant part of the bulk of the building is the original chapel to the south of the sanctuary. This giant chapel became a parish hall. A new ceiling reduced the height of the main area by half. In an interesting innovation, Calvary became the first church in Cleveland with a gym. In the sanctuary, John Severence donated the organ.

Calvary is a fine example of late Victorian Romanesque Revival architecture, especially considering its rock-faced coarse finish set in an asymmetrical pattern, its large front and side gables pierced by deep-set, rounded stained-glass windows, its wide arch over the entranceway, and its squared-off bell towers crowned by battlements. The church was not far from Schweinfurth's own proto-modernist house located on East 75th Street just south of Euclid Avenue.

The beautiful wood sanctuary with its monumental windows, great beamed ceiling, and wonderful original Tiffany light fixtures was carefully restored in 1985. Because founding minister and architect were both associated with the Old Stone Church, it is not surprising that the churches' interiors are similar. "On the interior of Calvary," Johannesen wrote, the scheme used in Old Stone was elaborated further by Schweinfurth. Each set of arches is supported by slender clustered columns making a traditional three-aisled division of the nave, although the seating is arranged in the curved auditorium fashion. The effect of these two interiors is to create an increasingly light and airy atmosphere that belies the fortress-like character of the massive exterior walls, towers, and Romanesque arches. In this respect, the new eclecticism of the period, achieved by combining different styles and spatial effects, was expressed in the churches as well as the homes of Euclid Avenue.[54]

10. Liberty Hill Baptist Church, originally Euclid Avenue Temple (see also Fairmount Temple [Anshe Chesed], p. 350) (1912; 1923)
Architects: E. W. Willingale of Lehman and Schmidt (1912); Joseph Weinberg (1923)
Builder: Louis Wolsey
Location: 8206 Euclid Avenue

A succession of dynamic clerical leaders have led Liberty Hill Baptist Church from the home of a congregant in 1917 to, almost a century later, the grandeur of its current surroundings.[55] The congregation's first permanent home was the Kinsman Congregational Church, first rented and then purchased in 1919. Over the next six years, the congregation paid off its debt and increased from forty to four hundred. Under the Reverend M. F. Washington of Birmingham, Alabama, Liberty Hill purchased the seventy thousand dollar German Missionary Society building, also on Kinsman Road, in 1929 and proceeded to grow out of that, increasing membership from 450 to 2,200. After several years spent looking for adequate space, the Liberty Hill trustees finally reached an agreement with Rabbi Barnett Brickner to purchase the Euclid Avenue Temple for $250,000 (its original cost). Liberty Hill moved in after spending another $90,000 to adapt the building to Baptist worship. This church has the significant array of programs that one would expect from such a large congregation. Of particular note, however, is its participation in the Church Square Apartments on Carnegie Avenue for the physically impaired and the Church Square Shopping Center, twenty businesses directly across Euclid Avenue from the church. The giant church auditorium, christened the Liberty Hill Performing Arts Center has, over the years, hosted the Ohio Chamber Orchestra, the Morehouse College Glee Club, and performers such as Lionel Hampton.

Although the Euclid Avenue Temple would become known as "Brickner's Temple" to distinguish it from "Silver's Temple," the other prominent Reform temple in Cleveland (see Temple Tifereth Israel, p. 44), Louis Wolsey planned and built this building. Wolsey had become rabbi of Anshe Chesed in 1907—a low point in its fortunes. The oldest Jewish congregation in Cleveland had by that time dwindled to 186 members in their (now destroyed) 1,500-seat neo-Romanesque building on Scovill Avenue. During his eighteen-year rabbinate, Wolsey increased membership from 186 to 1,300. Five years after his appointment, a reinvigorated Anshe Chesed stormed out here. Ten years later, with their children crammed into the basement school of their relatively new building, the congregation dedicated the immense adjoining Temple House with its giant supplemental auditorium. When he moved to Cleveland, Wolsey taught a conservative view of Reform Judaism. During his first ten years of tenure Wolsey was frequently at odds with the more liberal "Classical Reform" of Moses Gries at Tifereth Israel. After Gries's death, however, Wolsey would lead Anshe Chesed so far that, when Wolsey left Cleveland for a temple in Philadelphia, Anshe Chesed had become one of the major reform temples in the United States. Wolsey was succeeded by Barnett Brickner, who planned the move of Anshe Chesed to the suburbs (see Fairmount Temple, p. 350).

Liberty Hill is one of the five large religious buildings (True Holiness Temple; Calvary Presbyterian Church, p. 32; Anglican Church of the Transfiguration, p. 36; and East Mt. Zion Baptist Church) clustered along eleven blocks on the north side of Euclid between East 77th Street and East 100th Street. In the shadow of the Cleveland Clinic, it remains to be seen whether the development of the Euclid Corridor at their front doors will mean their revival or their extinction.

There are about as many descriptions of the style of the Euclid Avenue Temple as there are describers—Byzantine, Moorish, even Romanesque. Moorish Revival temple architecture in the United States derived from the 1853 Leopoldstädter Tempel in Vienna. Later, Hitler destroyed all examples of similar architecture in Germany. The first Moorish Revival temple in the United States, significant for Euclid Temple's Reform roots, was the Plum Street (now Isaac M. Wise) Temple in Cincinnati. The roughness and irregularity of this building's extraordinary brick work stimulate the eye and make the great massive surfaces on the temple's exterior come alive with color. At construction, the brickwork was described as "Oriental tapestry" or "rainbow brick" because the many shades of red were laid as they came to the site. The rich tone coloring results from the slightly different brick reflecting the sunlight in different ways. The rough bricks, furthermore, were laid with rough, thick mortar to produce a "mosaic-like" effect. Arcaded windows are Romanesque-style, trimmed with burned terra-cotta and pink marble. Huge piers at the corners of the building authenticate the size of the dome and reflect the way it is supported.

This is a big building. The original 1912 building has twenty-six classrooms, twelve bathrooms, and six showers with a mezzanine and second and third floors. In the front of the temple is a long vestibule. At each end, staircases lead up into the gallery. An elevator goes from the basement to the second floor.

The giant 1923 Temple House is attached to the back of the original building. When the immense 1,400-seat (now 1,200) Temple House auditorium was completed, it was, reportedly, the largest Jewish space in Cleveland. (This was in addition to the thousand-seat main auditorium in the original building.) Temple House also includes recreational space, twenty-eight classrooms, a library, an assembly hall, the school office, and a kitchen.

The main auditorium, with one thousand individual seats arranged in a semicircular pattern, has a canted floor. The massive ornamental coffered dome has been repainted by the Baptist congregation. Original light fixtures are identified by their Star of David. The choir and organ loft are behind the pulpit. This main auditorium originally included a fifty-five-stop Moeller Organ, the second-largest pipe organ in Cleveland. Richly carved oak woodwork and paneling decorate the front of the sanctuary. The original ark, composed of Hunterville marble inlaid with Tiffany glass mosaics, was renovated in 1997. The Baptist congregation installed a baptistry on the second floor in the front of the sanctuary.

Half of the famous windows were given in memory of members of the Halle family. Conceived by Wolsey and designed and executed by Tiffany, they represent Jewish history with words and symbols (following the Jewish tradition of refraining from the use of human figures in a house of worship). The windows were left behind when Anshe Chesed moved to Fairmount. The Jewish congregation's prolific architect, Percival Goodman, was famous for incorporating modern art into his buildings and he did so on Fairmount. In Goodman's high modern imagination, however, there was no place for Tiffany windows. The windows have been carefully protected by their current owners.

11. Anglican Church of the Transfiguration, originally Emmanuel Episcopal Church (1902)
Architects: Ralph Adams Cram and Bertram Goodhue
Builder: Wilson Stearly
Location: 8604 Euclid Avenue

One hundred years after its design and partial construction by America's premier Gothic Revival architects, in a burst of enthusiasm and optimism at the beginning of the twentieth century, this building is now largely abandoned.[56] Emmanuel Episcopal's famous neighborhood food distribution center no longer exists.

Frederick Brooks established Emmanuel as a mission of St. Paul's Episcopal Church (see pp. 28 and 329). St. Paul's, as a memorial to Brooks following his tragic death in 1874, continued to support the parish after Emmanuel became independent in 1876. Brook's original frame Gothic-style building was enlarged and moved slightly west to the present site in 1880. Despite religious disputes within the congregation that eventually resulted in the formation of a second Episcopal parish, the Emmanuel congregation continued to grow. It established a new parish school in 1890 and built a chapel in 1892.

Wilson Stearly, rector from 1899 to 1909, conceived of the present building as the major Episcopal landmark of upper Euclid Avenue. This was at a time when the parish of St. Paul's was leapfrogging into Cleveland Heights from East 40th Street at Euclid Avenue and when Trinity Parish (see p. 21) was inventing itself as the Episcopal Cathedral at East 22nd Street at Euclid. Before leaving Cleveland to become bishop of Newark, Stearly summoned from Boston the Anglo-Catholic grandmasters of collegiate Gothic—Ivanhoe's answer to Frank Lloyd Wright—Ralph Adams Cram and Bertram Goodhue. They never finished the building, although the original six bays of the nave and a temporary chapel were completed in 1902. The remaining two bays and the interior of the church were finished in 1904. The bell tower, more than a century later, remains to be completed. Emmanuel-Transfiguration is interesting because it serves as an architectural parallel to the Cleveland Museum of Art's unfinished *The Sacrifice of Isaac* by Andrea del Sarto. Like the del Sarto painting, the structure of Emmanuel-Transfiguration is complete. The trimming is missing.

The Boston Gothic Revival junta believed that decoration constituted an important part of building, and, thus, they spent a lot of time, effort, and other people's money in designing derivative decorative doodads for their buildings. This was greatly disparaged by the modernists. Adolf Loos would say, "Ornament is Crime."[57] As waves of destructive iconoclasm have demonstrated, great historic buildings do prevail despite (or to some sensibilities, because of) the absence of their decoration; however, this does not seem to be the case in revival buildings. Without glass and without furniture, it is difficult for the Boston architects' bare bones to exert their intended effect. Without decoration, Emmanuel-Transfiguration is not an undecorated Gothic Revival building, it remains an uncompleted church.[58]

The ordination of homosexual Eugene Robinson in 2003 as Episcopal bishop of New Hampshire caused—what St. Ambrose would have called—a major tumult. Some conservative parishes withdrew from the Episcopal Church. Five parishes in the Diocese of Ohio, including Emmanuel-Transfiguration, took this as an opportunity to join the Anglican Diocese of Bolivia and, in 2008, move to the Convocation of Anglicans in North America, a mission of the Anglican Church of Nigeria. Four of the dissident parishes departed because of differences concerning doctrine, including the sexuality of priests. Emmanuel-Transfiguration, however, left not because of differences concerning belief or practice but because the bishop of Ohio had decided to close the parish because the building was falling down. In the Episcopal Church, the diocese, not the parish, holds title to the real estate. Emmanuel-Transfiguration and the diocese were at odds concerning whether the city had or had not condemned the building (in the nave, the second pillar on the left is severely cracked and has shifted on its foundation). Beneath the rhetoric about saving the church lay a traditional real-estate dispute about which party might profit from sale of the property to the adjacent Cleveland Clinic. Over the years, the diocese had invested substantial resources in attempts to keep this struggling parish afloat while, over those same years, members of this parish had also invested substantial resources in their attempts to do the same. On April 15, 2011, Judge Denna Calabrese of the Cuyahoga County Court of Common Pleas ruled in favor of the diocese that has put up the building for sale.

For two reasons, Emmanuel-Transfiguration is the least conspicuous of the great religious institutions lining the south side of upper Euclid Avenue. In the first place, one hundred years of pollution have so stained its masonry that the building melds into its unprepossessing surroundings. The glory of Gothic revival is difficult to appreciate through the environmental contamination. Second—as a major Cleveland religious landmark—Emmanuel-Transfiguration remains unique due to the absence of its tower. Those who would disparage the importance of a tower on a Christian religious building as an unnecessary economic extravagance, at odds with the humble message of Christ, should examine Emmanuel-Transfiguration.[59]

Inside, this is a large, almost empty, sanctuary. Although the gate into the chancel is elaborate, the altar is simple. A limited amount of carving decorates the choir stalls and the organ case. The organ no longer functions. The windows are plain except for a small window over the baptistry. One of the pillars, as noted above, is severely damaged. Whatever happens to this institution, it remains a monument to Christian fortitude and economic sacrifice.

12. Euclid Avenue Congregational Church (1887)

Architects: Forest Coburn and Frank Barnum
Builder: Henry Ladd
Location: 9606 Euclid Avenue

In 1828, the widowed Sarah Cozad Mather and her three children tried to live quietly in her little brick house on the road to Buffalo (Euclid Avenue), then in the midst of the forest.[60] Unbroken woods stretched north to Lake Erie and south to the foothills of the Alleghenies. The sublimity of the wilderness immediately to the west, however, was noisily interrupted by the raucous carryings on of teamsters overnighting at the neighboring tavern and hotel established by Nathaniel Doan. Mrs. Mather felt the need to establish a Sunday school. When, two years later, she moved to Bath Township to marry Jonathan Hale and raise her children and his five on his farm, neighbors took over the school. Its neighbors—the Fords, the Cozads, and the Posts—would keep the institution alive until it would finally flower sixty years later, after many tribulations, as one of the great foundations of Cleveland. The leadership of the Ford family in this institution for five generations, originally from their 1841 farm on the site of University Hospitals, is unparalleled in Cleveland church history.

Reformed congregations (see the Old Stone Church, p. 12) do not go in for hurriedly constructed flimsy frame churches and, after renting around Doan's Corners, the community began building a brick building as their first church in 1846 on the northwest corner of Euclid at Doan (105th).[61] On moving in, they described themselves as "the First Presbyterian Church and Society of East Cleveland."[62] Six years later, led by Horace Ford, the congregation pulled out of the Presbytery in opposition to slavery and became an Independent Presbyterian Church. A decade later, as Cleveland expanded during the Civil War, the frontier settlement of Doan's Corners rapidly became part of the metropolitan area, and, in 1866, the community moved into a new church at its present location. In the second year of the Civil War the congregation had become "the First Congregational Church of East Cleveland," and Congregational it remained thereafter. It is unclear whether this second building, of which only one photograph has survived, was poorly designed or never completed or both. Heating, for example, consisted of wood-burning box stoves in the basement. Such heat as they produced circulated into the main worship space through cracks in the floor, an arrangement that even then was considered primitive. Despite their unpromising surroundings, the congregation thrived, attracting such prominent neighbors as Liberty Holden, publisher of the *Plain Dealer*. When the congregation moved into the 1887 building, Liberty Holden's paper described the structure as "handsome, homelike and attractive."[63] Johannesen writes of Coburn and Barnum as "one of the two or three architectural firms that dominated" the 1880s in Cleveland.[64] At the end of the twentieth century, Euclid Avenue Congregational was one of their few surviving important buildings.[65] After Coburn's death, Barnum became superintendent of buildings for the Cleveland Board of Education. In this capacity, following the death of 172 children in the North Collinwood School fire, he revolutionized American school construction in eighty-six fireproof schools.

Between 1901 and 1902 Herbert Briggs, an architect in Barnum's office, built a three-story "education wing" as a seamless addition to the south end of the church. In addition to a dining room, classrooms, parlors, the pastor's study, a library, and an auditorium, there was a drill room for boys in the basement next to an armory lined with gun cases.[66] Euclid Avenue Congregational continued to outgrow its building and established five satellites—East Madison Congregational, Hough Avenue Congregational, Park Congregational, Lake View Congregational (originally in Little Italy[67]),and the "Reservoir Mission."

By the early part of the twentieth century, Doan's Corners had become a now hard-to-imagine "second downtown" for Cleveland, an affluent entertainment district of residential hotels, theaters, and restaurants. As a schoolboy, Bob Hope lived in this neighborhood while his stonemason father worked on the Church of the Covenant (see p. 52). Doan's Corners was devastated by the Great Depression. By the mid-1930s it had become a neighborhood of gas stations, boarding houses, used-car lots, and auto-repair shops. Hathaway Brown School and Laurel School, both once across the street from Euclid Congregational, had moved to Shaker Heights. A bowling alley stood next door to the church. Ferdinand Blanchard, pastor from 1915 to 1950, saw these changes in the neighborhood. Before Blanchard, Euclid Congregational's pulpit had been a revolving door. The congregation's major challenge in the nineteenth century was the abrupt departure, for one reason or another, of clerical leadership. Blanchard changed this. He saw his institution as the Congregational Church's downtown equivalent of First Presbyterian (Old Stone), First Methodist, Trinity, and St. John Cathedrals. From time to time he exchanged pulpits with his friend Barnett Brickner at Euclid Avenue Temple down the street.[68] A major voice in Cleveland, Blanchard rose outside the city to the position of moderator of the General Council of Congregational Christian Churches in the United States and would play a leading role in his denomination's 1957 union with the Evangelical and Reformed Church to form the United Church of Christ (UCC).

Euclid Congregational's struggle to maintain a voice in the city of Cleveland is recounted by Miller.[69] In no other book is the passion of a great Cleveland church, its internal and external struggles, described so eloquently and frankly. Many of the religious institutions in Cleveland have suffered the ordeal of neighborhood transformation. Only that of Euclid Avenue Congregational is so well documented. Miller tells in detail the story of the changing neighborhood and the tantalizing chimera of the University-Euclid urban renewal project that was sacrificed to the ill-fated Erieview project farther downtown. She recounts the church's attempt to reach out to its new community. There was the Congregational Church in Cleveland's "pilot project." There was Euclid Congregational's Hough House community center. There was the Hitchcock House treatment center for addicted women at Euclid Congregational for two years before it moved to St. Mary Seminary on Ansel Road (see p. 88). All this took place, while members voted down an attractive proposal to move to Pepper Pike.

Calvinist churches commonly make up for their lack of paintings and statues with their music. This has been the case at Euclid Congregational since Jarvis Hanks offended the Methodists at Doan's Corners by playing his violin at Congregational services in their borrowed building. Vincent Percy, concurrently organist of Public Auditorium (1922–61) and the Cleveland Orchestra (1922–46), served at Euclid Congregational for forty-six years (1919–65). If he did not like the way his choir was singing, "he would crank up the [organ] volume . . . to drown them out."[70] He knew how to work space. When his choir performed in Municipal Stadium, other church choirs could not sing loud enough to be heard well in the massive, open area; however, Euclid Congregational had prerecorded its offering and, as it played through the audio system, the Euclid

Congregational choir lip-synched. In the realm of music, the church was fortunate in its instruments: a 3,505-pipe Austin that, on its installation in 1920, was "one of the best church organs in the country,"[71] and its replacement—the giant Ford Memorial tracker organ—installed by Karl Wilhelm in 1981.

Although much larger than it appeared from the street, this Romanesque-style Amherst sandstone building was an exceptionally compact, rectangular block of masonry, particularly when seen from the east. This was a building all of one piece. The rough masonry surfaces were clearly and cleanly conceived. Windows were regularly spaced. Parts of this building did not wander off as in most religious structures. The entrance was between two imposing square towers capped by pyramidal roofs.

The inside featured a lofty, light and open, almost square auditorium-style sanctuary. Seating was semicircular. The trim was oak with a timber ceiling. A massive semicircular wraparound balcony dominated the back of the sanctuary. There was some carved ornament on the ceiling beams and wonderful plaster capitals on the columns in the front of the sanctuary, but this was a Reformed church with a minimum of decoration. The plain walls were plastered. In front, the massive Ford tracker organ, rising toward the ceiling, dominated a simple dark wood choir. Beautiful nineteenth-century windows featured Congregational saints, and there was a great north window of opalescent glass. One found generous administrative and educational rooms behind the sanctuary in space designed to appear incorporated within the main block of the building.

Before dawn on March 23, 2010, fire destroyed the Euclid Avenue Congregational Church and its precious organ. As the congregation tried to decide what to do next, the Methodists invited them to meet in the vacant sanctuary of First Church (see p. 26).

13. Uqbah Mosque Foundation
(1999)
Architect: Mohamed Barak
Builder: Ramez Al Islambouli
Location: 2222 Stokes Boulevard

Because of its location, beside the major pathway between University Circle and the eastern suburbs, the Uqbah Mosque is the best known of the more than fifteen mosques in Greater Cleveland.[72] Because of its leadership, which has always been based in the academic environment of Case Western Reserve University, Masjid Uqbah is also the most accessible Islamic community to other religious traditions.

Uqbah Mosque began as a student organization at CWRU in the early 1980s,[73] the Cleveland branch of the national Muslim Student Association (MSA). The Malaysian Islamic Study Group and the Muslim Arab Youth Association played major roles in the original organization, many of whose members had been active in overseas revivalist Islamic groups such as the Muslim Brotherhood in Egypt, Algeria's *Front Islamique du Salut,* and Tunisia's *En-Nahda.* The students began to hold Friday prayers in a variety of campus locations, finally settling into a consistent weekly worship and Islamic education program in the University Student Center. In 1987–88, the students bought the flower shop below the Fairhill Road Baldwin Reservoir for the MSA Mosque as the organization broadened its focus to include Cleveland State, Cuyahoga Community College, and the Islamic community in general. The North American Islamic Trust (NAIT) holds the title to the property.[74]

By the early 1990s, this mosque was no longer a student organization. It had become a community institution. Renamed the Uqbah Mosque Foundation, under the leadership of President and Imam Ramez Al Islambouli and with substantial financial help from the United Arab Emirates, the community acquired an adjacent building and merged and rebuilt the two buildings into the present structure. About half of the congregation it serves are—or were—associated with the academic community. The other half are local orthodox African American Muslims.[75]

The mosque shares a largely abandoned neighborhood along Petrarca Road with the church of the tiny former Italian parish of St. Marian, established from 1905 to 1975 by immigrants from the little town of Rionero Sannitico in Campobasso Province.[76] Uqbah Mosque is identified as an Islamic religious building by its minaret, topped with a large stylized crescent, and the blue trim of the doors and windows. Exterior walls are of rough ivory stucco. This is a Sunni mosque with separate entrances for men and women. The women's entrance leads to a second floor nursery and women's prayer quarter, linked to the downstairs by television. The men's entrance leads to a foyer with offices, a small library, bookstore, a room for prayer with moderately large skylights, and a large community room for the food and clothing distributions of the foundation. All this is simple and without decoration but well maintained and meticulously kept.

14. Pentecostal Church of Christ, originally Fourth Church of Christ, Scientist (1918)
Architects: Briggs and Nelson
Builder: Unknown
Location: 10515 Chester Avenue

Pentecostalism is a Christian religious movement that puts special emphasis on the direct personal experience of God through the Holy Spirit.[77] Worship is spontaneous, demonstrative, and energetic. Pentecostalism includes many different organizations and viewpoints and encompasses almost a quarter of the world's two billion Christians. The Pentecostal Church of Christ is the oldest Pentecostal congregation in Cleveland and the "mother church" of "apostolic assemblies" in Cuyahoga County. Its senior pastor, Bishop J. Delano Ellis, formerly served as head of the United Pentecostal Churches of Christ and continues to direct the Joint College of African American Pentecostal Bishops, an educational institution.

Dr. Chelcie France organized the Pentecostal Church of Christ ("the PCC") in 1935 in his mother's house. It was active at several locations on the east side of Cleveland until 1980 when it purchased its current building. Bishop Ellis has directed the congregation since 1989. In 1994 he purchased the Park Chester office building, located to the east of the church. It was formerly the physicians' offices of Women's Hospital when the hospital was located southwest across Chester. Now, as the J. D. Ellis Plaza, the office building houses the church's national responsibilities. The church was beautifully restored in 2000.

The First Church of Christ, Scientist, in Cleveland was established in 1877 (see pp. 62 and 127). The Second Church was organized in 1901. The Third Church was organized in 1903 on the west side. The Fourth Church was founded in 1914 and held its services in the Woodward Masonic Temple before moving to this building in 1920. At that time, between World War I and World War II, this location was part of Cleveland's second-largest commercial district. The Fifth Church was established in 1915.[78]

The powerful presence of this church dominates East 105th Street at its Chester Avenue intersection. The Pentacostal Church of Christ announces, to those traveling eastbound on a major artery out of downtown Cleveland, that they are about to enter University Circle. Two sets of doors flank the central entrance with its semicircular arch. Diamond details, varied brick patterns, and corbelling below the gable ends give a human scale to this large building. Sixty years after building one block north of Euclid Avenue, the Christian Scientists sold their building to the Pentecostal Church of Christ. The building had been vacant for some time.

The church's main sanctuary seats 1,600 people, and the Sunday school auditorium downstairs seats an additional one thousand. The sanctuary should not, but does, surprise the visitor.[79] Oriented east and west, as would be expected from the main church entrance on East 105th Street, the main worship area is wide and shallow—about three times as wide as it is deep. A complete half circle of plain, dark, beautifully stained wood pews provide seating. A relatively small balcony extends back over a spacious narthex; this is now blocked off from the street and used as a gathering area. Great areas of stenciled, painted canvas decorate the walls and ceiling. Crisp, bright, gilded molding further decorates the beautifully restored ceiling. Dramatic early twentieth-century patterned nonfigurative glass lights the sanctuary from north and south. The worship area is quite plain except for the ceiling and the windows, but they are so large and powerful that the sanctuary makes an immediate impression. In the shallow front of the sanctuary, two gold Corinthian columns stand in front of a generously carved, elevated, finished wood chancel.

15. Temple Tifereth Israel, otherwise referred to as "the Temple" (see also Friendship Baptist Church, p. 130, and the Temple Tifereth Israel East, p. 344) (1924)
Architect: Charles R. Greco
Builder: Abba Hillel Silver
Location: University Circle and Silver Park

When Temple Tifereth Israel was dedicated in 1925, Calvin Coolidge telegraphed congratulations.[80] Some would say that even then, the unassuming president was dwarfed by the larger-than-life figure of Rabbi Abba Hillel Silver.[81] Silver not only built his, "Silver's," mammoth temple (1,886 seats in the sanctuary, twenty-seven classrooms on three floors, a library, a museum, and a hall seating another thousand), he was, in the fullness of time, the force behind the creation of a country. In 1943, Silver took control of the American Zionist Emergency Council, "the most important Zionist organization of the war years."[82] After the war, Silver became president of the Zionist Organization of America, and it was in this capacity that he delivered his famous address to the United Nations in May 1947, demanding a vote on the partition of Palestine. Because of his role in establishing the Jewish state, many anticipated that Silver would leave Cleveland and settle in Israel. Thus, they must have been surprised when the dynamic rabbi, although he continued to support the new country, withdrew from Zionist politics and decided to remain in Cleveland.

As active as Silver had been in the world beyond Cleveland, he never lost his focus on his temple and its spiritual role: "worship, religious education, and ethical guidance."[83] In contrast to the secular enthusiasms of Moses Gries, who preceded him as rabbi of the Tifereth Israel community, Silver "had no difficulty in persuading the congregation to abandon the plan for a gymnasium, play court, and swimming pool" in the temple they were building.[84] Before Silver's arrival his congregation had concentrated on "Americanization" and, as part of this, strongly opposed the establishment of a Jewish homeland in Palestine. It is a measure of his charisma that they would be so enthusiastic about their young Zionist rabbi from West Virginia. On Silver's side were the changing demographics of temple membership. There had been an influx of non-German Jewish immigration into the United States in the later nineteenth century. Central European, Russian, and Polish Jews were more conservative than the Germans who had initially settled in Cleveland. The newcomers were also more likely to be Zionist. Their presence affected Jewish practice not only at Tifereth Israel but also at Reform Anshe Chesed, the original German congregation in Cleveland, at that time on Euclid Avenue (see Liberty Hill Baptist Church, p. 34) and soon to be in the suburbs (see Fairmount Temple, p. 350). Within a year of his appointment, Silver began to reverse some of his predecessor's more radical reforms. He restored Hebrew to the school; he read the Torah at services (Rabbi Gries had read from a codex in English); he reinstated Friday evening and Saturday morning religious services.

Congregation Tifereth Israel was a well-established part of the greater Central Avenue–East 55th Street Jewish neighborhood; yet, within fifteen years of the construction of its new temple there (see the now padlocked Friendship Baptist Church, p. 130), the new building could no longer accommodate its congregation. For thirteen years after 1907, Tifereth Israel searched for a new home, finally settling on a difficult site overlooking Wade Park. The gradual movement of the congregation from East 55th Street to Wade Park and Cleveland Heights also prompted the move. Overlooking Rockefeller Park to the east, the golden colored tile dome of the temple acted as a gateway to the Jewish neighborhoods that then encircled the park and its cultural gardens. Between World Wars I and II, this area served as the center of Cleveland's Jewish community.

Boston architect Charles Greco designed the new temple in the "Byzantine-Romanesque" revival style he had used two years before in his equally gigantic new home for congregation B'nai Jeshuran in Cleveland Heights (see the New Spirit Revival Center, p. 318). Greco is known in Boston as the architect of seven important Roman Catholic churches, including his "Italian Renaissance Revival" Church of the Blessed Sacrament. Elsewhere he designed Jewish temples—Cleveland, Hartford, and Miami Beach. He was also known in Cleveland as a residential architect, designing several important colonial and Tudor Revival houses in Ambler Heights, the far western part of Cleveland Heights.

The temple was carefully placed into an unusually narrow, triangular site. Armstrong thought that Greco's juxtaposition of Byzantine design and Romanesque detailing stimulated the visitor's vision.[85] The exterior cladding of Indiana limestone is set in alternating tall and thin courses. The exterior presents a satisfying bulk that announces it is here to stay. Although it is a prominent landmark in this area of Cleveland, its appearance, from close up, is not overwhelming.

Inside, the surface play between the seven prominent ribs that support the main dome and the dome skin is exciting, as is the color play of the dark walnut of the balcony, pews, and ark against the lighter Tennessee marble walls. The awe-inspiring seven-sided main sanctuary rises eighty-five feet from the floor and is ninety feet in diameter. Corner columns reach from the floor to the spring of the dome. It has a carved walnut arcaded choir loft/gallery behind the ark. Lighting is indirect so that the immense sanctuary has a warm, intimate character, in part the result of the prominence of the balconies that reach down and embrace those seated on the first floor. Two programs in glass in two distinct historical styles enhance the space—the upper clerestory is contemporary with the building while the lower clerestory was brought over from the 55th Street Temple.

The Temple Museum of Religious Art, dedicated in 1950 in a space initially intended for a gymnasium, is the fourth oldest museum of Judaica in the United States. The main collection remains in University Circle and can be seen by appointment. To facilitate appreciation of the museum, the curator displays parts of the collection at the Temple Tifereth Israel East. Additional public access is provided by the Maltz Museum of Jewish Heritage in a generous permanent area dedicated to the collection. In the early 1930s Miriam Leikind began her forty-four-year reign as temple librarian. By 1938, she had assembled six thousand volumes, and the library was on its way to becoming one of the most important libraries of Judaica in the United States.

The Gries Memorial Chapel recognizes the 765 men and women from the temple who served in the armed forces during the Second World War and the twenty-two who lost their lives. Twelve memorial windows (for the twelve tribes of Israel), inscribed with the names of the dead, are in the chapel itself. The three famous 1947 windows of Jewish warriors (Gideon, Samson, and Judah Maccabee) by Arthur Szyk are located in the War Memorial alcove leading to the chapel.

When Eleanor Roosevelt came to speak at a Temple Women's Association program in 1937, she was so popular that the meeting had to be moved to Public Auditorium's Music Hall. By 1955, the congregation had grown to the point where Severence Hall had to be leased to accommodate everyone on high holy days. Children were being bused in from the suburbs. The neighborhood was changing. The staff was expanding (including the addition of Daniel Jeremy Silver in 1956). Anshe Chesed, the other large Reform congregation, was moving from Euclid Avenue to Fairmount Boulevard in Beachwood.

Faced with a decision to move or to build, the congregation—heavily influenced by Aba Hillel Silver ("The great cathedrals of Europe do not move to the suburbs."[86])—decided to build a new wing designed by the large Chicago architectural firm of Perkins+Will. The wing included ten classrooms, a larger library to accommodate fifteen thousand volumes, office space, and a 750-seat auditorium. Although the size of the congregation peaked in 1957, the cost of expanding the building proved to be enormous: George Szell and the Cleveland Orchestra, *inter alia,* were engaged to play a benefit at Severance Hall. Large anonymous donations finally reduced the temple's debt to manageable proportions and the congregation moved into the new wing in 1959. Four years later, everything changed—Abba Hillel Silver died preparing a commemorative service for John Kennedy. Thereafter, no number of philanthropic programs in the inner city could obscure the obvious—the congregation had moved to the suburbs and the temple as an institution would die if it did not move as well. The final straw was the Highway Planning Commission's proposal to build a "Bedford Freeway" through the temple parking lot and the costly park the temple had built to improve its location. In 1966, Daniel Silver asked his board to form a committee "to examine pressing problems concerning the location of Temple property" (see the Temple Tifereth Israel East, p. 344).

On March 19, 2010, Tifereth Israel and Case Western Reserve University announced a partnership to preserve Silver's Temple. The scrolls will remain in the building for occasional Jewish services. CWRU will raise $25 million, of which the Maltz family has committed $12 million, to renovate the temple as a performing arts center. Improvements will include air conditioning, more comfortable seating, and enlargement of the bimah into a stage.

16. University Circle United Methodist Church, originally Epworth-Euclid United Methodist Church (1926)
Architects: Bertram Goodhue; Walker and Weeks
Builder: L. C. Wright
Location: 1919 East 107th Street

"The Church of the Holy Oil Can"[87] may compete with the Cleveland Museum of Art, Severence Hall, or Frank Gehry's Peter B. Lewis Building in the minds of Clevelanders as the most distinguishing building in University Circle, but—for visitors—the church is in a league of its own.[88] Soaring 233 feet above the street beside the Fine Arts Lagoon, the copper spire and fleche of Bertram Goodhue's posthumous masterpiece remains an incredibly distinctive landmark. With the lights out inside its great octagon, the quiet apparition of the blue, purple, and green east rose, combined with what appear to be tiny blue lancets in the fleche, turn its interior into one of Cleveland's most awe-inspiring religious spaces.[89] As Eric Johannesen hints,[90] University Circle Methodist, a modern building in superficial historical dress, is an aching reminder of what the fifty-five-year-old Goodhue might have done and where American architectural modernism might have gone on a road not taken.

Bertram Goodhue's twenty-four year partnership with Ralph Adams Cram put them at the center of archaeologically informed Gothic Revival in early twentieth-century America. They built West Point and, after their separation, the loquacious Cram would carry on with his dream Gothic commission at the Cathedral of St. John the Divine in New York. It is easy to glance at Epworth-Euclid and dismiss it, as many do, as another bizarre product of a Connecticut Yankee in King Arthur's court.[91] Johannesen attempted to disabuse us of this idea by tracing the progression of Gothic Revival in Cleveland religious architecture. This begins with Patrick Keely's 1848 Cathedral of St. John the Evangelist, a large hall with a few Gothic trimmings (see p. 16). During the nineteenth century, trimmings became more exuberant and the underlying plan, space, and decoration more archaeologically correct, culminating in the work of Cram (see the Church of the Covenant, p. 52, and Transfiguration, p. 36), Charles Schweinfurth (see Trinity Episcopal Cathedral, p. 21), Henry Vaughan (see the Amasa Stone Chapel, p. 51), and J. Byers Hayes (see the first part of St. Paul's Cleveland Heights, p. 329). Then, in Hayes's First Baptist Shaker Heights (see p. 337), Johannesen identified a "modernistic simplification" that reaches a climax in Cleveland in the simple strong planes of University Circle Methodist.[92] In 1918, Goodhue had said, "I dream of something very much bigger and finer and more modern and more suited to our present-day civilization than any Gothic church could possibly be."[93] Goodhue's "modernistic simplification" reached a secular climax in his 1924 Nebraska State Capitol, the only modern state capital in the United States.[94] Goodhue died at fifty-five and we do not know where his genius—dueling with Frank Lloyd Wright, Eric Mendelsohn (see Park Synagogue, p. 315), and the German internationalists—might have led us. After his death, Goodhue's integration of art and architecture was frowned on by the international style and his students, while important, were of the second rank.[95]

University Circle Methodist is in the middle of that rare and treasured Cleveland phenomenon of a neighborhood on the rise. The church has always been sheltered to the north and east by the Wade Park museums, the lagoon, and Case Western Reserve University. Now, to the west, the upscale presence of Judson Manor, the affluent promise of the Park Lane Villas, and the solid, well-maintained Pentecostal Church of Christ complex (see p. 43) dominate the area. To the immediate south, the previously tawdry neighborhood has been spruced up with a new Cleveland Police station, a Cleveland Public Library branch, and the increasing presence of the Cleveland Clinic. This transformation has made Epworth-Euclid's historic missions to the poor and to the university more credible and more manageable.

There is no evidence that Goodhue was inspired by the Mont St. Michel Abbey in France, however, the massing of his building—with its central fleche and the grouping of the various rectangular blocks of chapel, offices, minor towers, stairways, and basements—suggests the giant fortified monastery on the mountain in the sea. University Circle Methodist and Mont St. Michel have in common their towers and the gathering of a variety of activities into one constructed mass. Both churches are seen as a contiguous unit with chapels, education, and administrative spaces integrated into the upper stories, and the sanctuary positioned high over social and recreational spaces down below. University Circle Methodist's sloping site above Liberty Boulevard and the Wade Park Lagoon reinforces this impression. The simple masses of the exterior, constructed of a warm, golden, Plymouth, seam-faced granite, contribute greatly to its monumental character. Goodhue designed University Circle Methodist with a massive space under the central spire as the controlling architectural element. Additional space in the form of nave and transepts around the high, vaulted crossing under the fleche form a cruciform plan. The tapering tower and fleche of the church are so dominant that one tends not to realize that the structure is a nave church that widens into a great octagonal crossing.

In spite of his spire and the use of pointed arches, Goodhue kept Gothic detail to a minimum. The structure does not have any flying buttresses, crockets, or finials, and it has little tracery. The art deco–patterned copper in the lower part of the spire contrasts with other elements in the traditional French Gothic style. Art deco continues in the cast stone sculptures by Leo Friedlander, the New York sculptor whose work includes four pylons at the entrance of the RCA Building in New York City. In Cleveland, the Friedlander-Goodhue ornament follows the pattern that was so successful on the Nebraska State Capitol and that anticipated the Lorain-Carnegie Bridge pylons. Massive blocks of masonry terminate in sculptured figures that grow out of the architectural mass, becoming more three-dimensional and less planar as they rise.

University Circle Methodist has a wonderful, wide, spacious, hospitable narthex and a gym downstairs.[96] The Cleveland Institute of Music (CIM) uses the ninety-seat chapel with its beamed barrel ceiling for recitals (CIM maintains the Steinway). The chapel balcony holds a tracker organ. The chapel rose was given to memorialize the Epworth League. It was transferred, with its original tracing, from Epworth Memorial Church on East 55th Street. Off the chapel is a beautiful bride's chapel and an exquisite small prayer room.

The sanctuary seats 950 downstairs and 450 in the balcony. The nave is one hundred feet from front to back and one hundred feet from the floor up to the base of the fleche. The interior octagonal vaulting is said to be patterned after that of Ely Cathedral in England and the painted ceiling after those in East Anglican churches, although no evidence exists that Goodhue was following these historical precedents when he designed the building. The Carrara font is from Epworth Memorial on East 55th Street. Chandeliers and the beautiful wood reredos have been restored. The transept glass and the famous rose above the intricate organ screen are original; the nave glass was completed after the Second World War. The tracery around the rose is a rare example of this kind of architectural ornament in this modern building. The 1928 Skinner organ was rebuilt in 1954 by Holtkamp and modified in 1978 by Hemry. The Schulmerich Carillon was installed in 1971 and replaced in 2002.

University Circle Methodist represents the union of three of the largest and oldest Methodist communities in Cleveland, one in University Circle and two from downtown. A permanent Methodist class was established at Doan's Corners in 1831 and, as Doan Street Methodist Episcopal, built its first church on Doan (East 105th Street) in 1837. They built a second church in 1870, and they took it down in 1885 when they moved into a substantial medieval revival church at East 93rd Street at Euclid with the new name—the Euclid Avenue Methodist Episcopal Church.

Meanwhile, another class was established downtown in 1827; they built their first church in 1841. The subsequent history of the many little Methodist parishes downtown was extremely complex until Bishop Jesse Peck rode through in 1882 and identified the need for a large, central Methodist church.[97] The result was the Prospect Avenue at East 55th Street Central Methodist Episcopal Church. Here, in 1889, five Methodist youth groups united into the Epworth League, which grew over the next ten years into one of the most influential religious youth groups in the world with 1.75 million members in 19,500 chapters.[98] When Central Methodist rebuilt in 1893, it was logical to rename their congregation Epworth Memorial Methodist Episcopal Church. Before its removal, this was one of the great religious landmarks of Cleveland. Sidney Badgley's auditorium and connecting Sunday school were similar in plan to those of his Pilgrim Congregational Church in Tremont (see p. 202) with the addition of a monumental exterior dome. Badgley became known for his use of steel domes unsupported by columns. Epworth was the most notable example. Its central dome was the largest known of its kind. Badgley's design for Epworth Memorial was called "modernized Byzantine"; it was actually Romanesque and Renaissance.[99] It became known to less pretentious Methodists in Cleveland, because of the dome, as "the Mosque of Ohmar."[100] Epworth occupied what was then considered a remarkably ecumenical neighborhood in the late nineteenth century—adjacent, on East 55th Street, to Tifereth Israel Temple and to Schweinfurth's now demolished Ursuline College and Convent. In 1920 Epworth and Euclid Avenue merged and built their University Circle church.[101] The resulting Epworth-Euclid Methodist Church merged in 2009 with First Church, Cleveland (originally the First United Methodist Church; see p. 26) to form today's University Circle United Methodist Church.

17. Amasa Stone Chapel (1911)
Architect: Henry Vaughan
Builder: Flora Stone Mather[102]
Location: Euclid Avenue opposite
Wade Park

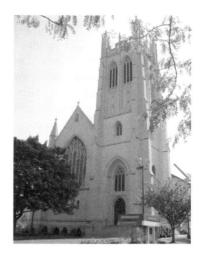

Built to remember the Cleveland entrepreneur Amasa Stone, who paid to move Western Reserve College from Hudson to Cleveland before his tragic death, this chapel has become a memorial to the beneficent daughter who built it.[103] At the head of the chapel is a great south window by Charles Eamer Kemp, given by Clara Stone Hay, wife of John Hay—President Abraham Lincoln's secretary and later secretary of state. Mrs. Hay gave the window to remember her sister, Cleveland's greatest resident philanthropist. Her sister's portrait marble looks on from the back, above a life-sized marble of "Philanthropy." The space in between has become the CWRU Valhalla, lined with plaques remembering the presidents and chancellors of Case Western Reserve University, and CWRU graduates who died in the First and Second World Wars—as well as a plaque memorializing Jerry Tracy of Battery A, First Ohio Voluntary Artillery, who died on August 12, 1898, "for Cuban freedom."

Walter Leedy pointed out that the Stone Chapel is important because of the way Henry Vaughan adapted "a space for Anglican worship to a collegiate chapel by lowering the end window, replacing the altar and reredos with oak stalls, and placing the pulpit on axis with the central aisle (later moved to the side)." Stone Chapel was a precedent, Leedy wrote, for the great Gothic college chapels of the 1920s at Princeton and the University of Chicago. Flora Stone Mather and Clara Hay had chosen Vaughan because of his chapels at Groton and St. Paul's Schools and his Washington Episcopal National Cathedral. Vaughn was, with Ralph Adams Cram (see the Church of the Covenant, p. 52 and Church of the Transfiguration, p. 36) and Bertram Goodhue (see University Circle United Methodist Church, p. 47) one of the great "Boston Gothicists."

Located on the campus of Case Western Reserve University across Euclid Avenue from the Cleveland Orchestra's home in Severence Hall, the chapel, with its 140-foot tower, is a point of orientation in University Circle, in part defining the urban wall surrounding the Wade Park Lagoon in front of the Cleveland Museum of Art. The asymmetry of the finished Indiana limestone chapel with its flanking fliers, pointed windows, and crockets, typifies English West Country Gothic Revival. The tower, constructed without a spire, is similar to that seen in Magdalen College, Oxford.[104]

United in eternity by the merger of their educational institutions, Amasa Stone and Leonard Case were not, in this life, good friends. Some say that the

Stone daughters commissioned their famous spitting gargoyle on the tower of the chapel to face Case Institute. The rest of the tower is decorated with angels.[105] A bust of Stone, moved from his Bank Street Railroad Station to a position above the choir entrance to the chapel, faces his college and turns its back to Case. The chapel has four entrances—public, student, choir, and one for the president of the institution. Stone appears again, in another bust, in the foyer of the public entrance to the chapel.

The interior appears Tudor. The narrowness of the building is said to have been occasioned by the original narrow site. The center aisle barely accommodates two marchers in academic regalia. The lateral aisles are arcaded. The balcony and the choir feature beautiful woodwork. The horizontally ribbed wood ceiling is unique to Cleveland. A continuous Gothic pointed arch runs down the ceiling from front to back. None of the vaulted, Gothic ceiling segments so common in Roman Catholic religious buildings appear here. The Gothic arch is much more apparent when one looks at either end of the ceiling than when one looks straight up. In the front the chapel has a relatively small choir with elaborate three-pew choir seating on both sides. Single-row choir seating is along the south wall. An imposing but restrained organ case occupies the east side of the choir. Before the choir is a wonderful wrought-iron waist-high screen encircling the lectern, now moved to the right from its original central position.

Of particular interest is the south window memorial to Flora Stone Mather. Rich in ornamentation and painted details, it is the only authenticated Cleveland work by Charles Eamer Kempe, the English arts-and-crafts stained-glass artist. Although the sisters spent lavishly on the stone tracery, they gave no glass except the memorial of one to the other, assuming that others would give memorial windows. This has not happened and, except for the south window, the elaborately traceried windows remain opaque.

18. The Church of the Covenant
(1909; 1972)
Architects: Ralph Adams Cram;
Richard Fleischman
Builders: Henry Lyman and Albert
Jeandheur
Location: 11205 Euclid Avenue

In Cleveland, all Presbyterian roads lead back to the Old Stone Church (see p. 12), and the Church of the Covenant is no exception.[106] The Church of the Covenant is a merger of three Presbyterian churches—Second Presbyterian, Fourth Presbyterian, and Beckwith Memorial. Second and Fourth Presbyterian were established by the Old Stone Church to manage its overflow.[107]

Second Presbyterian was attempted in 1837, only two years after Old Stone became a permanent institution. The attempt failed and, after returning to Old Stone, the congregation tried and succeeded a second time in 1844. Initially they moved into a former Congregational frame church, also on Public Square. In 1852, Second Presbyterian built an imposing brick and sandstone Romanesque Revival church on the corner of Superior Avenue at East Third Street designed by Old Stone architects Heard and Porter. At that time, Second Presbyterian was the largest church building in Cleveland. When this church burned in 1876, the congregation rebuilt on the northwest corner of Prospect Avenue at East 30th Street, across the street west of what is now First United Methodist (see p. 26) and across the street north of what is now Zion Evangelical Lutheran (see p. 24). This 1,300-seat, cream-colored "Norman-style" building became, by the 1890s, "the strongest Presbyterian Church of the city."[108] For nine years, this church could offer Cleveland *le Culte Français*, Presbyterian services in French. In 1915, its Men's Club, led by Dr. Dudley Allen, founded what became Cleveland's prize-winning Karamu settlement house. The neighborhood, however, was becoming commercial and the congregation was departing. By 1920, Second Presbyterian shared the intersection of East 30th at Prospect with the Lutherans, the Methodists, and, on the southeast corner, the Mafia, who were selling almost everything the Presbyterians were against from Mafia headquarters in the Sterling Hotel. In 1905 eleven Presbyterian churches stood between Public Square and East 107th Street, twenty-five years later five remained. For Second Presbyterian, merger loomed as a possibility—with either Fairmount Presbyterian (see p. 327) or Euclid Avenue Presbyterian. Second Presbyterian chose the latter.

For Fourth, later Euclid Avenue Presbyterian, in contrast, the mid-nineteenth century was a continuous struggle. Its clergy kept changing and its growth was inhibited by the completion of a new, larger Old Stone Church in 1855. For two decades Fourth Presbyterian's overly ambitious building on the corner of East 14th Street at Euclid stayed unfinished. In 1887 Samuel Sprecher arrived and made Fourth Presbyterian a success.

The third leg of the stool was established by the will of dry-goods merchant T. Sterling Beckwith.[109] The Beckwith Presbyterian Church was established in 1885 in a small brick chapel at Doan's Corners on the site of the present Children's Museum. This was replaced in 1892 with a substantial Romanesque stone building. Although Beckwith Presbyterian would establish one branch in Little Italy and another that would become Forest Hill Presbyterian, the church did not do well in University Circle. Beckwith and Euclid Avenue Presbyterian merged in 1906, took the name Euclid Avenue Presbyterian, and held services at Beckwith for four years as they planned their new church nearby. The congregation purchased a parcel of land adjacent to the Woman's College at Western Reserve University. They converted Euclid Avenue Presbyterian's substantial nest egg from the sale of its downtown property into the construction of the new church. Adjacent to the upscale neighborhood of Wade Park, some described the result as the finest Presbyterian church in the United

States. Bob Hope's British stonemason father worked on the project while Bob grew up down the street in Doan's Corners.

In 1920, Euclid Avenue Presbyterian, with its splendid new quarters, merged with the movers and shakers of Second Presbyterian down on Prospect Avenue, naming this new congregation the "Church of the Covenant." Both of its previous pastors, Paul F. Sutphen of Second Presbyterian and Alexander McGaffin of Euclid Avenue Presbyterian, initially served the new congregation.[110] As would be expected, it took some time before the two congregations were truly united. Philip Smead Bird accomplished this; he led the combined congregations to greatness (after summoning Cram back for some alterations to the sanctuary) from 1928 until his unexpected death in 1948. When the first two pastors stepped down because of illness, the search committee settled on Bird in meetings at the Union Club. The Church of the Covenant, a merger of two powerful Presbyterian congregations into a national institution, had become Cleveland's Old Stone Church for the twentieth century, with energy and funds directed toward the needs of university students, foreign missions, and the poor and oppressed of Cleveland.

An important mission and powerful exercise of influence, with a tragic outcome, involved civil rights. The Reverend Bruce Klunder, a graduate of the Yale Divinity School and associate executive secretary of the Student Christian Union housed at the Church of the Covenant, was killed by a bulldozer during a civil rights demonstration at a construction site in 1964. The intense reaction to this tragedy led to the resignation of the pastor and the departure of the mayor, Ralph Locher, who had been a church elder.

It is the nature of this church to be open in discussion, and in subsequent years it was particularly torn by the controversy surrounding the Vietnam War, even as it attempted to reach out to both its immediate academic and its largely suburban residential communities. The Church of the Covenant has historically been an unusually dynamic and responsible community. It has also been hard on its pastors.

This massive, Indiana limestone, Gothic Revival church on the north side of Euclid Avenue is almost surrounded by CWRU and its University Hospitals. Cram designed the Church of the Covenant in the style of English Gothic. He described his adaptation as "severe, massive and restrained," making a point that "the disposition of parts, the proportions and the symbolism that would be appropriate to a Roman Catholic or Episcopal church would of necessity fail to adapt themselves exactly to the impulses and the requirements of a Presbyterian church."[111] The main facade is massive and simple. It consists of a single deeply recessed doorway below a large rose window framed by two large octagonal turrets with crocketed spires. For a Gothic structure, typically light and airy, the amount of stone seems excessive. This may, in part, be explained by the plainness of this Presbyterian building with sheer walls, no statuary, little trim, and little other exterior decoration (except for the odd buttress). The buttresses in combination with accentuated waterlines and window tracery struggle to lighten the structure. The smooth finish Indiana limestone is structural; the church does not have a steel or brick skeleton. This is unusual for such a large building and may also explain the massiveness of the structure. The 140-foot tower with four tall, graceful corner finials divides the parish house from the sanctuary.

Fleischman's brutalist 1972 community Education Building extends to the east of Cram's original educational, social, and administrative Beckwith Church House. The new addition is a contemporary, contrasting complement to the original, traditional design. Its brutalist style with wonderful cast cellular ceilings has been, after much controversy, softened with several coats of paint. The new addition was originally designed to enlarge the church's pioneering 1947 Monday, Thursday, and Friday morning day-care program. This program earned the church a special nickname from socially ambitious mothers in Cleveland: "the Church of the Convenience." The upper story of the addition has now become home to an interfaith campus center. The new addition originally extended eastward toward a CWRU-owned ecumenical religious plaza with separate but integrated Jewish, Roman Catholic, and Protestant campus ministries. This innovative joint ministry has collapsed for reasons having to do with finance, the character of the ministries, and the physical inadequacies of the buildings. Only the Hillel Jewish Student Center remains; the Roman Catholic and Protestant missions are abandoned. The Muslim Student Association, the Newman Catholic Campus Ministry, and the United Protestant Campus Ministries have moved into the second floor of the Church of the Covenant community education building—where they appear to be flourishing.

Cram's stonework inside the sanctuary is also Indiana limestone. The ends of the open-timbered hammerbeam ceiling, patterned after Wymondham Abbey in Norfolk, England, are carved to represent angels and monks. The organ was located originally at the head of the choir. When Cram returned to Cleveland, in 1931, he divided the organ between both sides of the choir and installed a limewood-against-mahogany Covenant reredos of his design, framing it with the carved woodwork he had originally designed for the organ case. He reoriented the east transept into a north-facing chapel. An ornamental iron screen made by Cleveland's Rose Iron Works sets off this Christ Chapel from the nave.

Presbyterian churches do not incorporate pieces of saints in their altars (they usually do not have altars). Consistent with Cram's Gothic Revival, however, the Church of the Covenant has a treasured piece of stone from St. Giles in Edinburgh, the mother church of Presbyterianism, beneath the "altar table." Cram's elaborate canopied pulpit is modeled after the pulpit used by John Calvin in St. Pierre, Geneva, Switzerland. Particularly notable are the deep, dark mahogany pews. The Church of the Covenant is known for its glass by Gorham, Burnham, Connick, Wright, Willet, Tiffany, and Phillips and for Cram's elaborate tracery. Truly Presbyterian, all the figures in the glass are Biblical except for St. Cecelia, patron of music, clutching her miniature Holtkamp organ with its exposed pipes. The Worthington Jesus window in the east gallery was from the Euclid Street Church. The Tiffany Good Shepherd window in the south gallery is from Beckwith Church. Cram patterned the Gorham Lamb of God south rose after the west rose at Chartres. (There are twelve Gorham transept windows and two roses.) Modern Phillips glass decorates the narthex, which extends across the full width of the building. The ashes of deceased Presbyterian parishioners are rising from the old choir rehearsal room in the sub-basement to a new Columbarium in the west transept. The Aeolian-Skinner-Holtkamp organ is now the largest church organ in northeast Ohio and is a descendent of the original 1911 Möller that occupied the north end of the choir. Skinner replaced most of the Möller when the organ was moved to either side of the choir. There were further organ additions and revisions in 1958, 1996, and in 2003, when Holtkamp built a new movable console for concerts. A second organ in the balcony blocks the original five lancet windows beneath the south rose. The forty-seven-bell Eijsbouts carillon has recorded with the Cleveland Orchestra.

19. Florence Harkness Chapel (1902)
Architect: Charles Schweinfurth
Location: Bellflower Road

What the Harkness Chapel has in common with Frank Gehry's Peter B. Lewis Building, built across the street almost one hundred years after the chapel, is that both were the result of lots and lots of new money put to good use. Florence Harkness was the daughter of Stephen Harkness, the second-largest shareholder in the Standard Oil Company. On his own, Florence's brother, Edward Harkness, completely transformed the campuses and the student life of Yale and Harvard. Following the model of the colleges at Oxford and Cambridge, Edward Harkness gave Yale ten residential colleges, each with a dining common room, kitchen, social rooms and halls, classrooms, library, faculty offices, and at least one squash court. He did the same for Harvard, establishing the "houses" there. Although the finances of the Standard Oil junta in Cleveland were intentionally murky, Florence Harkness—when she died—was one of the wealthiest women in the United States. For the details of her tragic life, see Diana Tittle's recent *The Severances: An American Odyssey.* Florence devoted her life in Cleveland to good works directed primarily to the relief of the immigrant poor. Then, at the late age of thirty, Florence found romance. In 1894 she married Louis Severance, the hardworking treasurer of Standard Oil of Ohio. Ten months later, she died, leaving her husband "unimaginably rich."[112] Her estate financed philanthropies around the world—from a medical school in Korea to Severance Hall in Cleveland.

The entrance to this rough stone building with rubble coursing and stone trim is through an elaborate finished stone porch on the west side. A one-story classroom projects to the south. The width of the building is increased by the lateral extension of the first floor space out to the faux buttresses (capped by finials). This extension, as seen from the outside, mimics a series of lateral chapels. Gothic pointed windows are inserted in the Romanesque coursed ashlar wall surface. Small, deep-set windows in the classroom projecting to the south and the heavy exterior buttresses give the building a Romanesque fortress-like appearance.

Whatever the religious or spiritual intension of the donors, their chapel, in contrast to the University's Stone Chapel, has evolved into a teaching and performance space. This is emphasized inside by the breadth of the auditorium and the width and depth of its stage. The stage, occupying one-fifth of the first floor, extends across the full width of the auditorium. Accessed by steps beside the wall on either side, the stage commands the front of the main interior space of the building. There is no balcony. Arcades on each side of the central hall support the upper exterior walls and provide access to the lateral undivided "chapel" areas so obvious from the outside. Seating in these side areas was originally in pews facing the center of the auditorium. The lateral area on the west has been closed. On the east only one pew remains.

Johannesen identified the "elegant hammerbeam arches" of the ceiling, with their highly polished trusses, as the first phase in the late nineteenth-century reliance on sixteenth-century Tudor Gothic as the primary source for collegiate Gothic.[113] Wood wainscoting and a wood wall behind the stage warm the interior. Elaborate period wrought-iron chandeliers hang from the ceiling, supplemented by marvelously fanciful electric fixtures with bare bulbs in front and in the rear. The nineteenth-century glass windows are glazed with opalescent glass as befits an educational space where students need to see to take notes. The large north window has scattered stained glazed inserts and the side windows have only stained glazed edges.

20. Mt. Zion Congregational Church (1955)

Architects: Carr and Cunningham
Builder: Richard Andrews
Location: 10723 Magnolia Drive

In 1864 a small group from Shiloh Baptist Church (see p. 132) decided they would be more comfortable in the Congregational Church.[114] Under the auspices of Plymouth (see p. 335) and supported by all of the Cleveland Congregational churches, they organized the first African American Congregational church east of the Mississippi. Although the subsequent history of the parish has not been without challenge,[115] Mt. Zion Congregational has always, according to David Van Tassel and John Grabowski's *Encyclopedia of Cleveland History,* enjoyed a reputation as the church most appealing to the upper reaches of Cleveland's African American society.[116] While many other African American churches might dispute this preeminence, Mt. Zion Congregational is the only institution in this guide that was bombed during the civil rights period. At approximately 12:30 A.M. on Friday, March 26, 1954, soon after the congregation had moved into the former Robert Grandin mansion in Wade Park, and as they were planning a permanent church next door, two bombs were thrown into the basement through a broken window. Mt. Zion Congregational stayed, and Mt. Zion Congregational rebuilt.

Mt. Zion Congregational built its first meetinghouse on East Ninth Street opposite Webster Avenue just south of Carnegie Avenue. That site is now under the tangle at the intersection of Interstate 77 and the Interstate 90 Innerbelt. Unforeseen mortgage expenses forced Mt. Zion Congregational to leave this building and move to a new, less expensive structure on East 31st Street directly south of Cedar Avenue. Andrew Carnegie provided the organ. Mt. Zion remained here until a fire destroyed their church in 1923. Here on East 31st Street, the famous Mt. Zion Congregational Church Lyceum was established. The Lyceum met to discuss and debate issues important to African American society. On East 31st Street, the congregation established the first African American Girl Scout troop in Cleveland and the first day nursery for children of working women.

After the fire, the congregation decided to purchase the immense Temple Tifereth Israel building at the corner of Central Avenue and East 55th Street (see p. 130). The cost of maintaining this gigantic building, together with the Great Depression, was too much for the congregation, which gave up the former temple in 1938 and moved to another church on Cedar Avenue. As their congregation grew after World War II, they sold this church before they found a new home and had to move to the Cedar Avenue branch of the YMCA until

1954. The congregation then purchased the seventeen-room Grandin mansion on Magnolia Drive and used it for their church. Within a year, plans were unveiled for a new sanctuary.

A walkway joins the renovated Grandin mansion, which is still used for administrative and educational purposes, to the new church. In the center of the walkway is a one-and-a-half-story foyer, glass-walled to the south, which provides entrance to the sanctuary. On the outside of the new church, uniform brick surfaces are coordinated with plain windows and doors to create a well-balanced, well-proportioned building.

The sanctuary is open arched and spacious—simple, plain, and impressive. Great wood arches spring from the walls and support the wood ceiling—the most striking feature of the worship space. A 1988 Hemry organ stands behind the altar with open pipes in front of a wood screen. Seating for the choir, the lectern, and the pulpit flank an elevated podium. Decoration consists of the brick lower walls and the magnificent ceiling. Beneath the sanctuary is a social hall and kitchen. On the outside above the sanctuary towers a lighted spire, a signal of hope to patients entering the large Veterans Administration Hospital next door.

21. Holy Rosary Roman Catholic Church (1905)
Architect: William P. Ginther
Builders: Antonio Gibelli and Joseph Militello
Location: 12021 Mayfield Road

Holy Rosary is the center of one of the most vibrant, and certainly the most widely recognized, nationality parishes in Cleveland.[117] Is there anyone younger than forty-five in Cuyahoga County who has never been to Holy Rosary's Feast of the Assumption?[118] Are there art lovers, bocce enthusiasts, or serious eaters in northern Ohio who have never been to Little Italy? Holy Rosary and its congregation, in part because of their unique location and in part because of the high quality of their cooking, have maintained their nationality parish in Cleveland when so many others have failed.

This is ironic because, in the beginning, Italian parishes in Cleveland were notable for their limited means and their notorious *campanilismo*,[119] the former partly resulting from the latter. Early immigrants from Italy originally settled in "Big Italy" along Woodland Avenue and organized their first parish, St. Anthony of Padua, in 1886. Although they could never afford a school, they put up a substantial brick Romanesque church in 1904 (see p. 119). At one time, St. Anthony celebrated twenty-two feasts a year—with twelve street processions—in honor of the patron saints of the congregation's different societies and hometowns. In 1938, St. Anthony merged with St. Bridget because St. Bridget had a school. St. Anthony-St. Bridget was torn down in 1961 to make way for the Innerbelt.

As the Italian community moved eastward, they established Holy Rosary in 1891 for those living east of East 55th Street. Additional Italian nationality parishes were subsequently established in University Circle (St. Marian in 1905) and in Collingwood (Holy Redeemer in 1924). Parishes established farther east, for example, the 1944 St. Clare in Lyndhurst, may have had large numbers of Italian members but were not nationality congregations (for West Side Italian parishes, see St. Rocco [p. 236] and Mount Carmel [west; p. 249]).

St. Marian, on the other side of the CWRU–University Hospitals campus from Holy Rosary, was quite a *campanilismo* parish, drawn almost exclusively from former inhabitants and their descendants of Rionero Sannitico, a small town in Italy's Campobasso Province. Even so, St. Marian was the first Italian parish in Cleveland with a school. In spite of its close and extended association with Holy Rosary, St. Marian finally succumbed to a growing University Circle and a shrinking congregation, closing in 1975.

Although its parish now includes all of University Circle, Holy Rosary has traditionally benefited from a tightly circumscribed geographic neighborhood. "Little Italy" is hemmed in by Lakeview Cemetery on the east and north, CWRU on the south, and the former Nickel Plate Railroad on the west. This physical isolation, protected from encroaching non-Italian commercial, industrial, or residential neighborhoods, has been its salvation. The employment opportunities of the adjacent two-hundred-acre Lake View Cemetery, together with those generated by the subsequent affluent building spree in Wade Park and the Heights, attracted Italian stonecutters to this little enclave beginning in 1880.

Holy Rosary was organized in 1891 by the Scalabrini (Missionaries of St. Charles Borromeo), an order founded four years earlier by Giovanni Battista Scalabrini, bishop of Piacenza, to "maintain Catholic faith and practice among Italian emigrants in the New World." The Scalabrini administered the parish for the next sixteen years, and their last missionary, Father Gibelli, planned and began building the permanent church in 1905. When the parish ran out of money, they postponed construction and converted the basement into a temporary church. Gibelli died in 1907, and the church was completed two years later by Father Joseph Militello. This may explain the church-over-school form of the current building.

It is not uncommon for Roman Catholic pastors to serve more than thirty years. Holy Rosary is unusual in having had sixteen pastors, in part because of illness and death. Philip Racco, the current pastor, installed in 1989, is its longest-serving pastor. Opened in 1954, the school closed in 1993, but reopened two years later as the independent Montessori School at Holy Rosary. Although nonsectarian and without formal association with Holy Rosary Parish or the diocese, the Montessori movement in Cleveland has always had a strong association with the Roman Catholic Church. Ruffing Montessori, the second Montessori school in the United States, originated in a John Carroll University–Ursuline College study group and began teaching in the basement of St. Patrick Church on the West Side (see p. 189). Its East Side branch is located on the campus of Catholic Beaumont School in Cleveland Heights. (The Montessori movement also has a strong association with Park Synagogue; see Ratner Montessori School, p. 347.)

Holy Rosary is an unusual church, perhaps because of the hesitancy of its construction. The brick church on a generous stone foundation is sited directly on a busy street in a busy Italian-American commercial neighborhood overflowing with small shops and restaurants. Flanking steps lead up from the sidewalk on the street to a restrained masonry entrance. Statues of Matthew, Mark, Luke, and John surround the statue of Our Lady of the Holy Rosary standing in the central bay. The facade, with its flanking volutes, is taken from Giacomo della Porta's Il Gesù of 1568, the mother church of the Jesuits in Rome, and the pattern for innumerable Catholic Baroque mission churches in the Americas. It has a superficial resemblance to Ginther's St. Adalbert (see p. 134), constructed five years later. Within the church, in the narthex, a second set of stairs leads up from the entrance doors to the sanctuary that—unlike most Roman Catholic churches—has a low and shallow barrel ceiling. Close inspection reveals that the floor of the basement, now a community space, is only a few feet below the level of the ground, allowing tall windows in the basement walls to illuminate the interior from the sides. Therefore, although from the outside and particularly from the street, this church initially appears much like what one would encounter in Rome; in fact, the sanctuary is set almost like a second story on a slightly sunken first story. The impression in the sanctuary appears to be a glorified version of what one might have expected to see in the second story of a nineteenth-century, temporary Roman Catholic school-and-church in Cleveland—the first building erected by a parish, where the school was on the ground floor and the church on the second. Such a sanctuary obviously presents problems with modern access, and these are cleverly addressed with an elevator from street level to the sanctuary built outside (to the east) of the building, similar to the elevators giving access to the Centro de Arte Reina Sofia in Madrid.

The interior of the sanctuary reveals several remarkable features. Because of lack of funds, the ceiling was originally surfaced with tin sheets rather than plaster. Today, of course, what was an economical move a hundred years ago is now crisply painted and part of the charm of the building. Furthermore, the metal ceiling—together with the stone floor—creates remarkably clear and crisp acoustics. The pastor says, "When people sing they can hear themselves, so they sing louder." At the back of the church is an unusual room designed for Reconciliation (Confession), which is open and inviting in contrast to the traditional confessional. Also at the back of the church is a wonderful polychromed statue of the martyred Bishop St. Blaise, from the original church of St. Anthony, in papier-mâché. Two fine pieces of modern sculpture flank the altar: the *Meeting at Emmaus* on the left and the *Baptism of Christ* on the right. In a small rose at the west end are images of Pius X, who ruled when the church was built, and Sister Lucia Filippini, who founded a teaching order active in the parish from 1936 to 1980.

Because of the security of its neighborhood, this church does not need the locks and alarms so characteristic of other Cleveland religious buildings. Father Racco opens Holy Rosary early in the morning and closes it late at night. In between, scattered students, staff, and families from University Circle medical and academic institutions come and go. Holy Family remains one of the few religious institutions in Cleveland where people are free to wander in to pray.

22. Nottingham Spirk Design Associates, originally First Church of Christ, Scientist (1930)
Architects: Walker and Weeks (Dana Clark; 1930); City Architecture (2005)
Builders: Unknown (1930); John Nottingham and John Spirk (2005)
Location: 2200 Overlook Road

On March 15, 2009, the Roman Catholic Diocese of Cleveland closed twenty-nine parishes and merged thirty-nine. In the resulting uproar, the public lost sight of a diocesan strategy that preferred to close a church and then attempt to convert it to some other purpose by sale or destruction than the alternative—leave insolvent and abandoned buildings to painfully succumb to the elements. Bracketing Cleveland, two former Christian Science churches vividly illustrate the alternatives. On the West Side, across West 117th Street from Lakewood, the derelict, abandoned, and deteriorating Fifth Church of Christ, Scientist, has become a frightening burden on a fragile neighborhood. On the East Side, across the street from Cleveland Heights, many consider the beautifully restored Nottingham Spirk Design Associates to be the poster child of church renovation for a nonreligious purpose.[120]

John Nottingham and John Spirk graduated from the industrial design program of the Cleveland Institute of Art in 1972. They design and develop consumer products, for which they now hold more than 464 patents. Their products, including, for example, the world's largest-selling electric toothbrush, have generated more than $30 billion in sales. Nottingham Spirk is unusual in its field for its vertical integration. Although it may become involved with a product at any stage of development, Nottingham Spirk is capable of thinking up an idea and carrying it through design and prototype to production and sale. In 2006 John Nottingham and John Spirk won the Cleveland Arts Prize in Design.

In 2003, Nottingham Spirk rescued the First Church of Christ, Scientist, from developers who intended to level it and replace it with condominiums. They asked the design firm City Architecture for, and got, "a dramatic and compelling work environment."[121] Fifteen million dollars later, the former church has a new roof, new floors, new heating, cooling, plumbing and electrical systems, forty-two miles of Internet cable, and a ten-thousand-square-foot addition discretely hidden so as not to detract from the historic building. The sanctuary/auditorium is now the design studio. The former Sunday school gathering room accommodates the engineering/prototype shops. The sanctuary balcony has been reconfigured into offices for incubator companies (while keeping one row of pews and the balcony railing, together with the pews in the choir loft, to retain a strong sense of its original purpose). Nottingham Spirk likes the building because its sixty thousand square feet over five floors keeps its design and laboratory facilities in one place. The restoration is of the quality expected of a successful twenty-first-century business. Nottingham Spirk restored the organ and wired it for whatever music would inspire its younger designers. In 2006, they departed from this program to play "Rule, Britannia!" for a visit from a British client. It caused him to brush a tear from his eye.

The First Church of Christ, Scientist, was incorporated in Cleveland by the Reverend George A. Robertson in 1888. It received its charter from the state of Ohio in 1891. Services were held at various locations, including (ironically, for what was to come) the Nottingham Building and the Pythian Temple,[122] until the congregation moved into its own church building at the corner of Cedar Avenue and present-day East 46th Street in 1901. This building is now the home of Lane Metropolitan Christian Methodist Episcopal (CME) Church (see p. 127). In 1914 the Christian Science congregation moved into the Duchess Theater, where they remained until 1915, when the group purchased the former Euclid Avenue Methodist Church at Euclid Avenue at East 93rd Street (now the Euclid Avenue Church of God; see also University Circle United Methodist Church, p. 47).

First Church of Christ, Scientist, then purchased the property now occupied by Severence Hall from the Roman Catholic Diocese of Cleveland in 1926. Bishop Schrembs had decided to keep his cathedral at East Ninth Street at Superior Avenue (see p. 16). The Christian Scientists commissioned Walker and Weeks to design a church in University Circle. Before construction began, however, they sold their property for $600,000 to John Long Severance for the Musical Arts Association. That $600,000 was more than enough, in 1928, both to purchase the residence of Mrs. Howell Hinds with its surrounding four acres of land on the west side of Overlook Drive and to construct this building.

The sale of their lot to the Musical Arts Association explains the striking similarity between the exterior and interior of First Church of Christ, Scientist, and Severence Hall. Dana Clark designed both buildings in succession for Walker and Weeks (first the church and then the hall). Johannesen writes that Clark found certain aesthetic solutions discovered in the church so satisfying as to be irresistible for reuse . . . Both [buildings have] neoclassical exteriors and . . . modernistic interiors . . . the church is the more classical [building]. The octagonal shape of the First Church is a clearly defined geometric solid, and the portico of four columns is a true classical temple front, instead of being elevated on an entrance podium [like the hall] . . . The similarities between the [church] sanctuary interior and the grand foyer of Severance are . . . remarkable. Although the foyer is elliptical and the church circular, both spaces are bounded by a colonnaded gallery with Ionic columns [in restoring the church, City Architecture maintained the nineteen marble columns of the balcony]. An oculus opening of a painted sky dome in the [church] sanctuary . . . became a circular ceiling motif in the [hall] foyer, and the lacy filigree ornament of the church ceiling is closely echoed in the Severance Hall auditorium.[123]

First Church of Christ, Scientist, moved to their new house of worship in 1931. Fifty years later, the congregation left the building, and, by 1995 the structure was threatened with demolition. In 1998 part of the north facade of the church was ripped away to facilitate the plugging of an abandoned gas well that was leaking beneath the building.

On its elevated site at the edge of the Allegheny escarpment, Nottingham Spirk Design Associates stands, adjacent to the old mansions and new apartments of Cleveland Heights, atop a hill overlooking the city. From here, looking west, one can see most of the buildings in this guide along the Downtown-University Circle Dual Hub Corridor and most of those in north and south-central Cleveland.

This is a robust eight-sided masonry building—clean, majestic, solid, and symmetrical. Monumentally grand, this is not obviously a religious institution. It could as well be a school, an auditorium, a library, or a design center. The two-story portico with its enlarged triangular cornice is supported by four modified Corinthian pillars. A Palladian window dominates the center of the second story over the entrance. The other second-story facades around the octagon have three large non-Palladian windows. It has a new eight-sided metal roof. As a religious structure, the building's chief distinguishing feature was its giant flanking "campanile," which is atypical of Christian Science churches.[124] This open tower was long used as a chimney and thus known throughout University Circle as "the smoking minaret." It is not obvious to drivers climbing Edgehill Road to the north behind the church (who, one hopes, are keeping their eyes on the road) that this building rests on a three-story Sunday school extending down the hill behind the church. At the bottom of the hill, adjacent to Edgehill Road, is a park and day care center for Nottingham Spirk employees.

The octagonal auditorium is a form often used in Christian Science churches. Robert Mills in his Richmond, Virginia, Monumental Church, introduced this plan in the United States as a means of housing large congregations in a comfortable auditorium with good sightlines. The pews on the ground floor of the sanctuary are now replaced by the desks and apparatus of the large design studio. Nottingham Spirk gave the pews to replace those of a church that burned. Restored original chandeliers hang from a wonderful and wonderfully restored plaster ceiling.

23. Garfield Memorial Monument
(1890)
Architects: George Keller and John S. Chapple
Builders: Jeptha Wade, Henry Payne, and Joseph Perkins
Location: Lake View Cemetery

James Garfield—preacher (see the Federated Church, p. 364, and Franklin Circle Christian Church, p. 187), teacher, soldier, and congressman—was briefly the twentieth president of the United States. Shot by a deranged office-seeker four months after his inauguration as he tried to put together a government amid national struggles over patronage issues, Garfield's assassination became the catalyst for the development of the civil service in the United States.[125] In addition to the stimulus that the circumstances of his death gave to the cause of good government, it generated an outpouring of national sympathy for the slowly dying president and for his family.[126] The national outrage following his death resulted in a large subscription for a memorial in Lake View Cemetery, high on a hill overlooking Lake Erie and the city of Cleveland.[127] This hill is said to be the beginning of the foothills of the Allegheny Mountains. The observation deck of the memorial provides a spectacular view of eastern Cleveland down to the Lake Erie. The granite Rockefeller spire down the road is the tallest in the world.

Henry Payne, Joseph Perkins, and Jeptha Wade established the Garfield Memorial Association. In 1883 they sponsored a design competition won by George Keller of Hartford, Connecticut. John S. Chapple of London assisted Keller in the design by supervising the work on the mosaics and the stained-glass windows. Construction of the monument began in 1885, and it was dedicated on Memorial Day 1890, with President Benjamin Harrison, former President Rutherford Hayes, and Vice President Levi Morton in attendance.

The castlelike round main tower, with its conical-shaped dome and secondary octagonal towers, is Romanesque. Constructed of rough-cut Ohio sandstone, the structure is both a tomb and a memorial. The three-tiered circular central tower, 180 feet high and fifty feet in diameter, rises from an extended square base and terrace area approached by a wide flight of steps. Around the exterior of the base, life-size reliefs of Garfield show five periods of his life—as teacher, soldier, congressman, president, and in death. One can find the caskets of Garfield and his wife and two urns containing the ashes of his daughter and son-in-law in the crypt beneath the base of the tower.

On the main level, a three-foot-thick circular wall supports the vaulted floor above. A perimeter aisle is spanned by arched buttresses. The buttresses, along with the point openings in the entrance portal and surrounding porch windows, are Gothic. At the center of the Memorial Room is a larger than life Carrara marble statue of President Garfield standing in front of a marble replica of the chair he used in the White House. At the time the memorial was built, its builders considered it the first true mausoleum in the United States combining a tomb and memorial. They claimed that it was the fourth such structure in the world after the Mausoleum at Halicarnassus and the Mausolea of Metellus and of Hadrian in Rome. The "soul" and the "central thought" of the memorial was the statue of Garfield. While such ideas may be "light years rather than decades"[128] away from the twenty-first century, such extravagant memorials were typical of the High Victorian period.

Upper galleries surround the central rotunda. Stone mosaic panes depicting various allegorical mourning processions decorate the inside of the chamber below a dome. Several winding stairways (closed to the public in 1994) lead to the observation deck and upper spaces. The first space, above the rotunda, is a large chamber with a circumferential ambulatory. In the center of this space, which occupies the entire tower, is the top of the rotunda dome, separated from the ambulatory by a large wall reaching almost halfway to the brick-dome ceiling of this space. Another story up is the great circular room of the memorial's famous "ballroom." The ceiling of the "ballroom" is a vast brick beehive dome that supports the conical masonry roof of the monument. The ballroom was never used as such. Its social use would have been severely restricted by the narrow spiral stairways leading up to it, too narrow for either dresses or food. Johannesen reminds us that "the Memorial is a massive engineering work";[129] the outward thrust of the roof is counteracted by an iron tension ring whose spokes, extending out above the ballroom, are embedded in the stonework of the dome.

The memorial, and the Wade Chapel down the hill with its famous Tiffany glass, is maintained and staffed by Lake View Cemetery and is open from nine in the morning to four in the afternoon from April 1 to November 19 (Garfield's birthday).

24. Wade Memorial Chapel (1900)
Architects: Hubbell and Benes
Builder: Jeptha Wade II
Location: Lake View Cemetery

Cleveland is fortunate in having two nationally famous ensembles of glass in two quite different styles in two quite different parts of town—the 1906 Mayer windows at St. Stephen on the West Side and the 1900 Tiffany glass and mosaic glass ensemble in the Wade Memorial Chapel.[130] The Tiffany spectacular (more than seventy-five linear feet of glass) was assembled by Jeptha Wade II in honor of his grandfather, Jeptha Wade, one of the founders of Western Union. In common with his grandson, Wade was one of Cleveland's major philanthropists. The Wades gave their estate of more than seventy-five acres and a great deal of money to the City of Cleveland and the institutions around University Circle.

Understanding the physical peculiarities of their little neoclassical chapel and the iconography of its decoration involves an understanding of its function and of Jeptha Wade the elder. No one is buried in Wade Chapel. The Wades are buried on Wade Hill farther back in the cemetery. The chapel was built as a temporary repository for the dead and a place for funerals. Remains were transported to the crypt below the chapel.[131] Family and friends gathered in the chapel above, together with imported clergy. This explains the front portico, which embraces a carriage driveway similar to those in front of turn-of-the-century homes. Inside the chapel, the architects designed an elevator, complete with rollers for the casket, which brings the departed up to the front of the chapel from the crypt below. The unique and not-quite-Christian exuberance of Tiffany's funereal decoration is explained in part by the fact that Jeptha the elder was a Unitarian (nonpracticing).[132] The chapel is rarely used for funerals but, because of the classic beauty of the building, its setting, and the extravagance of its decoration, it has become a favorite site for weddings.

The chapel sits on a small rise at the bottom of the hill below the Garfield Memorial. It is sited so that the complex of small rooms in the crypt are hidden from the front driveway. The crypt is in a giant order, rock-faced, light tan, sandstone platform at the back of the chapel, slightly below the top of the rise. The marble-lined crypt overlooks a pond fed by a spring welling up in its center. The pond is so peaceful and quiet that one may be disappointed to find that no one is buried in the crypt.

Designed by Hubbell and Benes, who were also architects for the Cleveland Museum of Art, the neoclassic architectural elements of the granite upper chapel include the extended front portico supported by four fluted columns and topped by Ionic capitals, a low-slung pediment roof, and a wide, unadorned frieze below a dentilated roof cornice. The classical style was not rigidly copied. This is not at all a Roman temple. For example, the driveway width determines the spacing of the half-round columns on the sides of the building, and there are half as many as one would expect on an ancient building.

The marble interior, probably inspired by Louis Comfort Tiffany's personal Egyptian tour, includes two sets of large bronze doors, floor tiles symbolizing the "Voyage of Life," Lebanese cedar benches, and Islamic chandeliers. Designed by Tiffany and Frederick Wilson and executed by the Tiffany Studios, these were beautifully restored in 1986–87. The large stained-glass window, set in a gold-glass tesserae wall opposite the entrance, portrays *The Consummation of the Divine Promise*. Based on William Blake's 1783 painting of Christ, experts have hailed this as one of Tiffany's finest windows. Before installation, it was exhibited at the 1900 World Exposition in Paris.

Unoccupied walls and ceiling are marble. Each side wall is covered with an eight-foot-high, thirty-two-foot-long glass mosaic mural. These, with their many allegorical figures and oarsmen, straining beside symbolic shields, also represent the "Voyage of Life." Although the subjects are different, the walls parallel each other with corresponding oarsmen and other figures. On the left is *The Prophecy and Law of the Old Testament,* alternatively known as the wall of *The Law and the Prophets.* The prophets are rowing toward the front of the chapel. Women represent various aspects of Judaism. All move toward an Angel of Sacrifice. On the right is *The Fulfillment and Light of the New Testament,* also known as the wall of *Fulfillment.* Here, saints are rowing and the women represent the gifts of the Holy Spirit. They are moving toward an Angel of the Eucharist. In summary, Johannesen wrote that "The Wade Memorial Chapel combines the late nineteenth-century desire for symbolic representation, a free adaptation of classical architectural style, and the important principle of collaboration between architects and artists that would continue in force until the 1930s."[133]

The chapel, like the Garfield Monument up the hill, is maintained and staffed by Lake View Cemetery and is open from nine in the morning to four in the afternoon from April l to November 19 (Garfield's birthday). (Since the chapel is also used for weddings and funerals, out of town visitors should confirm that it will be open to the public during their visit by calling 216-421-2665.)

CHAPTER TWO

North Central Cleveland

Three neighborhoods make up North Central Cleveland: Goodrich-Kirtland, Hough, and St. Clair-Superior.

The Goodrich-Kirtland neighborhood, originally the home of Irish and German immigrants, was largely made up of small shops and houses. The construction of the Pennsylvania Railroad transformed this area into two distinct districts: north of St. Clair Avenue became industrial and south of St. Clair became industrial-commercial. A few of the old and influential neighborhood institutions remain scattered along Superior, hinting at the area's former character. Cleveland's Asian community clusters along Payne, Rockwell, and St. Clair Avenues.

Tour

Begin the tour at the Innerbelt-Superior Avenue interchange and travel east on Superior. Modern St. Nicholas Parish (Croatian) (25) stands on the northwest corner of the intersection at East 36th Street. There, visitors enter the church from a small, secluded plaza, approached from the back and screened from the street by a hedge.

Continue on Superior to East 40th Street. North Presbyterian Church (26) occupies the northeast corner. The building resembles a school more than a church. Turn left (north) onto East 40th. On the right (east), in the middle of the block, is St. Paul's Croatian Church (27). At St. Clair, turn right (east). Turn right again (south) onto East 41st Street. At Superior, turn left (east). On the northeast corner is Immaculate Conception Parish (28), a large Gothic building with Victorian gables above its entrances. Drive east on Superior. On the left, at East 51st Street is the former location of St. Andrew Roman Catholic Church, taken down in 2009.

Turn left (north) at East 53rd Street. Travel on East 53rd for only one block and then turn right (east) at Spencer Avenue. At the end of Spencer turn right (south) onto East 55th Street. On the corner is St. Paul Lutheran Church. Travel south on East 55th. The east side of East 55th, south of Superior, lies in the Hough neighborhood; the west side lies in Goodrich-Kirtland.

Named after early landowners Oliver and Eliza Hough, the Hough neighborhood, by the mid-1870s, had become a fashionable residential district characterized by large single-family homes. Between 1920 and 1950, Hough remained a predominantly white, working-class neighborhood. Hough's African American population—5 percent in 1950—had grown to 74 percent in 1960. Riots in July 1966 reflected the city's and the nation's racial tensions and frustrations. Over a one-week period in Hough, four died, thirty were injured, three hundred were arrested, and there were 240 fires.[1] Willson United Methodist Church, a Romanesque Revival building, is located south of Superior on East

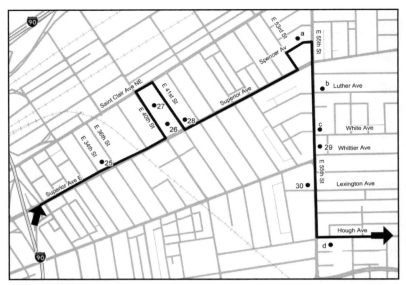

GOODRICH–KIRTLAND

25. St. Nicholas Parish (Croatian)
26. North Presbyterian Church
27. St. Paul's Croatian Church
28. Immaculate Conception Parish
   a. St. Paul Lutheran Church

b. Willson United Methodist Church
c. Corinthian Baptist Church
29. St. James Church
30. Fellowship Missionary Baptist Church
   d. Emmanu-El A.M.E. Zion Church

55th, on the northeast corner of the East 55th Street–Luther Avenue intersection. Continue on East 55th. Corinthian Baptist Church stands on the northeast corner at White Avenue. Built in 1894 as White German Baptist, the building has belonged to the Corinthian congregation since 1979. On the left, south of Corinthian Baptist is St. James Church (29), a small stone-and-frame building that would look more at home in a small English village than on East 55th. Fellowship Missionary Baptist Church (30) lies farther south on the right, on the corner of Lexington Avenue at East 55th. A German Lutheran congregation built this church, located in the Goodrich-Kirtland neighborhood.

A few blocks farther south, at Hough Avenue, turn left (east). Emmanu-El A.M.E. Zion Church is to the south. Travel east on Hough, past the Salvation Army, to East 65th Street. Bethel Church of Christ Bible Way (formerly the Hough Avenue United Church of Christ) stands on the northwest corner of the intersection. This sandstone building, built in Richardson Romanesque style, has a unique lantern. Continue east, past Martin Luther King High School on the left, to East 79th Street. Turn right (south) onto East 79th. Drive on East 79th toward Chester Avenue. Gethsemane Baptist Church is located on the left, opposite Home Avenue. Turn left (east) onto Chester Avenue. Travel on Chester to East 89th Street.

Turn left (north) onto East 89th Street. The modern University Church of Christ lies on the right. Drive north on East 89th Street and cross Hough

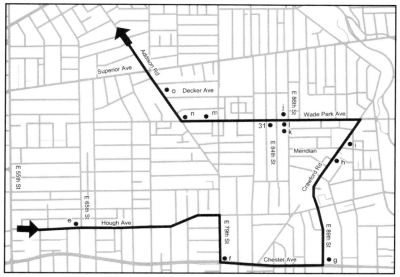

HOUGH

e. Bethel Church of Christ Bible Way
f. Gethsemane Baptist Church
g. University Church of Christ
h. Crawford Road Christian Church
i. Star of Bethel Missionary Baptist Church
j. Nazarene Baptist Church Inc.

k. Christ Church
l. St. Matthew United Methodist Church
31. Fidelity Baptist Church
m. Greater Avery A.M.E. Church
n. Bethel Seventh Day Adventist Church
o. New Jerusalem Baptist Church

Avenue. To the left is the large campus of the Thurgood Marshall Recreation Center. When East 89th crosses Hough, it becomes Crawford Road. Continue on Crawford. Shortly after passing Meridian Avenue on the left, Crawford Road Christian Church appears on the right. Built in 1907, it evolved from the Cedar Avenue Christian Church, which had been founded in 1883. The Star of Bethel Missionary Baptist Church occupies the northeast corner of Crawford at Kenmore Avenue. Continue northeast on Crawford to Wade Park Avenue.

Turn left (west) onto Wade Park. After passing East 86th Street, the Nazarene Baptist Church Inc. (built as Church of the Holy Spire in 1893) lies to the north, Christ Church lies to the south of East 86th at Wade Park, and St. Matthew United Methodist Church (constructed in 1907) lies to its north. On the southeast corner of East 84th Street at Wade Park stands Fidelity Baptist Church (31), Sidney Badgley's only frame church, constructed in 1891. Continue west on Wade Park. After crossing East 79th Street, you first see Greater Avery A.M.E. Church, followed by Bethel Seventh Day Adventist Church on the right at the corner of Wade Park and Addison Road.

Turn right (north) onto Addison. After two blocks, New Jerusalem Baptist Church stands on the northeast corner of Addison at Decker Avenue. After Addison crosses Superior, enter the St. Clair-Superior neighborhood. Continue on

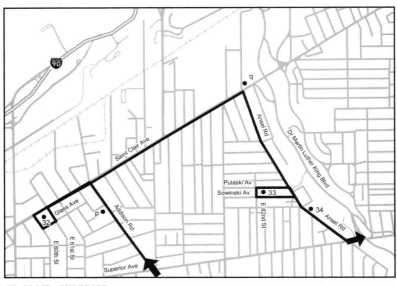

ST. CLAIR–SUPERIOR

p. Fair Temple Church of God
32. St. Vitus Church
q. St. Philip Neri Roman Catholic Church

33. St. Casimir Church
34. Hitchcock Center for Women

Addison past the white-painted frame Fair Temple Church of God on the left. At St. Clair, turn left (west) and continue to East 61st Street. Turn left (south) on East 61st and travel for one block. On the right corner lies St. Vitus Church (32). The St. Vitus school, on the left, has become the award-winning St. Martin de Porres High School. Turn right (west) onto Lausche-Glass Avenue, and travel past the entrance to St. Vitus for one block. Turn right (north) onto East 60th Street. After one block on East 60th, turn right (east) back onto St. Clair. This area became ground zero for the 1944 East Ohio Gas Company explosion, which killed 130 and leveled the neighborhood—except for St. Vitus.

Travel east on St. Clair to its intersection with Ansel Road. At Ansel, turn right (south). When turning, note the contemporary church and modified rose window of St. Philip Neri Roman Catholic Church on the northeast corner. Drive south on Ansel and then turn right (west) onto Sowinski Avenue. Turn right again (north) onto East 82nd Street. On the right, behind the new elementary school on Ansel, stands St. Casimir Church (33) with its tall twin brick towers. After passing the church, turn right (east) onto Pulaski Avenue and return to Ansel. Turn right one more time back onto Ansel. South on Ansel, the Hitchcock Center for Women (formerly St. Mary Seminary) (34) is on the left.

Continue on Ansel Road to Superior. Here this tour ends. One block to the left (east), Martin Luther King Jr. Drive provides easy access to the Shoreway via Rockefeller Park.

25. St. Nicholas Parish

(Croatian) (1972)
Architect: Berj A. Shakarian
Builder: Unknown
Location: 3431 Superior
Avenue

St. Nicholas was the first (1901) and now the only remaining Byzantine Croatian Catholic Church in the United States.[2] The Eparchy (Diocese) of Krizevci in central Croatia encouraged the establishment of this church. In 1901 the eparchy sent Mile Dolubic to the Croatian communities in Pittsburgh, Cleveland, and Chicago to follow up on efforts by an 1894 missionary in Pennsylvania. Between World Wars I and II, the eparchy was responsible for all Byzantine Catholics in Yugoslavia and abroad; however, in 1938—perhaps anticipating the tumult that was about to envelope the Balkans—the Vatican transferred the relatively few American Byzantine Croatian Catholics to the Apostolic Exarchate of the United States for the Ruthenians. St. Nicholas's supervision and much of its support now comes from the Eparchy of Parma (see the Cathedral of St. John the Baptist, p. 310).

Although most Croatians are Roman Catholic (see St. Paul's Croatian Church, p. 76), Cleveland is the beneficiary of an extremely robust Croatian population. Thus, the Croatian Byzantine Catholics also established a vigorous, if relatively small, religious community here. Their church is in the heart, with St. Paul's Croatian Church, of what used to be Cleveland's Croatia. Croatian Byzantine Catholics located their first church in a former Protestant church at the corner of St. Clair Avenue at East 41st Street. They bought an existing church at their present location in 1913. In 1973 (at the same time that other Croatians acquired one hundred acres on Mulberry Road in Chesterland for a Croatian center) they defiantly replaced their old building. Berj A. Shakarian's interesting modern church became the first ethnic church built in Cleveland in more than a decade. Shakarian is best known as the Cuyahoga County government architect.

This small church deserves its reputation as an important, urban religious landmark. Cleverly tucked into a neighborhood of large commercial buildings, it turns its back, of necessity, on the weekday uproar around it and focuses on a small, secluded, gracious entrance courtyard.[3] This court—circumscribed by church, rectory, and street—is not as isolated from Superior Avenue as it appears. Only a low wall separates the court and the street, although two large trees and other landscaping screen it from the outside. This more-or-less hidden court faces the ceremonial entrance to the church—a broad wall of glass flanked by narrow, two-story mosaics of *Angels*. From the court, three steps up take one to the glass wall of the narthex.

Built using large tan bricks, the church provides a marked contrast to the

Roman brick of the rectory. The church remains a building of wonderful modern planes and masses highlighted by its elaborate and famous scalloped bell tower on Superior. The facade on Superior appears as a series of smooth unbroken brick planes. These planes both step down and step back, separated by narrow continuous slit windows.

Inside, the church has a center aisle Orthodox worship space with two side aisles and small transepts. The south wall, toward Superior, is built of plain brick. The north wall, paneled with wood ribs, features reproductions of more than forty small icons. There is no real iconostasis: the sanctuary is defined by four large and two small, freestanding icons. The large icons are of *Mary, Jesus, Nicolas,* and *John the Baptist.* The sanctuary wall, behind the altar, displays a wonderful mosaic of *Mary* with a symbolic roundel of *Jesus* in front of her. On either side of the central mosaic hang a row of small icons. A shrine of the Crucifixion lies to the left of the altar and a shrine of the Resurrection lies to the right. The wall behind the chancel is composed of plain plaster articulated with stained frame ribs. Pews are constructed from a warm, stained wood, and there is a large balcony with a low ceiling. This proves an innovative church for a small ethnic congregation.

26. North Presbyterian Church (1887)
Architects: Forest Coburn and Frank Barnum
Builder: William Gaston
Location: 4001 Superior Avenue

As the neighborhoods around Public Square became less residential during the middle of the nineteenth century, the Old Stone Church (see p. 12) drew its congregation from two directions: affluent Presbyterians on Euclid Avenue along Millionaire's Row and middle-class Presbyterians on St. Clair and Superior Avenues into the Goodrich-Kirtland neighborhood.[4] The year before the Civil War began, Old Stone planted a Sunday school, known as the Wassonville Mission, at East 41st Street at St. Clair Avenue.[5] Eight years later, this branch moved to East 36th Street north of Superior Avenue, and—after three more years, in 1870—the mission became a permanent institution as North Presbyterian Church.[6] Anson Smythe became North Presbyterian's first pastor. He had served previously as both Ohio's commissioner of education and the superintendent of the Cleveland Public Schools, and he subsequently became known as "the father of the Cleveland Public Library."

Long after organizing the mission as a permanent institution, Old Stone Church continued to furnish workers, support, and most of the funds for the present building, with the omnipresent Presbyterian philanthropist Flora Stone Mather as the largest contributor. In 1887, the congregation moved into this extremely unusual, 1,130-seat Akron Plan church. At first the congregation was successfully running one of the largest children's Sunday schools in Cleveland. By the late nineteenth century, however, Goodrich-Kirtland had become a largely Roman and Byzantine Catholic neighborhood with a large influx of Slovenian, Lithuanian, Croatian, German, and Polish factory workers. By the 1920s the population was only 25 percent Protestant. Then, as the neighborhood became industrial and commercial, almost everybody left. The population of Goodrich-Kirtland fell from 29,000 in 1910 to 4,500 in 1990. This resulted in North Presbyterian, which had been vigorously committed to a variety of programs benefiting the less fortunate, becoming less fortunate itself. Except for a brief solvent interlude from 1945 to 1960, North Presbyterian has been an aided congregation since 1918.

From the outside, this unusual religious building with its businesslike rows of windows may appear more like a school than a church. This is not a coincidence. In 1887 Forest Coburn and Frank Barnum were also building the superficially similar, no longer extant, Case Western Reserve University Medical School at East Ninth Street at St. Clair. Eight years later Barnum won appointment as the superintendent of buildings for the Cleveland Board of Education. In this capacity, he built eighty-six public schools.

North Presbyterian is trimmed with a combination of Victorian Gothic and Romanesque detail. Gothic are the pointed arches, a restrained central rose window, finials, and spires. Romanesque are the rounded arch entranceway with jamb shafts and the squared-off bell tower with pyramidal roof. The short belfry above the main entrance from Superior does not convincingly identify the building as a church, and the substantial dome above the sanctuary remains mostly hidden from the street level by the high, fenestrated walls.

The sanctuary, elevated almost a full story above the street, sits on top of a first story containing administrative, social, and educational space. One accesses the church now from the parking lot behind the building, rather than from Superior as first planned. The stairs originally giving access to the second story sanctuary from Superior divide inside the entrance and lead up on both the left and the right to the worship space. These divided stairs at North Presbyterian are a larger version of the 1891 entrance to St. Timothy's on Chester (see p. 31), also built as a Presbyterian church.

From the austere exterior of this building, it is difficult to know what to expect on the inside. The sanctuary offers a surprise. North Presbyterian is a variant of the Akron Plan (see chapter 7, note 41, concerning Pilgrim Congregational Church). The North Presbyterian version, although popular in small-town nineteenth-century Protestant churches, is relatively rare in Cleveland. North Presbyterian does not have a separate Sunday school assembly area as in the Sidney Badgley–designed Akron Plan churches most common in Cleveland.[7] At North Presbyterian, the classrooms open into the main sanctuary.

The architecture of the building, by the arrangement of the Sunday school rooms around the sanctuary and their expression on the exterior, clearly announces this church's interest in education. The windowed walls that—from the outside—make the building look like a school, flood the Akron Plan educational space with light.

Even with these Akron Plan Sunday school doors up and increased seating for 1,130, the sanctuary would appear much smaller than one might expect when looking at the outside of the church. Because the metal doors dividing the classroom spaces from the central sanctuary are now pulled down (probably permanently), the relative smallness becomes accentuated. This turns the sanctuary, even with its wraparound balcony, into a small semicircular area. This smaller worship space soars up more than three stories into the sixteen-sided dome. This height, as in an Orthodox church, helps contribute to the impression of relative smallness.

This Presbyterian congregation spent—or asked Flora Stone Mather to spend—on brick and mortar construction rather than the decorative luxury of stained glass. The glazing has little ornament and is not figurative. The frontal screen is plain, stained wood.

27. St. Paul's Croatian Church
(1903)
Architect: Gerhard Tenbusch
Builder: Milan Sutlic
Location: 1369 East 40th Street

The bustling, animated, decidedly non-English atmosphere of the old-fashioned but bright and freshly painted St. Paul's Croatian rectory takes a visitor back one hundred years—back to a time when ethnic Roman Catholic parishes in Cleveland served the economic, social, and educational, as well as the spiritual, needs of their newly arrived immigrant populations.[8] Today's Croatian newcomers still visit St. Paul's Croatian seeking work, housing, advice, and companionship from clergy and staff fluent in Croatian. Yet this historical parallel is, of course, not completely accurate: St. Paul's Croatian also serves as the cultural and spiritual center of one thousand Croatian families in northeastern Ohio, many of whose roots here, like their church, go back more than a hundred years. Nevertheless, economic and political turmoil in the Balkans has continued to drive a stream of Croatian immigrants to Cleveland, who, in turn, look to their church for help adapting to life in the United States.

Cleveland has the fourth-largest Croatian population in the United States (after Pittsburgh, Chicago, and New York) and, as a result, has always been a center of Croatian cultural and political activity. Croatian immigration into Cleveland began in the 1860s and peaked about 1910. In Cleveland, the Croatians have been closely associated with their old-country neighbors, the Slovenians. The Slovenians the Croatians had known in Europe helped attract them to Cleveland. Croatians settled together with Slovenians along St. Clair and worked with them in the heavy industry located along the lake. Croatian immigrants originally worshiped in the Slovenian congregation of St. Vitus (see p. 85).[9] The Croatian Union of Fraternal Lodges served as the catalyst for a church of their own. In 1901, the community purchased property and petitioned the bishop of Cleveland and archbishop of Zagreb for a Croatian priest. Construction began shortly after Father Milan Sutlic's arrival the following year, and they celebrated the first Mass in 1904. St. Paul's is an unusual—but not unique—Roman Catholic church in three ways. First, the parishioners largely built the building themselves instead of hiring workers. Second, the current building remains essentially unchanged from what it was when first constructed more than one hundred years ago. Third, the parish did not begin construction of a school until five years after moving into the church.[10] When Sutlic went back to Croatia, Father Niko Grskovic from Chicago took his place. In 1917, Father Grskovic went on to lead the Yugoslav Committee in Washington, D.C., and publish the only daily Croatian newspaper outside of Croatia.

St. Paul's Church established Christ the King Parish as a mission in Akron in 1935. Croatian immigration continued during the interwar period because of many Croatians' opposition to the way their nation had been incorporated into the Yugoslavian state. During World War II, forty-seven parishioners and one priest from St. Paul's died serving in the armed forces. By the 1950s, half a century after the initial economic wave of Croatian immigration to Cleveland, a second, political wave of immigration arrived, composed of thousands of young and often highly educated Croats fleeing the Communists. They reenergized the Croatian neighborhood around St. Clair and its churches.[11] While St. Paul's parishioners have now spread to eight counties in northeast Ohio, they continue to find their cultural and spiritual home on East 40th in Cleveland.

This modest, well-maintained, and well-proportioned Gothic meetinghouse lies in the middle of a heterogeneous industrial, commercial, and residential neighborhood. Gothic style elements include pointed arches over entry doors with shallow jamb shafts, pointed stained-glass windows, and a louvered belfry capped by a conical copper spire surrounded by finials. However, the corbel brick effect beneath the gabled edge of the roof is Romanesque, and the squared-off bell tower is classical. Above the entrance looms a commanding, white, larger-than-life-sized statue of St. Paul created by the Croatian sculptor Josip Turkalj. It is enough to keep the hands of king or commissar off this congregation. Turkalj founded and served as the longtime leader of the art department at Gilmour Academy. He also crafted, in a modern representational style, the dramatic shallow-relief panels installed in the sanctuary and the narthex in 1981.

The interior—a simple hall—has retained its original appearance. Most of the glass is early twentieth century, except for a small round window above the altar showing St. Paul and Pope Paul VI in anachronistic equality. Above the windows are large paintings on the concave lateral ceilings located below a central flat ceiling. Like the Sistine Chapel before Michelangelo, the central ceiling has been painted with stars in a blue field. On the balcony at the rear of the sanctuary stands the original tracker organ.

28. Immaculate Conception Parish
(1873)
Architects: Koehler and Lane
Builder: Thomas Thorpe
Location: 4129 Superior Avenue

The great (geographical west) bell and (geographical east) clock towers of Immaculate Conception dominate views of Superior Avenue along the mile from the Innerbelt to East 55th Street.[12] Described by Foster Armstrong as "one of Cleveland's finest examples of a Victorian Gothic-style church," Immaculate Conception is a magnificent masonry shell embracing a large and carefully restored Gothic Revival sanctuary and little else. It has few of the appurtenances usually associated with such a large religious building—only recently installing a bathroom. It still does not have a bride's room. The floor space of the breathtaking two-story baptistry is relatively small, and the sacristy is tiny. The apse/chevette at the head of the sanctuary is shallow; the chapel is small and the narthex is narrow. Yet Immaculate Conception has a tall, commodious, beautiful, and well-proportioned sanctuary with a thin layer of Gothic clothing.

The history of this parish intertwines with that of the Cathedral of St. John the Evangelist. The location of the first Catholic church in Cleveland, Our Lady of the Lake (generally known as St. Mary-on-the-Flats), was too distant from the Roman Catholic population. The first Catholic bishop, Amadeus Rappe, decided to build a second church—a cathedral—on the present site of the Cathedral of St. John the Evangelist. They built a small frame "chapel of ease,"[13] called the Chapel of the Nativity because of its first use on Christmas Day 1848, on the construction site to accommodate the congregation of the under-construction cathedral. When the congregation moved into the new cathedral, the parish used the Chapel of the Nativity as a school for three years, then dragged it thirty blocks up Superior, and installed it—still as the cathedral's chapel of ease—on Immaculate Conception's present site. Ten years later the chapel became a permanent parish, but in that interval it had acquired a new name, Immaculate

Conception, certainly reflecting the excitement surrounding Pius IX's definition of this dogma in 1854. Five years after Immaculate Conception became a parish, its first priest, a Canadian, was needed by a French-speaking parish; Thomas Thorpe arrived as the replacement. Within two years, Thorpe had replaced the old chapel with a new, temporary church and began the current building the following year. Construction stalled when the Diocese established the parish of St. Columbkille in between Immaculate Conception and the cathedral. As soon as Thorpe had managed to restore Immaculate Conception's fortunes and push forward with the building, he was transferred to the cathedral as rector (dean). His departure coincided with an economic downturn in Cleveland, and construction moved forward slowly or not at all. At last, twelve years into the project, the great church was dedicated, minus its clerestory and towers. On the death of Thorpe's successor as Immaculate Conception's pastor, Thorpe, after serving seventeen years as Rector of St. John the Evangelist, asked to return to Immaculate Conception. There, despite another economic depression and the inroads of newly formed St. Agnes, the redoubtable Thorpe completed his church—including the bell tower—in 1898, installed eleven bells in 1899, and completed the clock tower in 1900.

Immaculate Conception played an important role in diocesan education. For decades its school served as the observation school and teacher training center for the Sister's College of Cleveland, subsequently St. John's College, established in 1928 for the education of teaching nuns. The church has long enjoyed a somewhat specious reputation as being one of the great Irish parishes of Cleveland. Early in its history, a majority of the parish claimed they were from County Mayo: the men, who had originally come to dig the Erie Canal, worked on the docks; women worked as domestics along Millionaire's Row. In fact, Immaculate Conception lost its Irish feel early in its history and has had an international flavor for more than a century. In 1989 the parish began celebrating weekly Tridentine Latin Masses.

The massive rough masonry of the church makes it a powerful presence along the commercial neighborhood on both sides of Superior. Pointed arches above the window and door openings, a large front gable with niche and statue, and recessed portals with gables and jamb shafts are Gothic in style, as are the modified crenellation with finials on the taller tower and the triangular gables and crockets on the shorter tower. Unlike most neo-Gothic churches, the buttresses along the walls are not decorative. They actually function to counter the outward thrust of the roof on the walls.

Like a Gothic cathedral, everything in the sanctuary seems vertical, directing the eye upward to the distant ceiling and toward the gorgeous, high-quality Bavarian glass windows, installed during one of the church's infrequent prosperous periods of the late nineteenth century. In contrast to the rough, stained, and weathered exterior of the building, the inside is plastered, clean, light, graceful, and airy.

29. St. James Church (1890)
Architect: H. B. Smith
Builder: Theodore Foote
Location: 1681 East 55th Street

Even for Episcopalians, who are used to variations in worship, St. James is different—so different, in fact, that it is no longer Episcopalian.[14] More than thirty years ago, it left the Episcopal Diocese of Ohio and—with other like-minded conservatives—formed the Anglican Catholic Church. This branch of the church organized in St. Louis in 1978 in protest of the revision of the 1928 Episcopalian Book of Common Prayer and the ordination of women. The Anglican Catholic Church has its own bishops, and its primate is the Metropolitan and Archbishop in Athens, Georgia.[15] St. James is part of the Diocese of the Midwest in Indianapolis.

Trinity Church, which became the Episcopal Cathedral (see p. 21), was briefly large enough—or Cleveland was small enough, that it could house all Episcopalians in worship. By 1846, however, Trinity had fallen under the influence of the Oxford movement. This Anglo-Catholic movement in the Church of England promoted a more sacramental, medieval, "High Church" style of worship of "smells" (incense) and "bells" (sounded during the service to tell people what to do). The second bishop of Ohio, "obsessed with the dangers of ritualism," established St. Paul's (see pp. 28 and 329) as a "Low Church" to keep the Oxford movement in Ohio at bay.[16] In contrast, Trinity had always had degrees of Anglo-Catholicism; it eventually settled into a "Middle Church" pattern that would prove compatible with becoming a cathedral representing everyone in the diocese. St. James, established in 1857 to provide, in part, a haven for the more conservative Anglo-Catholics, remains so today. At this point, short of a Tridentine Latin Mass, St. James—with its reserved Sacrament and its confessions—is as or is more sacramental than any of the most liturgically conservative parishes in the Roman Catholic Diocese of Cleveland.

St. James's original frame building was replaced with a brick church, built in 1865 at the corner of Superior Avenue at East 26th Street, a lot now occupied by the west Superior exit off the Innerbelt. This church, in turn, was replaced in 1890 by the present stone church, never finished. Under the influence of English Benedictines, the parish enlarged the church in 1938 to better accommodate the "High Church" Mass. They greatly expanded the area behind the communion rail in a large addition to the east.

This is a challenging, difficult neighborhood and the church gives—probably intentionally—an initial impression of modest circumstances. From East 55th Street, St. James appears a humble, hundred-year-old masonry structure, identified as a religious building only vaguely by the massing of the simple structure and the weathered small masonry cross at the peak of its front gable. From this busy but poverty-stricken thoroughfare, only a small paved parking lot is visible behind the church's carefully locked chain-link fence. Only an opaque and rather unpromising hedge is visible from Whittier Avenue, the street beside the church. The chain-link fence opens, however, to reveal that, behind the church, there nestles a carefully tended garden, shaded by two handsome trees, with well-kept flower beds and two peaceful tabernacle shrines—one of the *Virgin* and one of the *Crucifixion*. Across the garden stands a nicely painted (all this is at odds with the neighborhood) building, also shaded from the street, used as the church office, educational, and social space with an apartment for the Rector. Even the bars on the windows are painted and attractive.

The church features a good-sized worship area with a timbered roof. The entrance from the street, as originally designed, is composed of a small, completely undecorated, narthex at the side rear with a step up to the level of the nave. (Worshipers now enter through the sacristy from a back entrance on the parking lot.) The back of the nave is filled with a Holtkamp organ (Walter Blodgett played here) and seating for the choir. A large, 2005 west window, featuring a brightly colored, compatible, conservative style, is dedicated to *St. James* and the four parts of the United Kingdom. The window's presence is not obvious from the outside. This window replaced an original window that had disintegrated and then had been dismantled and replaced with brick. It is now gloriously reopened. The rest of the church glass is lozenge patterned, dating from the original construction. The area around the altar is much larger than that typical of a church of this size. On either side of the altar stand brightly polychromed half life-sized statues installed in 1917: *St. James* on the left and *St. Michael* on the right. The wall behind the altar is paneled beautifully and plainly with stained wood. A large stained wood baldachin arches up over the altar from the wall. The church features a good deal of carved and sculpted decoration, some polychromed, all around its interior. This gives the nave its "High Church" atmosphere. Over the baptismal font in the back is a delightful, small *della Robbia*-style blue and white ceramic *Annunciation*. The quiet and surprisingly hidden garden outside and the immaculate and tastefully decorated interior make this a private, but not a secret, landmark.

30. Fellowship Missionary Baptist Church, originally Grace Lutheran Church (see p. 324, then First Assembly of God) (1908)
Architect: Bonard and Parsson
Builder: H. P. Eckhardt
Location: 1754 East 55th Street

Fellowship Missionary Baptist Church is the sixth institution to evolve from Shiloh Baptist Church (see p. 132), the oldest African American Baptist church in Cleveland.[17] In 1962 approximately 160 Shiloh members began meeting on Sundays next door to the Shiloh church at the House of Wills Funeral Home. Later moving to the Phillis Wheatley Association,[18] the congregation—within two years—had grown to more than five hundred under the leadership of A. Henson Jarmon when it purchased its present building from the First Assembly of God.

The First Assembly of God had purchased the building in the 1920s from the Grace Lutherans. From 1951 to 1952 Thomas Zimmerman served as the Assembly of God Pastor. He would go on to serve as the national general superintendent of the Assemblies of God from 1959 to 1985. The Assembly of God congregation sandblasted and waterproofed the entire building in 1953. After selling the building to the Baptists, the Assembly of God moved to their present location on Richmond Road in Lyndhurst, two blocks north of Mayfield Road.

The initial construction of this church by Cleveland Lutherans constituted an important step in the Lutheran break from the German liturgy to worshiping in English. Cleveland remains a center of the conservative Lutheran Missouri Synod with its historic preference for the German language. Zion Evangelical Lutheran Church (see p. 24) played an instrumental role in founding the Missouri Synod in 1847. About half of Cleveland Lutheran congregations belong to the Missouri Synod. The founders of Grace Lutheran Church were determined that their Americanized children would have the opportunity to worship as Lutherans in English. They first met with like-minded Lutherans from the West Side to found an English-speaking religious school. The school rapidly evolved into a church and then two churches when the West Siders wanted to worship closer to home. One pastor shuttled back and forth between them. In 1898 the East Siders laid the cornerstone for the first English Lutheran church in Cleveland, a small frame building on the corner of Lexington Avenue at East 55th Street. Within ten years the congregation had built this brick church on the same site.[19] Over the next decade, four pastors served in short succession. In the 1920s things settled down. Gathering its forces, Grace planned to move to its current location on Cedar in Cleveland Heights. This move was not without drama, because the Assembly of God moved into

Grace's old church before Grace's new church was completed. As a result, the Lutherans spent six months worshiping in the Cedar Lee Theater.

Occupying the northwest corner of East 55th at Lexington, Fellowship Missionary Baptist Church, along with St. Paul Evangelical Lutheran on the corner of Superior Avenue at East 55th, defines the eastern edge of the Goodrich-Kirtland neighborhood. When built, this church stood in a quietly prosperous middle-class neighborhood lined with trees and filled with purposeful residents hiking back and forth from the trolleys. Today, this neighborhood has become a blighted commercial area scattered with unkempt, vacant lots. Despite, or perhaps because of this, Fellowship Baptist has become a substantial presence along East 55th, visible for many blocks on either side of this four-lane thoroughfare. The building, brick with Gothic cast stone trim, has a crenellated square tower over the front entrance that is short by Cleveland standards. A three-story brick addition to the back of the building offers space for education, administration, and socialization.

The dominant feature inside is the sanctuary's magnificent hammerbeam ceiling. The beams are not solid; instead, each is constructed of six great timbers held together with massive exposed bolts giving them an appearance of strength and power. At the back of the sanctuary, in place of a narthex, a tiny balcony hangs over an interior stairway up from the street. The worship space is a wide-open area that slopes down to the chancel under the self-supporting roof. Walls are plain plaster and transepts are shallow. Restrained cast limestone tracery outlines undecorated windows. For more than one hundred years, various denominations have been comfortable in this plain, large, open space with its wonderful ceiling.

31. Fidelity Baptist Church (1891)
Architect: Sidney R. Badgley
Builder: Unknown
Location: 8402 Wade Park Avenue

Fidelity's frame building is interesting because it incorporates many of the features that one would expect in a giant, masonry, Sidney Badgley-designed, Akron Plan church.[20] This church is Badgley's only existing frame building in Cleveland.[21] Here, relatively small in both structure and frame, is the characteristic Badgley worship space angled toward a corner, separated from its Akron Plan assembly area by a large movable wall. One finds it unfortunate that the early history of this building and its congregation is clouded. Armstrong and his *équipe* concluded, after examining the Cleveland Landmarks Commission file concerning Fidelity Baptist Church, that the church, founded in 1892, constructed their building in 1911.[22] A Lakewood historian particularly interested in Victorian era architects, Craig Bobby has concluded—after examining building permit applications and printed accounts published at the time of construction—that this building was constructed in 1891,[23] a date obviously inconsistent with Armstrong's.

Fidelity Baptist Church is one of a series of small churches lining Wade Park Avenue in this residential neighborhood. Cleveland religious buildings seem to come in two kinds: those that appear smaller on the inside than on the outside and those that appear smaller on the outside than on the inside. Fidelity Baptist falls into the larger-on-the-inside category. This church may be Sidney Badgley writ small, but it remains a substantial building.

Particularly attractive is the high-pitched roof with its multiple gable dormers. Two charming, short, octagonal towerlike bay projections at both north corners of the building flank the frame porch, so much like those at St. John A.M.E. The building, which gives the initial impression from the street of having a simple meetinghouse plan, is actually L-shaped with an administrative-educational wing to the east of the assembly area behind the sanctuary. The assembly area is now used as a gym. The assembly area's second story walkaround was built only on the south and east sides, although this may reflect a modification since the original construction.

Like Badgley's Pilgrim Congregational in Tremont and his St. John A.M.E. in the Central neighborhood of Cleveland, the sanctuary is oriented on an angle—in the case of this building, toward its southeast corner.[24] The retractable wall on the right of the congregation, the south wall of the sanctuary, originally opened into the Akron Plan assembly area. (It is no longer used.) The sanctuary seats about three hundred in a semicircle divided by two aisles. Because of its angled orientation, the worship area is much wider than it would appear from the outside. (The assembly area to the south also gives the building, from the outside, a misleadingly long and narrow appearance.) The ceiling of the sanctuary is painted with two large rosettes in the center with gilded decoration. Painted beams outline this central ceiling decoration. A large wooden organ case stands behind the lectionary. A curtain screens the baptistry—to the left at the front of the chancel—from the congregation when not in use. Dark-stained wood trims the unglazed windows, which admit so much light that the sanctuary has a bright and lively character. There is a narrow narthex.

32. St. Vitus Church (1932)

Architect: William Jansen
Builders: Bartholomew Ponikvar and
Joseph Boznar
Location: 6019 Lausche-Glass Avenue

In 1910, Cleveland was the third-largest Slovene city in the world. The neighborhood north of St. Clair between 24th and 87th Streets was the largest Slovene settlement in the United States. Its cultural center, just south of St. Clair, was St. Vitus, the largest Slovenian Church in America.[25]

Slovenes had originally settled much farther south, in the Newburgh neighborhood around East 80th Street, between Union and Broadway Avenues. There they had come under the leadership of the multilingual and omnipresent Stefan Furdek, pastor of Our Lady of Lourdes (see p. 166). Furdek, among everything else, "knew some Slovenian."[26] He also knew enough to travel to Ljubljana and recruit a Slovene seminarian, Vitus Hribar, to take his place ministering to the growing Slovene community moving north in Cleveland to St. Clair.[27] Like almost everyone else in Cleveland, Hribar began his new nationality parish at Historic Saint Peter (see p. 18). In little more than a year, his congregation had moved into a little frame building on the current campus of St. Vitus.

The community on St. Clair grew so explosively that tensions developed within the parish.[28] The situation was exacerbated by divisions between Catholic and anticlerical elements in the Slovene community, divisions that would culminate after the Second World War.[29] Dissidents imported a Franciscan Slovene, the charismatic Kazimir Zakrajsek, to replace Father Hribar as pastor. Bishop Ignatius Horstmann attempted to calm the Slovene community by dividing it at East 55th Street. Those west of 55th were reorganized as Our Lady of Sorrows; those east of 55th continued at St. Vitus. This did not work. After seven months the parish was reunited under a new pastor, Bartholomew Ponikvar. In addition to inheriting a deeply divided congregation, Ponikvar found that the frame school on the property required immediate replacement. While St. Vitus School grew to become the largest elementary school in the diocese (in 1922 Sister Akaija had 106 children in her second-grade classroom), the demands of the parish educational program kept delaying the construction of a permanent church. Arguments raged concerning the location of the new church. Finding frontage on commercial St. Clair prohibitively expensive, the parish finally settled in its current location, a block south. Construction began in 1930 in the teeth of the Great Depression and completed in 1932. In 1944, this parish suffered from the 1944 East Ohio Gas Company explosion, three blocks north of the church, which killed 130 people in the surrounding area.[30]

As one would expect from such a large and vigorous parish, St. Vitus has produced a significant number of leaders. Frank Lausche, for whom the street in front of the church was renamed, served as Cleveland's mayor (1941–44), Ohio's governor (1944–46, 1948–56), and a U.S. senator (1957–67). Lawrence Bandi, abbot of the Abbey of Holy Cross in Colorado, grew up in the parish. So did Edward Pevec, rector of Borromeo College and auxiliary bishop. Bishop Pevec had served the parish as pastor during a particularly critical time in the aftermath of the Hough Riots from 1975 to 1979. The current pastor, Joseph Boznar, undertook a major renovation of the church, completed in 1993. In this renovation, the congregation is particularly proud of the painting and traditional stenciling done by Slovene artists and of the fact that their daily prayers were answered by completion of the $2 million project without injury to any of the workers.

The 1,500-seat church, designed by the architect of St. Casimir (see p. 87) and St. Aloysius (see p. 99), is constructed of pale yellow Falston brick in a "Romanesque-Lombard" style. Octagonal cupolas top twin one-hundred-foot ornamental towers. Undecorated pilasters with ornate capitals visually support the terra-cotta molded pediment. The spare but precisely carved marble trim is particularly notable in the bas-reliefs flanking the entrance. The bells, a toll and three others, hang in the west tower. Across the street sits a large Slovenian retirement home. St. Vitus's large former parish school is now Cleveland's St. Martin de Porres High School, part of the Jesuit-influenced Cristo Rey Network of schools that has had such spectacular results in this and other inner cities.

St. Vitus proves an unusual Roman Catholic church in that it has a large, wraparound balcony that extends forward over the one-hundred-foot transepts on either side.[31] These deep balconies at St. Vitus, despite being ramped, turned out to be an unfortunate innovation—the altar cannot easily be seen from the side balconies by anyone not in the first row.

Everything inside this church looks brand-new with its marvelous Slovene stenciling on the ceiling and gilded square Slovene carved capitals. Fourteen beautiful square marble columns alternate with round columns marching down the nave. The arches between columns are gilded and nicely detailed. Much of the interior had been whitewashed in the middle of the twentieth century, and this white paint has now been removed. The large choir at the front of the church and an impressive baldachin both feature a great deal of marble. An attractive antiqued Vatican II marble altar marks the crossing. (The altar from the original frame church is installed as a side altar.) To a greater degree than is usual in a Cleveland religious building, some of the art in this church features our contemporaries. Large-scale murals on either side of the apse include portraits of Bishop Pevec and Fathers Ponikvar and Boznar. Medallions along the nave include portraits of figures from recent Slovene history and Mother Teresa as well as two of the 1980 El Salvador missionary martyrs, Jean Donovan and Sister Dorothy Kazel.

A beautiful rose window and eight Mayer Munich windows in the side balconies let in light. The window under the west tower features the stained-glass figure of a Boy Scout, given by members of Troup 250. A chapel at the southeast rear of the church holds an elaborate and attractive shrine to St. Bernadette with a wonderful modern window based on a photograph of the saint. On the east of the nave hangs an Infant Jesus of Prague.[32] There is a fine Holtkamp organ. Out of immediate public view, dark wood paneling lines passageways around the sanctuary and the dark wood staircases.

33. St. Casimir Church (1918)
Architect: William Jansen
Builders: Carl Ruszkowski and John Solinski
Location: 8223 Sowinski Avenue

Looming between Sowinski and Pulaski on the eastern edge of the St. Clair-Superior neighborhood, St. Casimir Church towers defiantly over a neighborhood that no longer exists.[33] One of the three major historic Polish neighborhoods in Cleveland—Warsawa along Broadway (see St. Stanislaus, p. 172, and Immaculate Heart of Mary), Kantowa in Tremont (see St. John Cantius, p. 209), and Pozan (St. Casimir)—Pozan houses the fewest number of Roman Catholics. Flanked at one time along Ansel Road by St. Thomas Aquinas (five blocks to the south, demolished in 1975) and St. Philip Neri (seven blocks to the north and for sale since 2008), St. Casimir carried on for more than twenty years behind a chain-link fence in front of its imposing entrance. At the front of the nave, the flag of Solidarity (Solidarność) proudly waved unfurled beside a copy of the monument honoring those who died for the Church and for Polonia in the dockyard at Gdansk.

St. Casimir formed the center of a neighborhood of families drawn by the factories along the railroads. The parish shared the turbulent history that characterized the Cleveland Polish community, yet, between episodes of turmoil, it erected a magnificent building. Father Ruszkowski planned the current church, but the project came to a halt when he died in 1918. His assistant, Father Solinski, then took up and completed the project. The arrival of Father Andrew Radecki brought harmony to the parish in 1924—many describe his forty-three year pastorate as the "Golden Years" of St. Casimir. The church was not only at peace but also at its zenith in number of parishioners and students.[34] On September 19, 1969, the parish welcomed Krakow's then cardinal, Karol Wojtyla. The parish became the Solidarity Center of Cleveland in 1985 in spiritual and material support for the Gdansk dockworkers who stood against the Communist government of Poland, contributing to the events that would eventually culminate in the dissolution of the Soviet Union.

The entrance of St. Casimir faces west, the way all churches should. The surrounding vacant lots and devastation only enhance the power and the majesty of the building. The church shares a campus with an immaculate and well-maintained modern school, parish center, and convent, all of which remain locked. The church's imposing red brick building has two symmetrical tall and elegant, although massive, towers. Both open belfries are boarded shut. The limited stone trim over the three entrance doors contrasts with the generous, well-designed and well-executed brick trim that is particularly striking in the pilasters and emphasizes the height and strength of the towers.

The interior is large. Beautiful rectangular and octagonal marble pillars support a painted barrel roof. Polish saints look down from a large painting over the church's famous white altar. An uncompromising marble altar rail separates the nave from the sanctuary. To the left, a shrine surrounds an imported copy of the painting of Our Lady of Czestochowa. To the right stands the copy of the shrine in Poland to the Gdansk dockworkers. Polish flags modestly share equal billing with those of the United States. The good windows include a large rose with dominant cross tracery. Wall stenciling is generous and beautiful. There is a traditional baptistry. In the narthex a bronze plaque commemorates the gallant exile Poles of Gen. Stanislaw Mazek's First Polish Armored Division that closed the Falaise Pocket around the German Army behind Normandy.

On March 15, 2009, Bishop Richard Lennon announced the closing of St. Casimir. On November 8, he celebrated the final Mass. St. Casimir has been merged with Our Lady of Perpetual Help Church, more than two miles east on Neff Road. Our Lady of Perpetual Help has been renamed St. Casimir. It remains to be seen when the Poles will stop demonstrating in front of old St. Casimir and be welcomed by the Lithuanians of what used to be Our Lady of Perpetual Help. On March 1, 2012, the Vatican Congregation for the Clergy ruled that Bishop Lennon had failed to follow church law and procedure in closing St. Casimir.

34. Hitchcock Center for Women, originally St. Mary Seminary (1924)
Architect: Franz Warner
Builder: Joseph Schrembs
Location: 1227 Ansel Road

In treating substance abuse, it becomes important to separate the patient from the environment associated with the abuse. However, this presents a challenge when treating women with children. Even if they can be separated from their children, women usually cannot be effectively treated if their children remain behind in an abusive environment, one where the women logically return upon completion of their inpatient treatment. The

Hitchcock Center is one of the few treatment centers that addresses this problem.[35] It welcomes and supports its patients' children during treatment and then provides a subsequent substance-free environment for several months while its patients attempt to build a new life. This explains why the Hitchcock Center can make such good use of this former seminary with its more than fifty-five private rooms for students and faculty, social spaces, library, gymnasium, classrooms, eating facilities, and enclosed and protected cloisters.

A nurse from the now demolished Women's General Hospital at East 101st Street and Chester Avenue founded the Hitchcock Center in 1978. Jane Mazzarella organized a ten-bed halfway house in a large residence on Magnolia Drive; the Hitchcock family, founders of Reliance Electric, had donated this home. Ten years later the Center moved to the Euclid Avenue Congregational Church (see p. 38), operating there for three years before purchasing St. Mary Seminary from the diocese in 1992.

Bishop Amadeus Rappe had established St. Mary Seminary in a remodeled stable at East Sixth Street and St. Clair Avenue in the first year of his episcopate. Within two years he had to purchase the Spring Cottage Bath House at Hamilton and Lake Avenues to accommodate the need for priests in his dramatically expanding diocese. In 1853 and again in 1856, additional buildings were built and another new structure was built in 1859 that required a subsequent addition in the 1880s. By 1922 the facility was so inadequate that postgraduate seminarians had to study in Cincinnati. Bishop Joseph Schrembs then directed construction of the present building on an eleven-acre site on the western rim of Rockefeller Park. By 1954 this building, too, was inadequate and the diocese established Borromeo Seminary in Wickliffe, which now houses all diocesan clergy programs.

St. Mary Seminary sits at the edge of Rockefeller Park, which is part of a long chain of parks extending south from Gordon Park on the lakefront to Shaker Lakes Park in Shaker Heights. St. Mary overlooks Doan Brook, one of the most picturesque areas in the city. The building is of buff-colored tapestry brick in a "Spanish Mission" style. The plan of the seminary complex is that of an "H" on its side, and enclosed at both ends. On either side of the central chapel (the bar of the "H") is a cloister surrounded by rooms. Today, treatment facilities are concentrated around the south cloister while the north cloister provides housing for patients in transition to an outside life.

The central pavilion of the complex, which projects west onto Ansel Road, has a curved Rococo gable. The pediment outline is similar to Johan Fiscurt's Zwiefalten Church in Bavaria. Flanked by octagonal twin towers with decorative urns on the twin belfries, the richly decorated stone entranceway is Italian Renaissance. Byzantine pendentives support the central dome. The Ansel Road entrance of this unusual combination opens into a generous and impressive vestibule that, in turn, opens into the chapel. St. Mary's famous library, with space for forty thousand volumes, is located on the floor above the entrance vestibule. This library has been a Cleveland literary landmark for almost a century.

The books have been dispersed, although the magnificent space remains. The outside entrance dome, with its twelve glazed windows, soars above the library rotunda. Five great, carved-wood bookcases surround the visitor. A wrought-iron screen offers a view toward the chapel. The library and main vestibule are to the west of the chapel, balanced to the east by a social solarium that looks out through generous windows into Rockefeller Park. The view from the solarium at dawn is one of the most dramatic in Cleveland. Beneath the solarium lies the refectory, served by a dumbwaiter from the kitchen below.

The chapel, now used by a neighborhood congregation, has choir seating with worshipers seated in rows of stalls parallel to the long axis of the chapel on either side of a wide center aisle. An open timbered ceiling tops travertine walls. The stations are gilded cast bronze. Twenty-four Munich Zettler stained-glass windows show figures intended to inspire the seminarians: the Evangelists, major prophets, Latin and Greek fathers, and Doctors of the Church. Confessionals are located at the back with the organ housed in the balcony above. Although the main altar has been removed, flanking altars to Mary and Jesus remain.

CHAPTER THREE

Northeast Cleveland

Located along the edge of Lake Erie, northeast Cleveland consists of Glen-ville—Forest Hill, North and South Collinwood, and Euclid Green. Glenville, originally an Irish settlement, incorporated as a village in 1870. The City of Cleveland annexed it in 1904. Glenville derived its name from its woody landscape and many streams. Located next to the lake, it was a popular location for well-to-do Cleveland at the end of the nineteenth century. As the city's industrial base expanded east along the railways during the twentieth century, however, many of Glennville's prosperous Jewish families moved to the eastern suburbs, and, as a result, Glenville's character began to change. By 1950, 90 percent of Glenville's population was African American.[1] During the 1960s and 1970s this neighborhood, like Hough, suffered from racial tensions.

Forest Hill was the summer home of the John D. Rockefeller family.[2] The house and most of the estate were located south of Euclid Avenue, in East Cleveland and Cleveland Heights—not in Cleveland proper. The Forest Hill neighborhood of Cleveland has come to mean the area surrounding Cleveland's Forest Hill Park.

Tour

Begin this tour at the intersection of Martin Luther King Jr. Drive and Superior Avenue, traveling east on Superior. Turn right (south) onto East Boulevard. When turning, the Garden of Prayer Cathedral (originally St. Mark Presbyterian Church) lies to the left. Located across from the Cultural Gardens in Rockefeller Park, this church was built in 1911. Continue on East Boulevard and then turn left (east) onto Ashbury Avenue. Crossing East 105th Street, continue on Ashbury to East 110th Street.

At East 110th, turn left. North of Orville Avenue, on the left, is Beth-El A.M.E. Zion Church, founded in 1940 and rebuilt in 1958. Farther north, on the right, just opposite Hull Avenue, is Burning Bush Evangelistic Ministries (formerly the New Wood Missionary Baptist Church). Continue on East 110th and then turn left, back onto Superior. Traveling west on Superior, the Calvary Holiness Cathedral (formerly the Calvary Church of God and Christ) occupies the southeast corner of the East 108th Street intersection. Stay on Superior and then turn right (north) onto East 105th.

Drive north on East 105th to the Bethany Baptist Church at the corner of East 105th at Hampden Avenue. Farther north, the Greater Abyssinia Baptist Church and its new addition sit on the right at Tacoma Avenue. Stay on East 105th to Drexel Avenue. Turn right (east) onto Drexel around the giant Cory United Methodist Church (35), originally built as the Cleveland Jewish Center by the Anshe Emeth Congregation.

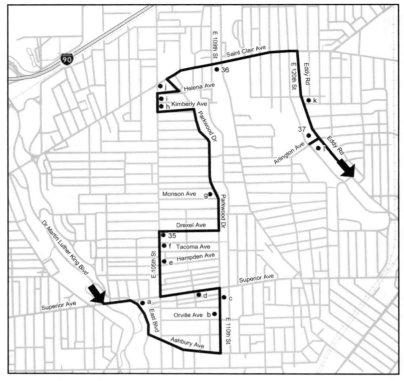

GLENVILLE—FOREST HILL

a. Garden of Prayer Cathedral
b. Beth-El A.M.E. Zion Church
c. Burning Bush Evangelistic Ministries
d. Calvary Holiness Cathedral
e. Bethany Baptist Church
f. Greater Abyssinia Baptist Church
35. Cory United Methodist Church
g. Parkwood C.M.E. Church

h. Glenville Seventh Day Adventist Church
i. Glenville New Life Community Church
j. Central Christian Church
36. St. Aloysius Church
k. Second Mt. Olive Baptist Church
l. True Churches of the Apostolic Faith
37. Greater Friendship Baptist Church

Traveling east on Drexel, turn left (north) onto Parkwood Drive. On the left, at the Morison Avenue intersection, is the Parkwood C.M.E. Church, another former synagogue. Continue on Parkwood and then turn left (west) onto Kimberly Avenue. Traveling on Kimberly turn north (right) back onto East 105th. The Glenville Seventh Day Adventist Church is at the corner of East 105th at Elgin Avenue. Turn right (east) at Helena Avenue. Glenville New Life Community Church occupies the southeast corner of the intersection. The Central Christian Church is to the northeast. Travel on Helena back to Parkwood and turn left. Then turn right (east) onto St. Clair Avenue.

On the southeast corner of St. Clair at East 109th Street stands St. Aloysius Church (36). Continue on St. Clair and then turn right (south) onto Eddy

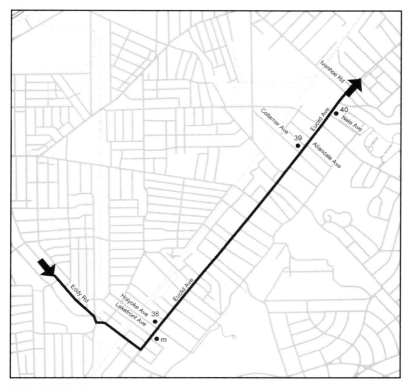

EAST CLEVELAND

m. St. Philomena Church
38. Windermere United Methodist Church

39. Antioch Christian Fellowship
40. First Presbyterian Church of East Cleveland

Road. On the other side of Gray Avenue, on the left, is Second Mt. Olive Baptist Church, originally built as Sieb Sachs Evangelical Lutheran Church. Continuing on Eddy, turn right onto Arlington Avenue. True Churches of the Apostolic Faith (formerly Christ Temple Apostolic Faith) lies to the left and Greater Friendship Baptist Church (37), built as the First Evangelical and Reformed Church in 1926, sits to the right. This Gothic Revival church looks out over Forest Hill Park.

Turn right back on Eddy Road. Drive one mile southeast on Eddy, jogging left and then right under the railroad tracks, to Euclid Avenue and turn left. This is East Cleveland. When John D. Rockefeller summered here, he shared East Cleveland with some of the most beautiful churches in America. Almost immediately on the right of Euclid Avenue is the Late Gothic Revival St. Philomena Church. Across the street on the left stands the monumental Windermere United Methodist Church (38), almost entirely (except for its famous tower) destroyed by fire in 1946 and rebuilt in 1949. Continue on Euclid, past Shaw High School, for somewhat more than a mile. On the left is the Antioch

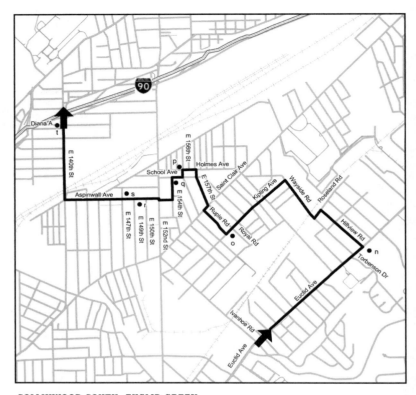

COLLINWOOD SOUTH—EUCLID GREEN

n. Good Shepherd Baptist Church
o. Holy Redeemer Roman Catholic Church
p. St. Mary of the Assumption Church
q. Freedom Christian Assembly
r. Greater New Calvary Baptist Church
s. Aspinwall Church of God Mountain Assembly
t. Golden Rule Church of God

Christian Fellowship (39), built as St. Paul's Episcopal Church of East Cleveland. Three blocks farther on the right is the First Presbyterian Church of East Cleveland (40). Established in 1807, this was the oldest religious community in Cuyahoga County.

Drive east on Euclid, entering Cleveland's Euclid Green neighborhood. Continue on Euclid to Hillview Road. Here, opposite Hillview, is Good Shepherd Baptist Church. Although it fronts Euclid, this church is only accessible from Torbenson Drive to the west. Built in 1958, the church rests on the side of a hill, and its open glass sanctuary looks out onto its landscaped setting.

Turn left (north) onto Hillview. Take Hillview until it ends at Roseland Road. Turn left (west) onto Roseland. Follow Roseland for one block and then turn right (north) onto Wayside Road. Take Wayside, crossing the tracks,

COLLINWOOD NORTH
41. St. Jerome Church
  u. Tabernacle Baptist Church
42. St. John Nottingham Lutheran Church
43. St. Casimir Parish
  v. Beachland Presbyterian Church

for three blocks and then turn left (west) onto Kipling Avenue, entering the Collinwood South neighborhood. Annexed to the City of Cleveland in 1910, Collinwood was home to large Italian, Irish, and Slovenian communities. Its proximity to the railroad switching yards made Collinwood an important industrial center during World War II. At that time, the Five Points area—around the intersection of East 152nd Street, St. Clair, and Ivanhoe Road—was some of the most valuable commercial land in Cleveland.

Follow Kipling to Ruple Road. Before turning right on Ruple, note Holy Redeemer Roman Catholic Church, built in 1959. Stay on Ruple for one block and then turn right (east) onto St. Clair. After going one block on St. Clair, turn left (north) onto East 157th Street. Take East 157th for two blocks and, passing over School Avenue, turn left (west) at Holmes Avenue. St. Mary of the Assumption Church is at the northwest corner of the Holmes-East 156th intersection. The congregation's original structure, built in 1908, is located directly east of the current building. This 1957 church's copper-clad bell tower is a local landmark.

Turn left (south) onto East 156th Street. Travel on it for one block and then turn right (west) onto School Avenue. Take School for one block and then turn left (south) onto East 154th Street. The Freedom Christian Assembly (originally the Collinwood Christian Church) is on the southeast corner of the intersection. Organized in 1878, this was the second church in the original village of Collinwood.

Take East 154th Street to Aspinwall Avenue and turn right (west). After two blocks, Greater New Calvary Baptist Church occupies the southwest corner of Aspinwall at East 150th Street. Built in 1893 of buff-colored sandstone in the Richardsonian Romanesque style, this church first housed the First Congregational Church of Collinwood. Organized in 1876, First Congregational was the village's first church. The building became Greater New Calvary Baptist Church in 1971.

Continue on Aspinwall, past the Aspinwall Church of God Mountain Assembly on the corner of East 147th Street. At Aspinwall and East 140th Street turn right (north). Drive on East 140th north to Diana Avenue. Just west of East 140th is the Golden Rule Church of God. This church, opposite Longfellow Elementary School, is scaled to match the context of the surrounding residential neighborhood. Continue on East 140th, under Interstate 90, to Lake Shore Boulevard. Turn right (east) at Lake Shore. Drive on Lake Shore to East 151st Street. On the right sits St. Jerome Church (41).

When Lakeshore turns north, continue east. You are now on Macauley Avenue. Continue on Macauley for one block. The Tabernacle Baptist Church (originally the Immanuel Presbyterian Church) stands on the left. Built in 1924, this church is connected at the transept to the earlier church constructed in 1906. Turn right (south) onto East 156th Street. After one short block on East 156th, turn left (east) onto Arcade Avenue. Travel on Arcade until it ends at East 167th Street.

Turn left (north) onto East 167th Street and travel on it to Grovewood Avenue. At Grovewood, turn right (east). At East 176th Street, turn left (north). Stay on East 176th Street, past the Salvation Army, until East 176th Street intersects with Nottingham Road. Dominating the view to the north is St. John Nottingham Lutheran Church (42). Founded in 1890, the present church building was dedicated in 1954. The building wraps around itself to create an inner courtyard garden. Opposite the church stands St. John Nottingham Lutheran School. Both of these buildings are landmarks in this pleasantly scaled neighborhood.

Turn left (west) onto Nottingham. After going one block, turn right (north) back onto Lake Shore Boulevard. Continue on Lake Shore as it curves into Marcella Road. Bear right on Marcella to Reese Road. Take Reese left one block. Then turn left again onto Neff Road. Opposite Sable Road is the newly renamed St. Casimir Parish (43). Continue on Neff back to Lake Shore Boulevard. Turn right (northeast) onto Lake Shore and continue on it to Cornwall. On the point of land created by the intersection of Cornwall and Canterbury Roads with Lake Shore sits Beachland Presbyterian Church, a small Wren-Gibbs building. Its style could easily blend with that of a small New England town.

The tour ends here, only a few blocks west of Cleveland's boundary with the City of Euclid. Travel east on Canterbury or Cornwall to East 185th Street, then turn right (south) on East 185th to access Interstate 90, more than ten blocks farther south.

35. Cory United Methodist Church, originally the Cleveland Jewish Center/ Anshe Emeth Synagogue (see also the Park Synagogue, p. 315 and Park Synagogue East, p. 345) (1921)
Architect: Albert S. Janowitz
Builder: Samuel Benjamin
Location: 1117 East 105th Street

Cory United Methodist Church was one of the first African American congregations in the city of Cleveland.[3] Founded in 1875 and originally known as Union Chapel, the community was renamed in honor of J. B. Cory. Cory, an itinerant Methodist missionary whom some say founded eleven churches in Cleveland, gave his life to the poor and made his way about Cleveland with a basket to collect and distribute handouts. The congregation named for him held services in private homes and public halls until it purchased a building at the corner of Central Avenue at East 37th Street in 1890. Twenty-one years later the congregation moved to a larger building at the corner of Scovill Avenue at East 35th Street. A fire in 1921 required the renovation of the entire building. After the Depression the congregation grew from several hundred to more than three thousand, and the Scovill Avenue church proved to be too small. Oliver B. Quick began a long-term fund-raising campaign, which by 1946 had accumulated enough to purchase the million-dollar Anshe Emeth Synagogue for $135,000. Later, in 1961, as the church began to sponsor a boy's football team, the City of Cleveland Division of Recreation took over most of Cory's athletic facilities, which the city now operates as the Cory Recreation Center. Cory United Methodist Church continues to be responsible for the library, credit union, day care center, and the Cory Kitchen, a hunger center that feeds all comers during the last seven days of every month.

Our post–World War II image of the Park Synagogue, the largest Conservative synagogue in the United States, is one of an orderly succession of distinguished long-serving rabbis and powerful patrons, a world-famous building in Cleveland Heights, and a striking new annex in Pepper Pike. It is difficult to reconcile this with the boisterous congregation that built and occupied what is now Cory before selling it to the Methodists in 1946. Anshe Emeth was founded as a Polish Orthodox congregation in 1869 and went through the usual struggles between Orthodox and Reform. It remained small until it built a brick synagogue at East 37th Street at Scovill Avenue and brought on its first full-time rabbi in 1903. This was the remarkable Samuel Margolies, born in Russia, raised in the United States, and then educated back in a Russian Yeshiva before returning to the United States and graduating from Harvard. Margolies quickly made his congregation preeminent in the Cleveland Orthodox community, in Jewish education, and in Zionism. He laid the foundation for Anshe Emeth's eventual construction of the Cleveland Jewish Center. Margolies resigned in 1917 to enter the insurance business and tragically died the same year in an automobile accident.

After two years without a rabbi, Anshe Emeth called Samuel Benjamin, "another fiery orator both in English and Yiddish." Benjamin "galvanized the congregation with his dream of . . . the Cleveland Jewish Center," with educational, social, recreational, and cultural activities in addition to worship services. With its two giant auditoriums, swimming pool, and basketball and handball courts, "the *schul* with the pool" became the center of Jewish life in Glenville, then one of the two Jewish neighborhoods in Cleveland. The Cleveland Jewish Center was one of the most imposing landmarks on the southern end of what from 1900 to 1930 was known as the "Gold Coast," the most dynamic commercial neighborhood in Cleveland. In 1922, the year of the Cleveland Jewish Center's dedication, "Rabbi Benjamin resigned abruptly . . . amid a stormy clash of wills and temperaments, and left for Palestine."[4]

Benjamin was replaced by the "very controversial" Solomon Goldman, who himself had resigned from B'nai Jeshurun[5] in part because of its resistance to building a Jewish center of its own. Goldman "led the congregation into the ranks of Conservative Jewry" before leaving for Chicago in 1929, "partly because he was unwilling to share the leadership of Cleveland Jewry with Rabbi Abba Hillel Silver."[6] Things quieted down over the next five years under Harry Davidowitz, but then Davidowitz left for Palestine. He was replaced by twenty-six-year-old Armond Cohen, who would pay off the almost overwhelming debt on the Cleveland Jewish Center, move Anshe Emeth to Cleveland Heights, hire Eric Mendelsohn, and lead the congregation for fifty-four years.

This block-long brick building, with its massive front portico supported by four freestanding columns and its memorable frieze just below the roofline, inscribed with the names of Jewish prophets and scholars, remains one of the largest religious landmarks in Cleveland. It is a worthy predecessor to Mendelsohn's building up the hill. With its worship, athletic, and educational facilities, Cory is a vast building. The second floor of the south wing includes a significant and beautifully maintained ballroom that features a large stage and comfortably seats one thousand diners. An industrial-strength kitchen supports their efforts at the table.

The northern auditorium, capped by a circular dome, seats 2,400. It has been large enough to accommodate the Cleveland Orchestra with plenty of seats left over for attendees commemorating Martin Luther King Jr.'s birthday. This main worship space is a large cube defined by four massive arches upon which, and on whose squinches, rests a massive dome. Plasterwork animals decorate the great dome like a gigantic piece of Wedgwood jasperware. One finds clerestory windows in the drum of the dome and a circular walk beneath the dome with miniature pilasters. The Methodists were attached to a large Star of David that hung from the dome for many years. It has since been removed. The rear of the dome features a large balcony, supplemented by generous lateral balconies on either side, to accommodate women in a congregation that was moving from Orthodoxy to Conservatism. To the left and right of the main worship space are stationed large, early twentieth-century windows. The Methodists have installed a wood communion rail. Behind the large platform stage (bimah) with its authoritative pulpit (Torah reading table) stands a beautifully carved wooden screen. Recently restored bronze menorah light fixtures encircle the sanctuary.

36. St. Aloysius Church
(1922)
Architect: William Jansen
Builder: Francis Malloy
Location: 10932 St. Clair
Avenue

Driving through the blighted neighborhood of Glenville along St. Clair Avenue, the campus of St. Aloysius suddenly appears at the border of Forest Hills as an unexpected oasis: a substantial building beside a comfortable rectory surrounded by a crisply cut lawn and carefully tended garden presided over by a calmly assertive statue of the Virgin.[7] When it was built, this church played an important role in the neighborhood. Glenville, at one time the "garden spot of Cuyahoga County" because of its numerous vegetable farms, had been nationally known as a center of horse racing until the track moved to North Randal in 1908. In the early twentieth century the wealthiest Glenville residents made way for middle-class Irish, but John Rockefeller continued to summer around the corner in Forest Hills until 1917.

Seeing opportunity, Bishop Ignatius Horstmann established St. Thomas Aquinas parish in 1898. (This 1,400-seat church was located on the corner of Superior Avenue at Ansel Road; St. Thomas Aquinas was demolished in 1975.) St. Thomas's first pastor studied his parish more carefully and concluded that it would support two churches. As the St. Thomas pastor began construction of his first temporary church in 1898, he also helped construct a small frame St. Aloysius church on East 105th. The St. Thomas pastor then helped the new parish purchase its current lot on St. Clair. Constructing a three-story brick church-and-school (now the Parish Center) in 1902, St. Aloysius began construction of its current church in 1922. The new bishop, Joseph Schrembs, strongly discouraged the construction of grandiose new churches that he considered an unnecessary financial burden on Cleveland parishioners. It is said that when the bishop came to visit the construction site, the pastor of St. Aloysius, Francis Malloy, instructed the workmen to pile trash and construction materials over one end of the rising church to conceal the size of the building. The bishop reportedly grumbled about the messy scene but continued on his way. Although Malloy would serve St. Aloysius for thirty-four years, his ambitions would be more than realized by his successor. By the Second World War, St. Aloysius was one of the largest parishes in the diocese, filling its 1,250 seats to overflowing.

William Jansen also designed St. Casimir (1918) and St. Vitus (1932). His design here has been described as Italian Renaissance: rounded arches above the windows, paired pilasters with modified Corinthian capitals flanking the simple but dignified main entrance, and an enlarged triangular pediment above the second-floor facade. St. Aloysius is a good-sized, straightforward, no-nonsense red brick building with modest composition trim, supplemented with simple but clever brick decoration. A composition balustrade separates the building from the street.

Some churches look bigger on the outside than they seem on the inside. St. Aloysius looks substantial on the outside. Inside it is gigantic and impressive. The immense barrel vault runs the length of the nave. Both side aisles have neo-Gothic vaulting. The impressive span of the barrel vault rests on well-proportioned pillars with carved Corinthian capitals. Although the columns appear capable of carrying the load, they provide relatively unimpeded sight lines for the congregation. Leaving the old altar in place, a Vatican II altar stands on a platform under the crossing to create a handsome choir. An impressive marble baldachin hangs over the elaborate marble altar in front of a false ambulatory. The marble communion rail and the carving that separates the first pew from the chancel have been retained although moved back into the nave. The sacristy features a full complement of windows and a fireplace.

St. Aloysius has had to be big to accommodate the parishes that found shelter under its vault in the second half of the twentieth century—St. Agatha (1974), St. Joseph (1994), and St. Philip Neri (2008). Of interest, St. Aloysius's incorporation of St. Joseph went against the grain of parishes struggling in the inner city. Usually the school struggles and then closes and the parish continues. In this case, the parish of St. Joseph in Collinwood closed and left the school to operate in connection with St. Aloysius. St. Aloysius (Luigi Gonzaga), the Jesuit novice who died of complications of plague at twenty-three, is the patron of Roman Catholic youth.

37. Greater Friendship Baptist Church, originally First Evangelical and Reformed Church (1926)
Architects: Corbusier, Lenski, and Foster
Builder: J. C. Hansen
Location: 12305 Arlington Avenue

The construction, maintenance, and, when necessary, renovation of sacred landmarks can be summarized in one word: leadership. Religious leadership stands out on every page of this guide. Leaders, usually—but not always—clergy, organize religious communities, raise money, hire architects, argue with contractors and, when the buildings are up, raise more money, hire other architects, and encourage more workers to keep them standing. When this does not happen, communities fail and buildings fall. This guide largely focuses on the first part of the process: the original builder-leader, the first architect, the building as originally conceived. Implicit in this account, however, is the obvious: sacred landmarks still stand because someone cares for them. The story of the Howard family of Greater Friendship Baptist Church serves as an important illustration of this theme.[8] This Baptist community began like most religious communities—small, poor, and struggling. Organized in 1955, it met in three progressively more ambitious buildings before buying this church from the Lutherans in 1969. Its first years here were not easy. When the third generation of Baptist pastors in the Howard family (the fourth generation has begun preaching at Greater Friendship) took over the parish, he was faced with the usual problems: the roof, the mortgages, and the heating system. A response by the Cleveland Fire Department to a dramatic malfunction of the jury-rigged and not-to-code furnace interrupted his installation. Now, more than thirty years later, he has retired the mortgages and replaced the roof twice and the furnace three times. Congregants are now baptized in a pool in the apse instead of in the municipal swimming pool across the road, and Larry Howard has shared his pulpit with Martin Luther King Sr.

Early in its history, the Protestant reformation divided between the more traditional (more Roman Catholic) Lutheran followers of Martin Luther and the less traditional Reform followers of John Calvin and Huldrych Zwingli. Differences between the Lutherans and the Reformed were only exacerbated in Germany by various government efforts to unite the Protestants into one denomination. This struggle within the Protestant German community was played out in Cleveland in the Schifflein Christi congregation. Eventually, as the First Evangelical and Reformed Church, it would build this building in 1926. Zum Schifflein Christi (the Little Boat of Christ), established in 1835, is usually considered the first Lutheran congregation in Cleveland but it included strong Reform elements. The more orthodox Lutherans departed in 1842 to found Zion Evangelical Lutheran Church (see p. 24). The more Reformed remained in Schifflein Christi. This congregation, uniting with other Reformed communities, became progressively more Reformed and less German until it ultimately sold this building to the Baptists and found a home with the Fellowship United Church of Christ (UCC) in Wickliffe, whose residual recognition of national heritage is its annual sausage and sauerkraut dinner.

The powerful stone masses of Greater Friendship grace a neighborhood overlooking Forest Hills Park with the aplomb expected of a building from the office of John Corbusier. Corbusier, who built more than thirty churches in the United States, designed the Church of the Saviour (see p. 325) and was the Cleveland architect for Cram's Church of the Covenant (see p. 52). As would be expected, Greater Friendship's medieval and picturesque appearance originally harmonized well with the park; today, however, the park is increasingly taken up by school construction and recent municipal recreational facilities and playing fields. Although the church stands immediately adjacent to a busy automobile repair facility on the east, this remains largely a neighborhood of reasonably well-kept houses.

The random coursed, subtly rock-faced Briar Hill Sandstone has acquired a dark patina with time. This well-proportioned, solid, eclectic structure has an impressive Gothic entry and rose window. The building is set off by a single tall bell tower with louvered Romanesque-style openings. The church serves as the center of its community. The gymnasium, which has a large stage, is equipped to seat four hundred and contains showers, individual lockers, and a six-lane bowling alley. The basement houses dining rooms, a kitchen, and additional space for club rooms.

With the dark heavy beams of its wood ceiling and its plain plastered walls, the 650-seat worship space has an English country look. As originally planned, the sanctuary had a cruciform plan with five-pew transepts, an ample balcony at the rear, and a generous balcony in the apse above the chancel for organ and choir. To accommodate the Baptist congregation, the choir moved to the south transept and was replaced by a baptistry pool still surrounded by a screen of organ pipes. The north transept originally opened through a retractable wall into a large educational gathering room; this increased seating to one thousand. Gothic stone trims the doors and arches. Dark church furniture is plain but beautifully stained. A low and comforting wood-beamed ceiling embraces an ample narthex. Three large, African American–themed windows illuminate the sanctuary from the south. At night the windows can be illuminated from inside so that the images become dramatically vibrant to passersby.

38. Windermere United Methodist Church (1909)
Architects: J. C. Fulton (1909);
Travis Gower Walsh (1949)
Builder: Ner Stroup
Location: 14035 Euclid
Avenue, East Cleveland

Created to be a model municipality, East Cleveland was the first suburb of the city of Cleveland and one of the first incorporated suburbs in the United States. An incorporated village after 1895, East Cleveland is believed to owe its continued existence to Charles E. Bolton, who, as mayor from 1899 to 1901, successfully defended his community from annexation by the City of Cleveland.[9] After a vacation in the English Lake District, Bolton assigned names from that area, including "Windermere," to East Cleveland Streets, and Windermere Street gave the neighborhood its name.[10]

Windermere United Methodist Church was established in 1899.[11] Every parish has its founding myth. For St. John Cantius, it was the car barn. For Our Lady of Peace, it was the pool hall. For the teetotaling Methodists of Windermere, it was the roadhouse—established for the convenience of those who needed a drink on their way to Buffalo. The parish rented the roadhouse and then bought it in 1902. Their tavern was a block northwest of "Forest Hill," John Rockefeller's six-hundred-acre summer estate straddling East Cleveland and Cleveland Heights. In an era in which sobriety, industry, and honesty were religious virtues that parish leaders often urged the general public to pursue, the second Windermere pastor would preach a sermon in 1908 urging Theodore Roosevelt to remain in office while comparing him to St. Paul.

In late 1906 and early 1907 this pastor, Ner Stroup,[12] and his famous evangelist wife, the suffragist Emma Cartwright, were given a four-month sabbatical to study at Magdalen College, Oxford. They came back with a child and plans for a church.[13] Many of Cleveland's sacred landmarks are imaginatively said to be patterned on famous buildings. Windermere's tower is, in fact, quite similar to that of Magdalen College. Although smaller than the English original, and never hung with bells, Windermere's tower is much more visible, up and down Euclid Avenue, than that of Magdalen from the cramped streets of Oxford. Windermere tower is the only part of the church that has survived intact. The 1909 church had a large, octagonal 850-seat sanctuary separated by Akron Plan folding doors from a 650-seat lecture room. There was a Skinner organ and a large art glass dome supported, without pillars, by the walls and ceiling of the main worship space. Three Tiffany windows were visible, when illuminated, from the outside. A year after building this church, Stroup became superintendent of the Cleveland District of the Methodist Church. Four years later he was killed in a gruesome automobile accident and, for the first time, the folding doors were drawn back to accommodate 1,500 mourners. Although severely disabled, Emma Stroup would survive the accident to head the campaign to make East Cleveland the first city east of the Mississippi to give the vote to women.[14]

Fire destroyed the 1909 church in 1946, and it was rebuilt in 1949 with the help of the Austin family (of the Austin Construction Company, see Broadway United Methodist Church, p. 168).[15] Only the Magdalen tower and the marvelous entry room at its base survived the fire. The extent of the damage can best be appreciated from the east, where the new brick of reconstruction contrasts with the Hummelstone brownstone of the original building. The Akron Plan auditorium church was replaced with an axial processional church, perhaps more in character with Magdalen's medieval tower, but certainly at odds with the architect and builder's original intention. Nevertheless, Windermere was rebuilt as a large program church. The mass of the new building dominates its neighborhood as much as the old building did before the fire.

The building has room for an acre of fellowship hall in the basement, flanked by a modern kitchen that feeds five hundred to eight hundred of East Cleveland's hungry every month. The immaculately restored gym accommodates a full-size basketball court, generous dressing facilities, and a large Tiffany-style window of *Christ Teaching* with gorgeous blue glass in the sky. Separate, but alongside the sanctuary, is the Austin Chapel with its exquisite woodcarving. There is a seemingly unending procession of other chapels, classrooms, and a pastor's study with a working fireplace. The surviving small entrance room under the tower is lined, in honor of the Austin family, with beautifully carved apostles, a wonderful wrought-iron door, and two windows of outstanding modern glass. Classrooms are occupied during the day by a day-care program of the Methodist-associated Berea Children's Home.[16] In an environment of urban ruin and destitution this church, inside, presents a picture of vitality and promise.

The new construction completely transformed the main worship area. It is now an axial nave seating 1,200. The space is plain and emphasizes its structure—massive simple Gothic arches march down from the ample balcony to the chancel. The high open-timbered ceiling creates a great space. The walls of the nave are completely plain but the large, traditional choir is paneled in wood. In contrast to the decay beyond the bounds of the church, the sanctuary is a refuge of order and dignity.

39. Antioch Christian Fellowship, originally St. Paul's Episcopal Church (1845 and 1894)
Architects: Unknown (1845); Coburn, Barnum, and Benes (1894)
Builders: Unknown (1845); Howard Ingham (1894)
Location: 15837 Euclid, East Cleveland

Some would say that the former pastor of this church,[17] Francis Sayre, was the most illustrious Ohio Episcopal churchman since Bishop Philander Chase.[18] Others would say that the unusually named bishop set a ridiculously low bar, one that the Olympian Sayre cleared with aplomb. Sayre (1915–2008), the grandson of Woodrow Wilson, was the last person born in the White House. After serving as a chaplain on a warship in the Pacific during the Second World War and as "the Industrial Chaplain of the Diocese of Ohio" responsible for factories and union halls, he was assigned to St. Paul's East Cleveland. In 1951 Sayre was named dean of Washington National Cathedral, and in this capacity for the next twenty-seven years, he led the battle against nuclear proliferation, apartheid, the Vietnam War, segregation, and, most famously, Joe McCarthy.

The Antioch Christian Fellowship was established by Pastor Kevin Hannah in 1996 as a nondenominational church drawn from his home Bible study group. They originally met in the Lee Heights Community Church. Three years later, they moved to Notre Dame College in South Euclid. The congregation then established the Bridge to Abundant Life Outreach Center as a mission in East Cleveland. In 2002 they moved entirely to their mission. For two years they struggled to fit into this storefront. When St. Paul's East Cleveland, one hundred yards away, became available, Hannah drove downtown to the Episcopal diocesan Church House to meet with the diocesan treasurer. On the way, the Lord told him, "Ask him to sell you the church for one dollar." When he did, the treasurer replied, "That sounds like a great idea." After reviewing what the Antioch Christian Fellowship intended to do with their building, the Episcopalians decided to waive the dollar. In addition to the usual spiritual and feeding ministries, the Fellowship administers a serious clothing ministry.

This is a building of parts, and its separate parts have been assembled over almost 170 years. Not all the parts are visible from Euclid Avenue, but one has a clear impression of distinct architectural pieces put together like an assembly of children's architectural blocks arranged on a rug. From the street, one sees two dominant pieces. On the left (west), atop a high-ceilinged masonry piece, a large, white-plastered, half-timbered gable reaches up to a high roofline. This is the original 1845 church, now used as a chapel, and believed to be the oldest standing building in East Cleveland. On the right is a similarly sized, entirely masonry piece with a contiguous masonry gable reaching up to a roofline at the same height as its fraternal twin on the west. This is the 1894 church. On its gable one can see the tracery of its famous south window and, from the outside, a hint of the glass to be seen from inside. A battlemented connecting hall unites these two dramatically gabled pieces. One enters both this hall and the adjoining 1896 church through traditional red Episcopal church doors. Three full-length lancet windows decorate the front of the original church. Three small windows are positioned over the door of the connecting hall. The tracery of the great south window is also divided into thirds. Masonry in both buildings is constructed of large blocks. To the west of these buildings is a large adjoining brick building, erected in the 1960s—the time of St. Paul's greatest prosperity—to house what was reportedly the largest Episcopal Sunday school in the United States. A brick Akron Plan assembly room is hidden from the street behind the original church. As all this suggests, this is a large institution masquerading as a little English country church, or perhaps, since there is no tower, a castle.

Entering the building from the street, one finds, on the left, an ample narthex the width of the original sanctuary with a modern east window. Behind the original church is the 1922 Akron Plan assembly area with second story classrooms around a U-shaped balcony with a wrought-iron balustrade. The first and second churches are joined at the front of the lot by the crenellated hall visible from the street and by the sacristy behind. These two connecting elements, with the two churches, enclose an interior court. The church has a good-sized gym in the basement adjacent to a large kitchen.

The sanctuary is a simple, large hall with plastered walls. A magnificent ribbed, dark wood, paneled ceiling is articulated with substantial timbers. It features wonderful dark wood pews, reportedly brought up from either the cathedral or its predecessor, Trinity Parish, on Superior Avenue. Each side of pews is farther halved longitudinally with a wood divider. The unsigned great south window, vaguely visible through elaborate tracery from the street, is beautiful cold process opalescent glass in the school of Tiffany. In its center is a large, bloodred, opal glass cross. The side windows are figurative and of lesser quality, those on the east date from the 1960s and those of the west date from the 1970s. It has small semi-lancet windows around the apse. Pastor Hannah describes the sanctuary as "ark-style" because it is, with its timbered ceiling, like an inverted ship. Three steps lead up to the chancel and another two steps lead up to the apse. The original wood altar is now pulled forward from its original place in the apse into the center of the chancel.

40. First Presbyterian Church of East Cleveland (1893)
Architect: W. W. Sabin
Builder: Dormer Hickok
Location: 16200 Euclid Avenue, East Cleveland

The First Presbyterian Church of East Cleveland ("Old First" to distinguish it from Old Stone) was the first organized religious community in Cuyahoga County.[19] Unlike their Pilgrim and Puritan forebearers who fled England for religious reasons, the settlers of the Western Reserve of Connecticut were drawn to northern Ohio by what they perceived as economic opportunity. They were relatively slow to establish religious institutions. The first church in the Western Reserve was established in Youngstown in 1797, followed by churches in Hudson in 1804 and Austinburg (eight miles southwest of Ashtabula) in 1805. Around this time, settlers began meeting for religious exercises led by Nathaniel Doane in his cabin in what is now University Circle. Doane was an entrepreneur who had been a member of Moses Cleaveland's surveying party. In 1807 the East Cleveland pioneer group formalized their organization as the "Euclid Church."[20] "Old First" was the first site of the Grand River Presbytery, which would later become the Cleveland Presbytery and then, in 1973, the Presbytery of the Western Reserve, the governing organization of the local Presbyterian Church.

This rural community continued to meet in cabins until securing a two-acre site for a church and cemetery on a hill beside Nine-Mile Creek (it was nine miles from Cleveland). They would occupy this property for more than two hundred years, being one of the few early churches in the Greater Cleveland area to continue in an original location. Their lot fronted on what was then known as "Center Highway." This road ran due east from Cleveland to the Pennsylvania line. Their first church was on the same level as the highway. Now known as Euclid Avenue, this thoroughfare has been lowered three times, in part the result of excavations for trolleys, so that First Presbyterian is now "the church on the hill" overlooking the street.[21] In 1810 the community built a thirty-by-twenty-foot log church on the northeastern corner of their lot, the corner now occupied by their cemetery. Although their log cabin had windows on both sides and behind the pulpit, there was no chimney and no heat. Worshipers brought foot warmers to services that they replenished at noon from neighbors' homes. Sin was always a concern in the wilderness; therefore, the church was attentive to such misbehavior as "soaking hides to add weight and gain more money from their sale, inability to control the behavior of children, [and] selling whiskey on the Sabbath to Indians."[22] Dancing was a perennial problem.

Following the War of 1812, their pastor rode to the East Coast to solicit funds for a new church. He returned with $800, and in 1816 the community began construction of a white frame building. Although this church had three doors, thirty-four windows, a tower, and a steeple (but no spire), the windows had not been glazed at dedication. The dedication was interrupted by half an hour of lightning, thunder, squalls, high wind, and torrential rain. The congregation huddled under umbrellas in the center of the sanctuary. By the time the dedication had resumed and then concluded, fifteen trees had fallen around the church without having damaged the new building. In 1823 the parish added the spire and the three-by-eight-foot Meriam window depicting St. Paul. This window would subsequently be incorporated into a large north window when the stone church was built in 1893.

During this period the parish was still a mission of the Board of Missions in Connecticut. The pastor was paid partly in money and partly in kind—one load of hay, six sheep, eighteen pounds of honey, one pair of shoes, twelve and a half pounds of butter, and one cheese.[23] In 1835 one of the original church founders, John Shaw, who was the third settler in Cuyahoga County, died and left his property to establish an academy. His farm would become Shaw High School; Shaw held its graduation exercises in the church for several years after 1900. In 1840 the founder of the community, Nathaniel Doane, was summoned to answer for "frequent and habitual participation in worldly amusements."[24] Remaining in his corners, Doane ignored the summons.

William H. Beecher, brother of Henry Ward and Harriet Beecher Stowe, served an unsuccessful two-year term as pastor in the 1840s.[25] In the endless discussion of whether to build a masonry church, it was finally decided to divide the frame sanctuary with a ceiling, putting the church above and the Sunday school below. Like all Reformed denominations, the congregation repeatedly was torn apart by slavery. Whether First Presbyterian East Cleveland was part of the Underground Railroad remains unknown. Some evidence suggests it was, but such activity was unlikely to have been well documented given that it was illegal at the time.

When Dormer Hickok, who would build the stone church, was called to the pulpit of First Presbyterian, his compensation was $1,000 and "the use of the manse excluding"—in conformity with the teetotaling practice of the church—"the vineyard."[26] His stone church was built with the support of Flora Stone Mather, who advanced $30,000 toward construction of the $36,000 building. The severe financial depression of 1892 almost stopped construction. It was resumed with the use of oak pillars to support the roof instead of a more expensive freestanding roof, and the use of pine instead of oak for wainscoting and sheathing. During construction, the original frame building was moved onto an adjacent lot and, when the stone church was occupied, the frame building was given to the owner of the lot. In return, he gave $250 to the building fund and recast the bell that, hanging in the east tower, is still rung by a pull hanging down into the twin east narthex. Charles Brush, inventor of the arc light, had become an Episcopalian although his parents and grandparents had belonged to First Presbyterian; he was approached for a five-thousand-dollar donation for an organ for the new church. He is reported to have replied that it was a high price to pay for having parents who were Presbyterian.[27] As originally built, there was a rectangular, one-story, stone educational wing, broader than the church, built south of the sanctuary. The church describes this as an Akron Plan but it did not communicate with the sanctuary. The classrooms did open into a central assembly area, separate from the sanctuary, surmounted by an octagonal clerestory floor.

In the first part of the twentieth century, First Presbyterian was greatly energized by neighborhood residents working in Nela Park, the ninety-two-acre Georgian Revival headquarters of General Electric Lighting next door, the first industrial park in the world. The loyalty of General Electric employees and their children, dispersed into the suburbs, may explain why, despite its location in a predominantly African American neighborhood, First Presbyterian of East Cleveland continued into the twenty-first century as one of the few truly integrated churches in the United States. In 1923–24 the south end of the church was rebuilt as a two-story rectangle, the size of the original first story, and the octagonal clerestory disappeared. The parish built a home for the pastor on the south border of the church's lot in 1924. It was razed in 1974. In 1933, in an attempt to cope with the Great Depression, First Presbyterian rented a 120-acre farm near Chardon. Every day, using an old Dodge truck the church had purchased for $50, unemployed members drove out to the farm to tend the two pigs, three ponies, three sheep, one goat, and fruit and vegetables the church sold in five-dollar lots.

In 1962 the church completed an administrative-education wing to the east, designed by Damon, Worley, Samuels, and Associates. The Akron Plan addition to the south of the stone church had been completely reorganized in 1948 by the addition of a ceiling that divided the assembly area into two floors. A church parlor and the Wells chapel within the original educational wing were reconstructed in 1962 as part of the new administrative-education wing to the east. A proposed fellowship hall associated with the new addition, to run to the south of the present building, was never completed. In 1972 the two-hundred-member Windermere Presbyterian Church merged with First Presbyterian. The Windermere building became the East Cleveland Community Center before its purchase by the East Cleveland Theater.

"Old First" is an imposing stone structure on what appears to be a hill overlooking Euclid Avenue from the south. Looking out at the large General Electric plant across the street, the church complex backs into the residential neighborhood between the church and Nela Park. At the far east end of Euclid Avenue, as it runs through East Cleveland, the church's location adjacent to industry, rather than commerce, spares it partially from the urban blight to its west.

First Presbyterian, on the far East Side, like another former country church, St. Patrick's West Park on the far West Side (see p. 271), somewhat uncomfortably shares its campus with a cemetery. Like St. Patrick's, First Presbyterian's plans to expand its building into the cemetery were initially frustrated although, unlike St. Patrick's, the Presbyterians eventually prevailed in court. They were allowed to build their 1962 brick education-administrative addition out to the east over the graves. The displaced headstones, including that of John Shaw, are displayed in a shelter on the east border of the cemetery. The cemetery embraces the remains of three veterans of the Revolution, two of the War of 1812, and five from the Civil War. The East Cleveland Memorial Day parade, for many years, began at the East Cleveland City Hall and ended with speeches and gun salutes around a flagpole, given by the East Cleveland Parent Teacher Association at the First Presbyterian cemetery.

Built on four massive thirty-by-seven-foot cornerstones, this is a Romanesque Revival building with a steeply gabled roof, pointed arches, picturesque silhouette, towers and battlements, leaded glass, crenellation, and wooden scrollwork at eaves and gables. A slate roof has survived more than a century.

Each of the two tower entrances from Euclid Avenue admits to two separate small narthexes, each the size of the tower base. A right angle turn from each narthex enters the sanctuary. Each narthex also has a stair down to the basement. The sanctuary is a broad, open, and expansive space seating about five hundred. Sight lines are not significantly interrupted by the wooden pillars (see above). The apse is slightly recessed. One finds light brown pews and a Moeller organ. The timbered ceiling is beautifully crafted under stained paneling. The large St. Paul window, now almost two hundred years old, dominates the north end of the sanctuary. After November 3, 2009, when they held their final service, St. Paul could no longer look down on the first religious community established in Cuyahoga County.

41. St. Jerome Church (1950)
Architect: William Koehl
Builder: Leo Hammer
Location: 15200 Lake Shore Boulevard

The 1876 decision of the Lake Shore & Michigan Southern Railway (which became the New York Central) to establish a roundhouse and repair shop in Collinwood brought many Irish and German families to a neighborhood previously known as the largest shipping point in the nation for grapes. Within a year, the mission that would become St. Joseph (Collinwood) celebrated Mass in a new frame church. Unfortunately, the enterprise that had made St. Joseph necessary soon divided the parish—the giant Collinwood Rail Yards became an almost impassible barrier between North and South Collinwood.

The assistant at St. Joseph, Leo Hammer, established St. Jerome on the north side of the tracks in a tent in 1919.[28] A Thanksgiving Day storm blew away the tent, and the congregation began meeting in the basement of its unfinished church.

William Koehl, who had designed St. Dominic (see p. 338) in Shaker Heights in a completely different style two years before, completed this modern interpretation of an English Gothic church in 1950. St. Jerome is sited on a busy thoroughfare in a commercial-residential neighborhood now in transition. Although, like so many post–World War II churches, this is a light brick building, the street facade is faced with multicolored Tennessee quartzite. Trim is Indiana limestone. The 850-seat church has a slate roof, a large, pointed neo-Gothic narthex window with elaborate tracery, neo-Gothic buttressed walls, robust, carved wood lintels, and an impressive statue of St. Jerome.

The tower is a memorial to parishioners who served and died in World Wars I and II. At the base of the tower, accessible from the nave, is a chapel named for the militant St. Joan of Arc with glass depicting her life. All of the glass in this church was created by the Burnham Studio of Boston, considered by the Smithsonian Institute to be one of the four best glass studios in the United States.[29] The Burnhams were closely associated with America's premier neo-Gothic architect, Ralph Adams Cram, and were responsible for the clerestory windows of Riverside Church in New York and much of the glass program of Trinity Cathedral in Cleveland. St. Jerome's Burnham Studio windows include fifteen *Rosary* windows along the nave and a magnificent west window of the four *Doctors of the Church*. Other important decorations in this church are the Stations produced by the Vatican Mosaic Studio, the gold two-story mosaic of the *Trinity* behind the altar, an alabaster statue of *Our Lady of Fatima* with gold mosaic, a handsome, shallow, modern marble baptismal font, and an unusual wrought-iron screen behind glass panels separating the nave from the narthex.

There are two unusual features of this church. It has, for a Roman Catholic church, an unusually generous narthex.[30] Second, instead of a series of neo-Gothic quadripartite vaults marching down and across the ceiling or a continuous barrel vault, St. Jerome has a ceiling arching across the nave, running along the long axis of the building. The ribs supporting the ceiling each rest on a large, wooden lion head in honor of St. Jerome.

42. St. John Nottingham Lutheran Church (1954)

Architects: Ward and Conrad
Builder: Walter Luecke
Location: East 176th Street and Nottingham Road

In 1839 Martin Stephan led 1,100 conservative Saxon Lutherans across the Atlantic (350 were lost at sea) to establish a community in and around St. Louis; this became the Lutheran Church–Missouri Synod. It is now the eighth-largest Protestant denomination in the United States (see also Zion Evangelical Lutheran Church, p. 24, Trinity Evangelical Lutheran Church, p. 192, and Immanuel Evangelical Lutheran Church, p. 234). One must distinguish this branch of the Lutheran Church from the more liberal Evangelical Lutheran Church in America, which is the fourth-largest Protestant denomination in the United States (see Grace Lutheran Church, p. 324).[31] Missouri Synod Lutheran churches frequently have parochial schools, maintaining two high schools in the Cleveland area. Historically, the Missouri Synod has been closely associated with the German-speaking American population, although by the 1880s the majority of Missouri Synod young people were English-dominant bilingual. Anti-German sentiment during the First World War enabled the younger generation to "Americanize" the denomination, and Missouri Synod membership doubled between the World Wars.

Lutheran services began among German rail workers in Collinwood in 1883. What would become St. John Nottingham was established in 1890.[32] It built its first frame church in 1891 and a school the following year—where the pastor was the teacher. This church was on what is now East 159th Street. Later, St. John Nottingham moved around a good deal. The congregation bought property on Holmes, south of the railroad tracks and the interstate that now divide Collinwood. Then it moved back north to property across the street from its present location. By 1907 the parish maintained two teachers, but on the day after Christmas their church was partially destroyed by fire. Ten parish children died a year later in the Collinwood School fire.

In 1918 the congregation began English-language services on Sunday, and in 1924 the church constitution was rewritten in English and German. By 1950, when the congregation purchased their current eleven-and-a-half-acre lot on the triangle between Nottingham Road, East 176th Street, and Lake Shore Boulevard, the congregation had grown to 1,300 with 195 students in the school. In the 1940s St. John Nottingham played a major role in the organization of the Cleveland Lutheran High School Association that opened a secondary school in 1948. When the first high school was demolished to make way for the Innerbelt, St. John Nottingham promoted the construction of Lutheran High School East on Mayfield Road and mounted successful campaigns in the early 1980s and late 1990s to keep that high school open.

Perhaps because of its commanding modern tower and sprawling site, St. John Nottingham appears much larger from the street than from inside. It is a surprise that the sanctuary seats only five hundred. The church, with its smooth planes of light-colored brick and simple unadorned openings, has a contemporary appearance. With little historic ornamentation, except for the smooth-cut stone lintels and sills around the windows and the stone caps along the roofline, the overall design is horizontal. The freestanding, high, slender tower is its most characteristic feature. A generous portico faces east and draws attention to the main entrance to the sanctuary.

Inside, the sanctuary is plain, much in the style of the 1960s. Trim is stainless steel, and the sanctuary is separated from the narthex by clear glass. The sanctuary has a plain wood ceiling and a well-proportioned balcony. The asymmetry of the sanctuary is unique in Cleveland. The center aisle divides the seating approximately into one-third and two-thirds, so that the south pews are much shorter than are those to the north. The large windows to the south are modern patterned glass. To the north, the glazing is clear and looks out into a charming courtyard that separates the church from part of the school. A large vernacular window of *Christ* dominates the front of the sanctuary. This window is lit from inside, making it visible at night. The principal historic element in the sanctuary is the baptismal font, brought over from the previous church.

43. St. Casimir Parish,
originally Our Lady of Perpetual Help Church (1952)
Architects: Michael Boccia and Stasys Kudokas[33]
Builder: Juozas Angelaitis
Location: 18022 Neff Road

Cleveland is a big place, and although the Lithuanian population has always been comparatively small, it has been substantial in absolute numbers; it had between ten thousand and twelve thousand members by 1930 and grew by another four thousand after the Second World War. In exile, their attachment to their occupied homeland has been fierce. The Lithuanians first settled, like all immigrant groups, in the inner city near their industrial jobs. They worshiped in a variety of locations. Only after Lithuania first became independent at the end of the First World War did the Cleveland community become large and affluent enough to build their first church of St. George on Superior Avenue in 1921. The community grew rapidly, moved east along the lake, and thought, in 1929, that they needed a second parish, Our Lady of Perpetual Help.[34]

The new parish had difficulty getting started. Pranas Kundrota made the first large donation to the parish: twenty-five dollars. The congregation bought the Hillgrove Inn, which then stood on their present location. The transaction included kitchen fixtures and dishes, chairs, carpets, and an old piano. For a decade the parish struggled, ever deeper in debt, until the appointment of Juozas Angelaitis as pastor. Father Angelaitis was a serious money raiser. The parish dealt in scrap metal, recyclable newspaper, returnable bottles, old furniture and appliances, and sales-tax stamps. Vegetables and chickens were raised for sale. "After Mass, the altar was covered over, refreshments were served, card parties and other forms of fund raising activities were held to add to the treasury."[35] This paid off a $65,000 debt in two years so that Father Angelaitis could settle down to building a church, auditorium, school, convent, and rectory. He completed the present church in 1952, the remainder of the campus in 1961, paid off the debt in 1972, and retired in 1974.

Ethnic parishes historically struggle with two problems: first, a shortage of priests who speak their language, and, second, a greater shortage of priests who speak it well. The diocese seemed to have solved this problem for Our Lady of Perpetual Help in 1974. An agreement with the Lithuanian Jesuit Vice Province in Chicago brought the provincial, Gediminas Kijauskas, to Cleveland with three of his staff. In 1987, celebrating the six-hundredth anniversary of the Christianization of Lithuania,[36] Father Kijauskas vigorously renovated and redecorated the church.

Our Lady of Perpetual Help has an interesting campus. The buildings, which share a similar style, continuously wrap around a forecourt embraced by the church to the south, the school to the north, and the other buildings to the west. In the center of the forecourt is a 1973 shrine to the *Pensive Christ* carved by Ramojus Mozoliauskas.[37]

This plain brick church with a tile roof has clean lines and strong forms. The few openings in the smooth wall planes are generously outlined in light-colored stone that contrasts with the color of the darker brick building mass. It features unusually exaggerated stone sills beneath the windows. A simple, restrained, and dignified tower to the south of the entrance identifies this as a religious building. An authoritative figure of the Virgin standing behind Christ as a young boy looks down from above the double doors.

The interior is quiet and simple. The spare columns do not significantly interrupt the large open space. Nine large pieces of modern statuary, also by Mozoliauskas, dominate the interior. His figures are representational in a modern style. This is a church dedicated to the Virgin, and this is clear in the selection of the figures. Lithuanians have always been known for their dedication to Mary, "*Terra lituana—terra Mariana.*" Four of the figures are of the best-known Madonnas of Lithuania: Our Ladies of Siluva, of Vilnius, of Pazaislis, and of Kalvarija. Over the altar stands a statue of *Our Lady of Perpetual Help,* patterned after a fourteenth- or fifteenth-century painting by an unknown artist in Crete, now in Rome.[38] In this representation, Christ is seen having jumped up into the arms of the Virgin, fleeing an image of his Passion, with the sandal of his right foot askew. A metal relief on the front of the altar details the Hill of Crosses in Lithuania.[39]

For most ethnic churches, the struggle goes on. Long ago, they brought themselves up from the depths of immigrant poverty, built the school and then the rectory and then the convent and then the church, and then they dealt with the divisions inherent in successive waves of their later immigrants who had different objectives from the original settlers, both here and in the home country. Now, their affluent congregations have departed to the suburbs, leaving them to struggle with a declining staff, a declining membership, an empty school, and a declining neighborhood. Although it too once struggled with the usual problems of an ethnic parish, Our Lady of Perpetual Help, with its well-kept, immaculate campus in the middle of a prosperous neighborhood of well-maintained homes thought it was different. Then, at the beginning of the twenty-first century, the bishop changed the name of the parish and invited in the Polish refugees from the shuttered St. Casimir, two impoverished miles to the west.

CHAPTER FOUR

South Central Cleveland

The south central region of Cleveland is composed of three neighborhoods—Central, Fairfax, and Kinsman.

Among the oldest residential neighborhoods in the city, Central changed significantly with the advent of public housing, urban renewal, and the construction of the interstate highway system following World War II.

Tour

Begin the tour at Progressive Field, traveling east on Carnegie Avenue. One block east of the stadium, on the left, is St. Maron's Catholic Church (44). Before reaching the church, note its three-story parking garage topped with life-size white religious statuary. This church does a brisk business on game days. Turn right at East 14th Street and, going under the Innerbelt, bear to the left, following the signs to East 22nd Street. Cross East 22nd as the road you are on becomes Community College Avenue. On the left is St. Vincent Charity Hospital. On the right, before reaching the complex of its main buildings, is Cuyahoga Community College's "Parking Lot B," all that remains of the once mighty St. Joseph Franciscan Roman Catholic Church, the mother of so many eastern European Roman Catholic parishes in Cleveland.[1] Passing the community college—John Bonebrake's masterpiece of urban planning and design—turn left at East 30th Street. On the right in succession are, first, the Jane Addams Business Careers Center—a Cleveland Metropolitan Schools cluster high school—second, the Murtis Taylor Adult Behavioral-Health Care Center—an important source of help in Cleveland for the emotionally ill—and, third, St. Philip's Christian Church (45)—another modern masterpiece but this time on a small scale.

At the corner turn right onto Central Avenue. On the northeast corner of the intersection is the Marion Sterling Elementary School. Travel on Central to East 38th Street and turn right (south). Travel on East 38th to Community College Avenue and turn left (east). Triedstone Baptist Church (46) occupies the southwest corner. This landmark was built for an Orthodox Jewish congregation.

Stay on Community College Avenue for two blocks and then turn left (north) onto East 40th Street. At Kenard Road, on the left side of East 40th, is the Pilgrim Baptist Church. St. John A.M.E. Church (47) stands the northeast corner of East 40th Street at Central Avenue. St. John A.M.E. is one of the oldest religious communities in Cleveland. Continue on East 40th for one more block and then turn right (east) onto Cedar Avenue. Travel on Cedar to East 46th Street. On the northeast corner of this intersection is Lane Metropolitan C.M.E. Church (48), originally the First Church of Christ, Scientist. Continue on Cedar for one more block and then turn right (south) onto East 49th Street.

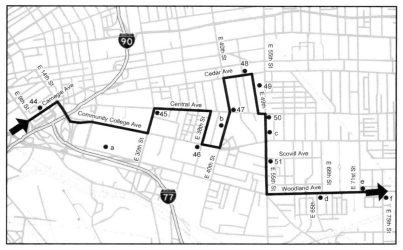

CENTRAL

44. St. Maron's Catholic Church
   a. St. Joseph Franciscan Roman Catholic Church site
45. St. Philip's Christian Church
46. Triedstone Baptist Church
   b. Pilgrim Baptist Church
47. St. John A.M.E. Church
48. Lane Metropolitan C.M.E. Church

49. St. Andrew's Episcopal Church
50. Friendship Baptist Church
   c. St. Paul A.M.E. Zion Church
51. Shiloh Baptist Church
   d. New Bethlehem Baptist Church
   e. 4 Real Church
   f. Mt. Sinai Baptist Church

St. Andrew's Episcopal Church (49) sits on the left. Travel south on East 49th Street to Central Avenue. Turn left (east) onto Central for one block.

At East 55th Street turn right (south). Friendship Baptist Church (50) occupies the southeast corner. This church was built for the congregation of Temple Tifereth Israel. Continue south on East 55th, past St. Paul A.M.E. Zion Church on the left. On the northeast corner of Scovill Avenue at East 55th stands East Tech High School. Opposite, on the southeast corner, stands Shiloh Baptist Church (51) built by Congregation B'nai Jeshurun. Continue on East 55th and then turn left (east) onto Woodland Avenue.

Travel east on Woodland, past the New Bethlehem Baptist Church on the right at East 65th Street. In the middle of Woodland Cemetery, on the left, is the twin-towered 4 Real Church (formerly Holy Trinity and St. Edward Roman Catholic Church). Mt. Sinai Baptist Church sits on the right (south) at East 75th Street. Continue on Woodland, entering the Fairfax neighborhood. At East 83rd Street, turn left (north). The Open Door Missionary Baptist Church occupies the northwest corner of the intersection. Travel north on East 83rd past Quincy Avenue. On the right, opposite the recreation center, is St. Adalbert/Our Lady of Blessed Sacrament Church (52), which resembles

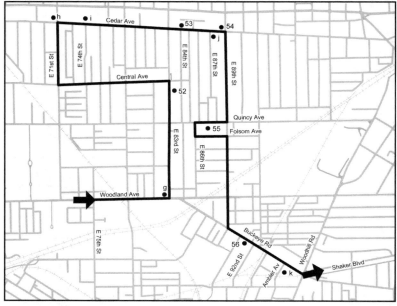

FAIRFAX–KINSMAN

g. Open Door Missionary Baptist Church
52. St. Adalbert/Our Lady of Blessed
Sacrament Church
h. Mt. Gillion Baptist Church
i. Messiah Baptist Church
53. St. James A.M.E. Church

j. United House of Prayer for All People
54. Antioch Baptist Church
55. Olivet Institutional Baptist Church
56. St. Elizabeth's Church
k. Calvary Apostolic Assembly

the cathedral in Salzburg, Austria. Continue on East 83rd to the end of the block and then turn left (west) onto Central Avenue.

Travel west on Central and then turn right (north) onto East 71st Street. Travel north on East 71st and then turn right (east) onto Cedar. Mt. Gillion Baptist Church stands on the northwest corner of the intersection. Drive east on Cedar. Opposite East 74th Street is Messiah Baptist Church. Continue on Cedar. Across from East 84th Street is St. James A.M.E. Church (53), originally built as Trinity Congregational Church. Continue on Cedar to East 89th Street. On the right lies the recently built United House of Prayer for All People. Turn right (south) onto East 89th. Antioch Baptist Church (54) is located on the northwest corner of this intersection.

Travel south on East 89th for a long block and then turn right (west) onto Quincy. Travel on Quincy beside the Olivet Institutional Baptist Church (55), opposite East 87th and East 88th Streets. Continue on Quincy to East 86th Street and turn left (south). Drive on East 86th for one block and then turn left (east) onto Folsom Avenue. Travel on Folsom for one block and then turn right (south) back onto East 89th Street. Continue on East 89th, entering the Kinsman neighborhood.

Drive south on East 89th past Woodland until East 89th intersects with Buckeye Road. Turn southeast (left) onto Buckeye. On the southwest corner of Buckeye at East 92nd Street is St. Elizabeth's Church (56), an Italian baroque style church built by the Hungarian immigrants who once dominated this neighborhood. This ends the tour of South Central Cleveland.

To leave this neighborhood, drive uphill on Buckeye Road for several blocks, passing Calvary Apostolic Assembly on the right. At the top of the hill, Shaker Boulevard veers off to the left. To begin the tour of Buckeye-Woodland (Chapter 5), continue east on Shaker Boulevard.

44. St. Maron's Catholic Church,
formerly St. Anthony Parish (1904)
Architect: Unknown
Builder: Umberto Rocchi
Location: 1245 Carnegie Avenue

Progressive Field, the prize-winning home of the Cleveland Indians, opened to the public in 1994. For St. Maron's, a long half-block away, it was a miracle.[2] St. Maron's probably has more riding on a good season for the Cleveland Indians than any church in Cleveland.[3] Its three-deck parking lot—distinctive for its religious, white, life-size statues on the upper story that greet sports fans— combined with its game-day specials seems to have hit a home run no matter the record of the Indians. St. Maron's had another reason to replace its social hall with an impressive parking garage—its parishioners had difficulty parking on game days.

St. Maron was a fourth-century Lebanese solitary. His followers built a monastery in his memory and this became the Maronite Church. When the patriarch of Antioch was martyred in 602, the Maronites elected John Maroun as their first native leader. Surviving almost every conceivable disaster in the mountains of Lebanon, the Maronites were thought to have disappeared until contact with Europe was reestablished by Raymond of Toulouse during the First Crusade. Maronite communion with Rome dates from 1182. Maronites retain their Antiochene (somewhat Orthodox) tradition with a unique liturgy, discipline, and hierarchy. Maronite difficulties in Lebanon continue and have led to a worldwide diaspora. Approximately half of the community now lives outside the Middle East.[4] The president of Lebanon is, by agreement, a Maronite Christian. The widow of Senator Edward Kennedy, Victoria Reggie Kennedy, is a Maronite Christian. The Maronite patriarch of Antioch, Mar Nassrallah Cardinal Boutros Sfeir, has his see north of Beirut. The American primate has his seat at the Eparchy of St. Maron of Brooklyn. St. Maron's in Cleveland is in the Eparchy of Our Lady of Lebanon of Los Angeles, headquartered in St. Louis.

In Cleveland, a St. Maron Society organized in 1914. The following year it purchased and remodeled a two-story brick apartment house for a church and rectory on East 21st Street. In 1939 the parish acquired and renamed the first Italian church in Cleveland. There was an extensive renovation in 1955, including three new altars, windows, and paintings. The church was remodeled and renovated again in the 1980s. In 1997 an addition was added to the west, and in 1999 they added a parallel addition to the east. These additions explain the unusual configuration of the nave.

This is one of Cleveland's most historic religious buildings. Before it was St. Maron's, it was St. Anthony. Before it became the Cleveland mother church of Maronite Christians, it was the Cleveland mother church of Italians—the religious center of "Big Italy." In this era of church closings, St. Anthony is the only church in Cleveland to have been closed twice.

The Haymarket neighborhood was Cleveland's first slum. It was a place where the residents, besieged by unrelenting temperance workers, sat on the curbs and drank beer out of a pail. By 1900 it was 93 percent Sicilian. St. Anthony, the first Italian parish in Ohio, had been established in 1887 to serve them. The parish acquired and renovated a little frame hall, where the Indians' field now stands, across East Ninth Street from the Erieview Cemetery.[5] In 1904 the constantly struggling parish built the present church on Carnegie. The impoverished community could never afford a school. In 1896 the Ursulines had begun a Sunday school to provide religious instruction for the children, and this remained the available instruction until 1938. The parish was plagued with *campanilismo,* the Old World parochialism that affected all of the Cleveland Italian community. Although some have estimated that by the First World War St. Anthony had ten thousand parishioners, the community was firmly divided along the regional fault lines of Italy, to the despair of its clergy and bishops. At one time St. Anthony celebrated twenty-two regional feasts per year and organized twelve annual street processions honoring regional saints.

When the Irish moved out of St. Bridget on Perry Street in 1938, the diocese closed St. Anthony for the first time, giving the brick Gothic Revival St. Bridget church to the Italians. Ten thousand countrymen, women, and children turned out to help the regional societies carry the statues and paintings of their patrons to the new church. They now had a school, but not for long. The Innerbelt stamped out St. Anthony-St. Bridget in 1961, closing the parish for the second time.

St. Maron's is an urban establishment in the middle of a busy commercial area. Across the street, the church faces a large auto parts distributor and an eleven-story Hilton Inn. One can find the nearest grass in the Erie Street Cemetery and the Indians' outfield. The ceremonial entrance to the church faces Carnegie, and one enters the church office through the parking garage. The original brick church, with its twin towers and stone columns and portico was, before the flanking additions of the late 1990s, quite narrow.

One enters up twin outside stairs from the street. There is a small narthex, reflecting the width of the original narrow building. A small chapel is located on the left. Stairs to the ample balcony are on the right. The additions have created a square nave, with an extension to the back under the balcony and to the front for the chancel and apse. The nave is divided longitudinally into quarters. In the central two quarters, on either side of the center aisle, march the pews of the original church. On either side of them, elevated up three steps, are the two lateral additions. The new additions are further divided from the original nave by rectangular pillar arcades. Down the ceiling of the original nave, toward the front of the church, are six distinctive large, shallow, oval domes, oriented at right angles to the center aisle. Relatively small lighting fixtures, with beautiful metalwork, hang down from the center of each dome. Gilded garlands run from the center of the nave down to the rectangular pillars that divide the nave from the elevated lateral additions. The borders of the domes and the ribs of the vaulted ceiling are outlined in blue. The lateral additions each have four smaller shallow oval domes from which hang crystal chandeliers. An elevated marble chancel appears in front, and in back one finds a deep open area under the balcony.

This is a church, like Hungarian St. Elizabeth's on Buckeye (see p. 142), that puts its patron over the altar. The large painting of *St. Maron,* under a large crystal chandelier, dominates the apse. To the right is an altar to St. Sharbel and to the left an altar to the Masabky brothers.[6] The altar of mixed marble has small columns supporting the tabletop. Several windows on the east and one on either side of the chancel have been blocked off by outside buildings. They are not illuminated, but their leading is still visible. The chancel windows can be identified as *St. Anthony of Padua* on the left and the *Virgin and Child* on the right. The church features conventional molded stations topped with the three bars of the Maronite cross. The cedar of Lebanon is painted on the marble lecterns to left and right.

45. St. Philip's Christian Church

(1968)
Architect: Frederick S. Toguchi
Builder: Gordon Majors
Location: 2303 East 30th Street

St. Philip's Christian Church, the smallest religious building in this book, is a gem.[7] Apart from its imaginative modernist form and its wonderfully clever plan,[8] it has gleamed for almost half a century as a symbol of what little light shines upon the West Central neighborhood of Cleveland. Bounded by Euclid Avenue on the north, East 55th Street on the east, Woodland Avenue on the south, and East 22nd Street on the west, West Central is "one square mile of depression."[9] Crime, poor housing, inadequate education, the absence of health services, hunger, unemployment, slum clearance, freeways, and expanding education and health institutions have decreased the population from 78,000 in 1920 to fewer than 12,000. West Central has "the highest concentration of public housing in Cleveland, the highest rate of unemployment, the highest incidence of homicide . . . and the highest number of people on welfare."[10] Gunshots are heard once or twice a week in a neighborhood almost without hope.[11]

Four young people, who had just graduated from the prestigious Union Theological Seminary, drove to Cleveland in an old converted milk van in 1954. They came to establish the Inner City Protestant Parish, patterned after the East Harlem Protestant Parish, which was an experimental ministry that had successfully dealt with neighborhood as well as spiritual issues while they were students in New York. Beginning in a storefront on Woodland Avenue (a location now obliterated by the freeway), moving to another storefront east of East 30th Street at Central Avenue, their effort settled at last on the southeast corner of Central at East 30th. Raising money throughout Cleveland for a permanent home, the Inner City Protestant Parish evolved into St. Philip's. It became associated with the Christian Church (Disciples of Christ) and acquired a full-time pastor and a parsonage. Over the years, St. Philip's would work closely with a much older inner-city landmark, the Fidelity Baptist Church (see p. 83). For more than twenty years after his hiring in 1970, the remarkable Alan J. Davis served St. Philip's while also serving as the executive secretary of the Cleveland City Club. Davis led St. Philip's into an effective and active role in community development. He has described his experience in *Second Chance: White Pastor, Black Church*.

Physical efforts to improve West Central surround St. Philip's. To the immediate north, across Central Avenue, is the Marion Sterling Elementary

School. Immediately south is the Murtis Taylor Adult Behavioral-Health Care Center, which cares for the emotionally ill. Next to Murtis Taylor is the Jane Addams Business Careers Center, a high school specializing in vocational education. Next to Jane Addams is the sprawling yet award-winning campus of Cuyahoga Community College. West, across East 30th Street, stand the renovated Sterling Public Library and the massive fourteen-story Cleveland Metropolitan Housing Authority Bing Center for senior citizens. Behind the church to the east are eighty-seven townhouses built in the early 1970s by Interfaith Housing. Although the immediate neighborhood functions as a microcosm of greater society's physical attempts to deal with its problems, the troubled 640 apartments of the 1935 Works Progress Administration's Cedar Estates, the oldest public housing complex in the United States, sprawls to the northwest and dominates St. Philip's neighborhood.

St. Philip's called upon Fred Toguchi, winner of the Cleveland Arts Prize for Design in 1965,[12] to design a home for a small, poor congregation on a limited budget contributed by others. They built small not only out of necessity, but also because they believed their mission should be outside, carrying their message to their neighborhood, rather than within the protection of their building. The building was assembled, not built, of precast concrete slabs attached to a preset concrete foundation. The articulation of the great slabs is the external decoration of the church. Walls are without ornament except for the anchor plates for the tie rods that hold the building together. The rough surface of the concrete has held up well for more than forty years, and its strong muscular forms, divided by deep-set vertical doors and windows, have retained their freshness. The church has no historic ornamentation except for the detached bell tower.

The previous edition of this guide delicately noted that "St. Philip's is an example of contemporary design intended to withstand the tensions of urban living"—a nice way of saying it was designed to survive a riot. Although its sheer concrete walls do not invite vandalism, it does not give the impression of being a fortress. St. Philip's has made a point, over the last four decades, of being an institution open every day of the week, and it has been rewarded over this period by an absence of vandalism and graffiti.

Inside, architect and congregation created a rethought religious institution in miniature. Every square foot on three small floors is cleverly utilized while retaining an atmosphere of openness and dignity. The building, as a church should be, is defined by its unforgettable sanctuary, so often described as "the length of a bowling alley and three lanes wide."[13] With its plain plaster walls and simple modern spherical hanging lights, two memorable features define the space. In the ceiling, asymmetrical interlocking wooden support beams crisscross from one side to the other, somewhat like the extended interlocking fingers of two praying hands. On the second floor of the sanctuary, two-thirds of the way back from the altar, hangs St. Philip's famous balcony, entered from a stairway hidden in the interior wall. The balcony is more than an elevated platform for worshipers and musicians. When a movable wall closes off the space below, the balcony becomes part of an area for educational or social purposes, now oriented toward the rear of the little building. By dividing the space into two large areas, the balcony acts as a central focal point for each.

46. Triedstone Baptist Church, originally Oheb Zedek Hungarian Orthodox Synagogue (1905)
Architect: Albert S. Janowitz
Builder: Unknown[14]
Location: 3782 Community College Avenue

"Triedstone Baptist," Armstrong wrote, "faces a field of vacant, deteriorating houses near the city's center."[15] What a difference fifteen years can make. These years have been unkind to many of the neighborhoods surrounding the buildings described in this guide. Many poor neighborhoods have deteriorated. Neighborhoods have frequently disintegrated into almost unimaginable destitution. All too frequently, at best, fire and demolition have clear-cut these churches' surroundings. In contrast, although it is in the poorest and most crime-ridden area of Cleveland, Triedstone Baptist is surrounded on the south by bright, spanking-new Cleveland Metropolitan Housing Administration residential construction. This has physically transformed the neighborhood. The transformation is less dramatic across Community College Avenue to the north, but the proliferation of new individual private homes there have largely eliminated the physical blight. The Greater Cleveland community looks to Triedstone Baptist and similar sacred landmarks to help address the social blight.

Triedstone could be called "The House of Splits." It was built by a group that split from one of Cleveland's historic congregations, and then, only fifteen years later, another group that split from another of Cleveland's great congregations acquired it.

A group that parted from B'nai Jeshurun built Triedstone. B'nai Jeshurun, at that time in the old Eagle Street Synagogue, would go on to build Shiloh Baptist Church (see p. 132) and the New Spirit Revival Center (see p. 318) before settling in Pepper Pike (see p. 349).

After B'nai Jeshurun, a group from Antioch Baptist Church, which had split from Shiloh, acquired this synagogue. At that time, they were meeting in the church built with Rockefeller's help that was later destroyed by the projects. Antioch later moved out to East 88th Street (see p. 138). In any case, it is significant that Triedstone's Baptist congregation has now been comfortably in this church for six times longer than its original congregation had been there.

The first Jewish Hungarian immigrants to Cleveland were solidly Orthodox, thus, they founded an Orthodox synagogue, B'nai Jeshurun, in 1866. As they acculturated to the United States, however, the Hungarians became more liberal and, by the time they moved out to East 55th Street in 1906, their practice had evolved into the Conservatism that we associate with B'nai Jeshurun today. Later-arriving Hungarian immigrants found it difficult to adapt rapidly to such innovations as the mixed or family seating that B'nai Jeshurun adopted in 1873. In 1904 the more conservative of the Hungarians established Oheb Zedek and built this building. Ten years later the congregation had a branch in Glenville, and in 1922 Oheb Zedek consolidated its operations into a gigantic 1,200-seat synagogue in Glenville. Within another thirty years, Oheb Zedek would move on to Cleveland Heights where, as the Taylor Road Synagogue, it united with five smaller congregations into Cleveland's largest Jewish Orthodox institution.

The dissident Baptist Antiochenes settled comfortably into Triedstone in 1921 with a minimum of fuss. They built a baptistry into what became their chancel and subsequently replaced it with a larger, more stylish, and more visible baptistry above their lectionary-pulpit. In 1958 they added a handsome international-style glass courtyard to the west of the original building to improve access from their large parking lot behind the church. This interior court connects an ambitious education and recreation building to the century-old church. The major thing, inside the building, that did not survive the transition from synagogue to church is Triedstone's distinctive facade. The carefully balanced outer three stories of triple tower windows, the handsome large double windows on the outside gable, and the three tastefully proportioned entrance doors that carefully gather in the broad ascending exterior staircase from the street are somehow lost in the interior of this painted brick building.

The building was built as a relatively big Orthodox synagogue. The two-aisle first floor sat eight hundred men, and the well-designed balcony could accommodate two hundred women. The wraparound balcony extends forward on both sides to the chancel. Despite its capacity, the plain sanctuary has the character of a small, intimate space. The plain, undecorated ceiling is articulated in three planes. Below the baptistry there is a large area for the choir in a square, recessed apse behind the lectern. Windows are plain except for one modern window on the west side and a large *Road to Calvary* window above the baptistry. The two large gable windows are visible from the balcony but their impact is muted. The other exterior windows are lost in the towers.

47. St. John African Methodist Episcopal Church (1908)
Architects: Sidney Badgley and William Nicklas
Builder: Ira Collins
Location: 2261 East 40th Street

St. John African Methodist Episcopal Church is singular in many ways.[16] It is the oldest African American congregation in Cleveland and, not surprising, has played an important role in its community for almost two hundred years. Along the way, it built Cleveland's first frame African American church. Now, unlike many other large congregations, it does not occupy a historic building built by another denomination or faith, it occupies a building it built itself. St. John is the first substantial church, and the first substantial building, put up by Cleveland African Americans. Its dedication in 1908 was cause for community parade and celebration. St. John, the center of a neighborhood from which people have been leaving, has become the center of a neighborhood to which people are returning.

St. John is one of the oldest churches in Cleveland. It was probably established after the Episcopalians (Trinity, 1816), the Presbyterians (Old Stone, 1820), the Catholics (St. Mary's-on-the-Flats, 1826), and the other Methodists (First Methodist, 1827) but before the Baptists (First Baptist, 1833), the Lutherans (Schifflein Christi, 1834) and the Israelitic Society of Cleveland (1839). In 1830 the remarkable William Paul Quinn recruited six former slaves into a Cleveland branch of the relatively new A.M.E.[17] The A.M.E's first church in Cleveland, on the corner of Bolivar Street at Prospect Avenue, was dedicated in 1850 (the Bolivar Street A.M.E.). They moved to Ohio Street (the Ohio Street A.M.E.) and then, after a fire, to Erie Street (as St. John's A.M.E.),[18] before finally moving to East 40th Street. This location, in the center of the early twentieth-century African American community in the Central neighborhood of Cleveland, made St. John a pivotal institution and attracted a large membership. St. John was where Booker T. Washington and W. E. B. Du Bois spoke and where Marian Anderson sang.

On a large, well-kept campus, across East 40th from a large, undeveloped park, in the middle of a once devastated residential district now rebuilding with new house construction, St. John finds itself in the midst of a large internal renovation. Robert Madison, a graduate of the École des Beaux Arts who has built churches all over the eastern United States but only two in Cleveland,[19] is supervising the $1.3 million renovation.

With its white stone trim, this is an imposing and unusual-looking brick building. A brick rectory to the rear is undergoing renovation as well. What appear to be flat transepts are actually the back and sides of the main worship space (later this chapter). The building's main perpendicular-style windows, parapets, and front and side porticoes give it an English country Tudor appearance. Hoodmolds and reverse corbiesteps are Romanesque. Two towers of differing heights, a common feature in Romanesque Revival churches in the United States at the turn of the century, break up the overall horizontal effect of the main block.

The unusually oriented sanctuary and its educational wing are located on the floor above a large social hall that runs almost the entire length of the rectangular building. The square sanctuary is plain and well designed. It is oriented at a forty-five-degree angle toward the northeast so that the chancel, with its organ, pulpit, lectionary, and altar rail, occupies the northeast corner, and the back of the sanctuary occupies the southwest corner. Thus, the entrance wall and the north wall of the church form the left side of the sanctuary, and the south wall of the building and a retractable wall to the east form its right side and divide the sanctuary from the educational wing. A large balcony wraps around the sanctuary from the retractable east wall to the north wall. There are no pillars. When the giant sliding wooden east wall is retracted into the ceiling, the sanctuary opens into the square educational wing on its right. This Akron Plan education area centers on a two-story education gathering room. Around this are Akron Plan classrooms with retractable or movable dividers on both floors. When the gathering room and classrooms are opened up, the worship space is almost doubled; the capacity of the sanctuary increases from 1,200 to 2,000. A large plaster dome dominates the sanctuary. It features early twentieth-century symbolic glass.

48. Lane Metropolitan C.M.E. Church, originally First Church of Christ, Scientist (see also Nottingham Spirk Design Associates, p. 62) (1900)
Architect: George Hammond
Builder: Unknown
Location: 2131 East 46th Street

Diagonally across the street from the nine-story Phillis Wheatley Association, the massive, dark, symmetrical, stone bulk of Lane Metropolitan C.M.E. conceals one of the most unusual church plans in Cleveland.[20] The exterior of this church is loosely patterned after the Pantheon in Rome. Although things are quite different inside, the plan of Lane, in its way, is as startling and surprising as that of its two-millennia-old exterior prototype.[21] One enters from the shorter side of the church on East 46th Street. The entrance is, as into the Pantheon, under a giant order classical portico. The large, undecorated pediment is supported by four three-story

Corinthian columns resting on a stepped-front podium. The front doors admit into a relatively small anteroom, the left side of which is now occupied by a credit union. Continuing to the right, members enter a long, beautifully plastered gathering room running most of the length of the building from west to east. To the north, parallel to and overlooked by this gathering room, is a large fellowship hall. Symmetrical double-helical staircases in the center of the first floor lead up into the sanctuary. The rectangular, two-story, eight-hundred-seat worship space, oriented toward the north, occupies most of the second and third floors. The staircases emerge in the middle of the semicircular seating.

This main hall is remarkably well lit through early twentieth-century windows. The off-white walls are articulated with white pilasters, again with Corinthian capitals. The dome, visible from Cedar Avenue on the outside of the building, is composed of Byzantine translucent glass, which further explains the light flooding into the sanctuary. The floor slants down to the north. Plasterwork is plain, simple, and elegant. What most distinguishes this space, however, are the stairs rising into the middle of the seating.

Christian Science, established by Mary Baker Eddy in Boston in 1866, came to Cleveland eleven years later via one of her students, who is usually referred to as "General" Erastus N. Bates. Bates, who had been captured and then exchanged at Charleston in 1864, ended the war as a lieutenant colonel in command of the Eightieth Illinois Volunteer Infantry, a unit that saw service at Kennesaw Mountain. After trying several locations, Cleveland's Christian Scientists found a home in the Pythian Temple until they built this church in 1900. The neoclassical style of this building is characteristic of most Christian Science churches of its period in Cleveland.[22] Classicism was considered a style based on reason, just as Christian Scientists considered their religion to be an explanation of life that appealed to reasonable people. George Hammond designed this church; he was also the architect for the original 1885 Hollenden Hotel, Cleveland's nineteenth-century luxury hotel with electric lights and one hundred bathrooms. In 1917, sixteen years after moving into this building and as the Second Church of Christ, Scientist, was moving into its much larger building at East 77th Street at Euclid Avenue, this congregation moved into a theater for a year before purchasing the Euclid Avenue Methodist Church.[23] In 1928 First Church of Christ, Scientist, moved to the top of the hill overlooking University Circle (see p. 62). After selling that building to Nottingham Spirk, First Church of Christ, Scientist, moved to the northwest of the four "holy corners" of Cleveland Heights at the intersection of Fairmount at Lee.[24]

49. St. Andrew's Episcopal Church (1916)
Architect: Charles Schneider
Builder: B. W. Paxton
Location: 2171 East 49th Street

With much of their residential and commercial neighborhoods clear-cut by fire, it is much easier to see the gathering of spiritual power clustered around the intersection of East 55th Street and Cedar Avenue, including Shiloh and Friendship Baptist churches (see p. 132 and p. 130), St. John A.M.E. (see p. 126), Lane Metropolitan C.M.E. (see p. 127), and prosperous and historic St. Andrew's Episcopal Church.[25] By reputation, St. Andrew's is another church of the aristocratic element of the Cleveland African American community, descendants of the Caribbean population who settled in Ohio in the early nineteenth century long before the massive migration north from the southern United States began in the 1890s. In fact, although St. Andrew's has been a prosperous parish since its beginning, the members of the congregation who have made it famous were primarily self-made women and men, born in Cleveland or making their way here from the south. Some of its most illustrious members have included Garrett Morgan—who invented the traffic light, the gas mask, and the respirator—and John Patterson Green—attorney, Republican politician, and "Father of Labor Day." St. Andrew's, under a series of distinguished rectors, including Solomon Jacobs and Austin Cooper, has played a disproportionally large role in the Episcopal Diocese of Ohio, the national Episcopal Church, and the local Cleveland community.[26] H. Irving Mayson, a son of the parish, was suffragan bishop of Michigan.

St. Andrew's was established in 1890 as a mission of Trinity Episcopal Cathedral (see p. 21) and in 1899 purchased the Swedish Evangelical Lutheran Bethlehem church at East 24th Street at Central Avenue. When that building was demolished in 1915 to make way for St. Vincent's Charity Hospital, the parish moved to East 49th Street.

Rising unexpectedly adjacent to East 55th, St. Andrew's, because of the destruction of its neighborhood, now looms much larger than it probably appeared immediately after its construction. This will change with the reconstruction of the George Washington Carver Elementary School next door to the south.[27] St. Andrew's is one of those substantial brick buildings that is larger than it appears from photographs of the outside (and appears smaller than expected on the inside). Detailing is Tudor, and it features large east and west perpendicular-style windows. There is no tower, and what one sees from the outside, aside from the adjacent 1953 parish house, is the volume of the sanctuary expressed in its exterior brick walls. The two arms of an addition embrace a courtyard to the north.

The sanctuary is rectangular. Admission is from the side, in both the back and in the front, from both wings of the addition. Stone shoulders support an open timber ceiling from which the original chandeliers hang. The stations of the cross line the warm brick walls (unusual but not unknown in an Episcopal church). The seating for the choir runs along either side of the chancel. Decoration of the apse is wood paneling with limited carving. Furniture is solid and simple. One has an impression of quiet simplicity with the decoration consisting primarily of the comforting brick walls and the timbers of the open ceiling.

50. Friendship Baptist Church, originally Temple Tifereth Israel (see also Temple Tifereth Israel, "the Temple," p. 44, and Temple Tifereth Israel East, p. 344) (1894)
Architects: Lehman and Schmidt
Builder: Aaron Hahn
Location: 5600 Central Avenue

The imposing dark-stone presence of Friendship Baptist Church looms over the southeast corner of Central Avenue at East 55th Street.[28] A chain and padlock now bar the door of this building, so important to the history of Protestant and Jewish Cleveland.[29] One wonders, has Friendship Baptist/ Tifereth Israel gone the way of the 1928 Fifth Church of Christ, Scientist, the abandoned eyesore on the border of Cleveland and Lakewood, now owned by an increasingly desperate City of Cleveland? Will it go the way of St. Joseph Franciscan Roman Catholic Church, now transformed into Cuyahoga Community College Parking Lot B?

When the Jewish community began to organize in Cleveland in 1839, their members were divided between Orthodox and Reform.[30] Orthodox held to tradition, and Reform sought to adapt aggressively to life in the United States. Jewish immigrants brought this division, dating from the middle of the eighteenth century, with them from Europe. In 1850 Reform in Cleveland established Tifereth Israel. In 1854, the congregation received enough funds from New Orleans philanthropist Judah Touro to build a temple, completed in 1855, at the corner of Huron at Miami Streets. This temple soon established itself as the Cleveland leader of Reform Judaism and began to be referred to as "the Temple."

What was happening in Cleveland paralleled developments in other areas of the United States. The Reform movement, inspired by Rabbi Isaac Mayer Wise, was based at Hebrew Union College in Cincinnati and subsequently in Cincinnati's famous Plum Street Synagogue. Orthodoxy was led by Rabbi

Isaac Leeser of Philadelphia. Both men came to Cleveland in 1855, in what was called the Cleveland Assembly, and met with fifteen other Jewish leaders, including Rabbi Isidor Kalisch of Tifereth Israel. The Assembly was the first and last general Jewish synod in the United States. Although unsuccessful in uniting American Jewry, one positive result of the Cleveland Assembly was Reform agreement on the *Minhag America* (American Ritual), the Reform prayer book written by Wise and Kalisch.

As the nineteenth century progressed, the Reform movement accelerated at Tifereth Israel under the leadership of Rabbi Aaron Hahn. Hahn was responsible for construction of this building and led the first services here; however, he resigned shortly before the building was dedicated. Hahn's place was taken by Rabbi Moses Gries. Gries, "an outspoken anti-Zionist," represented the height of Reform in Cleveland and, perhaps, in the nation.[31] Under Gries, Tifereth Israel became a major congregation in "Classical Reform." In his *The Jewish Community of Cleveland,* Gries approvingly quoted an article in the *Jewish Encyclopedia* by a Dr. Wolfenstein: there was "almost an entire abolition" of tradition at Tifereth Israel. "The Temple congregation worships on Sunday, a large number of its attendants being non-Jews. It has abolished the reading of the Torah and practically all Hebrew from its service and Sabbath School."[32] Bare-headed rabbis without yamakas, dressed in business suits conducted services. Instead of a cantor accompanying them, an organ played and a choir sang hymns composed for nineteenth-century Protestants. Tifereth Israel became a "programmatic" religious institution. In addition to the choir and a nonsectarian program of weekly lectures, there was an orchestra, a junior orchestra, Boy Scouts, Camp Fire Girls, a drama club, a debate team, and active use of the Temple's gymnasium. By the time Gries resigned because of ill health in 1917, Tifereth Israel had become one of the largest Jewish congregations in the world. Tifereth Israel, and in a larger sense the United States, experienced the high tide of Classical Reform in this building. Gries's successors at Tifereth Israel, like twentieth-century rabbis throughout the United States, would carefully nudge his temple in a more traditional direction until, in 1999, Tifereth Israel again had a cantor.

Tifereth Israel built a huge, rugged, masonry, square stone structure on the southeast corner of East 55th Street and Central Avenue. The west facade on East 55th Street is an arcaded porch flanked by two Richardsonian picturesque round towers. From Central Avenue the building looms as a massive fortress. Dominating its neighborhood is its great Mansard-like square lantern with its conical roof. In the late nineteenth century Tifereth Israel shared its immediate neighborhood with Sidney Badgley's 1893 Epworth Memorial Methodist Church and Charles Schweinfurth's 1893 Ursuline College and Convent. These three great Cleveland buildings were said to be an ideal example of American comity.[33] Now the Methodists and the Catholics and the Jews are gone.

51. Shiloh Baptist Church,
originally Temple B'nai
Jeshurun (see also New Spirit
Revival Center, p. 318, and
B'nai Jeshurun Congregation,
p. 349) (1906)
Architect: Harry Cone
Builder: Sigmund Drechsler
Location: 5500 Scovill
Avenue

Mighty Shiloh rises from East 55th Street to remind drivers headed north on I-77 that Cleveland sacred landmarks visible from the interstates are not all located on the West Side.[34] Perhaps patterned after the Panthéon (St. Genevieve) in Paris, neither Shiloh nor any other Cleveland landmark could duplicate the size of that French monument to the glory of itself. Driving down East 55th Street, it is difficult to realize that Shiloh's massive portico is a much smaller version of anything, including the Panthéon portico that launched neoclassicism in Europe. Nor is it easy to imagine, driving up I-77, that Shiloh's great dome with its distinctive lantern is a smaller copy of the French landmark's dome that, in turn, was patterned after Bramante's *Tempietto* in the courtyard of San Pietro in Montorio in Rome. Neither can the interior of Shiloh, inspiring as is its great glass dome, match the magnificence of the French holy of holies. Nevertheless, Shiloh, with its stunning interior and dominating exterior, is one of the largest and most impressive worship spaces in Cleveland.

Shiloh Baptist Church is the oldest congregation of black Baptists, and the second-oldest black church in Cleveland. Michael Gregory organized it in his small grocery store on East Ninth Street sometime before 1850.[35] It was subsequently engulfed by the First Baptist Church, which established Shiloh as a mission on East 14th Street. Moving to Central Avenue near East 22nd Street, Shiloh became an independent church in 1869. Moving again to East 30th Street near Scovill Avenue and energized by the flood of migrants from the South after the Civil War, Shiloh, by the 1890s, was the largest black church in Cleveland. Then, in 1893, almost half of Shiloh's membership left to found Antioch Baptist Church (see p. 138). Shiloh resumed its growth and gathered its resources to buy this building on East 55th Street in 1925. The building had been a synagogue for only twenty years. The Baptists have now occupied the building more than four times as long as it had been occupied by its original Jewish congregation.

The sixteen men who became the B'nai Jeshurun community of Orthodox Hungarians, Cleveland's third-oldest Jewish congregation, began meeting in the home of Herman Sampliner in 1866. Moving to Gallagher's Hall on Erie Street at Superior Avenue and then into Halle's Hall, where the BP building now stands, the congregation moved to the German Theater on Michigan Avenue in 1882 and filed for incorporation with the state. In 1887 the congregation purchased the famous Eagle Street Synagogue from Anshe Chesed and soon thereafter hired Sigmund Drechsler, their first ordained rabbi. Drechsler would build this splendid synagogue. Seven rabbis led B'nai Jeshurun during the tumultuous two decades it occupied this Scovill building while the congregation negotiated its turbulent passage between the *Scylla* of Reform and the *Charybdis* of Orthodoxy, finally emerging on the Heights of Cleveland as a staunchly Conservative congregation in 1926 (see the New Spirit Revival Center, p. 318). During its time at East 55th Street, the dynamic Solomon Goldman served B'nai Jeshurun for a stormy five years; then, unable to realize his ideas here, he resigned in 1923 to take over the Cleveland Jewish Center (six years later Goldman would storm off to Chicago; see Cory United Methodist Church, p. 97). B'nai Jeshurun moved to Pepper Pike in 1980 (see p. 349).

Flanked along the east side of East 55th Street by the House of Wills to the south and East Tech High School to the north,[36] Shiloh, together with the equally substantial and quite different Friendship Baptist Church (see p. 130), two blocks north, dominates its neighborhood. The massively symmetrical presence of its main rectangular block and the giant-order columns of its great portico command East 55th Street.

Shiloh's light and bright 1,500-seat auditorium was beautifully restored, in 2005, in a prize-winning $700,000 campaign.[37] Its great dome window dominates the church. This breathtaking circular expanse of brown and tan opalescent glass, almost fifty feet in diameter, is lighted partially by the clerestory windows in the dome's Tempietto and partly by artificial lighting. With its purple ornamental center, ten feet in diameter, this great expanse of glass is one of Cleveland's most inspiring religious objects. The dome is encircled by a border of plasterwork and supported by arches and pendentives decorated by additional elegant plasterwork. LED lights with thirty-five-year bulbs have been embedded in the plaster. This space is so big that, in the course of restoring its plaster walls, two lost windows were uncovered over the chancel. The great space dwarfs the large Wren-Gibbs wraparound balcony. The first floor is so large that it requires five aisles to seat the congregation in its forty-five-degree circular seating. Giant-order pilaster columns with powerfully elegant capitals define each corner of the sanctuary. Except for the richly paneled wall behind the chancel, walls are plain but beautifully painted. A baptistry in the upper part of the chancel faces worshipers. Side windows are decorated with early twentieth-century patterned glass with Jewish symbols.

At the beginning of the twenty-first century, this Baptist congregation debated the fate of their deteriorating one-hundred-year-old building. Alternatives included sale of the building or its lot and purchase or construction of a smaller church at a new location. They elected to stay where they were and restore the building.

52. St. Adalbert/Our Lady of the Blessed Sacrament Church (1911)
Architect: William P. Ginther
Builder: John Malecha and John Becka

Our Lady of the Blessed Sacrament is the oldest African American Roman Catholic church in Cleveland.[38] It developed from discussions following the First World War among African American veterans who had been greatly influenced by their Roman Catholic chaplain in France. Encouraged by Joseph Smith, pastor of St. Philomena, the parish was established in 1922 with the St. Philomena assistant as pastor. He convinced St. Katharine Drexel, the second American-born Roman Catholic saint, to establish an educational presence of her order at Our Lady of the Blessed Sacrament. St. Katharine frequently visited the parish during the next ten years. Although the parishioners had begun to call their community St. Monica, it was renamed Our Lady of the Blessed Sacrament when their brick church was completed in 1923. John D. Rockefeller, a friend and neighbor of Smith, donated the organ. Established to evangelize the African American community, the parish grew rapidly—so rapidly that it outgrew its resources during the Great Depression. Although the convent was temporarily rescued from a sheriff's sale, the banks finally foreclosed on the parish three days before Christmas in 1936. The parish was saved when Monsignor Smith refinanced the debt and the parish was taken on by the Brothers of the Precious Blood Community from Cincinnati.

This was a new mission for the brothers, part of a Swiss contingent that had come to Ohio in 1843 to minister to mostly rural German immigrants. Nonetheless they made a great success of Our Lady of the Blessed Sacrament, as they had across town at Our Lady of Good Counsel, now Mary Queen of Peace (see p. 222). As Our Lady of the Blessed Sacrament continued to grow, the brothers established a satellite mission closer to downtown. This mission, however, was unsuccessful because rationing during the Second World War made it impossible to heat its building. The brothers then moved into Irish St. Edward Church, where they established the second Cleveland African American parish in 1943. Although the nuns were delighted with the improvement in their living quarters, St. Edward Church did not prove as successful as hoped, and the brothers eventually withdrew when St. Edward merged with the formerly German Holy Trinity Church. Meanwhile, Our Lady of the Blessed Sacrament, although it had lost half its parishioners to St. Edward, had continued to grow and was bursting from its increasingly decrepit seams. In 1961 Our Lady of the Blessed Sacrament moved into St. Adalbert.

Czechs originally settled in Cleveland in the Croton district along Kingsbury Run in an idyllic suburban community of small homes, orchards, vineyards, and gardens. Here they established their mother church of St. Wenceslas. When the Standard Oil Company built refineries along Kingsbury Run, it disrupted this idyllic community. Many of the Czechs fled the resulting pollution for the more rural north Broadway area around Our Lady of Lourdes and the central Broadway area around St. John Nepomucene, although both of these areas were soon industrialized by steel mills. Some reinforced the West Side Czech community around St. Procop. A minority moved into the area of the East 70s at Quincy and established a parish in 1883.[39] Although this parish would complete a relatively small but substantial church in 1912, with the requisite school, rectory, and convent, St. Adalbert was always something of a marginal parish, having only 250 families at its height (1910–13). Things had gotten off to an inauspicious start in 1886 when, after building a temporary school-church and a rectory and then furnishing both buildings down to altar cloths, bell, and candles, the bishop reassigned the Czech seminarian whom the parish had identified as their first pastor to a parish south of Toledo. Two years later, St. Adalbert got its priest back from Toledo only to have him die at a young age after a prolonged illness. With the exception of John Becka, who served the parish for thirty-seven years and finished the present building, St. Adalbert was usually only a temporary way station for the Czech priests the diocese kept shuffling among its larger Czech parishes. By the end of the Second World War, the school had closed and the parish was declining. Thus, the arrival of the vigorous Our Lady of the Blessed Sacrament and its energetic order became a cause for general celebration.

Our Lady of the Blessed Sacrament, with its linden trees behind a historic iron fence, remains one of the architectural and social anchors of a modest residential neighborhood. The church bears a resemblance, albeit in miniature and in brick, to the Cathedral of Salzburg, the seventeenth-century, Italian baroque building where Mozart was baptized. Our Lady of the Blessed Sacrament has symmetrically balanced open bell towers with copper crowns and two large bells installed by the original congregation. A large, two-story central pavilion is topped by a decorative gable. Classic columns that support a niche containing a statue of St. Adalbert flank the tripartite entrance.

Inside one finds a charming and intimate five-hundred-seat worship space generously decorated with statuary that tastefully identifies this church as African American. The worship space is open and without columns. Our Lady of the Blessed Sacrament is a Roman Catholic Cleveland parish church written small. Its smaller size has made the church easier to decorate and the congregation has taken full advantage of this opportunity. The church is not that small; Our Lady of the Blessed Sacrament seats approximately the same number of worshipers as Trinity Episcopal Cathedral on Euclid Avenue (see p. 21). It has a complete ensemble of windows from Chicago.

On March 15, 2009, Bishop Richard Lennon announced the closing of St. Adalbert/Our Lady of the Blessed Sacrament Church. He celebrated the final

Mass on June 6, 2010. On March 1, 2012, the Vatican Congregation for the Clergy ruled that Bishop Lennon had failed to follow church law and procedure in closing Our Lady of Blessed Sacrament.

53. St. James A.M.E. Church, originally Trinity Congregational Church (1894)
Architects: Knox and Elliot
Rebuilders: Joseph Gomez, Hurbert Robinson, and Donald Jacobs
Location: 8401 Cedar Avenue

As they filed out of the former Cleveland Play House complex and drove their cars out of its parking lot on the north side of Carnegie, not all playgoers realized that the brightly colored panels of the modern structure rising up behind a one-story commercial building across the street in front of them, on the south side of Carnegie, is the most recent part of St. James A.M.E.[40] Its building is Cleveland's most architecturally cosmopolitan church. Disastrous fires and dynamic leadership have produced an astonishing assembly of styles that make this building a living monument to 125 years of architectural history, from H. H. Richardson to Walter Gropius.

In the beginning, the Congregationalists built a conventional Richardson Romanesque church on Cedar Avenue in 1894. Rock-faced, sandstone, ashlar courses are sturdy and muscular. The Syrian arches, which frame an extended front portico and side entrance, emphasize a powerful medieval Revival presence. Although close study reveals that the short towers are a little shorter and a little more squared off than originally designed, the towers have more or less survived a succession of disasters. As seen today, one can imagine them as a provincial imitation of Richardson's late nineteenth-century architectural language. This Richardson Romanesque building, with its curved and Congregational auditorium, is what the St. James congregation purchased in 1926.

Twelve years later, fire destroyed this first building. Only the facade survived. The congregation rebuilt the main building in brick. Then, another twelve years later in 1950, an equally disastrous fire again destroyed the building. The facade survived this fire, too, and the congregation again rebuilt in brick. The sanctuary that emerged from these twin catastrophes is now axial, with a center aisle. Then, Donald Jacobs led St. James to its dominant role in the civil rights movement in the late 1950s and 1960s. The congregation's new role required more administrative and educational space. This prompted the 1963 construction of a contiguous, modernist, brightly paneled Educational Annex to the north, reaching out toward the former Cleveland Play House.

St. John African Methodist Episcopal Church and St. James A.M.E., forty-five blocks apart, bracket their inner-city neighborhood on the west and the east. St. James's projecting entrance porch bears an eerie resemblance to the signature porches of its great A.M.E. mother institution downtown. Inspired by a tempestuous religious revival at St. John, one of the first churches in Cleveland, St. James was established in 1894 as the East End Prayer Meeting. This evolved into the St. John's East End Mission at a time when the African American population of Cleveland was approximately seven thousand. Originally meeting in private homes, the parish began gathering publicly in 1894 at the Wigwam, the Republican meeting place on Cedar Avenue near East 110th Street. They moved into their own new church on Hudson Avenue in 1899. During its first years, a rapid succession of recent graduates sent up from the Payne Theological Seminary in Wilberforce served St. James. St. James began its reach to prominence in 1925 when Joseph Evans, its longest-serving pastor up to that time, purchased this Trinity Congregational Church for $57,000.[41] Evans's immediate successor, Ormonde Walker, established St. James as a national institution. He started the St. James Literary Forum, and—as an occasional political candidate himself—he began to move Cleveland African Americans out of the Republican Party. A succession of dynamic pastors thereafter not only kept rebuilding the church after its successive catastrophic fires but also kept St. James at the forefront of both the civil rights movement in Cleveland and efforts to cope with the problems of its neighborhood.

Surrounded by parking lots, this well-kept and well-landscaped building is set back across a lawn from Cedar. From the side, the building looks like successive layers in an archaeological dig—first, the even-coursed, rough-cut sandstone of the original Richardson Romanesque facade, then the sturdy brick and brick trim of its vernacular replacements, and, last, the deep blue panels and modern ribbon glass windows of the international style 1963 addition.

The sanctuary is a rectangular space with a pentagonal ceiling and a wide center aisle. With its ample side balconies and large back balcony, the central worship space seats 1,200. It features a wide rectangular apse for choir and organ. A new window is installed above the much-restored street entrances. In the building behind the sanctuary is a large junior church, also used for small weddings, with an attractive balcony and an organ. A large historical quilt decorates this chapel.

54. Antioch Baptist Church, originally Bolton Avenue Presbyterian Church (1892)
Architect: William Warren Sabin
Builder: Unknown
Location: 8869 Cedar Avenue

The Great Commission,[42] in other words, the idea that congregations should draw others into their community, is central to the practice of religion in the United States. Ideas about who should be targeted and the style in which this should be done differ, but every institution in this book is an evangelical institution. Some are more successful than others. Lack of success has caused many to fail and many are struggling, but this is not for lack of trying. Antioch is not trying harder than anyone else, it is just more successful.[43] It brings powerful advantages to this daily struggle—a long tradition of leadership and success, substantial resources, and an ability to innovate. However, many of the institutions in this book that are now struggling to repair the roof or that no longer answer the telephone, whose schools are closed or that sold their building to someone else, once enjoyed similar advantages.

Antioch also faces substantial challenges. It is in the poorest area of Cleveland; this poverty nourishes crime, decay, and disorder. Most Antioch members who continue to pay the big bills live and work elsewhere. Antioch's membership keeps coming back, in part, for the usual reasons—good preaching, compelling music, a supportive community atmosphere. However, Antioch's membership also comes back because of its attention to other aspects of a religious experience. Their members can see and hear what is going on, they worship in an immaculate and attractive environment, and they can expect to find their cars intact at the end of the service.

Antioch is unusual in Cleveland because it moved downtown before it moved uptown.[44] Beginning in a division of Shiloh (see p. 132), Antioch started as a prayer meeting in the modest frame home of Henry Myers on East 29th Street in 1893. Within six months, the community, the second African American Baptist congregation, had moved into a much more substantial frame building they had remodeled on East 24th Street at Central Avenue. As the congregation continued to grow, it developed particularly cordial and helpful relations with other institutions in Baptist Cleveland. In 1905 John D. Rockefeller agreed, as was his wont,[45] to match the congregation, dollar for dollar, to build a substantial neo-Gothic building at East 24th Street at Central. This building was destroyed by the federal government for the construction of the Cedar-Central public housing projects in 1934. The community moved out to East 89th Street.

This church has always had a large number of community ministries together with a seemingly overwhelming number of church programs. In 1959 the congregation constructed an unobtrusive but large education building west of the church, adjacent to the main building. The Antioch Credit Union, now one of the largest Protestant credit unions in Ohio, was begun in 1947 (with a capitalization of $174) to assist returning veterans. Antioch's most spectacular physical projects have had to do with credit and housing—namely, its 1968 Antioch Credit Union building, the 1968 Kenmore-Randalls Estates in the Hough Area, and the 1975 twelve-story Antioch Towers built with Forest City Enterprises and the Cleveland Clinic. Part of Antioch's success has obviously been the result of a succession of gifted pastors, although occasional gaps in leadership and sudden departures suggest that, like other great religious institutions, it has been capable of surviving the occasional lapse. In general, Antioch's pastors have been exceptional: Horace Bailey (1903–23), Wade McKinney and Ruth Berry (1928–61), Emmanuel Branch (1964–83), and, after 1987, Marvin McMickle. Before his recent retirement, Dr. McMickle served as president of both the Cleveland National Association for the Advancement of Colored People (NAACP) and the Shaker Heights School Board. He had been a candidate for the U.S. Senate and House of Representatives. Three decades before, Mrs. McKinney had been an important part of a leadership team, not uncommon in African American churches, in which the pastor's wife is an important preacher (see, for example, Drs. Darrell and Belinda Scott at the New Spirit Revival Center, p. 318).

This building was built in 1892 for the Bolton Avenue Presbyterian Church. In 1934 the Presbyterians sold their building and moved in with the congregation of Calvary Presbyterian at East 79th Street at Euclid Avenue (see p. 32). Their Cedar Avenue church was purchased by Antioch. The asymmetrical design, the massive bell tower, the rusticated Syrian arches, and the deep-set rounded window headers were features of church architecture popular at the end of the nineteenth century. Antioch does not give the impression of being, however, so much a beautifully restored Romanesque Revival extravaganza as it does of being a well-maintained solid brick building with stone trim. The tower is not as tall as it appears in pictures. The building does not overwhelm the intersection nor appear as big as its historical reputation would suggest.

The entrance doorways lead to simple stairways into the sanctuary. In the immaculate sanctuary, the Gospel meets *Star Wars* meets Richardson revival. A parishioner with a professional background in national news broadcasting, who moved to Cleveland to establish a television consultancy, has designed, built, and now directs an audiovisual system (installed in 2008) of several cameras and multiple flat screens, allowing every worshiper an unobstructed, clear, and close-up view of the service together with access to a high-tech sound system. The control system for this is discretely screened from worshipers behind wooden barriers at the back of the sanctuary. All this is in a beautifully maintained, late nineteenth-century Romanesque Revival religious interior, complete with the massive beams of a great wood scaffold ceiling held together with powerfully evocative giant tie rods at the crossing. The polished complexities of the wood ceiling are reminiscent of the Old Stone Church (see p. 12). The ceiling, after the audiovisual system, is the great wonder of the sanctuary.

The exterior of the building suggests a complex sanctuary but, except for the balcony and ceiling, the worship area is a simple rectangular space with modest transepts that bow out at their end. The transepts appear bigger than they are. The right transept contains seating. The left transept has an elevated platform for the choir. Seating on the first floor is in a quarter circle. Although the 240-seat balcony extends only to the transepts, it so completely reaches out over the six-hundred-seat first floor that the space of the sanctuary, although quite large, appears small and intimate. Minimal wood columns support the steep balcony. The nooks and crannies above and below are all within sight and hearing of the television system. In front of the sanctuary is a podium-stage below the obligatory Baptist baptistry. The front platform is large enough for dance. New furniture has been designed for rapid reorganization to accommodate different church programs. Walls are plain and plastered. The chancel arches have minimal decoration, largely chevrons and modified egg and dart. The early twentieth-century glass is simple and nonfigured. The windows are wonderfully bright but are supplemented with theater lighting. Antioch has two organs, including a large Hemry.

The worship space is comfortable and not overwhelming. This is a beautiful and careful restoration of a late nineteenth-century building with early twenty-first-century technology.

55. Olivet Institutional Baptist Church (1954)
Architect: Unknown
Builders: Eugene Ward and Odie Millard Hoover
Location: 8712 Quincy Avenue

Three thousand people do not belong to Olivet because they appreciate great architecture, or sculpture, or painting, although the church could certainly afford it.[46] They flock to this largely undecorated, vernacular, inner-city brick building to hear Martin Luther King Jr., Andrew Young, Jesse Jackson, Al Sharpton, Tavis Smiley, Johnny Cockran, Naomi Tutu, Coretta Scott King, Oprah Winfrey, Jimmy Carter, Bill Clinton, Hilary Clinton, and Al Gore. Above all they came to hear the message of Otis Moss Jr., described on the front page of the *New York Times* on March 15, 2009, in its article "Without a Pastor of His Own, Obama Turns to Five," as "a graying lion of the civil rights movement." Moss, aide to King and associate of King's father, preached until 2008 from one of the great pulpits of African America. Physically unpretentious, modest—almost painfully simple, Olivet sits at the epicenter of American Christian power.

Olivet has come a long way with the forty refugees from the Triedstone Baptist Church (see p. 124), who met in 1931 in a small building on Quincy Avenue to organize another Baptist congregation. Founded as the New Light Baptist Church, the congregation changed their name to Olivet (derived from Jesus's ascension from the Mount of Olives) only to find there already was one and that it had to suffer the indignity of being the "Second" Olivet Baptist Church. At its low point in 1937, without a pastor and with membership down to thirty-five, the little group met in an upstairs back room in the former Temple Tifereth Israel (see p. 130), then owned by Mt. Zion Congregational Church (see p. 58). Olivet was rescued from the back room by Eugene Ward, the "boy preacher" from Detroit. Within a year they were renting in the Bohemian Hall at East 88th Street at Quincy from the Czechs of St. Adalbert (see p. 134). They liked the hall so well that they bought it. By 1950 Ward was planning the current building. He left two years before it was completed.

Ward was replaced by Odie Hoover from Montgomery, Alabama. Hoover changed the name to its final form: Olivet Institutional Baptist. He inspired the church to become actively involved with the civil rights movement. Hoover was such a close associate of Martin Luther King Jr. that he traveled with him to Stockholm when King accepted the Nobel Prize. Hoover completed the church in 1954 and then the adjoining Christian Community Center, with its gym and educational space, in 1966. When Hoover died in 1973, after twenty-one years as pastor, his place was taken by Otis Moss Jr. Although Dr. Moss has put more effort into the life of his congregation than into building projects, he has built the $2 million Otis Moss Jr.-University Hospitals Medical Center across the street from his church.

In addition to the Medical Center, Olivet shares the intersection of East 89th Street at Quincy with Karamu House. This theater, day care, and cultural arts center launched the career of Langston Hughes. It is the oldest African American theater in the United States. The three institutions, and the large parking lots they require, are about all this devastated neighborhood has left. Not even Moss's Olivet Housing and Community Development Corporation can put it entirely together again.

The church is a simple brick vernacular building. Since everyone in Cleveland knows where and what it is, a great deal of symbolism and signage is unnecessary. The building is identified by a small conventional church inscription modestly engraved in stone, "Olivet Institutional Baptist Church." This is unobtrusively embedded into the brick wall facing Quincy. The large community center is distinguished by slightly lighter brick.

Simplicity is carried inside into a simple, meticulously maintained, rectangular sanctuary seating 1,200. One finds a modest wooden apse behind a simple lectern/pulpit. Above is a curtain across the obligatory baptistry. Walls are plaster. Pews are comfortable but plain. Small windows run down either side of the sanctuary and feature simple religious symbols. Smaller windows above are patterned in blue. Olivet has a large balcony. Everything is simple. Olivet is not a place to look. It is a place to listen.

56. St. Elizabeth's Church (1918)
Architect: Emile Uhlrich
Builder: Julius Szepessy
Location: 9016 Buckeye Road

In the twentieth century, Cleveland was the second-largest Hungarian city in the world, and Greater Cleveland continues to be the largest Hungarian city in the United States. St. Elizabeth was the first Hungarian church in this country, organized by the first Hungarian priest to come to America.[47] It is "one of the premier spiritual centers of the Hungarian-Catholic community in the United States."[48] This explains why St. Elizabeth is a necessary stop whenever the primate of Hungary visits the United States, including János Csernoth in 1926 (to celebrate the fiftieth anniversary of the ordination of St. Elizabeth's pastor), József Mindszenty in 1947 and 1974, and László Paskai in 1989.

When Hungarian founders and other metalworkers began to congregate along Woodland and move into the Buckeye neighborhood in the 1880s, the omnipresent Czech priest, Stephan Furdek from Our Lady of Lourdes, was there to organize them, together with the Slovaks, into St. Ladislaus Parish. This combination did not survive Furdek's departure in pursuit of other central European Roman Catholics. The Hungarians asked for a parish of their own. They were awarded $1,000 as compensation for their contributions to the building of St. Ladislaus and the calling of the remarkable Charles Boehm from Hungary. Boehm would be the apostle of Hungary to America. Within ten months of his arrival in Cleveland, he had organized the parish and put up a substantial brick neo-Gothic church and the first of many schools. He expanded the parish bulletin into a national weekly Hungarian Catholic newspaper and began his travels establishing other Hungarian parishes. In 1907 Boehm resigned to pursue his missionary work more actively. In addition to Ohio, he was active in Indiana, Pennsylvania, Connecticut, Louisiana, and Virginia. Father Boehm was noted for his skill as a financial manager and for his ability to solicit funds to support his missionary enterprises, in particular, it is said, from breweries. In 1922 Father Boehm returned to St. Elizabeth after a sixteen-year absence to find that the building he had discussed in Rome with the Holy Father had been built. He served it for another five years.

Over the years St. Elizabeth has been plagued with all the problems endemic to a nationality parish. Are the parishioners here to stay or will they go back home? How much time and treasure should they invest in what may be a temporary parish? What is the proper balance between tradition and American citizenship? What side should they take in the battles back home? How much support should they offer? How can successive waves of immigrants, of quite different social, economic, and educational backgrounds and quite different reasons for leaving the homeland, adapt to each other? How can the parish maintain itself as its members prosper, marry outside the community, and age? St. Elizabeth is fortunate in parishioners who have written sensitively about these problems, and they should be consulted.[49]

It is difficult to say whether St. Elizabeth has been fortunate or unfortunate in its location. On Buckeye, it is at the bottom of the hill up to the Heights. At the bottom of the hill are the foundries and other factories where the Hungarians worked. The surroundings of St. Elizabeth continue to be industrial. After they became established, much of the Hungarian population lived up the hill, and this is where they had their stores and shops. The population at the top of the hill is no longer Hungarian, and, because of its location down the hill, St. Elizabeth is spared some of the distractions of the new neighborhood on the top of the hill.

This is a massive 1,344-seat, smooth-faced, ashlar, Indiana limestone presence on a busy thoroughfare. It is unlikely that most of those speeding past toward work in the morning or toward home in the suburbs in the evening have any idea of the vitality and richness inside, much less give its exterior any attention. Both are full of surprises. Open bell towers and a pedimented gable with side scrolls on the front facade flank the two-story central pavilion. The classical Baroque Revival facade is disproportionately wide in comparison to its height. This reflects the proportions of the interior sanctuary but is unexpected in a major Roman Catholic building. This broadness is "cleverly disguised" by compressing the three entrance doors into a narrow space in the center of the facade and by appearing to detach the imposing flanking towers from the body of the structure.[50]

Entering from the street (most now enter from the parking lot behind the building), one finds a delightful, generous, well-proportioned Gothic-vaulted narthex extending across the width of the building (in contrast to the narthex of most Roman churches that appear to be cramped afterthoughts between the baptistry and the broom closet). Instead of the traditional long, narrow nave with central and side aisles that one could expect based upon the towers and narrow entrance, one discovers a glorious broad auditorium with a columned central aisle. The openness and the width of the interior have the clarity of a classical space. The Baroque elements are largely decorative. The elaborate but powerful and sedate horizontal painted ceiling, with its ambitious giant molding and segmentation, is supported by only four large Indiana limestone cylindrical pillars. Their capitals are beautifully gilded and restored. Great iron lighting fixtures hang from the ceiling. Limestone pilasters line up in a well-nuanced progression down each side. Interesting windows, not surprisingly, dwell on the religious history of Hungary. Most of the main and two side altars are imitation, or painted, "art marble." The use of faux marble is an old Hungarian tradition.[51] Presiding over this, from her position over the main altar, is Elizabeth of Hungary, not to be mistaken for the Virgin who is so often the central figure in Roman churches. (It is common for Hungarian churches to have their patron, instead of one of the Divine figures, over the altar.)

CHAPTER FIVE

Southeast Cleveland

Southeast Cleveland is composed of six neighborhoods—Buckeye-Woodland, Shaker, Mt. Pleasant, Lee-Miles, Corlett, and Union.

Known as Cleveland's Little Hungary by the end of the nineteenth century, the composition of the Buckeye-Woodland neighborhood has shifted considerably since then. During the civil unrest of the 1960s and 1970s, the neighborhood's crime rate increased alarmingly, and many of the Hungarian immigrants, as well as other residents, left the area.

Tour

This tour begins at the intersection of Shaker Boulevard, Woodhill, and Buckeye Roads. Calvary Hill Church of God in Christ (COGIC) stands to the left on the northeast corner, between Woodhill and Shaker. Morning Star Baptist Church (formerly the large Qua Buick Agency) occupies the eastern triangle between Shaker and Buckeye. Drive east on Shaker and turn right onto Martin Luther King Jr. (MLK) Drive. At the top of Buckeye Hill, notice how the First Hungarian Lutheran Church (57) and then the Full Gospel Evangelistic Center (formerly the First Hungarian Reformed Church) (58) frame Buckeye Road to form a view of downtown Cleveland. Immediately south of the Full Gospel Evangelistic Center, turn right (west) into a drive that runs beside St. Benedictine High School. This drive leads to the small, parklike enclosure of St. Andrew Abbey (59). Its interior is one of the most moving modern sacred landmarks in Cleveland. After visiting the abbey, return to MLK Drive.

Turn right (south) onto MLK Drive and continue on it for one block. Turn right (west) at Lamontier Avenue. On the northwest corner stands the imposing gray-stone Cathedral of God in Christ (COGIC) (formerly St. Benedict Roman Catholic Church) (60). Continue on Lamontier until it ends at Woodhill Road.

Turn right (north) at Woodhill, past Olive Grove Missionary Baptist Church on the left side of Woodhill, and continue to the five-point intersection of Shaker, Woodhill, and Buckeye. Turn right (northeast), but not hard right, back onto Shaker. Passing Calvary Hill COGIC and the Morning Star Baptist Church for the second time, continue on Shaker. At East 116th Street, turn left (north) onto MLK Drive, crossing the Shaker Rapid Transit tracks and, one block farther north, turn right onto Buckingham Avenue, entering the Shaker neighborhood of Cleveland. Buckingham curves right, going through the campus of Our Lady of Peace (61) before it intersects with Shaker Boulevard. Turn right (west) onto Shaker and drive back to MLK Drive. Cross the Shaker Rapid tracks once again and then turn left proceeding east on Shaker.

Enter Shaker Square, built as an early shopping center in conjunction with the development of the municipality of Shaker Heights to the east. Transformed

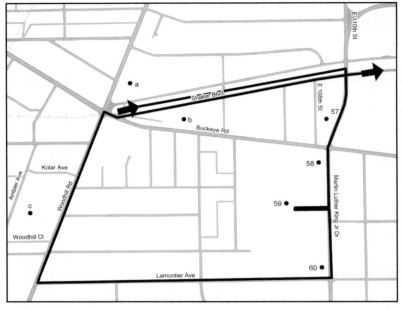

WOODLAND HILLS

a. Calvary Hill COGIC
b. Morning Star Baptist Church
57. First Hungarian Lutheran Church
58. Full Gospel Evangelistic Center

59. St. Andrew Abbey
60. Cathedral of God in Christ (COGIC)
c. Olive Grove Missionary Baptist Church

from an early twentieth-century traffic circle, architects Philip Small and Carl Rowley created an octagonally enclosed space based on Amalienborg Square in Copenhagen. Central pavilions flanked by lower wings are located in each quadrant.

Leaving the southwestern quadrant of the square on South Moreland Boulevard, travel on South Moreland for one block and then turn right (west) onto Drexmore Road. Stay on Drexmore for only one block and then turn left (south) onto East 130th Street. Midway down the street, Holy Grove Baptist Church sits on the right. Built in 1930, it was originally the Shaker Square Baptist Church. After one block on East 130th, turn right (west) onto Buckeye. Stay on Buckeye to East 126th Street and then turn left (south). On the southeast corner are the elegant proportions of the small, brick Grace Fundamental Baptist Church. Designed by the Cleveland architectural firm of Hamilton and Waterson, it was built as First Hungarian Baptist in 1918.

Continue south on East 126th Street for one block; then turn left (east) onto Forest Avenue for two blocks before turning right (south) back onto East 130th. On the left, in the block south of Abell Avenue, is the Quinn Chapel A.M.E. Church (62). Designed by Robert Madison, who has been so active in church architecture outside of Cleveland, the Quinn Chapel is his only active

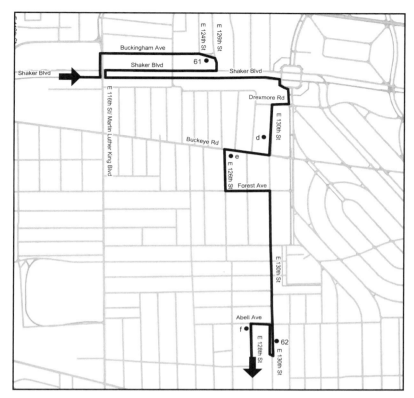

BUCKEYE–SHAKER

61. Our Lady of Peace
  d. Holy Grove Baptist Church
  e. Grace Fundamental Baptist Church
62. Quinn Chapel A.M.E. Church
  f. Mt. Pleasant United Methodist Church

complete design in Cleveland.[1] Returning to and turning left (west) onto Abell Avenue, drive one block before turning left again (south) onto East 128th Street. Mt. Pleasant United Methodist Church stands on the corner. This is the northern edge of the Mt. Pleasant neighborhood.

Take East 128th to Kinsman and turn right (west). Providence Baptist Church is located on the corner. At the intersection of East 119th Street at Kinsman is the Covenant Community Church of Cleveland. Continue on Kinsman and then turn left (south) at East 116th Street. Travel on East 116th for one block and then turn right (west) onto Regalia Avenue. On the right is the contemporary St. Philip Lutheran Church in a residential neighborhood. Staying on Regalia to East 113th Street, turn right (north). Take East 113th back to Kinsman and turn left (west). Zion Hill Baptist Church stands west on Kinsman, on the right, just east of Luke Easter Park.

Turn right (north) off Kinsman onto MLK Drive. Stay on MLK Drive for

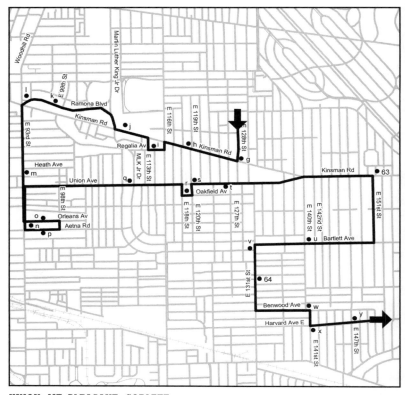

UNION–MT. PLEASANT–CORLETT

g. Providence Baptist Church
h. Covenant Community Church of Cleveland
i. St. Philip Lutheran Church
j. Zion Hill Baptist Church
k. Damascus Missionary Baptist Church
l. Hayes Temple COGIC
m. St. Catherine Roman Catholic Church
n. Harvest Missionary Baptist Church
o. City Church
p. Christ Temple Missionary Baptist Church

q. Mt. Haven Baptist Church
r. Epiphany Roman Catholic Church
s. Second Tabernacle Baptist Church
t. Union Avenue Christian Church
63. New Freedom Ministries
u. St. Peter's A.M.E. Zion Church
v. Grace Missionary Baptist Church
64. Hope Academy Chapelside
w. Fifth Christian Church
x. Zion Pentecostal Church of Christ
y. Unity Faith Missionary Baptist Church

only one block and then bear left to follow the line of the park on Ramona Boulevard. Travel on Ramona for two blocks. On the northwest corner of the intersection with East 99th Street is the Damascus Missionary Baptist Church (formerly Incarnation Episcopal Church). This little building fits in beautifully with its residential setting overlooking the park. Follow Ramona for another block and at the northwest corner of Ramona and East 94th Street notice the large brick building of Hayes Temple COGIC that dominates the intersection. Bear left at the intersection to follow the curve to East 93rd Street. Crossing

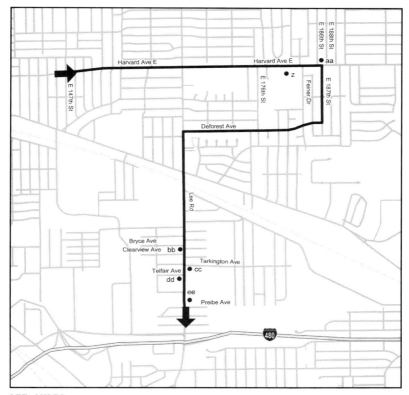

LEE–MILES

z. St. Henry Roman Catholic Church
aa. Good Shepherd Lutheran Church and Harvard Avenue COGIC
bb. Lee Heights Community Church
cc. Southeast Seventh-Day Adventist Church
dd. St. Paul United Methodist Church
ee. Lee-Seville Baptist Church

Kinsman, take East 93rd eight blocks south. On the southeast corner of the intersection with Heath Avenue was the site of the former St. Catherine Roman Catholic Church.

Continue south on East 93rd and turn left (east) at Orleans Avenue. On the southeast corner is the Harvest Missionary Baptist Church. On the left (north), farther east on Orleans, is the dominant structure of the City Church (formerly the Greater Zion Hill Baptist Church and originally built by the St. Joseph Byzantine Catholic parish), a ruin now sadly open to the elements. Take Orleans for one block and turn right (south) onto East 98th Street. Stay on East 98th for one block and turn right (west) onto Aetna Road. Midway down the block on the left is the Christ Temple Missionary Baptist Church (formerly the Church River of Living Waters and built as the Nativity of the

Blessed Virgin Mary Roman Catholic Church). At the end of the block, turn right (north) back onto East 93rd.

Backtrack on East 93rd and then turn right (east) at Union Avenue. At Union's intersection with MLK Drive sits the elegant, gray-stone building of Mt. Haven Baptist Church on the northwest corner, originally built by the congregation of Concordia Evangelical Lutheran Church. Continue on Union to East 118th Street. Turn right (south) at East 118th for one block. Turn left (east) onto Oakfield Avenue and travel on it for one block. Turn left (north) onto East 120th. On the left is the former Epiphany Roman Catholic Church. Epiphany's property has been divided into three parcels. At the request of the community, one parcel was donated to the Thea Bowman Center, which provides social services to the homeless and needy. Another parcel was sold to a provider of day-care services. The remaining parcel is for sale. At the end of the block, turn right (east) back onto Union. To the left is the Second Tabernacle Baptist Church on the north side of Union.

Continue on Union four more blocks. On the right is the Union Avenue Christian Church of the Christian Missionary Alliance on the corner of Union's intersection with East 127th Street. Continue on Union to its three-point intersection with Kinsman. Travel east on Kinsman to East 151st Street. On the left (north) are the New Freedom Ministries, formerly St. Cecilia's Church (63). Turn right (south) at East 151st Street.

Stay on East 151st for two long blocks and turn right (west) at Bartlett Avenue. At Bartlett's intersection with East 140th Street sits St. Peter's A.M.E. Zion Church. Stay on Bartlett for two more blocks and then turn left (south) onto East 131st Street to enter the Corlett neighborhood. On the right, immediately after turning is the Grace Missionary Baptist Church (formerly the Holy Trinity Baptist Church). Keep on East 131st. On the left is Hope Academy Chapelside (originally Holy Family Roman Catholic Church and School and then Mt. Pleasant Catholic Elementary School) (64). Stay on East 131st and turn left (east) onto Benwood Avenue.

Stay on Benwood for two blocks. Here, opposite East 141st Street, in a residential neighborhood, stands the Fifth Christian Church. Turn right (south) onto East 141st Street. Turn left (east) onto Harvard Avenue. At the turn is Zion Pentecostal Church of Christ (formerly St. Mary of Czestochowa Roman Catholic Church) on the right side of Harvard. Drive east on Harvard. On the northwest corner of East 147th Street at Harvard is the Unity Faith Missionary Baptist Church.

Continuing on Harvard, enter the Lee-Miles neighborhood at East 154th Street and cross Lee Road. On the right side of Harvard are the extended modern campuses of John F. Kennedy High School and Whitney Young Junior High School. Opposite East 183rd Street, also on the right, to the east of the Whitney Young playing fields, stands St. Henry Roman Catholic Church and its Archbishop Lyke Elementary School, named for the African American Franciscan who was auxiliary bishop of Cleveland before his appointment as archbishop of Atlanta. Stay on Harvard to East 187th Street. On the left of the intersection is the building that formerly housed two churches—Good Shepherd Lutheran Church and the Harvard Avenue Church of God in Christ (COGIC).

Turn right (south) onto East 187th Street. After two blocks, turn right (west) onto Deforest Avenue and take it to Lee. At Lee turn left (south), crossing Miles Avenue. On the northwestern corner of Lee's intersection with Clearview Avenue is the Lee Heights Community Church. Farther south on Lee, on the southeast corner of the intersection of Lee at Tarkington Avenue, is the Southeast Seventh-Day Adventist Church. Stay on Lee for another block and look to the right to see the octagonal St. Paul United Methodist Church at Telfair Avenue. Continue one more block on Lee to the Lee-Seville Baptist Church on the left.

This ends the tour of the Southeast neighborhoods. Lee intersects with Interstate 480 a few blocks south of Lee-Seville Baptist Church.

57. First Hungarian Lutheran Church (1940)
Architect: R. Orr
Builder: Andor Leffler
Location: 2830 Martin Luther King Jr. Drive

Although only 3 percent of Hungarians are Lutherans, they hold a special place in the history of their country. The great nineteenth-century Hungarian patriot Lajos Kossuth, governor-president of Hungary following the unsuccessful wave of revolutions that swept Europe in 1848, was a Lutheran. Bishop Lajos Ordass, Lutheran primate of Poland, continued this heritage of resistance in the twentieth century with his public opposition to, first, the Nazis and, next, the Communists. Lutheran Hungarians in Cleveland maintained a presence disproportionate to their number by founding the first Hungarian orphanage in the United States and then by welcoming more than 200 displaced Hungarians after the Second World War and another 150 families following the unsuccessful 1956 Hungarian Revolution.[2] This church is not only the first Hungarian Lutheran church in Cleveland but also the first Hungarian Lutheran church in the United States.[3] As once staunchly independent nationalities meld into the general population, Cleveland, at one point the second-largest Hungarian city in the world, now supports the only two remaining Hungarian Lutheran churches in North America.[4]

Organized in 1905, the Hungarian Lutherans purchased a frame church at 8021 Rawlings in 1907. This church, which is still standing, had been built in 1893 by Hungarian Greek Catholics who sold it to the Lutherans when they built a larger church on the corner of Buckeye at Ambler Avenue.[5] By 1913, the Lutherans had established the Hungarian orphanage at their church. In 1921 the parish was instrumental in moving the Lutheran Seminary in Hungary to Budapest. The parish began construction of the present building on the northwest corner of Buckeye Road and today's Martin Luther King Jr. Drive in 1940. It was completed during the Second World War, a war in which sixty-six members served and thirteen died.[6] English was introduced into the liturgy during the war. In 1954, First Hungarian Lutheran moved its parsonage south to Buckeye Road to make way for the parish's new educational center, Kossuth Hall.

Located at the top of the Buckeye Road hill, the First Hungarian Lutheran Church and the Full Gospel Evangelistic Center (formerly the First Hungarian Reformed Church, see below), located across the street, frame, to the west, a magnificent view of downtown. Described as "Transylvanian Gothic," this simple church has, when viewed from Martin Luther King Jr. Drive, the look of a country church. Its rustic appearance is charmingly unpretentious. This impression is even more pronounced in the simple 280-seat interior. Decoration consists primarily of the relationships the architect established between the plain, plastered, ivory-colored walls and columns and the dark wood timbers of the ceiling. The plain rectangular columns are particularly striking. The interior has a small balcony. Choir seating is to the right in the chancel. Windows include a large vertical apse window, a small window over the entrance, and glazed panel inserts in the windows on each side. A marble *Last Supper* is inserted into the altar. Christian symbols on the surface of the center aisle lead up to the chancel.

58. Full Gospel Evangelistic Center, originally First Hungarian Reformed Church (1948)
Architect: H. W. Maurer
Builder: Stephen Szabo (and Joseph Herczegh)
Location: 2856 Martin Luther King Jr. Drive

The Full Gospel Evangelistic Center, despite its size and prominent location on the southwest corner of the intersection of Buckeye Road and Martin Luther King Jr. Drive, is so screened by the trees on its ample lot that, from the street, it does not make the impression it deserves.[7] Motorists are distracted by, first, the other important religious institutions in the center's immediate vicinity,[8] second, the magnificent view of the city of Cleveland looking west down Buckeye Road, and, last, the need to attentively navigate the intersection. This good-sized church with its prominent tower deserves close inspection.

The Full Gospel Evangelistic Center began in a storefront on Union Avenue in 1977. This is an independent church, unaffiliated with the Full Gospel Baptist Church Fellowship headquartered in New Orleans. Moving to East 80th Street south of Kinsman Avenue and then to the Civic in the late 1980s (see New Spirit Revival Center, p. 318), the congregation purchased this building in 1993.

Hungary became almost completely Lutheran at the time of the Reformation but by the middle of the sixteenth century it was a Calvinist country and Debrecen, Hungary's second city and sometime capital, became known as the "Calvinist Rome." In the middle of the sixteenth century the Jesuits entered Hungary and initiated a counter-reformation that converted Hungary into a predominantly Roman Catholic country. Today, about 52 percent of Hungarians are Roman Catholic and about 16 percent are Reformed (Calvinist).

The Hungarian Reformed Church began in Cleveland on the West Side. Its first services, in 1890, were temporarily held in a church on West 32nd Street near Lorain Avenue. All Cleveland Reformed Hungarians worshiped there until 1894, when the East Siders built a wooden church on the corner of East 79th Street at Rawlings Avenue in the Hungarian neighborhood of eastern Cleveland at the bottom of Buckeye Road. Because they were the first to build, they carried the name of the early community with them to the East Side. Their First Hungarian Reformed Church of Cleveland was the first Reformed Hungarian church in the United States.[9] Five years later they replaced their first frame church with one of stone. This masonry building was rebuilt and expanded in 1904 and in 1929. As it became clear that this church was not big enough, the pastor, Dr. Joseph Herczegh, purchased land at the corner of Buckeye Road at MLK Drive in 1925. In 1932, the community completed the Bethelen Hall Education Center on this lot. The nave of the present church was built into the south end of the Bethelen Center in 1948. Credit for constructing the current building is given usually to Herczegh's successor, Dr. Stephen Szabo, although Herczegh served as pastor until 1947.

In 1914 the congregation had divided. One group remained at the First Hungarian Reformed Church. The other group established the First Magyar Presbyterian Church. After selling the present building in 1993, the remaining Reformed congregation reunited with the Hungarian Presbyterians as the First Hungarian Reformed Church of Walton Hills. They built a church in 1996 on a twenty-acre site. The reunited community is determined to maintain itself as a center of Hungarian civilization in Greater Cleveland. A highlight of its liturgical year is the annual all-you-can-eat stuffed cabbage dinner.

Much of the Buckeye-MLK building, because of the surrounding trees, is difficult to appreciate from the street. This includes the great tower, so obvious for almost a mile up and down Buckeye, but not so obvious from right next to the church. The nave of the present church is joined to Bethelen Hall by this brick tower with its commanding marble open belfry and spire. The conjoined buildings are sited back from the corner behind "the courtyard." The resulting complex is a somewhat traditional building from the second half of the twentieth century. Its multicolored brick is more flavored than defined by restrained stone trim.[10] The interesting nave windows are framed in a double arcade. The roof is that clay tile, so irresistible to the Northern American traditional religious architect, and so impractical for the annual accumulation of ice in the Cleveland climate. The lateral projections of the nave, which appear to be chapels from the outside, turn out to be, on the inside, no-nonsense Reform side aisles.

The 1948 sanctuary is a large box basilica seating six hundred on the main floor and another hundred in the balcony. The Reformed tend not to sit close together, so the sanctuary could probably accommodate a larger number of worshipers. The walls were built of composite block with stone trim and have been painted a warm color that makes them comforting and welcoming and invites worshipers into the space. Arcades down both sides define the side aisles. The open-timbered roof has narrow timbers. Beautiful windows, flanking the nave, appear more first-half than second-half twentieth century. The church features both a great east rose and great west rose. Arches are decorated with brick trim.

Extending northward from the nave, like a giant transept, is the former gathering room of the original Bethelen building. It is a half story above the floor of the 1948 sanctuary so that the 250 worshipers in this space look down into the nave. Following Reformed tradition, walls are plain; however, the four large, glazed windows to the east enliven the space. The building has apartments for the pastor and for the sexton, along with the usual classrooms and social spaces.

59. St. Andrew Abbey
(1986)
Architect: Evans Wollen
Builder: Roger Gries
Location: 2900 Martin Luther King Jr. Drive

In the early 1900s, Cleveland was the largest Slovak city in the world. Led by the indomitable Stephan Furdek, the pastor of Our Lady of Lourdes—who seemed to have a hand in every eastern European parish in Cleveland—Slovaks spread over Cleveland in the same manner as the Florentines had spread over Europe in the thirteenth century. Slovaks, the people without a country, were on the march, founding St. Ladislas in 1885, St. Martin in 1893, Saints Cyril and Methodius in 1902 (see p. 279), the Nativity of the Blessed Virgin in 1903, St. Wendelin in 1903, St. Andrew in 1906, and St. Benedict in 1928 (see p. 156). As the fortunes of European Slovakia waned and waxed, Cleveland became one of the principal cultural centers of Slovakia in exile. The Slovak Institute was established in Cleveland in 1952. The institute and a companion institute at Sts. Cyril and Methodius in Rome became the Slovak libraries in exile and the centers for the publication of books in Slovak—books that would be smuggled into Communist Czechoslovakia. The institute in Cleveland, which includes a museum, occupies most of a floor of the abbey.[11]

Then, before Slovakia achieved independence and economic affluence following the "Velvet Divorce" from Czechoslovakia in 1993, the African American wave of immigration from the southern United States broke over Cleveland Slovakia. St. Martin closed in 1960, St. Ladislas in 1971, St. Benedict and the Nativity of the Blessed Virgin in 1993, St. Andrew in 2008, and St. Wendelin in 2010. In the midst of this tumult, only the peaceful Slovak Benedictines remained upright, deciding in 1979 that it was their mission to keep their large abbey, with its Slovak Institute and its high school, where it was in Cleveland.

The Benedictines have maintained a close relationship with the Cleveland Slovak community since 1921, when they were asked to start a high school—originally for Slovak young men—at St. Andrew parish (hence the name of the abbey) on Superior Avenue. St. Andrew is now the only Slovak abbey in the United States. Monks from Illinois began arriving in Cleveland in 1922. By 1927, they had established Benedictine High School. The following year, the first monk to arrive in Cleveland, Father Stanislaus Gmuca, became the pastor of the newly established St. Benedict's Parish off upper Buckeye Road. The community moved there and moved its high school into a newly purchased Roman Catholic school. In 1934, with thirty-five monks, the community became an abbey; Father Stanislaus was elected the first abbot. The monks built a new high school in 1940, and, in 1952, the community—now grown to seventy-eight—moved into a new abbey. Basil Cardinal Hume, archbishop of Westminster, Roman Catholic primate of England, and regularly named Britain's most popular religious figure in opinion polls, visited the abbey in 1980 to ordain one of the monks. In 1986 the abbey was rebuilt and the current chapel, constructed within the complex, was dedicated by the international Benedictine Abbot Primate.

St. Andrew Abbey, one of only two Benedictine abbeys in the United States located in a major urban neighborhood, is nestled in a parklike area back from Martin Luther King Jr. Drive and to the north of the order's high school. From here monks fan out during the day to teach or to perform pastoral responsibilities in the high school, dependent parishes, convents, retirement homes, and hospitals, or they remain to staff the monastery. This is a proper abbey with a cloistered residence for the monks, offices for the abbot and his staff, work and storage rooms, a cloister, a kitchen, a laundry, a library, a refectory, and a calefactory (literally, where the monks keep warm; in modern use, where they gather socially and watch television). In this new structure designed by Evans Wollen, such traditional architectural forms as the classical portico are amalgamated with such modern spaces as the soaring, skylit chapel. This is a simple brick building with stone trim and an elegant arcade at the entrances to the chapel and to the abbey proper.

The center of monastic activity is the dramatic modern chapel, accessible from the abbey for services throughout the day and night. The abbot describes the large, hexagonal space, with its scalloped front wall, as being "like a tent gathering people in." By convention, the monks are seated in two formally ordered groups facing each other across an inverted "V" space. A Benedictine cross defines the front of the chapel before a massive, plain, roughly cut marble altar. The laity is welcomed into the third space in the chapel, adjacent to the chapel's public entrance. The interior of the chapel is of plain composition bricks, and the massive steel beams supporting the structure are exposed and painted in a primary color. The floor is brick. Foster Armstrong loved this space for its "suggestion of procession created by the central axis that runs through the Romanesque-style portico, exterior entry, altar, and scalloped rear wall, alluding to the energy of the early church. Perhaps more than any other sacred landmark, the abbey church successfully combines the tradition of procession while encouraging participation among its worshipers."

60. Cathedral of God in Christ (COGIC), originally St. Benedict Roman Catholic Church (1952)
Architect: J. Ellsworth Potter
Builder: Leo Rehak
Location: 2940 Martin Luther King Jr. Drive

This building is now called the *Cathedral* of God in Christ and is the seat of one of its denomination's bishops.[12] It belongs to the denomination of the *Church* of God in Christ, commonly referred to by its acronym—COGIC. COGIC is a large African American Pentecostal church. Martin Luther King Jr. gave his final "I've Been to the Mountaintop" address from the pulpit of the Mason Temple in Memphis, headquarters of COGIC. Established as a separate church by Pentecostal Baptists, COGIC was the mother institution of the now larger Assemblies of God. Originally divided by racial issues, these two Pentecostal denominations have been edging toward union over the last two decades. Bishop F. E. Perry Jr. purchased this five-building campus from the Diocese of Cleveland and established it as his seat after the Roman Catholic parish closed in 1993. Initial efforts of the new congregation to operate the parochial school as a Christian academy were not successful, and the school buildings are now the Cathedral Campus of Hope Academy. Bishop Perry has established an amicable relationship with the adjacent Benedictine High School and the Abbey of St. Andrew to his north.

The apparently omnipresent Stefan Furdek, pastor of Our Lady of Lourdes (see p. 166), purchased property at the bottom of Buckeye in 1885 to establish a school. This evolved into St. Ladislas on East 92nd Street. St. Ladislas, in turn, purchased property up the hill at the corner of Lamontier at East Boulevard in 1924 for both a $240,000 expansion of its school and a parish hall.

Meanwhile, down on Superior, another Slovak parish, St. Andrew (also established by Stefan Furdek), invited Slovak Benedictines from Illinois to establish a school. Their high school for Slovak young men opened at St. Andrew in 1927. In 1928, three-fourths of St. Ladislas parish and all of its new school were given to the Benedictines, who moved their high school and priory up the hill and established the parish of St. Benedict. The large St. Ladislas parish hall became the church. This Slovak parish immediately thrived. By 1929 there were 1,200 students in the parish school. St. Benedict would send one thousand sons and daughters off to the Second World War. Stymied by the Great Depression and World War II, the parish only began building in 1950. Their church would accommodate 1,300 worshipers and nine marble altars in a style they imagined was similar to St. Peter in Rome. Dedicated in 1953, it was one of the largest Slovak churches in the United States. Then, the neighborhood changed. As "tension . . . quickly escalated . . . amid the community's turmoil and neighborhood violence, . . . it . . . became painfully clear, the parish and school could not continue."[13] In 1993, before a crowd of 1,500, Bishop Pilla celebrated the final Mass. Benedictine High School and its abbey (see p. 154) continue.

The massive limestone church stands on the corner of a residential area at the south end of the Benedictine complex of high school and abbey that extends along MLK Drive. The church is embraced by four substantial auxiliary brick buildings—two schools, a convent, and a rectory. While the monumental ashlar square and octagon of the church are imposing, passersby will struggle to reconcile their image of it with their memory of St. Peter. This building is a giant masonry square, articulated on both street sides by severe classic entablatures. On this cube rests a large octagon that, in turn, supports an eight-sided roof. The church is oriented toward the west, and its west end is a round apse. The east end extends toward MLK Drive to accommodate a giant-order three-window nave and narthex. Thus, in its unusual plan, St. Benedict shares with St. Peter an extension that creates a more conventional nave and cruciform design.[14] Beside the building stands a robust sandstone tower with a pyramid roof and a partially open, tall belfry. The style of this ensemble is severely classical, more reminiscent of the Escorial than of St. Peter.

The interior is a large rectilinear and then, going upward, octagonal space. The fifty-three-foot-in-diameter dome, sixty feet above the floor, has had to be closed because of acoustical problems. One reason the nave was extended out toward the street to the east was to allow for two additional chapels on each side. The marble altars, which departed with the Roman Catholic congregation, have been replaced in their chapels along the nave by monumental Chinese vases, so large that they comfortably fill the space of the absent altars. The building has a large narthex and ample balcony. An attractive altar rail, on either side of a great new lectern pulpit, survived the change in ownership. The original church glass is now elsewhere, replaced by one window—the COGIC seal in the east rose.

61. Our Lady of Peace (1951)
Architects: Stickle, Kelly, and Stickle
Builder: Edward Reilly
Location: 12601 Shaker Boulevard

All parishes have their mythical beginnings. For St. John Cantius it is the streetcar barn converted into school-church-rectory-convent. For Our Lady of Peace it is the pool hall.[15] As in a page from Henry Morton Robinson's 1950 novel, *The Cardinal,* Bishop Farrelly in 1919 sent James Cummins, a recently discharged army chaplain, out to organize a new parish in Woodland Hills, the area at the east-central border of Cleveland and Shaker Heights. Thirty-five-acre Luna Park, "Cleveland's fairyland of pleasure," with its midway and thousands of electric lights, was an important part of this neighborhood.[16] The prosperity of Luna Park largely depended on the availability of beer within its grounds; thus, Prohibition would later drive it out of business. Cummins successfully persuaded Luna Park's owner to make its billiard room available for Our Lady of Peace's first Mass. Although the roller rink—the last building of Luna Park—burned in 1938, the billiard room lives on via the website of Our Lady of Peace, where it is listed as the first building in the succession of the parish's places of worship.

Within four months, the parish began construction of a frame church on the corner of Buckingham Avenue at East 121st Street and, two years later, began construction of a highly ambitious school-and-church on Shaker Boulevard at East 126th Street. The sanctuary of this building, west across East 126th from the current church, is now the school gym. Although the interior of the school-and-church was kept "extremely simple" with a barrel-shaped roof carried by undecorated wood arches, these arches ended with angel heads carved in stone, and the liturgy was supported by a Holtkamp organ.[17] A succession of elegantly designed columns, topped with shield capitals, march along the exterior of this building, interrupting the brick walls. Extending to the north of the former sanctuary stands a handsome school. At the onset of the Great Depression, the parish unfortunately still had a one-hundred-thousand-dollar debt from the construction of this large project, and it took the decade of the 1930s to pay off the debt and accumulate the hundred thousand dollars required to begin construction of a permanent church. The parish purchased a lot for this purpose across the street in 1938. Construction was then stymied by the Second World War.

The present building was finally completed in 1951. The architects did better here than with their widely criticized restoration of the Cathedral of St. John the Evangelist downtown. Edward Reilly, who paid off his predecessor's debt and then organized, planned, and saved for a permanent church, died before its dedication. His Funeral Mass was the first service in his new building.[18] Reilly patterned his building after the 1924 Notre Dame Chapel at Trinity College in Washington, D.C., a worship space large enough to accommodate a papal visit in 1979.[19]

Separated from the Hungarians, who used to live along Buckeye Road to its immediate south (see pp. 151 and 152), by four lanes of Shaker Boulevard and the sunken double tracks of the Rapid, Our Lady of Peace is in the residential neighborhood between Shaker Square to the east and what used to be St. Luke's Hospital to the west. The character and the scale of this church seem to change depending on the direction from which one views it. Driving west on Shaker beside the church, its plain, satin-finished Indiana limestone suddenly appears—large, dominant, soft, and comforting. Looking east at the entrance of the building from its school across East 126th, the four Doric columns, all of one piece, appear cold, severe, and pinched. Inside, in contrast, the sanctuary is large, warm, and welcoming.

Father Gary Chmura, who is not an enthusiast of modern architecture, describes his sanctuary as a happy combination of twentieth-century architectural engineering without the eccentricities of twentieth-century style. The great space, designed to seat one thousand, is free of supporting columns, a marvel of the magic of the cantilever. The floor slopes from back to front fifteen inches to improve sight lines. The sanctuary, beautifully restored for the seventy-fifth anniversary of the parish in 1995, has four elegant but simple transept chapels. The generous marble chancel is crowned above with a large glass mosaic from the Vatican Studios, patterned after a painting of *Lady of Olives* by Nicolo Barabino. Above the altar is a giant baldachin supported by four large solid Breccia Stazzema columns with Bottocino capitals. The *Crucifix* of bronze and white marble is spectacular. The front altar is from the former church of St. Mary of Czestochowa. Two wonderful marble angel torches decorate the chancel. Side altars are not in the front but in the transepts. The figure of *St. John* holding his baptismal shell on the bronze cover of the baptismal font looks, to the delight of all children and the amusement of their elders, as if he were about to throw his Frisbee. Ceiling and arches are carefully stenciled. The wainscoting around the nave has 902 pieces of Breccia Aurora marble. Stations of the cross are made of glass mosaic. From the Burnham Studios in Boston is a wonderful ensemble of glass, with roses in both transepts. The main program for the glass is the *Rosary; The Five Joyful Mysteries* are on the right, *The Five Glorious Mysteries* are on the left, and *The Five Sorrowful Mysteries* are in the chancel. The parish is particularly proud of the two flanking frescoes of *Our Lady of Lourdes* and *Our Lady of Fatima* in the transepts.

62. Quinn Chapel A.M.E. Church (1965)
Architect: Robert Madison
Builder: H. L. Smith
Location: 3241 East 130th Street

The Quinn Chapel descended from St. John African Methodist Episcopal Church (see p. 126) and was named for the founder of that congregation. Bishop William Paul Quinn was present at the organization of the A.M.E. (African Methodist Episcopal) church in Philadelphia in 1816. Ordained a deacon in 1818, he became famous as a missionary on the frontier, particularly in Ohio and Indiana. In 1830 he organized the A.M.E. Society in Cleveland. Its six members would become St. John, the fifth oldest church in Cleveland. Quinn was elected an A.M.E. bishop in 1844 and the A.M.E. senior bishop in 1849, a position he held for the next twenty-four years.

The chapel honoring Bishop Quinn was designed by Robert Madison and is one of only two churches he has built in Cleveland, although he is known nationally for his religious work in Pittsburgh; McKeesport, Pennsylvania; Little Rock; Cincinnati; Philadelphia; Stamford, Connecticut; and Tuskegee, Alabama. In Cleveland, Madison is known primarily for secular commissions—the Browns' Stadium, the Louis Stokes Wing of the Cleveland Public Library, and the Great Lakes Science Center.

The Quinn Chapel is the only nonresidence in a neighborhood of modest homes. The congregation's parking lot is to the north of the church. Madison added his building to the west, toward the street from the original church, which is a composition stone building now used for administration and education. The present A-frame church is also composition stone. A diamond pattern is cut into the blocks, and the entrance and sides of the building each feature high, glass block windows. Painted-wood panels decorate the exterior walls. The composition roof over the A-frame is prominent.

Strong, slender wood arches hold up the A-frame from the inside. They are beautifully stained and finished. The glass blocks at the front of the church, which appear clear from the outside, are actually colored on the inside. Quinn Chapel has a center aisle, elevated podium, and transparent glass along both sides. The wood ceiling on the inside of the A-frame is also beautifully finished.

63. New Freedom Ministries,
formerly St. Cecilia's Church (1916
and 1942)
Architects: Schneider and Potter;
Joseph Miller
Builders: John Farrell, Edward
Kirby, and John Ruffing
Location: 3476 East 152nd Street

New Freedom Ministries, the nondenominational congregation that
purchased St. Cecilia's after it closed in
2009, was established in 2000 by former Methodist minister Tonya Fields-
Brooks. Beginning with thirty members, she rented three successive
spaces before settling in a former Methodist church in Chester Township. New
Freedom had grown to 200 members when it took over this church. St. Cecilia's
had 700 members when it closed. The new congregation intends to continue St.
Cecilia's ambitious program of feeding, clothing, addiction counseling, and
community building.

Mt. Pleasant, now the most residential neighborhood in Cleveland,[20] was a
rural area before it was subdivided for housing in 1921. Eight years before that
happened, a group of Roman Catholics had taken the first steps to organize
a parish.[21] They dedicated a 450-seat white frame church in 1915. From the
beginning, St. Cecelia was a "Pentecostal mission": it was open to all races and
nationalities. Unlike any other neighborhood in Cleveland, Mt. Pleasant had,
early on, a significant African American population—one hundred families in
1907. At first the only non-nationalistic parish serving eastern Cleveland and
Shaker Heights, St. Cecilia grew exponentially. In 1942 the church was completely transformed to seat one thousand, but it still could not accommodate
the parish. The parish was repeatedly divided—Epiphany (1944), St. Dominic
(1945), and St. Henry (1946). Twelve hundred men and women left St. Cecelia
to serve in World War II.

The expansion of the building during the first part of the Second World
War left the original roof in place. Pillars were put up to support the ceiling.
All four walls were pulled down and expanded outward, doubling the size
of the church. This created new seating to the outside of the side aisles and
expanded the front and the back of the building. The result was wrapped in
the brick veneer with white trim that the parish thought was more in keeping
with the neocolonial architecture of Shaker Heights.[22] On examination of the
facade of the present building, the lateral additions are obvious and charming
in their unobtrusive way.

With its back parking lot running up against the stout chain-link fence
separating this part of Cleveland from Shaker Heights, the front facade of

New Freedom Ministries occupies a decidedly unpretentious commercial area of Kinsman. The symmetrical composition, central gable, and rose window topped by a plain square bell tower with belfry louvers and simple spire are Georgian. This utilitarian building looks as if it were built by a nation at war.

Inside there is a peaceful expansiveness in the simple open space of the enlarged church. The interior is freshly painted, freshly plastered, well kept, and quite plain. It has a full complement of modest 1958 Winterich-Bedford Eisenhower-style windows with saints representing the different backgrounds of this parish. This is not a highly decorated church. The only exception is a Tiffany-style window of St. Cecilia, salvaged from St. Agnes, and now used as a door for a confessional.[23]

On March 15, 2009, Bishop Richard Lennon announced the closing of St. Cecilia. He celebrated the final Mass on April 25, 2010.

64. Hope Academy
Chapelside, originally Holy Family Church and School and then Mt. Pleasant Catholic Elementary School (1920)
Architect: William Koehl
Builders: Francis Faflik and Joseph Kresina
Location: 13205 Chapelside Avenue

This building is now occupied by the Hope Academy Chapelside.[24] The Hope Academies, established by Akron industrialist David L. Brennan, are the elementary school branch of his White Hat Management. White Hat, which employs more than 1,700 teachers, staff, and administrators, is the third-largest charter school organization in the United States and the largest in Ohio. In eastern Cleveland, in addition to Chapelside, Hope Academies now operate in the former parochial schools of St. Benedict (see p. 156), Our Lady of Lourdes (see p. 166), and Sacred Heart, and, on the West Side, St. Procop (see p. 238), Corpus Christi, St. Rose of Lima (see p. 246), and Annunciation.

The building was originally built for the Czech parish of Holy Family. Holy Family was established in 1911 by the omnipresent Stephen Furdek as a mission of his Our Lady of Lourdes (see p. 166). It was characteristic of the Czech population to move out of central Cleveland into neighborhoods accommodating their residential gardens. Annexed by the City of Cleveland in 1909 and 1917, the Corlett neighborhood population increased from 1,200 in 1920 to 20,000 in 1930. Corlett was a center of the Czech community in Cleveland. The Sokol Tyrs Hall, a gymnastic, cultural, and educational community center, was dedicated in 1927, six short blocks up East 131st Street from Holy Family.

The parish constructed a frame building in 1912. Father Faflik planned and raised money for, and Father Kresina completed, their imposing L-shaped brick church-and-school in 1920. A subsequent permanent church was never built. By 1970, with Czech parishioners moving to the suburbs, even the school was threatened. The diocese decided to maintain the impressive school as the Mt. Pleasant Elementary School. This was a joint project that included St. Cecelia (see p. 161), Epiphany, and St. Mary of Czestochowa and opened the school to students "beyond the Catholic community."[25] In 1988 Bishops Pilla and Lyke closed the parish, and the sanctuary became a chapel for the school. In 1997 all the students were transferred to Archbishop Lyke Elementary School at St. Henry.

The 1942 Diocesan guide to *Parishes of the Catholic Church* describes the church-and-school as "a low L-shaped red brick building in Mission Style."[26] However this building is described, it is a much more impressive monument than its pictures suggest. One distinguishing feature of the plain brick building, with its limited simple stone trim, is the broad formal stair up from the street to the three doors of the entrance. The building was also designed with the low-profile extended eves generally associated with the Prairie School style made popular by Frank Lloyd Wright. This style is carried farther in the grouped windows below the roofline and the protruding waterlines. This would have been up to date in 1920.[27]

In addition to the church and the twelve-room school, the building originally accommodated an auditorium, gymnasium, and lunchroom. The *Parishes* continues:

The interior of the church . . . is simple, with its plain white brick walls relieved by a vaulted ceiling of plaster. Back of the main altar is a statuary group of the Holy Family, supported on either side by an angel. Where the side altars are usually found are a bas-relief of a priest offering sacrifice of Mass for souls in purgatory, who are being released by angels, and, on the other side, a reproduction of the Grotto of Lourdes. The church bell is in a cupola surmounting the corner of the building where church joins school.[28]

White Hat has reconfigured the sanctuary as classrooms below a dropped ceiling with offices in the space above. The cupola is also a memory.[29]

CHAPTER SIX

The Broadway Corridor

The Broadway Corridor is made up of two neighborhoods along State Route 14: Broadway to the northwest and Miles Park to the south and east.

Tour

Begin this tour at the intersection of I-77 and Fleet Avenue, traveling east on Fleet. Immediately on the right stands St. John Nepomucene Roman Catholic Church. Visible from I-77, this church, with its tall tower and dark brick exterior, serves as the gateway to Slavic Village, the old Warszawa Polish neighborhood. Continue on Fleet to East 55th Street and turn left (north). Take East 55th north over the tracks. The great spire of Our Lady of Lourdes Parish (65) rises to the north at the corner of the Hamm Avenue intersection. Stay on East 55th to Broadway Avenue and turn left (northwest) onto Broadway.

On the left is the Broadway United Methodist Church (66). Turn right (northeast) onto McBride Avenue. Continue on McBride, past the vacant site of the former St. Alexis Hospital, to East 55th Street. Turn left (north) onto East 55th and cross over the tracks. Turn right (east) onto Francis Avenue. On the right side of Francis sits Elizabeth Baptist Church, formerly St. Hyacinth Church. Located in an older, secluded neighborhood off Broadway and separated by railroad tracks, St. Hyacinth was an integral part of its community for many years. Continue on Francis and then turn right (south) onto East 65th Street. Travel on East 65th until it ends at Union Avenue. Turn left (east) onto Union and stay on it to East 80th Street. Turn right (south) onto East 80th for one short block. Turn left (east) onto Mansfield Avenue. After one block turn right (south) onto East 81st Street. St. Lawrence Church (67) stands on the right (west).

Continue south on East 81st. Turn right (west) onto Aetna Road and, joining Broadway, continue for one block to East 65th Street. Turn left (south) at East 65th. The Shrine Church of St. Stanislaus (68), one of the largest churches in Cleveland, looms on the left. Continue on East 65th, over Fleet Avenue, and then turn left (east) at Lansing Avenue. On the right lies Immaculate Heart of Mary Church. Continue on Lansing until it ends at East 71st Street. Turn left (north) onto East 71st. Turn right (east) at Fullerton Avenue and stay on it to Broadway.

Turn right (southeast) onto Broadway. On the left (east) is South High School. Just down Broadway on the right sits a small brick church, the former Holy Trinity National Polish Cathedral. Rising up in the distance down Broadway to the south is the great tower of Holy Name Church. Stay on Broadway. Before reaching Holy Name, turn right onto Jones Road. Jones Road Church (69) is located on the left. Return to Broadway. Turn right (southeast) back onto

THE BROADWAY CORRIDOR

a. St. John Nepomucene Roman Catholic
  Church
65. Our Lady of Lourdes Parish
66. Broadway United Methodist Church
b. Elizabeth Baptist Church
67. St. Lawrence Church
68. Shrine Church of St. Stanislaus
c. Immaculate Heart of Mary Church
d. Holy Trinity National Polish Cathedral

69. Jones Road Church
70. Holy Name Church
e. New Life Fellowship
f. Pentecostal Determine Church of God
g. House of Our Redeemer Baptist Church
h. Triumph Church
i. Apostolic Church of God
71. Shaffer United Methodist Church
j. East Mt. Vernon Baptist Church site

Broadway. After passing under the railroad tracks, Holy Name Church (70) sits on the right. Continue on Broadway to Miles Park Avenue and turn left.

After turning onto Miles Park, on the right stands the former Miles Park Presbyterian Church, more recently the New Life Fellowship, and now closed. Miles Park is the heart of what used to be the Village of Newburgh. The park and commons, created when the village was plotted in 1850, were the site of the town hall in 1860. Annexed to Cleveland in 1873, the square was named Miles Park in honor of Theodore Miles, who donated the land to Newburgh.

At East 93rd Street turn left (north) and then left again (west) just before Miles Park Elementary School. On the right as you drive west is the Pentecostal Determine Church of God, formerly the Allen Chapel-Missionary Baptist Church. Turn right (north) at East 91st Street and then left (west) onto Harvard Avenue. On the southwest corner stands the House of Our Redeemer Baptist Church, formerly Calvary Episcopal Church (and Grace Episcopal before that).

Having completed a circle around Miles Park, turn left (south) back onto Broadway. After negotiating the complicated ramp and following the signs to Miles Avenue (east), the Triumph Church stands on the right on Miles Avenue. Continue east on Miles Avenue. On the northwest corner of East 110th Street is the Apostolic Church of God. Continue on Miles Avenue until it intersects with East 120th Street. On the right is Shaffer United Methodist Church (71). One block farther east on Miles is the site of the now destroyed East Mt. Vernon Baptist Church, located on the northwest corner of the East 124th Street intersection. This ends the tour of the Broadway Corridor. Continue east on Miles to East 131st Street and turn right (south). On the left (east) is Holy Spirit Catholic Church, opposite Cranwood Park. Several blocks south turn left onto Broadway and follow the signs to Interstate 480.

65. Our Lady of Lourdes Parish
(1891)
Architects: Emile Uhlrich and
Bernard Vandervelde
Builder: Stephen Furdek
Location: 3395 East 53rd Street

The magnificent and imperious metal-sheathed spire of Our Lady of Lourdes commands the attention of anyone driving north on East 55th Street or northwest along Broadway Avenue into what was known a hundred years ago as "Little Bohemia."[1] In the early twentieth century, Cleveland was the fourth-largest Czech city in the world.[2] Most ethnic populations arrived in Cleveland in several waves. The Czechs, one of Cleveland's oldest and largest national groups, were no exception. The original settlers stopped off on their way to Nebraska in the 1870s and stayed. As Willa Cather explained, the first Czech immigrants were unusual because of their high level of education and because they consisted primarily of family groups who intended to settle permanently. Like everyone else, however, they initially settled in the Near East Side. The Czechs soon moved out because they preferred to build settlements on the outskirts where they could garden. They moved to the north Broadway neighborhood on the East Side and the Clark-Fulton neighborhood on the West Side (see St. Procop Church, p. 238). As these areas became industrialized, Czechs began working in the steel mills; they were joined by a second wave of immigration from 1900 to 1914. Czech immigrants were remarkably literate. Their literacy rate of 98.5 percent was greater than that of most other Americans in the early twentieth century. By the time of the third wave of immigrants, fleeing the devastation of the Second World War and the Communists, "Little Bohemia" was increasingly a memory.

The diocese welcomed its first Bohemian priest, Anthony Krasny, in 1858. Cleveland Czechs originally gathered to worship with him at Saint Peter (see p. 18). Nine years later, Father Krasny established St. Wenceslaus, on the corner of East 35th Street at Woodland Avenue, as the first Czech parish in Cleveland. In 1872 Anthony Hynek established St. Procop as the second Czech parish and then, following the death of Krasny, returned to St. Wenceslaus as pastor. In 1886 Hynek purchased land on the corner of East 37th Street at Broadway (where Interstate 77 meets Interstate 90) and prepared to move, with his expanding parish, into "Little Bohemia." A few years earlier, in 1882, Hynek had purchased property for a new Czech parish on the corner of East 55th Street at Hamm Avenue. The bishop recruited a seminarian from Prague to establish that parish. The seminarian, Stephen Furdek, visited the Shrine of Our Lady of Lourdes in southwestern France on his way to the United States and promised the Virgin that he would name an American parish for her if he had the chance. During its first year, the parish built a frame church-and-school. The rapid growth of the parish led to the construction of this giant church, begun in 1891 and completed in 1902.

East 55th at Broadway became, in the early 1920s, one of Cleveland's most active retail districts. Father Furdek went on to found the First Catholic Slovak Union of the USA and Canada (he also spoke Slovak), a $142 million insurance organization. Furdek also published its newspaper as well as a reader for Slovak students. Furdek became active organizing Slovak parishes for miners and industrial workers in Pennsylvania, Illinois, New York, Virginia, and elsewhere in Ohio. In Cleveland, Furdek seemed to be everywhere as he organized other middle-European nationality churches. He frequently staffed his Slovak parishes with Czech priests because of the unavailability of Slovak clergy.

Furdek was succeeded at Our Lady of Lourdes by Oldrich Zlamal, who had previously organized Saints Cyril and Methodius in Lakewood (see p. 279). Like Furdek, Zlamal was active politically, in Europe as well as the United States. Zlamal was an important organizer and an inspiration to Czechs and Slovaks when they established their new country after World War I.

Our Lady of Lourdes Parish lies one block south of the now weathered commercial intersection of Broadway at East 55th Street. This is a brick building of immense bulk. Trimmed in stone, it contains details typical of Victorian Gothic churches—the tripartite entrance with double points and the large rose window. Unusual features include the polychromed statue of Our Lady of Lourdes above the rose window, the oculus windows on the south tower, and the clock beneath the spire on the north tower. The rectory is well kept and well decorated. An outdoor shrine beside the entrance of the church was built in 1965.

Inside, what distinguishes this sanctuary is its bright blue and white decoration and its lively polychromed statuary. It features more than fifty statues. They are not to everyone's taste. Originally polychromed, the statues were whitewashed in the middle of the twentieth century by a priest who believed that white statues were more fitting in a place of worship. They have now been restored to their glorious polychromy, and they impart a bright cheeriness to the interior of the church. In particular, at the front of the church around the altar, the interior atmosphere contrasts with the building's somewhat morose exterior, the result of spending too much of its life beside steel mills. The interior has a much smaller and more intimate feel than one would expect from the great mass of the exterior. This is a traditional Cleveland neo-Gothic plastered sanctuary with the usual plain Gothic arches soaring beautifully to the ceiling. One finds a charmingly elaborate grotto shrine to St. Bernadette on the south side of the nave balanced by the baptistry on the north. A full program of large stained-glass windows was purchased in Munich in 1915 and installed in 1920. At the crossing, the ceiling is nicely painted with the four archangels and the four evangelists.

66. Broadway United Methodist Church (1918)
Architect: Unknown
Builder: Oliver Stafford
Location: 5246 Broadway Avenue

This charming late Gothic Revival church is much like its more affluent contemporaries in form and unlike them in its complex history.[3] Broadway United Methodist Church is improbably plunked down in an unprepossessing commercial neighborhood across the street from the former St. Alexis Hospital. St. Alexis was transformed into St. Michael's Hospital. Neither hospital exists today. From its beginning, when this church was established to promote the spiritual, economic, and social welfare of the immigrant Czech population, Broadway United Methodist was deeply involved in ministering to the less fortunate, the newly arrived, and the marginalized. In the early twentieth century, this church enjoyed a national reputation for its outreach to newly arrived immigrants. It reached more than 1,200 every week in seven languages through its Sunday school. No sooner had it stopped bilingual services in Czech in the late 1940s than the Koreans arrived.

Formed as the Broadway Union Mission Sunday School, probably as a mission of First Church (see p. 26), the community acquired a small frame house "beside Morgan's cow pasture on the old plank road" in the neighborhood now obliterated by the intersection of I-90 and I-77. The Methodists then moved south on Broadway Avenue into a substantial frame carpenter's Gothic building on Gallup Avenue, where I-77 now goes over Broadway. At last, the community settled, in 1918, into this masonry building with its gym, showers, game rooms, and auditorium with stage. Oliver Stafford, who is given credit for the construction of this church, insisted that the new building be open seven days a week "as a social and service center for the community."[4] From 1890 to 1947, Broadway Methodist had a Bohemian Department, directed by six Czech pastors—the last of whom, V. J. Louzecky, served for thirty-five years. Recently, Broadway Methodist hosted the offices of the North Coast Methodist District, which includes Cuyahoga, Lorain, and Medina Counties. This district, headed by a Methodist district superintendent, is one of several districts in the East Ohio Conference, which, in turn, is directed by a Methodist bishop.

After the modification of immigrant quotas in 1970, Koreans began entering the United States in substantial numbers. Syngman Rhee, first president of an independent South Korea from 1948 to 1960, was a Methodist. In 1981 these new immigrants established the Korean-American United Methodist Church in Cleveland. It first found a home at the Seven Hills United Methodist Church. In 1987 the community joined with Broadway United Methodist Church in a joint ministry called the St. Andrew Joint Parish. By 1995 no Koreans lived within ten miles of McBride Avenue at Broadway. The Korean community, renamed the Han Madang United Methodist Church, moved out into the building of the Covenant United Methodist Church in Parma.[5]

The vigorous mission activities of Broadway United Methodist were supported for more than a century by many of its more fortunate members. Among these are the Austin family. Samuel Austin was an English carpenter who came to the United States in 1872 to find work rebuilding after the Chicago fire. Waylaid in Cleveland he worked as a carpenter and then became an important local Broadway contractor. Joined by his son in 1901, they perfected the Austin Method—by which one company designed, engineered, and constructed a building. The Austin Company would grow to forty offices in ten countries. Samuel Austin's son married the pastor's daughter, and the family's support of Broadway United Methodist was long-standing. The Austins are also major supporters of Windermere United Methodist Church in East Cleveland (see p. 103).

This ashlar, Indiana limestone church is a well-kept and maintained exception to its modest neighborhood. It has a large parking lot to the south. Overlooking the street is a large square crenellated bell tower. To the rear is a moderately large vernacular brick addition with a tall chimney. The final building originally included an Akron Plan Sunday school—that could seat two thousand—behind the sanctuary to the west. The beautifully polished wood partitions of the Sunday school's lower story have been retained, although they no longer retract. The second story of the assembly space has been closed off with a ceiling.

The small intimate sanctuary seats six hundred people but appears smaller. This appearance of a relatively small space is surprising compared to the apparently large size of the church as seen from the outside. The sanctuary is an open, wide space with a white, plain, barrel-vaulted ceiling supported by arched ribs. It has two aisles. At the back, an ample balcony hangs over a comparatively large narthex. The chancel is wood paneled. In 1922, while reportedly standing in front of a copy of Leonardo's *Last Supper* in the Louvre, of all places, a member decided it was just the thing for the chancel. A full-size copy of Leonardo's painting by Armando Vandelli, one of two in the United States, just fits onto the west wall.[6] The magnificent windows, now much in need of costly repair, are by R. Toland Wright. It has one window of modern glass between the narthex and the sanctuary.

On November 17, 2010, the seventeen members of the congregation voted to close Broadway UMC after the Sunday service on December 26. The North Coast District headquarters intended to remain in its offices behind the sanctuary.

67. St. Lawrence Church (1939)
Architect: George S. Voinovich Sr.
Founder: John Jerome Oman
Location: 3547 East 81st Street

The Slovenes originally settled in the St. Lawrence neighborhood of Newburgh in the 1880s to work in the huge American Steel and Wire Works. The first known Slovene settler in Cleveland, Joseph Turk, initially lodged, apparently by accident, with a Slovak on Marble Street in the immediate vicinity of what would become St. Lawrence.[7] The Slovenes were immediately befriended by the infatigable Stephen Furdek who drew them into his parish of Our Lady of Lourdes (see p. 166). When the majority of Slovenes departed for the mills farther north along Lake Erie, Furdek followed in hot pursuit. He sailed to Slovenia in 1890 to recruit the Slovenian seminarian Vitus Hribar. Hribar established the first Cleveland Slovenian parish at St. Vitus just south of St. Clair. St. Vitus would become the center of Slovenian life in Cleveland and those Slovenians who stayed behind in the Broadway neighborhood walked up or rode the trolley to St. Vitus for a decade before convincing the diocese, and an assistant at St. Vitus, to establish a parish back in the area of original settlement.

The congregation attended services in the basement of Holy Name Church (see p. 175) until St. Lawrence's combination church-and-school on East 81st Street was completed in 1902. This temporary building was greatly enlarged in 1924 by Cleveland architect William Jansen. The church was converted into a school when the new church was constructed in 1939. A newer, modern entry to the school covers the facade of the earlier church.

St. Lawrence evolved into the center of a small, quiet, and well-kept residential neighborhood. It has "never been one of the larger parishes of the diocese."[8] What excitement there was, Monsignor John Jerome Oman provided. He served the parish for forty-seven years, got his name on the street beside the church, and got the father of a future mayor, governor, and senator to design the permanent church in 1939. Gregory Rozman, bishop of Ljubljana and metropolitan of Slovenia, visited St. Lawrence in the 1930s. After World War II, fleeing the Communist government of Yugoslavia, the bishop was taken in by the parish as a refugee and is remembered fondly for the time he lived in the St. Lawrence community from 1948 until 1959.

George Voinovich Sr. designed an elegantly proportioned box for St. Lawrence. Located between Union Avenue and Aetna Road on East 81st Street, the church must be approached via Mansfield Avenue and East 80th Street because of the Union Street bridge over the Erie Railroad line. The brick exterior, with its simple, straightforward tower, is plain, clean, and attractive. Windows are rounded and buttresses subtly suggested, identifying the building as religious without any fussy distracting details.

In the interior—also tan brick—less is more. There are no columns and no side aisles. This is a simple open space. It has a wood semi-coffered ceiling. Spare trim is dark brick. Large ceramic blocks are combined with standard bricks. Like the exterior, the interior is a box, but a big box. It features a balcony for the choir and a proper chapel in the left rear. The Mary and Joseph altars at the front are plain and flat. Dark marble stairs lead to a simple altar that tastefully occupies the sanctuary and is framed with simple hangings.

On March 15, 2009, Bishop Richard Lennon announced the closing of St. Lawrence. He celebrated the final Mass on June 20, 2010.

68. Shrine Church of St. Stanislaus (1886)
Architect: William Dunn
Builder: Anton Kolaszewski
Location: 3649 East 65th Street

St. Stanislaus, the largest neo-Gothic Roman Catholic church outside New York City (St. Patrick Cathedral) when it was built, is the physical and spiritual anchor of Polish Cleveland and of Polish Cleveland's geographical epicenter, the Warszawa ("Little Warsaw") neighborhood (now officially known as Slavic Village).[9] It is this central location that makes it—geographically, socially, culturally, and spiritually—a place of pilgrimage and, thus, led to its designation as a shrine in 2004 on the 750th anniversary of the canonization of St. Stanislaus.

Poles first came to northeast Ohio to work in the Berea stone quarries, the source of so much of the material for Cleveland's religious buildings.[10] When they began working in the Newburgh steel mills, the diocese asked their pastor, Victor Zareczny, to establish a satellite parish of St. Stanislaus. The new parish began, like almost all the new nationality parishes, by meeting at St. Mary-on-the-Flats from 1873 until 1879. In 1881 they purchased land for a new church, and their dynamic new pastor, Anton Kolaszewski, began building five years later.

The Polish community in Cleveland had a close association with the Franciscans.[11] From 1879 to 1883 a friar was in charge of St. Stanislaus, walking back and forth every day from the friary at St. Joseph Church on Woodland. In 1906 the parish was taken on again by the Franciscans, most recently by the Friars of the Assumption of the Blessed Virgin Mary from Pulaski, Wisconsin. Originally established to minister to Polish congregations in the United States, this branch of the order broadened its mission in 1952 to include the African American population of Greenwood, Mississippi, and established another mission in the Philippines.

When the Franciscans took over St. Stanislaus, the mighty building was one of Cleveland's most conspicuous landmarks. A generation of immigrant Poles, when they got off the train in downtown Cleveland, were reportedly directed to find their way to Warszawa by walking toward St. Stanislaus's two gigantic 232-foot spires. In 1909 a tornado swept away the spires, the organ, much of the glass, and almost destroyed the church. When the city would not allow the parish to rebuild to its former grandeur, the towers were rebuilt as crowned belfries approximately half as tall (122 feet) as before. Another whirlwind, then Cardinal Archbishop Karol Wojtyla, made St. Stanislaus the first stop in his 1969 visit to the United States. He was followed to St. Stanislaus thirty years later by Lech Walesa, the leader of the Solidarity movement and former president of Poland.

It is not unusual for the Roman Catholic Church to play a major role in attempts to keep struggling communities afloat.[12] The Pulaski Franciscan Community Development Corporation, in addition to keeping St. Stanislaus open, solvent, and thriving has become a major player in efforts to vitalize education, culture, food, shopping, and housing in Slavic Village. An important part of this has been the St. Stanislaus parish school and the consolidated Cleveland Central Catholic High School on the St. Stanislaus campus.

The absence of the giant spires coupled with their stubby replacement, if anything, increases the impression of bulk projected by this immense brick building. The monumental size of the schools and other buildings crammed onto St. Stanislaus's generous block farther enhances the apparent size of the building. Last, of course, the fact that this church towers over its modest residential and commercial surroundings, rather like a medieval cathedral over its town, only enhances its monumentality.

What distinguishes the soaring vaulting of the sanctuary, in fact what distinguished the "extravagant" building at its dedication,[13] is the sumptuousness of its decoration. No plain plaster neo-Gothic vaulting here. The gilded arches are lined with floral and geometric designs. It is said that St. Stanislaus is second only to St. Stephen (see p. 256) in the generosity of its statuary.[14] St. Stanislaus imported its statues primarily from France. More than forty-five life-size statues decorate five major altars and, *inter alia,* the ten major columns of the sanctuary. A recent addition is the figure of Maximilian Kolbe, the Polish Franciscan prior and publisher who volunteered to die in the place of a stranger at Auschwitz. This building is so large that it seems to overwhelm the eight hundred places in its pews. The high-quality, plain, polished red oak church furniture, including the almost overwhelming altarpiece with its seemingly endless life-sized statues, was made in Salem, Ohio. The complete program of glass, repaired following the 1909 tornado, is "Berlin style," imported from Innsbruck. As anticipated, a place of honor is given to the display of a miter worn by Karol Wojtyla, later John Paul II, when Wojtyla was bishop of Kraków. The interior was beautifully restored in 1998 by Conrad Schmitt and Van Dijk Pace Westlake, winning a 1999 Honor Award for Restoration from the Cleveland Chapter of the American Institute of Architects. The 1909 Schulke organ has been restored by Holtkamp (1930) and Leek (2001). The church has a complement of six bells in the towers.

69. Jones Road Church
(1876)
Architect: A. D. Kent
Builders: David and John Jones
Location: 8000 Jones Road

A lot of Welshmen named Jones were involved in the steel industry in the nineteenth century in the United States, but only two, David and John, were involved in establishing the Cleveland Rolling Mill Company and the Jones Road Congregational Church.[15] These Jones brothers began working in the mills in Wales, emigrated to Pennsylvania about 1845, and subsequently moved to Cleveland in 1856. They were the central figures in a Welsh community in Newburg that established the steel industry along the Cuyahoga River. The brothers should not be confused with their first partner, J. W. Jones, or the William Jones in whose home the Welsh community organized a Congregational Church in 1858, or the Thomas D. Jones in whose home the congregation then met for two years and who led the singing, or with the George M. Jones who was the congregation's first secretary, superintendent of the Sunday school, and preacher, or with the Reverend John Jones who was the pastor when the current church was built.[16] Any, or none, of these could explain the naming of Jones Road. In any case, the Jones brothers came forward in 1876 and paid for most of the current building. Until this point, the community had been worshiping in a small church erected in 1860 on Wales Street and subsequently enlarged. Their new church, dedicated on July 4, 1876, was known, for this reason, as the Centennial Welsh Congregational Church.

Although a Welsh settlement continued around Broadway Avenue and Jones Road into the 1960s, Welsh workmen in the mills were being replaced a hundred years before—first by the Irish, then by the Czechs, and, last, by the Poles. Welsh owners were replaced by Scots. By the end of the twentieth century there were few Welsh members of Jones Road Congregational, and now they are no more—although the 150th anniversary of the church was celebrated in 2008 with a *Cymanfa Ganu* and a *Te Bach*.[17] Led for more than thirty years by Peter and Ione Parry, the Welsh have been replaced by vigorous new neighbors. In 2003 the congregation voted to change its denomination affiliation from the United Church of Christ to the Conservative Congregational Christian Conference (CCCC). The CCCC was organized in 1948 as a conservative alternative to the Congregational Christian Church that merged with the Evangelical and Reformed Church in 1957 to form the UCC.[18]

This well-kept and modestly—but nicely—landscaped church on a relatively narrow lot is somewhat larger than it appears in photographs. It is surrounded by neighbors unimagined when it was built—a large used truck agency to the east and a metal plating firm to the west. Three large houses on small lots face the church across narrow Jones Road. The brick building with Victorian stone trim, resting on a stone foundation, appears to be elevated on a terrace above the street; however, it originally stood at street level—Jones Road had later been dug out to make way for trolley cars. The church features decorative brick corbeling.

The sanctuary is a simple rectangular space entered from the street through a small narthex with a small Roman Catholic-sized balcony. Pews are canted on either side of two aisles to face the chancel. It has a twenty-foot attic between the ceiling and the roof. The chandeliers hang down for gas and electric lighting. Early twentieth-century plain patterned glass with one Christian symbol per window celebrates a memorial cacophony of Welsh names—Jones, Llewellyn, Griffiths, Thomas. A large north window memorializes David Jones. The chancel includes a small stage accessible by four steps on the left and center right. Walls are plastered white, and a large clock at the back faces the center pulpit to prompt long-winded clergy.

70. Holy Name Church (1881)
Architect: E. Malone
Builders: Joseph Gallagher and John Carroll
Location: 8328 Broadway

Holy Name, one of Cleveland's largest religious buildings, rises powerfully above the industrial-commercial jumble along south Broadway at the southern city limits of Cleveland.[19] Mighty Holy Name is not a presence from another era; it is a presence from before the era before that. The church that time forgot, it rumbles on with new missions into the twenty-first century.

Newburgh, with its waterpower and much more healthful climate, was the predominant community along the Cuyahoga River in the early nineteenth century. Newburgh was much more prosperous than the malarial settlement of Cleveland at the mouth of the river. As early as 1799, sawmills, carding mills, and flour mills sprung up at the cataract of Mill Creek. Mills bred mills, and shortly before the Civil War the Cleveland Rolling Mill established itself here. The railway that would become the Pennsylvania Railroad had come through a decade before. The Irish who had built the nearby Ohio Canal began to gather until, at the beginning of the Civil War, one of them—the explosive Eugene O'Callaghan—purchased two lots for a church at first named "Holy Name of Mary" and later changed to "Holy Rosary."[20]

As the mills grew in number, so did the Irish community. In 1881, the beloved principal officer of the Cleveland Rolling Mill died and was replaced by his unpopular son. In May 1882, a few months before the dedication of their community's new church, many members of the parish walked out of the mill seeking a union wage and a closed shop. The strike was broken by Polish and Czech workers (see St. Stanislaus, p. 172 and Our Lady of Lourdes, p. 166); three years later, they, in turn, walked out even more violently when their wages were cut. Although the resulting industrial warfare would embitter the Broadway Corridor for a generation, Irish, Czech, and Polish clergy all played major roles in reconciling their warring congregations.[21] By 1882, the Irish had constructed, outgrown, remodeled, and again outgrown a substantial masonry church together with three schools and the expected rectories and convents. Moving to their present location, they dedicated the present church—with another name change—"Holy Name," in September 1882.[22] Eventually the great Holy Name church would be completed in 1887 by John Carroll after the death of Joseph Gallagher. Its schools, convents and rectories would multiply, and by 1914 the parish needed its own power plant. Satellite parishes were established—St. Catherine (1898), St. Mary, Bedford (1910), St. Timothy, Garfield Heights (1923), and St. Therese, Garfield Heights (1927).

Holy Name, surrounded by a much different neighborhood today, is particularly proud of its vigorous school—an unusual feature in the twenty-first century for what had been a great nationality parish in the nineteenth. The school is beautifully cared for, well attended, and staffed with a substantial number of industrious staff. It particularly prizes its library, packed with computers. One hundred and fifty years after its founding, Holy Name's rectory parish office is today alive and crowded with parish missions.

Holy Name now stands, with its parochial outbuildings, almost alone on Broadway between the railroad tracks and Harvard Avenue. Its mass and its great 220-foot steeple slowly loom up as one drives south on Broadway. Side buttresses, elongated pointed windows with tracery on the north and south facade, and the recessed main door with jamb shafts are Gothic; the corbels are Romanesque. The church's louvered belfry topped by four gables, each with an oculus, is Victorian. From the front, its triangular massing and sharply peaked roof with massive tower are, as one would expect, similar to that of Irish St. Patrick–Bridge (see p. 189), designed ten years before. Holy Name's dark, somber brick is consistent with its neighborhood. Closer examination reveals beautiful brick work in the details of this massive building with its masonry trim.

The interior is a beautiful example of Victorian design and, in the absence of supporting columns, an awe-inspiring example of Victorian engineering. This is a great space. Light and playful, it contrasts with the church's dark, somber exterior. Elaborate plaster work decorates both the great gilded ceiling and the sills below the windows. The monumental woodwork at the front of the church was taken out in 1951 and replaced with more modest marble. The only piece saved was a wonderful dark wood chair for the presider that had been hidden away for half a century in the rectory. Holy Name has a Holtkamp organ. Among the statuary stands the life-size figure of St. Cecelia holding *her* Holtkamp organ.

71. Shaffer United Methodist Church (1914)
Architect: Maurer and Mills
Builder: H. R. Whiting
Location: 12002 Miles Avenue

In 1899 a group of New-burgh Methodists organized a church they named the Mars Hill Methodist Episco-pal Church. It was named so because St. Paul was said to have preached on Mars Hill in Athens, but this name would change. Indeed, eighteen years before, an Ohio Methodist minister named Hiram Shaffer had died. His daughter offered six hundred dollars to any congregation willing to name their church in honor of her father. The Newburgh Methodists took up her offer and built a church at the corner of Ferris Avenue and East 131st Street. Fifteen years later, they moved five blocks to Miles Avenue and built a building that stands here today.[23] To celebrate the fiftieth anniversary of the founding of their congregation, in 1949 they laid down new carpet in the sanctuary and redecorated every room. Just nineteen days after their celebration, a fire destroyed their updates as well as the organ, the skylight, the other windows, and much of the floor of the sanctuary. The congregation set things to rights in four months. Eight years after the fire, the congregation completed an addition to be used for education.

Along with the corresponding but now destroyed East Mt. Vernon Baptist Church (one block farther east), Shaffer Memorial anchored the east end of the Miles Park neighborhood. Shaffer UMC, which sits on an extremely weathered commercial thoroughfare, stands across the street from a quite large municipal gardening area. In the summer, gardeners in Shaffer's neighborhood turn the block into an oasis of order, bounty, and civility.

This well-proportioned brick building, trimmed with light stone quoins and waterlines, was built high off the ground to provide light for social and education rooms on the lower level. Wide stairs rise from the street to a beautifully detailed portico supported by Doric columns. What, to passing drivers, appear to be doors are actually two large windows at the back of the sanctuary. Rather than face the street, the real entrances face each other on the porch on either side of the portico. The gable end above the dentilated entablature contains a single oculus.

The 425-seat square sanctuary is white with ivory-painted wood trim. The elevated choir and central lectern are recessed under a plain, painted arch and behind a painted wooden barrier. One finds an elegant, white-painted ceiling, without decoration except for the crisp lines of geometrically dividing cross members and a round translucent window in the center of the sanctuary ceiling. Pews are slightly curved but all face in a forward direction. The plain white frame decoration makes a Congregational first impression but, on closer examination—because of its width—this church is clearly Methodist. One presumes that Charles Wesley would have been at ease with the translucent orchid-tinted windows. This is a bright, open space with a spacious feeling, although it is actually smaller than the outside of the building would suggest. The clarity and elegance of the sanctuary contrasts with the darkness on the streets outside. It has a relatively large right transept with seating. Admission to the sanctuary is on the left and right from two small narthexes on either side of the entrance portico. Aisles at the back and on the sides are narrow. Two main aisles between the pews are more generous. The floor has a modest cant forward. Except for painted wood trim, the walls remain undecorated.

CHAPTER SEVEN

The Near West Side

The Near West Side is composed of two neighborhoods—Ohio City and Tremont. Ohio City is one of Cleveland's oldest neighborhoods. Until 1854 it was an independent municipality that extended west from the Cuyahoga River to West 58th Street. After its annexation by the City of Cleveland, the area became home to many German, Hungarian, and Irish immigrants. By the 1980s, more than fifteen ethnic groups claimed Ohio City as their home.

Tour

Begin this tour at the west end of the Detroit-Superior Bridge heading west. At the first intersection, Detroit Avenue at West 25th Street, St. Malachi Church (72), topped by a Celtic cross, lies to the right. At the intersection, turn left (south) onto West 25th Street. After one block, turn right (west) onto Church Avenue. One block west stands Cleveland's oldest existing sacred building, the shuttered—one hopes temporarily—St. John's Episcopal Church (73).

Continue on Church for another block and then turn left (south) on West 28th Street. West 28th meets Franklin Boulevard at Franklin Circle. To the southeast is Lutheran Hospital. To the southwest is Franklin Circle Christian Church (74). Bear to the right between the church and the hospital onto Fulton Road. Turn right (west) off Fulton onto Bridge Avenue. St. Patrick's Church (75) sits on the right, opposite the park and a branch of the Cleveland Public Library.

Continue on Bridge. At its intersection with West 38th Street is the West Side United Church of Christ. Continue on Bridge to West 44th Street. On the southeast corner of this intersection is the Primera Iglesia Metodista Unida Hispana (the First Hispanic United Methodist Church), first built as St. Mark's German Methodist Church in 1916. Turn left (south) onto West 44th Street and travel on it through its intersection with Lorain Avenue to its intersection with Bailey Road. At the southwest corner of the intersection stands Dios es Bueno Iglesia Emmanuel, formerly the Independent Evangelical Lutheran Church, with its asymmetrical entrance tower and Gothic Revival details. Continue on West 44th, go over I-90, and turn left (east) onto Train Avenue. After going back under I-90 on Train, turn left (north) onto Fulton. On the northwest corner of the intersection with Chatham Avenue stands the Iglesia de Dios Pentecostal Church M.I.

Drive north and turn right onto Lorain. The third intersection on the right is West 30th Street. Turn right where Trinity Evangelical Lutheran Church (76), once the west side center of Lutheran *Germania,* now finds itself in the middle of Jesuit St. Ignatius High School, something not predicted in the nineteenth century. Return and turn left back onto Lorain driving west. At

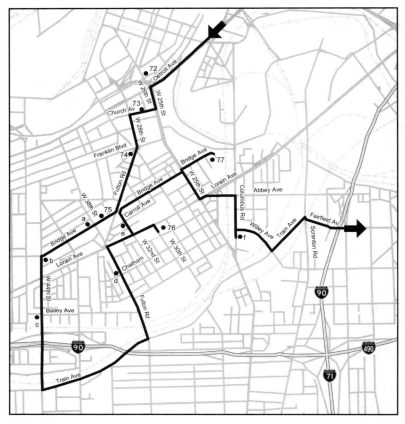

OHIO CITY

72. St. Malachi Church
73. St. John's Episcopal Church
74. Franklin Circle Christian Church
75. St. Patrick's Church
    a. West Side United Church of Christ
    b. Primera Iglesia Metodista Unida Hispana

c. Dios es Bueno Iglesia Emmanuel
d. Iglesia de Dios Pentecostal Church M.I.
76. Trinity Evangelical Lutheran Church
    e. Christian Fellowship Church
77. St. Emeric Church
    f. St. Wendelin Church

the next intersection, with West 32nd Street, turn right. At its intersection with Carroll is the Christian Fellowship Church, with its copper-capped tower, formerly the Iglesia Católica Parroquia San Juan Bautista and before that the West Side Hungarian Reformed Congregation. Continue north on West 32nd Street to Bridge. At Bridge, turn right (east) and, crossing West 25th, continue on Bridge until it curves along the high west bank of the Cuyahoga River and ends at St. Emeric Church (77). When entering the church's turnaround, notice the magnificent view of downtown Cleveland to the northeast. Backtrack west on Bridge and turn left (south) onto West 25th Street. At its intersection with Lorain, at the West Side Market, turn left (east) onto Lorain. After one block, turn right onto Gehring Avenue and immediately left onto

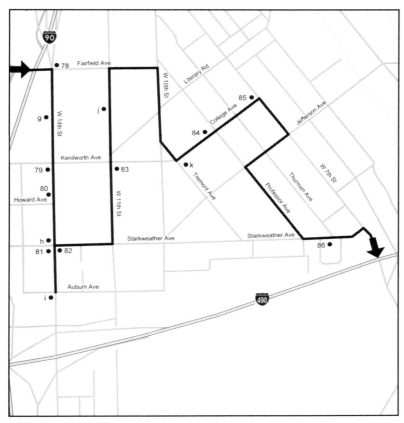

TREMONT

78. Greek Orthodox Church of Annunciation
  g. St. Andrew Kim Korean Catholic Church
79. Holy Ghost Byzantine Catholic Church
80. St. Augustine Church
  h. Iglesia El Calvario
81. Pilgrim Congregational Church
82. St. George Orthodox Church
  i. Zion United Church of Christ

83. Our Lady of Mercy Church
  j. Iglesia Hispana Asambleas de Dios
  k. Iglesia di Dios Pentecostal
84. St. John Cantius Church
85. Saints Peter and Paul Ukrainian Catholic
Church
86. St. Theodosius Orthodox Cathedral

Abbey Avenue. Crossing over the tracks, turn right at the next intersection onto Columbus Road. Three blocks down Columbus, on the left, stands closed St. Wendelin Church. Turn around and drive back north on Columbus. The first intersection is Willey Avenue. Turn right onto Willey, cross tracks again and turn left onto Train Avenue. At its intersection with Scranton Road, drive through the intersection and turn right onto Fairfield Road. Fairfield goes under I-90 and enters the Tremont neighborhood.

Tremont was originally part of Ohio City. In 1850, Cleveland University was founded in what was to become Tremont. Closed just five years later, the university left a legacy of once-fashionable streets, such as College Avenue, Literary

Road, Professor Street, and University Road. Tremont's location, on the western edge of Cuyahoga's industrial valley, offered a home to many immigrants. Ethnic groups included Irish and Germans in the 1860s, Poles in the 1890s, Greeks and Syrians in the 1900s, Ukrainians in the 1950s, and Hispanics in the 1960s. By 1985 a total of thirty nationalities were represented in Tremont.

Entering Tremont on Fairfield Avenue, notice the bright blue domes of the Annunciation Greek Orthodox Church (78) on the corner of Fairfield and West 14th Street. Turn right (south) onto West 14th. St. Andrew Kim Korean Catholic Church stands on the right side of West 14th. At the next intersection, Holy Ghost Byzantine Catholic Church (79) occupies the southwest corner.

Continue south on West 14th. Where West 14th intersects with Howard Avenue is St. Augustine Church (80). One block farther south, on the corner of West 14th Street at Starkweather Avenue, are three churches that frame the green space of the southwest corner of Lincoln Park. Iglesia El Calvario (formerly Cleveland Baptist Temple) occupies the northwest corner. Pilgrim Congregational Church (81) occupies the southwest corner. St. George Orthodox Church (82) occupies the southeast corner.

Continue south on West 14th Street to Auburn Avenue. On the right side of West 14th, just before the bridge, stands Zion United Church of Christ with its tall steeple. Turn around and drive back (north) on West 14th to Starkweather. Turn right onto Starkweather and then left onto West 11th Street. On the northeast corner of this intersection is located the Roman Catholic Church's Merrick settlement house.

On the right of West 11th, facing Lincoln Park, is Our Lady of Mercy Church (83). Drive north on West 11th through the Kenilworth Avenue intersection. On the left is the yellow-brick Iglesia Hispana Asambleas de Dios, formerly St. Vladimir Ukrainian Orthodox Church. Continue north on West 11th to Fairfield.

At Fairfield, turn right and travel east for one block. At West Tenth Street turn right again (south) and travel on West Tenth past Literary Road. Angle to the left onto Tremont Avenue. Travel southeast on Tremont for one short block. Turn left onto College Avenue. Iglesia de Dios Pentecostal occupies the east corner of the intersection. Continue on College. At the intersection of College at Professor Avenue sits the large, yellow-brick St. John Cantius Church (84) on the northwest corner. Continue on College to West Seventh Street. On the northwest corner of the intersection stands Saints Peter and Paul Ukrainian Catholic Church (85).

At West Seventh turn right (southeast) for one block and then right again onto Jefferson Avenue. After two blocks, turn left onto Professor and then left again onto Starkweather. On the right one can see the multiple domes of St. Theodosius Orthodox Cathedral (86) on top of the hill. At the bottom of the hill, on Starkweather, turn right (south) back onto West Seventh. Continue on West Seventh to I-490 and then choose an access to the east or west onto that interstate.

72. St. Malachi Church
(1945)
Architect: George Stickle
Builder: James Molony
Location: 2459 Washington
Avenue

St. Malachi was established in 1865 as a church for the Irish working in the port of Cleveland.[1] The new parish, separated from the more affluent Irish remaining at St. Patrick–Bridge (see p. 189), ministered to immigrants working on the ore docks and neighboring mills, foundries, and distilleries. The Irish huddled along the west side of the Cuyahoga River in miserable housing on Whiskey Island, in the "Angle" (the area, surrounded on three sides by water, north of Detroit Avenue and east of West 28th Street), and in "Irishtown Bend" (south of Detroit and east of West 25th Street). Meeting at first in St. Mary-on-the-Flats, the "Angle Irish" laid their cornerstone in 1867 and completed their church in 1871. St. Malachi (named for the eleventh-century Irish Bishop Malachy O'More but always spelled like the fifth-century BCE Hebrew prophet) quickly became, literally, a beacon of hope. Prominently sited on a hill overlooking the port and its lake, the cross on the tall spire of St. Malachi was illuminated at night as a guide to nineteenth-century seamen. Today the Shoreway (which runs right through the "Angle," dividing it in half) hides St. Malachi from the lake (or hides the lake from St. Malachi), but the tradition lives on—the Green Celtic (or Ionic) cross at the top of the tower is illuminated at night to greet those coming or going along the Shoreway.

At the beginning of the twentieth century, industrialization, commercialization, and road and bridge construction destroyed the community's housing and almost extinguished the parish. Merger with French-speaking Annunciation parish brought little more than a statue of St. Patrick. The salvation of St. Malachi was Cleveland's world-famous 1937 Lakeview Terraces (just under the Shoreway north of the church). Approximately one half of the tenants of Lakeview were Roman Catholic. Then, in 1943, three days before celebrating the renovation of their substantial Gothic Revival building, it burned down. Only the altar, baptismal font, and some of the renowned statuary (including St. Patrick) were saved.

After the war, Bishop Edward Hoban contributed enough Tennessee Crab Orchard stone from his restoration of the cathedral (see p. 16) to finish St. Malachi (and to coat Tremont's 1948 Our Lady of Mercy [see p. 207]). Tennessee Crab Orchard was popular, the bishop liked it, and maybe he got a good deal in Tennessee. In any case, St. Malachi and Our Lady of Mercy look like 1940s offspring of the cathedral. The bishop may also have contributed the architect. Stickle's St. Malachi is, of course, a much smaller building than the cathedral. If it resembles anything in Greater Cleveland, it resembles St. Peter's in Lakewood (see p. 286). In contrast to the rugged urbanism of its neighborhood and the large-scale institutionalism of most Roman Catholic churches, the 524-seat St. Malachi has—somewhat incongruously—the small, warm, comforting, humane scale of an English country church.

The people of St. Malachi stress that their rebuilt church is a "memorial church," rebuilt in memory of the parishioners and staff who worshiped there before. Bright and cheery windows celebrate the name-saints of previous rectors and nuns. A large Good Shepherd window, with its rectilinear English tracery, dominates the entrance. A rather startling life-size, white-painted wooden replica of Michelangelo's *Pieta*, displayed at the 1893 Chicago World's Fair and restored and repaired after the fire, dominates the north rear of the nave.

The area around St. Malachi is thinly populated and extremely poor. It has, however, two considerable assets. "The 'Angle Irish' were considered the most chauvinistic of Cleveland's Irish community,"[2] and although warehouses eventually forced the dispersion of the community in the 1910s, their traditional loyalty to St. Malachi's continues so that the parish still receives substantial support in material and in numbers from the suburbs. Second, the Community of St. Malachi, originally a group of people interested in understanding and implementing Vatican II, began meeting at the 11:00 A.M. Mass at St. Malachi in 1967. The community was recognized as a personal, nonterritorial parish in 1975. Supported by the parish and the community, St. Malachi pursues an extremely ambitious ministry to the poor. Its programs include: St. Malachi Center, a community center in a renovated trucking warehouse; Malachi Mart, which provides household items and staple foods at discount prices and serves as a job-training site; Malachi House, four row-houses providing shelter and food to the terminally ill poor; Backdoor Ministry, which provides coffee, a donut, and a sandwich to anyone who asks; the "Monday Night Meal;" Sunday brunch; and a variety of programs concerned with substance abuse, including Stella Maris, the Samaritan Ministry, and the legendary Thursday Night Angle Alcoholics Anonymous meeting.

73. St. John's Episcopal Church (1836)

Architect: Hezekiah Eldredge
Builder: Unknown
Location: 2600 Church Avenue

As the oldest standing church in Cleveland, St. John Episcopal Church is an important local landmark.[3] It is also an important national landmark. Priorities are slippery when discussing religious architecture, but St. John's probably shares the distinction with the First Unitarian Church in Salem, Massachusetts, of being the second-oldest-existing Gothic Revival church in the United States.[4] Armstrong believed that local builder and parishioner Hezekiah Eldredge copied the concept and many of the details for St. John's out of John Henry Hopkins's 1836 *Essay on Gothic Architecture,* said to have been the first publication in the United States concerning ecclesiastical Gothic architecture.[5] St. John's would have been up to date in the 1830s. The Oxford movement's *Tracts for the Times* established the intellectual foundation for the Anglo-Catholic High Church movement in the English-speaking world and were being published in England from 1833 to 1841. St. John's was built in the first phase of the Gothic Revival in the United States. Unlike the more "archaeologically correct" final phase Gothic Revival buildings built along the outer reaches of Euclid Avenue (see the Amasa Stone Chapel, p. 51, and the Church of the Covenant, p. 52), St. John is in the "Gothicized meetinghouse" style. It is a masonry New England meetinghouse decorated with the Gothic trimmings suggested by Bishop Hopkins—buttresses, lancet windows with tracery, and a tower with a pointed enclosed belfry.

Episcopalians have been unrelenting in their efforts to maintain this landmark. Although there have been glimmers of hope over the last half century, St. John's, over time, has resisted every effort. Now empty, its dwindling last congregation was unable to maintain either itself or its building and, thus, had to move to another church. The building is structurally shaky. The altar has been removed from the still immaculately maintained sanctuary with its historic glass. The thin, tired men and women waiting in line down the street behind the rectory of St. Malachi for their daily sandwich, donut, and cup of coffee have not proved to be crypto-Episcopalians. Diocesan hopes for St. John now rest on Cleveland's eternal hope for Ohio City. If Ohio City can in some way be induced to rise, St. John's will be resurrected.

For its first decade, the *via media* of the Episcopal Church in Cleveland was the Cuyahoga River. Trinity Parish, established in a log cabin in Brooklyn (Ohio City) in 1816,[6] is the oldest organized religious body now in the city of Cleveland.[7] From its beginnings, in the sixteenth-century Elizabethan Settlement of the Church of England, Anglicanism has been a faith of compromise. Early Cleveland Episcopalians were no more decisive than their forebearers were. Although organized in Ohio City, the new community spent most of its first four years in Cleveland. In 1820 it decided to move permanently back across the river to Ohio City. Then, in 1825, Trinity decided to move back across the river to Cleveland. When Trinity made its last move, the West Siders decided they had had enough of this and founded St. John's in 1834. When they built their stone church in 1836, the Trinity East Siders were still worshiping in the frame affair they had put up in 1829. Despite their Anglo-Catholic Gothic Revival building, St. John's—along with St. Paul's on the East Side (see p. 28 and 329)—remained a bastion of the "low church," eschewing the "smells and bells" of "high church" Trinity Parish.

Unlike Cleveland's Presbyterians and Congregationalists—torn apart by the controversy over slavery before the Civil War—Cleveland's Episcopalians were much more concerned with North-South political issues (as distinguished from social issues like slavery). Episcopal bishops continuously reminded their priests not to discuss politics from the pulpit. Although slavery was not a subject of public discussion for Episcopalians, it was an important subject of private action. St. John's "Station Hope" was one of the most important as well as one of the last stops on the Underground Railroad. It was the last destination before the boat to Canada.

In the middle of the nineteenth century, Franklin Circle rivaled Euclid Avenue as a center of social and economic power in Cleveland and the United States (see Franklin Circle Christian Church, p. 187). St. John's played a role in this, a role epitomized in the window at the right front commemorating the 1864 marriage of Marcus Hanna to Charlotte Rhodes. The Rhodes-Hanna clan, dominating U.S. coal and iron ore production, ruled Franklin Circle. At the end of the nineteenth century, some even said that Marc Hanna, after he installed William McKinley as president in 1896, ruled the United States as well. Such was the church's relationship with these families of prominence, that, when an 1866 fire gutted the church—leaving only the exterior walls standing—it was rapidly rebuilt on a more medieval cruciform plan with transepts and a steepened roof. An elaborate carpenters' Gothic parish house was added around 1875.

Reconstruction was not so rapid following the 1953 tornado that ripped off the roof and the north end of the church.[8] This rebuild restored the interior to its original rectangular plan, without the transepts. After the Second World War, in an attempt to strengthen the parish, an interdenominational Inner City Protestant Parish had been invited to share the church. That interdenominational group later merged with the Episcopalians. Structural deterioration forced the congregation out of the building in 1981. As the Episcopalians raised money throughout the diocese to restore and maintain the building, a recording company came to the rescue. The rent they paid to use the parish house, with its large assembly room, paid, in part, to prop up the building. This assembly room has a much more elaborate ceiling than the sanctuary. The assembly room ceiling is articulated by its open timber supports.

The church shares a mixed neighborhood with commercial, industrial, and early nineteenth-century residential buildings. St. John's is a much larger building than its photographs suggest. The church building is of irregular, roughly tooled Berea sandstone, partly coursed and partly random. The layers of mortar between the blocks are particularly thick. For more than a century and a half, this building has proved extremely durable, surviving the 1866 fire that destroyed the roof and interior and largely surviving the 1953 tornado. The tornado damage is apparent. The parish replaced the missing wall using brick and added an enlarged chancel.

The well-kept sanctuary comes as a surprise in a church without a congregation. It is rectangular with the large 1953 chancel projecting to the north. It has a modest hammerbeam ceiling, largely confined to the sides. The ceiling is plastered. The tracker organ with its giant wood case and the choir occupy a central position in the back, on the same level as the congregation. The musicians are separated from the congregation by a stained-wood barrier that gives the worship space the character of a medieval Spanish cathedral in miniature.[9] Beautiful dark-stained furniture fills the church. It has two aisles. The center pews, numbered of course, are farther divided in two by central barriers. The original weathered baptismal font is almost two hundred years old. This is a large but not overwhelming space, and its grace is largely the result of its splendid dark-stained pews that also look as if they have survived for almost two hundred years. St. John's has a charming brick narthex.

74. Franklin Circle Christian Church (1874)
Architects: Cudell and Richardson
Builder: Alanson Wilcox
Location: 1688 Fulton Avenue

Franklin Boulevard, running through the center of Franklin Circle, was, at the end of the nineteenth century, the West Side's Euclid Avenue. After Rockefeller moved from Euclid Avenue to New York, the influence of Franklin Circle on national life probably eclipsed that of its East Side rival. Franklin Circle's prominence resulted from the clustering, in this neighborhood, of the Rhodes-Hanna clan. Aside from their ownership of local newspapers, their control of a large fraction of American iron and coal production, and their prominence in letters and the arts, one of them, Marcus Alonzo Hanna, was considered by many to be the most powerful man in the United States.

Begun as a farmer's market and evolving into a gracious park with fountains and pavilions, Franklin Circle, within the memory of members of this church, was a place where the sun shone and children safely played. The physical integrity of the circle was destroyed by the 1969 sale of a portion of the circle to Lutheran Hospital for construction of an addition. The encroachment of the hospital destroyed what was left of the recreational character of the circle. Franklin Circle Christian Church now shares its side of the circle with the almost-abandoned former West Side Masonic Temple whose only activity, apparently, is the weekly "Fight Night" it advertises on a tired banner pinned up on its west end.[10]

Franklin Circle Christian Church is, like St. Philip's Christian Church (see p. 122), a congregation of the Disciples of Christ. This denomination is quite close to the Congregationalists of the UCC (United Church of Christ), so close that both denominations claim as a member President James Garfield, who was briefly pastor at Franklin Circle Christian Church before the Civil War. The principal difference between the Disciples and the Congregationalists involves subtle distinctions among the British peoples—the Disciples developed among the Scotch-Irish of western Pennsylvania, and the Congregationalists descend from the English Puritans of New England. Franklin Circle Christian Church was organized in 1842 by a Disciples preacher who led his flock back and forth across the Cuyahoga River until they settled in Ohio City in 1846. Two years later, the community put up a 64-by-40-foot frame building that they affectionately called "God's Barn." This was the church where Garfield preached. "God's Barn" was located north of the present church, approximately where the "Fight Night" former Masonic Temple now stands.

Franklin Circle Christian Church, the first Reformed Protestant presence west of the river, would become the parent of five West Side Disciple congregations. The church on Franklin Circle identified, in particular, with merchant officers of the port of Cleveland. At one time, it counted seven ship captains as members. Growth of the congregation after the Civil War, and the presence of the Rhodes-Hannas, dictated impressive surroundings. Such were designed by Cudell and Richardson in 1874 after they had designed St. Stephen in 1873 (see p. 256) and the now destroyed St. Joseph Franciscan Roman Catholic Church in 1871. Franklin Circle Christian is interesting because it shows what two architects, otherwise associated with liturgical Roman Catholic buildings for German parishes, could do for an Anglo-Saxon Protestant congregation.[11] The ecclesiastically famous tornado of 1953 toppled a chimney and destroyed one of the north windows.[12]

This church, across the street from sprawling Lutheran Hospital, is a massive presence: large and brick on a solid stone foundation. Behind the church, on the other side of its parking lot, sparkling new Cleveland Metropolitan Housing Authority town houses, demarcated by a white Tom Sawyer-style picket fence, compete with the lonely temple of the departed Masons. In 1916 a religious school was attached to the west side of the church. Its central feature was an Akron Plan Sunday school, now used as a chapel. Its retractable walls have long since gone up or gone down for the last time. One finds a moderately large baptistry in the front of the chapel for immersion baptism.

Offices, kitchen, meeting rooms, classrooms, and a gym are also in the 1916 addition.

Franklin Circle Christian Church has some extremely unusual elements. To the south, beside the church, stands a squared-off bell tower with Yorkshire battlements. The eastern entrance tower, facing Franklin Circle, has a pitched and gabled roof. The church does not have a proper narthex. Interior steps under the entrance tower lead directly up from the street.

The main worship space is a Greek square. Transepts, chancel, and balcony extend out from the center. The great vault overwhelms the seating. The four-hundred-person auditorium is not as large as its exterior suggests. The worship space was built, like an Italian medieval church, with decorated metal tie rods to keep the exterior walls from spreading. The decoration of this church is a nineteenth-century ode to polished black walnut. The shallow transepts are articulated by walnut columns in an enlarged Palladian configuration. Pews and window trimming are beautifully finished walnut. Walnut columns support the balcony. Stained wooden arches appear to support the ceiling. Brightly colored, beautifully preserved glass is partly patterned, partly figured, and partly symbolic as is appropriate for a denomination that originally, back in Pennsylvania, gently sought to unify the American church around biblical fundamentals.

75. St. Patrick's Church (1871)
Architect: Alfred Green
Builders: James Conlon, Vincent Conlon, Eugene O'Callaghan, and Timothy Mahoney
Location: 3602 Bridge Avenue

"St. Pat's," "the mother church of Irish Catholic Cleveland," is the second-oldest parish in Cleveland.[13] It was established in 1853, four months after its German East Side rival, Saint Peter. It has been more than fifty years since St. Patrick's could accurately be described as an Irish parish,[14] but the tradition continues. The Cleveland St. Patrick's Day Parade would not be the St. Patrick's Day Parade without the St. Pat's float.

Amadeus Rappe, the first Catholic bishop of Cleveland, effectively divided the Irish community between the West Side Irish of St. Patrick's and the East Side Irish when, in 1854, he established the parish of Holy Name (see p. 175) in Newburgh. The division continued, with the East Side Irish largely assimilating into the "Yankee" community while the West Side Irish fiercely maintained their ethnic identity. The first pastor of St. Patrick's, the immigrant

James Conlon, who was also the first vicar general of the Diocese, "encouraged the isolation of the Irish by helping form exclusive Irish societies, allowing the community to remain intact" until the middle of the twentieth century.[15] St. Patrick's is unusual for a Cleveland religious building in that it has had a succession of leaders responsible for its construction. After building the first six-hundred-seat brick church in 1854, Conlon purchased lots, made plans, laid the cornerstone, and began construction of the current building before he died in 1875. Construction was greatly slowed by the recession of 1873 and limped along under James Conlon's successor and cousin, Vincent Conlon. The colorful Eugene O'Callaghan got things moving again by arranging for the men of a parish seriously in debt to quarry, haul, and lay free "blue limestone" that they transported from Sandusky in a hearse. O'Callaghan left St. Patrick's two years before the church was completed to establish another Irish parish at St. Colman's. The community effort that O'Callaghan focused to get St. Patrick's built continued to sustain the parish as Irish until the end of the Second World War. In 1981 the current rector, Mark DiNardo, began an innovative "restoration drawing" (raffle) that earns approximately $35,000 every year for restoration of this historic landmark.

As a community built around a church, St. Patrick's developed many of the features now associated with a "program church." The first of these, of course, was education. Three months after the parish was established, the Ursulines began teaching parish children. More than a century and a half later, they continue teaching at St. Patrick's successor, Urban Community School. The parish constructed a two-story school in 1863, girls on the first floor, and boys on the second. A second brick school building went up right after the Civil War. In 1891 B. F. Vandevelde designed a mammoth High Victorian school for one thousand students that was demolished in 1978. In the early twentieth century, this school was reputed to be the largest parochial school in the United States. The school combined with St. Malachi's in 1968 and, in 1976, St. Wendelin joined the consortium to form the Urban Community School at West 49th Street and Lorain Avenue. In 1959 Mary Ruffing established the second or third Montessori School in the United States for forty preschool students in a rented room in the basement of St. Patrick's School. A residence was built for the Brothers of Mary (Marianist) teaching in the school in 1873. This is now the Catholic Worker building. The Catholic Worker group currently runs the Urban Plunge program out of St. Patrick's. This program introduces undergraduates from such colleges as Northwestern, Creighton, and St. Louis University to the realities of inner-city life in an intensive year-long experience. In 1903 St. Patrick's built a large Catholic Club complete with bowling alley, swimming pool, and gym on the corner beside the church. This building survived a major fire in its lower hall in 1983. Restored, it now houses outreach ministries and has become one of the most frequently used structures on the Near West Side, in part due to St. Patrick's significant feeding program.

The parish of St. Mary's of the Assumption merged with St. Patrick's in 1945, bringing with it the Society of Jesus. Bishop Rappe had created St. Mary's as the West Side German church in 1854 and had dedicated its substantial neo-Gothic masonry building in 1865, six years before the Irish laid the cornerstone for the present St. Patrick's. Bishop Gilmour gave St. Mary's to German Jesuits in 1880 to be the center of a college in Cleveland. St. Mary's became the victim of two disastrous fires, German assimilation (disappearance) into the general population, and Slovak and Hungarian invasion. The church was demolished in 1968 to erect a science center for St. Ignatius High School. St. Patrick's returned to diocesan priest management in 1980. Since the 1950s there has been a growing Hispanic presence in the congregation, and this continued even after Bishop Hickey established the Parroquia San Juan Bautista in 1975, two blocks away on West 32nd Street. The growth of the Hispanic congregation at St. Patrick's has been sustained and increased by the subsequent incorporation of San Juan Bautista into La Sagrada Familia out on Detroit (see p. 248).

Now standing in one of the poorest areas in Cleveland, St. Patrick's occupies most of the block across the street from the triangular park that surrounds the exaggerated Italian Mannerist rustication of Edward Tilton's famous—and remarkably well-designed—Carnegie West Library. St. Patrick's size and distinctive style make it an equal landmark.

The base of the building, the trim, and the top of the tower are of the warm, tan Berea sandstone—the predominant stone used in Cleveland religious buildings. Most of the rest of the building, almost uniquely, is of Father O'Callaghan's free "Sandusky blue limestone."[16] This was blue or blue-gray when freshly quarried, and originally the building presented an interesting contrast between the "blue stone" and the Berea Sandstone. The blue stone has long since faded into a light gray but the contrast can still be seen between the limestone of the lower tower and the sandstone of the upper tower. The fascination of the Sandusky limestone today, as it must have been for generations of parochial school children, is the multiplicity of fossils, some up to two centimeters long, imbedded in the stone. The uneven coursing of the masonry reflects the enthusiasm of the amateur masons who so heroically labored over so many years to erect this church. Structural elements behind the masonry are wood. This building does not have a steel framework.

St. Patrick's rough ashlar surfaces, pointed openings, and square-shaped bell tower with parapet and finials are Gothic in style. The unusual north end of the church is explained by a major addition to the building in 1913. The original church was eight bays long and the sanctuary ended in a flat wall. In 1913 they added an additional bay and installed a polygonal apse. The apse was flanked by shed roof additions over the side altars and a one-story ambulatorylike enclosure for the sacristies.

Three aisles divide the church. The steeply pitched roof is reflected in the interior. Quadripartite blue vaulting gives the interior a particularly lofty appearance. The light golden oak trim and walnut pews have been beautifully restored. Floors are quarry stone. The church has a full complement of windows, including one dedicated to major league baseball catcher Paddy Livingston—notable both for his play against Ty Cobb and for his disputed major league record of least strikeouts.[17] The altar is unusual for its deep relief of the *Offering of Melchizedek*. One window and the baptismal font remain from the first 1853 church. The sacristy has a good modern window. A chime of eleven bells, the largest on the West Side, was installed in 1899 and rang out again after restoration of the tower in 2002.

76. Trinity Evangelical Lutheran Church (1873)
Architects: Griese and Weile
Builder: Unknown
Location: 2057 West 30th Street

At West 30th Street and Lorain Avenue, Reformation meets Counter Reformation. Here the mighty brick mass of Trinity Lutheran—whose splendid, apparently cyclone-proof, spire announces its Reformation presence to more than twenty blocks up and down Lorain—is almost surrounded by the playing fields and sports complex of St. Ignatius High School.[18] The intersection of West 30th and Lorain once served as the epicenter of West Side German religious culture. Here, in 1853, Henry Schwan, pastor of Zion Evangelical (see p. 24), the first Lutheran church in Cleveland, established the mission that became Trinity Lutheran; his goal was to serve the twenty members of his parish who lived in Ohio City. Bishop Amadeus Rappe immediately countered in 1854 with St. Mary's of the Assumption on the north side of Lorain. Thus it went, through fires and reconstructions. Now, along with the Germans, St. Mary's is gone, replaced by a brand-new science center for the Jesuit high school. Trinity survives, now surrounded by teams of uniformed adolescents with Irish, Polish, and Italian names.

Zion Evangelical was one of the national founders of the conservative and German Missouri Synod branch of Lutheranism. The mission it established on the West Side in 1853 fell firmly under the control of Schwan. Two years before, he had scandalized Cleveland by introducing what local Yankees considered a pagan Christmas tree into his East Side church and eventually into American religious, family, and commercial practice. The West Side mission, calling its first pastor from Germany, built a frame church at its present location. This building, now a residence, was subsequently moved to the southwest corner of West 32nd Street and Chatham Avenue.

A substantial brick building just south of the present church later replaced the first frame church. This second church is still used as a chapel and community center for Trinity's many ministries. At one time it had a four-lane bowling alley in the basement. The principle room of this building, originally the main sanctuary, is remarkable for the steel beams that support the roof. Behind the church and chapel stands a good sized school building, once used as a Lutheran parochial school and now used for a variety of public and church educational activities.

Trinity Lutheran's elegant and authoritative spire, with its 175-foot hipped steeple, now duels with the wonderfully imaginative Victorian fantasy tower that Father Wipfler designed for St. Ignatius College across the street in 1888. In 2003 the Lutheran congregation celebrated its 150th anniversary with the repair and lighting of its steeple. This was made possible by a twenty thousand-dollar award from the Cleveland Foundation through the Steeple Lighting Program of the Cleveland Restoration Society. Other projects of this program lit St. Patrick–Bridge (see p. 189) and Pilgrim Congregational (see p. 202). In announcing this project, the Restoration Society noted that "the lighting design uses metal halide fixtures, a white light source that will differentiate the church from its neighbors" (read: St. Ignatius).[19]

The outside entrance wall of Trinity Lutheran is a magnificent expanse of brick. The church, a tall entrance tower in front of a sharply angled roof, takes the general form, somewhat incongruously, of a giant eighteenth-century New England meetinghouse reimagined in brick.[20] This is a form that Trinity Lutheran most dramatically shares, also in brick, with Holy Name (see p. 175) and, in masonry, with St. Patrick–Bridge. These churches all appear to be overgrown mutations of St. Christopher's in Gates Mills (see p. 366). This form was obviously popular with some congregations and architects in the middle of the nineteenth century for large urban churches. In its defense, North American colonial builders had adapted the original early eighteenth-century design (largely in frame, sometimes in brick) from James Gibbs's large 1721 masonry St. Martin-in-the-Fields on Trafalgar Square in London.[21] The present building, with its modest stone trim and dirt floor basement, has become the oldest Lutheran church in Cleveland, antedating its mother church—the 1902 Zion Lutheran building on the southwest corner of East 30th Street and Prospect Avenue.

The sanctuary is a simple rectangle with a center aisle. This is a great hall sanctuary. The space is divided longitudinally into three parts by tall, thin, clustered iron columns. Designed for 1,500, it now seats about 700. The balcony originally ran around three sides of the auditorium in a Wren-Gibbs configuration, cutting the columns vertically in two. Most of the anterior parts of the galleries were removed when a wall was built to support the rear gallery for the first organ. Above the sanctuary one finds a gigantic attic.

The reredos is set into a recessed rectangle. It is a startling wood extravaganza with the four evangelists painted white, and only somewhat more restrained than that of Zion Lutheran. The reredos is matched with a pulpit in similar style. The god of communion rails may have been banned by Vatican II but his spirit lives on in Trinity Evangelical's beautifully crafted Lutheran wrought-iron rail before the altar. Windows are tall lancets with nonfigured geometric patterns in clear, light colors against translucent white. Along the walls on either side of the sanctuary are six small paintings surrounded in elaborate frames, almost like stations of the cross, but here of the pre-*via dolorosa* life of Jesus. The back of the church, on West 30th, is unusual in having two narthexes. The largest one is immediately behind the sanctuary. The smaller narthex to the west leads from the street entrance into the larger narthex.

The congregation originally sang to a brass choir. Now, the 1957 Becherath organ dominates the church sanctuary.[22] Containing approximately 3,467 pipes, it was the first large tracker organ in North America.[23] Associate organist Florence Mustric is noted for her transcription of Mussorgsky's *Pictures at an Exhibition,* as remarkable in its way on a famous Baroque organ as Edwin Arthur Kraft's famous performances of *The Ride of the Valkyries* at Trinity Episcopal Cathedral.[24]

Trinity is making a valiant attempt to survive by again reaching out aggressively to those within walking distance. Initiating four services every Sunday, including an African immigrant service in the afternoon, it has been increasing in membership 12 percent a year since 1992. It has a parking lot for the Wednesday noon organ enthusiasts who are not walkers.

77. St. Emeric Church (1925)
Architect: Unknown
Builder: Joseph Hartel
Location: 1860 West 22nd
Street

St. Emeric (*Szt. Imre*) was the religious and only surviving son of St. Stephen, first king and patron of Hungary. Imre is the Hungarian version of the German name Heinrich or the English name Henry. St. Emeric was popular in Italy, and, when one of the Vespucci family was baptized in Florence in 1454, he was named *Emericus* in Latin or, in Italian, *Amerigo*. In 1938 St. Emeric parish launched a monthly news booklet called the *Emerican.*

Getting to St. Elizabeth, at least five miles away from the West Side Hungarian population working in the flats, was a major challenge. In 1904, with the encouragement of Charles Bohm, the energetic missionary pastor of St. Elizabeth, the West Side Hungarians purchased a commercial frame building at Bridge Avenue and West 24th Street, applied a wood tower to its entrance, and dedicated their new church in January of the following year.[25] Ten years later, after fire destroyed their church, Bishop John Farrelly arranged for the parish to buy Annunciation, a few blocks away.

The first Roman Catholic bishop of Cleveland, the French-born Amadeus Rappe, hoped that other immigrants from France and Canada would establish a vigorous community in Cleveland. To support this vision, he purchased land for a French church, Annunciation, just to the south of the present location of St. Emeric. The bishop's hopes for a robust French community were never realized.[26] Although the parish dedicated an imposing brick French neo-Gothic permanent church in 1898, Annunciation struggled with a rapidly decreasing French population, a slowly increasing Irish population, and pastors who could not speak French. Eventually, the declining number of French-speaking parishioners made continuing this struggle no longer necessary. What was left of the French parish moved—taking its statue of St. Patrick—to St. Malachi, and the Hungarians moved into Annunciation's building.

In 1921 fire destroyed the school and damaged the church they had just bought. They had hardly renovated their new church when it was found that the building blocked the western approach to Terminal Tower. In 1924 the Van Sweringen brothers purchased the church and the congregation moved, again, in 1925 into this church-and-school. They brought with them the old Annunciation altars, communion rail, statues, pulpit, stations, confessionals, windows, pews, and bell.

St. Emeric was an ethnic parish, the main services on Saturday and Sunday were, in 2009, still in Hungarian. It prided itself on "the beauty of [its pastor's] Hungarian expressions, brought from the heart of the Hungarian communities of Transylvania."[27] As one would expect, a high point in the twentieth century for St. Emeric was the visit of Joseph Cardinal Mindszenty in 1974. The parish played a major role in creating the cardinal's memorial in downtown Cleveland.

The surrounding Hungarian community was decimated by urban "planning" and "renewal." Particularly devastating were the Riverview Apartments—a fifteen-story federal housing unit of 639 suites for the elderly with adjacent three-story buildings for 140 other families—and the huge parking lot for the West Side Market, immediately south of the church.

Located high above the banks of the Cuyahoga River, St. Emeric offers a splendid view of downtown Cleveland. The 450-seat building serves as a combination church-and-school. In an unusual configuration, the church occupies the center of the building (the nave is over a communal hall) with symmetrical wings on either side for school, administration, and social gatherings. Steps lead up to the church proper allowing ample room for a naturally lighted basement with a social hall, a stage, and a series of club rooms. Exterior Gothic-style details include pointed arch openings, perpendicular-style front windows, and a squared-off bell tower topped by large finials. The great bell transported from Annunciation occupies the open belfry.

As designed, the nave was one large space under a central barrel ceiling with the lateral ceilings cantilevered out from the sides. The 1953 West Side tornado so damaged the roof and weakened the structure that the sanctuary was condemned for two years in 1959 (services were held in the basement) while the open sanctuary was reinforced with the present thin columns. The new columns do not significantly obstruct the space. The splendid white altar is well proportioned to the apse of the church. At the left of the nave, an unusual wall painting commemorates the one thousandth anniversary of the introduction of Christianity into Hungary. The painting features, underneath an image of Christ flanked by American and Hungarian flags, a large reproduction of the Apollo 8 commemorative postage stamp. The significance of the stamp is that the astronauts recited from the Bible as they circled the moon on Christmas Eve 1968, beginning with "In the beginning God. . . ." The church has a full complement of windows. St. Emeric was repeatedly redecorated over its eighty-five years. The interior is colorfully painted.

On March 15, 2009, Bishop Richard Lennon announced the closing of St. Emeric. The last Hungarian Mass was held on June 27, 2010. The final Mass on June 30 was canceled. On March 1, 2012, the Vatican Congregation for the Clergy ruled that Bishop Lennon had failed to follow church law and procedure in closing St. Emeric.

78. Annunciation Greek Orthodox Church (1918)
Architect: Unknown
Builder: Unknown
Location: 2187 West 14th Street

Annunciation Greek Orthodox Church, so well known to travelers and commuters, has served as the center of the Cleveland Greek community for almost one hundred years.[28] Its familiar blue-roofed twin towers, on the east side of I-90, greet incoming motorists just before the interstate crosses the Cuyahoga River into downtown Cleveland. The Greek community in Cleveland is unusual among local immigrant groups because there was only one wave of immigration—those who came seeking economic opportunity before 1920. Although there has always been a good deal of traffic to and from the homeland, the Greek community has grown largely from natural increase. Other immigrants typically came to Cleveland in pulses—waves of new immigrants coming in different generations for different economic and political reasons. The way the Greek community has steadily grown has given it a strong sense of cohesiveness. At the center of Greek society has stood its church; in Cleveland, this is the Church of Annunciation.

The first immigrants in the 1890s were largely men. They intended to make their fortune in America and then return to Greece. Their interest in religion was sporadic and involved itinerant priests and gatherings in coffeehouses, communal apartments, and St. Theodosius Orthodox Cathedral (see p. 212). The men organized a Pan-Hellenic Union and, beginning in 1910, engaged a priest who commuted monthly from Pittsburgh. Two years later they had collected enough to purchase a house for worship at West 14th Street and Fairfield Avenue in Tremont. In 1914 they moved back to rented quarters in the original Greek neighborhood downtown. Then, with the arrival of women and the institution of families, they began building the present church in 1918 on the site of their house in Tremont. Their pastor from 1924 to 1928 not only presided, he also painted. Father John Zografos completed eighty-five icons for the church. As the Greek community expanded, Annunciation followed, establishing Saints Constantine and Helen in Cleveland Heights in 1956 (see p. 314) and St. Demetrios in Rocky River in 1961 (see p. 291). Until 1967, when the daughter parishes became independent, all three institutions functioned as one parish—the American-Hellenic Community of Greater Cleveland. Numerous priests circulated among all three campuses. A fourth institution, St. Spyridon on East 65th Street at Addison Avenue, which followed the Julian calendar, was absorbed into the American-Hellenic Community in 1950.

Built of yellow brick with louvered bell towers topped by the Greek cross, Annunciation has the advantage and disadvantage of being right beside the busy interstate. It has an unparalleled view of downtown Cleveland across the Cuyahoga River Valley. In 1996 Annunciation added a substantial education addition to the east of the historic church.

Entering the church on a weekday, the visitor is greeted with the delicious, lingering aroma from a century of incense. The four-hundred-seat, three-aisle worship space has the tight, enclosed, integrated character of St. Mark's in Venice. Like St. Mark's, Annunciation appears smaller inside than out because of its larger than expected balcony. Resting inside four large columns, the balcony wraps around on either side halfway up to the chancel. The balcony makes the ground floor appear smaller than it really is. There is a general impression of being inside an elaborate jewel box. The double eagle of the Ecumenical Patriarchate of Constantinople is inlaid in mosaic into the front of the marble center aisle leading up to the marble chancel. Large gilded icons line the iconostasis. The walls of this church are covered with gorgeous iconography—*The Death of the Virgin, The Resurrection, The Baptism, The Entrance into Jerusalem, The Transfiguration,* and *The Presentation.* In front of the worshipers, the *Virgin* is surrounded by saints and angels. Above, the *Pantocrator* is in the dome, the evangelists on the pendentives, the apostles on the lower drum, and saints between the windows on the story above. Giant order pilasters with gilded Corinthian capitals frame the nave. The simple glass is patterned, the better to see the iconography. Chancel furniture is beautifully and intricately carved. All this is illuminated at night with three great crystal chandeliers.

79. Holy Ghost Byzantine Catholic Church (1910)

Architect: M. E. Wells
Builder: Emil Burik
Location: 2420 West 14th Street

"Eastern Catholic Churches" is the current popular way to describe religious communities that preserve liturgical, theological, and devotional traditions different from Roman Catholicism but are also in full communion with the pope. These churches were frequently the result of the principle of *cuius regio, eius religio,* whoever governs determines the religion of those governed. *Cuius regio, eius religio* ended the Reformation wars in western Europe in the 1555 Peace of Augsburg. In eastern Europe and in the Middle East, however, when the ruler was Roman Catholic and the people were Greek Orthodox, *cuius regio, eius religio* often resulted in an Eastern Catholic Church in which the ruler determined religious governance but the people tenaciously maintained their traditional Christian practice. Eastern Catholic churches in this book include St. Elias Church (p. 298), St. Helena's Catholic Church (p. 252), Cathedral of St. John the Baptist (p. 310), St. Josaphat Ukrainian Catholic Cathedral (p. 308), St. Maron's Catholic Church (p. 119), St. Mary Byzantine Catholic Parish (p. 221), St. Nicholas Parish (Croatian) (p. 73), Saints Peter and Paul Ukrainian Greek Catholic Church (p. 210), and Holy Ghost Byzantine Catholic Church.[29] To the outsider, things beneath the surface of these denominations appear extremely complicated. The collegial and welcoming character of many of these communities has encouraged different ethnic and national groups in Cleveland to shift from one institution to another. The unity of these eastern European communities was sometimes disrupted in the twentieth century by the Cold War. Readers are directed to the excellent article by Nicholas Zentos on "Byzantine Rite Catholics" in the *Encyclopedia of Cleveland History*[30] and articles in that encyclopedia concerning individual churches and ethnic and national communities.

Within these reservations, Holy Ghost was generally considered the center of the Ruthenian, or the Rusin, or the Byzantine Roman Catholic community in Cleveland in the middle of the twentieth century. "Ruthenia" is a politically charged word in eastern Europe, but in this sense Ruthenians were people who spoke Rusyn,[31] who came from the part of the Carpathian Mountains that was in Czechoslovakia, and who are not Ukrainians. The Ruthenians are one of those people, like the Kurds, who have had a strong ethnic identity but have always been part of someone else's country. The Ruthenian community is the largest Eastern Catholic Church community in Cleveland; it is slightly larger than the Ukrainian Byzantine Catholic community. At first settling in the inner city, in the area of Quicken Loans Arena and the Indians' stadium, the Ruthenians worshiped at St. John the Baptist on Scovill.[32] As they moved into Tremont, the West Side Ruthenians organized Holy Ghost in 1909. Completing this building in 1910, Holy Ghost would become, by the 1950s, the largest Ruthenian church in Cleveland with three thousand members. In 1918 the parish sadly had to establish an orphanage for the children of victims of the great influenza epidemic. Holy Ghost's dynamic pastor for forty-four years, Joseph Hanulya, wrote the first English history of Rusyn. When Hanulya built the Holy Ghost School in 1958, he also wrote the required Rusyn readers, catechism, and grammar. A major physical crisis occurred in 1969 when one of the towers came down in a severe storm. It would be ten years before the towers could be restored.

Holy Ghost stands across West 14th Street from Lincoln Park and south, across Kenilworth Avenue, from the Cleveland Catholic Charities' (Our Lady of Angels) OLA/St. Joseph Center for disabled children. The facade and towers of Holy Ghost Church are of yellow brick. The body of the church is red brick. The church is identified by the cross with three cross bars on each tower. The supposed parallel of the facade to Brunelleschi's Santo Spirito in Florence, even when one blanks out the two towers, is difficult for non-Italians to appreciate.

The six-hundred-seat worship space is a simple rectangle with two shallow transepts in the middle of the nave. The floor has an obvious forward cant. The simple space is liberally but not lavishly decorated. The walls showcase a good deal of Roman-style painting—over the transept arches, on the ceiling and on the side and back walls.[33] It also features a good deal of attractive stenciling. A painting of *David* decorates the small balcony. A large picture of the *Trinity* is painted on the ceiling of the nave and, as one would expect, an image of the dove of the *Holy Ghost* is painted on the ceiling behind the iconostasis. The *Virgin and Child* are painted on the back wall of the sanctuary. Simple altars, to Mary on the left and to the Sacred Heart on the right, flank a magnificent iconostasis imported from Budapest in 1924. The iconostasis is one piece—the forty-eight paintings were not acquired separately but designed and executed as an ensemble. The paintings are not all of individual images of saints; some are narrative paintings taken from the Christian story.

When Holy Ghost was built, everyone wore a hat to church. Men took off their hats when they went in. Women left them on. Since men, of course, sat separately from women, there were hat clamps on the back of the pews to the right so that the men did not have to listen to the liturgy with their hats in their hands or on their laps. A large rose of the *Baptism of Christ* over the entrance matches the style of the transept windows. Other windows along the sides of the nave are patterned.

80. St. Augustine Church,
originally Pilgrim Congregational
Church, see p. 202 (1864)
Architect: Joseph Blackburn
Builder: William Brewster
Location 2486 West 14th Street

Most religious institutions provide, more or less, some kind of charity. Throughout almost all of its history, St. Augustine's principal purpose has been to provide for the less fortunate—recent immigrants, the hungry, the deaf, the blind, the emotionally troubled, and frequently all of the above.[34] Like the Salvation Army, St. Augustine has always offered some salvation along with the soup, but it has also always offered help to all who ask. The City of Cleveland most recently recognized this by naming the corner of West 14th Street and Howard Avenue, in front of the church, after Sister Corita Ambro, who has fed the poor from St. Augustine for more than forty years, and Father Joe McNulty, pastor of St. Augustine since 1977.

St. Augustine, one of the oldest parishes in Cleveland, was established in 1860 for the Irish immigrants who were Cleveland's first steel workers. The original church, on the other (east) side of Lincoln Park, was located closer to the mills than the other Roman Catholic parishes. Too poor to support a pastor, the parish was staffed as a mission of the cathedral until 1867. Four years thereafter, their first pastor died of smallpox that he contracted on a sick call. A plaque in his honor hangs in the current church. Although the short-lived Cleveland University, which was more a real estate speculation than an educational institution, was quickly gone, much of Tremont in the nineteenth century was reasonably prosperous. The area around Lincoln Park supported one of the highest concentrations of religious institutions in the United States.[35] When Pilgrim Congregational Church (see p. 202) had to move to accommodate its rapidly growing congregation, it put its building up for sale. An impoverished Irish Roman Catholic parish was not what Pilgrim had in mind, but "after protracted and, at times, contentious negotiations,"[36] Pilgrim Congregational became St. Augustine in 1895.

Since then, St. Augustine has continued to be a landmark for the needy. Tremont serves as a magnet for new immigrants and for countrymen left behind when new immigrants become old immigrants and move to the suburbs. In 1964 Father John Wilson brought the Catholic Deaf Community to St. Augustine. Wilson was initially appointed administrator, rather than pastor, because it was anticipated that I-90 would be the end of St. Augustine. It is said that Wilson went to Columbus and got the interstate rerouted to spare his church. Instead, relocated to St. Augustine's backyard, the interstate spared the church but not the parish. In the early 1970s the Catholic Blind Community came to St. Augustine. Since then, St. Augustine has also become a center for the emotionally disturbed, and it now headquarters some of the Catholic Services Disabilities Services. Feeding the hungry is a major mission. In 1975 the parish began a holiday meal program that has grown to serve between ten thousand and twelve thousand meals at twenty ecumenical sites during Thanksgiving, Christmas, and Easter. For this, St. Augustine begins roasting and freezing turkeys every year on the first day of October. The weekly soup program, begun in 1975, has grown to a twice-daily meal program with special attention to the last two weeks of the month when the need is greatest.

Although it sits across the street from idyllic Lincoln Park, St. Augustine is next door to an automobile collision body shop. It is that kind of eclectic neighborhood. From the street, the freshly painted, well-kept six-hundred-seat building looks, perhaps because of its superficially vernacular appearance, like a much smaller building than it really is. This is a simple mid-nineteenth-century church with a few decorative trimmings—Gothic pointed arches and Romanesque pilasters, large extended gables, and a corbel table below the roofline. The styles blend together to create a human-scaled structure typical of the time in which it was built. The 1953 tornado, which caused such havoc among church steeples, took down this one too. The original Congregational bell cannot be removed from the remnants of the tower without destroying the roof.

After such a simple, utilitarian exterior, the elaborate Gothic hammerbeam ceiling of the interior is a surprise. If the nineteenth-century flavor of the exterior is Congregational, the interior, with its generous transepts and cruciform orientation, seems Roman. The width of the nave, however, suggests this might once have been something other than a Roman Catholic church.[37] Statues and stations are from the original frame church on the other side of Lincoln Park. Consistent with the historic mission of St. Augustine is much of the hand-me-down church furniture—the pews from St. Malachi and the organ from St. Vitus. Inconsistent with the St. Augustine mission to the neediest is the glass. Except for two figured Roman Catholic windows, the Congregationalists left behind (why do communities always do this when they move?)[38] a full program of good-quality mid-nineteenth-century patterned glass and, above the beautifully maintained altar, a wonderful Tiffany-style window.

81. Pilgrim Congregational Church (1893)

Architect: Sidney R. Badgley
Builder: Charles Mills
Location: 2453 West 14th Street

Pilgrim Congregational Church, Sidney Badgley's masterpiece,[39] is to the West Side as Eric Mendelsohn's Park Synagogue is to the East Side.[40] Why is Pilgrim so famous? First, Pilgrim's plan, now almost a hundred years out of date, is universally cited as a prime example of the "Akron Plan," and as such it influenced the building of thousands of American churches in the nineteenth and early twentieth centuries.[41] Second, Pilgrim's Richardson Romanesque style confirmed a historical revivalist idiom that swept the United States at the end of the nineteenth century. Third, Pilgrim's concept and image of itself as an "institutional church," internally developing the potential of its members while also reaching out to those around it, proved enormously influential to the idea of what an American church should be.[42] Pilgrim is a Cleveland landmark. Now fighting for survival in an impoverished neighborhood, Pilgrim was built as an international landmark. Someday it may be seen as such again.

Pilgrim was organized in 1859 as the University Heights Congregational Church and originally met in the Brooklyn Township schoolhouse before moving to the assembly hall of the Humiston Institute.[43] At that time Tremont was known as University Heights. It had been home to Cleveland University from 1850 to 1853. The Pilgrim congregation was ecumenical from the beginning, established by eight Congregational, six Methodist, six Wesleyan Methodist, and three Presbyterian members—a "union" congregation on a "congregational platform." Changing their name to the Jennings Avenue Congregational Church, they completed their first church in 1869 on the corner of West 14th Street (then Jennings Avenue) at Howard Avenue.[44] The Pilgrim congregation added transepts to their first church in 1877.

Pilgrim has a long tradition of helping the less fortunate in Tremont.[45] While still in the old church, before building their present building, Pilgrim established recreational rooms in 1873 to keep young men in the neighborhood out of saloons. In 1874 this became the Friendly Inn, with a parallel sewing school established for young women in 1876.[46] Pilgrim helped parishioners Carlos and Mary Jones establish their children's Jones School and Home in 1886.

The Pilgrim Institute, similar to a settlement house, was established immediately after the completion of the present church. It responded to community needs for education and recreation. The institute embraced the church's health, welfare, and social service societies. The Pilgrim Institute offered classes in music, languages, photography, stenography, bookkeeping, penmanship, mechanical drawing, and gardening in addition to Bible study. Pilgrim opened the first library on the West Side. It started the first kindergarten, the first cooking school, and the first Boy Scout Troop in Cleveland. At first, Pilgrim avoided merging its library with the developing Cleveland Public Library because of the secular nature of the public collection; however, eventually Pilgrim gave its library to Cleveland. Like Euclid Avenue Congregational on the East Side (see p. 38), there was an armory in the basement complete with rifles and helmets for drilling adolescents, an activity seemingly so at odds with the present character of the Congregational church. The present building was designed to be open all the time. The lower floor was built with separate entrances for men and women to place them closer to their respective recreational areas. The wood wainscoting around these halls, rooms, and stairways has been beautifully restored.

Membership peaked in 1924 with 1,297 members. Pilgrim has been served by a succession of particularly dynamic pastors, including Charles Mills who built the current church, Dan Freeman Bradley who led it through its greatest period of growth and, more recently, Laurinda Hafner, who restored its vitality at the end of the twentieth and the beginning of the twenty-first centuries.

Pilgrim is located opposite the southwest corner of Lincoln Park. It is the largest of the three churches on this corner.[47] Romanesque characteristics include a rough ashlar finish, a prominent round arch at the front entrance, and pyramidal roofs atop square-based towers. Pilgrim was built of brownish-red quartz sandstone, known as "brown stone," a favorite of architects building Richardson Romanesque churches. The church's main 150-foot northeast tower sometimes is compared to that of Richardson's 1872 First Baptist Church ("Brattle Square Church") in Boston, although the similarity is limited to the fact that both churches have big towers.

This was the first building west of the Cuyahoga in Cleveland to use electricity. Bare light bulbs once lined each arch in the sanctuary to celebrate this exciting innovation.[48] The electricity was produced by a steam power plant in the basement that, through a complex of cables, also provided the motor power to raise and lower the massive wall dividing the sanctuary from the Akron Plan assembly area. This assembly area—coffered with oak beams, lit through glass ceiling panels for natural light, and surrounded by twelve gallery rooms—is now used as a theater. A second, smaller theater, is just east of the balcony of the sanctuary to which it also communicates through movable walls. The highlight of this "little theater" is the large east rose. A visit to this church is not complete without a tour of the immense attic with its huge wooden beams and roof trusses. A dramatic catwalk above encircles the glass sanctuary dome. The original electrical wiring and complicated counterweights to move the walls are still in place. A southern addition to the main building was added in 1919 to house another "community" gymnasium and a four-lane bowling alley. The current building has had at least two major renovations. The first, in the 1950, sought to modernize its appearance. Visitors can be thankful that another renovation in the 1990s restored the building's original style and beauty.

Whatever kind of Akron Plan church this is, the main sanctuary is certainly a spectacular example. Retraction of the two-story half-block-long south wall, attached with its cables to the steam engine in the basement, must have paralleled the first paragraphs of Genesis. The main auditorium was designed to seat 1,200, and raising the wall to the Sunday school provided seating for another 1,200. The sanctuary is square and, like Bagdley's St. John A.M.E. and his Fidelity Baptist, oriented toward a corner but on a much larger scale. At Pilgrim, orientation is toward the southwest corner.[49] A small, elevated chancel occupies a small apse with a hemispheric dome. The chancel was restored to its original appearance in 1995 and its original furnishings reinstalled. Luxurious pews extend back in a quarter-circle from this southwest corner. The seating is thus able to fan out from the pulpit in an unimpeded sweep. One may find it remarkable that the hundred-year-old mohair-kapok pew cushions, although refurbished, are original. Slender columns support the balcony.

Four massive semicircular arches support a twenty-four-foot diameter central glass dome—designed by Elizabeth Parsons—forty-four feet above the floor. This magnificent glass, now illuminated by artificial light, was, like the glass dome at Shiloh (see p. 132), originally sunlit through windows in the attic. The ceiling hangs from a roof more than twenty feet above. The church features a great rose to the north and a smaller and less distinguished rose to the east.

In 1992 Chris Holtkamp restored Pilgrim's historic 1894 Ferrand-Votey organ that had previously been renovated by Moeller in 1936.[50] It is one of three Ferrand-Votey organs still working in the United States. Restoration included the regilding of a statue of *Gabriel* found lying on its side in a storage room. *Gabriel,* reinstalled above the organ, holds a cast-off horn found on the steps of the Music School Settlement. Two Maitland Armstrong windows, both of St. Cecelia,[51] flank the organ.

82. St. George Orthodox Church,
originally Lincoln Park Methodist Episcopal Church (1892 and 1935)
Architect: Sidney R. Badgley (1892)
Builders: W. C. Endley (1892); Elias Meena (1935)
Location 2587 West 14th Street

Although 90 percent of Arabs worldwide are Muslim, 77 percent of Arabs in the United States are Christian.[52] The earliest Christian Arabs in the United States were predominantly from Lebanon and came in two waves. The first, paralleling most European immigrant groups, came seeking economic opportunity and settled in Cleveland before the 1920s. The second wave, also paralleling European immigration to Cleveland after the Second World War, came to Cleveland for political reasons as refugees from the disturbances that convulsed the Middle East.

Christian Arabs in Cleveland are divided into three main groups—Orthodox, Maronite, and Melkite.[53] Since 1928, the Orthodox have been on the corner of West 14th Street at Starkweather Avenue.[54] Maronites, the largest Christian group in Lebanon and the largest Lebanese group in Cleveland, worship at St. Maron's on Carnegie (see p. 119). At first part of the Roman Catholic Diocese of Cleveland, St. Maron's now falls under the Eparchy of Our Lady of Fatima of Los Angeles.[55] The Melkites, who come to the United States from several Middle Eastern countries, built St. Elias in Brooklyn in 1964 (see p. 298). St. Elias also first belonged to the Roman Catholic Diocese of Cleveland; St. Elias is now part of the Melkite Greek Catholic Eparchy of Newton, Massachusetts.

Unlike other immigrant groups in Cleveland, the Arabs, and in particular the Lebanese, rapidly assimilated into the general population and tended not to gather in distinct neighborhoods. Their churches, although central to their national life, were not the geographic focal point of an ethnic neighborhood. This strengthened their religious institutions so that they have been relatively unaffected by the changing character of their surroundings. St. George, for example, is an island of well-kept prosperity in a generally challenged neighborhood.

As was the case with many Methodist congregations, the community that became the Lincoln Park Methodist Episcopal Church and then sold this building to the Antiochian Orthodox Church went through several moves and many name changes. During its beginning, when it met in a home and then in a rented room on West 11th Street in Tremont, the community identified itself as the Methodist Episcopal Mission. After worshiping in a tent, the congregation, now the University Heights Mission, moved into a room in the former Cleveland University building. In 1871 the Methodists built a frame church on West Tenth Street (Pelton Avenue) and became the Pelton Avenue Church. The community changed its name to Grace Church in 1879. Four years later they moved their frame building to Starkweather at 14th Street (Jennings Avenue). In 1885 this became the Jennings Avenue Methodist Episcopal Church. It was as Jennings Avenue Methodist that the community commissioned Sidney Badgley to build the present church in 1892. This became the Lincoln Park Methodist Episcopal Church in 1914. After the sale of this building to the Orthodox, the Methodist community moved out to Parma as the Ridgewood United Methodist Church. Ridgewood would establish three daughter churches on the west side including Pleasant Hills United Methodist Church (see p. 301).

A treasured memory of the Orthodox Lebanese community in Cleveland mixes the smoke of cigars with the odor of incense. The community met for liturgy in the billiards room of Gray's Armory soon after the armory's construction in 1893.[56] The Orthodox were then warmly welcomed by the Melkites of St. Elias. The official history of the parish begins in 1911 with the establishment of the St. Nicholas Syrian Orthodox Christian Church, the arrival of a full-time priest from Lebanon, and rental of a worship space on Bolivar Road. The parish struggled before the arrival of Father Elias Meena in 1927. During the next twenty-five years, he would transform his community.

In 1928 the parish purchased this good-sized Methodist church. Sidney Badgley had built it directly across the street from his monumental Pilgrim Congregational Church (see p. 202). The Orthodox renamed their new church for St. George. After four years of remodeling and acquiring icons from the Middle East, fire almost completely destroyed their church on May 7, 1933. The interior and roof were incinerated together with the smaller south tower and a substantial chapel built on the south side of the present building. The fire destroyed the fourth story of the existing north tower and, of course, the spire.[57] The Orthodox community elected to rebuild within the northern shell of Badgley's building. The destruction of most of the southern half of the original building explains the asymmetry of the current church's facade. So much of Badgley's building was destroyed that it is unwise to ascribe to him what little remains, although a hint of the original plan remains in the unusual width of the worship space. The construction of the current church should be credited to Meena who, together with his parish over the next two years, did much of the physical work of clearing away the wreckage and reconstituting the church.

After a succession of more than four priests in the 1950s, the parish was taken over by Philip Saliba. During eight years as pastor, Saliba built the 1964 educational and cultural center to the east of the main building. He left St. George to study at St. Vladimir's Orthodox Seminary in Yonkers, New York. Saliba emerged two years later with a master of divinity and the chair of the archbishop of New York, primate of the Antiochian Orthodox Church in North America. He has served as primate for more than forty years. Saliba was replaced as permanent pastor by Gibran Ramlaoui who became, beginning in 1969 and continuing for thirty years, Antiochian Orthodox bishop of Australia, New Zealand, and the Philippines. Elias Meena's oldest son, James Meena, a tank platoon leader with the Fourth Armored Division, was killed in France in 1944. He had graduated from the Cleveland Institute of Music and was studying for the priesthood when he was drafted. His younger brother took James's name when he was ordained in 1950 and served as pastor at St. George's from 1970 to 1984.

The reconstruction of this physically reduced church is enhanced by its meticulous maintenance and careful landscaping. Although steps, doors, windows, and the educational building are immaculate, the parish has elected not to remove the century-old effluvium of the steel mills from the masonry of the church, preferring the character of the darkened and weathered stone.

Whatever Badgley planned for the interior was destroyed by the fire. The main worship area is now approximately square. The square is divided into thirds with the anterior third occupied by a generous sanctuary, separated by an iconostasis from the two-thirds area of the nave. The walls on either side of the nave are covered by two large murals of *The Last Supper* and *The Resurrection,* illustrated with Latin, rather than Greek, imagery. Although this style may not agree completely with the twenty-first-century proclivities of the congregation, several paintings on the iconostasis are also more Latin than Greek. The iconostasis is articulated by large round pillars. The interior has a small balcony in the rear. The *Pantocrator* fills a small dome. Paintings of individual angels are on the walls. The nave is lit by an immense hand-cut crystal chandelier designed by Elias Meena. This building has the character of something reconstituted during the Great Depression by a thrifty, energetic, and highly motivated congregation that had seen a great architect's dreams go up in smoke and felt no reason to repeat the experience.

83. Our Lady of Mercy Church
(1948)
Architects: Stickle, Kelly and Stickle
Builder: John Krispinsky
Location: 2421 West 11th Street

Our Lady of Mercy represented, in miniature, the joys and sorrows of the Roman Catholic nationality church in Cleveland.[58] Our Lady of Mercy did not enjoy the operatic triumph and despair of the great Cleveland nationality congregations—St. Patrick's (see p. 189), St. Stephen (German; see p. 256), St. Stanislaus (Polish; see p. 172), St. Procop (Czech; see p. 238), St. Anthony (Italian; see p. 119), St. Vitus (Slovenian; p. 85), and St. Elizabeth's (Hungarian; see p. 142), to name just a few. The history of Our Lady of Mercy was the history of the nationality church writ small. It probably should not have been founded in the first place. Hints of solvency were rare and brief. This was a story of almost unending struggle, to pay the bills and to attract even a semblance of interest on the part of religious superiors. In 1922 Our Lady of Mercy School had 150 children in two classrooms. Despite its modesty, the school was an unremitting financial burden. It closed in 1973. Yet, whatever the merits of carrying the banner of Slovakia into Tremont, Our Lady of Mercy proved, for more than eighty years, to be the spiritual lodestone of a devoted community willing to sacrifice a great deal for its faith, and this drew—most of the time—devoted clergy to serve that community.

Bishop John Farrelly refused the little Slovak community of Tremont's 1915 petition to establish a parish. They petitioned because they believed it was too dangerous for their children to walk across three street-car lines and then the railroad tracks to reach St. Wendelin's school. It was, of course, out of the question for the children to walk across Lincoln Park to Irish St. Augustine's

School or a couple of blocks to the new brick school of Polish St. John Cantius. When the bishop refused to dismantle St. Wendelin Parish, the Slovaks bought a store and three houses on the east side of Lincoln Park anyway. They organized themselves as the parish of St. John the Baptist. Remodeling the store into a church and one house into a school, the community invited in the Polish National Catholic Church.[59] This did not work out as well as hoped and, in 1921, the community asked for reinstatement in the Roman Catholic Diocese of Cleveland. This was granted after a year's probation and a name change to Our Lady of Mercy. Under a succession of vigorous pastors, the community slowly prospered and was large enough to send 178 men off to World War II, seven of whom did not return. By 1948 the parish had put aside a third of the cost of a permanent church and construction began.

The church shares its Tennessee Crab Orchard stone exterior with the Cathedral of St. John the Evangelist (see p. 16) and St. Malachi (see p. 183), both of which were either built or reconstructed at about the same time. Trim is buff Indiana limestone. The church's semicircular entrance portal and corbel table in the large central gable are Romanesque in style. The fifty-six-foot octagonal bell tower with copper cupola is later Renaissance in style. Both styles work together to form a simple, well-proportioned structure. A bell, cast with the Slavic name "Stefan," is from the original church. The building, which looks like an English country church, is nicely scaled to its setting and can be enjoyed close up or from St. Augustine on the other side of Lincoln Park.

Large arches in the five-hundred-seat nave reach upward without pillars to support the ceiling. The Marian name of the church is reflected in windows that illustrate the life of the Virgin. The decorative character of the church is Slovak with appropriate color and designs painted onto the walls. Parishioners took pride in the ribbon effect of the painting, "like peasants in a dance."[60] On the front of the oak lectern is a large, unpainted, carved figure of St. John Vianney, patron of parish priests. Behind the altar is a striking Venetian glass mosaic of *Our Lady of Mercy* surrounded by her seven sorrows, said at its installation to be one of the largest mosaics in the United States. This is important to a Slovak congregation because the Sorrowful Mother is the patroness of Slovakia. The sanctuary is surrounded by a walnut parqueted wainscot. At the front of the church is an unusual screen behind the altar composed of walnut panels and pillars. There was to have been, behind the screen, a choir as in some Protestant churches. A large and colorful Slovak tester canopy hangs over the altar. To the left is a large enamel plaque/shrine to *Cyril and Methodius* and an unpainted oak *Infant of Prague*. To the right is a statue of *Joseph* with T-square and mitered workbench before a mural of the working life of the Slovak people.

On March 15, 2009, Bishop Richard Lennon announced the closing of Our Lady of Mercy. He celebrated the final Mass on May 9, 2010.

84. St. John Cantius Church (1925)
Architects: Potter and Gabele
Builder: Joseph Kocinski
Location: 906 College Avenue

St. John Kanty (Cantius)[61] stands on the "broad corners" of Professor and College Streets, in what was once intended to be a university neighborhood. Down the block is the Polish Veterans Alliance Inc.'s Gen. T. Kosciuszko Post 1. St. John Cantius is the central landmark in what was once the densely populated Polish section of Tremont.[62] The parish was organized in 1898 to accommodate the growing number of immigrant Polish Roman Catholic steel workers and their families settling in the area. Every parish has, somewhere in its history, an incident of mythical proportions. For St. John Cantius, this is the car barn. Father Hipolit Orlowski organized his poor immigrant congregation, at its present location, in a renovated car barn cleaned up for a temporary school church. Faded and poorly focused photographs of the car barn are now proudly displayed in obvious contrast to the splendid 1913 church and school and the magnificent 1925 present building. The rear of the refurbished barn was used as the school and as quarters for the clergy and for the Polish Sisters of St. Joseph of the Third Order of St. Francis—who took over the school in 1909 and labored subsequently "to serve Christ, His church, and Polonia."[63]

After fifteen years in the barn, the parish built a new combination church and school in 1913 with the church above and the school below. This imposing brick Victorian building, north of the present church, is itself a major landmark. A new parish house and convent quickly followed. In the early 1920s Father Joseph Kocinski began a fund drive with the intention of erecting a larger church. Designed by Potter and Gabele, the new building, seating one thousand, was completed in 1925. Kocinski, educated in Cleveland at St. Ignatius and St. Mary Seminary, had organized Polish St. Josaphat Parish on East 33rd Street between Superior Avenue and St. Clair Avenue and built the church there, now a gallery and performance space. From St. Josaphat he came and to St. Josaphat he eventually returned.[64] During his pastorate, a devout and quiet parishioner, Helen Pelczar, unbeknownst to most of the congregation, experienced stigmata from 1917 until her death in 1926.

Things settled down with the arrival of Marion Orzechowski, who had proven himself such a master at dealing with difficult Polish parishes that he had been promoted to domestic prelate while pastor of the sometime schismatic Immaculate Heart of Mary. Under his leadership, St. John became, by the late 1930s, the second-largest Polish parish in Cleveland. Orzechowski managed to shoehorn 1,800 Polish families into Tremont and serve them with six Masses every Sunday. Outside the church, things were not so orderly. Under the leadership of Robin Hood Joe Filkowski, Tremont had become one of the most spiritedly lawless neighborhoods in Cleveland.[65] The parish has written movingly and sensitively about its subsequent decline.[66]

This large, imposing yellow-brick and stone-trim church rises unexpectedly from a modest two-story frame residential-commercial neighborhood in eastern Tremont.[67] Trim is limited but is of high quality. The building's mass and detailing, its simple lines and modern ornamental buttresses are more contemporary than most of the churches in Tremont. Although the great modern south tower with its open belfry has become the most identifying characteristic of this building, the profile of the main entrance suggests that two towers may have originally been considered.[68]

The simple straightforward space of the interior is light, bright, and well maintained. The coffered barrel ceiling is gilded. The relative modernity of the building is emphasized by the over-life-size art deco angels with widespread wings and outstretched arms that emerge from pillars to line the arcade of the nave. Above the angels are medallions of Polish saints. A wonderful false clerestory arcade with little marble pillars in front of a blue field runs down either side of the nave. In 1992 the great high altar was salvaged from St. Joseph Franciscan Church and installed here but slightly reduced in size. The wall of the apse is brightly painted with Polish saints. The oak pews, unstained, have been recently restored. One finds a great deal of statuary. Wonderfully bright vernacular windows are unabashedly identified with the names of their Polish donors. It has only one statue of *John Cantius,* on the outside, and one window of him visible from the inside.

85. Saints Peter and Paul Ukrainian Catholic Church (1910)
Architect: Stephen Paliwoda
Builder: Wolodymyr Dowhowycz
Location: 2280 West Seventh Street

When the Ukrainians first settled in Cleveland at the end of the nineteenth century, they worshiped with the Ruthenians at St. John the Baptist, now buried by the Innerbelt.[69] As these communities moved up into Tremont, they divided. In 1902, twenty-six Ukrainian members of the Ruthenian National Association formed a separate Brotherhood of Saints Peter and Paul and petitioned the Ukrainian bishop in Philadelphia to organize a parish that would become the Ukrainian "Mother Parish" of Cleveland.[70] Seven years later the bishop came to Cleveland and celebrated the first Ukrainian liturgy in the hall of the German Association at Jefferson Avenue at West Tenth Street.[71] The group had been meeting in the St. John Cantius car barn (see p. 209). The following year the Ukrainians moved two blocks down the hill from St. John Cantius and built this brick church.

The parish grew quickly. In 1915 the Ruthenian Savings and Loan was established to promote home ownership among parishioners. An orphanage was established following the influenza epidemic of 1918. Under the leadership of Father Dmytro Gresko, the Ukrainian community, although never quite as large as the Ruthenian, greatly expanded, their numbers augmented by waves of political immigration after the First and Second World Wars. Gresko established an all-day parish school at Saints Peter and Paul in 1947 and a new convent in 1953. The *Ridna Shkola* (Native School), described as "one of the largest and best organized nationality schools" in Cleveland,[72] was organized at Saints Peter and Paul in 1950 to teach children the Ukrainian language and Ukrainian history and culture. Two years later the *Ridna Shkola* moved to Merrick House and then on to Parma in 1959.[73]

In 1956 Gresko completely renovated the interior and exterior of Saints Peter and Paul. He took down the onion dome and replaced it with a bell tower. Extensive changes were also made in 1978 when the stained-glass windows commemorating the millennium of Ukrainian Christianity were added. For the Ukrainians, Saints Peter and Paul Ukrainian Catholic Church played a role parallel to the Ruthenians' Holy Ghost Byzantine Catholic Church (see p. 198). Saints Peter and Paul was the center of Ukrainian Catholic Cleveland until the community largely moved out to Parma in the 1960s.[74] As the Ukrainians moved out of central Cleveland, Gresko established three additional Ukrainian parishes—St. Mary on Kinsman (which moved to Solon), St. Andrew, and St. Josaphat (which became the cathedral, see p. 308) in Parma.

From 1949 until 1968 Myroslav Ivan Cardinal Lubachivsky, a scholar in exile, served here. He subsequently returned to teaching in Washington, D.C., Philadelphia, and Stamford, Connecticut before being elevated to the American Ukrainian Catholic primacy as bishop of the Archeparchy of Philadelphia in 1979. John Paul II appointed Lubachivsky to succeed the Ukrainian Catholic primate in 1979, and he returned to his country in this capacity after the Soviets lifted the ban against the Church in 1989.

Saints Peter and Paul sits on the side of a quite substantial hill that runs north and south parallel to and overlooking West Seventh.[75] This is a neighborhood that is—unusual for Cleveland—transitional in the best sense of the word. Things are getting better. The east side of West Seventh is now occupied by new residential construction. On the Saints Peter and Paul west side of West Seventh, the push and pull of a residential renaissance appears—lots of fresh, mixed with lots of peeling, paint. This church is a substantial, yellow-brick building with spare stone trim. The building has a good deal of Romanesque (as distinguished from Byzantine) decoration—building and tower buttresses, semicircular arches over window and door openings, a parapet screen located above the roofline in the gable, and a front rose window.

Saints Peter and Paul's commanding position on the hill overlooking West Seventh makes the building, from the outside, appear larger than it really is. The interior space is open, without columns, under a barrel roof. The nave is modest but immaculate: bright and freshly painted. The church is decorated in a mixed style derived from the 1956 renovation. Gresko liked Roman ("academic") decoration as much on the inside as on the outside. This is now being replaced by iconography of a more Byzantine style by the Ukrainian painter Christine Hasigan. She has painted a wonderful chapel on the right dedicated to Peter and Paul. The ceiling has limited iconography, but a large image of the *Virgin* shines from behind the iconostasis. Figurative painting is supplemented with beautiful stenciling. Paintings specifically designed for the screen decorate an all-of-one-piece iconostasis. The central royal door of the iconostasis consists of a sculpted, gilded *Tree of Jesse*. Side balconies are narrow, but the rear balcony for organ and choir is large. Glass is simple.

86. St. Theodosius Orthodox Cathedral (1911)
Architect: Frederick Baird
Builder: Vasili Lisenkovsky
Location: 733 Starkweather Avenue

"But you must visit St. Theodosius," the priest said. "It is the mother church of Orthodoxy in Cleveland."[76] St. Theodosius is a Cleveland institution larger than life in several ways, including the physical prominence of its location (it looks down at the remnants of Cleveland's twentieth-century economic power from the heights of Tremont across Interstate 490), its history as the oldest Orthodox institution in northern Ohio, the stature of its towering priests who seem physically larger than life, the lavishness and peculiarity of its decoration with its mid-twentieth-century "neo-Byzantine" iconography and its great *iconostasis*—perhaps a gift of the Czar, the oddness of its architecture—an American architect's Anglo-Saxon translation of the Church of Our Saviour in Moscow, and, last, its place in the cultural soul of Cleveland as the site of the 1978 Academy Award–winning film, *The Deer Hunter*, America's Vietnam War version of *All Quiet on the Western Front*.[77]

Although always associated with the Russian Orthodox Church, St. Theodosius has never been a strictly Russian institution. This is not a congregation that began, like the typical Cleveland ethnic religious community, as a relatively homogeneous national group. St. Theodosius developed in its heterogeneous way for two reasons.

In the first place, there have never been many Christian Great Russians in Cleveland. Most Great Russians came to Cleveland in one of three groups. The first consisted of radicals fleeing the czar before the revolution, of whom there were never many. The second consisted of highly educated or skilled refugees from the Communists who rapidly assimilated into the general population. The third consisted of Jewish refugees who arrived beginning in the 1970s.

Second, St. Theodosius has always been associated with Orthodoxy in its greater sense, rather than its Russian sense. The Orthodox Church of America, of which St. Theodosius is a member,[78] was established on Kodiak Island, Alaska, in 1794. The first Orthodox church in the continental United States was established in New Orleans in 1864. In the heterodox way that St. Theodosius would develop in Cleveland, this New Orleans church was founded by Greeks with a large admixture of Slavs and Arabs (and not many Russians). Following the 1867 Russian sale of Alaska to the United States, the Russian Diocese of Kamchatka, the Kurile and Aleutian Islands, was divided, and the American part became a separate diocese in 1870. The bishop moved to San Francisco in 1872 and to New York in 1905. Although division into its ethnic parts, of what, by then, had become known as the *Metropolia,* had been proposed by Archbishop Tikhon (Vasily Ivanovich Bellavin) before the First World War, this only occurred after the revolution—the Ukrainian Greek Orthodox Church in Canada (1918), the Greek Orthodox Archdiocese of America (1922), and the Serbian Orthodox Church (1926). The *Metropolia* itself, as a result of the Revolution, became independent of the Russian Orthodox Church in 1920.

It is in the Orthodox community of the *Metropolia*—multiethnic, multinational, but always associated with the Russian Orthodox Church—that the founding of St. Theodosius is best understood. Its founding in Cleveland was farther complicated by the struggle of Orthodox Eastern Catholics to find a home in either the Roman Catholic Diocese of Cleveland[79] or one of the national Orthodox congregations.[80] In the mid-1890s a variety of eastern Europeans, Lemkos (non-Ukrainian Galician Rusyns), and Hungarian Rusyns, began meeting. Attended by Russian priests dispatched by the bishop at increasingly regular intervals, these Rusyns (not Russians) formed a Society of St. Nicholas as a prelude to a parish. In 1886, in the course of a visit, the bishop ordained a member of the group a deacon and two days later a priest. The archbishop insisted the new parish be named for the recently canonized St. Theodosius rather than St. Nicholas.[81] During construction of their first frame church, on the corner of Literary Road at West Sixth Street, the site had to be guarded at night to prevent Orthodox middle Europeans attached to the Roman Catholic Diocese from breaking the windows and stealing the lumber. In 1902 the first pastor of St. Theodosius was replaced by Jason Kappanadze, a towering Georgian priest who initially served in Alaska and then in Pennsylvania. When Kappanadze arrived in Cleveland, he is reportedly to have been surprised to find no Russians in his initial congregation of about fifteen families.[82] Almost immediately after arriving, Kappanadze arranged for the purchase of the thirty-acre enclosed Convent of St. Joseph. Although the nuns had moved out because there was not enough room for them,[83] the "huge" stone convent provided more than ample space for the church of St. Theodosius, Kappanadze and his family, a school, a social hall, and temporary housing for new immigrants.[84] Kappanadze put two streets through his purchase and subdivided the property among thirty families for homes and gardens before he returned to Georgia in 1908.[85] Parishioners' payments for their lots would finance the new church.

In 1910 Father Basil Lisenkovsky began planning the present cathedral. Frederick Baird designed the building using photographs of the Church of Our Saviour acquired by Lisenkovsky. Jason Kappanadze returned as pastor from 1922 to 1957.[86] The year after his retirement, a service was introduced on Sunday in English. Today all services are in English and, in preparation for St. Theodosius's one hundredth anniversary in 1996, the Slavonic inscriptions on the walls of the church were replaced with English. Kappanadze's son, Jason Jr., would become pastor in 1988.

In the early 1950s the interior of the church was frescoed by the Russian expatriate painter Andrej Bicenko. Bicenko, exiled from Russia after the Revolution and then from Yugoslavia after the Second World War, is best known for his religious painting in Serbia from 1924 to 1941. He decorated St. Theodosius in a personal style he called "neo-Byzantine" that combined Byzantine postures and clothing with Latin anatomy and perspective.

The great central onion dome representing Jesus, and the twelve surrounding smaller cupolas symbolizing the apostles, occupy the commanding heights of Tremont to the immediate north of motorists driving west on I-490 through the Cuyahoga Valley. At the top of the hill, the Tremont neighborhood around St. Theodosius has been greatly rehabilitated over the last decade. Across Starkweather stand bright new homes. Along Starkweather, beside the cathedral, renovated shops are opening.

The basic plan of the cathedral is a Greek cross with shallow transepts. The chancel extends farther toward the south but is screened by the czar's large, perhaps legendary, iconostasis from Kiev. The space behind is private and cannot be seen well through the iconostasis or through the holy doors when they are closed. What little can be seen hints at generous painting in the sanctuary. The iconostasis is decorated with large Latinate paintings. The Greek cross plan is extended to the rear for the balcony and narthex. The central space, within the arms of the Greek cross, is a cube whose arches and pendentives support a flat ceiling. This ceiling is pierced by a relatively small cylindrical interior tower that reaches up to a relatively small dome from which the *Pantocrator* looks down. This interior cylindrical tower and dome are independent of the large central exterior onion dome except that the cylinder is illuminated from the outside by windows in the drum. A tremendous crystal chandelier is suspended from a chain coming down from the dome. The public worship space is defined by pilasters capped by magnificent gilded capitals. Pews were installed after the Second World War and in 2000 were rearranged and opened up to promote the circulation of worshipers. At that time seating was decreased by half and the pews refinished in a light stain. One finds now a wide center aisle and generous side aisles with traditional seating in benches attached and parallel to the side walls. All of the walls are painted with Bicenko's neo-Byzantine iconography. Brightly colored symbolic glass lines the second story. Saints are illustrated in the glass of the first story. Floors are marble and the chancel is elevated three steps. There are several inscriptions on the walls, all in English.

CHAPTER EIGHT

The West Side South

West Side South is composed of three neighborhoods—Old Brooklyn, Arch-wood-Denison, and Fulton-Clark.

Old Brooklyn was incorporated as the Village of Brighton in 1838, and, until the twentieth century, it was an important market for the surrounding agricultural community. In 1905 the area was annexed by the City of Cleveland.

Tour

Begin the tour of this neighborhood at the intersection of Broadview and Brookpark Roads. Travel north on Broadview. Immediately after crossing the bridge over I-480, look to the left at the sweeping roof of the Church of St. Leo the Great located opposite Broadview Gardens, a community of modest, well-maintained apartments. Continue north on Broadview. At the intersection of Broadview with Alvin Avenue, St. James Lutheran Church occupies the southeast corner. Turn right (east) onto Alvin for one short block. At the first intersection, turn left (north) onto South Hills Drive. Continue on South Hills Drive until it intersects with West Schaaf Road. On the southwest corner of this intersection is the Brooklyn Heights United Church of Christ.

Turn left (northwest) onto Schaaf. Schaaf intersects with Broadview. Turn right onto Broadview and continue north on Broadview to Saratoga Avenue. Turn left (west) and travel on Saratoga to State Road. At State turn left (south). On the crest of the hill, on State Road at Biddulph Avenue, opposite the Brooklyn Cemetery, is St. Mary Byzantine Catholic Parish (87), with its large central window over the doors. Continue south on State for two blocks and then turn right (west) onto Germaine Avenue. Travel on Germaine for two blocks and then turn left (south) onto West 45th Street. Drive on West 45th to Archmere Avenue and turn right (west). Continue west on Archmere for one block to Pearl Road. On the southeastern corner of this intersection is the Korean American Presbyterian Church of Cleveland. Corpus Christi Parish is located directly west, across Pearl. In 2010, Corpus Christi merged with Mary Queen of Peace, formerly Our Lady of Good Counsel (see p. 222), one mile northeast on Pearl Road.

Turn right (northeast) onto Pearl and continue on it past the Lutheran Cemetery on the left. Directly north of this cemetery is Unity Lutheran Church. Farther northeast on Pearl, and again on the left, is St. Mark Lutheran Church. Continue on Pearl. Opposite its intersection with Spokane Avenue stands Mary Queen of Peace (88) on the right. Continue northeast on Pearl. On the other side of its intersection with Memphis Avenue is St. Luke's United Church of Christ (89). Just beyond St. Luke's, also to the west, is the Pearl Road United Methodist Church. It is a large church, but the part facing Pearl Road across a lawn north of St. Luke's is small. Continue on Pearl.

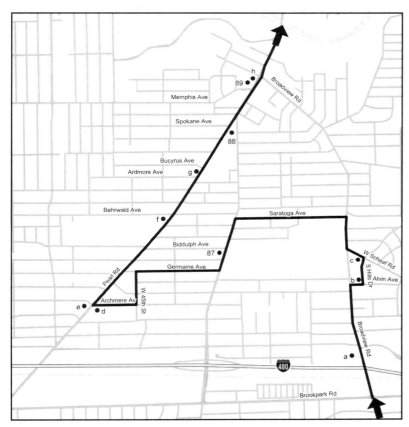

OLD BROOKLYN

a. Church of St. Leo the Great
b. St. James Lutheran Church
c. Brooklyn Heights United Church of Christ
87. St. Mary Byzantine Catholic Parish
d. Korean American Presbyterian Church of Cleveland

e. Corpus Christi Church
f. Unity Lutheran Church
g. St. Mark Lutheran Church
88. Mary Queen of Peace
89. St. Luke's United Church of Christ
h. Pearl Road United Methodist Church

Cross the large bridge over Big Creek (where the zoo is) to enter Archwood-Denison. Continue north on Pearl to its intersection with Denison Avenue. Turn right (east) onto Denison and drive to its intersection with West 15th Street. St. Barbara's Church is located on the south side of Denison, on the rim above the Cuyahoga Valley. Backtrack west on Denison through its busy intersection with Pearl. At West 33rd Street is the Rivers of Living Waters Apostolic Church, formerly St. Philip the Apostle Episcopal Church and the Episcopal Church's St. Agnes Mission for the Deaf. Turn right (north) onto West 33rd Street. After one block turn right again (east) onto Archwood Avenue and enter the Archwood historic district.

Driving east on Archwood, to the left (north) is the neo-Georgian Archwood United Church of Christ (90). Almost opposite, on the right, but a little farther east, is the newly closed Brooklyn Memorial United Methodist Church (91) with its high lantern. At the end of Archwood Avenue is the neighborhood's new fire station.

Turn left (north) onto Pearl. At the corner of Mapledale Avenue at Pearl is the small Bethlehem Temple of Praise Church, formerly the Third Church of Christ, Scientist, with its Greek Revival portico. On the other (right) side of Pearl is Riverside Cemetery, planned by landscape architect E. O. Schwagerl in 1875. Riverside attracts visitors because of its fine, recently renovated gatehouse, its view of the Cuyahoga Valley, and its Victorian chapel. Although it is now hemmed in by the construction of new expressways and its lakes have been drained, the cemetery is an interesting place to visit because of its scenic beauty and because it is the burial place of the old West Side aristocracy, including the Brainards, the Lamsons, the Sessions, and the Rhodeses. It is also reported to be the burial site of Chief Blackhawk's mother.[1] After visiting the cemetery, continue driving north on Pearl Road, crossing over Interstate 71.

Entering the Fulton-Clark neighborhood, jog right at the intersection of West 25th Street at Scranton Road, just north of the Pearl Road bridge over Interstate 71. Travel north on Scranton. The church on the left, directly opposite the Jones Home on West 25th, was formerly Trinity United Church of Christ. It is now rented to the Iglesia Emmanuel (92). Beside it is the Mother of God of Zyrovicy Church with its raised central entrance framed by two huge blue spruce trees. After driving through the ever-expanding Metro-General Hospital, one can see the Iglesia de Cristo Misionora Sinai on the left. Located at the intersection of Meyer Avenue at Scranton, Iglesia Sinai was built in 1900 as the St. Matthew German Evangelical Lutheran Church.

Continue north on Scranton. The buff-colored stone of St. Michael's School, on the left, has darkened with age so that it now matches the exterior of the church (93) that so dominates the southwest corner of Scranton Road at Clark Avenue. On the north side of the Clark Avenue intersection, a gateway is formed by the Scranton Road Baptist Church on the right and the South Branch of the Cleveland Public Library on the left. Traveling through this gateway note the Immanuel Evangelical Lutheran Church (94) on the southwest corner of Seymour Avenue at Scranton. Turn left (west) onto Seymour and continue to Fulton Road.

At Fulton, turn left (south) and continue through the busy intersection of Clark at Fulton. St. Rocco's Church (95) is farther south of this intersection, on the left. Continuing south on Fulton, the former Church of the Blessed Sacrament lies to the left at Sackett Avenue. Blessed Sacrament is now an inner-city mission of suburban Bay Village's Bay Presbyterian Church (see p. 292). Staying on Fulton, the Faith United Methodist Church, built in 1909 as the Evangelical Tabor Church, can be seen on the right side of West 41st Street between Daisy and Bush Avenues. Continue south on Fulton.

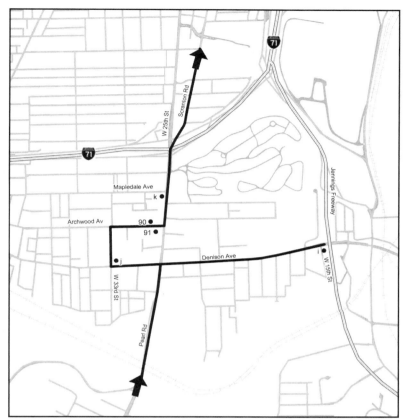

ARCHWOOD–DENISON

   i. St. Barbara's Church
   j. Rivers of Living Waters Apostolic Church
90. Archwood United Church of Christ
91. Brooklyn Memorial United Methodist Church
   k. Bethlehem Temple of Praise Church

After crossing the bridge over I-71, turn right (west) onto Denison. After five blocks, turn right onto West 54th Street. At the corner is the campus of St. Boniface Church. The church is located behind the school in a peaceful setting. Drive north on West 54th Street to Storer Avenue. Turn right onto Storer and continue to West 41st Street. On the southwestern corner of the Storer-West 41st intersection stands Bethany United Church of Christ. Turn left (north) onto the one-way West 41st Street. One block north, at Sackett Avenue, turn left (west). At West 43rd Street, turn right (north). Two blocks north, at the intersection of West 43rd at Robert Avenue is the large impressive Christ Lutheran Church, a Gothic Revival building typical of neighborhood churches built around 1900.

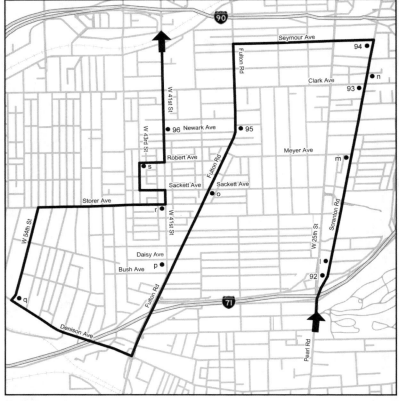

FULTON–CLARK

92. Iglesia Emmanuel
  l. Mother of God of Zyrovicy Church
  m. Iglesia de Cristo Misionora Sinai
93. St. Michael Church
  n. Scranton Road Baptist Church
94. Immanuel Evangelical Lutheran Church

95. St. Rocco's Church
  o. Church of the Blessed Sacrament
  p. Faith United Methodist Church
  q. St. Boniface Church
  r. Bethany United Church of Christ
  s. Christ Lutheran Church
96. St. Procop Church

Turn right (east) onto Robert. Travel back to West 41st Street and turn left. At the intersection of Newark Avenue and West 41st is St. Procop Church (96). Continue north to the intersection of West 41st at Clark. On the northeast corner of this intersection lies St. Mary's Cemetery. A few blocks north of the cemetery is an intersection with I-90. This ends the tour of the West Side South neighborhood. To get to the next tour, take I-90 west to the West 117th Street exit, turn left (south), and then left again (east) onto Lorain Avenue.

87. St. Mary Byzantine Catholic Parish (1949)

Architect: Unknown
Builders: Daniel Ivancho and Nicholas Elko
Location: 4600 State Road

St. Mary Byzantine Catholic Parish was built, in succession, by two unusually dynamic priests whose exciting lives, sometimes more exciting than anyone intended, characterized major issues within the Eastern Catholic churches in the United States.[2] The parish was actually founded by two other priests, Edmund Tabakovich and Stephen Petrick, just before the Second World War. They were soon replaced by Daniel Ivancho. Ivancho purchased the present site, built a rectory, and began planning and raising money for the current building. This was delayed by the war. Ivancho was unexpectedly called from the parish by the Vatican in 1946 (he had not been considered to be a leading candidate) to become bishop of the Greek Catholic Exarchate of Pittsburgh, the American primate. Bishop Ivancho subsequently resigned over issues having to do with married clergy, a historic controversy between the celibate Roman Catholic clergy and the Eastern Catholic clergy who, in eastern Europe, are generally married. Meanwhile, back at St. Mary in Cleveland, Ivancho was succeeded as pastor by Nicholas Elko. Elko raised the rest of the money, built this church, and dedicated it in 1950. In 1952 Ivancho called Elko to Pittsburgh to be rector of the new seminary, and then, rector of the cathedral in 1954. Succeeding Ivancho in 1955, Elko would build more than a hundred Byzantine Catholic churches in the United States but became entangled in controversies involving Latinization of these Eastern Catholic churches. Elko ended his career as an auxiliary bishop of the Roman Catholic Archdiocese of Cincinnati.

St. Mary, flanked by its ambitious schools and community center, is a much larger institution than it appears from State Road. It must be seen from Biddulph Avenue, which runs beside it on the north, to appreciate its size. The two large tall towers on either side of the entrance give this plain-finished masonry building, largely undecorated from the outside, a verticality that suggests a narrowness that is inaccurate and deceiving. The towers have honeycombed copper cupolas and are topped with the three-bar Byzantine cross. Between the towers rises a large, distinctive, two-story arch. The stone gives the building a much warmer appearance in life than it has in black-and-white photographs. The building is not entirely without decoration. Around and above the entrance are its famous, raised, painted, narrative stucco reliefs. Nonetheless, the even masonry courses, the almost overbearing height, and the severity of the finish and design give St. Mary, like the Escorial, a somewhat formidable exterior appearance.

On either side of the narthex are two small chapels with icons and candles but without chairs. Like many Eastern churches, a marked contrast exists between what is seen outside and what is inside. Inside, the bright and cheerful, colorful, naturalistic, figured glass creates an atmosphere of warmth and welcome. Columns with elaborate gilded capitals along the side aisles support the wide but shallow central barrel vault. The columns also support the vaulted lateral aisle ceilings (with the central aisle, there are four rows of pews). Transepts are shallow. All seating faces the front. Above the entrance, a small rear balcony for cantor and musicians hangs underneath a great window of the *Virgin and Child*. Walls along the nave are plain with limited stenciling. There is no iconostasis; four large icons, each an independently mounted painting, separate the sanctuary from the public worship space. The altar is elevated five marble steps above the level of the chancel. Over it hangs a generous hemispherical baldachin supported by four marble columns. The impression is somewhat Roman. The altar stands in front of an elaborate menorahlike candelabra. A great and wonderful iconography of *The Virgin and Child with Angels* is in the apse behind the altar. The arch over the apse is stenciled. The niches behind the side altars are a beautiful blue. To the right of the altar is an icon of *The Dormition* and to the left is an icon of *The Resurrection*.

88. Mary Queen of Peace, originally
Our Lady of Good Counsel (1930)
Architects: Henry A. Walsh and Erwin
O. Lauffer
Builders: Luke Rath and Sebastian
Kremer
Location: 4423 Pearl Road

For such an imposing and comprehensive twentieth-century institution, Our Lady of Good Counsel's nineteenth-century beginnings were surprisingly modest and uncertain.[3] From its commanding presence overlooking Old Brooklyn, Our Lady of Good Counsel—OLGC to its intimates—would become a mighty parish with giant church, giant school, giant convent, giant rectory, and giant parish center. As a measure of its size, by 1973 it had produced forty-six vocations to the priesthood and sixty-eight of its young women had become nuns; eight of its parishioners served and died in World War I, forty-one in World War II, one in Korea, and four in Vietnam. In the twentieth century, OLGC embraced almost every conceivable parish organization and activity down to the gas station it owned and leased to the Shell Oil Company in 1934, realizing 1.5 cents on each gallon sold. All this from uncertain beginnings.

During most of the nineteenth century, Old Brooklyn, then the village of Brighton, was isolated from Cleveland by Big Creek Valley, where the zoo now is. Brighton was an area of gardens feeding Cleveland, and, by the 1920s it was one of the nation's leading producers of greenhouse vegetables with more than one hundred acres under glass. For reasons unknown, considering what happened later, this was not an area hospitable for developing a Roman Catholic parish. In 1873 a small congregation, originally calling itself the Sacred Heart of Mary, began meeting monthly in the shavings and straw of a cooper shop. Within a year the parish began a substantial brick building that was dedicated in 1875. Things did not go well. For months at a time services were not held. Mass, at best, was said every other Sunday and on holy days. Priests, discouraged by poor attendance, left. At last, in 1890, a Jesuit appeared and "infused . . . life into a mission which had almost ceased to exist."[4] By 1891 there was a school building, and by 1894 there was a resident pastor. Then in 1907 an altar boy hung his cassock on a hook over an incense censer that still contained burning charcoal; during the ensuing conflagration, the cross on the steeple fell into the front yard in flames. The bishop turned to the Society of the Precious Blood, based in southern Ohio. The brothers, financed in part by their order, moved the parish to its present location. The society's first pastor changed the name of the parish from Sacred Heart of Mary to Our Lady of Good Counsel and, among his other projects, began construction of a permanent church. His successor completed the current building in 1930. The Sisters of the Precious Blood staffed the school.

A mile southwest down Pearl Road, Corpus Christi parish was established in 1935 by Poles. They had originally settled in Tremont as part of St. John Cantius (see p. 209) before moving to south Brooklyn. For some time the Sisters of the Third Order of St. Francis had been teaching Polish at Our Lady of Good Counsel. Corpus Christi met in the Pearl Road Recreation Center before dedicating its first church in 1937. A new church and school were dedicated in 1954. The school closed in 2006.

This large church, now Mary Queen of Peace, and the large buildings associated with it occupy an enviable location. On the crest of the hill on Pearl Road, at the southern edge of the center of Old Brooklyn, Mary Queen of Peace dominates its neighborhood with its size and height. Flights of elaborate formal steps leading up from the street to the massive portico only emphasize the size of this building. This was one of the last buildings in Cleveland to be built in the classical tradition.[5] This style was popular between Chicago's Columbian Exposition in 1893 and the rise of modernism in the 1930s. During this period architects, especially those trained in the tradition of the École des Beaux Arts in Paris, borrowed from classical styles of all types. It was, thus, not unusual to see here a Roman temple portico in front of an Italian Renaissance facade attached to a Georgian building that was placed on a modern base adjacent to a 140-foot copy of an early sixteenth-century Florentine bell tower. Armstrong, however, was right when he said that these seemingly disparate elements seem to come together comfortably. In front of the smooth-cut, three-story stone entrance portico, four monumental Indiana limestone columns with composite capitals support an imposing triangular pediment with its several-feet-high carved announcement of "Our Lady of Good Counsel." The plain and light stone frieze, dentilated cornice, stone cupola of the tower, and its short copper spire contrast well with the dark brick of the main structure.

The interior is a gigantic 168-feet-by-69-feet open space unimpeded by columns—a dramatic example of what architectural engineers were capable of in the first half of the twentieth century. The size of the nave is amplified by the unusually high, flat ceiling. It has a wonderful tile and wood floor. The left altar features a large painting of *St. Gaspar del Bufalo,* founder of the Society of the Precious Blood, with the Virgin and Child in front of a view of Cleveland complete with Terminal Tower, smoke stacks and, of course, Our Lady of Good Counsel Church. On the right, the altar of Joseph, patron of workers, has a painting of *Leo XIII,* author of *Rerum Novarum,* the papal encyclical that first dealt with labor relations. The pope is seen overlooking St. Peter's Square. In the nave are fifteen excellent windows of the seven joys and sorrows of the Virgin plus her marriage. Between the windows are framed icons of modern saints relevant to the United States or the New World. The church has a large *Last Judgment* painted across the width of its west wall. This parish has an electric organ. Father Moreeuw, the former pastor, said he liked organ music, and the quite large speakers in the balcony look like they are capable, even in this large space, of blowing the socks off the congregation.

After serving this parish for more than one hundred years, the Missionaries of the Precious Blood withdrew from Our Lady of Good Counsel in 2010. On April 25, 2010, Bishop Richard Lennon celebrated a Mass opening the new parish of Mary Queen of Peace. This merger of Our Lady of Good Counsel and Corpus Christi Parish will be served by diocesan clergy.

89. St. Luke's United Church of Christ (1903)
Architect: Herman Stuhr
Builder: Otto Rusch
Location: 4216 Pearl Road

St. Luke's United Church of Christ was organized by forty German families in 1839 as the German United Evangelical Protestant Church of Parma.[6] The German Evangelical Synod of North America evolved in the middle of the nineteenth century among German Protestant congregations of mixed Lutheran and Reformed heritage in the midwestern United States. The denomination reflected the 1817 union of these traditions in Prussia. In keeping with this background, these evangelicals were joiners, with strong ecumenical interests. This led to their merger with the German Reformed Church into the Evangelical and Reformed Church in 1934 and subsequent merger with the Congregational Christian Church in 1957 into the United Church of Christ (UCC).

The thrifty Germans purchased a schoolhouse in 1841 for twenty dollars and moved it to a farm at the corner of Broadview at Schaaf Roads.[7] Furnishings cost another sixty dollars. In 1853 the majority of the congregation wanted to move down the hill into Brighton (Brooklyn), and they did, leaving the minority behind. This majority built a new frame church on the lot of the present church. In the next twelve years, they tried out nine pastors and eventually got a pastor to stay for eleven years. Two more pastors later, Otto Rusch arrived. He served for forty-one years and built the present church. On his retirement, Rusch was replaced by F. H. Mittendorf, superintendent of the Evangelical Deaconess Hospital across the street.[8] Mittendorf built the educational building onto the north of the church in 1925. German language services survived the First World War but were largely discontinued in 1935. St. Luke's school served as the first home of the Old Brooklyn Montessori School from 1998 to 2002.

Despite the retirement of Deaconess Hospital, the church faces an exceptionally busy intersection. The squared-off tower topped by a crenelated parapet, the corner and side buttresses, and the wide central gable are Romanesque. Pointed arches above window and door openings are Gothic. The adjacent school, built of similar brick, also has pointed arches in its main window. The two symmetrical entrances to the church, under square lateral twin towers, flank three windows. These windows illuminate the back of the nave that is recessed back against the street wall. The entrances embracing this recessed nave both rise up from the street on stairways inside the building. The church does not have a narthex.

The current pastor, Jerry Madasz, points out that the Evangelical ecumenical impulse does not extend to a compulsion to worship in a Congregational Wren-Gibbs New England colonial-style, white frame meetinghouse. Evangelical churches, he says, maintain a distinctly "eastern European (German) flavor." There is an absence of Congregational white paint and a predominance of German stained wood. St. Luke has a traditional church feeling in addition to having (in the Evangelical and Reformed tradition) the pulpit on the left and the lectern on the right—in contrast to a Congregational right-handed pulpit and left-handed lectern. The sanctuary is an open square space with two aisles. Powerful wood arches support great wooden rafters. One finds an ample balcony for the migratory choir. The sanctuary is separated from the parish hall in the educational "annex" by three large sliding panels. Beautifully maintained, carefully stained, and functional, they suggest what Akron Plan movable walls might have looked like in a time when they were more attentively cared for than is now usually the case. Since the sanctuary floor slants down from the back of the nave to the chancel, each sliding panel is progressively larger as they march down to the front. The glass, of which the congregation is particularly proud, is beautifully patterned, late nineteenth-century opalescent and illuminated from the inside at night. The beautifully stained pews are in the ecumenical German tradition of fine woodwork.

90. Archwood United Church of Christ (1929)
Architect: Daniel Farnham
Builder: Lawrie Sharp
Location: 2800 Archwood Avenue

Despite its mid-twentieth-century appearance, Archwood United Church of Christ is one of the oldest churches in Cleveland.[9] Archwood was established in 1819 in a log cabin shared with the Methodists.[10] Archwood might have preceded the Old Stone Church, established in 1819 or 1820. In any case, Archwood called its first permanent pastor in 1834, the same year that Samuel Aiken became the first permanent pastor of the Old Stone Church. In the meantime, the community had erected a frame church at the corner of West 25th Street at Willowdale Avenue, a block northeast of their present location. In 1831 the Presbyterians, who had founded this Plan of Union congregation, decided they were really Congregationalists, and Archwood became the First Congregational Church of Brooklyn.[11] "In the 1840s the church was dormant for a period, partly due to disease" and partly due to theological differences.[12] By 1851 the community was sufficiently restored to move their building six blocks to a lot on the corner of West 33rd Street at Dennison Avenue. Six years later they crowned their efforts with a steeple. By 1879 they were able to purchase their present lot and put up a Gothic Revival brick building and a frame parsonage. A gym and Sunday school annex were added in 1914. As membership grew to more than a thousand, the present sanctuary was begun in 1923 and completed in 1929. In 1967, ten years after the mergers that created the UCC, Archwood itself merged with the Fourth Evangelical and Reformed Church that had been on the corner of West 32nd Street at Woodbridge Avenue, across the street from MetroHealth Medical Center, eight blocks north across I-71. Fourth Evangelical and Reformed had been established in 1869 as a mission of the First German Reformed Church then on the corner of West 32nd Street at Carroll Avenue, across the street from St. Ignatius High School.

Archwood rises abruptly out of a mixed neighborhood of two-story apartment complexes interspersed with the elegant porches of crisply repainted late nineteenth-century frame homes. The church towers over a neighborhood it shares with the gigantic Brooklyn Memorial United Methodist Church diagonally across the street. A half-block east on Archwood is the busy commercial area along West 25th with its large and modern Cleveland fire station. This is not an affluent neighborhood, but neither is it decrepit.

The large Georgian Revival building and its equally large, three-story educational-administrative addition are sited on a relatively small lot. This increases the impression of a building that overpowers its surroundings. The building was built of beautiful varicolored brick with white frame portico, pediment, and louvered bell tower. The pillars are thin in proportion to the height of the portico but could not have been built wider without blocking the three doors into the building. It has a graceful copper spire.

The bright, white 250-seat sanctuary is surprisingly small in plan, compressed by an ample narthex that has spare but well-executed plasterwork. What the main worship space lacks in the size of its plan is more than made up for in its elevation. The plain, flat, painted ceiling towers above the congregation. It rises above two-story plain translucent windows that are trimmed by giant-order, extremely elegant, grooved, ivory pilasters. The seating area appears small—compared with the bulk of the exterior of the building—but the space, because of its high ceiling, appears as a large, open rectangle. A relatively small balcony at the back does not wrap around the nave in the usual Wren-Gibbs configuration. The organ occupies the elevated choir behind the chancel. There is a low tulip pulpit on the left without a sounding board and a simple movable lectern on the right. On either side of the center aisle, the ends of the stained-wood pews are painted white. There are six large hurricane-lamp chandeliers with a small seventh above the choir. Over the baptismal font is a graceful broken pediment.

91. Brooklyn Memorial United Methodist Church
(1911)
Architect: Ray Fulton
Builder: Edward Warner and Arthur Smith[13]
Location: 2607 Archwood Avenue

The oldest Methodist congregation in Cleveland was around for a long time.[14] It was the only Cleveland religious community eventually in its fifth building. Forming a class in 1814, the church was formally established in 1818 in a 16-by-24-foot log cabin near the corner of Denison Avenue at West 25th Street. On Sundays the Methodists shared their primitive church with the Presbyterian-Congregationalists.[15] Weekdays the building doubled as the town hall. The church was remembered for its long wood benches, sawdust floor, table and chair serving as pulpit and lectern, and, of course, separate entrances and seating for men and women. The Methodists became the sole owners of the multitasking cabin and replaced it with a small frame building in 1827.[16] Twenty-two years later, in 1849, they replaced their second simple church with a handsome two-story frame building. It had a large bell in a sturdy, open belfry topped by a no-nonsense, little shingled roof of its own. The congregation continued to believe that Methodist women needed to be separated from Methodist men.

The third church was subsequently moved to a lot on Archwood Avenue adjacent to Pearl Road. (At its intersection with Archwood, West 25th becomes Pearl.) In 1881 the community moved into a substantial neo-Medieval brick church on the corner of Archwood at Pearl, just east of the present building. This fourth building, demolished in 1992, was somewhat similar to the building the Immanuel Evangelical Lutherans had built twenty blocks up Scranton two years before (see p. 234). When Brooklyn Village was annexed by the City of Cleveland in 1896, the community could no longer, according to the tenants of the Methodist Church, call itself the Brooklyn Methodist Episcopal Church since there was no longer any Brooklyn. Things were set to rights by renaming the institution "Brooklyn Memorial." In the first decade of the twentieth century, a new lot on Archwood—west of the fourth church—was finally purchased and the present sanctuary dedicated in 1914.

Many suburban religious communities sponsor evening Alcoholic Anonymous meetings to accommodate their working neighbors. Brooklyn Memorial sponsored a large morning meeting. It is that kind of neighborhood. Across the street from Archwood UCC and just down the corner from the splendid new Cleveland fire station on the east side of the Archwood-Pearl intersection, Brooklyn Memorial has a massive physical presence. Its great size is magnified by the narrowness of its lot so that it seems to almost spill out of its foundations onto the street. Property in this neighborhood used to be highly prized. Robust square towers with louvered belfries, lancet windows, and pointed arches above the doors dominate the street facade with its square projecting bays. Large perpendicular-style stained-glass windows and a crenelated parapet on the side tower are Gothic. A remarkable, six-sided lantern tower with arched dormer windows rises over the crossing of the bays. Two entrances—separated by a large perpendicular window toward the back of the sanctuary—lead into two small, separate, square, well-proportioned narthexes. Separate stairs from each narthex lead to the balcony.

The sanctuary, square including the balcony, is an Akron Plan auditorium oriented, like a Badgley building,[17] on a forty-five-degree angle toward the southeast. The interior does not seem as large as the immense exterior would suggest. A generous elevated stage in the southeast corner, about four feet above the main floor, supports a pulpit/lectern. Surrounding the stage at floor level is a quarter circle stained-wood communion rail and kneeler. Two aisles radiate outward through the pews, supplemented by a central aisle extending from the back of the worship space halfway to the front. The sanctuary floor slopes toward the southeast. Side aisles are narrow. The ceiling is decorated with large painted ribs supporting a great, translucent, milk-glass center dome. The interior sanctuary ceiling is shallow. It does not conform to the elaborate lantern above it that is such a prominent feature of the exterior of the building. The interior ceiling ribs and dome are outlined by the open bulbs in rosettes that would have been such a feature of modernity when the church was built. The worship space has large translucent glass chandeliers. The square sanctuary is interrupted by a single transept on the left (east) for choir and 1949 Austin organ. The musicians were on the same level as the pulpit/lectern. The church has a large, semicircular, wraparound, four-pew balcony. Beautiful, brightly colored, early twentieth-century, Tiffany-quality figured glass includes a window toward the back dedicated by the "WCTU" (Woman's Christian Temperance Union).

The Akron Plan assembly area was designed to open into the sanctuary by a retractable wall on the right (south) of the main worship space. The assembly area, which has its own smaller but impressive glass dome, outlined by more plain bulbs in rosettes, is remarkable for its state of preservation. It represents one of Cleveland's best examples of what an Akron Plan assembly area would have been like when inaugurated. With its thick, painted ribs that appear to support the ceiling, the assembly area mimics the main sanctuary. The second floor has a circular 270-degree balcony with railing. Two levels of classrooms radiate off the assembly area, from the main floor and from the balcony. The movable walls appear in good condition but are no longer retracted. Like the main auditorium, the assembly room is also oriented on an angle, in this case toward the northeast. It also focuses on an altar rail and pulpit, although more modest in size. On the first floor of the assembly area, approximately 150 seats in curved rows are directed toward the front. They appear to be original and are permanently attached to the floor. These seats are unique in Cleveland. In other Akron Plan Cleveland churches the first level of the assembly area is open and without permanent seating (unless, as at North Presbyterian, see p. 74, the main sanctuary is used as the assembly area).

Brooklyn Memorial United Methodist Church closed at the end of 2010.

92. Iglesia Emmanuel, originally Trinity United Church of Christ (1925)
Architect: Albert E. Skeel
Builder: August E. Kitterer
Location: 3525 West 25th Street

Trinity United Church of Christ was established in 1911 as an English-language mission of the German Evangelical Synod of North America.[18] This was the same Lutheran/Reform denomination that had established a German-language parish at St. Luke's United Church of Christ (see p. 224) in 1839. The synod was concerned, in the early twentieth century, that its young people, no longer comfortable in the German language, were drifting off into the English-speaking churches of other denominations. Like St. Luke's, Trinity would merge, as an Evangelical congregation, with the Reformed Church in 1934 and, subsequently, with the Congregational Christian Church in 1957 to form the UCC. Like St. Luke's, Trinity would remain, in the UCC, more of a conservative "Old World" congregation—in its practice, in its decoration, and in its architecture—than one of the whitewashed New England Congregational communities.

Trinity's original young parishioners, no less thrifty than their elders had been in the construction of St. Luke's, built their first frame 275-seat church on the present property for $130, the cost of materials. All labor was contributed by members and the pastor in what became known nationally as the "Romance of the Frame Church." The congregation, all of German extraction, dedicated their church on October 11, 1914.[19] Growing membership encouraged construction of the present building, dedicated in 1926. Trinity barely made it through the Great Depression. Its debt kept increasing because of unpaid interest. Things improved in the late 1930s. The congregation celebrated its thirtieth anniversary in 1941 with an eighty-five-pound cake in the shape of a cross that they cut into five hundred pieces. An educational wing was dedicated in 1948. That year a large lot adjacent to the church was purchased and leased to a used-car dealer. When the debt was retired in 1960, so was the dealer. The church resurfaced their lot for parking. In the 1950s the church purchased a restaurant behind the building, and this was used as an educational and administrative "annex" until it was torn down in 1966. It was replaced by a striking, high modern addition, to be used for a parlor, offices, and an entrance from the parking lot.

The construction of the interstate in the 1960s drastically affected members living in the vicinity of the church.[20] As their leadership fruitlessly explored merger opportunities in the suburbs, Trinity developed ever closer cooperation with Archwood UCC (see p. 226). For eleven years from 1977 to 1988, Trinity was also home to the Korean Central Presbyterian congregation before the Koreans completed their church in Brecksville. In 1983 the building was renovated to accommodate the offices of the Western Reserve Association, the regional headquarters of the UCC. Trinity's last service in this building was in 2008 when the congregation merged into Brooklyn-Trinity UCC on Memphis in Brooklyn. This West 25th Street building is now leased to the Iglesia Emmanuel, a fourteen-year-old Full Gospel Pentecostal community. Iglesia Emmanuel was previously located in the Independent Evangelical Church on West 44th Street, where this Hispanic community continues to maintain its Central Christian Academy.

The modern 1966 entrance from the parking lot to the south replaces the twin former entrances located well back from West 25th, on the north and south sides of the sanctuary. Armstrong identified the building on West 25th as unique because of the small battlement details at the top of the bell tower.[21] The new entrance is now through a magnificent high modern arcade into a large space with a large parlor to the left and a majestic staircase up to the sanctuary. This is the most impressive Christian narthex, if it can be called that, in Cleveland.[22]

The four-hundred-seat sanctuary is the kind of traditional space that one would expect in a former Evangelical church. The style is Tudor Gothic, reinforced by the traditional windows. The worship space is completely open without pillars. It is not clear whether the tie rods of the ceiling are functional or decorative. Stained pews are marked with the Trinity. The walls feature beautiful plasterwork, some of which is gilded. This is particularly notable on the chancel arch. The most interesting features of the sanctuary are the eight bronze light fixtures extending about twelve feet above the floor. Unique in Cleveland, these light fixtures are like residential stand-up lamps, only much larger. Choir and organ are behind the lectern toward West 25th Street.

93. St. Michael Church (1889)

Architect: Adolph Druiding
Builder: Joseph Koudelka
Location: 3114 Scranton Road

St. Michael is a Cleveland landmark.[23] During the day or illuminated every night, its 232-foot north spire (with an additional fourteen-foot cross), the tallest object in Cleveland when it was built and still Cleveland's tallest religious structure, can be seen for miles throughout the Cuyahoga Valley. The enormity of this gigantic structure shrugs off the unprepossessing character of its neighborhood. Seating 1,500 parishioners, for many years St. Michael was the largest church in Cleveland. Now reborn, yet again, as a bilingual congregation, St. Michael the Archangel/San Miguel Arcángel, is a community as well as a civic landmark. For such an impressive institution, St. Michael had a modest beginning. The Germans who settled in the Clark-Fulton and Tremont area were late to establish themselves in Cleveland. Worshiping two miles across the river at St. Joseph Franciscan on Woodland or more than a mile north at the original West Side German church of St. Mary's of the Assumption, they had a difficult time getting their children to trudge that far to school. In 1882 they convinced the Jesuits, who had taken over St. Mary's two years before, to help establish a school in their neighborhood. A Jesuit began saying masses in their school building, and, within a year, Bishop Gilmour established a parish and installed the remarkable Joseph Koudelka as its first pastor. Koudelka, who apparently was comfortable, and highly regarded, in every European language spoken east of the Rhine, was a Czech. His first assignment in Cleveland was seven years at St. Procop (see p. 238). When he left for St. Louis to edit the influential Bohemian publication *Hlas,* the rambunctious Czechs at St. Procop refused to accept any other pastor so that Bishop Gilmour had to close the parish for eighteen months. Koudelka's German, however, was so compelling that, when he returned to Cleveland, the sensitive and suspicious people of St. Michael took him to their heart. When their first frame church-school-rectory-convent burned on the current site of the south branch of the Cleveland Public Library, Koudelka moved the parish across Clarke and built this great church and its equally impressive high neo-Gothic adjacent school.[24] Building something like St. Michael was a major enterprise, and Koudelka was a no-nonsense money raiser, going about his parish regularly with his black collection bag. In addition to his work as pastor at St. Michael, Koudelka proved extremely useful in helping the Scots and German Bishops Gilmour and Horstmann maintain a veneer of order over their unruly nationality parishes. In 1908 Koudelka was consecrated the first auxiliary bishop of Cleveland. When, in 1911, Koudelka, who had continued to live at St. Michael, was named auxiliary bishop of Milwaukee, the greatest bell of the greatest church cracked irretrievably.

St. Michael survived the First World War as a German parish. It was 1925 before English hymns were introduced. By the Second World War, however, only one quarter of the parishioners were German, and Bishop Hoban made St. Michael a territorial (instead of a nationality) parish. Like so many religious communities, St. Michael suffered greatly when the interstates mowed down hundreds of its homes. Then, at the same time, Hispanic immigrants revitalized the parish so that it has become, again, a bilingual institution. On Good Friday, the community processes more than two miles to La Sagrada Familia and two miles back with stopovers at St. Patrick. St. Michael/San Miguel is a large congregation, and it has a large Hispanic presence. It would be inaccurate, however, to characterize this church as Hispanic as it has retained a vigorous non-Hispanic membership.

Bishop Gilmour took a direct hand in plans for this neo-Gothic church and selected Adolph Druiding as its architect. Druiding also designed the strikingly similar St. Patrick in Toledo. The church's exterior was finished with rock-faced Berea sandstone in a random coursed pattern. This has darkened with pollution from the mills and traffic. The congregation likes it that way. The roof is slate with copper trim. Two bell towers housing four tons of bells flank the church's recessed tripartite entrance. The open north tower is unusually thick and massive above the building and below the spire. Bernard Shildmacher, a local sculptor, did the three archangel statues on the facade. Raphael stands on the right. Gabriel stands on the left. On the apex above the deeply set rose window that forms the basic motif of the facade stood a four-times-life-size figure of St. Michael pointing upward with his sword. In 1969 fragments from the weathered statue of St. Michael began to threaten those passing below, and the statue had to be taken down. A shrine on the lawn preserves the statue's massive head.

In contrast to the stern dark exterior, the doors of the church open into a colorful wonderland of statuary conceived by Bishop Koudelka. The Czech in him liked bright colors and he repainted some of the imported statues himself. The nave features more than fifty polychrome statues, including a statue of *Our Lady, Mother of Divine Providence,* patroness of Puerto Rico, *Our Lord of Miracles* for members of the Peruvian community, and, from St. Mary's on Carroll Avenue in recognition of that church's role in establishing St. Michael, *St. John Berchmans,* the seventeenth-century Jesuit seminarian who is the patron of altar boys. On the pillars of the colonnade between the central nave and the side aisles are a parade of saints, women on the left, men on the right. This reflects the gender division in the pews—hat hooks on the right; no hat hooks on the left. (For a discussion of the importance and gender specificity of hat hooks and clamps, see p. 199.) The imposing altar, alive with statuary, is modeled on an altar in Italy. Koudelka built his church in 1889 with a skylight that illuminates the altar without artificial light. Unusual, large, three-dimensional stations are by Meyer Family Studios of Munich. Magnificent plaster reliefs on the walls were by Shildmacher, who sculpted the three great figures outside. This church has 109 images of angels.

The vestibule, nave, and side aisles are groin vaulted with a multiplicity of gilded ribs against a blue background. The floors are marble, and wainscoting is red Tennessee marble. In 1889 the Germans installed an image of the *Lamb of the Seven Seals* in the center of their great entrance rose window. This recognized the role of Bishop Gilmour in establishing the parish. The sacrificial lamb was his coat of arms. Today the image of the *Lamb of the Seven Seals* is also the center of the *escudo* (the commonwealth seal) of Puerto Rico. The new congregants took it as a welcoming gesture.

94. Immanuel Evangelical Lutheran Church (1879)
Architect: Charles Griese
Builder: Henry Weseloh
Location: 2928 Scranton Road

Immanuel is the kind of congregation where, when you ask the pastor whether it is Missouri Synod, he looks at you blankly and ignores the question. (What other kind of Lutheran Church is there?)[25] As inner-city ethnic congregations struggle to come to terms with their changing neighborhoods a few, like Immanuel (*Evangelisch-Lutherische Immanuels Gemeinde*), while attentive to the manageable needs of their surroundings, focus on the strength of their ethnicity. Immanuel coped with the interstate that crushed its traditional neighborhood by building a bigger parking lot. For more than a century, it has reached out to the different groups that surround it—in the nineteenth century to Latvians and English, in the twentieth century to its Hispanic neighbors. The industrious Germans of Immanuel established a successful Hispanic congregation that now has a building and two missions of its own. But Immanuel draws its strength, as it has for more than 125 years, from Cleveland *Germania*.

Immanuel sees itself as "an inner-city church with a suburban parish"—an inner-city German church with a suburban German parish.[26] Sunday services continue in English and German. For a generation, from 1958 to 1978, Immanuel produced a weekly German radio program that eventually reached an audience of 33,000. Bells and organ prelude were multinational. Hymns, introit, epistle, Gospel, prayers, and sermon were in German. The radio program became a major evangelical tool—Immanuel's congregation increased in size and decreased in age. In 1959 Immanuel inaugurated a twenty-six-member *posaunenchor* (brass choir) led by its trumpet-playing pastor. Brass choirs were a particular characteristic of the Evangelical Lutheran Church in Germany, where there were approximately three thousand church brass bands. In 1980 Immanuel discovered a German colony in Solon, and responded to its needs with a new Missouri Synod congregation (Our Redeemer Lutheran Church), initially staffed by Immanuel's pastor. Joining a German Roman Catholic priest, Immanuel's pastor is a fixture at the annual Kirchweihfestgottesdienst of the Donauschwaben German-American Cultural Center.[27] When Crown Prince Ferdinand, the Hohenzollern pretender, visited Cleveland, the Immanuel pastor was naturally included in the festivities. In 1964 Immanuel's Estey organ was replaced with a thirty-eight-rank tracker action instrument built by Friedrich Weissenborn of Braunschweig. The flavor of the music at Immanuel can be appreciated by considering the ensembles that perform—

the Cleveland *Maennerchor,* the German Orchestra, the Cleveland Lutheran A Cappella Choir, and *Der Deutsche Musik Verein.*

From its first settlement around West 30th Street at Lorain Avenue in the 1830s, West Side German Cleveland expanded exponentially in the middle of the nineteenth century. At its center stood 1,500-seat Trinity Lutheran (*Deutsche Evangelisch-Lutherische Dreieinigkeits Gemeinde;* see p. 192) and St. Mary's of the Assumption (which became St. Ignatius High School). As West Side Cleveland *Germania* expanded, Immanuel was established in 1880[28] together with German Roman Catholic St. Michael, founded two blocks south and two years later (see p. 231).

Trinity Lutheran built its school in 1853, prior to building its permanent church. Trinity subsequently found that so many of its members lived in Brooklyn that it should start a second school on the corner of Scranton Road at Seymour Avenue.[29] The assistant at Trinity, Henry Weseloh, was given responsibility for the school with the idea that he might establish a parish in Brooklyn. He established the parish. He built the church. He stayed for forty-five years.[30]

By 1881 the parochial school, taught by three teachers, had increased to 403 students. Three years later the congregation had grown to 2,354 members and was divided at Clark Avenue. Immanuel remained north of Clark. For those on the other side of Clark, St. Matthew's, about twelve blocks south (now Iglesia Sinai) was organized on the corner of Scranton at Meyers Avenue. Immanuel continued growing, and the following year, 1895, the balcony was built to handle the overflow. The 1909 tornado took off much of the upper part of the building.[31] Although photographs show that the tower and spire survived intact, they were so damaged as to be structurally unstable and had to be taken down and the tower reconstructed.

The first English services began in 1918. To celebrate its fiftieth anniversary in 1930, the church installed a three-manual Estey organ. The last German minutes were recorded in 1942. Parishioners who did not return from the Second World War had names like Schwanke, Hein, Teske, and Schultz. On Immanuel's seventy-fifth anniversary, in 1955, a white oak wall with glazed windows was installed below the front of the rear balcony to provide for lavatory space in an enlarged narthex. Construction of Interstate 90, two blocks to the north, resulted in a shift in the subterranean water table that so affected the church's foundations that the building threatened collapse. The congregation was determined to stay, although the cost of reconstruction eventually reached $100,000. Over the last fifty years, Immanuel has, through its Lutheran Chaplaincy Service, baked and distributed approximately ten thousand pounds of Christmas cookies, making it—with respect to Christmas cookies—what St. Augustine Church in Tremont is to Thanksgiving turkeys.

This remains a residential neighborhood with two-story apartment houses to the north, an eight-story modern apartment house to the south, and a line of well-kept nineteenth-century homes with full porches across the street. With its original 144-foot steeple, Immanuel was an overgrown brick meetinghouse like Trinity and Holy Name (see pp. 192 and 175). After the 1909 tornado, the spire came down and the tower above the roofline was reconstructed. The original louvered belfry was replaced with an open belfry. It has two bells. The spire was replaced with a short square upper tower with battlements and finials. As with other early Gothic Revival meetinghouses, one finds Gothic-style detailing around windows and doors. On either side of the original narthex, in from the street, are stairs to the balcony.

Inside, plain plaster walls contrast with the polished German woodwork. The worship space is open, without pillars. The large balcony, with its wonderful stained-wood column balustrade, wraps around the main worship space on either side up to the chancel. There are three aisles. Behind the nave is the 1955 wooden wall creating two narthexes. Windows are glazed with nineteenth-century patterned glass. In front of the congregation, behind the altar, are the four traditional, Missouri Synod, white, life-size apostles.[32] Made from carved wood, their original painted surface has mellowed over 125 years into a golden ivory. The altar is the same mellow color. Above the altar is an ivory-painted *Vera icon*. The altar stands in front of a plain, painted, small, square apse. A quite high, plain masonry arch vaults over the altar. Over the altar, carved masonry capitals sit on the rise of masonry. Of the same delicious ivory color and material as the altar is the pulpit that began at balcony level and has, as the result of serial revisions, now descended to three feet above the main floor. As the pastor has descended, the organist has ascended. Behind the congregation, the Weissenborn tracker organ is displayed in the loft above the narthex.

95. St. Rocco's Church (1949)
Architect: Michael G. Boccia
Builder: Sante Gattuso (see also his role in the closely associated parish of Our Lady of Mount Carmel, p. 249)
Location: 3205 Fulton Road

Visiting St. Rocco at nine on a Wednesday morning during the fall is like going to the movies.[33] Long lines of inattentive school-children emerge from the school behind the church, and, shepherded by pleasantly purposeful nuns in full habit—including wimples, they dutifully trudge into St. Rocco where the nuns corral them into the pews. When the nave is full of uncomfortably silent grade-schoolers, a nun in the narthex lights the candle-torches of the acolytes, a young priest in chasuble takes his place, the music begins, and all process down the center aisle to the altar. It is a world that many thought no longer existed.[34] The only touches this scene is missing are Bing Crosby and Ingrid Bergman.[35]

All of this had uncertain and unusual beginnings. At the beginning of the twentieth century, "American help" was important to many small, poor churches in Italy. In the southern half of the peninsula in particular, inscriptions identify altars, towers, and statutes as the gift of "Americans"—the emigrants who left. For many years before 1914, the little immigrant community around Trent Avenue and Fulton Road, originally from Noicattaro, a small town about eight miles southeast of Bari on the east coast of Italy,[36] had been sending back a collection to support the Feast of Our Lady of Mount Carmel. In 1914 there was belated thanks for the usual help, along with a hint that Americans had misappropriated some of the money. Deeply offended, the Cleveland community decided in 1915 to spend their money in Ohio on a celebration honoring St. Rocco, patron of Noicattaro. Stands were set up and decorated, the Iannone band played, and a small picture of St. Rocco was framed and carried in a procession-parade down Trent Avenue before being enshrined on a small altar in a tent. The next year, the pastor of the Italian East Side church celebrated Mass, the Lodge Giuseppe Mazzini joined the parade, and they had fireworks. In 1917 the community purchased a statue of St. Rocco to be carried in the procession. In the off-season, they stored the statue in a coal bin behind a neighboring church and dusted it off the following year. By 1918 much dissension had developed with those who had immigrated from Coreno, Petrula, and San Cosma e Damiano and now lived along Clark Avenue. Because of this tension, the priest, whom Bishop John Farrelly had assigned to minister to the West Side Italian community, decided the situation was so hopeless that he left. The community completed their small church and, apparently without the knowledge of the diocese, continued on their own for the next four years with traveling imposter "priests." The bishop became aware there was a church in the neighborhood in 1921 when an Illinois church supply house threatened to sue him for an unpaid bill from "St. Roch's Church." During this difficult period, the only parish function that flourished was the annual festival in honor of St. Rocco.

At last, in 1921 when Bishop Schrembs arrived from Toledo, he appointed an assistant at Italian St. Anthony on the East Side to oversee the parish. Three years later, he persuaded the Fathers of Our Lady of Mercy (the Mercedarians) to take over responsibility for the West Side Italians, and comity was restored. There was much to do. Father Sante Gattuso's first collection was $5.19. The chronic nationality parish complaint, that their priests do not speak the language or they do not speak it well, was never a problem at St. Rocco. The Mercedarians have staffed their Cleveland parishes with brothers who have usually been Italian. The first assistant at St. Rocco sat in the back of Sister Catherine's second grade for three months to learn English, and the second assistant became bishop of Alghero in Sardinia. The Mercedarians at St. Rocco have promoted an assistant to pastor whenever there has been a transition in the parish (as, for example, when Gattuso became master general of his order in Rome). Since 1924 there have been only three pastors, and this may explain why, in addition to their ambitious building program, the Mercedarians have maintained stability and order on the

West Side where before there was confusion. Gattuso's greatest legacy was not what he built but what he held together. When he was appointed, he not only took on the Clark Avenue Corenese, Petrulese, and San Cosma e Damianese but he and his assistants also established the mission among the Italians of East 70th and Detroit that became Our Lady of Mount Carmel.

Located opposite the intersection of Newark Avenue and Fulton Road, the flat brick facade of St. Rocco's overlooks a small and attractive plaza, an oasis of civility in this modest commercial neighborhood. The church terminates the view from the southwest on Fulton Road. Because of the simplicity of its front facade, the 750-seat church presents a modern appearance. Romanesque details, such as corbeling below the parapet, compound arches in the entrances, and a squared-off bell tower with arcading around the empty belfry, have all been abstracted into simplified forms. The rose window and tower with a pyramidal roof are simple and without detail.

Leading from an attractive and generous narthex, the main worship space is unusual for a Cleveland church. The broad nave appears wider than it is long, and its breadth is emphasized by four large chapels on the outside of each side aisle. These eight chapels reach laterally deep under the side eaves of the church. Packed with statuary, the chapels compete with the windows above and draw the eye down to the horizontal. There are no columns. The painted ceilings slant upward on either side and meet at a narrow flat center strip running the length of the nave. It features a large rectangular painted apse between flat nonrecessed Mary and Joseph altars. A relatively small but gracefully scaled mosaic of *St. Rocco* is over a similarly scaled altar. The quantity of statuary is breathtaking.

96. St. Procop Church (1902)
Architect: Fugman and Ulrich
Builders: Wenceslaus Panuska
and Peter Cerveny
Location: 3182 West 41st Street

St. Procop,[37] once the largest Czech church in the United States, reinvented itself in the twenty-first century as a small, self-sufficient, diverse congregation reflecting and ministering to its immediate neighborhood.[38] While one might have stretched the truth to call it prosperous, St. Procop earned a reputation for paying its bills, maintaining its buildings, and successfully scrounging around to support ministries important to the inner city—feeding the poor, educating the handicapped, supporting those struggling up from misery, and, at the end of the day, offering a spiritual beacon on the Near West Side. All this came from rowdy middle European beginnings.

Father Anthony Hynek established St. Procop in 1872 to serve West Side Czechs. Centered in the area south of Ohio City, the Czech community moved progressively westward into the area of West 41st at Clark Avenue as the Near West Side industrialized. For two years the congregation met in St. Mary-on-the-Flats. In 1874 the church built a two-story frame school-church-rectory on West 41st Street near Clark. Hynek was also assigned St. Wenceslas, the first Czech parish in Cleveland, and he managed both parishes until 1875. St. Procop then became a temporary home for two titans of the nineteenth-century church in Cleveland. Hynek was succeeded by Joseph Koudelka, initially a deacon from Wisconsin. It was for the St. Procop school that Koudelka developed his famous Bohemian readers, subsequently used in Czech parishes throughout the United States. After seven years at St. Procop, Koudelka left Cleveland to edit a national Bohemian publication based in St. Louis. This proved unfortunate as not even the omnipresent Stephen Furdek could calm down the parish after Koudelka's departure. The ongoing uproar forced Bishop Gilmour to close the parish.[39] Comity was restored in 1885. Fifteen years later the present 1,300-seat building was begun by Wenceslaus Panuska and, following his resignation in 1901, completed by Peter Cerveny. A mammoth fourteen-room brick-and-stone school was erected near the church in 1908, with a giant stone rectory added as well in 1908 and a large convent for twenty nuns added to this city-block complex in 1925. In 1926 both assistants were in a severe automobile accident; one was killed.

Thirteen hundred Czechs, however, could not resist the changes wrought by the second half of the twentieth century on the Near West Side of Cleveland. In the 1960s the poorly designed deteriorating dome and most of the two towers in the front of the church had to be taken down when the parish could no longer afford the high cost of their repair. In 1993, what was left of the entrance towers was dismantled. The high school closed in 1965 and the primary school in 1975. Then, at the beginning of the twenty-first century, St. Procop began to show surprising signs of life as a small inner-city parish. The first two floors of the magnificent school were leased to the award-winning West Bridge Positive Education Program, the government- and foundation-supported program located in a variety of sites in Cuyahoga County that provides for children with behavior and learning problems. The resulting rent, in the sparklingly renovated school, stabilized the St. Procop budget. The top floor housed a Lutheran program and Bay Presbyterian's (see p. 292) "Kids Church," a mission that provided lunch, classes, and activities for neighborhood children. St. Procop's spacious and abandoned convent was transformed into Procop House to provide affordable living for men transitioning out of homelessness after prison or Twelve Step programs. In 1990 the parish began providing a hot meal every Friday to between one hundred and two hundred poor and elderly. Twenty-five churches and five schools contributed food for distribution from St. Procop's pantry. St. Procop sponsored three Alcoholics Anonymous meetings a week for two to three hundred people. All of this was presided over by a dynamic nun who, as "parish life coordinator," had been entrusted by the bishop with the pastoral care of the parish.

The original concept of this church as "an attractive blending of the Italian and Byzantine architectural trends, symbolic of the Czecho-Slovakian culture shaped under European and Near East influences" is now difficult to appreciate.[40] Where the dome came down, it now has an unprepossessing peaked roof. Without its dome and two entrance towers, the attenuated brown masonry building defiantly crouches down like a wounded animal. With its blank walls of windows on the street, the rock-faced Berea sandstone makes the church look like a medieval fortress.

The drastic truncation of the exterior is not apparent inside. The worship space is a giant, broad room without the pillars so characteristic of the Victorian Gothic Revival style of most Roman Catholic churches of its time. Great arches span the nave in ribs across the ceiling. Transepts are present but shallow. Two altars on either side of the chancel project slightly into the nave. New marble altars and statuary were installed in the late 1920s, and the east side of the interior reconstructed again in 1949. In 1995 the altar and furnishings were again refinished, and the front pews realigned to focus on the Vatican II altar. The elaborate eastern altar with beautiful marble columns featured St. Procop on one side and St. Wenceslaus on the other. The ceiling is beautifully stenciled and the side walls showcase gilded painted decorations. The glass is quiet, nondominating, and brings a good deal of illumination into the nave. In the balcony stands St. Procop's famous Votteler-Hettche organ.[41]

On March 15, 2009, Bishop Richard Lennon announced the closing of St. Procop. On August 30, he celebrated the final Mass. On June 10, 2010, investors linked to the charter school company White Hat Management purchased St. Procop. The breathtaking woodwork and Mayer Munich glass at St. Stephen's, which the diocese had clustered with St. Procop in attempting to reach a closure decision, was spared. Sister Annette was right (see preface, xiii), all they wanted to talk about was stained glass.

CHAPTER NINE

West Central Cleveland

The West Central community is composed of three neighborhoods—West Boulevard-Lorain, Edgewater-Cudell, and Detroit Shoreway.

Tour

Begin this tour at the intersection of West 117th Street at Lorain Avenue just south of the interchange of I-90 at West 117th. Travel east for one block and then turn right (south) onto Bosworth Road. Drive south on Bosworth, past Bosworth Elementary School. At the intersection of Bosworth at Flower Avenue, to the left stands the Iglesia de Dios Pentecostal M.I., formerly the Bosworth Road Presbyterian Church. Continue south on Bosworth. On the northeast corner of Bosworth at Adeline Avenue is the closed Sts. Philip and James Church, now a charter school. Continue south on Bosworth to Bellaire Road and turn left (east). Continue on Bellaire as it curves north and turns into West 105th Street. At the intersection of West 105th Street at West Boulevard, bear right onto West Boulevard. Continue northeast on West Boulevard to its intersection with Lorain. On the southwest corner sits St. Ignatius of Antioch Church (97).

Turn right onto Lorain and then turn left (north) onto West 98th Street. Drive north on West 98th, entering the Edgewater-Cudell neighborhood after passing under I-90. On the left at the intersection of West 98th Street at Cudell Avenue stands the Iglesia de Jesucristo "Monte Moriah" Inc., formerly Christ United Church of Christ. Continue north on West 98th until it intersects with Madison Avenue. At Madison turn left. On the right at West 99th is the Trinity United Methodist Church. At the intersection of Madison at West Boulevard, look south at the West Boulevard Christian Church. Tucked in a curve of West Boulevard and shaded by trees, this church completed its front addition in 1959.

Turn right onto West Boulevard. At the corner of Detroit Avenue at West Boulevard, turn left (west) onto Detroit. On the southwest corner of the West 114th Street at Detroit intersection lies closed St. Rose of Lima Church (98). Sold to a charter school company, St. Rose is identified by its giant-order statue of the saint against a blue background. Continue on Detroit to its intersection with West 117th Street and turn right (north). West 117th Street separates Cleveland and Lakewood. On the southeast corner of the intersection of Lake Avenue at West 117th are the remains of the former Fifth Church of Christ, Scientist, now owned by the City of Cleveland.

Turn right and drive east on Lake past West Boulevard. East of this intersection, on the right side of the street, stands St. Thomas Evangelical Lutheran Church. This small church is located on a well-maintained residential street facing Edgewater Park and Lake Erie. Continue on Lake Avenue. Passing under the railroad, enter the Detroit Shoreway neighborhood.

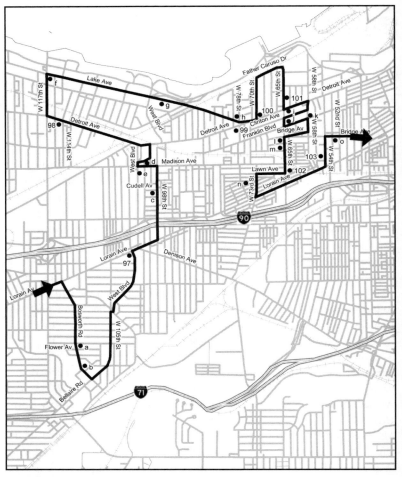

WEST CENTRAL CLEVELAND

a. Iglesia de Dios Pentecostal M.I.

b. Sts. Philip and James Church

97. St. Ignatius of Antioch Church

c. Iglesia de Jesucristo "Monte Moriah" Inc.

d. Trinity United Methodist Church

e. West Boulevard Christian Church

98. St. Rose of Lima Church

f. Fifth Church of Christ, Scientist

g. St. Thomas Evangelical Lutheran Church

h. St. Luke's Episcopal Church

99. La Sagrada Familia Church

100. Our Lady of Mount Carmel Church

101. St. Helena's Catholic Church

i. Cleveland Public Theatre

j. Bethany Presbyterian Church

k. Iglesia Adventista del Septimo Dia

l. People's Hope United Methodist Church

m. Calvary Reformed Church in America

102. St. Colman's Church

n. St. Paul Evangelical Lutheran Church

103. St. Stephen's Church

o. Enterprise Full Gospel Church

On the northeast corner of Lake at West 78th Street, is the small frame St. Luke's Episcopal Church. Continue on Lake until it ends at Detroit. Across the street, on the south side of Detroit, is La Sagrada Familia Church (99), consecrated to celebrate the 150th anniversary of the Roman Catholic Diocese of Cleveland. Turn left (east) onto Detroit. Travel east on Detroit to West 70th Street. On the northeast corner of West 70th at Detroit is Our Lady of Mount Carmel Church (100), an important institution in the redevelopment of its Detroit Shoreway neighborhood.

Turn left on West 70th and note the housing for the elderly built by Our Lady of Mount Carmel. Stay on West 70th until it ends. Turn right onto Father Caruso Drive (named for the second pastor of Our Lady of Mount Carmel). At West 65th Street turn right again (south). Before West 65th Street's intersection with Detroit, on the left, is St. Helena's Catholic Church (101), a traditional Transylvanian Maramures-style church. At Detroit, turn left (east). On the right side opposite West 61st is the Cleveland Public Theatre, built as St. Mary Romanian Orthodox Church and then becoming Holy Resurrection Russian Orthodox Church. This was originally a predominantly Romanian neighborhood. At the intersection of West 58th Street at Detroit turn right onto West 58th and then, one block later, turn right again (west) onto West Clinton Avenue. On the southeast corner of West Clinton at West 65th is Bethany Presbyterian Church.

Turn left (south) onto West 65th Street and travel on it for one block. Turn left (east) onto Franklin Boulevard and travel on it for one block. On the northeast corner of West 58th at Franklin is the Iglesia Adventista del Septimo Dia. Turn right (south) onto West 58th Street. Then turn right (west) onto Bridge Avenue and travel for one block. On the southwest corner of Bridge at West 65th Street is People's Hope United Methodist Church. Turn left (south) onto West 65th. Between the intersections of Fir Avenue and Wakefield Avenue, is Calvary Reformed Church in America. Built in 1972, this modern building serves a congregation established in 1880. Continue south on West 65th to Lawn Avenue. On the left side of this intersection sits the giant St. Colman's Church (102).

Turn right (west) for one full block on Lawn Avenue and then turn left (south) onto West 73rd Street. Travel one block south. To the west stands St. Paul Evangelical Lutheran Church. Located on a point of land, this small church is both beautifully crafted and scaled to suit a neighborhood of small residences. Continue south on West 73rd until it intersects with Lorain.

At Lorain turn left (east) and travel past the Michael Zone Recreational Center, until Lorain intersects with West 54th Street. At West 54th turn left (north). On the left one finds St. Stephen's Church (103). Beautiful woodwork and glass make St. Stephen's interior one of the most important in Roman Catholic Cleveland. Turn right (east) onto Bridge. On the corner of Bridge at West 52nd Street sits the Enterprise Full Gospel Church, formerly the Cleveland First Enterprise Baptist Church.

This ends the tour of the West Central neighborhoods. To gain access to the regional highway network, continue on Bridge to West 45th Street and turn left (north) to get on the Shoreway, or take Bridge east to West 44th Street and turn right (south) to gain access to I-90.

97. St. Ignatius of Antioch Church
(1930)
Architects: Edward T. P. Graham and
F. Stillman Fish
Builder: Thomas Hanrahan
Location: 10205 Lorain Avenue

Across the street from a commercial district, St. Ignatius used to adjoin a gracious neighborhood of comfortable two-family homes.[1] Much of this has been blotted out by I-90. What the interstate took away, however, it may now give back in providing unparalleled access to the church for its suburban parishioners. Boston architects Graham and Fish also designed St. James Parish Lakewood (see p. 284) and Our Lady of Peace on the border of Shaker Heights in eastern Cleveland (see p. 158). St. Ignatius is an immense building on a large educational and administrative campus. During the Second World War, St. Ignatius, with a parish population of approximately twelve thousand, had more than one thousand parishioners in the service. One Sunday in 1959 more than three hundred children made their first Holy Communions.

This parish was organized in 1902 as an additional responsibility of the then part-time pastor of St. Patrick West Park. It was one of the first non-nationality parishes in the Diocese of Cleveland although it has always had something of an Irish flavor. There was the usual succession of schools and churches. The parish grew so rapidly that the first pastor, after being assigned to St. Ignatius full time, resigned, asking for a smaller parish. A smaller parish was not what the second pastor, the energetic Thomas Hanrahan, had in mind. He rapidly paid off the debt and left for Rome to survey the architectural possibilities offered by the Eternal City's great pilgrimage churches. Hanrahan began his American version of a great early Christian basilica in 1925. He did not live to see his building completed. Bishop Schrembs gave a hurried special blessing to the almost completed church in 1930 to allow Hanrahan's funeral to be the main sanctuary's first service.

Only a handful of Cleveland religious institutions are blessed with first-rate histories. Of these, only St. Ignatius is favored with an outstanding physical description and Timothy Barrett's splendid article should be consulted concerning this church.[2] What follows is only a brief parse of Barrett's masterful description. Barrett begins by reminding us that mighty St. Ignatius—with its great campanile—was once one with the Terminal Tower and Cleveland downtown's world-famous "Group Plan." St. Ignatius was built, Barrett points out, during "the seemingly endless period of national optimism" when "Cleveland was the fifth-largest city in America" and "enjoyed a reputation for being one of the most progressive and beautiful cities in the nation."

As Barrett explains, the interior of St. Ignatius is a particularly powerful modern adaptation of the early Christian basilica church. Patterned by its architects and builder after St. Paul's Outside-the-Walls (A.D. 385–400) and influenced by St. Maria Maggiore (begun 432–40), St. Ignatius, with its great beamed ceiling, is probably as close as one can get to one of the ancient Christian basilicas without crossing the Atlantic. Barrett goes on to describe the sumptuous decoration of the interior: the arches, the arcade of columns (some of which may be Roman *spolia*), and the wonderful glass. Early Christians, who did not have stained-glass windows, would have had to forgo the great nave glass and the fifty-two gorgeous little clerestory windows.

Barrett explains that the exterior of this building displays several notable departures from an early basilica church—the Romanesque rose window over the entrance, the elaborate Islamo-Byzantine frieze around the church under the eaves, and the imposing facade—with its distinctive, recessed tripartite entrance supported by slender columns—which is so much a creation of the early twentieth century. Most out of character for an early Christian basilica, but the feature that most vividly characterizes St. Ignatius today, is its amazing 210-foot-tall campanile, much taller and more narrow than any European prototype. Four tower bells sound the Angelus at noon and at six every day. Frequently described as a mosquelike minaret, the Ignatius tower is visible on the south side of I-90 for miles driving east or west. Built in an era when aircraft were smaller and flew closer to the ground, it was thought important that the tower be lighted at night for the safety of airplanes landing in Cleveland.

On March 15, 2009, Bishop Richard Lennon announced the closing of St. Ignatius of Antioch. The parish appealed and the bishop relented.

98. St. Rose of Lima Church (1957)
Architect: Anthony Ceresi
Builders: Patrick O'Connell and
Edmund Kirby
Location: 11411 Detroit Avenue

An offshoot of St. Colman's, this parish was named for St. Rose of Lima—a Dominican solitary contemplative and the first canonized saint (1671) from the Western Hemisphere.[3] The growing parish built a substantial two-story frame school-church within seven months. The size of the first temporary building may explain the twenty-five year wait before the foundation of a permanent church was dedicated in 1927. The parish gathered for another twenty-five years in the basement of the current building before moving into a completed 1,100-seat church in 1957. This prolonged transition should not obscure the vigor with which this rapidly expanding parish pursued, with the appropriate schools and convents, its robust educational program. St. Rose's dynamic second pastor was thought by many parishioners to have miraculous healing powers.[4] The third pastor, who had previously been chancellor of the diocese, is remembered for his "dread of debt," and this probably explains the prolonged hiatus in building the permanent church.[5] Father Kirby's economies apparently did not discourage the growth of the congregation; by the time of his death, St. Rose numbered 6,500 parishioners. Edward Cardinal Mooney presided at Kirby's Requiem Mass.

Located on Detroit Avenue, the Edgewater-Cudell neighborhood's busiest commercial street, St. Rose sits at a transitional point between the working-class neighborhoods to its south and the more prepossessing homes found along Lake Erie to the north. In the last quarter of the nineteenth century, the area north of Detroit was one of the wealthiest in Cleveland—home to Marcus Hanna among others. By 1920 the great estates had been subdivided but the neighborhood retained an elegant character. Manufacturing in the early twentieth century, in particular of automobile and paper products, followed the railroad south of Detroit. This neighborhood lost 450 houses to I-90.

Begun in 1927, the original permanent church design was by Edward T. P. Graham of Boston and his Cleveland associate F. Stillman Fish. They designed some of the Cleveland area's greatest churches—St. Ignatius of Antioch (see p. 244), St. James (see p. 284), and Our Lady of Peace (see p. 158). The basement of their design served the congregation until 1957, when the present building was constructed to plans drawn up by Anthony Ceresi. Ceresi's plain brick structure is composed of three simple elements—base, auditorium, and bell tower. Three glass-door entrances under segmented arches originally relieved the simplicity of the masonry base. An entry portico projects from the subsequently constructed upper auditorium. Above this portico is a monumental ten-ton, twenty-foot statue of *St. Rose,* designed by Ceresi and executed by the Cleveland sculptor Joseph Motto. The commanding presence of St. Rose on the facade of her church, such a marked contrast to the retiring manner of the historical St. Rose, makes this building a compelling monument. Her statue dominates the busy thoroughfare in front of her. A dark blue screen mounted with early Christian symbols in cast aluminum serves as a backdrop to the statue. A plain but gold-leafed 125-foot bell tower is capped by a simple cross that is mounted on a similarly colored, dark blue base.

Although traditional detail is noticeably absent inside, the building maintains a wonderfully warm human scale with its plain surfaces and strong color contrasts. There are no pillars. The nave is a plain open space. Undecorated sheets of beautiful Roman brick, interrupted by narrow plaster walls, dominate the interior. A twenty-four-foot cast-aluminum altar screen decorated with religious symbols had been an important part of the interior of this church; however, this was removed in 1975, as was much of the other metal trim in the interior, including the screen between the narthex and nave. A marble sanctuary with black marble stairs and marble altar and attractive modern marble altar rail remain. One finds a wonderful plaster dove in the ceiling above the sanctuary. Striking modern windows are dedicated to relatively modern saints such as *Peter Claver, Frances Xavier Cabrini, John Neumann, Thomas More, Edmund Campion, Martin de Porres,* and, of course, *St. Rose.*

The baptistry became a library and then a study room. In the basement beneath the worship space, massive pillars topped with gilded Celtic capitals support the floor above. This is not a cement or linoleum church basement floor; this floor is made of terrazzo and marble. Their fiscally conservative pastor may have kept them in the basement for twenty-five years—but he kept them in style.

On March 15, 2009, Bishop Richard Lennon announced the closing of St. Rose of Lima. He merged St. Rose with Saints Cyril and Methodius Church in Lakewood (see p. 279) to form Transfiguration Parish. On June 25, 2010, investor groups associated with White Hat Management bought St. Rose for a charter school.

99. La Sagrada Familia Church (1998)

Architect: Zarzycki-Malik
Builder: David Fallon
Location: 7719 Detroit

La Sagrada Familia, consecrated to celebrate the diocese's 150th anniversary, was the first Catholic church built in Cleveland in half a century.[6] It was built as a "transitional" parish to assist Hispanic newcomers to Cleveland make the transition from a foreign to an American environment. The assumption was that, after some time in the parish, members would move on and be replaced by newer arrivals. Now, however, the parish is considering introducing more English into its liturgy. Its younger members are settling into the parish as well as settling into Cleveland and becoming more comfortable in English than in Spanish.

The initial Hispanic presence in Cleveland came from Mexico and Puerto Rico during the 1940s and 1950s. Mexicans tended to settle all over the city. Puerto Ricans clustered in the Superior and Lexington areas on the Near East Side. In the late 1950s both groups began to congregate on the Near West Side, and in the 1980s they were increasingly joined by refugees from Central and South America. Alarmed by the difficulty these groups had finding a home in existing parishes, the diocese began to offer Spanish-speaking alternatives, establishing the Capilla de Cristo Rey and the parish of San Juan Bautista. In 1980 Dennis O'Grady, an assistant at St. Michael on Scranton Road, celebrated a Spanish mass in Ricardo's Restaurant on Fulton Road. When O'Grady became pastor at St. Michael, it seemed natural to continue as a community, San Miguel, within the larger parish of St. Michael. They now make up a majority of the parishioners at St. Michael.

In 1987 the Capilla de Cristo Rey moved into a church on the corner of West 34th Street at Clark Avenue. San Juan Bautista moved into the church built by the West Side Hungarian Reformed Congregation on the corner of West 32nd Street at Carroll Avenue, across the street, west, from St. Ignatius High School. When the Hispanic community decided to merge into a new parish, San Miguel decided to remain at St. Michael. The new parish that became La Sagrada Familia was the result of the merger of San Juan Bautista and the Capilla de Cristo Rey, previously separated by Interstate 90.

The diocese provided the new congregation and its architect with a difficult, narrow, sloping site squeezed into a commercial area beside St. Augustine Nursing Home (previously St. John Hospital before it moved to the new hospital of St. John's West Shore on Center Ridge Road in Westlake). The principal advantage of the site was the large parking lot behind the church belonging to the former hospital. A vacant lot when construction began, the site had been the location of the Altenheim Nursing Home, razed many years before, a German retirement community belonging to the diocese.[7]

The style of the church, Southwest mission, suggests its Hispanic basis. It was built consistent with a limited budget. Unable to stucco the concrete block walls because of Cleveland weather, the appearance of stucco was mimicked by spraying the walls with "SkidProof," an acrylic paint mixed with sand. The design takes advantage of the pronounced downward slope of the site by placing administrative and educational space on the first floor, opening onto the street. (The main entrance to the church is on the side, off the street, away from the former hospital.) Putting the worship and meeting spaces on the second floor not only takes advantage of the site but provides a more impressive presence from the street. A simple tower with an open cupola contains the bell from the original church (now activated electronically from the sacristy instead of, as before, with a rope). The facade is made more dramatic by sheathing the bottom half of the first floor with split blocks painted a salmon-reddish color.

Entrance is from the side into a large interior space called "the plaza" that separates the sanctuary to the north from a parish hall with stage and kitchen to the south. The one-and-a-half-story building, with its entrance road on the east, occupies most of the site. The Vatican II sanctuary has the members of the congregation facing each other. Around the periphery of the sanctuary is statuary brought by the people from their former parishes—*St. John the Baptist* and *Our Lady of Divine Providence*.[8] Penetrating the north wall is a locally designed and produced small window of the *Holy Family* with Christ as an older child.

100. Our Lady of Mount Carmel Church (1952)
Architect: William Koehl
Builder: Sante Gattuso
Location: 6928 Detroit Avenue

In the Diocese of Cleveland, the two West Side Italian parishes of Our Lady of Mount Carmel on Detroit Avenue and St. Rocco's (see p. 236) on Fulton Road have a uniquely close association.[9] Both were established at about the same time (St. Rocco's in 1922 and Our Lady of Mount Carmel in 1926) by the same priest, the remarkable Sante Gattuso. After a long struggle, Gattuso was also responsible for building a permanent church for each, again, at about the same time—St. Rocco's in 1949 and Our Lady of Mount Carmel in 1952. Both parishes have managed to continue to maintain vigorous schools for immigrant young people. Until recently these two parishes were staffed continuously by the same orders—the Sisters of the Most Holy Trinity[10] and the Mercedarians.[11] Their parallel success at St. Rocco's and Our Lady of Mount Carmel became a self-fulfilling prophecy. Gattuso and his Mercedarians were brought to Cleveland by Bishop Joseph Schrembs in the hope that, where others had failed, they could do something with the notoriously sensitive and desperately poor West Side Italians. It was not easy. Before the parishes were established and the permanent schools and churches built, the fathers spent years "without housing, taking up residence in cars and later unused classrooms."[12] "The Sisters had no permanent convent for two years, they slept in one room of the school and cooked in the basement," and they "commuted by streetcar from St. Rocco . . . to Mount Carmel."[13]

Initial efforts among the Italian population of Detroit Avenue were painfully slow and difficult. When Gattuso invited himself to his first meeting with the Detroit Avenue Italians in February 1924, "the cold, snowy weather was nothing when compared to the freezing reception he received inside the meeting room."[14] His first success was with the women of the community. With the permission of the bishop, who was "pleasantly surprised at Father Sante's success,"[15] Gattuso celebrated Mount Carmel's first mass at St. Helena Romanian Byzantine Church (see p. 252).[16] Major events in the founding included a parishioner setting aside a room in her house for a chapel and then the parish moving from there into a rented saloon.

However, in the fullness of time, success arrived. In 1961, a Lady of Mount Carmel school principal—the Venerable Reverend Mother Mary Santina (Beatrice Villella)—would become the provincial and, thereafter, the mother general of her order. In 1977, the Mount Carmel school became the first school in the United States with a television set in every classroom. In 1998, the Trinitarian Sisters, who had labored under such difficult circumstances for the school, were forced to withdraw. They were replaced by the Mercedarian Sisters, whom Gattuso had first asked to come to Cleveland seventy-five years before but who had been unable to respond at the time because of responsibilities in Italy and the lack of English-speaking sisters. In 2002 the Mount Carmel School, with its white-robed brothers and nuns in full habit, became one of the first private year-round schools in the United States (five-week summer vacation and longer breaks during the year). With children from twenty-two countries, Mount Carmel School finds the year-round schedule particularly helpful for its many students who do not hear English spoken at home.

It is inaccurate to give Gattuso credit for all this. His assistant at St. Rocco's, Vincent Caruso, gave his life to Mount Carmel—assistant for five years, vicar for twenty-three years, and then, after Gattuso left for Rome to become master general of his order, pastor for fourteen more. Caruso prepared for his responsibilities at Mount Carmel by sitting in the back of Sister Catherine's second grade at St. Rocco's to perfect his English. After forty-five years at Mount Carmel, Caruso had improved his English to the point where he was named major superior of his order in the United States.

Careful reading of the parish histories of Our Lady of Mount Carmel and of St. Rocco's suggests that Gattuso did not establish St. Rocco's first and then establish Mount Carmel as a mission; instead, he spread his efforts over the whole West Side Italian community. When Vatican II abolished the Latin mass and introduced the vernacular, Our Lady of Mount Carmel, of course, began celebrating in Italian.

Sited along commercially busy Detroit Avenue, Mount Carmel has been an important player in efforts to revitalize its neighborhood. In 1967 Father Marino Frascati, at that time an assistant at Mount Carmel, hosted the first meeting of the Neighborhood Rehabilitation Project. It would become in 1973, after Frascati became pastor and coined the term "Detroit-Shoreway," the Detroit Shoreway Project. As founder and first president of the Detroit Shoreway Businessmen's Association, Father Frascati purchased the area north of his school for the U.S. Department of Housing and Urban Development (HUD)-subsidized 152-apartment Villa Mercede (as in Mercedarian) senior high-rise. Mount Carmel pressed forward with more HUD subsidized townhouses, and then the eighteen-unit condominium complex called St. Peter's-by-the-Lake (for St. Peter Nolasco, founder of the Mercedarian Order), and, at last, the Nolasco Housing Corporation that has rehabilitated or constructed more than seventy-four housing units.

The six-hundred-seat, plain brick, permanent church is, like St. Rocco's, an example of simplified Romanesque-style design. They look much alike. Romanesque details include round arches above the window and door openings, a recessed double door at the main entrance set in a plain portico, and buttressed side facades. The flared stone parapet front gable, modified rose window, and square bell tower with its modified arcade and low hip roof are also Romanesque. The statue of *Our Lady of Mount Carmel* draws attention toward the tower while the accentuated cut-stone waterlines in the tower and on the main sanctuary provide a visual contrast to the building's plain brick veneer.

The hall-nave, unencumbered by columns and with its square apse, is bright and cheery. A statue of *Our Lady of Mount Carmel* is over the altar. The Italian love of expressionist sculpture is not as overwhelming here as in St. Rocco, but Our Lady of Mount Carmel has many statues. The same sensibility is expressed in the polychromed, three-dimensional stations. The glass is modern and figurative with a window to *John XXIII*. The school's gym-cafeteria may have been the first building in the United States dedicated to that pope. One finds a nice relief of the *Baptism of Christ* over the baptismal font. The shield of the Mercedarians is everywhere.

101. St. Helena's Catholic Church

(1906)

Architect: Unknown

Builders: Epaminonda Lucaciu (frame),
George Babutiu (brick), and Mircea
Toderich (rebuilt)

Location: 1367 West 65th Street

For the architecture and decoration of their churches, the Romanians of Cleveland get first prize (see also St. Mary Romanian Orthodox Cathedral, p. 265, the most dramatic religious building in Cleveland). St. Helena's Catholic Church, built in 1906, is not at all what it seems.[17] Impeccably recast in 1965 and subsequently redecorated with exquisite taste, St. Helena's is the Cleveland poster child for what transformation of a building, as distinct from historic restoration, can accomplish.[18] St. Helena's was built as a modest frame first church in 1906. Subsequently it was enlarged and resurfaced in brick just before the Second World War. The original building was reborn in its current traditional-modernist form in 1965, following the lines of churches in Transylvania.[19] Since then it has been decorated with restrained religious contemporary art and, as a final touch, had its sanctuary behind the iconostasis repainted in a breathtaking blue in honor of the Virgin.

More Romanians immigrated to Cleveland than to any other city in the United States; thus St. Helena's was the first Romanian Catholic church in this country. The Romanian Catholic community, which originally settled on the Near West Side among the Saxons who had arrived earlier from Transylvania, has always enjoyed a particularly cordial relationship with the Roman Catholic Diocese of Cleveland. Charles Boehm, "the apostle of Hungary to America" and first pastor of St. Elizabeth's (see p. 142), played an important role as a catalyst for the organization of the Romanian Catholic community. Boehm convinced Bishop Ignatius Horstmann to call Epaminonda Lucaciu, son of the Romanian nationalist Vasile Lucaciu, from Rome to found a parish. The dynamic Lucaciu was the first Romanian Catholic priest in the United States and would later edit the first Romanian newspaper in this country. After serving for three years at St. Helena's, Lucaciu established three parishes in Illinois and New Jersey before returning to Romania. Bishop Horstmann, fondly remembered by a congregation that may appear to outsiders as an Orthodox community except for its governance, advanced $1,800 to establish the parish and another $5,000 to build the church. Members were so excited about their new 450-seat church that they had "St. Helena 1906" spelled out in darker slates on the lighter slates of half of their roof, an innovation thankfully obliterated by subsequent reconstructions. Until John Paul II established the Apostolic Exarchate at St. George in Canton, St. Helena's was part of the Roman Catholic Diocese of Cleveland.

St. Helena's continues to get administrative help from the Diocese of Cleveland in things like insurance. Visits by the Roman Catholic bishops of Cleveland are warmly remembered. The congregation was particularly devoted to Cardinal Hickey when he was bishop of Cleveland and to Bishop Pilla. The second pastor at St. Helena's was Alexandru Nicolescu. On a leave of absence from Blaj Seminary, Nicolescu returned there after two years at St. Helena's. He subsequently became bishop of Lugoj and ultimately archbishop and metropolitan of the See of Alba-Iulia and Fagaras, the Romanian Byzantine Catholic primate. The third pastor, Aurel Hatiegan, established St. Theodore's in Alliance, St. George's in Canton, St. Basil's in Lorain, and Most Holy Trinity in the east part of Cleveland—all, at that time, part of the Roman Catholic Diocese of Cleveland.

The Romanian Greek Catholic Church suffered terribly when the Russian Communists took over its country. In 1948, the 250th anniversary of the union between the Romanian Greek Catholic Church and the Roman Catholic Church, the Communist government dissolved the church and transferred its communicants and property to the Romanian Orthodox Church, except for what the state kept for itself. In an unexpected result, St. Helena's in Cleveland became "the mother church" for Romanian Greek Catholics worldwide. During the ensuing suppression of the Church in Romania, six hundred clergy were arrested and three hundred were murdered, including seven bishops. Concerned that the Greek Catholic Church in Romania would be eliminated, Rome established the Apostolic Exarchate in Canton in 1982 and elevated it to a diocese responsible for the United States in 1987. The number of Greek Catholics who survived underground in Romania, until the 1989 revolution overthrew the Communists, is debated. At most, 50 percent of the 1948 church survived. The number may be as low as 10 percent.

On a little side street off Detroit, St. Helena's does not enjoy the broad campus and lengthy approach that gives Romanian Orthodox St. Mary such a dramatic presence four miles to the southeast. Nevertheless, St. Helena's clean sharp Transylvanian lines and beautifully proportioned modernist tower and spire, crowned with an elegant traditional cross, dominates a small-scale commercial neighborhood that seems, at last, to be coming back to life. Daytime visitors are surrounded by the vans and equipment of workmen involved in a variety of restoration projects on neighboring businesses. Although lots are cramped in this part of Cleveland, this church takes effective advantage of the space it has created for itself. Its community center is located on one side. On the other, the rectory connects to the church by a brick arch spanning the driveway.

Through tasteful wrought-iron doors, the worship space focuses on the gorgeous blue of the sanctuary, with its fine modernist crucifix behind the iconostasis. The worship space is relatively small. The ceiling is peaked, ribbed stained wood. Artificial illumination is by wonderful thick wire candelabras. The figurative iconostasis paintings were by the Cleveland painter Douglas Phillips in his own style. They combine Greek and Roman tradition with the twentieth century. Compelling paintings of *St. Helen* and *John the Baptist* flank *Mary and Jesus* on either side of the altar. Iconography on the walls is also from Cleveland. Attractive, brightly colored, modernist glass figures of twelve saints in twelve windows line both sides of the nave. The windows are from Rome, as are the modernist stations. The church has a marble-elevated chancel. Pews have been reduced in number and moved back to open up the chancel.

102. St. Colman's Church (1914)
Architects: Count Lenore and
Schneider and Potter
Builder: James O'Leary
Location: 2027 West 65th Street

The classical twin towers of St. Colman's are a landmark on the north side of I-90 just past, going west, the exit for West 44th Street.[20] The highway unfortunately cut through and consumed much of the middle of the parish. The interstate has been the death of St. Colman's school, and now it seriously threatens what was Cleveland's longest-lasting Irish parish. St. Colman's was established by Eugene O'Callaghan in 1880, just as he was completing St. Patrick's, the mother church of West Side Irish Catholicism (see p. 189). O'Callaghan obviously liked to build, and he was good at it. In 1880 he started all over again at St. Colman's in an abandoned school on Pear Avenue. Within two years he had built a new frame church on the current St. Colman's campus. One year later this was expanded to accommodate seating for one thousand. Two years later there was a new school-and-hall combination, but it fell to his successor, James O'Leary, to plan and complete the 2,900-seat behemoth that now serves the parish. St. Colman's is big, but it was never big enough. After it was completed—without a mortgage—the staff still had to use the basement as a lower church to accommodate part of the congregation. Build it, and more will come.

Among the residential and commercial structures located along West 65th Street, St. Colman's stands out—apart from its size—because of its color, material, and architectural quality. In 1914 a Roman aristocrat, with the assistance of Cleveland architects Edwin Schneider and J. Ellsworth Potter, designed the present church, constructed of thick blocks of Indiana limestone, in a classical style. A two-story central pavilion supported by four monumental paired fluted columns with Corinthian capitals dominates the central portion of the west-entry facade. Symmetrically placed 130-foot bell towers frame the portico. The smooth ashlar exterior accentuates the plain block form of the building. St. Procop has a similar form and mass, but it is made of rough rather than smooth stone, and its central form does not include a portico.

In the interior, the relatively narrow narthex contains three bays. One might expect, therefore, that the nave would be similarly divided into the typical three-aisled arrangement. This is, however, not the case since the nave has no interior columns. In the main worship space and in the basement below, St. Colman's is a miracle of the twentieth-century cantilever. The space nevertheless alludes to a cruciform shape with a coffered ceiling in the shape of a cross. The long axis of the cross follows the central aisle, and the short axis projects between the side shrines.

An ambulatory behind the apse embraces an interesting semicircular baptistry together with the elaborate sacristy complex required by such a large establishment. In the nave, flat stations are encased in large red and white alabaster frames. The Italian marble communion rail, baptistry font, and freestanding pulpit were made in Dublin, Ireland, under the eye of O'Leary, to prove the worth of Irish craftsmen. He let Italians carve the rest. Together with its towering three-story altar, its flanking Mary and Joseph altars, and its side aisle altars, the church is an extravaganza of marble—Verde antique, mottled red, light gray, mottled gray, light purple, white, Vermont, red, green, Connemara, Verona, onyx, Siena, orange, golden, and yellow. Black marble steps lead to an exquisite transparent marble communion rail with Eucharistic carving. The marble goes up and up and up as marble is piled on marble, figures follow figures, and reliefs follow reliefs. After all of this marble, the Tiffany-style milk glass windows are relatively restrained. Nave walls and the basilicalike ceiling are painted simply.

St. Colman's is so big that parts of it get lost. Sometime after the Second World War, two large grottos on either side of the immense basement space disappeared. Dedicated to the Virgin, each complete with finished marble statuary, their marble altar rails were sledgehammered and each space plastered up. They had been an important part of parish life during the Second World War as the congregation prayed for peace and the return of their men. Now, one or both of these grottos may be reborn outside as a memorial to those who fought in all wars.

On March 15, 2009, Bishop Richard Lennon announced the closing of St. Colman's. The parish appealed and the bishop relented.

/3. St. Stephen Church (1873)
.rchitects: Franz Cudell and John
.Richardson
Builder: Casimir Reichlin
Location: 1910 West 54th Street

St. Stephen Church has, as Armstrong wrote, some of the most important ecclesiastical artwork in the United States.[21] The church's interior was considered one of the finest in the world in the 1890s and was officially recognized in 1893 at the Columbian Exposition in Chicago, where the freestanding oak pulpit with its finely detailed canopy (rising more than twenty-five feet above the floor) was displayed. The carved oak, polychromed statues, imported from Munich in 1893, are exceptional because most Victorian statues were made of plaster and cast in molds. Critics of the sculpture love to point out that the figures have Germanic facial features. They are invariably enamored by the blond, rather than brunette, hair of the Virgin. Among the throng (more than thirty major figures), scholars consider as the most outstanding the one-third of life-size statues of Christ and four Doctors of the Church encircling the speaking platform of the pulpit.

The glass, commissioned in 1906 through the Bavarian Institute of Art and imported from the Mayer Studio in Munich, is also of the highest quality. The Mayer Studio, established in 1848, is now in its fifth generation. Mayer glass has been used in more than one hundred major religious buildings, including St. Peter in Rome. In 1953 a tornado severely damaged a dozen windows and completely destroyed the three windows behind the main altar. The church was closed for five months for repairs. One of the technicians sent over by the Mayer Studio had worked on the original windows in 1906. In 1993 the three windows behind the altar were partially replaced with three Mayer windows from St. Joseph Franciscan.

In 1853, after the cathedral was completed, the bishop gave the first Roman Catholic church in Cleveland, Our Lady of the Lake (commonly known as St. Mary-on-the-Flats), to the Germans. Germans living on the East Side promptly began building Saint Peter Church (see p. 18) and soon moved out. West Side Germans, organized as St. Mary's of the Assumption, struggled to build a church of their own and did not move into it until 1865. Four years later, as the West Side German community expanded, the bishop asked the pastor of St. Mary's to build a two-story mission school-church (worshipers up, children down). The following year, newly ordained Casimir Reichlin was appointed first pastor of St. Stephen. Three years later Reichlin began the present building.

St. Stephen was designed by Cudell and Richardson, who were also responsible for St. Joseph Franciscan and Franklin Circle Christian (see p. 187) Churches. St. Stephen appears as their "most massive and permanent" building.[22] Although they became famous for the use of iron columns in commercial buildings, the pillars and soaring vaults of St. Stephen are made entirely of stone. The importance of the church's decoration should not detract from the elegance of its interior and the massiveness of its Berea sandstone exterior, although the massiveness did not protect the Gothic finials (now replaced) that also fell victim to the tornado.

Somewhat incongruously sited in a quiet street of modest homes, the sumptuousness of the high-style interior decoration of this large cruciform building contrasts with its vernacular neighborhood surroundings. Lancet windows, decorative buttresses, and the attractive square bell tower are Gothic in style. So are the corner finials. The streets of St. Stephen have not always been as quiet as they appear today. In the late twentieth century, the neighborhood served as the epicenter of the West Side's heavy drug culture with its crime and violence. Social disorder reached the point where neighbors were afraid of each other, and neighborhood meetings were poorly attended for fear of violence. The church that every Christian should visit before going to heaven was surrounded by social disaster. As Father Michael Franz tried to make his neighborhood habitable, children in the parish schools, sprawling over the St. Stephen campus from 54th to 57th Streets, began reporting that his life was in danger. He persisted and prevailed, and the old law-abiding German community has become a new law-abiding Hispanic community where people can walk safely to the Rapid.

Despite the powerful forty-foot-high weight-bearing exterior walls, generous windows give the interior a bright and airy feeling, even through the Mayer glass. On each side of the main aisle, six great, plain, plastered pillars sweep up to support the subtly painted vaulted ceiling seventy-five feet from the floor. In this Gothic Revival church, the tall aisle arcade, the great proportion of open space to the supporting columns, and the absence of a clerestory give St. Stephen the effect of a hall church. Shallow transepts are decorated with painted oculi. Glazed rose windows in this location would be out of place in this relatively early Victorian Gothic building. Oak pews constructed by furniture-making parishioners harmonize with the imported woodcarving of the altars and pulpit. Sanctuary and aisles are surfaced with basket-weave marble tile but the worshipers' feet rest on oak flooring. The original 1886 tracker organ was rebuilt and redesigned by Holtkamp in 1938 as an electropneumatic instrument. The organ was severely damaged by the 1953 tornado and is currently being rebuilt for the second time.

CHAPTER TEN

West Park

The West Park community is composed of the four Cleveland neighborhoods located west of West 117th Street and includes Jefferson, Kamm's Corners, Riverside, and Puritas-Longmead.

Tour

Begin this tour at the eastern edge of the Jefferson neighborhood on Lorain Avenue, just south of the interchange of West 117th at I-90. Drive west on Lorain. At the intersection of West 128th Street, Mt. Calvary Lutheran Church occupies the northwest corner. The former church, now used as a school, lies to the west while the new contemporary sanctuary lies to the east.

A little farther west, on the northwest corner of the intersection of Lorain at Berea Road, is located St. Vincent de Paul Church, a modified Prairie School-style building of dark brown brick. Drive to West 138th Street, just past the shopping center on the left side of Lorain, and turn left (south). The large, gray-stone, Gothic Revival Christ United Methodist Church (104) dominates the triangular intersection formed by West 138th Street at Fairwood Drive. Keeping to the right of the church, drive one block south on West 138th. Turn right (west) onto San Diego Avenue. After two blocks, turn left (south) onto West 140th Street. After two blocks turn right (west) onto Carrydale Avenue. The small neighborhood church of the West Park Evangelical Friends stands at the southwest corner. At the end of Carrydale, turn right (north) onto West 143rd Street and return to Lorain Avenue.

Turn left onto Lorain and pass under the Rapid Transit bridge to enter the Kamm's Corners neighborhood, an area of well-kept homes bordering the Rocky River Reservation of the Cleveland Metropolitan Park System. Beyond the intersection of West 150th Street at Lorain, make a sharp right turn onto Triskett Road. On the left, at the intersection of Rockport Avenue, stands the traditional Bethany English Lutheran Church. It contrasts with the contemporary building of St. Mark's Episcopal Church located diagonally across the street on the right.

Proceeding northeast on Triskett, another little contemporary church, the West Park Christian Reformed Church, sits opposite the intersection of West 152nd Street. Continuing on Triskett, the large, plain brick St. Mel Church, with its deeply recessed entry, is located on the left side of Triskett just before the intersection of Orchard Park Avenue. Turn left onto Orchard Park, follow it to the left, and then, at the first intersection, turn right onto Westland Avenue. At the end of Westland one finds St. Mary Romanian Orthodox Cathedral (105), formerly located in the Detroit Shoreway neighborhood. The church doors do not face Warren Road, as one might expect, so take the drive-

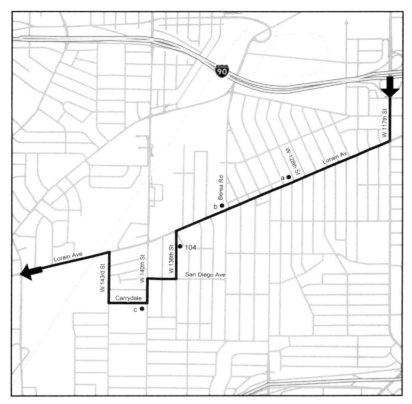

JEFFERSON
  a. Mt. Calvary Lutheran Church
  b. St. Vincent de Paul Church
104. Christ United Methodist Church
  c. West Park Evangelical Friends Church

way on the north side of the building to see the cathedral's dramatic entrance. Return to the street and turn left (north) onto Warren Road. At the first intersection turn left (west) onto Montrose Avenue and follow it to West 159th Street. The modern brick St. Mark's Parish was erected here in 1959. At the end of Montrose turn left (south) onto West 159th Street. After two blocks, passing Impett Park on the left, turn right onto Edgecliff Avenue and drive west until Edgecliff dead-ends at Rocky River Drive.

Turn left onto Rocky River Drive and proceed south. After a few blocks, enter the "Holy City." On the right is St. Joseph Academy and the Sisters of St. Joseph, set in an expansive campus. A little farther south, on the left (east) side of Rocky River Drive, is the Monastery of Poor Clares. Notice the beautiful little circular pavilion in the front. Within a short distance on the right is another Roman Catholic institutional complex centered on Our Lady of Angels

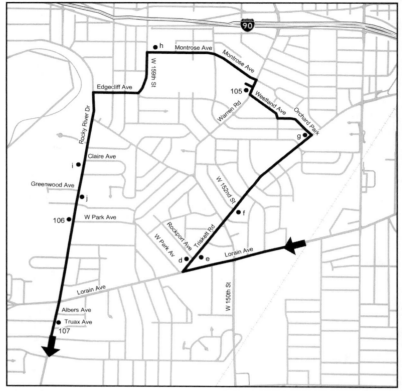

KAMMS CORNERS

   d. Bethany English Lutheran Church
   e. St. Mark's Episcopal Church
   f. West Park Christian Reformed Church
   g. St. Mel Church
105. St. Mary Romanian Orthodox Cathedral
   h. St. Mark's Parish
   i. St. Joseph Academy and the Sisters of St. Joseph
   j. Monastery of Poor Clares
106. Our Lady of Angels Church
107. West Park United Church of Christ

Church (106). The church, schools, hall, rectory, and the Franciscan Village elderly housing development extend across this third large campus. Continue on Rocky River Drive. Shortly after passing the Kamm's Corners Shopping Center at Lorain Avenue, West Park United Church of Christ (107) appears on the left at the northeast corner of Truax Avenue at Rocky River Drive.

Continuing south on Rocky River Drive, enter the Riverside neighborhood. After a few blocks on Rocky River Drive, the long, low, contemporary Holy Cross Lutheran Church appears on the right. Built in 1957, this church has a porte cochere between the educational building to the south and the

RIVERSIDE

k. Holy Cross Lutheran Church
108. St. Patrick's Church West Park
109. Masjid Al-Islam/Ihsan School of Excellence

sanctuary to the north. Parking is located behind the building and hidden from the street.

On the northeast corner of the intersection of Puritas Avenue at Rocky River Drive is St. Patrick's Church West Park (108). A few blocks south of this, on the northwest corner of Ferncliffe Avenue at Rocky River stands Masjid Al-Islam/Ihsan School of Excellence (formerly Riverside Community Church) (109). It was remodeled in a modified Prairie School style after being moved here from another location. Across the street is Riverside Homes, the community that originally housed the Lewis Research workers of the National Aeronautics and Space Administration (NASA), who created the Riverside Community Church congregation. This is the last church in the Riverside Neighborhood.

To get to the Puritas-Longmead neighborhood, turn right (west) onto Ferncliffe. After one block turn right again (north). After four short blocks turn right once more (east) onto Puritas Avenue. Drive east past Rocky River

PURITAS–LONGMEAD

l. Hungarian Reformed Church West Side
m. Ascension Catholic Church
n. Puritas Lutheran Church
o. Second Calvary Missionary Baptist Church
p. Annunciation Church

Drive and St. Patrick's Church and under the I-71 and Rapid Transit bridges to enter the Puritas-Longmead residential neighborhood.

The western section of the Puritas-Longwood neighborhood is characterized by newer houses, built in the 1950s, while smaller homes built around 1920 are clustered around West 130th Street.

On the left side of Puritas between West 154th Street and West 152nd Street, one finds the brick neo-Modern Hungarian Reformed Church West Side, erected in 1977. It has a striking central bell tower. Continuing east on Puritas, the Ascension Catholic Church is located on the northwest corner of Puritas at West 140th Street. The Puritas Shopping Center is across the street to the right. Across the street to the east is the Rockport Branch of the Cleveland Public Library. Ascension Catholic Church is a large, plain, modern brick building that contrasts with its older, smaller frame predecessor that remains on the corner. At West 139th Street, Puritas continues east and Bellaire Road curves to the north. Bear left onto Bellaire and note, on the left, the large sprawling Puritas Lutheran Church built in a modified Georgian style in 1955.

Drive northeast on Bellaire through its intersection with West 130th Street. Continue on Bellaire to the Second Calvary Missionary Baptist Church, located at the corner of Brookfield Avenue at Bellaire. Then backtrack to West 130th by turning left onto Brookfield, going west. Turn left (south) onto West 130th. Crossing Bellaire, after several blocks, pass Annunciation Church on the left, on the corner of West 130th at Bennington Avenue. To gain access to I-480 continue south for a few more blocks.

104. Christ United Methodist Church (1938)
Architect: Unknown
Builders: Ernest Knautz (1938) and Virgil Jump (1956)
Location: 3578 West 138th Street

Christ United Methodist Church resulted from the merger of the Bethany German Methodist Church and the West Park Methodist Church during the Great Depression.[1]

A historic relationship between Methodism and German immigrants began in 1735. During their voyage to Georgia to help James Oglethorpe establish his colony, the Wesleys were greatly influenced by twenty-six Moravians (German speakers from what is now the Czech Republic).[2] In the middle of the nineteenth century, the Methodist Church launched a major missionary effort directed toward Germans. An important base for this in northern Ohio was Wallace College. It was established in 1863 on what is now the south campus of Baldwin-Wallace College. At one time there were eight Methodist churches in Cleveland belonging to the Zentral Deutsche Konferenz.[3] The conference was dissolved in 1933, and the German parishes became part of their regional English Methodist organization.

A Baldwin-Wallace student founded Bethany German as a mission in 1893, locating it in a tent at the intersection of Lorain Avenue at Clark Avenue. His congregation moved two blocks east on Lorain to a real wigwam at West 86th Street before settling into a permanent home at West 91st Street and Willard Avenue in 1894. This served the congregation until 1938, when they sold the building to the Immanuel Pentecostal Church.

The West Park Methodist congregation was established in 1908 as a storefront mission by J. F. Hecker, also of Baldwin-Wallace College. In 1909 this congregation moved to the corner of Lorain at West 135th Street. The congregation constructed a main sanctuary there in 1915.

During the Great Depression, the two congregations decided to merge and construct the first portion of the present church. On a Sunday morning in June in 1938, members of Bethany Church met at their church for the last time and, forming a motorcade with police escort, drove out to join the members of West Park Methodist. They held groundbreaking ceremonies that August followed by vesper services under the large oak tree on the east side of their new property. They hung the bell from Bethany Church in the belfry of the new church. By 1954 Christ United Methodist had more than two thousand members. In the course of a major 1956 building campaign, the community greatly enlarged and changed the configuration of their first building. In 1976 the City of Cleveland designated the oak tree a historic site; however, on a Sunday morning in 1990, a great wind blew down the tree, destroying a car.

Located on a point of land where Fairwood Avenue curves into the commercial intersection of Lorain at West 138th Street, Christ Methodist's lawn provides a refreshing green space in an otherwise busy and worn commercial neighborhood. Behind the church is a well-kept residential area. This building is a handsome and imposing medieval revival church. The extremely unusual plan reflects its two distinct campaigns. The first campaign, in 1938, resulted in a conventional 1930s Gothic Revival building with window tracery, pointed arches above windows and doors, plain ashlar wall surfaces, and an entrance through the present east tower. In 1956 this building was substantially enlarged in the same style. A west tower was constructed so that both short two-story towers, each with an entrance toward Lorain, are located astride the south end of the original building. The south third of the nave, inside the building, was elevated three steps and extended past the towers, both of which now provide access to the sanctuary from the outside. The back of the original building, behind the towers, was enlarged. Behind the sanctuary, to the south, one finds a large parlor to the east, the large Stocker chapel (oriented toward the south) to the west, and classrooms in between.

The result of the 1956 rebuilding is a large, if unusual, sanctuary. The peaked ceiling follows the roofline. It does not have an attic. Ceiling and walls are plaster. The ceiling is articulated by stained wood beams between which are smaller stained stringers. High cross ties pull the large beams—but not the thin stringers—together. Each cross tie is decorated with a simple shield on which a cross is imprinted. The high, peaked ceiling makes this a large space. A center aisle and narrow side aisles define the space. The elevation of the rear one third of the nave, while unusual, greatly improves the sight lines for those in back of this axial church. This overcomes the difficulty a Methodist community might have following what is going on in a worship space different from that of a traditional, Methodist, semicircular, auditorium church. Despite the towers straddling the church, there are no transepts; the towers simply provide access into the nave. The antiphonal choir at the front of the church is of light stained wood and matches the altar, frontal, and other church furniture. It features symbolic traditional glass along the walls, a rather small symbolic rose on the south wall, and three lancet windows with one figure of Christ on the front wall.

105. St. Mary Romanian Orthodox Cathedral (1960)

Architect: Haralamb H. Georgescu
Builder: Vasile Hategan
Location: 3256 Warren Road

St. Mary Romanian Orthodox Cathedral, the most dramatic religious building in Cleveland, turns its back on our world and lives in its own.[4] This is a world, in the middle of Cleveland, of fields and trees, a garden and a fountain. The church faces west, away from Warren Road. To appreciate this remarkable building, turn west off Warren, onto the driveway east of the church, between the building and its adjacent playing field. Get out and approach the entrance to Georgescu's masterpiece through its garden, past its fountain, between the two rows of trees framing the building. The architect-in-exile who crafted this building was a figure of such stature that he could command, and knew how to use, a great site for a great building.

Haralamb Georgescu (1908–77) was the Romanian Eric Mendelsohn (see Park Synagogue, p. 315). Like Mendelsohn, Georgescu was an internationally famed European architect (Romania was a smaller pond than Germany) forced into exile at the height of his career—in Georgescu's case, by the post-war Communists. Georgescu, like Mendelsohn, attempted to rebuild his life in the United States. The Romanian architect is best known for his high modern 1958 Pasinetti house in Beverly Hills. His 1959 St. George Orthodox Cathedral in Southfield, Michigan, the seat of the American Romanian Orthodox primate, is slightly smaller than Cleveland's St. Mary. The Cathedral of St. George in Michigan is a different historical style than this church in Cleveland. The tradition from which the cathedral in Michigan draws is of Bucovina.[5] To twenty-first-century eyes, this historical style is not as striking as that of Transylvania, from which Georgescu's Cleveland church descends. Both St. Mary and Romanian Catholic St. Helena's on Detroit (see p. 252) are "Maramures-style churches"—derived from the Transylvanian country church tradition.[6] St. Helena's is somewhat closer to this tradition. St. Mary is Georgescu's vigorous transformation of an Old World tradition into a monument of modernism.

Romanians, a majority of whom are Orthodox, were economically one of the most heterodox Cleveland immigrant communities. Although they would make Cleveland the largest Romanian city in the United States, most immigrants were single men, with no intention of staying in the United States. They came individually at the urging of Hungarian, Saxon, Swabian, and Jewish neighbors in Transylvania and Bucovina. Over time, however, some brought families to this country and began to gather around West 60th Street at Detroit

Avenue. However, after the First World War when Transylvania and Bucovina became part of Greater Romania, half of the immigrants in Cleveland returned to Europe. After the Second World War a modest number of political refugees settled in Cleveland.

Organized as a religious community in 1904, the Orthodox Romanians immediately built the first St. Mary Church. It was the first Romanian parish in the United States and the seat of the bishop before he moved to Michigan. This church went up a year before Romanian Catholic St. Helena, two blocks west on Detroit. The first St. Mary is a charming small brick building in a mixture of Romanesque, Gothic, and Byzantine styles. The church parallels Detroit. Its entrance is off the street to the west to keep the altar at the east end of the building. In 1954 the parish sold this first church to Holy Resurrection Russian Orthodox Church.[7] This precious building is now no longer used for religious purposes—it is the Cleveland Public Theatre.

At the beginning of the twentieth century, things did not go well for the new Romanian parish. Its second pastor died on board a ship from Romania and was buried in New York. In 1909 the bank took possession of their church, and it took a year and a half of strenuous fund-raising for the parish to regain control of the building. Serious fires in 1918 and 1932 burnt parts of the church.

Forty-three parishioners from St. Mary served in American forces during the First World War, in which Romania, at great cost, joined the allies. Prince Carol visited the parish in 1920 but "many" parishioners returned with him to Romania.[8] Prince Nicholas came over when the community built a "national home" for religious and social purposes in 1927 next to the first small church. As the congregation became more Americanized, pews were installed in 1933 and two collection plates began to be passed around—one for the church and one for the pews. Fifteen parishioners from St. Mary died fighting for the United States in the Second World War, although Romania was on the other side.

Like Polish St. Stanislaus (see p. 172), Hungarian St. Elizabeth's (see p. 142)—and, before the Second World War, Italian Holy Rosary—St. Mary serves as an important stop in America for politicians and clerics from the old country. In 1995 the postmaster of Romania unveiled a stamp, illustrated by Georgescu's building, to commemorate St. Mary's ninetieth anniversary as the first Romanian parish in the United States. The parish's ninety-fifth anniversary was celebrated by its elevation to a cathedral. The president of Romania visited the cathedral in 2003.

Romania had an elaborate house and pavilion at the 1939 World's Fair in New York. As the turmoil of the Second World War enveloped the country, a decision was made to keep the exhibition artwork in the United States. St. Mary, the largest Romanian community in this country, was the logical place to store the orphaned material. It remained in storage at St. Mary until, in the depth of the Cold War, it was decided to display this heritage in the rebuilt campus on Warren Road. St. Mary's current collections are partly from the World's Fair and partly from subsequent donations. A substantial amount of the collection was brought surreptitiously out of Romania during the Communist period. The collection now includes that of Anisoara Stan, who willed her collection of Romanian art to the St. Mary community in 1963.[9] Two large rooms in the education building are devoted to a variety of art, clothing, and cultural artifacts. Some of the material is associated with the Romanian royal house. Paintings and drawings are of a high quality. Most of the material is of greater interest to Romanian specialists, but one finds good-quality drawings by Brancusi. Two major items from the 1939 World's Fair are featured elsewhere on the St. Mary campus. The education building has a large fresco in its entrance lobby illustrating Romanian culture. A two-block-long hammered copper relief history of Romania with life-size figures surrounds the principal gathering room of the community center. In the courtyard between the community center and the education building stands a statue of U.S. Civil War General George Pomutz, the Romanian émigré who subsequently, as American consul in St. Petersburg, negotiated the purchase of Alaska.

The buildings on St. Mary's substantial acreage have been cleared away, leaving fields, trees, garden, the church, its attached educational buildings, and the community center. The spacious campus is surrounded by a well-kept residential neighborhood. Warren Road, in front of the church, is a relatively busy street. Trees screen the building from the street and, although the building can be seen from Warren, the church cannot be entered from that direction.

Georgescu's interpretation of a Transylvanian country church is a large A-frame building. Its commanding modernist tower is surmounted by its famous 176-foot-tall, nine-ton modern spire. This spire, in turn, is capped with a large slender aluminum cross. One enters under an imaginative conical canopy supported by four diagonal struts. This canopy supports another thin, tall, elegant cross that corresponds to the main spire of the church behind it. Above the entrance canopy, on the north wall of the church, appears a large enameled icon of Christ, one of the famous enamels on the outside of this church by Edward and Thelma Winter of Cleveland. The enameled figures consist of sixty-two distinct sections fused together by an intense heating process.

The interior of this building is not an anticlimax. On the south wall of the church, above the apse, is a twenty-four-foot Italian mosaic of the Virgin. The handsome iconostasis was designed in one piece by Ilie Cristoloveanu. The imitation stained glass was beautifully painted by Ilie Hasigan. At the rear is a two-level balcony for communicants and choir. The cathedral has seating for only six hundred, but the high ceiling and generous decoration make it a dramatic space.

Most of the inside of the large A-frame was decorated by the Canadian iconographers Niculai and Ioana Enachi, a five-year project completed in 2003.[10] This iconography includes a complete program in the sanctuary behind the iconostasis. Painting after painting appears within the worship space, the narthex, and the sanctuary. Although the ceiling, following the outline of the exterior, is peaked, it has room for *The Pantocreator*. Even the vestibule of the church is lavishly decorated. The iconography there includes a portrait of Policarp Morusca, the first Romanian Orthodox Bishop of North America, who lived for a time in a house the parish provided on Detroit. This bishop holds a miniature of the 1905 church. Beside Morusca stands Archbishop Valerian Trifa holding a miniature of this Georgescu church that he consecrated in 1960. The current pastor, Remus Grama, says that his worship space is "the *Sistina* of west-side orthodoxy." Rather, it is the *Sistina* of Cleveland.

106. Our Lady of Angels Church (1941)
Architect: William Koehl
Builder: Linus Koenemund
Location: 3644 Rocky River Drive

Our Lady of Angels is the church at the center of what is sometimes called the Holy City along Rocky River Drive on the far west border of Cleveland.[11] The immediate campus of Our Lady of Angels, in addition to the church and rectory, includes three substantial school buildings and a large early twentieth-century former Franciscan monastery that, in turn, is the center of the three-building, 176-unit Franciscan Village retirement complex. Across the street from Our Lady of Angels is the ten-acre campus of the cloistered Poor Clare (Colettine) Religious.[12] Two blocks north along Rocky River Drive, within walking distance when the nuns began teaching at Our Lady of Angels School, is the forty-four-acre campus of the Sisters of St. Joseph. Located here is their American mother house and the 670-student St. Joseph Academy, the only all-girl Catholic high school in Cleveland.[13]

Our Lady of Angels began in a Franciscan seminary. The German Franciscan Friars of the Province of the Sacred Heart were brought to Cleveland by Bishop Amadeus Rappe in 1868 to staff St. Joseph Franciscan. Also teaching in schools and ministering to congregations all over Cleveland (see St. Stanislaus, p. 172), these Franciscans began a seminary in 1904 on Rocky River Drive to prepare their friars for ordination. As frequently happens, local Catholics began attending the seminary chapel, known originally as the Church of the Stigmata of St. Francis. It evolved, led by the Franciscans, into the parish of Our Lady of Angels in 1923. The community built its schools and its large church adjacent to the seminary (the dedication of the church was scheduled, and proceeded on December 8, 1941, despite the tragedy of the Japanese attack on Pearl Harbor the day before). In 1964 the Franciscans transferred their seminary students to Our Lady of Angels Seminary in Quincy, Illinois. HUD lent $6.2 million in 1979 to reopen three floors of the seminary and build a five-story building behind it as a one- and two-bedroom, 135-unit Franciscan Village retirement community. Former First Lady Rosalynn Carter attended the dedication in 1982. They received a $2.2 million grant in 1995 for another building and forty-one additional units.[14] In 1987 the Franciscans withdrew from Our Lady of Angels and, since then, it has been led by diocesan clergy.

Overlooking the Rocky River with its Emerald Necklace Rocky River Reservation and among the gracious homes along Rocky River Drive, Our Lady of Angels sits in the middle of one of the last affluent neighborhoods in Cleveland. The church stands between the church's substantial, high-tech school and the large and noisy 1955 gym-and-cafeteria that shields Our Lady of Angels's 1964 kindergarten and first-grade building from the street. The unassuming, low-slung, rambling church has a vaguely South American feeling. The patterned brick masses are simple. Trim is sandstone. Prominent anterior and lateral buttresses, of course, have nothing to do with the structure of the building. A modern complex of offices and classrooms attaches the church to the almost hundred-year-old Franciscan friary (and its brightly renovated retirement complex). Our Lady of Angels's seventy-foot tower with its arcaded open belfry and low, hipped roof appears short and stocky.

A large, gracious hundred-seat chapel, originally the brothers' oratory and now used for daily services, small weddings, Lenten programs, and as a cry-room for mothers on Sundays, is separated from the south side of the sanctuary by a glass wall and Venetian screens. The chapel is decorated with Franciscan-themed glass. Angels are relegated to frescoes on the walls.

Behind the sanctuary is an exceptionally large sacristy, reflecting its long-time use by the many brothers in the seminary. To the south of the nave, in a separate room with a separate entrance, is the baptistry with the font behind a fine Irish wrought-iron screen.

In contrast to its appearance from the outside, this is a large church. The nave seats one thousand. Above the nave one finds a beautiful plain wood ceiling with great wood timbers. Walls are plain with more large Franciscan windows. The sanctuary with its beautiful wood altar of sacrifice under a great wood baldachin, is elevated above the level of the nave. The apse, with its tabernacle on the altar of repose, is elevated even higher. In the balcony, in front of a wheel window and above a large vestibule, is a 1943 Holtkamp organ. In front of the large Holtkamp, a statue of St. Cecelia holds her miniature Holtkamp in her right arm.

107. West Park United Church of Christ (1955)

Architect: Erwin O. Lauffer
Builder: Oliver Cowles
Location: 3909 Rocky River Drive

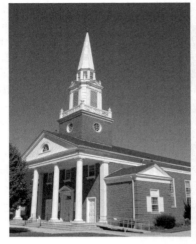

William Kennedy famously described the Plan of Union, the evangelical program in which the Presbyterians and the Congregationalists cooperated in founding frontier churches in Ohio, as a program in which the milk from Congregational cows was turned into Presbyterian butter.[15] West Park United Church of Christ is an exception to this.[16] Presbyterian minister Nehemiah Cobb founded West Park UCC in 1859 as Rockport Congregational Church. Congregational this church was, and Congregational it remains.

Rockport was created in 1819 as one of the most northwestern townships in the Western Reserve—divided almost in half by the Rocky River. The Rockport-Cleveland township border was approximately where 117th Street now divides Cleveland and Lakewood. At first meeting in the school house at Puritas Springs,[17] the Congregationalists established their version of Christianity in the local Methodist church before building their first church in 1861. This simple, small, white clapboard country church was dedicated by William Goodrich, second pastor of the Old Stone Church.[18] As Dr. Goodrich rose to deliver his remarks, his progress to the lectern was no doubt facilitated by the "slippery, black, haircloth sofa" that was such an important feature on the raised platform in front of the congregation.[19]

Rockport became known as West Park, and the church renamed itself accordingly. In 1905 the little frame building was turned ninety degrees so that it ran parallel to Rocky River Drive. An imposing, masonry, English Gothic extension of the worship space was added, toward the street, at right angles to the new orientation of the original small church. The new addition dwarfed the original building. In 1928 the community put up the large brick building now north of the church. With its large assembly room and stage adjacent to a kitchen, it continues to provide community and education space. At last, in 1955, the original frame church and its masonry addition were taken down and replaced with the present building. In 1977 a Shantz organ was installed.[20] The congregation voted to join the United Church of Christ in 1968.

Just a block down the street from Kamm's Corners, one of the busiest intersections in Cleveland, and sharing a property line to the north with a large drive-in bank, this church otherwise adjoins a tidy residential neighborhood to east, south, and west. Four unadorned columns support its extended entrance portico, with its large triangular pediment. Brick quoins and a bell tower capped by a classic balustrade and copper urns are Georgian. To the undiscriminating student of the Connecticut Western Reserve, it is extremely difficult to differentiate this building from Daniel Farnham's 1929 Archwood UCC on West 25th Street near Pearl Road. Differences between the exteriors of the buildings do exist, but they require careful examination to sort out.[21] The physical surroundings of the two buildings could not be more different. Archwood UCC is shoehorned into a cramped inner-city lot along a narrow street. West Park UCC, graciously set back from the street across a generous lawn, dominates its neighborhood up and down Rocky River Drive south of Kamm's Corners.

The interior of the two churches is also completely different. While Archwood is gracefully decorated, West Park is extremely and elegantly simple. Here the church is divided by a center aisle and narrow side aisles. The choir is elevated; there is a small balcony at the rear. West Park does not have Wren-Gibbs side balconies. White-painted pews match white-painted molding along the walls, in the back, and within the chancel. Other church furniture is also white. The ceiling is flat, plastered, and white. Despite all the white paint, the pale blue walls give the sanctuary a surprisingly warm character. Windows are encased in white framing with painted wood keystones. An occasional, faintly colored pane enlivens the otherwise clear antique glass windows. Ten elegant chandeliers light the space at night. The three windows at the back and five on each side provide strong illumination during the day. West Park has a small rose at the front over the exposed pipes of the organ. Everything has a simple, elegant, rational Congregational feeling.

108. St. Patrick's Church
West Park (1898)
Architect: Henry Hanks
Builder: Joseph Hoerstmann
Location: 4427 Rocky River
Drive

St. Patrick's West Park, originally a small community of mostly Irish farmers in the middle of nowhere on the Far West Side was, until it was closed in 2009, the oldest existing Roman Catholic parish in Cleveland.[22] Nine months before establishing the parish that would become his cathedral, Bishop Amadeus Rappe rode out on the Feast of St. Patrick to the home of Morgan Waters in the southern part of Rockport Township; there he baptized, heard confessions, and said Mass.[23] For the next six years the little community continued as a mission of the cathedral, personally tended during monthly visits by the bishop and then by his assistants. The country parish grew slowly. It would be sixty-two years before a successor bishop assigned a full-time resident pastor.

A family donated a half-acre on the corner where the church now stands, and the community put up a small frame building in a field on the site of the present graveyard. The community was assigned to the pastor of St. Mary's of the Falls in Olmsted Falls as a part-time responsibility; it continued as someone's part-time responsibility until 1910. As a growing number of Germans moved into Rockport, Bishop Rappe established St. Mary Rockport in 1860 (now Assumption, Brook Park). When he assigned a resident German pastor in 1865, the bishop transferred St. Patrick's to the new priest's care.[24]

St. Patrick's struggled along until 1896, when Bishop Ignatius Horstman suggested that the parish—still without a permanent pastor—build a church to accommodate a community twice its size. This would allow St. Patrick's to respond to the coming of the interurban and the streetcar. St. Patrick's built and people came. Between 1922 and 1924, seven new Roman Catholic parishes were established in Rockport Township, all taken out of St. Patrick's territory.[25] St. Patrick's still kept growing. There ensued the traditional wrangling between priest, parish, sisters, and diocese concerning the school. When the Great Depression hit the parish, the pastor was so concerned with the welfare of his parishioners that he invited them to help themselves from the coal pile in the parking lot. He almost lost the school to the bank. By the end of the thirties, St. Patrick's, despite the southern part of the parish being farmland, had financially recovered to the point where, in 1938 and 1939, the grand prize for the fall bazaar raffle was an airplane (in both years, however, the winning parishioner took the alternative prize of $1,000).

Wartime rationing ended the St. Patrick's Day roast beef dinners and forced the nuns to ride the streetcar back and forth from their mother house, but the Brook Park bomber plant (now the I-X Center), with its government housing, greatly expanded the parish. As the parish gathered its resources for further building, it also remembered those devastated by the war. Relief was collected for the French home parish of Amadeus Rappe, who had come to the aide of the little community of poor Irish farmers one hundred years before.

After the war, the population in southwest Cleveland exploded, and three more new parishes were carved out of St. Patrick's—St. Mel (1945), St. Mark (1945), and Ascension (1946). The parish continued to grow. Between 1945 and 1951 it more than doubled in size to 1,950 families. They kept busy. Ten years later, 1,600 students attended the school, and another eight hundred public-school children attended religion classes. In 1967 the school had a fourteen-thousand-volume library. By 1974, when the construction of I-480 together with the airport noise abatement program began to reduce the number of parishioners, there were more than 3,100 households at St. Patrick's, and its original area had been divided into twelve parishes.

St. Patrick's Cemetery, immediately south of the present church on the northeast corner of Rocky River Drive and Puritas Avenue, greatly complicated the construction of an adequate new building in 1951 and explains the unusual length and narrow width of St. Patrick's worship space. Because the parish was initially so far out in the country, it established a cemetery beside the church. When the first frame church and school were razed, their area was added to the cemetery. At last, in 1918, the diocese denied further expansion of the cemetery. In 1927 the parish defeated the City of Cleveland's plan to widen Puritas at the expense of the cemetery. Twenty-five years later, the parish defeated their clergy's plan to move the cemetery two miles away to the new Holy Cross Cemetery in Brook Park and build a new church. The solution, by the Cleveland architectural firm of Ward and Conrad, was to double the length of the nave to hold almost nine hundred worshipers.

In the middle of a mixed residential-commercial neighborhood, St. Patrick's sits on a large campus with a big school. As one would expect, from the way the original church was lengthened, St. Patrick's appears much larger from the south (from Puritas) than from the west (from Rocky River Drive). It is not clear how large this nearly nine-hundred-seat church is until an observer sees how large the school is. The 1951 addition, which doubled the capacity of the building by extending the nave east from the transepts, is much more obvious from the outside than from the inside of the building. Although some of the masonry of the original structure was extended east, the most eastern part of the building is brick. The church's crenelated battlement tower with its pointed louvered belfry and the opposite tower with its rounded turrets frame the pointed arch entrance.

In the interior, the long, narrow character of the nave is striking. The plain, wood-beamed ceiling towers fifty-four feet above the floor. The west window is beautiful. The figurative glass of the lateral windows presents an interesting selection of modern and biblical saints. The major window above the north transept features *St. Patrick with St. Columbkille and St. Bridget. The Marriage at Cana* appears above the south transept. An ambitious relief is over the baptismal pool. The main entrance doors display, in modern glass, *St. Patrick* on one door and *Ireland* (with the north in chains) on the other.

On March 15, 2009, Bishop Richard Lennon announced the closing of St. Patrick's. On March 1, 2012, the Vatican Congregation for the Clergy ruled that Bishop Lennon had failed to follow church law and procedure in closing St. Patrick's.

109. Masjid Al-Islam/ Ihsan School of Excellence, originally Parma–South Presbyterian Church then Riverside Community Church (1946)
Architect: (1946) Carl Droppers
Builders: Unknown
Location: 4600 Rocky River Drive

Sheikh Salih Nawash, one of the imams, and two executive members of the Islamic Center of Cleveland (ICC, see p. 300), resigned from the ICC in 1992 to found Masjid Al-Islam.[26] In 2000 this new Islamic community moved into this building.[27] The next year they established the Al-Ihsan School of Excellence as a kindergarten and first grade. It is now kindergarten to sixth grade. Graduates go to the public schools; there are no Islamic middle or secondary schools in Cleveland.

This interesting building has been the subject of several transformations. The present building, with its extended eaves, hip roof, and sliding horizontal planes, is widely known as one of Cleveland's relatively few institutional examples of Frank Lloyd Wright's Prairie style.[28] The original architect is unknown. The building began its life as a frame structure put up for the Parma-South Presbyterian Church on Pearl Road in Parma Heights in 1893. It would not have been built as a Prairie-style building.[29] This frame building was subsequently moved four miles to its present location and extensively rebuilt in 1946 by Carl Droppers. At that time, it acquired its squared-off bell tower with open belfry, its brick sheathing, and its Prairie-style character. Droppers rebuilt the building for the Riverside Community Church that had been organized in 1945. Most of its members lived in the Riverside Estates across the street. They were employees of the National Advisory Committee for Aeronautics (NACA) laboratory established in Cleveland in 1940 on land west of the airport that had been used previously for stands and parking for the National Air Races. In 1944 NACA built the most advanced wind tunnel in the world. The laboratory was renamed the Lewis Flight Propulsion Research Laboratory in 1948, and it became part of NASA when it was established in 1958.

This building's Islamic community has rebuilt the building a second time to support their religious and educational mission. The original sanctuary has been divided so that its eastern two-thirds is carpeted and transformed into the men's prayer area of the mosque. This prayer area faces east (the Riverside church sanctuary faced west). The original timbered framing of the sanctuary ceiling has been retained. It is the only decoration in the quiet and simple men's prayer room. To the side, in front, is the movable wooden *minbar*, or pulpit. The original simple spherical light fixtures remain. The previous main, eastern, entrance to the building from Rocky River Drive has been sealed off, and the elaborate multiple Prairie-style stairs and terraces, sliding out of the mass of the building, have been disassembled. The western third of the sanctuary is now an assembly area and provides access to the administrative space supporting mosque and school. The basement has been completely reorganized in an ambitious building program to adapt it more effectively to the needs of the school.

CHAPTER ELEVEN

Lakewood—Rocky River—Westlake—
Bay Village—North Olmsted

Tour

Begin this tour at the West 117th Street interchange of Interstate 90. Drive north on West 117th through Cleveland and turn left (west) onto Madison Avenue, entering Lakewood. A few blocks down, on the right side, stands Transfiguration Parish, formerly Saints Cyril and Methodius Church (110). Transfiguration is in the heart of the Slovak neighborhood of Birdtown (so called because of the names of the cross streets—Lark, Robin, and Quail). To the left (south) on Madison, you see an onion dome on top of the tower of Sts. Peter and Paul Russian Orthodox Church. Turn right (north) onto Alameda Avenue and drive two blocks north. Turn left (west) onto Detroit Avenue. Farther west, on the right, stands the Church of the Ascension. Founded in 1875, it is the oldest Episcopal church in Lakewood. Pass, also on the right, St. Edward High School with its new modern chapel. Farther on the right, just past the intersection of Detroit at Manor Park Avenue, sits Pilgrim Lutheran Church with its famous windows. Farther west, on the left side of Detroit, is the neo-Gothic Lakewood Baptist Church. On the northwest corner of Detroit at Marlowe Avenue stands Lakewood Presbyterian Church (111), with its sparkling, innovative education and entrance pavilion. Farther west on Detroit, the West Shore Assembly of God meets in the Classic Revival Lakewood Masonic Temple on the right, across the street from the Lakewood Public Library. Continuing west, on the left side of Detroit, is St. Paul Lutheran Church with the spire above its tower. Farther west, on the right, is the Lakewood United Methodist Church (112) where Jesse Jackson preached when he was running for president. Continuing on Detroit, on the right stands another neo-Gothic church, Trinity Lutheran Church. Visible down Detroit are the great twin Sicilian towers of Roman Catholic St. James Parish (113) where Detroit jogs slightly to the south. Across the street from St. James sits the contemporary Lakewood Christian Church beside the Beck Center for the Arts. Continuing on Detroit, on the left (south) appears St. Peter's Episcopal Church (114), across the street from the brick neo-Georgian Lakewood Congregational Church with six white pillars supporting its white frame portico.

Drive farther west on Detroit and cross the Rocky River. On the right, in downtown Rocky River, is the Rocky River United Methodist Church. Farther into Rocky River, spreading out from the southeast corner of Lakeview Avenue at Detroit is the campus of Roman Catholic St. Christopher Parish Community (115). Here, in the 1920s and 1930s, the pastor would have stopped you on the Feast of St. Christopher and given you a St. Christopher medal

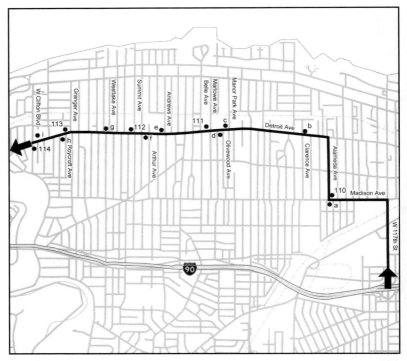

LAKEWOOD

110. Transfiguration Parish
  a. Sts. Peter and Paul Russian Orthodox
Church
  b. Church of the Ascension
  c. Pilgrim Lutheran Church
  d. Lakewood Baptist Church
111. Lakewood Presbyterian Church
  e. West Shore Assembly of God

  f. St. Paul Lutheran Church
112. Lakewood United Methodist Church
  g. Trinity Lutheran Church
113. St. James Parish
  h. Lakewood Christian Church
114. St. Peter's Episcopal Church
  i. Lakewood Congregational Church

along with a warning that St. Christopher would appear if you drove faster than sixty miles per hour. Continue on Detroit to Northview Road and turn left (south), behind Rocky River High School. Cross over I-90 and turn left (east) onto Hilliard Boulevard. On the right stands West Shore Unitarian Universalist Church (116), across the street from Our Savior's Rocky River Lutheran Church on the left side of Hilliard. Turn around in West Shore Unitarian's parking lot and pause to appreciate this institution's startling functional modernity. Go back (west) on Hilliard, past Magnificat High School on the right, turning left (south) onto Wagar Road. Rocky River City Hall occupies the northwest corner. Just before the Westgate Mall, turn right (west) onto Center Ridge Road. St. Demetrios Greek Orthodox Church (117) appears on the left just before the Rocky River-West Lake border. Even the exit and entrance signs to its parking lot are the blue and white of the Greek flag.

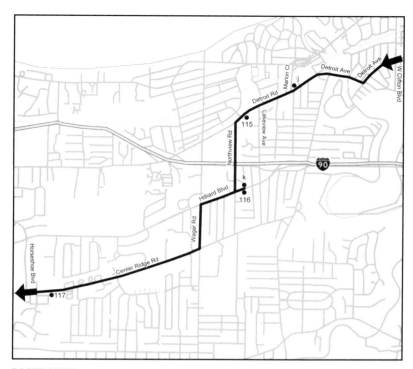

ROCKY RIVER

   j. Rocky River United Methodist Church
115. St. Christopher Parish Community
116. West Shore Unitarian Universalist Church
   k. Our Savior's Rocky River Lutheran Church
117. St. Demetrios Greek Orthodox Church

Continue on Center Ridge Road, past brick Grace Baptist Church Westlake on the right with its sprawling additions behind. Also on the right of Center Ridge Road is the expanding Church of the Redeemer, United Church of Christ. At Clague Road, turn right (north). Going past a Clague Park on the left, the Parkside Church of the Nazarene stands on the northeast corner of Hilliard at Clague.

Recross I-90 and drive past another Clague Park, this time on the right, to Lake Road and turn left (west). Bay Presbyterian Church (118) sits on the left at the intersection of Columbia Road. Before reaching Columbia Road, turn left into the church's parking lot to see its dramatic entrance. Leaving the parking lot, turn left (south) onto Columbia Road. Cross I-90 for the third time. On the left, south of Center Ridge Road at Columbia, stands the small but dramatic modern tower of the Hungarian Seventh Day Adventist Church.

Farther down, on the west side of Columbia, you first come upon the large metal building of the North Olmsted Assembly of God and then, well back

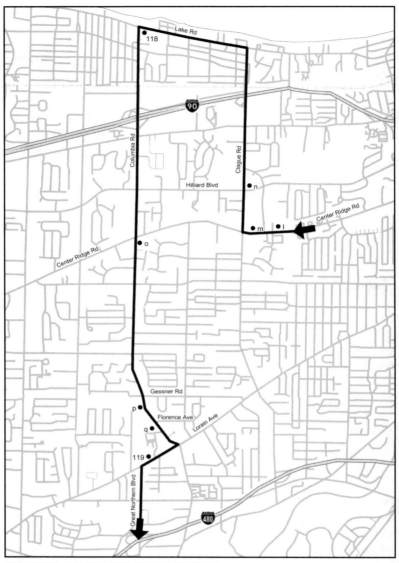

WESTLAKE—BAY VILLAGE—NORTH OLMSTED

   l. Grace Baptist Church Westlake

   m. Church of the Redeemer, United Church of Christ

   n. Parkside Church of the Nazarene

118. Bay Presbyterian Church

   o. Hungarian Seventh Day Adventist Church

   p. North Olmsted Assembly of God

   q. Columbia Road Baptist Church

119. John Knox Presbyterian Church

from the road, the Columbia Road Baptist Church. Turn right (west) onto Lo-rain Road. John Knox Presbyterian Church (119) is located on the right of the T-shaped intersection of Lorain at Great Northern Boulevard. Turn left and drive south on Great Northern Boulevard, passing the vast eponymous mall to the west, to the interchange of Great Northern Boulevard and Interstate 480.

110. Transfiguration Parish,
formerly Saints Cyril and Methodius Church (1929)
Architect: Potter-Gable and Co.
Builder: Francis Dubosh
Location: 12608 Madison, Lakewood

Saints Cyril and Methodius traditionally are given credit for inventing the Cyrillic alphabet and, thus, bringing literacy and Christianity to the Slovak people. Known as the "Apostles to the Slavs," they were obvi-ous potential namesakes for a church built for the large number of Slovaks who came to southeastern Lakewood at the beginning of the twentieth cen-tury. Many worked for Union Carbide across the border in Cleveland. When Union Carbide found it did not need the large acreage it had initially acquired in Lakewood, it sold lots to its employees. In organizing their neighborhood, they named their streets Quail, Robin, Lark, Plover, and Thrush. Saints Cyril and Methodius became the emotional center of "Birdtown."[1]

Establishing their parish in 1902, the Slovaks built a frame church in 1906. This still stands on Lakewood Avenue immediately to the north of the current church.[2] The deaths of thirty-six parishioners in the 1918 influenza pandemic temporarily closed the school. Recovering from this tragedy, the parish com-pleted its large, yellow-brick Carolingian church with stone facing in 1931. A single tower soars beside the apse. Two rows of ten columns support the beamed ceiling of the nave, with its wide central aisle.

Transfiguration is known in particular for its artwork. After the Second World War, Joseph Cincik found that Communist Czechoslovakia was not a supportive environment for religious art. He made his way to Cleveland. Here he was probably involved in three major projects on what had been the undeco-rated rough brown walls of Saints Cyril and Methodius. These include, first, a mural narrative running around the nave, above the arcade, concerning inci-dents in Slavonic religious history; second, a two-story mural on the south wall of the east transept (the church faces north) concerning *Cyril and Methodius;* and, third, another two-story mural on the south wall of the west transept of *The Sorrowful Mother,* the patroness of Slovakia.[3] Windows are decorated with inter-esting glass, including a good rose over the south main entrance to the church. In the apse one finds mosaics of *Cyril and Methodius* with other associated saints and *The Trinity*. The cover over the baptismal font is decorated with the symbols of each of the Slavic nationalities. A 1931 Moeller pipe organ has been recently restored.

On March 15, 2009, Bishop Richard Lennon announced the closing of St. Rose of Lima Church in Cleveland (see p. 246). He merged St. Rose with Saints Cyril and Methodius Church to form Transfiguration Parish.

111. Lakewood Presbyterian Church
(1908; 1918; 2007)
Architects: Unknown
(1907 and 1918); David
Krebs (2007)
Builders: Alfred Wright
(1908 and 1918) and
James Butler (2007)
Location: 14502
Detroit Avenue,
Lakewood

Lakewood Presbyterian's award-winning twenty-first-century addition added fifteen thousand beautifully conceived, designed, and executed square feet to a 25,000-square-foot, ninety-year-old building on a busy downtown commercial corner.[4] It deserves its awards as "the best large building renovation in 2007" in Lakewood and "the best addition to a historic building" in Lakewood. The new addition knits together and improves a 1908 building, a 1918 building, and the educational, administrative, and social responsibilities of a large, growing, and historic urban parish. This landmark building (1918) now has a landmark addition (2007). In a style consistent with the reserve that one associates with Presbyterians, this church has revitalized its neighborhood as it has revitalized itself.

Lakewood Presbyterian, known to its intimates as "LPC," had a much more humble beginning. It began in a parishioner's house as a branch of the Old Stone Church (see p. 12). Then it moved into a tent for six Sundays before the congregation leased a house. Alfred Wright held the title of "assistant pastor of Old Stone Church, in charge of the Lakewood Branch" in 1905. He became famous for riding his horse out to Lakewood from the Old Stone Church on Sundays and for riding around Lakewood greeting every parishioner, no matter what the weather, on New Year's Day. His efforts were so successful that the community had to lease larger quarters in a building on the second floor above a butcher shop. As, during the summer, the voices of the faithful rose to the heavens, so did the atmosphere of the shop downstairs rise to the second-floor worshipers. This prompted the purchase, in 1907, of the lot on which they built their substantial, if small, first church. This building is now incorporated into the fabric of their 2007 addition as the "Wright Chapel." Complete with a Ruggles tracker organ and restored glass, the pews have been taken out of the chapel to allow for more flexible seating.

LPC was organized, in 1912, as an independent church. By this time, the 1908 building was so crowded that men volunteered to stand in the aisles. The present sanctuary was dedicated in 1918. Since then LPC has been responsible for establishing two daughter churches: Grace Presbyterian in Lakewood (1920) and Rocky River Presbyterian Church (1955). An education wing beside the 1918 church was dedicated in 1951, and in 1961 the sanctuary was renovated with the installation of the current ensemble of glass. Richard Watts, pastor from 1973 to 1980, began work in 1979 on what became the Presbyterian Peacemaking Program. Dedicated to reversing the arms race, this now involves an office in the national church, a Presbyterian office at the United Nations, numerous meetings, publications, and subordinate organizations, and an annual peacemaking offering in many Presbyterian churches. Dr. Watts left LPC in 1980 to work full time on his national project.

On the other side of Detroit from the rambling Lakewood Hospital, LPC presents a hulking, formidable, urban presence. Lightness is not the first word that comes to mind to describe the massive, brick, neo-Gothic, ninety-year-old building. With its spare stone trim and ogival windows, it overpowers the downtown corner of Marlowe Avenue at Detroit Avenue. This impression is completely transformed at the entrance of the building. In 2007 the reportedly gloomy narthex was gutted and replaced with a bright three-story interior space leading down to the street. Illuminated with bright modern glass, separated from the sanctuary with more restrained pleated modern glass, the narthex is enlivened by the silent fleeting shadows of cars moving past on the busy street outside.

The sanctuary is also at odds with its exterior. Again, glass is the centerpiece. From the outside, the windows appear to be the usual dark, early twentieth-century affairs with their customary foreboding neo-Gothic tracery. Inside, the glass turns out to be something bright and cheery from the 1960s. No need for light box illumination here. The interior is as powerfully illuminated when it rains as when the sun shines. Interior brightness seems to be the mantra of this church, extending into the chancel, which is flanked by a divided and carved light wood screen. The altar is brought out from the wall into the center of the chancel. The 1963 Holtkamp organ is unusual for two reasons. First, the pipes are divided on either side of the chancel, and, second, the pipes are in organ cases and cannot be seen. In 1963 the congregation installed a Schulmerich carillon.

Although an attempt was made in 2007 to adapt the 1951 vernacular education wing to the needs of the congregation, this fifty-year-old brick addition ultimately was removed. It was replaced with what is called the Kilgore Ministry Center. In a brick postmodern style consistent with the 1918 building, the most important part of the thoughtful new Kilgore Center is a two-story atrium that unites the 1907 chapel, the 1918 main sanctuary, the parking lot, and a serious elevator—all of this plus a convenient meeting space in the atrium. Elsewhere in the addition are the social, educational, and administrative facilities required by a large programmatic church. In this mélange, a superb second floor conference room features floor-to-ceiling glass walls that overlook a wide swath of the attractive Lakewood neighborhood, away from the street, visually uniting LPC with its community.

112. Lakewood United Methodist Church (1913–14)
Architects: Sidney Badgley and William Nicklas
Builder: John Blackburn
Location: 15700 Detroit Avenue, Lakewood

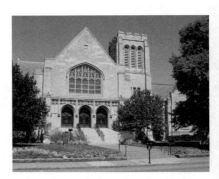

In their parish histories, Methodist churches frequently emphasize the rowdiness of their original surroundings and their role in bringing the calming balm of Methodism into their neighborhood. In Cleveland Heights, the predecessors of the Church of the Saviour (see p. 325) dampened down the exuberance of "Heathen Heights." In Lakewood, the founders of the Lakewood United Methodist Church poured the oil of temperance on troubled waters where previously (according to a parish history) "roadhouses sprang up like mushrooms along Detroit [Avenue] to quench the thirst of travelers."[5] In this promising evangelistic soil, four farmers' wives prodded their husbands into establishing a Methodist church. Borrowing against their farms, the couples purchased a lot where the third-consecutive Methodist church now stands. The farm couples designed and built a small frame church in 1876. Ten years later, a member of the church donated a bell to the church in her will. Purchased for $82 from the McShane Bell Foundry in Pittsburgh, her bell has rung from the Lakewood Methodist churches for more than 125 years. Its bell pull hangs seductively through the ceiling beside one of the current Sunday school rooms. Over the years the congregation gradually added to their lot, and their large, current church sits comfortably on a good-sized expanse in a commercial section of Lakewood. The little fruit farms of the original donors are long gone.

During the second half of the nineteenth century, Lakewood grew quite slowly. It took twenty years for the congregation to grow enough to warrant a permanent pastor. After the arrival of the streetcar and Lakewood's incorporation as a village in 1903, things began to happen in a hurry. A second church, designed by Badgley and Nicklas, was dedicated in 1905. This second church, an addition with two towers, was built in front of the original church. It increased the size of the first church by a factor of six. Within five years it was far too small, and so plans were drawn for the current building. The current sanctuary was completed in 1913 and the education wing in 1914.

Both the first and second churches, in turn, were sold together to the Collinwood United Methodist Church. Taken apart, pieces of the church (except the bell) were loaded on Nickel Plate Railroad flatcars and taken to the Collinwood Yards, where large sections were floated east on Lake Erie on a barge and then moved up East 152nd Street on rollers. Sixty years later, in 1973, this church in Collinwood was torn down.

Back in Lakewood, Badgley and Nicklas were also in charge of putting up the third church. Badgley and Nicklas were the designers of the now demolished Epworth Methodist Church on East 55th Street, the monumental Pilgrim Congregational Church in Tremont (see p. 202), and the Methodist Church in Fuzhou, China. Their modified English Gothic, third Lakewood United Methodist Church was built in two stages. First, they built the sanctuary to seat 1,100. Then, a year later, the congregation challenged themselves to put up the adjacent educational wing, with its kitchen and dining room capable of feeding five hundred. (Behind the church stands a vernacular brick and glass block second educational wing with a gym, class, and meeting rooms, completed in 1951.)

This massive neo-Gothic church faces the street through a three-tympanum entrance. Above the doors one finds a large English Gothic window with masonry tracery in its upper half. The 1963 window is of *Christ and the City,* with Lakewood Methodist in one of five lancets and Terminal Tower in another. Simulated Romanesque buttresses decorate the exterior. The large tower (with the bell) stands above the street entrance to the original educational wing.

The original sanctuary, with its wonderfully massive hammerbeam ceiling, followed an axial plan. There were no transepts. Where the east transept would be was a large Akron Plan gathering space (projecting into the education wing). Movable walls separated the gathering space from the sanctuary hall. This large educational space, in turn, could be farther opened up into two floors of classrooms.[6]

Ambitious plans were proposed in 1967 to convert the sanctuary from a linear to a central plan. The altar and the area around it would be moved toward the congregation to occupy a crossing in front of a large choir facing the congregation. A large east transept (with balcony) would extend into the 1914 education wing. Construction of a new large west transept (also with balcony), in the same style as the 1914 building, would, seen from the street, balance the education wing.

The west transept was never built. Its place was taken by a large *People's Window* with elaborate tracery and ten lancets of the life of Jesus. The large choir was completed in front of a dramatic preexisting twenty-six-foot-high wrought-iron *Apostles Screen* with ten-foot figures of each of the twelve. The altar was moved into the center of the church surrounded by communion rail, lectter, and pulpit. The original Akron Plan assembly room, occupying less than half of the proposed east transept, remains open to the nave so that current seating is in an inverted L.

The library and the Yoder Chapel in the educational building are illuminated by their ensemble of 1914 glass. There was a small organ to accompany the small choir in the original small church. Andrew Carnegie donated half of the Vottler-Hettche organ in the second building. A Moeller organ was installed in the third church. This was replaced in 1949 with a four-manual instrument built by the Austin Company of Hartford. Funding was inadequate to complete the project, and the top keyboard was left with only one stop. In 1972 Austin came back and finished the job.

113. St. James Parish (1925–35)
Architect: E. T. P. Graham
Builder: Michael Leahy
Location: 17514 Detroit, Lakewood

St. James is known for its style and, in particular, for its unusually sumptuous decoration.[7] St. James was established by Michael Leahy in 1908 to serve Lakewood. Subsequently, as people rapidly followed the trolleys, St. James mothered St. Clement's and St. Luke to the east in Lakewood and St. Christopher to the west in Rocky River, all in 1922. During his thirty-four-year tenure, Father Leahy began the first church, now the gym, in 1913 and completed the second church in 1935. The complex includes a large rectory, school, and convent. After St. James began participating, with St. Clement's and St. Luke, in the Lakewood Catholic Academy on Lake Avenue, St. James's school and convent began to be used for municipal education.

Begun optimistically in 1925 in hopes that it would become a national monument to the Roman Catholic faith, St. James was built the old-fashioned way—slowly. The parish moved into the basement of the new building in 1926 and began building the upper church on April 2, 1929. Construction never stopped during the Great Depression. It did not, however, proceed rapidly. All were amazed when the church was dedicated in 1935. In the interim, the parish worshiped in a remarkably finished basement where stout columns with capitals representing the Evangelists supported the columns being built a floor above. The basement sacristy would become the church kitchen.

The current church is E. T. P. Graham's interpretation of Norman Sicilian Romanesque. The exterior is patterned after the Cathedral of Cefalù, built in 1131 by Roger II, fifty miles east of Palermo on the northern coast of Sicily.

Cefalù may be the best church of its era. The interior of St. James is adapted from the better-known monastery foundation at Monreale—built six miles southwest of Palermo by William II. Cefalù is known primarily for its exterior and Monreale for its interior.

St. James is an encyclopedia of stone. The exterior is built of Indiana limestone with patterning in three colors of finely finished ashlar Ohio limestone. Steps and columns are Minnesota granite. The large columns at the entrance are made of "Rainbow Granite" (Morton Gneiss), a banded pink, light greenish gray, and black variegated stone quarried in the area of Morton, Minnesota."[8] The symmetrical bell towers reach up more than one hundred feet. Bells by the Dutch company of Petit and Fritsen were installed in 1955. Statues of the four Evangelists together with their symbols, in niches above the porch, suggest the opulence of the interior. The Evangelists overlook bronze doors, also decorated with their symbols. Roof tiles and colored ceramics unfortunately do not do as well in Lakewood as they do in the milder climate outside of Palermo. They required a million-dollar restoration in 1995.

By American standards, St. James is carefully and minutely detailed. One finds a great deal of wood and stone carving, bronze casting, gilding, enameling, and painting with a large vocabulary of Christian figures and symbols—animals, birds, stars, and crosses. The sword and the shell of St. James are everywhere. The church includes several series of symbols of famous religious women and famous religious men. A large mural on the vaulted ceiling of the chancel displays gold signs of the zodiac, the four seasons, the 365 days of the year, and the star of the Epiphany with the Holy Spirit. Another large mural behind the altar, patterned after Monreale or the Palatine Chapel in Palermo, shows Christ as Pantocrator (Ruler of All) with Mary, Joseph, the four archangels and the twelve apostles with their symbols. This mural is perforated by three stained windows illustrating the Rosary.

J. T. Hannibal, Cleveland's apostle of religious rock, wrote, "This church contains a variety of fine stone that is unparalleled in the Cleveland area."[9] Marble in eleven Italian varieties is everywhere—carved, polished, paneled, and inlaid. Eighteen marble columns in the nave with richly carved Rosata capitals support a blue, red, and gold timbered and trussed ceiling detailed with a wealth of symbolism. Eight of these marble columns are Porta Santa marble (*Holy Gate*, the marble around the door of St. Peter that is open during Holy Years). Quarried from Chios in Greece, these could be ancient *spolia*.[10] St. James has a complete complement of glass—three roses, a west clerestory range of Latin and Greek fathers, and an east clerestory range of patriarchs and prophets. Lower windows illustrate the narrative of Christianity.

On March 15, 2009, Bishop Richard Lennon announced the closing of St. James. He celebrated the final Mass on June 26, 2010. On March 1, 2012, the Vatican Congregation for the Clergy ruled that Bishop Lennon had failed to follow church law and procedure in closing St. James.

114. St. Peter's Episcopal Church
(1928)

Architects: John Wing and James Chrisford[11]

Builder: Daniel Goodwin

Location: 18001 Detroit Avenue, Lakewood

For such a precious building (remarkable plan, human scale, immaculate maintenance, careful restoration, and gorgeous glass), St. Peter's has had a most turbulent history.[12] Its multiplicity of rectors has included four of outstanding accomplishment. It has moved back and forth from poverty to prosperity to crushing debt to affluence. It has grown and withered and grown again.

St. Peter's was founded in 1906 as a personal crusade by William Attwood, then pastor of All Saints on Scranton Road. For unknown reasons, Attwood was determined to establish an Episcopal church in western Lakewood, despite the fact that Lakewood already had a thriving Episcopal church, Ascension. Attwood arranged a nine-hundred-dollar grant from the diocese, bought a lot, purchased an abandoned church, and hauled it sixteen blocks to his property. He then resigned from All Saints, loaned his new mission five thousand dollars, built an apartment for himself and his family onto the church, and then, after instructing his congregation to sing "Abide with Me, Fast Falls the Eventide" downstairs, he died in his room upstairs.

After four pastors in seven years, things settled down with the arrival of Daniel Goodwin. Goodwin had previously established himself as a successful rector in Illinois and Indiana and seems to have been drawn to Cleveland by nothing more than the plight of a struggling congregation. Not only did Goodwin inherit "a little church, on a little street, in a little neighborhood,"[13] but what was there was almost immediately threatened with extinction. Frederick Avery, rector of St. John's in Ohio City (see p. 185), "increasingly concerned over the deterioration of the neighborhood surrounding his church,"[14] had purchased a lot on Clifton and proposed moving St. John's, stone by stone, into Lakewood. Like St. Paul's on the East Side (see the saga of St. Paul Shrine [p. 28], St. Alban [p. 320] and St. Paul's Cleveland Heights [p. 329]), St. John's had an ambitious rector, a large endowment, and a socially prominent and economically affluent congregation moving into the suburbs. If, however, Bishop William Leonard could not keep St. Paul's from moving east, he could keep St. John's from moving west. Not only did the little Lakewood congregation keep St. John's at bay, but several handsome gifts allowed it to acquire a prime site at the corner of Detroit Avenue at Clifton Boulevard. At that time, trolley service on Detroit ran every two minutes in the summer and every five minutes during the winter. Construction began in 1926, and the current building was finished in 1928, complete with Holtkamp organ, its wonderful assembly of windows, and a large mortgage.

The Great Depression was a particular trial for St. Peter's, greatly exacerbated by the failure of the bank that held its mortgage. It took eighteen years before the debt was paid off and the church consecrated in 1946. In the meantime, the Sunday congregation shrank to sixty. On June 30, 1940, the treasurer reported cash on hand of $43.63 with the rector, organist, and secretary unpaid together with utility bills and taxes. The parish was fortunate that two particularly dynamic rectors and the postwar prosperity of Lakewood were able to keep the parish going. By 1961 it had 1,155 members.

St. Peter's occupies the north side of a short block on a busy thoroughfare. From Detroit, the "English Tudor country church,"[15] with its crenellated tower and rubble masonry, appears to settle down modestly over its lot like a hen protecting her chicks. From Clifton, on the side, it appears to be a substantial building but, in contrast to other landmark religious buildings, it does not project a commanding presence when viewed from the main street in front.

Inside, what makes St. Peter's so appealing, aside from its glass and its furniture, is its human scale, the result, in part, of the large size of its choir. The choir is so large that, now that the altar has been pulled out into the crossing, the sanctuary, with its generous transepts, almost appears to be a Greek cross (only almost, the nave is slightly long enough to form a Latin cross). Forward facing pews in the crossing and transepts were taken out to accommodate the altar. New transverse seating in the large transepts is now arranged so the entire congregation can comfortably see the altar. St. Peter's seats only 350, so parishioners enjoy an intimate space. Almost everyone looks at each other as in a post–Vatican II Roman Catholic church.

St. Peter's has a heavy, dark cross-beamed (not hammerbeam) wooden ceiling. Pews, pulpit, communion rail, other church furniture, arches, and wall trim are also in dark wood. A pretty, simple Mary chapel lies to the right of the sanctuary. An ambulatory behind the sanctuary leads to a large columbarium illuminated with outstanding modern glass. The predominant glass in the complete program in the sanctuary is by Von Gerichten of Columbus and then Munich,[16] supplemented by windows by Rossbach of Columbus.[17] It features a great *Te Deum* window at the head of the choir, major windows for each transept, and a *Peter* window on the north end. Aisle windows include one dedicated to *William Laud,* the archbishop of Canterbury martyred for his leadership of the Star Chamber.

115. St. Christopher Parish Community

Architects: Walker and Weeks, Horn and Rinehart[18] (1954)
Builder: Edmund Ahern
Location: 20141 Detroit Road, Rocky River

Richard Patterson established St. Christopher in 1922 in an area that had been part of the St. James Lakewood parish. St. Christopher would subsequently mother St. Raphael in Bay Village (1946) and St. Bernadette in Westlake (1950).[19] Patterson, who had been secretary to both the bishop and the bishop's predecessor, moved with his mother into an eighty-five-year-old farmhouse as a schoolhouse rectory on a seven-acre tract in rural Rocky River. Completing a school-church on the site two years later, Patterson acquired what was thought to be a relic of St. Christopher. With this, he blessed the long line of cars, trucks, and motorcycles that lined up all day in front of St. Christopher Parish on that then saint's feast day, July 25. Each driver received a St. Christopher medal, a written prayer, and a warning that St. Christopher would appear at speeds faster than sixty miles per hour. In some years, the parish gave out 1,200 medals. The event attracted national attention and became an important reminder, in the 1930s, to try to drive safely.

Although the parish rapidly grew in ten years to one thousand members, it put most of its resources into education. Patterson was a good friend of the bandleader Sammy Kaye, and Kaye would leave a hundred dollars in the collection plate when he visited Cleveland. Building a convent in 1939, St. Christopher did not seriously consider a permanent church until after the Second World War. The original church had been considered "temporary" from the beginning because engineers had informed the diocese that the lot and surrounding area were unsuitable for a larger structure. In 1948 the parish purchased twenty-one acres north of Hilliard Road and began raising money. The diocese, however, was trying at that time to establish high schools and induced St. Christopher to give its new property to what would become the Magnificat college preparatory school for young women. Then engineers were persuaded to move almost a quarter of a million yards of earth into a ravine north of the existing church. In 1954, an appropriately sized church was finally dedicated.

Described as "modified-Romanesque," this large ashlar masonry building, with its robust square tower, has more of the character of an early Christian basilica from the outside. The church is an imposing presence on Detroit Road, particularly when illuminated at night. Inside, the decoration is restrained. When he built the new church, Monsignor Ahern limited interior decoration to the stations of the cross and a large northern rose. Subsequently, the nave was decorated with the fourteen large lancet windows of the Passion that maintain its atmosphere of strength and simplicity. Walls and beamed ceiling are largely undecorated. A naturalistic life-size crucifix is almost invisibly suspended by wires in front of a plain semicircular apse. This apse is conservatively decorated with six short recessed lancet windows above shoulder-high wood paneling. There is an elegant, but relatively small, stone altar. The Marian niche to the left of the apse actually contains a tabernacle beneath two sculpted angels. The Joseph niche to the right encloses all of the Holy Family, emerging from a roughly outlined masonry block.

The choir visited Rome in 1992 and sang High Mass in St. Peter. In addition to its vigorous parochial school, St. Christopher maintains a joint Vacation Bible School with Rocky River Presbyterian Church.

116. West Shore Unitarian Universalist Church (1952, 1962, 2005)
Architects: Wallace Teare (1952 and 1962), Chris Auvil (2005)
Builder: Everett Moore Baker
Location: 20401 Hilliard Boulevard, Rocky River

According to parish legend, West Shore was established by accident.[20] In 1964, Frederick May Eliot, the national Unitarian leader, addressed a group of West Side Unitarians. On the way out the door as he left for the airport, he commented, "I congratulate you on starting the newest Unitarian church in the country," and left before he could be corrected. Perhaps more realistically, the congregation gives Everett Moore Baker credit for establishing a West Side Unitarian presence. Before Baker left Cleveland to become a much-revered dean of students at the Massachusetts Institute of Technology, he served as minister of the 82nd Street Unitarian Church from 1942 to 1947. Unsuccessful in his effort, while he was in Cleveland, to establish a suburban East Side presence, Baker's efforts on the West Side met with success, and he installed his 82nd Street assistant, Wayne Shuttee, as the first West Shore minister.

Unitarianism historically has been associated with what many religious Americans considered quite liberal ideas—such issues as abolition, birth control, and the repeal of prohibition. Although Unitarianism is a welcoming religious organization, it has usually been, since its Harvard days, most attractive to highly educated people. Many Unitarians are associated with institutions of higher learning, and West Shore is unusual for a Unitarian church in that it is not in close proximity to a college or university. Over the years, West Shore has drawn many of its members from the NASA Lewis Laboratory. Although the congregation has proved capable of erecting large buildings, they have a strong tradition of volunteerism with much gardening, painting, and handy work done by individual members.

West Shore's unconventional current building, on a three-acre site on a main boulevard through a residential area, was built in three campaigns, the first two managed by Wallace Teare. A parishioner, Teare is best known for his work on the internationally acclaimed 1937 Lakeview Terrace project at West 28th Street between Lake Erie and the Main Avenue Bridge. The first West Shore structure was a modernist, no-nonsense, super-functional, redwood "minimalist" cube for offices, classrooms, and an assembly hall. As educational wings metastasized about the site, Teare gathered steam ten years later with a utilitarian but wonderfully proportioned permanent sanctuary. With its blue brick exterior and unusual profile, the spectacularly innovative five-hundred-seat sanctuary has been described, because of the Sunday custom of parking small cars on the circular entrance drive in front of it, as "the Great Blue Whale giving birth." Inside, at the front of the sanctuary, a large, blank wall greets the congregation. The pastors have taken advantage of this to introduce new audiovisual material into their services, projected onto the wall from a digital projector on the ceiling of the sanctuary powered by a laptop in a pulpit to the side.[21] Utilitarian pews were designed for the space. To the side several rows of pews are half removed to allow wheelchair-bound parishioners to join their families during services. On either side toward the rear of the sanctuary, the terra-cotta brick walls are decorated subtly with two small areas of patterned recessed brick. At the rear of the sanctuary, carefully planned screens of thin wood strips flank a Holtkamp organ. The remarkable acoustics of the sanctuary, in part the result of the absence of sound-absorbing decoration, is much beloved by chamber music musicians. Behind the sanctuary is a "fireplace room" that overlooks an inner courtyard. In 2005 the original cube was renovated with a large addition for administration, education, and gathering behind the 1962 sanctuary. The new addition is integrated and organized around a dramatic modernist "rotunda," drawing congregants in from the parking lot on the side of the lot. Down a hall is a glass chapel for receptions and weddings, also looking into the courtyard.

117. St. Demetrios Greek Orthodox Church (1973)
Architect: Stickles International
Builder: Peter Metallinos
Location: 22909 Center Ridge Road, Rocky River

St. Demetrios is the most physically ambitious and the most richly furnished of the four Greek churches in Cleveland. It was established in 1960 as the West Side outpost of the American Hellenic Community of Greater Cleveland (that then also included Annunciation [see p. 196] and Saints Constantine and Helen [see p. 314]). Purchasing the old Rockport Methodist Church in Rocky River (now the Buna Vestire Romanian Orthodox Church), St. Demetrios was soon renting additional space as well as accepting the hospitality of the Methodists in their new church across the street. St. Demetrios became an independent parish in 1967. In 1968 the community began construction of their present Hellenic Cultural Center (administrative, educational, and social space) where they began worshiping in 1970. In 1973 they moved into their church. Later, they constructed a mammoth gym farther back on their lot, the Zapis Activity Center.

This beautifully landscaped campus in a wooded residential-commercial area is set back in a large property on the border of Rocky River and Westlake. The low buff-brick complex identifies itself with a calm, beautiful, shallow dome and a large mosaic of St. Demetrios, clearly legible from the busy street. The well-massed buildings are plain with occasional simple recessed brick decoration. Modest composition stone trims the windows and doors.

Mosaics beside the exterior entrance announce the narthex. The main worship space features a spectacular dome. The image of Christ as *Pantocrator* in the center of the dome was supplemented in 2002 by dramatic mosaics of twelve prophets on the inside of the dome, of the twelve apostles on the base of the dome, and of four angels on the pendentives. Although this "iconography" was done by an Italian artist, Bruno Salvatore, to non-Greek eyes it appears suitably severe in its Byzantine style. The iconostasis and the walls of the narthex, sanctuary, and communicating hallways feature a remarkable profusion of carefully arranged gold- and silver-plated icons. The use of marble in the sanctuary is particularly generous, most notably on the iconostasis and on the beautiful altar rail. St. Demetrios has nice glass around the altar and on the screen dividing the sanctuary from the narthex. The cultural center includes an exquisitely furnished chapel for daily use dedicated to St. Philothea of Athens.

St. Demetrios sponsors the service ministries expected of such a large parish. Of particular importance was its support for St. Mary of Egypt Orthodox Monastery and St. Herman's Monastery when they were Orthodox ministries to the homeless and needy of inner-city Cleveland.

118. Bay Presbyterian Church
(1955–59; 1989; 1998)
Architects: Ward and Conrad
(1955–59), Ellis–Meyers (1989),
and Carlton DeWolff (1998)
Builders: Floyd Ewalt
(1955–59) and Hu Auburn
(1989 and 1998)
Location: 25415 Lake Road,
Bay Village

No religious institution is without its challenges. The challenge at Bay Presbyterian has been to keep a roof over its head during periods of explosive growth.[22] Bay Presbyterian was established as a Sunday school in a rented schoolhouse at an intersection of dirt roads west of Cleveland in 1912. Organized as a Presbyterian church in 1917, the members purchased a condemned one-room brick schoolhouse, renovated it, expanded it, and called their first full-time pastor. When fire consumed their church in 1932, the congregation rallied with money, material, and labor, and they were back in the schoolhouse in six months.

Responding to the dramatic increase in the size of their community following World War II, Bay Presbyterian built their first church in 1955, seating 450. The congregation continued to build education, administrative, and social facilities around this second church. Its sanctuary eventually became the great hall of Bay Presbyterian's present two-story west wing. The current sanctuary was built in 1989. This sanctuary divides the west wing from the large 1998 east wing. The east wing supplements the educational, administrative, and social space of the west wing.

Presbyterians are by nature a solid, conservative people of the Book who tend to be more interested in the quality of their preaching and the extent of their mission outreach than in the drama of their surroundings. Bay Presbyterian reflects this nature. It is a collection of plain, brick, solid, well-designed, unostentatious buildings with a clear purpose and limited trimmings. One gains a sense that this affluent exurban congregation would rather invest in water purity in Guatemala than in *brise-soleil* in Bay Village. While they could not resist a striking, four-story, triangular glass entrance atrium or an imaginative massing of the undecorated exterior brick surfaces of their sanctuary, the overall appearance of their buildings remains consistent with a deep-seated, no-nonsense approach to religious surroundings.

Bay Presbyterian's most recent new ministry involves the purchase of the closed Blessed Sacrament Catholic church in Cleveland's lower West Side (see pp. 218 and 220). After investing $28,000 in the roof and $122,000 in a new boiler, hundreds of Bay Presbyterian volunteers swarmed over the complex of church, school, rectory, and convent applying 500 pounds of plaster powder and 73 gallons of paint. For a very nominal rent, Bay will rent space in Blessed

Sacrament to about fifteen inner-city poverty and social justice ministries, small nomadic churches and schools.

Over recent decades, the good-hearted but profound conservatism of Bay Presbyterian has been frequently at odds with the progressive liberalism of their national church. In November 2007, the congregation voted 1,196 to 113 to leave the Presbyterian Church (USA) and join a transitional presbytery of the more conservative Evangelical Presbyterian Church.

119. John Knox Presbyterian Church (1968)
Architect: Robert Gaede
Builder: Gordon Blasius
Location: 25200 Lorain Road, North Olmsted

John Knox Presbyterian Church was proposed in 1958 by Floyd Ewalt, minister of Bay Presbyterian (see p. 292), as a mission for members of his church living in North Olmsted, Westlake, and Fairview Park.[23] Organized in 1959, John Knox Presbyterian's first and longtime minister was Gordon Blasius, who had been an assistant at Bay Presbyterian when the new church was suggested. The area was growing rapidly. Acquiring their current six-and-a-half-acre site the year they were founded, the congregation moved into a new sanctuary (now a parish hall) and schoolrooms in 1962. Within seven years, the congregation had far outgrown their initial building and had erected their current sanctuary together with a second educational building. They subsequently built a third educational building and are now planning their fourth.

In a fifty-year career beginning with a commission involving the kitchen of Pilgrim Church (see p. 202), Bob Gaede would build more than twenty churches in northeast Ohio—ranging from the large, such as the Church of the Western Reserve on Lander Circle in Pepper Pike, to the relatively small, such as the Solon United Methodist Church (see pp. 355 and 356).[24] Although Gaede could be quite unorthodox as seen in his Chesterland Community Church, he was strongly influenced—even in his more traditional buildings—by Frank Lloyd Wright. Like Wright, Gaede attached his buildings securely to their site. However, as Gaede played with triangular forms and great sheets of plain brick, his churches characteristically hugged their plots, firmly bonded to the earth. Where Wright's buildings reached out over the plains of western Illinois, Gaede's held on tightly to the hills of eastern Ohio. Working at a succession of firms,[25] Gaede also developed an active practice in historic preservation and renovation, ultimately working for more than one hundred religious organizations. In addition to churches, Gaede also did residential and commercial work. He was, for example, involved in the restoration of the Athenaeum Hotel at Chautauqua, and Gaede became known in particular for his work in general restoration. In 1976 he founded the newsletter of the Cleveland Restoration Society and edited almost eighty subsequent issues. Gaede was awarded the 1989 Gold Medal of the Ohio American Institute of Architects.

John Knox Presbyterian was one of Gaede's favorite churches and one of his longest ongoing client-architect relationships; a firm of his built each of John Knox Presbyterian's components. The church occupies an unusually deep narrow lot at the top of the T intersection of two major thoroughfares—Lorain Road and Great Northern Boulevard (Ohio-252). At the intersection, northbound Ohio-252 abruptly stops at the exit of the church parking lot. This Presbyterian complex, nestling rather quietly back from the street beside a wooded lot, is immediately adjacent to one of the busiest and most prosperous commercial districts in northern Ohio, centered on Great Northern Mall. The lot is large enough that the buildings seem isolated in their space. Gaede's trademark copper-sheathed, tapered, obelisk spire on a tapered base surmounted by a narrow, recessed stem identifies—but does not loudly proclaim—the quiet grouping of buildings as religious. Beginning as an L-shaped sanctuary and educational building in 1961, the complex evolved into an inverted U with the addition of another educational wing and the present sanctuary in 1968. Subsequent additions have closed off the bottom of the inverted U with a generous gathering area that looks through plate glass windows into what became a central courtyard. Another educational wing added a tail to the U. Now an additional educational wing is planned. Each uniform, wood-trimmed, red-brick component, with its characteristic low-pitched gable roof, has progressively defined a series of outdoor spaces and courtyards.

The Wright influence, within the one-story complex, is emphasized by narrow, low-ceiling corridors emptying into broad flagstone public spaces connecting with the outside through carefully proportioned glass walls. Decoration is limited. Variety is expressed primarily by subtle differences in the shadows of carefully defined brick walls. Only at either side of the rear wall of the original sanctuary are there twelve outset bricks in a column.

One enters the sanctuary from the side of the complex, going into an atrium that opens into the back of the worship space. The sanctuary is extremely plain and appears small for such a large congregation. The brick walls are so well proportioned that they give a feeling of warmth, security, and as much intimacy as a Presbyterian congregation would allow. Wonderfully rich stained pews are complimented with two lateral strips of nonfigurative modern glass. The unpretentious, undecorated front of the worship space is a plain, low platform. The choir's space is undefined, but their simple rows of solid chairs seem much in character with the building.

CHAPTER TWELVE

Brooklyn—Parma—Middleburg Heights

Begin this tour at the Ridge Road interchange of Interstate 480. Drive north on Ridge Road. On the left looms the dramatic masonry tower of the postmodern Dr. Martin Luther Evangelical Lutheran Church. Turn left (west) at Memphis Avenue. On the left side of Memphis, on the other side of Memorial Park, west of City Hall, appears the elaborate facade of St. Elias Church (120). To the west, beside St. Elias, is the Lutheran Church of the Good Shepherd. On the right side of Memphis, behind the large John M. Coyne Recreation Center stands the giant St. Thomas More Church. Drive west on Memphis. Brooklyn Trinity United Church of Christ is located on the right side of Memphis. Turn left onto Tiedeman Road. On the left, south of the Memphis at Tiedeman intersection, stands the large Cleveland Baptist Church. Tiedeman merges onto I-480 West just south of the Cleveland *Plain Dealer* production plant.

Drive west on I-480 to the next interchange and, leaving the interstate, turn left (south) onto West 130th Street. Two and a half miles south on the left, just past Plaza Drive, is the entrance to the Islamic Center of Cleveland (121). Drive into the parking lot to see the beauty of the minarets and the golden dome of the mosque. Continue south down West 130th. South of Kathleen Drive on the right is the large brick and composition stone complex of the Immanuel Assembly of God. Farther south on West 130th, turn right (west) onto Bagley Road. Pleasant Hills United Methodist Church (122) is almost immediately on the right. Turn around in the church parking lot and go back, driving east on Bagley.

At West 130th, Bagley becomes West Pleasant Valley Road. Driving east on West Pleasant Valley Road, on the right appears the Bethel Temple Assembly of God with its large addition to the rear. Farther east on West Pleasant Valley Road stands the Parma Baptist Church, across the street from James Day Park and the West Campus of Cuyahoga Community College. On the northeast corner of York Road at West Pleasant Valley is the sensational and modern Holy Family Church of Parma. Continuing on West Pleasant Valley, the octagonal Han-Madang United Methodist Church stands on the left. The monumental brick and shingle A-frame of the Calvary Lutheran Church looks down on the intersection of West Pleasant Valley at Ridge Road from a hill to the northeast.

Turn right (south) onto Ridge Road. The Shiva-Vishnu Temple (123) is down the road on the left. Drive into the parking lot and then, to the right of the temple, continue driving downhill into the lower parking lot for a good view of the entrance to the building and the "bridge" that, running along the north of the building, leads to the entrance from the upper parking lot. Returning to the upper parking lot, turn to the right (north) back onto Ridge Road. Cross West Pleasant Valley and travel several blocks to see the large brick Ridgewood United Methodist Church on the left and the larger Parma Community Hospital

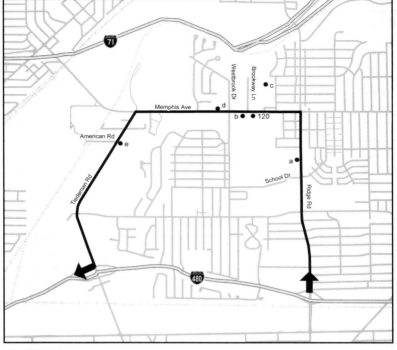

BROOKLYN

a. Dr. Martin Luther Evangelical Lutheran Church
120. St. Elias Church
b. Lutheran Church of the Good Shepherd
c. St. Thomas More Church
d. Brooklyn Trinity United Church of Christ
e. Cleveland Baptist Church

on the right. Farther north, the masonry Ridge Road United Church of Christ stands on the left—with a spire—while across the street, on the right side of Ridge, stands the masonry Bethany Lutheran Church—without a spire.

Farther north, on the right, lies St. Charles Borromeo Parish (124). Continue two blocks north on Ridge Road and turn right (east) onto Snow Road. The intersection of Snow Road with State Road is the heart of Ukrainian Cleveland, but the massive brick church on the southeast corner, with its giant order pillars, is the Roman Catholic St. Francis de Sales Church. Turn right (south) onto State Road. St. Vladimir's Ukrainian Orthodox Cathedral (125) is two blocks south on the left, across the street from the sturdy brick of Good Shepherd United Methodist Church. Turn around. Driving north past Snow Road, you will see St. Josaphat Ukrainian Catholic Cathedral (126), with its cluster of onion domes, in the second block on the left. This is the seat of the Ukrainian Catholic bishop of Parma. Driving past the cathedral and its school, turn left, beside the school, into the parking lot. (If the sign is up, continue

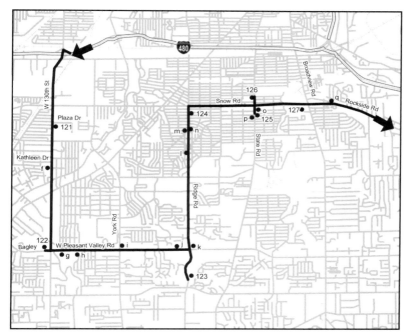

PARMA—MIDDLEBURG HEIGHTS—SEVEN HILLS

121. Islamic Center of Cleveland
  f. Immanuel Assembly of God
122. Pleasant Hills United Methodist Church
  g. Bethel Temple Assembly Of God
  h. Parma Baptist Church
  i. Holy Family Church of Parma
  j. Han-Madang United Methodist Church
  k. Calvary Lutheran Church
123. Shiva-Vishnu Temple
  l. Ridgewood United Methodist Church
  m. Ridge Road United Church of Christ

  n. Bethany Lutheran Church
124. St. Charles Borromeo Parish
  o. St. Francis de Sales Church
125. St. Vladimir's Ukrainian Orthodox Cathedral
  p. Good Shepherd United Methodist Church
126. St. Josaphat Ukrainian Catholic Cathedral
127. Cathedral of St. John the Baptist
  q. Church of Jesus Christ of Latter-day Saints

straight ahead to the great dome of the "astrodome" at the back of the campus and pick up some *pyrohy*.) To the west of the cathedral is its handsome court with a great mosaic of St. Josaphat above its entrance. Leaving the parking lot, turn back right (south) onto State Road and then left (east) onto Snow. After one mile (with the Midtown Shopping Center on the left), turn right into the parking lot in front of the Cathedral of St. John the Baptist (127). This is the seat of the Ruthenian Catholic bishop of Parma. Examine the six great mosaics on either side of the cathedral and the two mosaics over its entrance. Coming out of the parking lot turn right (east). After the first intersection, Snow Road becomes Rockside Road. Continue east on Rockside Road past the Church of Jesus Christ of Latter-day Saints on the left of Rockside close to Pinnacle Park Drive. Continue on Rockside to the complicated interchange at Interstate 77 that leads in any direction.

120. St. Elias Church (1964)
Architect: Sal Petralia
Builder: Ignatius Ghattas
Location: 8023 Memphis Avenue,
Brooklyn

The Melkite Greek Catholic Church is an Arab Eastern Catholic parish that maintains communion with the pope but whose practices remain similar to those of Eastern Orthodoxy. Melkite Arabs are more cosmopolitan than the Maronites (see St. Maron's Catholic Church, p. 119) who are almost exclusively from Lebanon. Melkites came to the United States from Egypt, Palestine, Jordan, and Syria as well as Lebanon. Before Nasser's 1952 Islamic and socialist revolution in Egypt, the richest Melkite community lived in that country. In 1945 the largest Melkite diocese was in Palestine. The Melkite patriarch of Antioch is now resident in Damascus. Melkites are one of many Christian groups who have made a home in the Middle East since the beginning. In the modern era, a 1724 controversy concerning the election of the patriarch of Antioch defined their denomination. In it, the pope supported the Melkites, and, thus, they parted ways with the Orthodox (see St. George Orthodox Church, p. 204). Although St. Elias is now in the Melkite Greek Catholic Eparchy (diocese) of Newton, Massachusetts,[1] Melkite churches in the United States at first fell under Roman Catholic diocesan bishops, and this remains a particularly close relationship. St. Elias's liturgy is celebrated in Arabic, English, and Greek.[2]

Although their churches largely define the Christian Arab community in Cleveland, Christian Arab immigrants did not tend to settle together in homogeneous neighborhoods. This resulted, for St. Elias, in a great deal of moving around as it tried to position itself where it would be accessible to its dispersed community. In 1901 a Basilian Salvatorian missionary came to Cleveland to organize the Melkites.[3] After meeting for five years at St. Joseph Franciscan and at the cathedral, they remodeled a building on East Ninth Street for a church. This became the first Melkite church outside of New York. Two years later, the community purchased two houses on Webster Avenue (now underneath the I-77 Innerbelt interchange) that they remodeled as a church and rectory. Their simple frame church was identified by its imposing frame open belfry. At this time, the community named itself St. Elias. In 1937 the parish purchased the small brick South Presbyterian Church on Scranton Road (just south of the St. Michael school). This building, with its American Protestant semicircular auditorium seating, frequently proved inadequate for major community events. When the patriarch from the Middle East visited Cleveland in 1955, the community celebrated at the Cathedral of St. John the

Evangelist. When the superior general of the Basilian Salvatorian Order vis-
ited in 1958, he was welcomed at St. Michael Church. When the pastor of St.
Elias died in 1964, the Liturgy of the Dead was offered by the archbishop of
Nazareth, again at the Cathedral of St. John the Evangelist.

St. Elias had become an important national Melkite church and, in 1964,
the parish began construction of the present church in Brooklyn. More property was acquired in 1979 and construction began on the community's strikingly modern cultural center, across the parking lot behind the church. When
the patriarch and superior general visited in 1996, St. Elias had room for them.
Ignatius Ghattas, the man responsible for all this physical building and the
community building that went with it, was elevated to the American primacy
in 1989 (proposed by the Holy Synod of the Melkite Church at Rabweh to
which the pope consented). Hardly had Ghattas's successor as pastor, Ibrahim
Ibrahim, been naturalized, than he was elevated in 2003 to the primacy of
Canada in Montreal. A major renovation of the church in 1998 included new
columns on its Memphis Avenue facade.

St. Elias's large, open, expansive campus occupies a gracious, sprawling
multi-institutional center in the middle of Brooklyn. The church itself is set
back, across a large lawn, from Memphis Avenue. To the immediate west lies
the moderately large complex of the Lutheran Church of the Good Shepherd.
To the east stands the Brooklyn City Hall, with its fire and police station, and,
surrounded by trees, the Brooklyn senior center and the Veterans Memorial
Park. North across Memphis is the large John M. Coyne Recreational Center.
Farther north, behind the recreation center, looms the gigantic cylinder and
dome of St. Thomas More Church. This whole suburban center, in turn, is surrounded by a well-kept and prosperous residential neighborhood. St. Elias is a
tall, rectangular brick building with unusual columns.

The interior of the church is another eastern Christian example of how a
high ceiling can dominate the pews and make the worship space appear smaller
than it really is. St. Elias has neo-Latin glass and a dome with the traditional
eastern-Christian large crystal chandelier. This creates a light, rectangular space.
Light wood pews are plain. The balcony is small. The narthex is large. The nave
ceiling iconography is of the *Dormition* and *Crucifixion*. The *Pantocrator* is over
the sanctuary, behind the iconostasis, looking out at worshipers. Except for the
ceiling, much of the decoration in this church is mosaic rather than paint.[4] A
great mosaic icon of the *Virgin and Child,* the *Platetera,* also looks out from the
sanctuary. A modern metal iconostasis has been backed with a gold curtain to
make its mosaic icons more visible. To the left of the sanctuary is a large mosaic
of the *Nativity.* To the right is the *Resurrection.* The holy doors are decorated
with a two-part mosaic of the *Annunciation.* On the left of the chancel is a life-
size mosaic of *St. Basil* and on the right is one of *St. John Chrysostom.* Dramatic
sheets of gorgeous marble decorate the back wall of the sanctuary. On either side
of the sanctuary behind the iconostasis, clear, glass-plated cough rooms allow
children to observe and become familiar with the ritual.

121. Islamic Center of Cleveland
(1995)
Architects: Mohammed Madjar and
Gerald Rembowski
Builder: Ahmad Ansari
Location: 6055 West 130th Street,
Parma

Islam is the fastest-growing religion in the United States. More than thirty thousand Muslims live in Greater Cleveland. Thirty-five percent of them are converts. Twenty percent of local Orthodox Muslims are African Americans, many originally drawn to Mohammed by the Nation of Islam. The Nation of Islam is not considered part of the Orthodox Islamic community. Since 1975, however, many Nation of Islam members, following the lead of W. Deen Mohammed, son of the founder, have become full members of the Sunni community. The first Cleveland Mosque, established in 1927 on Woodland Avenue, still exists on East 131st Street. Although Cleveland now has more than fifteen mosques (*masjid*), most are neighborhood institutions located in converted premises. Three masjid occupy buildings designed for this purpose—the Islamic Center of Cleveland (ICC),[5] Masjid Bilal on Euclid Avenue (the second newly built mosque in the United States when it opened in 1983), and the Uqbah Mosque Foundation at the base of Fairhill Road (see p. 41).

Muslims, many of whom were physicians and engineers at CWRU, began meeting in University Circle in 1963. In 1967, fifteen families established the Islamic Center of Cleveland—now the largest Cleveland Muslim congregation. They purchased and remodeled a duplex on Detroit Avenue in 1968. To bring the community into conformity with Islamic Sharia forbidding usury, King Khalid of Saudi Arabia paid off their remaining $26,000 mortgage in 1975. By 1986, membership had grown to one thousand, requiring rental of additional facilities; two years later the ICC bought land in Parma. Their mosque was completed in 1995. The ICC is considered unusual in the United States for having many Islamic nationalities worshiping together.

The Islamic Center of Cleveland occupies a large lot in a commercial/residential neighborhood of Parma. The mosque is approached by a long, tree-lined drive with parking spaces on either side. The golden dome of the mosque, framed by its two tall minarets, rises up dramatically at the end of the drive above a large, stucco, off-white building elegantly trimmed with bands of blue stucco. A small dome is above the entrance-atrium. Colonnaded loggia line each side of the main building. A large education and recreation building is connected to the rear of the central block of the mosque.

From the front, a columned entrance beneath a Palladian window leads to an atrium with the charm of a fountain surrounded by columns and blue tile.

Beyond the atrium is the sanctuary. The initial impression, there, is of a large, plain, undecorated space. Closer inspection reveals walls subtlety decorated with dark and light wood with sky blue trim. Quotations from the Koran appear in large calligraphed Arabic letters on some walls. Eight pillars within the sanctuary support the dome. They rest on truncated pyramidal bases and have capitals of unusual interlocking rectangles. An immense crystal chandelier hangs from the dome. The sanctuary is flooded with light during the day from unglazed clerestory windows in the drum of the dome and large windows in the upper part of the sanctuary walls. Niches around the walls hold a few books; sometimes during the day the niches are surrounded by a small group in study. The sanctuary is completely carpeted. Lines on the carpet line up worshipers toward the *qiblah*. The *qiblah* is the east wall opposite the entrance. The *mirhab* is a niche in the quiblah, farther orienting worshipers toward Mecca, men in front and women behind. A large women's gallery, used when the main floor is completely occupied by men, reaches out above from the back of the sanctuary over one fourth of the prayer space. A movable wooden *minbar,* or pulpit, is beside the mirhab.

122. Pleasant Hills United Methodist Church (2000)
Architect: Robert S. White
Builder: Ward Hines
Location: 13200 Bagley Road, Middleburg Heights

In addition to its impor-
tance as a spiritual community, Pleasant Hills United Methodist Church is known for two things: its architecture and its Boy Scouts.[6] Drawing from ten communities, Boy Scout Troop 636 (and its junior edition, Cub Scout Pack 636) has been, for a generation, one of the biggest and most active scouting programs in Cleveland—so big that it has exchange programs with scouting in Britain.

Pleasant Hills is a granddaughter of the Lincoln Park Methodist Episcopal Church (see St. George Orthodox Church, p. 204) and a great-granddaughter of the First United Methodist Church (see p. 26). Lincoln Park Methodist sold its building in Tremont to the Syrian Orthodox Church in 1928. Changing its name to Ridgewood United Methodist Church, it constructed and moved into the basement of its new church in Parma in May 1929. The move was ill timed. The Great Depression intervened, delaying the dedication of their church for twenty-three years. By the end of the 1960s, however, Ridgewood was packing 1,581 children every week into its Sunday school, and, within that decade, Ridgewood had founded three additional parishes—including Pleasant Hills.

Meeting in a school, as so many young parishes do, Pleasant Hills' first physical asset was a Hammond Spinet organ to replace its borrowed army field organ. Pleasant Hills moved into the shell of the original church, now part of its educational wing, in 1963. A new sanctuary was built in 2000. Judith Craig, the Pleasant Hills pastor from 1976 to 1980, later became the United Methodist bishop of Michigan from 1984 to 1992, and then served as bishop of western Ohio from 1992 until her retirement in 2002.

The new octagonal brick sanctuary addition is set back, across a generous lawn, from the street. It is separated from its neighbors by a wooded ravine. The eight-sided roof leads up to a clerestory, on top of which is a smaller octagonal roof with a modest spire. An educational-administrative complex spreads out behind the new sanctuary and includes the original church, now used as a parish hall. The main entrance on the side of the complex, between the sanctuary and the original building, leads into an atrium that accesses both sanctuary and educational-administrative space.

The simple but elegant eight-sided sanctuary, which seats about two hundred, is much smaller than its photographs would suggest. The walls are faced in plaster with wood trim. Plain clear windows on the first floor are screened from the outside by vertical semiopaque blinds. Large wood beams divide each of the eight walls and rise to support the dome. Three progressive levels of octagonal ceiling rise to the symbolic modern glass of the clerestory and a small modern chandelier. To the left, facing the front, one finds a simple but defined choir space. The principal feature of the chancel, with its beautifully segmented floor and well-designed wood pulpit and lectern, is an organ with exposed pipes (not a Holtkamp).

123. Shiva-Vishnu Temple
(1997)
Architect: Ganapathi Stapathi
Builder: Darshan Mahajan
Location: 7333 Ridge Road, Parma

Discussion of a permanent home for the Hindu community in Cleveland began in 1983 among a group meeting in the atrium of Cleveland State University.[7] They decided, as a means of bringing together all of the different Cleveland Hindu groups from all the different parts of the subcontinent, to name their institution the Shiva-Vishnu Temple. Shiva is the Supreme Deity of the large Hindu Shaivite sect. Vishnu is the Supreme Being for another large sect—the Vaishnavas. Other branches of Hinduism consider Shiva and Vishnu to be two of six manifestations of the divine. Hindu temples usually are dedicated to only one Deity, and this is reflected in their construction. However, there is a Shiva-

Vishnu temple in Madras, and temples are frequently dedicated to two Deities by the relatively small Hindu communities of the United States.

In Cleveland, the first Shiva-Vishnu Temple was established in 1985 in a closed restaurant on the corner of West 120th Street and Lorain Avenue. Plans for a future temple were flown for a blessing to India. Two years later, the community purchased a thirty-two-acre property in a mixed commercial-residential area in south Parma. The hilly property looks over miles of woods. A burned-out building on the property was found to be structurally sound and rehabilitated. It was dedicated as a temporary temple in 1989. The present temple was completed in 1997. In 2007, the Jain Community of northeast Ohio installed their own *murthis* (images) and began worshiping at the temple. A Balaji temple was added in 2008.

The sprawling 25,000-square-foot building overlooks a good-sized, rush-lined pond and a large wooded area. Steep steps lead up to the main entrance. The light tan composite blocks of the building are decorated with light horizontal limestone trim courses. Chocolate-colored blocks define the foundation and outline white frame windows. Twin towers over a flat roof identify the building from the east and west; eventually a much larger tower will define the entrance. The plane-glazed bridge from the west parking lot can be seen prominently from both the east and the north. The bridge opens through the east entrance into a large atrium divided from the spacious, brightly lit central worship area by interior glass windows. Four alcoves on each of the north, south, and west walls of the central hall accommodate secondary deities. Toward the west in the central hall are two large, glazed cubes under their respective towers for the principal Deities, Shiva on the south and Vishnu on the north. Worshipers circulate quietly among the Deities, sit on the large carpeted floor, or gather in small groups with a priest.

The Chennai (Madras) architect Ganapathi Stapathi designed the Greater Cleveland Shiva-Vishnu Temple. The *stapathis* belong to the Viswakarma community, craftsmen and architects traditionally believed to have descended from Viswakarma—who designed and built the divine architecture of the universe at the request of Brahma, Lord of Creation. *Stapathis* are particularly associated with the lost wax process of casting images. Their art reached its height from the tenth to the thirteenth centuries in the perfection of Chola bronzes of Shiva as Nataraja, the king of the dance. Stapathis are also experts in *Vastu Sastra,* the Hindu canon of the proportions of buildings and towns. Vastu, like the Chinese feng shui, deals with the design and building of environments that are in harmony with physical and metaphysical forces. Ganapathi Stapathi, who expresses his principles well in English,[8] taught Vastu for many years as principal of the College of Architecture and Sculpture at Marnallpuram. He has also designed other temples in the United States—one on the Hawaiian island of Kauai (Iraivan Temple) and another outside of Washington, D.C. (Siva Vishnu Temple).

Vastu locks every piece of the Greater Cleveland Shiva-Vishnu Temple together. These parts, in turn, are locked onto the site and into the universe. There is a canonical relationship between the size of the Deities, their location within the building, and the size and orientation of the building.[9] Because there are two Deities, there are two towers, one directly above each Deity. The Deities rest on the ground and their northern-India-style towers are open to the sky. They face east. The temple and its main entrance, at the break of a pronounced hill, also face east, a south-Indian characteristic. The temple overlooks the steep staircase rising up on the east side of the building. Shiva-Vishnu's largest parking lot, however, adjacent to Ridge Road, is west of the temple. Therefore, the community has constructed the bridge, a right-angled, glazed hall along the north and east sides of the temple. The bridge gives access to the east entrance from the western parking lot. Thus, the bridge, the entrance, and the parking lot are on the same level. Although worshipers have a supplementary parking lot at the bottom of the hill and east of the temple, the bridge provides access to the east entrance for members of the community who would find a climb up a steep staircase impossible or challenging. Thus, Ganapathi Stapathi's interpretation of the Vastu also locks the temple into twentieth-century American ideas of access to a public building.

124. St. Charles Borromeo Parish (1955)
Architect: Thomas Koehl
Location: 5891 Ridge Road, Parma

St. Charles Borromeo Parish is huge.[10] Forty-four hundred families—eleven thousand people—were part of the parish in 2008. During the 1960s, the 2,800 students in its school made it the largest private school in Ohio. In the 1980s St. Charles Borromeo celebrated fourteen masses every weekend. A good-sized church, two large school buildings, a sizable gym, a large rectory, and a large convent sprawl over an area of almost two square blocks, excluding the new parking lot.

The parish was established and a frame church built in 1923 on land at the intersection of Ridge Road at Charles Avenue in Parma. Twenty-five years later, the frame church, still considered temporary, was moved to make way for the Corrigan gym and additional classrooms for the school. The frame church was moved onto a foundation with a basement—but then moved again to make way for the Parish Hall. The original building was then used for six more years as a temporary classroom space before being finally dismantled in 1960.

Like many West Side Roman Catholic parishes, St. Charles grew so rapidly that the parish was hard-pressed to keep up with its educational responsibilities. During the 1950s, a hundred souls—many Roman Catholic—moved into Parma every week. As the diocese kept whittling away at parish boundaries, the people kept coming and the parish kept building. The school was given priority. A large permanent school building appeared in 1927, four years after founding the parish. There was a school addition in 1949 and another large school building in 1958. The Parish Hall appeared in 1960, and the large convent was completed in 1963.

At last, in 1954, a cornerstone was laid for a permanent church, completed in eleven months. It is characteristic of many of the large Roman Catholic churches that, when they did decide to build, they built rapidly. Thomas Koehl, who had also designed all of the educational buildings, designed this "American Romanesque" church. Other Koehl buildings are St. Philip Neri on the corner of St. Clair at Ansel Road, Our Lady of Angels on Rocky River Drive (see p. 268), St. Jerome in Collinwood (see p. 110), and St. Dominic in Shaker Heights (see p. 338). You can imagine this brick church on the Po River plain outside of Milan where St. Charles had been cardinal archbishop. Although the church is not dwarfed by its educational outbuildings, it does not overpower them. The nave seats 750 and the parish requires eight services every weekend including a "double header" at 10:00 A.M. on Sundays that also fills the gym.

Decoration is restrained and reflects the plain but imposing exterior of the building. The stations of the cross are glazed terra-cotta in the style of Lucca della Robbia. Three statues, the *Virgin, Sacred Heart,* and *St. Charles* are from the original church. Around the ceiling are large medallions of thirty-one saints and two statues of figures awaiting canonization, chosen by members of the parish to represent their ethnic heritage and personal devotional life. These men and sixteen women range from Mary of the Immaculate Conception—patroness of the United States in red, white, and blue—to Joanna Beretta Molla (1922–62)—patroness of the unborn. The west rose is of *Carlo Borromeo* in front of buildings signifying his role as the father of seminaries, with book and pen in hand, wearing the rope of penance over his red cardinal robes. Around St. Charles are medallions of the seven acts of mercy and the motto of the Borromeos: "Humility."

125. St. Vladimir's Ukrainian Orthodox Cathedral (1967)
Architect: Geary and Moore
Builder: The Ukrainian Orthodox Community[11]
Location: 5913 State Road, Parma

Greater Cleveland has two centers of liturgical church governance. The "Western European Christian center" sits on the Near East Side. The Cathedral of St. John the Evangelist, on the corner of Superior Avenue at East Ninth Street (see p. 16), is the seat of the Roman Catholic bishop of Cleveland. Trinity Episcopal Cathedral, on the corner of Euclid Avenue at East 22nd Street (see p. 21), is the seat of the Episcopal bishop of Ohio. The "Eastern European Christian center" is at the intersection of State and Snow Roads in Parma. One block north is St. Josaphat (see p. 308), seat of the bishop of the Ukrainan Catholic Eparchy of St. Josaphat. Three long blocks east is the Cathedral of St. John the Baptist (see p. 310), seat of the bishop of the Byzantine Catholic Eparchy of Parma. Three short blocks south is St. Vladimir's Cathedral, the seat of the metropolitan of the Ukrainian Orthodox Church of the United States. It hardly needs to be said that the intersection of State at Snow is also the epicenter of Ukrainian Cleveland.[12]

The history of Christianity in the large area historically associated with Ukraine is extremely complicated and best left to specialists. So is the history of Christian Ukrainians in the United States and in Cleveland. In the fullness of time, however, the history became simpler. In 1924 former Greek Catholic members of Saints Peter and Paul Ukrainian Catholic Church in Tremont (see p. 210) returned to their ancient Orthodox faith and formed their own parish. They dedicated their first church in 1933 on West 11th Street between Fairfield and Kenilworth Avenues. This imposing yellow brick building, with its onion domes, is now the Iglesia Hispana Asambleas de Dios, a community established in 1952 as the first Hispanic Pentecostal church in Cleveland. In 1959 the parish of St. Vladimir's purchased, renovated, and moved the old Parma City Hall to their present location on State Road at Marioncliff Drive. Their newly constructed 450-seat church was consecrated in 1967. Its magnificent eight-hundred-square-foot mosaic of the *Baptism of Rus-Ukraine* was installed, in 1988, over the main doors to celebrate their millennium of Christianity.[13] In 1993 the parish dedicated a monument, south of the cathedral, to the memory of the more than seven million Ukrainians who died of hunger engineered by the Communists after 1933. St. Vladimir's became the seat of the American metropolitan and the Cathedral of the Central Eparchy of the Ukrainian Orthodox Church of the United States in 1997.

Across State Road from the Good Shepherd United Methodist Church, St. Vladimir's shares their thoroughfare with a succession of prosperous, small Ukrainian businesses. The extensive, beautifully and lovingly tended St. Vladimir campus sits on a deep lot. It backs into a well-kept residential neighborhood. The cathedral is sited at the west end of the property. Behind the cathedral, across a parking lot hidden from State Road by the building, is a community center with conference and meeting rooms, historical and cultural displays, an eight-room school, a library, and church offices. Behind the community center, on Marioncliff, is another large parking lot and two rectories. The parish owns two additional homes beside the cathedral on State Road. In one of the homes are the offices of ZOE for Life, a program that provides a link between women in crisis pregnancies and couples wishing to adopt children.

In contrast to the usual verticality of Orthodox churches, St. Vladimir's has a horizontal appearance. The building plan is that of a Greek cross. The exterior walls of the cathedral are of large-piece flattened but unfinished rubble masonry. This exterior finish is repeated in the community center across the parking lot. St. Vladimir's has an elaborate central tower and a conspicuous lantern just above the roofline. The lantern appears to be illuminated through latticed windows. The cathedral was originally built with nontraditional (for the Orthodox Ukrainians) ball turrets. These have been subsequently covered up with the modified onion domes more representative of their tradition, but the result is that the lantern does not communicate with the inside of the cathedral.[14] The interior does not have the usual Orthodox dome with a *Pantocrator*. Instead, a large crystal candelabra hangs down from the center of a rather shallow ceiling. The *Pantocrator* is centered in front of the chandelier.

Two shrines face the entrance in the narthex—*Mother and Child* on the left and *Jesus* as an adult on the right. The worship space makes the point that it is dangerous to generalize about the distinctive characteristics of different denominations. The seating area is essentially square. It appears larger than the usual seating area in an Orthodox worship space because of the interior horizontality, resulting from the relatively low ceiling (the ceiling is high enough to accommodate the wonderfully gigantic chandelier comfortably). The cathedral has a small balcony for the choir. The parish is proud of its large iconostasis, carved by a parishioner and completed by a California painter. Forward of the *Pantocrator* is a large iconographic roundel of *Mother and Child*. What little can be seen of the sanctuary behind the iconostasis is a simple, plain blue. Iconography on the walls is not intrusive. Restrained stenciling is of high quality. Large, colorful windows brightly illuminate everything.

126. St. Josaphat Ukrainian Catholic Cathedral (1983)

Architect: unknown
Builder: unknown
Location 5720 State Road, Parma

St. Josaphat Cathedral is the most lavishly decorated religious building in the Cleveland area.[15] Entering its worship area, lined with mosaics, takes one's breath away. It is northern Ohio's Ravenna.[16] Mosaics appear everywhere in St. Josaphat. Most of the mosaic is neo-Byzantine. One finds some Roman naturalism in the portraits and a limited amount of contemporary design. Only occasionally does a little marble peek through. Mosaics not only wrap around the visitor on the ground floor, but also a complete program appears in the sanctuary behind the iconostasis and another appears in the balcony. As overwhelming as all of this craftsmanship is, part of its charm is its contemporaneity. Like Renaissance or medieval religious imagery, some of the mosaics are of religious figures and some are of historical and contemporary figures, of importance to the community or of importance to the congregation. Right there, sitting among those at the Last Supper, are figures of proud donors. Imagine being able to look up from a pew at a biblical scene and being able to recognize your grandfather. Federico da Montefeltro and Nicolas Rolin would be proud.[17] Figures from recent Ukrainian and Ukrainian-American history are spread out across a great mosaic stretching across the back of the balcony. For the uninitiated, the figures are identified by name on great floor to ceiling marble plaques flanking the mosaic.

Between narrative mosaics on the first floor are plaques of marble relief with cut-out designs, like *sgraffito,* in Botticino marble. One also finds rather small amounts of traditional 1960s glass. The iconostasis has four large paintings copied from Santa Sofia in Rome and two smaller paintings.[18] The iconostasis itself is a wonderful construction of thin, light, ivory Botticino marble columns. Additional elegant, light Botticino marble pillars flank the chapels to the left and right of the iconostasis. Beautiful bronze chandeliers and much Ukrainian writing decorate the interior.

As in St. Mark's in Venice, the basic structure of the worship space is somewhat overwhelmed by the decoration. Another reason why the seating appears so small, compared to the external size of the building, is the combined height of the ceiling with the height of the balcony. This is a conventional, somewhat square, Orthodox worship space—almost a cube. The balcony projects backward out of the cube, and the sanctuary projects forward behind the iconostasis. With all the decoration on the walls, it is easy to miss that the five domes, a large central and four smaller quadrant domes, are undecorated. This lavish project remains unfinished. The plainly plastered domes eventually will be painted. Modern building codes discourage mosaic on upside-down surfaces because the tesserae may rain down on those below.

Although the visitor is tempted to plunge immediately into this building to see the decoration, its exterior is a major presence in northeastern Parma. Driving south on State Road, while still in Cleveland, the large, clustered domes of the tan brick cathedral loom up more than a mile and a half away, on the other side of I-480. The cathedral, facing the east, is entered from the west, away from the street. Driveways lead to a spacious, quiet, well-proportioned courtyard in front of the back of the building. Over the entrance to the cathedral is a great mosaic of St. Josaphat, a hint of the mosaics inside the building. The cathedral shares a large campus with a school, rectory, convent, chancery, and an immense community center called the "astrodome." On Fridays, a train of cars turns off State Road into the complex, directed to the astrodome by a handwritten sign advertising "Pyrohy."[19]

The cathedral is the seat of the bishop of the Ukrainian Catholic Eparchy of Parma. The Ukrainian Greek Catholic Church is the largest of the Eastern Catholic churches and is led, under Rome, by Lubomyr Cardinal Husar, major archbishop of Kyiv-Halych in the Ukraine. His predecessor as major archbishop was Myroslav Ivan Cardinal Lubachivsky (1914–2000). Lubachivsky, in exile, served at Saints Peter and Paul Ukrainian Catholic Church in Tremont (see p. 210) from 1949 until 1968. John Paul II appointed Lubachivsky to succeed the primate in Kiev in 1979. As the result of the Communist period in Ukraine, twice as many Ukrainian Catholics live in "the West" as live in Ukraine. The American Ukrainian primate is the archbishop of Philadelphia. The Eparchies (dioceses) of Chicago, Parma, and Stamford, Connecticut, fall under his jurisdiction. The Eparchy of Parma includes Ohio, western Pennsylvania, and the American southeast. Saints Peter and Paul Church served as the center of Ukrainian Catholicism in Cleveland before the Ukrainian population largely moved to Parma. Although there are more Ukrainians in the United States than Ruthenians, there are more Ruthenians in Greater Cleveland than Ukrainians. Ukrainian Catholics in Cleveland maintained a close, intertwined, and edgy relationship with the Ruthenian Catholics until John Paul II definitively separated the groups in 1983.[20]

127. Cathedral of St. John the Baptist (1959)

Architect: Unknown
Builder: Unknown
Location: 1900 Carlton Road, Parma

The pope administers the Catholic Church worldwide through dioceses and eparchies. Most of the church—the Latin Church or the Roman Catholic Church—is organized into dioceses, as in the Catholic Diocese of Cleveland, led by its bishop, who has his seat at the Cathedral of St. John the Evangelist (see p. 16). Eastern Catholic Churches, such as the Ruthenian Catholic Church, are administered through eparchies, such as the Eparchy of Parma, led, at this writing, by Bishop John Kudrick, who has his seat at the Cathedral of St. John the Baptist.[21] His eparchy, established by Pope Paul VI in 1969, now includes most of the Midwest from Ohio to Kansas to North Dakota. In Cuyahoga County, the Eparchy of Parma oversees St. Stephen in Euclid, St. Eugene in Bedford, St. Joseph in Brecksville, St. Mary Magdalene in Fairview Park, St. Gregory in Lakewood, Holy Spirit in Parma, St. John in Solon, Holy Ghost in Cleveland (see p. 198), and St. Mary in Cleveland (see p. 221). The Eparchy of Parma also includes non-Ruthenian Eastern Catholic Churches that are too small in number to warrant a diocese of their own, such as St. Nicholas Croatian Catholic Church in Cleveland (see p. 73). With the Eparchies of Passaic (New Jersey) and Van Nuys (California), the Eparchy of Parma is part of the Metropolia of Pittsburgh. Bishop Kudrick's predecessor as bishop of Parma, Basil Schott (bishop of Parma, 1996–2002), was named metropolitan archbishop of Pittsburgh in 2002, reporting directly to Rome.

Measured by the hundreds of automobiles that assemble on its grounds and in its neighborhood for a major meeting of the eparchy, this is an important institution. Across Snow Road from the Midtown Shopping Center, the cathedral and the chancery spread out over a large area. The complex occupies most of the otherwise undeveloped area on the southwest corner of Snow at Broadview Road. Access to the chancery, beside and behind the cathedral, is from the east on Carlton Road. Admission to the chancery is behind the complex, through a simple but imposing entrance off the large parking lot at the end of Carlton Road.

The cathedral, set back more than a hundred yards from the street, faces Snow Road. Access is through a drive-through arcade at its entrance or through a garden, with fountain, between the Snow Road parking lot and the building. The religious orientation of the cathedral is announced by three onion domes above the entrance. Running along the exterior of the nave, on both sides of the cathedral, are three immense, two-story narrative mosaics. A large mosaic of the *Virgin* embraces the three arches of the lower part of the entrance arcade.

Farther up the main central tower is a two-story mosaic of the *Baptism.* Through the entrance is a generous narthex flanked by a small chapel with an iconostasis—seating eleven—to the east, and an elegant and formal parlor to the west.

The worship space is not as large as one might anticipate from the size of the complex. There is a wide center aisle. Lateral aisles run under an arcade that supports a wraparound balcony running on both sides from the rear balcony up to the chancel. Between nave and sanctuary is a one-piece, dark-stained wood iconostasis through which one may see figures in the sanctuary. On either side of the iconostasis are magnificent Byzantine-style paintings—*St. John Chrysostom* on the right and *Basil the Great* on the left. Iconography of *Mary and the Child* and of the *Last Supper* are in the sanctuary behind the iconostasis. Generous but restrained iconography decorates both sides of the nave under the balcony. In front of the choir on the back balcony is a *Dormition of the Virgin.* The *Pantocrator* is overhead, surrounded by angels in a shallowly recessed dome. Above the chancel hangs a giant chandelier, and bronze lights illuminate the pews. The impression is of a worship space that is elegant, simple, and well decorated without being lavishly ostentatious.

CHAPTER THIRTEEN

Cleveland Heights

Begin this tour at the intersection of Mayfield Road and Taylor Road in Cleveland Heights.[1] Driving west on Mayfield Road, Saints Constantine and Helen Greek Orthodox Cathedral (128) appears on the left. Beside Saints Constantine and Helen, to the west, lies the grounds of Eric Mendelsohn's Park Synagogue (129), the most famous religious building in Cleveland and perhaps the most famous building of any kind in northern Ohio. Turn left into its driveway and drive through the grounds to the parking lot to see this famous building. Returning to Mayfield, turn left (west). Beside Park Synagogue is the mammoth building erected by the other large Conservative Jewish community in Cleveland, B'nai Jeshurun. After difficult decades as an arts center—the Civic Center—the prospering New Spirit Revival Center (130) has returned this building to repair.

Continue down Mayfield Road for 1.2 miles, through Forest Hill Park with its recreational buildings and past Lakeview Cemetery on the right. At the main entrance to this large cemetery the road divides, with Mayfield veering right and Kenilworth Road branching to the left. Jog onto Kenilworth and, after two blocks, turn left onto Edgehill Road. After one block, turn right onto Euclid Heights Boulevard. St. Alban Episcopal Church (131), rebuilt in modern shingle after a 1989 fire, stands on the right at the corner. Drive one block southwest on Euclid Heights Boulevard and then turn left onto Berkshire Road. After one block turn right onto Norfolk Road. After two blocks turn left onto Cedar Road.

Cedar Hill Baptist Church is located on the left. Communion of Saints Parish, formerly St. Ann Church (132), is the large Classic Revival building that looks like a bank on the southeast corner of Cedar Road at Coventry Road. Continue east on Cedar. Grace Lutheran Church (133) is the sprawling Gothic Revival complex to the north. Continue on Cedar and turn right (south) at Lee Road. Cleveland Heights High School occupies the northeast corner. The massive French Gothic Revival Methodist Church of the Saviour (134) is located farther down Lee on the left. At the intersection with Fairmount, turn right into the Fairmount Historic District (for the four religious institutions on each corner of this intersection, see p. 331). West on Fairmount, on the east side of its intersection with Coventry Road, is Fairmount Presbyterian Church (135). West of Coventry is St. Paul's Episcopal Church (136).

This is the heart of "Pill Hill," where the leadership of the Cleveland Clinic and University Hospitals lived and sometimes worshiped. Here, within a mile-and-a-half radius, were the great Cleveland establishment religious institutions of the second half of the twentieth century: St. Ann (p. 321), Saints Constantine and Helen (p. 314), Fairmount Presbyterian (p. 327), Grace Lutheran (p. 324), Park (p. 315), St. Paul's (p. 329), Plymouth (p. 335), Church of the

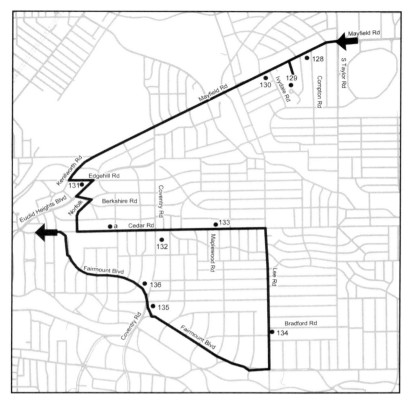

CLEVELAND HEIGHTS

128. Saints Constantine and Helen Greek
    Orthodox Cathedral
129. Park Synagogue
130. New Spirit Revival Center
131. St. Alban Episcopal Church
    a. Cedar Hill Baptist Church

132. Communion of Saints Parish
133. Grace Lutheran Church
134. Church of the Saviour
135. Fairmount Presbyterian Church
136. St. Paul's Episcopal Church

Saviour (p. 325), and the Temple on the Heights (p. 318). The First Baptists (p. 337) were two miles away in one direction and Abba Hillel Silver (p. 44) was two miles away in the other. This ends this tour. Continue down Fairmount to Cedar and to University Circle.

128. Saints Constantine and Helen Greek Orthodox Cathedral (1956, 1985)
Architects: Carr and Cunningham (1956) and Robert Yoder (1985)
Builders: John Geranios (1956) and Stephen Callos (1985)

Location: 3352 Mayfield, Cleveland Heights

Stairs lead up from a busy thoroughfare to the imposing but restrained Saints Constantine and Helen.[2] This church stands in one of the few residential neighborhoods along Mayfield Road. Most visitors, however, will enter from the parking lot behind and to the west of the church. Although the church is immediately adjacent to Park Synagogue, both institutions keep their distance and do not intrude on each other. The quiet, introverted exterior of this church is reminiscent of the great Byzantine churches of Ravenna—modest on the outside, dramatic on the inside. The plain exterior walls are of rough brick alternating with narrow string courses of a darker brick. It has modest brick treatment around the windows and stone trim around the entrance. The roof is plain tile. The only exterior decoration is a colorful but relatively small mosaic of *Constantine and Helen* on the tympanum over the front entrance. The front doors are perforated with Byzantine glass, desert-plate disks of crown, or spun, glass. Saints Constantine and Helen keeps its greatest treasures hidden until visitors go inside.

Foster Armstrong liked to say that purity of style was not a characteristic of Cleveland churches and, like many of them, Saints Constantine and Helen mixes several styles. The mixture at Saints Constantine and Helen is important because it reflects not the eclectic taste of some architect but, rather, the sympathy and inclination of a congregation alternating between the severity of symbolic Byzantine and the accessibility of more naturalistic Latin. In an interesting way, in their church, the parish is acting out the early Renaissance in Florence, when Cimabue and Giotto found themselves between the Greek of their tradition and the naturalization of their observation.

Saints Constantine and Helen is what its parishioners call "a basilica," not the traditional domed Greek church. Although this church does not have a dome, the image of the *Pantocrator* dominates the nave from the center of the ceiling. The *Pantocrator* is traditionally a severe Byzantine image of Christ as judge. In Saints Constantine and Helen, the iconic severity of Christ's expression is softened by a more naturalistic, Latin style. In a similar manner, on the iconostasis, the images of *Jesus, Mary, John the Baptist,* and the titular saints, separating the nave from the inner sanctuary, are naturalized. Light floods into the nave from the side through stained-glass figures instead of Byzantine crown glass. One finds not only the traditional desk on the right for the cantor but also a nontraditional organ on the left. Within this mixture of styles there remains, however, a powerful impression that this is a Greek church. It has an oversized cathedra for the bishop on the right, dramatized by a large lion at either hand. The ceiling is a wonderful dark Byzantine blue, and the side walls are painted striking yellow and red ochre.

The Church of Annunciation in Tremont (see p. 196), built in 1918, is the mother church of the Greek community in Greater Cleveland. Annunciation was legally organized as the Pan-Hellenic Union in 1910. In 1937 St. Spyridon was established to serve the East Side, but it was reabsorbed by Annunciation in 1950. East Siders, led by Father John Geranios, petitioned the Cleveland Pan-Hellenic Union in 1952 to establish what became Saints Constantine and Helen. In 1955 the union was reorganized into the American-Hellenic Community of Greater Cleveland. The first service in Saints Constantine and Helen was held in 1957, and in 1960 St. Demetrios (see p. 291) was organized on the West Side. At this time, all three Greek churches functioned as a single community with numerous priests circulating among the various churches. In 1967 the Hellenic Community was dissolved, and each parish became independent. At that time, Saints Constantine and Helen was designated as a cathedral by the Archdiocese of Pittsburgh.

129. Park Synagogue (see also Cory United Methodist Church, p. 97; The Lillian and Betty Ratner School, p. 347; and Park Synagogue East, p. 345) (1950)
Architects: Eric Mendelsohn (1950); Michael Gallis, Myron Manders, and Jack Alan Bialosky (1969)
Builders: Armond Cohen and Leonard Ratner[3]

Location: 3300 Mayfield Road, Cleveland Heights

Eric Mendelsohn's Park Synagogue is unquestionably the most important sacred monument in Greater Cleveland and probably the most important building of any kind in northern Ohio.[4] It is the largest and most ambitious synagogue that Mendelsohn built in the United States. Park Synagogue (one of the world's largest Conservative congregations) established modern architecture as a possible style for the construction of Jewish religious buildings. As an international landmark, it weaned Judaism away from the Near Eastern eclecticism of the "modernized Byzantine" style. Farthermore, Mendelsohn's plastic vision in Park Synagogue was an important step in introducing modern expressionism into the practice of Eliel and Eero Saarinen, Pier Luigi Nervi, and Frank Lloyd Wright.

As the Anshe Emeth congregation, uneasily ensconced in its monumental Cleveland Jewish Center (see Cory United Methodist Church, p. 97), drifted into insolvency in the Great Depression, it called, in desperation, the twenty-six-year-old Armond Cohen as rabbi. Raising enough to keep the banks at bay, in 1942 the young rabbi bought the twelve-acre defunct Park School as an eastern branch of the center. As Anshe Emeth was moving in, a 1945 fire destroyed several of the Park school buildings together with the congregation's library and all of its Torah Scrolls. Undaunted, Cohen and Leonard Ratner purchased another twenty-one wooded acres and called in Eric Mendelsohn.

Like Cohen, Mendelsohn had also been something of a prodigy. Coming back from the First World War, he designed the expressionistic Einstein Tower in Potsdam, a significant modern landmark. In Germany, Mendelsohn developed one of the first highly successful, modern architecture practices. With Ludwig Mies van der Rohe and Walter Gropius, he established the modern architecture group known as Der Ring. In 1933 his country turned him out with a pencil. Despite a 1941 retrospective at the Museum of Modern Art in New York (where he attracted the attention of Cohen), Mendelsohn never—in the United Kingdom, Israel, or the United States—regained the commercial success he had enjoyed in Germany. In the United States, he was known primarily as a teacher at Berkeley. In Cleveland, he proved to be a strong personality, surrounded by clients who also had strong personalities.[5] Had it not been for Leonard Ratner, a bust of whom Mendelsohn suggested for the synagogue, Mendelsohn's masterpiece might never have been built.

Like all architects, Mendelsohn was familiar with and probably took some of his basic concepts from others—Percival Goodman, Cecil Moore, and Joseph Hoffmann. Mendelsohn began with a great site, a thirty-foot-high triangular promontory defined by ravines in dense woods, set one thousand feet back from the street. Standing in the bed of a truck parked on Mayfield, Ratner recorded the results as Mendelsohn, waving his arms, moved about the site almost a quarter of a mile away. From his first sketches, Mendelsohn conceived of the synagogue as a large dome on the promontory. To the east (back) of the dome, Mendelsohn planned a lower-ceilinged, fan-shaped foyer and assembly hall, extending out from the dome. When opened up, it would accommodate three thousand for holy days. Mendelsohn subsequently used this plan in the other three synagogues that he designed in the United States. It is a different solution—with the same result—as the famous Akron Plan followed by many Protestant churches.[6] On a lower level, in front of the dome, Mendelsohn designed the triangular Miller Chapel and across the creek to the north an educational building with thirty classrooms, a nursery, and a basement auditorium. Immediately published,[7] the contractors bid the original plan at three times what the congregation could afford. Mendelsohn's revision relocated education to a two-story wing across a patio behind a smaller foyer and assembly hall. An administrative wing and library joined the educational wing to the main building. Mendelsohn's organic, expressionist style ties all these pieces together so that while worship, assembly, and learning areas are distinguished, they are also integrated and visually interlocked in a dynamic and rhythmic creation. Use of curved and rectangular shapes creates a dynamic tension that draws visitors through the flowing spaces. Like Mies, Mendelsohn used materials publicly associated with the vernacular architecture of the period, but with the greatest subtlety. Mendelsohn's modern organic style was an alternative to "the monotonous cubic austerity of most modern architecture of his period."[8]

The unornamented interior of the dome, one hundred feet in diameter and sixty-five feet high, was designed as an overwhelming visual experience. Every Jewish sanctuary is supposed to have a window to the outside, to signify that it is not hiding from the world. This 680-ton dome rests, not on the floor, but on six columns separated by fifteen-foot-high walls of clear glass that visually integrate and unite the interior of the worship space with the ever-changing environment outside the building. Constructed of alternating thin layers of acoustical tile, cork, steel reinforcing bar, sprayed concrete, felt, and copper, the dome is four inches thick; its thinness allows an identical interior and external profile. In 1950 it was the third-largest dome in the United States. Because of its position on the west point of the promontory, the ark and bimah, instead of directing the congregation east toward Jerusalem, as dictated by tradition, turns it west. "The earth," said Mendelsohn, "is round."[9] The circular plan, with its long rows of seats on a pitched floor, ensures visibility and brings a large congregation closer to the ark and bimah than would a long narrow rectangular plan. Each seat is individually and almost imperceptibly angled toward the focal point of the service, providing, in such a large space, a surprising feeling of intimacy between the congregation and its leader.

By the early 1960s, the congregation had grown to the point where it was renting the Richmond movie theater for the high holy days. Mendelsohn's original concept of a school on the other side of the ravine, tied to the main building by a bridge, was revived in 1969 by Michael Gallis, Mendelsohn's assistant, as Kangesser Hall. With its Stein Auditorium and Goldberg Assembly, tied to the main building by the Ratner gallery, the new addition equaled the size of the main building. Seating two thousand, it increased the capacity of the complex to four thousand. The congregation also began to transfer its aggressive educational program farther east, originally in 1986 to the Edward Durrel Stone B'rith Emeth Synagogue, purchased and renamed Park Synagogue East (see p. 347). Later, the Centerbrook group built a new Park Synagogue East (see p. 345) and the Edward Durell Stone building became the Ratner School.

130. New Spirit Revival Center (see also Shiloh Baptist Church, p. 132 and B'nai Jeshurun Congregation, p. 349) (1926)
Architect: Charles Greco
Builder: Abraham Nowak
Location: 3130 Mayfield Road, Cleveland Heights

In 1994, with four other members, Drs. Darrell and Belinda Scott organized the New Spirit Revival Center (NSRC) as a nondenominational Pentecostal/charismatic church in rented quarters in the huge (110,000 square feet) and increasingly decrepit building then known as "the Civic."[10] Nine years later, they purchased the entire building and initiated a campaign to maintain, renovate, and refurbish the structure. Within five more years, the roof was repaired, the windows restored, the basement was permanently dry, the summer and winter ventilation systems were in repair, and the enormous public spaces showed the result of several coats of paint and energetic use. By 2008, renovation of classrooms was far enough along that the Covenant Childcare Learning and Enrichment Center was well established. Radio 1000 (the first church-owned station in Cleveland) had been on the air for three years from modern studios next to the completely renovated Studio Theater, and Barack Obama was speaking in the sanctuary. All this in a building that, thirty years before, the City of Cleveland Heights had bypassed as too expensive to convert into its municipal headquarters.

This building was built by the Congregation B'nai Jeshurun when it moved here from the building now occupied by the Shiloh Baptist Church on East 55th Street at Scovill Avenue in Cleveland. By that time, almost a third of the Cleveland-area Jewish community lived in Cleveland Heights. B'nai Jeshurun adapted the English name of "the temple on the Heights" or "Height's temple" and, by 1926, was one of the largest conservative congregations in the United States with membership of 1,125 and school attendance of eight hundred. By the 1930s, the congregation had increased to two thousand families with 1,400 children in the religious school. After the Second World War, the congregation continued to grow and built the 1956 west wing.

The B'nai Jeshurun Torahs were walked out to Pepper Pike in 1980 (see p. 349), and this building was purchased by Temple Associates, a limited partnership that attempted to operate the building as a home for arts and civic organizations and events. The expense of maintaining the building, mortgage payments, and capital improvements always exceeded revenue. In the end, the partners transferred the building to the Civic Foundation Inc., a nonprofit corporation. They also transferred $1 million in unpaid taxes, bills, and bank loans. The estimated demolition cost was $550,000, so the bank faced a large loss if the foundation defaulted. An estimated three million dollars

318

was required to renovate major areas, repair the leaking roof, and upgrade the antiquated plumbing. Between eleven and thirteen million dollars would be required to renovate the building into the arts and civic center originally anticipated. The struggle continued with support from the bank, local foundations, and local, state, and federal governments until, providentially, the building was purchased by the New Spirit Revival Center in 2003.

Charles R. Greco of Boston designed this building; he designed the University Circle Temple Tifereth Israel (the Temple) in the same neo-Moorish/Byzantine style (see p. 44). Byzantine Revival architecture was particularly popular in Russia in the late nineteenth and early twentieth centuries. Important examples of this style in the United States are the campus of Rice University in Houston, the Roman Catholic basilicas in St. Louis and Washington, D.C., and, much more recently, Philip Johnson's postmodernist addition to the former Cleveland Play House. The exterior of the New Spirit Revival Center is red brick with Indiana limestone, polychrome terra-cotta, and colored marble trim. A red tile Byzantine roof covers the dome. The entrance is from broad stairs off Mayfield Road with five wooden doors alternating with stone columns. The columns, with Byzantine capitals, support arches from which hang marble slabs inscribed with the Ten Commandments.

The entrance lobby's polychrome, marble veneer walls, marble floor, and vaulted ceiling are flanked by monumental stairs to the left and right that both lead to the sanctuary balcony. Beside the sanctuary, to the east, was a 1,200-seat auditorium, now used for weddings, parties, and civic events. On the floor below are two giant rooms now used for a variety of parish activities; the room below the sanctuary originally housed four bowling alleys. There were thirty-one classrooms in three stories east and south of the main public spaces in the original building. In 1956 a west wing was added in the style common to commercial buildings of that time. This addition contained more classrooms, offices, and a chapel subsequently used as a theater.

Light floods into the sanctuary from arched windows ringing the dome and from windows in the side walls and above the balcony. The sanctuary originally seated two thousand. Now called the great hall, the center of NSRC worship, a lobby extension has reduced seating to nine hundred.

131. St. Alban Episcopal Church
(1892; 1992)
Architects: Unknown (1892), William
Morris (1992)
Builders: Unknown (1892), George
Landis (1992)
Location: 2555 Euclid Heights
Boulevard, Cleveland Heights

Fire—it is the scourge of historic
churches. They are old, dry, and flam-
mable. If a church's resources wither,
its electrical and heating systems become antiquated and poorly maintained. Temptation, frequently the
child of necessity, grandfathers historic buildings around modern fire codes.
Large and sometimes unpopular public landmarks, churches may attract the
attention of the unstable. As populations change, churches become isolated
from their communities. The list goes on. Considering how vulnerable historic
churches are, it is surprising how few burn.

The original St. Alban was built in 1892, in what would become Little Italy,
on the corner of Murray Hill Road and Fairview Avenue two blocks west of
Mayfield Road.[11] Five years later, the frame building was hauled by oxen up the
hill into Cleveland Heights; there it was transformed over the years into a traditional, stucco, Tudor-style church with dark wood trim.[12] St. Alban put on an
addition in 1926 and dedicated a parish hall in 1963. Although St. Alban was the
first Episcopal parish in the Heights area, it has always struggled because of its
location, too close to Lakeview Cemetery and too far from adequate numbers
of affluent Episcopalians. In 1901 it was reorganized as a mission of Emmanuel
Episcopal Church (see p. 36) and called St. Andrew's-in-the-East. In 1912 it
was taken over by St. Paul's Episcopal Church. During a turbulent period in the
1920s, the aggressive rector of St. Paul's, in defiance of his bishop (who wanted
him to merge with St. Alban), sold his church to the Romans (as the Conversion
of St. Paul Shrine, see p. 28) and stormed up into the Heights (see p. 329). At
the corner of Coventry and Fairmount, well within the established boundary of
the parish of St. Alban, the rector of St. Paul's established what he hoped would
become the Episcopal cathedral.[13] In the end St. Paul's did not become the cathedral. Because of the Depression, in fact, it struggled to complete its building.

St. Alban carried on until 1989 when an unknown arsonist torched the dry
oak and combustible varnish in three places. The original frame church was a
complete loss. The parish continued, using a borrowed tent, the partially damaged educational wing, and the First English Lutheran Church down the street.
The diocese, the City of Cleveland Heights, and the insurance company urged
the congregation to abandon everything and turn their lot into a park. Resisting
this advice, the parish decided to pull down what little was left and start over.

St. Alban designed a new building to accommodate the original Episcopal congregation and to share its space with an outpost of a Reform Jewish congregation based in Euclid. The Jewish community became the Congregation Etz Chayim. When Etz Chayim moved, the Episcopalians invited the Edgehill Community Church of God to share the space. Since 2006, this ecumenical community has had a third member—the Prospering Circle Baptist Church.

The brown-shingled new church, with a composition roof, has a smaller worship space and a larger educational and administrative space than the old church. From the church, white trimmed Palladian windows look outward at the street. Plain picture windows look inward into a garden, embraced by both wings of the simple, cleanly defined masses of the new building.

The wood and plaster sanctuary faces east where a large cherry "triptych," decorated on the outside with "the tree of life," divides in half. Opening the upper doors reveals a cross. Opening the lower doors reveals the arc for a Torah. A large cherry baldachin arches over the triptych and wooden altar. Marble inlays, salvaged from the old church, decorate the altar. Its carved crosses were covered with an altar cloth when the space was used for Jewish worship. The marble baptismal font, also salvaged from the old church, shows the flame-marks of the fire. The only decorative touch in the sanctuary is patterned blue tile covering the cement floor, given by a parishioner who had watched the fire from her house across the street. The siting of the sanctuary allows light to pour into the worship space from large, unglazed windows on either side of the triptych. These windows also allow the congregation a good view of the trees and parkway of this residential neighborhood. The sanctuary was an ecumenical affair—the Catholic Diocese of Cleveland gave the pews from a discontinued church, the Kulas Foundation gave the splendid semicustom tracker organ, and Trinity Episcopal Cathedral gave the two-hundred-year-old wooden altar in the permanent chapel.

132. Communion of Saints Parish, formerly St. Ann Church (1952)
Architects: Walker and Weeks and Horn and Rhinehart (1952)[14]
Builder: John Mary Powers
Location: 2175 Coventry Road, Cleveland Heights

Many of the imposing figures who built the sacred landmarks of our area are unknown or only dimly remembered (see Dedication). Few were fortunate enough to have their Boswells. John Mary Powers was such an out-sized personality that he inspired two Boswells—and they should be consulted concerning the life of this remarkable man and his remarkable church.[15]

Father Powers established St. Ann Church in 1915 with a specific agenda. He wanted to build and lead a stable, lasting Irish bourgeois parish. In his twelve years as an assistant at St. Thomas Aquinas in Cleveland, he had seen a dynamic, model parish be rapidly overrun and destroyed by the absence of residential zoning (it was said that he removed his collar and closed a saloon across the street from St. Thomas Acquinas one Sunday morning with his fists). He would see St. Agnes, "the most perfect parish church in America," doomed in a generation by the uncontrolled development that destroyed Euclid Avenue's Millionaire's Row.[16] Therefore, gathering a group of investors and families from St. Thomas Aquinas, Powers, like a latter-day Brigham Young, organized the Meadowbrook Land Company, purchased a large tract in Cleveland Heights, and planned a church, in what he imaginatively described in later years as a wilderness, to be surrounded by affluent, devout Roman Catholics. It worked . . . for fifty years.

Koehl and Van Renssalaer designed, in a domestic vernacular style, the first school-church, built between September and Christmas 1915. This "temporary" structure served as St. Ann Church for the next thirty-seven years. The original church was then converted into its current use, and likely its original intended role, as a recreational center. This included, by 1954, a roller rink and snack bar in the basement (but without the rumored swimming pool). The stone rectory, built in what was described as "the early Georgian Classic tradition," was begun in 1916. In 1918 St. Ann Church was responsible for the first public performance of the Cleveland Orchestra at a benefit for the church in Gray's Armory. The orchestra played Tchaikovsky, Liszt, and Bizet. The irrepressible Powers sang, to piano accompaniment, from "his vast repertoire of sentimental songs."[17]

After ten uncomfortable years in the "temporary" church, and even more temporary surrounding frame buildings, the school moved into permanent quarters in 1925. Designed in twentieth-century Beaux Arts style by George Hunt Ingraham, the school added rooms in the basement in the 1950s and opened a third floor in 1960. The area south of the church and school, now occupied by a large parking lot, at one time accommodated four professional-class, lighted tennis courts, a large formal garden, and four greenhouses (St. Ann Church was in the flower business until the florist at Shaker Square complained to the diocese). The parish was not responsible for the coincidentally named St. Ann's Hospital, the now demolished Catholic maternity hospital at the top of Fairhill Road across the street from the Cleveland Water Works, but it played an important role in founding the Beaumont high school for girls in 1942.

In 1925 Powers walked into the First National Bank in downtown Cleveland, which was being razed and consolidated into the Union Trust, in search of a used desk for the rectory. He walked out with a church. He bought ten massive fluted Ionic limestone pillars, many large marble slabs, two bronze balconies, several marble drinking fountains for holy-water fonts, an enormous clock, fourteen teller's lamps (each of which used three bulbs—fortuitously representing the Trinity) to illuminate the stations of the cross, and fourteen massive bronze chandeliers. In 1927 he commissioned Walker and Weeks to make something of all this and submitted their plans to Bishop Joseph Schrembs. The bishop torpedoed the project for three reasons. First, he did not like Powers. Second, he did not like "extravagant parish churches."[18] Third, he thought the plans looked more like a bank than a church. The bishop could stop construction but the collecting continued, including a twenty-five-year-old 3,173-pipe Steere-Skinner organ from the Piedmont Presbyterian Church of Worcester, Massachusetts, for $2,500 with a carillon thrown in; wood paneling from the Hanna mansion in Bratenahl to construct six confessionals and panel the sacristy; a copy—from the Van Sweringen brothers' liquidated board room in the Midland Building—of the Victoria and Albert Ardabil carpet for the sanctuary; the thousands of bricks for the interior of the new church's walls from the Murray Hill School; the marble lobby of the Ritz-Carlton in New York for the chapel; and, all from the Central National Bank of Cleveland, the marble steps for the altar and sanctuary, the wood and bronze railing separating bank officers from the public for the altar rail, and the bronze vault doors for the sanctuary doors flanking the altar. Walker, Horn, and Rhinehart wove all this into their dusted-off plans, and Powers's church was finally completed in 1952. The view from the altar is, except for pews seating eight hundred, a remarkable reconstruction of the business office of a large bank.[19] The result was generously, if variously, described by the architects as Roman, Grecian, Italian Renaissance or, most imaginatively, Romanesque. For the pews, Powers invented a noiseless kneeler as he was irritated by the banging of kneelers on the floor, but his parishioners were spared the retractable pulpit that Powers wished to rise from underneath the floor. Retired priests were spared his proposed retirement colony in the tower.

The smooth-faced Indiana limestone exterior with its great Ionic portico, pediment, and basilican profile reflects Powers's unusual combination of the Parthenon and Santa Maria Maggiore in Rome. One greenhouse survives on an upper level of the southeast corner of the building. The bell tower is somewhat blunter than the original 1927 plan tower. The proposed 1927 tower was identical to that built in 1929 for the First Church of Christ, Scientist (see p. 62).

In October 2009, Bishop Richard Lennon merged St. Ann Church, Christ the King Parish and St. Philomena Church in East Cleveland, and St. Louis Church in Cleveland Heights into a new Community of Saints Parish to be established at both St. Ann and St. Philomena.

133. Grace Lutheran Church
(see also Fellowship Baptist
Church, p. 82) (1927)
Architect: John W. C.
Corbusier
Builder: H. W. Bartels
Address: 13001 Cedar Road,
Cleveland Heights

The interior of Grace Lutheran is an exquisite example of the full-bore, early twentieth-century, late Gothic Revival style championed by the "Boston Gothicists."[20] Another example by Corbusier is the Church of the Saviour (see p. 325), also in Cleveland Heights, and Ralph Adams Cram's Church of the Covenant (see p. 52) in University Circle, of which Corbusier was the Cleveland assistant. To walk into Grace Lutheran during the day—with the lights turned out so that light streams in through the windows—and to look upon the masonry, the paneling, the carving, the metalwork, and the Moravian tile floor is to experience what was, to early twentieth-century American architects, the medieval world.

Corbusier described this 1927 church as Tudor Gothic, as distinct from the French Gothic of his 1928 Church of the Saviour. Both are quite different in style from the eclectic combination of Romanesque and Gothic of his 1926 Greater Friendship Baptist Church (see p. 101). In contrast to Grace Lutheran's ornate interior, its exterior, while recognizably Gothic Revival, is relatively restrained. This relative simplicity reflects the impact of modernism on the archaeological early twentieth-century medieval flamboyance of the Gothicists from Boston. Particularly good examples of the impact of the modern on the medieval in Cleveland are Byers Hayes's 1928 First Baptist Church of Greater Cleveland (p. 337) and, of course, Bertram Goodhue's 1926 posthumous masterpiece, the recently renamed University Circle Methodist Church (p. 47).

Grace Lutheran's sanctuary is ninety feet long and ninety feet high with a full complement of windows. An elaborately carved wood screen frames the altar. The 111-bell Schulmerich carillon was installed in 1976 and the fifty-two rank Moller-Kegg organ the following year. Voluptuous woodcarving continues into a large chapel and then into a large separate baptistry with its own complement of windows.

134. Church of the Saviour
(1928; 1952–59; 2008)
Architects: John W. C.
Corbusier (1928), Travis
Gower Walsh (1952–59), and
Gregory Goss (2008)
Builders: George Pickard and
Jeffares McCombe (1928),
Howard Brown (1952–59),
and Charles Yoost (2008)
Location: 2537 Lee Road, Cleveland Heights

The history of the founding of the Church of the Saviour is so complicated that it requires a full-page family tree in the church's recent history.[21] Perhaps the current pastor best sums this up: "A group of small congregations built this monument with the idea that 'If you build it, they will come.'" Eleven congregations came together, over the years, to form the present congregation; these were the Evangelical Association Mission (founded 1862), Fairmount Church (1875), the Warrensville Methodist Circuit (Warrensville, Orange Hill, Orange Center, Radcliffe Schoolhouse, Euclid Stone Schoolhouse and Centenary) (1875), Kinsman Heights (1912), Madison Avenue Trinity (1901), and Wesley Methodist (Ferncliff) (1906). Most of the small frame buildings that these pioneer Methodists and Brethren built, borrowed, or rented have long since disappeared. Fairmount Church, the core congregation, was the twenty-sixth Methodist church in Cuyahoga County and the first in Cleveland Heights. It began in a schoolhouse at the corner of Superior Road and Euclid Heights Boulevard, in the part of Cleveland Heights then known as "Heathen Heights," because of the after-hours carousing of the quarry workers living along the bottom of Heights Ridge near Lake View Cemetery.[22] This schoolhouse has since been rebuilt and is now the Cleveland Heights Historical Center at Superior Schoolhouse. The congregation built a frame church next to the Superior Schoolhouse and, in 1904, built the church on the corner of Superior at Hampshire Lane now occupied by Christ Our Redeemer A.M.E. Church. Outgrowing this, Fairmount Church rented the auditorium and classrooms of the now destroyed Roosevelt School on Lee Boulevard before moving to the Church of the Saviour in 1928. The Reverend Dr. George Pickard led the campaign to build the current church until he died in 1925—before construction started. The Reverend Dr. Jaffares McCombe succeeded him and laid the cornerstone in 1927.

John W. C. Corbusier designed this French Gothic Revival church; he also designed the English Gothic Revival Grace Lutheran Church (see p. 324). The Church of the Saviour is faced with light gray and yellow-brown Weymouth, Massachusetts, seam-faced granite, set in a random ashlar pattern that is darker and bluer at the base of the building, becoming lighter in color as the masonry rises.[23] This emphasizes the height of the building. Foundation and trim are of coarse-grained Old Gothic limestone alternating with fine-grained

Indiana limestone. This masonry building is built like a medieval cathedral, without a steel framework. A complex roof support system, visible above the congregation, supports sixty-six tons of Vermont slate shingles.

The interior pillars, arches, and window frames are of Indiana limestone. Rich detailing with crosses, inscriptions, and other carving is elaborate but not complete; eighteen stone pedestals await their figures. The sanctuary seats approximately 1,100. Travis Gower Walsh completed the original design including the three-story south wing and chapel (1952), the upper tower (1953), and the east wing (1959). Gregory Goss designed an elegant entrance in 1998 and, most recently (2008), a 24,000-square-foot south addition with a large great hall for contemporary worship, fellowship, and recreation. The new south addition features a rooftop playground for 150 daily preschool children.

Corbusier designed the imposing carved-wood church furniture, the elaborate ironwork, and the intricate Carrara carved marble baptismal font (one of the few in Cleveland) with its remarkable carved cover. Fourteen large, wood figures on the lectern represent the Beatitudes and Christian virtues. The wood pulpit with nineteen carved Old Testament figures was given in memory of the first mayor of Cleveland Heights. A spectacular Gothic Revival ensemble of glass around the sanctuary memorializes figures from Obadiah to Savanarola and others before, since, and in between. A great east chancel window summarizes the Christian story. It is complemented by a great west window and continued with glass in the slightly more restrained chapel. Completion of the tower had been stimulated by the gift of a forty-seven-bell, four-octave carillon in 1953. An elaborate windowlike mural of a cross in the tower vestibule is constructed from stone from around the world.[24]

The Church of the Saviour was a deliberate attempt by several congregations to come together so that they could offer an ambitious education and music program. This had to be done on a regional basis, and this monument serves a congregation in Cleveland, Shaker and Mayfield Heights, Lyndhurst, and Mayfield. This regional organization provides the resources for local as well as international mission activities.

135. Fairmount Presbyterian Church (1942)

Architects: Bloodgood Tuttle (parish house; 1924), Walker and Weeks (sanctuary; 1942), and Garfield, Harris, Robinson, Schafer (chapel; 1956)
Builder: Frank Halliday Ferris
Location: 2757 Fairmount Boulevard, Cleveland Heights

There was a dignified but energetic rush among the Protestant denominations to evangelize the Heights. Each separate denomination labored under the threat of the creation of a nondenominational Protestant church.[25] Such a community church was probably encouraged by the Van Sweringens, who may have been concerned that religious divisiveness would endanger property values in their development.[26] In the end, however, the Baptists, Congregationalists, Episcopalians, Methodists, and Presbyterians all established impressive independent physical establishments (as did John Mary Powers at St. Ann, see p. 321).

For Presbyterians, the Presbyterian Union, established in 1869, played an important role. It organized Sunday school classes in homes, then in a real-estate office on the corner of Wellington at Fairmount, and, finally, bought two lots and put up a small frame chapel on the corner of Fairmount at Coventry. Three months after the first service by the first permanent minister, lightning hit the chapel and the resulting fire destroyed the church. As was appropriate for a denomination with a sermon-dominated liturgy, only the pulpit survived. Undeterred and helped by their insurance, the Presbyterian Union, and their own limited resources, the congregation had another building up in three weeks. Thereafter Fairmount Presbyterian experienced an uneventful ascendancy to the top of "Pill Hill," so named because of its neighborhood's popularity among physicians at University Hospitals and the Cleveland Clinic. By 1921 their replacement church was so crowded that the elders seriously considered issuing tickets for worship services. Three years later, they completed their parish house, a complex of spaces that still provides for much of the educational, social, and administrative activity of the community. The picturesque assembly hall in the parish house, although charming, was soon inadequate for the growing congregation, and in the midst of war, the current sanctuary was dedicated in 1942. Fairmount Presbyterian sent 350 members off to the war and twenty-two did not return.[27] By 1950, the church, reportedly "in the heart of the most heavily Presbyterian section of the Cleveland area," had "one of the largest active memberships and Sunday schools" in the Presbyterian United States.[28]

In 1956 the large chapel was dedicated as an additional worship space, but things were changing at Fairmount Presbyterian. By 1958, ushers serving

327

communion were no longer required to wear tails, dancing was permitted on church property on New Year's Eve, and women were allowed to play bridge in the church as long as the prizes were gifts and not money. Reaching out to the greater community, the congregation constructed twenty-two garden apartments on East 90th Street between Chester and Hough in a development called "Fairmount Village."

Fairmount Presbyterian is built of three contiguous parts. While maintaining their formal and period identity, they each wrap around, and almost enclose, a central garden area called "the Garth." The parish house, built in 1924, now appears to have its main entrance on Scarborough, off Fairmount, and now most enter it from Scarborough. The parish house was built, however, with an imposing entrance on Fairmount. This entrance stood well back from the street and is now swallowed up by the Garth. The sanctuary, attached to the parish house in 1942, extends to Fairmount, and its entrance is usually associated with the present church. The chapel is the third element, and it, running approximately parallel to Fairmount, almost closed the encirclement in 1956.

The parish house, with its rubble masonry and its stucco walls with half-timber wood trim and slate roof, was designed as an English country church. In addition to its gracious two-story assembly hall that served as the main worship space for almost twenty years, the parish house contains a generous assortment of meeting rooms, classrooms, and offices.

The sanctuary was built to continue this style as "an English village parish church of simple lines and sound design."[29] The dimensions of the interior, however, are hard to discern from the street, and the large and spacious interior is more than a little at odds with the modest ambition of its exterior. The giant arches of the sanctuary are an inversion of the ribs of a ship hull and may be related to wartime steel fabrication. It features singular windows of the story of Jesus in almost *grisaille* (there are small patches of color) and a great west window. Woodcarvings cover the back of the church. The sense of the sanctuary is no nonsense Presbyterian; congregations come to hear the preaching and listen to the music, not to be distracted by the surroundings.

From the outside, the chapel appears stylistically consistent with the complex, but the chapel interior is high modern. One finds good modern glass at its west end, a striking baptistry, and a two-manual tracker organ.

When excavation for the sanctuary was underway, at the beginning of the Second World War, the discovery of a giant glacial boulder seriously interfered with construction. Blasting through the obstruction was either impossible or, given what else was going on in the world, inappropriate. In any case, while only a cramped part of the basement could be built over the stone, it was always said thereafter that Fairmount Presbyterian was built on a rock.

136. St. Paul's Episcopal Church

(see also Conversion of St. Paul
Shrine, p. 28) (1928)
Architects: J. Byers Hayes of Walker
and Weeks (1928 and 1951); John
Carr of Carr-Cunningham (1956);
and Bill Collins of Collins, Rimer and
Gordon (1990)
Builders: Walter Russell Breed
(1928); John Legare O'Hear (1951
and 1956); and Nicholson White
(1990)
Location: 2747 Fairmount Boulevard,
Cleveland Heights

St. Paul's stands in the center of the
Fairmount Historical District in Cleveland Heights, a residential neighborhood
that evolved from a golf course before onset of the Great Depression.[30] The parish moved from its late nineteenth-century location in the middle of what had
been Millionaire's Row on Euclid Avenue (see St. Paul Shrine, p. 28) in what
proved to be the final maneuver in a seventy-five-year struggle with Trinity
Parish for Episcopal primacy in northeast Ohio (see also St. Alban Episcopal
Church, p. 320, and Christ Episcopal Church, p. 340). In the beginning, the
struggle had to do with liturgical practice—Trinity was "high church" ("smells
and bells") and St. Paul's was "low church" (four-in-hand ties instead of clerical
collars). Passions ran so high in the middle of the nineteenth century that, when
arsonists burned down the original St. Paul's, a frame building on East Fourth
Street at Euclid, Trinity was suspected. In the end, Trinity became the cathedral
(p. 21), and St. Paul's moved out to become the largest Episcopal church in
Greater Cleveland and one of the most prominent Episcopal churches in the
United States. When St. Paul's moved out of Cleveland, only one parishioner
could still hear the church's bells on Sunday morning. In Cleveland Heights,
Sunday school attendance went from forty to four hundred.

St. Paul's Cleveland Heights was built in four campaigns. The first (1928),
in High Gothic Revival style, consists of the tower, large parish hall, offices,
and classrooms. Designed to be part of a monumental complex, Walter Russell
Breed probably hoped that his church would so dwarf Charles Schweinfurth's
1901 Trinity Episcopal Cathedral that a dazzled bishop would move his seat
out to Cleveland Heights and that St. Paul's would at last permanently seize
Episcopalian hegemony in Ohio from the grasping hands of Trinity parish.[31]
As originally designed, the nave, with twin balconied transepts, would seat
1,250. St. Paul's would have been similar to First Baptist farther out on Fairmount (see p. 337), only bigger. In an unfortunate decision, Breed determined
to save the best for last, thus, the Great Depression frustrated construction of
his great neo-Gothic nave.[32]

At last, after huddling in their glorious but relatively cramped parish hall for twenty-three years,[33] the main sanctuary was completed. Byers Hayes had to redesign and reduce the nave by half. The new design, without the balconied transepts, seated only 750. Hayes eliminated the elaborately vaulted ceiling of his 1927 design and replaced it with a lowered, flat ceiling suggesting an early Christian basilica. The ceiling rests, rather imaginatively, on his previously built neo-Gothic pillars (Hayes was a genius at working with what he had; see Good Shepherd Episcopal Church, p. 353). A simple clerestory replaced the originally planned tall neo-Gothic windows. Byers redeemed himself with two important innovations. First he pulled the altar far out from the wall in front of the church and, with the help of John Bonebrake, designed a great perforated wooden screen behind it, separating the choir from the congregation, which the choir now faced. In the early 1950s, this was a major innovation. Second, Hayes suggested to Walter Holtkamp Sr., that he design an organ with visible, freestanding pipes clustered by division. This kind of organ became so associated with the Holtkamp Company and modern organs in the United States that St. Paul's musical instrument is better known than Hayes's building. St. Paul's Holtkamp organ is the most famous organ in Cleveland; the 1958 Encyclopedia Britannica illustrated its article on organs with a photo of St. Paul's organ.

A third campaign constructed schoolrooms to the west of the original building (1956). The most recent addition (1990) adds additional education and conference space together with an art gallery.

Although, as a regional church, St. Paul's draws its congregation from twenty-one zip codes, much of its character derives from the continuing vitality of its immediate surroundings in Cleveland and Shaker Heights. St. Paul's, however, also shares the quality and vigor of its education and music programs with an audience beyond its parish family. Its tutoring program with inner-city Miles Park School has a long history, as does its after-school Open Doors program for students of Roxboro Junior High. St. Paul's helped found the Cleveland Ecumenical Institute. Apollo's Fire, the Cleveland Baroque Orchestra, has performed in St. Paul's sanctuary since the music ensemble was founded.

CHAPTER FOURTEEN

Shaker Heights—Beachwood—Pepper Pike—Lyndhurst

Begin this tour in Shaker Square. Leave the square heading east on Shaker Boulevard and turn right (south) at Coventry Road. In front of the next intersection is the canonical Shaker Heights, New England, Congregationalist, Wren-Gibbs style of Plymouth Church of Shaker Heights (137). Return to Shaker Boulevard and, turning right (east), continue for one mile, driving beside the Shaker Rapid. At Lee Road, turn left (north). Crossing over Horseshoe Lake Park on Lee Road, turn right onto Fairmount Boulevard. Four religious institutions occupy each corner of this intersection. On the southwest corner, its garden secluded by a wall but fronting a gracious lawn, stands the quiet masonry Holy Family Monastery of the Carmelite nuns. On the northwest corner stands the Cleveland First Church of Christ, Scientist, in a four-pillared neo-Georgian brick building with white frame trim and spire. On the northeast corner stands the Jewish philanthropic True Sisters Child Care Center, treasured by eastern suburb professional women of all denominations. On the southeast corner, behind high masonry walls, stands the expansive campus of Beaumont School, the Ursuline high school for women that is the oldest Roman Catholic school in Cleveland and the first Catholic high school.

After turning right, continue on Fairmount Boulevard for a little less than a mile. On the right appears the First Baptist Church of Greater Cleveland (138), Byers Hayes's masterpiece in the third and last style of American Gothic Revival. At the corner, turn right (south) onto Eaton Road. Continue on Eaton as it curves left and right. Cross the Shaker Rapid and bear right where Eaton becomes Torrington Road. Crossing South Woodland Road, Torrington twists to the right, through the Shaker Heights Country Club, before intersecting with Parkland Drive. Turn left onto Parkland and remain on Parkland as it curves beside the club. On the left, when Parkland crosses the Van Aken Rapid tracks, the pristine colonialism of the Church of St. Dominic (139) is magically transformed, at the insistence of the Shaker Heights building code, into a Roman Catholic church. Continue south as Parkland becomes Lynnfield Road. Crossing Chagrin Boulevard, turn left onto Lomond Boulevard. As Lomond curves to the left (north) and becomes Farnsleigh Road, the neat brick neo-Gothic Shaker Heights Community United Church of Christ stands on the right at Lytle Road, across from the school. Recrossing Chagrin, bear to the left behind the commercial area that backs onto the right (east) of Farnsleigh. Recrossing Shaker, skirt the parking lot of the Van Aken Shopping Center on the right and pause at the intersection of Farnsleigh Road at Warrensville Center Road. Christ Episcopal Church (140), another Georgian Revival building with another splendid white tower, stands to the southeast.

Turn north (left) onto Warrensville Center Road and, after recrossing South Woodland, slightly less than a mile north, turn right (east) onto Shaker

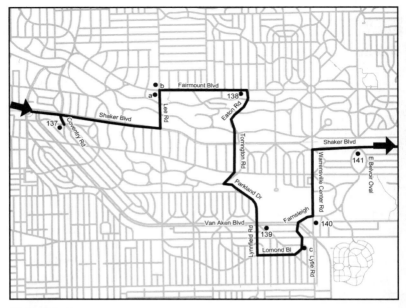

SHAKER HEIGHTS

137. Plymouth Church of Shaker Heights
   a. Carmelite Monastery of the Holy Family
   b. Cleveland First Church of Christ, Scientist
138. First Baptist Church of Greater Cleveland

139. Church of St. Dominic
   c. Shaker Heights Community United
     Church of Christ
140. Christ Episcopal Church
141. First Unitarian Church of Cleveland

Boulevard. On the right one sees the sprawling Byron Junior High School, the Shaker Heights middle school. East of the school, on the north cusp of Belvoir Oval is the First Unitarian Church of Cleveland (141), still another Georgian Revival building but this time one in a little closer synchrony with the New England origin of its denomination.

Continue east on Shaker Boulevard for one and a half miles and enter one of the largest concentrations of Jewish institutions in the United States. To the right, south on Richmond Road, is the Maltz Museum of Jewish Heritage. This stunning 2005 Westlake Reed Leskosky golden Jerusalem limestone building burrows into the ground and, from the street, presents mostly a lawn. Driving east on Shaker Boulevard, hidden from the street by its landscaping, is Perkins+Will's relaxed modern Temple Tifereth Israel East (142). On the right, farther east on Shaker Boulevard, is the Laura and Alvin Siegal College of Judaic Studies, the kindergarten through eighth grade Agnon School, the Akiva High School, and the Fuchs Mizrachi School. To the south, beyond Tifereth Israel and the schools, spreads the huge campus of the Mandell Jewish Community Center with its fields, courts, pools, play areas, and buildings. Continue one half mile east on Shaker Boulevard and drive under I-271. On the southeast corner of the Shaker-Brainard Road intersection is Centerbrook

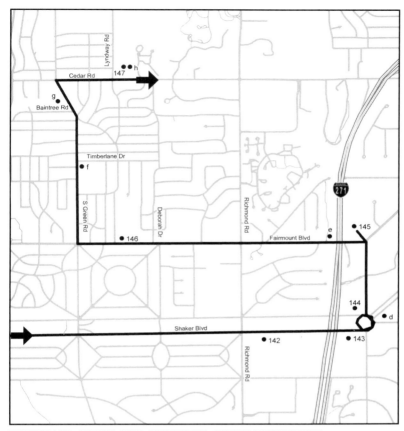

BEACHWOOD–PEPPER PIKE–LYNDHURST–UNIVERSITY HEIGHTS

142. Temple Tifereth Israel East
143. Park Synagogue East
  d. Bethaynu Congregation
144. Lillian and Betty Ratner School
145. B'nai Jeshurun Congregation
  e. Congregation Shaarey Tikvah

146. Fairmount Temple
  f. Green Road Synagogue
  g. John Carroll University Annex
147. Church of the Good Shepherd
  h. Kehillat Yaakov Congregation

Architects' 2005 Park Synagogue East (143) that manages to be large, beautiful, and environmentally friendly at the same time.

Some would say that the best is kept for last but, if so, the best requires two circumnavigations of the Shaker Boulevard-Brainard Road traffic circle. Continue east on Shaker Boulevard and, at the circle, past the low-frame neo-colonial Bethaynu Congregation, take the fourth exit leading back to Shaker Boulevard but now going west. On the right is the Lillian and Betty Ratner School (144), the splendid building—now a Montessori school—that Edward Durrell Stone designed as the B'rith Emeth Temple and that continues to announce the Jewish presence in Cleveland to everyone driving north around the city on I-271.

Continue west on Shaker Boulevard and turn left (south) at the first intersection and then immediately left again to get on Shaker Boulevard going east. Take another trip around the Shaker-Brainard traffic circle, but this time take the third exit onto Brainard Road. Half a mile north is B'nai Jeshurun Congregation (145) and its Gross Schechter Day School. Through the parking lot, at the entrance to the complex, is Don Hisaka's modern giant-order interpretation of Hebrew characters.

Returning to and turning right (west) onto Fairmount, just west of I-271 stands Congregation Shaarey Tikvah. This octagonal, modern brick building is set back from the street at the end of a long drive. In an inversion of the usual case in this book, where buildings originally built as Jewish centers of worship have now become Protestant, this building was built by the Parkside congregation, then called The Chapel, and subsequently sold to Shaarey Tikvah. Continuing on Fairmount, across Richmond Road, drive past the Beachwood municipal complex on the right with its library and swimming pools and Beachwood High School on the left (south). Farther on the right is the prolific Jewish architect Percival Goodman's Fairmount Temple (146), the oldest existing Jewish congregation in Greater Cleveland.

Continuing west on Fairmount, turn right (north) onto South Green Road. On the right (east) side of Green lies the extensive campus of the Green Road Synagogue with its Waxman Chabad Center and the Hebrew Academy of Cleveland's Beatrice J. Stone Yavne High School. On the left (west), just before the commercial area at the intersection of Green and Cedar Road is the John Carroll University Green Road Annex, formerly the Temple Emanu El. Turn right (east) onto Cedar. One half mile east on Cedar, on the left, stand the simple, imaginative masses of the Episcopal Church of the Good Shepherd (147). Drive into Good Shepherd's parking lot to appreciate this building, set far back from the busy thoroughfare. Beside the Cedar entrance to Good Shepherd stands the 2009 buff post-Modern Kehillat Yaakov Congregation.

This concludes the tour of the inner eastern suburbs of Greater Cleveland. Return to Cleveland by driving west on Cedar or access the interstate system by driving east. The Cedar-Richmond intersection to the east is one of the largest commercial centers of suburban Cleveland. On the southeast corner is the relatively compact La Place Fashion Center. Behind it is the immense Beachwood Mall. On the northwest corner of the Cedar-Richmond intersection is the large Legacy Village Shopping Center. Past the malls, the Acacia Country Club will appear on the left en route to I-271.

137. Plymouth Church of Shaker Heights (1923)

Architect: Charles S. Schneider
Builder: Charles Haven Myers
Location: 2860 Coventry Road,
Shaker Heights and Cleveland

Although Plymouth Church proudly traces its lineage to the nineteenth-century battle in Cleveland for the abolition of slavery, the congregation of the original Plymouth Society of Cleveland never made it from downtown to Shaker Heights.[1] In the middle of the nineteenth century, Cleveland had a reputation as a proslavery town. In 1850 a minority of thirty members of the Old Stone Church (see p. 12) walked out because of their opposition to slavery and to the Fugitive Slave Law. They organized the Free Presbyterian Church. Twelve years later, during the war, they changed their name to the Plymouth Society and their denomination to Congregational. In a letter to Harvey B. Spellman, Henry Ward Beecher had suggested the church be named "Plymouth," after Beecher's Plymouth Church of Brooklyn. Spellman, a church leader and a leader in the antislavery movement, was the father of Mrs. John D. Rockefeller.

When a company of slave rescuers from Oberlin, jailed for three months for aiding a runaway slave, were freed, it was natural that the church's Sunday school escort them to the station, with American flags waving and a band playing. Before the Civil War, Plymouth's path crossed that of the First Baptist Church, now up Fairmount in Shaker Heights (see p. 337). Plymouth was building a church on the corner of East Ninth Street and Euclid Avenue when financial pressure forced it to sell the building to the Baptists.[2] In 1882, after occupying various downtown sites, Plymouth settled into a church it built on Prospect Avenue at East 22nd Street. By 1913 their area had become firmly commercial, and the congregation was dissolved. The church and its site were sold for $140,000. This was deposited with the Congregational Union for the support of Cleveland-area Congregational churches, except that $30,000 was reserved for a new church that might adopt the name Plymouth (Plymouth Shaker Heights ultimately received $75,000).

At this time, the Van Sweringen brothers were organizing Shaker Heights. They decided to allocate a five-acre tract to churches. The Van Sweringens had an older brother, Herbert C. Van Sweringen, who was a trustee of the Congregational Union. Herbert and his sisters, Carrie and Edith, were members of the East Cleveland Congregational Church and the three of them helped arrange a new Congregational church on the border of Shaker Heights and Cleveland. Although the new Plymouth was always a Congregational church, financially and administratively supported by the Congregational Union, it did not emphasize its denominational affiliation. At that time, Shaker Heights had a strong community interest in a "union"—or nondenominational—community church, in contrast to the Presbyterians, Methodists, Episcopalians, and Roman Catholics who were organizing what was then known as "Heathen Heights." Plymouth intended to capitalize on this nondenominational feeling. In any case, since Plymouth was a more-or-less spontaneous development, instead of an organized congregation moving up to the Heights from the city, it had to appeal directly to its community for members; it used a printed invitation, dated June 15, 1916, addressed, "To the People of Shaker Heights."

Plymouth's first church in Shaker Heights was a small chapel dragged all the way from the Lakewood Congregational Church. This proved to be too small and too cold, and the congregation retreated to the high school auditorium. The remarkably durable little chapel was then moved to East 214th Street near Euclid; there it was used by the Euclid Congregational Church until sold to the Assembly of God in 1951. During the First World War, Plymouth's five acres were used by neighbors to grow vegetables. Work on a permanent structure, designed by Charles Schneider, began in 1919. The new eight-hundred-seat church would seat the 135 members from a variety of Protestant denominations then belonging to Plymouth with room to spare. The new institution aggressively evangelized; its members visited newcomers to the Heights as well as families not known to be attached to any other church. When the new church was dedicated in 1923, the congregation mailed invitations to every family in Shaker Heights. Eight hundred twenty-five people showed up.

They found a red-brick Wren-Gibbs structure with white-painted wood trim, including a classical pillared entrance and a tall steeple. Plymouth looked somewhat like a Congregational church transplanted to the Western Reserve from Connecticut. The unornamented white walls inside emphasized the beauty of plainness. A U-shaped, second-story balcony wrapped around the worship space. Proportions mirrored those Wren developed after the London fire to accommodate about a thousand people in one space within reach of an unamplified human voice (the church has since installed a modern sound system). By 1953 the congregation had grown, from its modest beginnings, to more than 2,500 members. Two wings were added, flanking the original building. It is the harmonious siting of the main building, with its two wings on the congregation's five-acre lot (with a rather small parking lot discreetly located to the west), that makes Plymouth such a striking icon of Shaker Heights (and Cleveland, since the municipal boundary runs through the church's property—one entrance is in Shaker Heights and one is in Cleveland).

Plymouth has long played an important role in the musical life of Cleveland. Like many other sacred landmarks, it has a magnificent Holtkamp organ. In addition, it has provided a home for the Cleveland Cello society, the chamber orchestra CityMusic Cleveland, and the Plymouth Trio (voice, oboe, keyboard), originally directed by John Mack.

138. First Baptist Church of Greater Cleveland

Architect: J. Byers Hayes of Walker and Weeks (1928)
Builder: Harold Cooke Phillips
Location: 3630 Fairmount Boulevard, Shaker Heights

On January 28, 1833, a small procession of Baptists marched down the banks of Lake Erie, broke a hole in the ice, and baptized four of their number. The following month they founded the First Baptist Church.[3] The next year they bought property on the southwest corner of the village green, where the Terminal Tower now stands, and built their first church. In 1849 First Baptist helped establish Shiloh Baptist Church (see p. 132), the first African American Baptist church in Cleveland. Two years later First Baptist helped establish Second Baptist, which later became Euclid Avenue Baptist Church.[4] Four years after that, in 1855, First Baptist established Third Baptist on the West Side and also purchased its second church on Euclid at East Ninth Street from the Congregationalists. First Baptist's third church was an imposing Romanesque Revival building constructed in 1889 as an enlargement of the Idaka Chapel on the corner of East 46th Street at Prospect Avenue. The Idaka Chapel had been built in 1874 by railroad entrepreneur Stillman Witt for use by First Baptist as a mission Sunday school. It was a memorial to his granddaughter, Idaka Fells. In 1919 twenty-five members of First Baptist established the Baptist Church on the Heights. Less than ten years later they were joined by the rest of the congregation when their old Prospect church was acquired by the City of Cleveland for the diagonal cut-through from Carnegie to Prospect Avenues.

The Baptists identified a desirable eight-acre site owned by the Van Sweringens. The congregation could only afford half of the parcel's $130,000 to $140,000 asking price, and the Van Sweringens did not wish to divide the property. Impressed, however, by initial plans and wanting a church on the property, the Van Sweringen's ultimately reduced the price to $75,000, requiring a $25,000 down payment, a $25,000 payment due in one year, and the remaining $25,000 due with interest in two years. When the Baptists' treasurer went to the Van Sweringens with the final payment, they told him that they had decided to waive the last installment.

Once the Baptists decided to move, they moved. The two congregations united in October 1927, laid the cornerstone in June 1928, and dedicated the new building in June 1929.[5] First Baptist is Byers Hayes's Gothic Revival masterpiece. With its richly carved symbolism and its large size, it is quite unlike most Baptist churches that tend to be simple and small.[6] First Baptist shares a simplification found in other Gothic Revival buildings of the late 1920s. Simple triangular oak trusses rather than masonry vaulting support the sixty-five-foot ceiling of the sanctuary. Its aisle piers lack the clustered vertical moldings of historic Gothic construction.[7] Its most distinguishing feature is the "beautifully geometric"[8] 130-foot Ambrose Swasey tower. The complex of sanctuary, schoolrooms, assembly hall, parlor, and offices are arranged like a cloister around an interior brick court decorated with masonry. An exquisite small balcony, projecting out from the pastors' offices, overlooks the interior court. The exterior of the complex is all masonry including a large classroom addition and another hall designed in 1958 by Ward and Conrad.

Although exterior and interior are replete with carved symbolism in stone and wood, the glory of the eight-hundred-seat sanctuary is a complete program of glass—four large windows for *Matthew, Mark, Luke,* and *John* on the east and another four for *Peter, Paul, Stephen,* and *John the Baptist* on the west. In the rear is an immense window of the *Life of Christ* given by Swasey. An elaborate two-story, pierced stone screen at the front of the sanctuary includes a tall cross, almost lost in a welter of other symbols and figures. Two small windows off the front of the sanctuary were given by Dr. Harold Cooke Phillips, minister for thirty years and the first to preach in the new church. Dr. Phillips was from Jamaica, and, when the original design proved to have such a beautiful echo that his accent could not be understood by the congregation, the ceiling had to be soundproofed in 1930. Two small rose windows from the East 46th Street building are visible only from the outside. First Baptist has always prided itself on its music program, now led by its Skerritt-Cumming organ.

139. Church of St. Dominic (1947)
Architect: William Koehl
Builder: Roy Bourgeois
Location: 19000 Van Aken
Boulevard, Shaker Heights

The most interesting thing about the Church of St. Dominic, now more than sixty years old, is how well this simple, crisp, and elegant Georgian Revival building has stood up over time.[9] Hurriedly put up in the midst of now legendary arguments with the Shaker Heights zoning board, St. Dominic has weathered beautifully, in contrast with some of its more trendy, high-modern contemporaries. Time can be unkind to modern buildings. They usually require unrelenting maintenance to maintain their just-minted appearance. Often, even in the most careful and affluent of hands, once "modern" buildings begin to show their age just as their once modern builders begin to show theirs. Fashion is fickle. Good design, in whatever style, is surprisingly enduring. It is a tribute to the priests and people of St. Dominic that they have not only painted over the chips and repaired the dings of their masterpiece and tastefully adapted it to the necessary changes of a half century, but that they have also resisted what must have been powerful temptations to change its character.

St. Dominic was established when Roman Catholics were beginning to be tolerated but not yet welcomed into Shaker Heights. Most Shaker Heights Catholics were crammed into St. Cecilia (see p. 161) or Our Lady of Peace (see p. 158) just across the border in Cleveland or gathered into the expansive empire of Father John Mary Powers in Cleveland Heights (see St. Ann, p. 321). The Shaker Heights zoning board, intent on maintaining their interpretation of the Western Reserve, laid down the law to discourage anything divisively "Roman" in their obsessively planned community. They required Wren-Gibbs Georgian Revival brick architecture with white frame trim and banned stained glass and bells. What they envisioned reflected their schools,[10] their public buildings,[11] and their Yankee churches.[12]

The remarkable result is a handsome, substantial, imposing—but not ostentatious—brick building. Brick stairways swell on either side of a tasteful two-story portico that supports a brick upper story and a well-proportioned brick tower topped with a white frame (bell-less) belfry. A cross on the tower and a whitewashed St. Dominic inside the portico announce that this is a Roman Catholic church but do not belabor the point. The church is flanked by a long avenue of parochial schools, also brick, also well proportioned, also by William Koehl. The rectory and convent are detached in residences across the street.

Entering the nave through an exceptionally small narthex, it is immediately obvious that, whatever style the city fathers may have insisted on, this is a Roman Catholic and not a Unitarian or a Congregational space. The nave, the sanctuary with its shallow apse, the symmetrical shallow transepts, and the balcony with space for musicians and their instruments (but not for parishioners) all give the space a strong Roman Catholic character. The interior is extremely simple, extremely plain, extremely well proportioned, and extremely beautiful. Trim is limited to white-painted wooden pilasters on plain mauve walls. Only a suggestion of decoration appears in the vaguely Corinthian capitals and a scroll over one door. The ceiling is plastered and without decoration. The large Palladian windows have no colored glass, the panes are translucent. One white statue stands on each wall on either side of the apse, *Mary* on the left and *Joseph and the Child* on the right. The side walls feature small metal stations. The main altars are white, frame, and undecorated. Three brass chandeliers hang down from the ceiling. Everything is plain, simple, and beautifully proportioned. Even the cry room and bride's room built into the back of the nave eight years ago are attractive and well proportioned. The style may be Yankee, but the character and the substance are Roman.

140. Christ Episcopal Church
(1959)
Architects: Monroe Copper
and Robert Wade
Builder: Maxfield Dowell
Location: 3445 Warrensville
Center Road, Shaker Heights

As Germans flooded into Cleveland in the 1860s, the Episcopal assistant bishop of Ohio hoped to woo them into his church. Frederick Brooks (see St. Paul's Shrine, p. 28) was the only Episcopal rector in Cleveland willing to help. A German-speaking Episcopal priest was called from Put-in-Bay and, under Brooks's supervision, he began recruiting the many Germans employed in the knitting mills around the intersection of Broadway Avenue at East Ninth Street. This "German church" was organized in 1869 as Christ Church, and a building was erected on the corner of East 29th Street at Orange Avenue, where the main post office is now, on the other side of Interstate 77 south of Cuyahoga Community College.[13] Prayer books, hymnals, the service, and the preaching were all in German. When the German colony moved eastward toward the end of the nineteenth century, the struggling congregation closed in 1909, its furnishings and assets turned over to the Episcopal Diocese.[14]

Thirteen years before, a small Episcopal congregation that included some Germans from the first Christ Church had established itself as the Mission of the Redeemer at the intersection of East 108th Street at Superior Avenue in Glenville. This parish agreed in 1909, when the downtown church closed, to change their name to Christ Church. The new parish built a Gothic Revival building, in part with the assets and furnishings of the first church. This was the first building in Cleveland constructed of concrete blocks.

The Glenville parish moved to Shaker Heights as part of the complicated maneuverings by which St. Paul's Church moved from Euclid Avenue to Fairmount Boulevard in Cleveland Heights (see p. 329). The vestry of St. Paul's agreed, as part of a bigger deal, for Christ Church to move to Warrensville Center Road, provided the diocese allowed St. Paul's to move up into Cleveland Heights.[15] With the help of the Van Sweringen brothers, Christ Church purchased a rectory and a lot on the southwest corner of Warrensville Center Road at Shaker Boulevard. As they prepared to build, Christ Church moved their religious services temporarily into the auditorium of University School. The Great Depression unfortunately intervened to such an extent that the parish lost their first lot to foreclosure.

When the parish moved south, farther down Warrensville Center Road, to their present location in 1934, they moved into the third country church built in the same place. The first church was built by people from the Island of Mann in 1819. This church was moved to another location in 1840 to make room for a larger church that, in turn, was destroyed by lightning. A third little country church was built in 1868. This building was abandoned when its Methodist congregation banded with other parishes to establish the Church of the Saviour in 1928 (see p. 325). By 1934 the roof leaked, the windows were broken, and the little church had been taken over by vagrants who cooked in bonfires on the floor. Neighbors and Methodists were relieved when the Episcopalians moved in and, over the next two decades, restored and progressively enlarged the original structure. In 1946 Christ Church's iconic white spire and tower were constructed as a memorial to parishioners who died in the Second World War. A substantial education and administrative parish house was dedicated in 1955. Then, a year later, the parish house and most of the church burned. After three years in Mercer School and then at Suburban Temple, the present building was dedicated in 1959. They salvaged several key elements from the burned church including the spire—lifted to the top of its new tower—the organ,[16] the pulpit, the lectern, the altar railing, and many pews.

Although Christ Church's complicated and roller coaster history is at odds with its image as the Episcopal church of the historically most prosperous residential municipality in northern Ohio, Christ Church has played an important role in the affairs of its wider church. Over the years, pastors have left to become deans of cathedrals in Cleveland, Atlanta, Wilmington, and Burlington. David Thornberry, rector from 1965 to 1969, became bishop of Wyoming. A son of the parish, Robert Dean, organized the Church of the Good Shepherd in Lyndhurst (see p. 353), an offshoot of Christ Church. The parish played an important role in establishing Alcoholics Anonymous in Greater Cleveland.

On a hill overlooking the busy commercial center where Van Aken Boulevard, Chagrin Boulevard, and Warrensville Center Road meet and where the Van Aken line of the Shaker Rapid ends, the red brick body and tall white steeple of Christ Church form a landmark to inspire a busy community. Christ Church has prided itself in maintaining an unusually close relationship with the bustling commercial area it overlooks. Although elevated, the church sits quite close to the street. It backs into a quiet residential neighborhood. The red brick mass of the building sits on a masonry foundation. Appearing from the distance to be a Wren-Gibbs style building, closer inspection reveals that the masonry tower rises beside, not above, the white wood pillared portico and plain pediment. The beautifully proportioned tower rises to a white, frame, lattice belfry. Christ Church has generous white wood framing around two-story windows.

Entering from the street, a large narthex divides the eight-hundred-seat sanctuary on the left from social, administrative, and education areas on the right. The quiet, peaceful, all-white frame sanctuary, at right angles to the entrance, parallels the street. This is a Wren-Gibbs interior with wraparound balcony. A sounding board crowns a freestanding pulpit. A large tracker organ and space for the choir are located behind the altar. A good-sized chapel is located off of the sanctuary away from the street. A kitchen, a music room, and a large gathering area with a stage are located in the basement.

141. First Unitarian Church of Cleveland (1955; 1959)

Architects: George M. White (1955); Gaede Serne (1959)
Builder: Robert Killam
Location: 21600 Shaker Boulevard, Shaker Heights

The Unitarian Universalist Association, which believes in a single personality of God in contrast to the orthodox Christian belief in a divine Trinity, has a long history in Europe, going back to Arius, Origen, and St. Gregory of Nyssa. Even after the Council of Nicea in 325, Arian ideas kept surfacing, particularly in Poland and Hungary during the Reformation and, more recently, in Massachusetts. Unitarianism in the United States developed out of liberal Congregationalism in the milieu of the Harvard Divinity School in the nineteenth century and is associated with Transcendentalists such as Ralph Waldo Emerson. Unitarianism was late in establishing itself in the Western Reserve of Connecticut, where Yale Congregational Church orthodoxy was dominant.

Although Unitarian meetings began, among a scattering of Massachusetts people, as early as 1836, Unitarians date their first permanent organization in Cleveland to 1867.[17] Their first church was a substantial masonry Gothic Revival structure dedicated in 1880 on the corner of Bolivar at Prospect Avenues. Typically, for a denomination with a strong tradition of progressive social involvement, the original church housed one of the first free kindergartens in Cleveland and offered domestic science classes to immigrants. Marian Murdoch and Florence Buck were joint ministers from 1892 to 1899. The Bolivar at Prospect Avenues building was sold to Episcopalians, and, in 1904, the Unitarians settled into another handsome Gothic Revival building at East 82nd Street at Euclid Avenue, which has since been taken down.[18] In the 1920s and 1930s membership increased to 1,500, making the Unitarian Church of Cleveland one of the three largest Unitarian churches in the United States. In the early 1950s, most of the congregation moved to Shaker Heights as the First Unitarian Church. A strong minority elected to purchase the 82nd Street structure and remain in Cleveland as the Unitarian Society. Now the Unitarian Universalist Society of Cleveland, they have moved to a former synagogue on Lancashire Road in Cleveland Heights.

Universalism, the belief that all will be saved, also has an ancient history going back to Clement of Alexandria and Origen. It was brought to the United States from England in 1770 by the Calvinist John Murray and over time became increasingly Unitarian. As a denomination in the nineteenth century, Universalism was particularly strong in small towns and rural areas. A Universalist Society was established in Newberry as early as 1820, and Universalist societies were founded in Aurora, Chardon, Burton, Bedford, Auburn, and Willoughby before 1850. The First Universalist Church in North Olmsted, a station on the Underground Railway, is the second-oldest religious structure in Cuyahoga County.[19] In Cleveland, All Souls Universalist Church was established in 1891 and dedicated a chapel in 1893. All Souls merged with the Unitarian Church of Cleveland in 1932, and in 1961 both denominations merged nationally to form the Unitarian Universalist Association.

The First Unitarian Church in Shaker Heights was dedicated in 1955. The church stands on four acres inside the northern ring of Belvoir Oval, across the street from the Shaker Heights Middle School. The church faces the eastbound and westbound dual lanes of Shaker Boulevard, a major thoroughfare on either side of the Shaker Rapid. The railroad tracks are sunken well below the surrounding level, and the one-hundred-yard-wide right-of-way is planted with lawn and shrubs. The Wren-Gibbs style of the church was selected as appropriate for Unitarianism's New England heritage. This is a beautifully sited, refreshingly plain, brick building with white frame trim, portico, and pillars below an undecorated pediment and spire. The church stands out as a landmark for many suburbanites driving in and out of Cleveland. It is enhanced by the relative calm of the affluent residential neighborhood and the broad playing fields surrounding the building. The public face of First Unitarian screens the large parking lot behind the building from which most people enter the church. The auditorium, decorated with blue Tuscan pilasters against a plain white plaster finish, seats four hundred with an additional one hundred in the balcony. The unpainted, varnished wood of the front of the sanctuary provides unexpected warmth and a human scale. In 1959 the addition of the Petersen wing to the south, in the same style as the main building, provided twenty-two additional classrooms. This addition was designed so that its asymmetry is not immediately apparent and the main structure superficially appears to be balanced at both sides.

First Unitarian has a powerful history of excellence in music. For fifty years, it shared a music director with Anshe Chesed. The Episcopalian composer James Rogers played at the Euclid Avenue Temple on Saturdays and at First Unitarian on Sundays while teaching at the Cleveland Institute of Music and serving as music critic for the *Plain Dealer*. Walter Blodgett, dean of the Cleveland Music School Settlement, music curator of the Cleveland Museum of Art, and music critic of the *Cleveland Press* was music director from 1941 to 1950. He was succeeded from 1955 to 1966 by Robert Shaw, the preeminent choral director who subsequently conducted the Atlanta Symphony Orchestra. More recently, to the joy of many driving parents, the church has been an eastern outpost of the Cleveland Institute of Music.

142. Temple Tifereth Israel East (See also Friendship Baptist Church, p. 130, and Temple Tifereth Israel, "the Temple," p. 44) (1970)
Architect: Perkins+Will
Builder: Daniel Jeremy Silver
Location: 26000 Shaker Boulevard, Beachwood

Temple Tifereth Israel's move to the suburbs was a tremendous undertaking.[20] It is a tribute to the resilience of the congregation that it managed to make the move at all. In addition to the gut-wrenching sorrow occasioned by moving much of their activity out of a beloved building and the tradition it represented, the congregation was faced with what must have seemed almost insurmountable practical difficulties. Tifereth Israel was financially exhausted from the recent construction of an ambitious new wing on their old University Circle building. They were struggling with declining membership, in part the result of their old location and in part the result of a general loss of religious enthusiasm among Americans in 1970s. Farthermore, the congregation did not follow the historical route of institutional movement—sell the old building to help finance the new. This meant not only the absence of capital to build a new building, but the ongoing expense of maintaining the old.

Nevertheless, they purchased twenty acres and rehired Perkins+Will, the architects of their large 1959 addition in University Circle. Perkins+Will is a large Chicago firm (1,200 employees, twenty offices) that has completed projects in forty-nine states and forty-three countries—including the Boeing International Headquarters and the Chase Tower in Chicago. Perkins+Will was asked to build what was originally described as a "branch religious school"— twenty classrooms, a library, an auditorium specifically for the school, a social hall, and a small kitchen. Dedicated in 1970, there was, at first, a valiant attempt to limit use of the branch to educational activities and keep all religious and administrative activities at University Circle. Within a year, however, two daylight holdups at the main temple office forced the temple's board to schedule its night meetings at the branch. Thereafter there was a steady movement of activity out to Beachwood. By 1980 the almost new religious school at the old building was leased to outside tenants.

The quiet, relaxed elegance of the new temple, nestled in the trees and set back and almost hidden from the street, makes a surprising contrast to its assertive predecessor in University Circle. The orange brick and the unpainted frame and copper sheathing of the new building has a laid-back character suggestive of California. The copper has now acquired its intended soft green patina. This is a rectangular, squared modernist building, but the copper sheathing, the brick, and the natural wood give it a softened edge. The massing of its elements and the carefully studied progressively rising slabs of the wood and copper sanctuary roof, nevertheless, define the building as an institution with a purpose. A brick colonnade across the front leads to entrance doors. The scale is welcoming, more human than institutional. From the outside, the purpose of the building is unclear. It could be more educational than religious. Rabbi Moses Gries would have approved.

Inside the building, architect James Herman continued the brick and light and dark unpainted wood warmth of the exterior and its human scale when he converted the original school assembly space into an elegant six-hundred-seat sanctuary, clearly a religious space. A quiet but imposing floor-to-ceiling white oak ark, carved with the tree of life by South Euclid sculptor Norbert Koehn, announces the sanctuary's purpose. The north wall is completely glazed from floor to ceiling, bringing the image of the wooded site dramatically into the sanctuary. The light from outside is supplemented by dramatic interior lighting. An elegant loggia frames the sanctuary on the left. Rabbi Abba Hillel Silver would have approved.

Consistent with its current use as the congregation's main building, the original temple branch keeps quietly growing. The elegant 1998 Hartzmark addition includes the temple library (complete with a historical replica of Abba Hillel Silver's study at the temple in University Circle) and a spacious meeting room. This room, like the sanctuary, opens out into the wooded lot through generous, clear glass. The Hartzmark addition is balanced by a large social and meeting area. Behind the building, across an attractive courtyard, stand the classrooms—some new and some dating from the 1970s.

West of the temple, on property it leases from Tifereth Israel, is the large, sunken, modernist, award-winning Maltz Museum of Jewish Heritage. The museum describes its light-filled Temple Tifereth Israel Gallery as one of its "crown jewels." This gallery features a rich selection from the Temple Museum of Religious Art's important collection of art and artifacts.

143. Park Synagogue East

(see also Park Synagogue, p. 315, and Cory United Methodist Church, p. 97) (2005)
Architect: Centerbrook Architects
Builder: Joshua Hoffer Skoff
Location: 27500 Shaker Heights Boulevard, Pepper Pike

The requirement of the *bar* (or, for women, *bat*) *mitzvah,* that all male (and now female) Jewish children be able to read from the Torah at age thirteen, and, thus, that all teenagers must be literate, has given the Jewish community a powerful cultural advantage over everyone else for millennia. It has also come at a steep price. In only one country in the world is Hebrew the official language. An emphasis on education, and the schoolrooms to support it, is as much a part of every temple and synagogue in the United States as the school and the convent were a part of every traditional Roman Catholic parish. For Jews, education is not a luxury—part of a religious institution's "program," like the guilds and the clubs. Indeed, education is what they do. Thus, while the imposing Park Synagogue East has a sanctuary that seats 190 and can expand to seat seven hundred when the walls slide away (up, for a change, instead of over), it remains primarily an educational institution—library, classrooms, and space to administer their ambitious education program.

The congregation of Anshe Emeth seems to have been building classrooms forever. When all the classrooms in their massive Cleveland Jewish Center on East 105th (now Cory United Methodist Church, see p. 97) proved inadequate, they purchased the Park School, and, when that burned down, they got into a battle royal with their world-famous architect Eric Mendelsohn about the number and the location of the classrooms in their famous synagogue (see p. 315). Mendelsohn's masterpiece was hardly finished before Anshe Emeth took over Edward Durell Stone's building (see the Ratner School, p. 347) for classroom space. This having proved inadequate, they have now moved into a new building designed by Centerbrook Architects. It has twenty-two classrooms on two floors. Centerbrook is an architectural practice outside of New Haven, Connecticut, that specializes in environmentally and energy-sensitive buildings. Many of Centerbrook's partners were students of Charles W. Moore, former dean of the Yale Architecture School whose 1978 Piazza d'Italia in New Orleans is an icon of postmodern architecture.

Park Synagogue East is the center for much of Park's educational activities, and its full parking lot on Sunday morning, adjacent to Interstate 271, is a source of wonder to many East Side Christians on their way to church. Centerbrook describes their building as "a simple steel frame box clad in a stick and panel mosaic of copper. Three large organic shapes burst from the box—a Jerusalem stone sanctuary and two great copper canopies leading to a two-story lobby." The canopies form the abstracted shape of two hands reaching out to equally welcome and bless those entering, on the east, the school and, on the west, the sanctuary, library, and offices. These hands are the sign of the "Kohan"—the second and third fingers are held together as are the fourth and fifth. There is a space between the thumb and the first finger and between the third and fourth fingers. The Kohan is also a prominent feature in the sanctuary of the Mendelsohn building. It was, understandably, much beloved by Armond Cohen, the rabbi who built the Mendelsohn building, and no one, Jew or Gentile, who ever saw Rabbi Cohen raise his hands in the Kohan and give his congregation a final benediction has ever forgotten it.

The relatively small sanctuary, really a chapel, is enclosed with gently curving Jerusalem stone walls in large, horizontal courses meant to suggest the primordial construction of early Jewish temples. Lighting is indirect, soft, and emphasizes quiet and calm. Blond wood trim lightens the atmosphere. A large curving canopy of interwoven wooden beams rises from the ark. This is functional—it reflects voices and music, and it is psychological—it forms a shelter for the congregation. A second canopy of wood slats covers the ceiling. These wooden canopies are designed to suggest the frame structure of the eastern European synagogues from which much of this congregation, originally Polish, came. Park shed its Polish character almost a hundred years ago and is now one of the largest Conservative congregations in the world.

In addition to the educational program required of an active Jewish congregation, Park has run a large summer camp for more than fifty years, originally located behind the Mendelsohn building and now run at Park East. The swimming pool beside the Mendelsohn building in Cleveland Heights has been filled in for safety reasons. It is replaced by what looks like an aqua park beside Park Synagogue East. Also replaced is the large Star of David that, for many years, confirmed the identity of the adjacent (on the other side of Shaker Boulevard) Ratner School building. This large aluminum symbol has been relocated beside the swimming pool.

144. The Lillian and Betty Ratner School, originally B'rith Emeth Temple and then Park Synagogue East, see p. 345 (see also Parkside Church, p. 362) (1967; 2008)
Architects: Edward Durell Stone (1967) and Jill Akins (2007)
Builders: Philip Horowitz (1967) and Barb Miller (2007)
Location: 27575 Shaker Boulevard, Pepper Pike

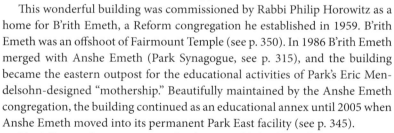

This wonderful building was commissioned by Rabbi Philip Horowitz as a home for B'rith Emeth, a Reform congregation he established in 1959. B'rith Emeth was an offshoot of Fairmount Temple (see p. 350). In 1986 B'rith Emeth merged with Anshe Emeth (Park Synagogue, see p. 315), and the building became the eastern outpost for the educational activities of Park's Eric Mendelsohn-designed "mothership." Beautifully maintained by the Anshe Emeth congregation, the building continued as an educational annex until 2005 when Anshe Emeth moved into its permanent Park East facility (see p. 345).

The Lillian and Betty Ratner School was established by Lillian (Mrs. Leonard) Ratner in 1963 at Park Synagogue.[21] Park Synagogue acquired its name from the Park School, a casualty of the Second World War, which Anshe Emeth purchased in 1942. The main Park School building burned in 1945 but several small frame classroom buildings survive. They continue being used for some of Park's summer camp and served as the original home of Ratner Montessori. In 1982 the Ratner School moved to the Anderson Road Primary School of the

City of South Euclid. When Park Synagogue moved out of the Edward Durell Stone building, the Ratner School moved in. Over the last three years, Ratner has embarked on an ambitious campaign to make the building more useful as a year-round school. Most of these renovations are subtle, including mechanical and electrical modifications to support teaching. Administrative and kitchen areas were improved. Small classrooms were merged into spaces more conducive to Montessori instruction. The school constructed a large gym to the east of the original building. It is sited so as not to detract from Edward Durell Stone's original structure.

Edward Durell Stone was an important late-modernist architect in the immediate second tier, of about the stature of Phillip Johnson. He is best known for his design of the U.S. embassy in New Delhi. He also designed the first Museum of Modern Art in New York and the Kennedy Center in Washington.

Stone's B'nai Emeth Temple is conspicuous for its shape, its color, and its location on a fifteen-acre tract just east of I-271 and Shaker Boulevard. Immediately recognizable as a Jewish religious structure, it was a dramatic announcement of the presence and the power of the Jewish community in the eastern suburbs of Cleveland to the tens of thousands who drove past it every day. At sixty miles an hour, however, they tended to keep their eyes on the road, and missed much of the subtle quality of the building. From the highway, the building appears to be a simple round structure. Closer (and slower) examination reveals that it is a central plan building circumscribed by a continuous tall portico. Within the loggia, actually separate from the building it encircles, six large, spindle-shaped, two-story "pods" organize the large white brick and concrete central structure. The walls between each pod are concave and come to an obtuse point at each pod. The plan of the building thus describes a scalloped circle.

Within the building, pods are used for entrances, staircases, or two-story rooms. Many of the original three small rooms between each pod have now been combined into larger classrooms. The original chapel features Stone-designed furniture and Ben Shan prints that have survived two changes in ownership. Although the walls of the classrooms, because of the circular shape of the building, are not rectangular, the building is so large that students do not have the feeling they are going to school in a piece of pie. A circular hall on each floor provides a central core flooded with light. About one-third of the central core is an auditorium. Lateral wood sliding walls separate it from the remainder of the core so that, when it was used as a worship space, the entire and quite large central area was available. Phillip Horowitz could be a rabbi in the round. Now the other two-thirds of the two-story central core are used as an immense terrazzo-floored indoor area for recess.

Although not strictly sectarian, the Ratner School is part of one of the nation's largest concentrations of Jewish facilities, which includes the Temple Tifereth Israel East (see p. 344), the Maltz Museum of Jewish Heritage, the Agnon (Jewish Day) School, the Siegal College of Judaic Studies, Park Synagogue East (see p. 345), and the Mandel Jewish Community Center (all adjacent to each other), and B'nai Jeshurun Congregation and its Gross Schechter School one-half mile to the north (see below).

145. B'nai Jeshurun Congregation (see also New Spirit Revival Center, p. 318 and Shiloh Baptist Church, p. 132) (1980)
Architects: Don Hisaka (1980) and David Gross (2000)
Builder: Rudolph Rosenthal
Location: 27501 Fairmount Boulevard, Pepper Pike

B'nai Jeshurun's move from Cleveland Heights to Pepper Pike was not easy. Although the board of trustees voted to build a new temple in 1969, it was eleven years before the Torahs were walked ten miles and the new building dedicated in 1980. John J. Boyle III has recorded the increasingly desperate and dispiriting efforts that members of the congregation made to save their magnificent old Cleveland Heights building.[22] Whatever their trials on Mayfield Road, the congregation was greeted with a splendid new modernist Jerusalem stone building in Pepper Pike. This building welcomes visitors with a monumental geometric gateway suggesting letters in the Hebrew alphabet. The gateway embraces a large court with a turning and waiting space for automobiles.

B'nai Jeshurun shares its twenty-two acre campus in a residential neighborhood with the Gross Schechter Day School. Gross Schechter is one of seventy-nine Solomon Schechter Day Schools in the United States. Solomon Schechter (1847–1915), rabbi, scholar, and educator, is generally given credit for establishing Conservatism in this country. Gross Schechter, founded in Cleveland in 1980, offers a religious-oriented education to 333 students from preschool to eighth grade. Previously located at Beth Am in Cleveland Heights, Greenview School in South Euclid, Park Synagogue, and Malvern School in Shaker Heights, Gross Schechter now rents the land for its permanent home, dedicated in 2002, from B'nai Jeshurun.

As one would expect in such a large congregation, several groups, over the years, have drifted in and out of B'nai Jeshurun. One group founded the Community Temple (Congregation Beth Am) in 1933; this eventually found a home in the exquisite neo-Gothic temple it purchased from the Trinity Congregational Church on Washington Boulevard in Cleveland Heights (now the New Community Bible Fellowship). Beset by a chain of catastrophes—including the unexpected death of their rabbi and the almost complete destruction of their building by fire—the congregation struggled on through intermittent attempts at reconciliation until 1999 (nineteen years after dedication of the new B'nai Jeshurun building), when the two congregations were at last reunited in Pepper Pike.

The Moskowitz sanctuary of B'nai Jeshurun seats 585 with an additional 180 in the balcony. When the north wall of the sanctuary is opened into the adjoining Rosenthal Auditorium, seating for the total worship area increases to two thousand. The simplicity and clarity of the sanctuary's off-white Jerusalem stone walls create a space of pervasive peace and tranquility. The warm, intimate Nickman Chapel seats one hundred. B'nai Jeshurun's ten-thousand-volume Mason library is computerized. The Bessie Hershey Religious School, completed in 2000, increased the education space to more than twenty classrooms.

146. Fairmount Temple,
or Anshe Chesed (see also Liberty Hill Baptist Church, p. 34) (1957)
Architect: Percival Goodman
Builder: Barnett Brickner
Location: 23737 Fairmount, Beachwood

Anshe Chesed is the oldest existing Jewish congregation in Greater Cleveland.[23] It has followed an orderly path through four buildings, from the first Jewish community in Cleveland and its small temple on Eagle Street to national prominence on Euclid and on Fairmount Avenues. Organized Jewish presence in Cleveland was established in 1839 by nineteen Germans and a Sefer Torah that emigrated together from the small Bavarian town of Unsleben. They were following Simson Thorman, who had immigrated to the United States from Unsleben in the 1820s, passed through Cleveland in 1832 in connection with the fur trade, and returned permanently to Cleveland as a merchant in 1837. The Bavarians established the Israelitic Society of Cleveland in 1839, and—when some walked out in 1841 in one of the seemingly inevitable divisions that plague American religious life—the majority left behind reconstituted itself as Anshe Chesed. The non-Jewish philanthropist Leonard Case gave Anshe Chesed land that the congregation, in turn, exchanged for another plot where they built the vaguely Gothic little Eagle Street Synagogue in 1846, the first Jewish religious building in Cleveland.[24] This Orthodox building had a "ladies' gallery" along three upper sides of the sanctuary. Dr. Michaelis Machol, leader of the congregation for three decades and the first rabbi in Cleveland to deliver sermons in English, led Anshe Chesed out of Eagle Street into a splendid new neo-Romanesque 1,500-seat building on Scovill, since torn down. At the turn of the twentieth century, the Czech synagogue in Cleveland merged with Anshe Chesed. Machol's successor, Louis Wolsey, developed the congregation into a national institution and, in 1912, moved it into the Euclid Avenue Temple (now the Liberty Hill Baptist Church, see p. 34). The Euclid Avenue Temple was vastly enlarged eleven years later with the construction of the adjoining Temple

House with its 1,400-seat auditorium. Later, the congregation was led up into the Heights in 1957 by Dr. Barnett Brickner. Brickner was so skilled a speaker that, shortly after arriving in Cleveland, he had bested Clarence Darrow (the man who made a monkey out of William Jennings Bryan) in a two-hour public religious debate listened to on the radio by an estimated 500,000 people. Brickner was tragically killed in an automobile accident in Spain two years after the congregation moved to Beachwood. Over the years, Anshe Chesed has been led by a number of nationally prominent rabbis, including Machol, Woolsey, Brickner, and more recently, Arthur Lelyveld. The community was also served by the Episcopal composer, James Rogers, who directed the music program at Anshe Chesed for fifty years while also playing on Sundays for the First Unitarian Church, teaching at the Cleveland Institute of Music, and serving as music critic for the *Plain Dealer*.

All this building and physical movement was accompanied by equally dramatic changes in religious practice. Anshe Chesed began as an Orthodox community. As the nineteenth century progressed, like many German congregations, it was increasingly influenced by the Jewish Reform movement coming out of central Europe and settling, in the United States, at Hebrew Union College in Cincinnati. Four years after moving into the Eagle Street Temple, Tifereth Israel (Silver's Temple), Cleveland's second Jewish congregation, split off. Although some dispute the reasons behind this separation, divisions concerning Reform versus Orthodox practice led, at least in part, to the split. This had also been behind the original division between Anshe Chesed and the Israelitic Society. In the middle of the century there was much coming and going of leadership. In 1861 the police had to take three worshipers away on charges of disturbing the peace. By 1876, however, when Dr. Machol began what would be a thirty-one-year rabbinate, things had settled down, and Anshe Chesed was firmly in the Reform camp. It has remained there, although subsequent leaders in the twentieth century slowly edged the congregation in a more traditional direction. Anshe Chesed had never gone as far in assimilating Yankee religious ideas as Tifereth Israel. In the turbulent world of Zionism, and Reform versus Orthodoxy, Anshe Chesed's progress during the past two centuries has been relatively serene.

Columbia professor and urban theorist Percival Goodman (1904–89) designed Fairmount Temple; his design of more than fifty synagogues has led him to be called "the most prolific architect in Jewish history."[25] His most famous building is B'nai Israel in Millburn, New Jersey, known for its integration of artworks by Herbert Ferber, Robert Motherwell, and Adolph Gottlieb. Here in Cleveland, on a large thirty-two-acre lot, Goodman discretely sited Fairmount Temple by setting it back from a busy four-lane thoroughfare running through a completely residential neighborhood. The siting may relate to the long, acrimonious, and ultimately unsuccessful lawsuit by which the municipality attempted to block construction of the building.

The angular high modernism of Goodman's Fairmount Temple strongly contrasts with the plastic expressionism of its competition three and a half miles to the northeast—Mendelsohn's Park Synagogue. Screened from the street by trees, Fairmount Temple, a brick building with stone trim, is a restrained, modernist statement. The butterfly roof of the chapel is the most dramatic part of the exterior building. From the outside, the long, narrow sanctuary is a quiet presence. A large atrium separates the sanctuary from the entrance to this large religious, educational, and social complex.

Like many Jewish buildings, Fairmount Temple is much larger than it appears from the street. The principal entrance to the worship space, flanked by unobtrusive but appealing one-story mosaic pillars, is from a large but unobtrusive parking lot on the west side of the building. One enters the large marble and Jerusalem stone atrium with wood trim through wide glass and aluminum doors. Originally designed by Goodman as an enclosed garden, the atrium now has a roof. A 1,200-seat auditorium to the left of the entrance is used for overflow during high holy days, for the school, as a lecture hall, and as a theater. It is much beloved by the Greater Cleveland community as home to the Cleveland Chamber Music Society. A balcony there accommodates lights, choir, organ, and a movie projector. To the right of the entrance is the chapel with its dramatic butterfly roof, so obvious from the outside. The chapel roof rests on four brick pillars surrounded by wonderful, modern, colored glass. The chapel seats 150 with the inevitable sliding door to the side that allows expansion to accommodate another 150. In the administrative area to the south of the atrium, a spacious office for the rabbi is used for private family services. Everywhere one finds generous Jerusalem stone trim. Throughout the building are beautifully articulated white monochromatic ceilings.

Goodman was known for his use of light, and this is particularly obvious in the majestic sanctuary. Five two-story banks of louvered windows on either side bathe the main worship space in light. The windows are on top of an unilluminated, brick, first-story wall that preserves an atmosphere of quiet decorum. At the front, a serried wall is pierced at unequal intervals with narrow windows of colored glass. Progressive step-levels rise to a stage. The front wall is plaster, flanked by modern wood screens. The eight-hundred-seat sanctuary is usually divided from the three successive social spaces to its rear by movable wood walls. The social spaces are accessible separately from the lobby. Sanctuary seating can be increased to 1,800 by opening the walls and using an ingenious continuous mechanical device that moves one thousand seats, identical to those in the permanent sanctuary, up from the basement in a matter of hours.

As one would expect in a Goodman building, several outstanding pieces by the American abstract expressionist sculptors Ibram Lassaw and Herbert Ferber and tapestries designed by the painter Abraham Rattner decorate Fairmount Temple.[26] Particularly notable is Lassaw's *The Wings of the Cherubim* containing the eternal light above the ark. Ferber's *Covenant II* and *Flood II* are considered among his finest work.

A large educational wing spreads out to the north behind the worship and administrative areas. Modernized in the 1990s, the educational wing includes courtyards, kitchens, one of the Tiffany windows from the Euclid Avenue building (the rest were left behind, see p. 34), an office complex for the rabbi emeritus, and libraries. There is a memorial to David Berger, the Israeli athlete murdered at the 1972 Olympic games in Munich. He had been a member of Anshe Chesed.

147. Church of the Good Shepherd (1958 and 1988)
Architects: J. Byers Hayes (1958) and Davison–Smith (1988)
Builders: Robert Dean (1958) and Graham Smith (1988)
Location: 23599 Cedar Road, Lyndhurst

The dramatic modernist planes and masses and the straightforward brickwork and undecorated wood trim of Good Shepherd, unlike that of many other relatively recent religious structures, retain the panache they had when this church was built fifty years ago. In part, this reflects the careful maintenance of the building and grounds by its leadership and congregation, despite both political upheaval during the Vietnam War and a neighborhood that, like most neighborhoods, has changed its character since the Eisenhower years. Good Shepherd is fortunate in having been built on a beautiful wooded seven-acre tract, most of which is located well back from Cedar Road. One accesses the parking lot in front of the church by a relatively long and narrow entry drive beside a synagogue completed in 2008. The church is farther buffered from its neighborhood by a deep ravine to the west and that ravine and a country club to the north. To the east, a new condominium residential area and part of a high-end residential neighborhood separate the church from a large commercial development.

Good Shepherd was also fortunate in its choice of architect—the amazingly versatile J. Byers Hayes. As principal designer during the 1920s for Walker and Weeks, Hayes was responsible for the Renaissance Revival style of the Cleveland Federal Reserve Bank and the technical grandeur of the 78,189-seat Municipal Stadium, at that time the largest amphitheater in the world. In church architecture he was responsible for the classicism of St. Ann's (see p. 321), the Lombard Romanesque of the Rockefeller's ill-fated Euclid Avenue Baptist Church, and the Gothic of both St. Paul's Episcopal (see p. 329) and First Baptist Churches (see p. 337). In later years Hayes was at home in the spare rectilinear international style, as in his stunning Lakewood High School Auditorium. The quality of his vision and the durability of his design are evident even in such a relatively modest commission as Good Shepherd.

Good Shepherd was established in 1952 to relieve the pressure inside Christ Church in Shaker Heights (see p. 340), a church that was bursting at the seams.

Meeting originally in the chapel of Hawken School, which fortuitously had an organ, expanding Good Shepherd then moved to the Hillcrest YMCA until their church was dedicated in 1959. After spectacular growth in the 1960s, the parish was severely tested by dissension concerning the Vietnam War. In 1977, when Graham Smith, assistant at St. Peter's Lakewood (see p. 286), was called to the parish, Good Shepherd was on diocesan aid. During Smith's fifteen years as rector, Good Shepherd again grew so substantially that it almost doubled its size with the addition of a chapel and a large, new education and social wing.

This building program was consistent with Hayes's original massing and retained Hayes's original brick and frame aesthetic. The sanctuary, the first educational-administrative wing, and the second educational-social wing (anticipated by Hayes but built thirty years later) all radiate from a small, elegant, plane-glazed atrium. Band windows and a two-story plane-glazed north wall in the second addition take advantage of the naturalism of the secluded site. Hayes articulated these functions with sweeping flat roofs, identifying this as a Christian church with a single thin tall tower (which also functions as a chimney).

Before he designed Good Shepherd in 1957, Hayes traveled in Europe. There he probably came in contact with several ideas about church architecture that were circulating in Roman Catholic circles before John XXIII convened Vatican II in 1962. Certainly Good Shepherd incorporates much of what is now associated with post-Vatican II Roman Catholic building (see Church of the Resurrection, 1973 and 2004, p. 360, and La Sagrada Familia, 1998, p. 248). Hayes's sanctuary-in-the-round configuration allowed all worshipers to be thirty feet from the altar and to see each other during services. He made room for 250 worshipers, whom he divided into three sections that face each other around a central altar and baptismal font. Several elements separate these three "slices" of seating, including a pulpit, a lectern, and the entrance to the sanctuary. Good Shepherd's freestanding altar was the first, for an Episcopal church, in Greater Cleveland. Overlooking all this was small balcony for organ and choir. Hayes limited sanctuary decoration to the pews and other church furniture that he designed, the plain carpeting, the subtly differentiated brick walls, a magnificently articulated chocolate-brown stained-wood ceiling, and the view out of unglazed windows. Perhaps because Hayes, drawing his plans in the 1950s, anticipated the style of the 1960s and 1970s, his design—now more than fifty years old—has retained its fundamental freshness into the twenty-first century.

CHAPTER FIFTEEN

Orange–Solon–Chagrin Falls–Gates Mills–
Highland Heights–Richmond Heights

Begin this tour at the Harvard Road exit off Interstate 271. Head east on Harvard approximately one-half mile to Brainard Road. Turn right (south) onto Brainard Road and continue for one mile. At the corner of Brainard Road at Emery Road is the recently built Temple Emanu El (148), designed by one of Cleveland's most promising young architects. Drive in to see this building's famous chapel. Continue eight-tenths of a mile south on Brainard Road and turn left (east) onto Miles Road. After seven-tenths of a mile on Miles Road, past the Miles Farmers Market—an eastern suburban gastronomic landmark—turn right (south), around an old country cemetery, onto Harper Road. Drive across the narrow green of the Hawthorn Parkway, part of the Emerald Necklace Park System encircling Greater Cleveland. One mile south of Miles, turn left (east) onto Cannon Road. On the southeast corner of Harper at Cannon stands Advent Lutheran Church. To the southwest stands the Chabad Jewish Center of Solon. A little more than a half mile east on Cannon sits the modern Church of the Resurrection (149) on the left. Drive into the parking lot. Set back from the street is the original 1973 high-modern church, now used as education, community, and administrative space. To the north, attached to the original building, is the new postmodern church, now the principal worship space. Leaving the parking lot, continue east on Cannon Road for another half mile and turn right (south) onto SOM Center Road. It derives its name from the municipalities of Solon, Orange, and Mayfield.

On the southwest corner of the Cannon-SOM Center intersection is the Solon United Methodist Church with its distinctive Robert Gaede designed spire. Driving south on SOM, on the left (east), at the back of a large parking lot, is the contemporary Solon Community United Church of Christ. Passing under U.S. 422, a major east-west divided highway, enter Solon on SOM Center Road. Immediately after going under the railroad, in downtown Solon, turn left (east) onto Aurora Road.

St. John Byzantine Catholic Church—with its onion dome, stained wood, and great exterior icon of *Christ and St. John*—occupies the northwest corner of Aurora Road at Liberty Road, a mile southeast of downtown Solon. Continue southeast on Aurora Road for another mile and a half and then, past the Grantwood Golf Course, turn left (east) onto Pettibone Road. In the distance to the left, the white spire of Parkside Church (150) is visible from the intersection. Drive into this church's parking lot and drive around the mega-church to appreciate its size and the size of its parking lot. Leaving Parkside Church, return to Aurora Road and turn right (west). At Liberty, turn right (north) and continue north on Liberty, passing back under U.S. 422.

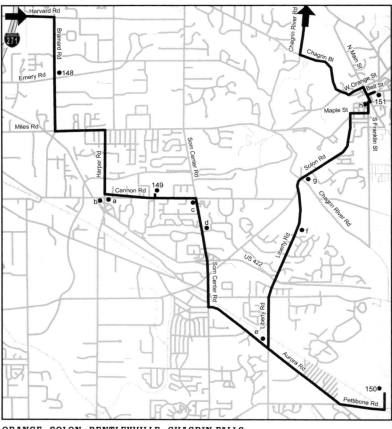

ORANGE–SOLON–BENTLEYVILLE–CHAGRIN FALLS

148. Temple Emanu El
   a. Advent Lutheran Church
   b. Chabad Jewish Center of Solon
149. Church of the Resurrection
   c. Solon United Methodist Church
   d. Solon Community United Church of Christ
   e. St. John Byzantine Catholic Church

150. Parkside Church
   f. Church of Jesus Christ of Latter-day
     Saints
   g. St. Martin's Episcopal Church
   h. United Methodist Church of Chagrin Falls
151. Federated Church

On the right of Liberty, at the border of the municipalities of Solon and Bentleyville, is a Church of Jesus Christ of Latter-day Saints with its identifying brick and white frame architecture. A half mile farther on, turn right at Solon Road. On the left of Solon Road, just past its intersection with Chagrin River Road, is the Bentleyville Village Hall. On the right is the white frame Colonial Revival architecture of St. Martin's Episcopal Church. Continue north on Solon Road for another mile, entering Chagrin Falls. Just past the traffic light marking its intersection with Miles, Solon Road turns right on its own. Continue east after the turn for four blocks and then turn left (north) at the

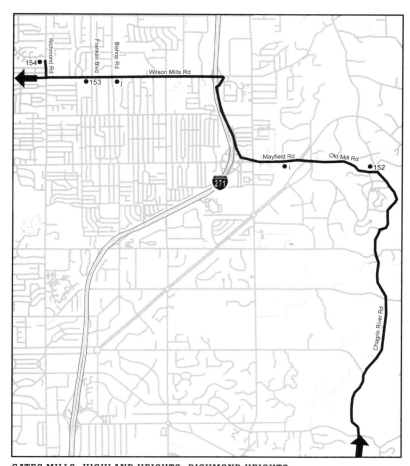

GATES MILLS–HIGHLAND HEIGHTS–RICHMOND HEIGHTS
152. St. Christopher's-by-the-River
  i. St. Francis of Assisi Church
  j. Highland Sixth Presbyterian Church
153. St. Paschal Baylon Parish
154. St. Gregory of Narek Armenian Church

traffic light onto South Franklin Street. On the left is the United Methodist Church of Chagrin Falls. After traveling two blocks on South Franklin Street, turn right and then immediately left onto Main Street, driving around the little square of this picturesque town. At the next traffic light, just before the park to the right, turn right onto Bell Street. The Federated Church (151) stands at the top of the hill on the right. At night, its lighted spire is visible across the valley.

Travel back down the hill to Main Street and turn right, passing the famous Popcorn Shop on the left where George and Laura Bush stopped during his 2004 presidential campaign to try the caramel corn. At the traffic light, turn left onto West Orange Street. As it leaves Chagrin Falls, West Orange Street becomes Chagrin Boulevard. Going down into the valley and crossing the Chagrin River, turn right (north) onto Chagrin River Road. For the next six miles, wind along the river through one of the loveliest semirural areas of Cuyahoga County, past manor houses, horse farms, and the polo field. Entering the reconstructed village of Gates Mills, pass the barns and staff housing of the Chagrin Valley Hunt Club. Turn left at Old Mill Road. St. Christopher's-by-the-River (151) stands on the right, across the street from the Hunt Club. Every year the rector of St. Christopher's, standing at the entrance of his church, blesses the horses, dogs, and riders of the club milling in the churchyard. Continue west on Old Mill Road, climbing the hill out of the valley. At the top of the hill turn right at West Hill Drive and immediately, after waiting for the traffic light, turn left (west) onto Mayfield Road. On the left (south) one can see the splendid white pillars in front of the large octagonal brick St. Francis of Assisi Church.

Driving past the buildings associated with Hillcrest Hospital and across SOM, turn right onto I-271 North. Exit the interstate at the next interchange (Wilson Mills Road) and turn left (west) onto Wilson Mills. Pass Mayfield High School and the Cuyahoga County Public Library on the left. The Highland Sixth Presbyterian Church is also on the left, just east of Bishop Road. Farther west on Wilson Mills, also on the left, is the sheer glass face of Richard Fleischman's unforgettable "Darth Vader" St. Paschal Baylon Parish (153). Continuing a half mile more on Wilson Mills Road, turn right (north) onto Richmond Road. A little less than a mile on the left, opposite the immense Richmond Town Square shopping mall, is the beautifully sited St. Gregory of Narek Armenian Church (154).

This concludes the tour of the far eastern reaches of Cuyahoga County. Return to Wilson Mills Road. Turn right (west) for the eastern suburbs of Cleveland. Turn left and travel east two and a half miles to access the thruways at I-271.

148. Temple Emanu El (2008)
Architect: Marc Cicarelli
Builder: Steven Denker
Location: 4545 Brainard Road, Orange Village

Temple Emanu El is the newest religious building in this book.[1] Studio Techne designed it; their firm is best known in Cleveland as the architects for the renovation and reconstruction of the Cleveland Heights Public Library and the spectacular bridge that unites that library, across Lee Road, with the new Heights Art Center. Steve Litt, architectural critic of the Cleveland *Plain Dealer,* has pointed out that while there is now little religious building in Cleveland, Marc Cicarelli seems to have a hand in what little there is.[2]

Temple Emanu El was organized in 1947 as a joint effort of the two major Reform Jewish congregations in Cleveland—Tifereth Israel (Silver's Temple, p. 44) and Anshe Chesed (Brickner's [Euclid] Temple, p. 34). Theirs was a campaign to reach out, after World War II, to the half of Cleveland's young Jews who were unaffiliated with a religious institution. The parent institutions provided six members from each of their boards to help organize the new congregation. They recruited Rabbi Alan Green and Cantor Irvin Bushman to develop an institution that would attract otherwise unaffiliated young families. They were successful. Initially meeting at Plymouth Church (see p. 335) the young couples of Emanu El moved to the chapel of the Bellefaire School on Fairmount before settling, in 1954, into a quietly modernist building on Green Road near Cedar. Cleveland architect Sigmund Braverman designed this space; he would go on to design more than fifty synagogues in the United States and Canada. Whatever local eminence the original members of Emanu El and their well-educated children eventually attained, by the twenty-first century, many of the children of the original members were well into retirement. This was no longer a congregation primarily made up of young families. In addition, their spirit of Reform was clearly out of step with many of their fundamentalist Jewish neighbors. Deciding to move, they landed in Orange in a building designed by one of Cleveland's most admired young architects.

This 37,000-square-foot building reaches out over a spaciously beautiful ten-acre campus surrounded by a prosperous, but less than aristocratic, outer-suburban neighborhood. The congregation and architect elected to limit parking in front of the building so as not to detract from its appearance. Most of their cars hide behind the complex. The entering road weaves past trees, lawns, gardens, and a generous pond with a fountain and ducks. The liberally glazed exterior walls are articulated by projecting limestone piers. These piers appear to go through the exterior walls and reappear inside the building.

The main entrance opens into a broad, open, irregularly shaped, multipurpose atrium from which the various worship, education, and administrative activities of this institution radiate. The lobby is designed for communal gatherings. Emanu El is a house of prayer, a house of assembly,[3] and a house of study. The importance of this congregation as a house of study is emphasized by its library, one that is not enclosed—as most libraries are—in a separate room, but instead reaches out into the large, multipurpose entrance space. Administrative space and a large complex for religion, language, and day-school education extend past and behind the library. Down a hall, at the front of the entrance-atrium, one finds the temple's fan-shaped principal worship space. This seats approximately 245 in substantial movable chairs. No one is more than nine rows from the front and no one is more than nine seats from a floor-to-ceiling window to the outside. The sanctuary can be opened on either side into a boardroom, a cry (or bride's) room, and a social hall to increase seating to approximately a thousand while maintaining good sight lines to the bimah and rabbi.

The chapel is the focal point of the building. From the outside, the chapel's cylinder, wrapped in warm wood panels, is what most identifies this as a religious building. From the atrium, worshipers enter the round chapel through a closed, half-circumferential, narrow hall faced on one side with glass from the Green Road Temple, illuminated by light boxes. This curved hall approach was designed to allow worshipers to pause mentally before entering the one-hundred-seat chapel. The wood ark and perpetual light are from the old temple, but the highlight of the chapel is the clear, inscribed, plain clerestory glass that runs in a complete circle in a band between the top of the chapel walls and the ceiling. Jewish faith is a belief in the Word and excerpts from the Torah, the Talmud, and other religious writing are inscribed on the glass in Hebrew. The transparent Hebrew letters are inscribed in frosted glass. This makes the inscriptions difficult to read. They become more or less legible depending on shifting light and the movement of the reader. Although this shifting legibility has been criticized,[4] it reminds users of an important part of the message: sometimes the Word is clear; sometimes it is not.

149. Church of the Resurrection
(1973 and 2004)
Architects: Richard Bowen (1973)
and Bill Beard (2004)
Builders: Louis Trivison (1973)
and Mark Hobson (2004)
Location: 32001 Cannon Road

The Church of the Resurrection is an important sacred monument because, in a religious context, it so accurately and so beautifully presents the two distinct architectural styles of the mid- and later twentieth century—modernism (1973) and postmodernism (2004).[5] Founded in 1971, Resurrection was one of the first Roman Catholic parishes in northeast Ohio established after, and reflecting the ideas of, Vatican II (1962–65). The parish was established following what the diocese described in its *People of Faith* as a "heated" meeting at St. Rita School. Approximately half of the members of St. Rita elected to join the new community.

Central to Vatican II was the vision of the church as the whole people of God. As *People of Faith*, the diocesan guide to its parishes explained, "Instead of the traditional pastor-based parish model, Resurrection . . . developed a pastoral staff, which, under the direction of its coordinator, Father Trivison, collaborated in making all community decisions."[6] Resurrection established a "parish council" to advise this clergy-lay pastoral team and make decisions concerning parish administration. For the first time in the Catholic Church in Ohio, women were invited to be meaningful public participants in administration.[7] The parish emphasized outreach over parochial services. There was no school, no gym, no separate building for social functions. Instead, partnerships were established with Epiphany and St. Cecelia (see p. 161) Roman Catholic Churches in the Mt. Pleasant neighborhood directly southwest of Shaker Heights.

The first Resurrection building reflected this spirit. All parish activities—worship, education, socialization, and administration—took place in one large, round, dogmatically pristine, modernist building. Built of off-white stone and covered and embraced by a single, large, round, shallow roof, Resurrection was identified as religious by a spare modernist tower (with a functioning bell) surmounted by a cross. Built in the middle of the first energy crisis, windows were small and the interior correspondingly dark. Beloved by (mostly non-Roman Catholic) modernists, the original building not only had begun to show its age by the beginning of the twenty-first century, but it severely cramped the worship and educational missions of the parish.

In 2004 the congregation completed an adjacent postmodern building to serve as a new worship space and to provide the support space necessary to fulfill more completely the church's mission (i.e., more bathrooms, a place to gather before going into church, a coatroom, a nursery, and a parlor). The new, octagonal worship space that dominates the new addition has no doors and is thus a constant presence reaching back into the original building. Large, clear windows are open to the woodland part of the church's fifteen-acre lot. This new worship space continues the circular concept of the original building but occupies its entire structure rather than a large piece of the pie—as in the old building.

Church furniture is contemporary and arranged in the spirit of the original congregation. The altar, made of wood instead of stone to celebrate the post-Resurrection supper at Emmaus instead of the pre-Resurrection stone of the tomb, stands in the center, surrounded by chairs instead of pews to emphasize the individuality of members of the parish. Chairs are in an "antiphonal" arrangement, patterned after a monastic choir, so that members of the congregation are more aware of each other than they would be if everyone faced the same direction. Also in the center is an ambo, or reading desk. At the entrance to the worship space is a spectacular, octagonal, mosaic baptismal font large enough to accommodate an adult for immersion baptism. Continuously running water swirls through the font, reminding those who enter that they enter Christianity through baptism and also reminding Roman Catholics, who bless themselves on entering, of their common baptism.

Around the periphery of the sanctuary are fourteen mosaic stations of the resurrection (the fourteen Franciscan stations of the cross are installed in the garden in back of the church). Contemporary objects reflecting the Resurrection and organization of the parish surround the sanctuary. It features a large, bronze *Christ Rising,* a bogwood lectern rescued from a prehistoric Irish swamp, and, in keeping with the role of women in the parish, three life-size recognizably feminine Marys emerge from a large block of Carrara marble to witness the Resurrection.

150. Parkside Church (1993 and 2000)
Architects: Denis Batty (1993) and Tony Paskevich (2000)
Builder: Alistair Begg
Location: 7100 Pettibone Road, Solon

With weekend attendance of about four thousand, non-denominational evangelical Bible-based Parkside has been a "mega" church for almost two decades. It began in 1968 as a small group of East Side businessmen meeting for a weekly prayer meeting. They invited their wives to join them for Sunday evening worship at Grace Episcopal Church in Willoughby and then the Church of the Western Reserve in Pepper Pike. Four years after their first meeting, they organized as "The Chapel" and called their first full-time pastor. Growing numbers forced the congregation to move to the B'rith Emeth Temple in Pepper Pike (see p. 347) and then to Orange High School. At last, in 1978, the group began worship in a building they built in Beachwood. Outgrowing this building in nine years, The Chapel sold its church to a Conservative Jewish congregation, Shaarey Tikvah, and moved to Solon High School. As they baptized members in the swimming pool, they built again. Changing their name to Parkside Church (in recognition of their new park-side location), they moved into their present home in 1993. Seven years later, they built a large addition to accommodate more classrooms, a bookstore and café, and a large area for fellowship, parish dinners, and conferences. Now, twelve years after the most recent addition, they are studying alternatives to accommodate their ever-increasing congregation. While most at Parkside would credit this phenomenal growth to the content of the church's Bible-based message, many within and without the institution would credit its expansion to the preaching, pastoral care, and administration of Alistair Begg, senior pastor since 1983.

In the twenty-first century, a church this large requires a lot of room—room, among other things, for a 1,300-space parking lot. Initially frustrated by a local building board concerned about the impact of such a large institution on its municipality, Parkside eventually located on forty acres in what appeared to be a rural area on the border of Solon and Chagrin Falls. The complex was far enough out in the country that Parkside had to maintain its own water and sewage treatment plant until the church hooked into Solon's municipal system. Their area is filling up with a large, although unobtrusive, commercial development across the street, a municipal golf course to the south, and houses around the periphery of the Parkside property. As homes are sold, seven have been purchased by the church as housing for visitors and temporary housing in the United States for the missionaries the church supports.

Dennis Batty, a Minneapolis architect specializing in churches—particularly large churches, designed the original building. The plain brick structure with white frame trim and brick quoins is almost vernacular. The church has three entrance porticos with plain white pediments; the central portico is stepped back. Zoning unfortunately limited the height of the steeple, one that everyone—except the zoning board—understood was much too small for the building. It is so small that one can only see it from the main road in the wintertime when the leaves are off the trees. The three entrances open into a main entrance-atrium that wraps around a semicircular sanctuary equipped for multimedia-assisted worship. Classrooms and administrative space are behind the sanctuary.

The large new addition was built north of the original complex and includes a "commons" that seats 850 for dinner and is otherwise used for concerts, commercial meetings, and overflow at Christmas and Easter. Additional class-rooms surround the "commons" and more are located below in the basement. Parkside now has thirty-three classrooms to accommodate, for example, the eight hundred children and three hundred adult volunteers in its week-long summer daily Vacation Bible School. Several classrooms have been converted into a radio studio that franchises 1,700 broadcasts each weekday and 1,500 on weekends through 1,081 radio outlets in seven countries and three provinces. Adjacent to the "commons" is a book store and café.

The fan-shaped sanctuary, which seats 1,600 and can be expanded to two thousand, is larger than any other gathering place in adjacent Geauga County. Thus, the church hosts graduations for West Geauga, Crestwood, and Kenston High Schools. Parkside's most spectacular secular public service took place in 2002, when a tornado blew the roof off the Solon Middle School. With no place in Solon capable of accommodating 850 students and their 75 staff members, the middle school moved into Parkside. For almost three months, until the middle school roof could be repaired, school met at Parkside during the week and then made way for the congregation every Sunday.

151. Federated Church

Architects: James Garfield
(builder; 1851); William
Hutchings (builder; 1875); ?
Hutchings (1885); architect
unknown (1928); architect
unknown (1957); Ward and
Conrad (1965); Peter van
Dyke (1997); and Braun and
Steidl (2000).

Builder: James Garfield and successors
Location: 76 Bell Street, Chagrin Falls

The Federated Church in downtown Chagrin Falls packs more church into less space than any religious institution outside of downtown Cleveland.[8] As its congregation grew after the Second World War, space was at such a premium that, in 1957, the church demolished the inside of its three-story 1928 administrative and education addition and transformed it into a four-story complex. At last, after a variety of other imaginative transformations, frustrated by a historical commission that refused farther increase in size, the church established a satellite Family Life Center on the outskirts of Chagrin Falls in 2000.

The Federated Church (United Church of Christ) is a federation of three denominations—the Disciples of Christ, the Congregational Church, and a Canadian denomination.

The Disciples of Christ (also known as the Christian Church) was founded in Pennsylvania in 1809 as a liberal offshoot of the Presbyterian Church. The Disciples of Christ is the largest indigenous American Protestant denomination. It continues as a denomination separate from the Federated Church.[9] A Disciples of Christ congregation was established in Bentleyville by the Reverend Adamson Bentley in 1831. When Bentley's flour mill, sawmill, woolen factory, and store failed to materialize into a town, his church moved out of its log cabin schoolhouse into Chagrin Falls. There, in 1851, James Garfield began scoring timber for a Disciples meetinghouse in which he subsequently baptized parishioners, performed marriages, and practiced his oratory between stints at Hiram and Williams College, the U.S. House of Representatives, and the White House. This building was torn down in the early 1930s.

The Congregational Church, the church of Connecticut and hence of the Western Reserve, was established in Chagrin Falls in 1835, four years after the Disciples of Christ organized in Bentleyville. The Congregational Church was the first church in Chagrin Falls. A building was put up in 1845 on the north side of the Chagrin River, north of the pond and park and east of the Chagrin Falls popcorn stand. This church was subsequently sold in 1893 and is now destroyed.

The Bible Christian Church was founded in Devonshire by William O'Bryan in 1815 as a denomination of Methodist belief and Congregational government. Its North American headquarters were located in Canada with two districts in the United States—Wisconsin and Ohio. In 1875 parishioners built what was considered a large church on the south side of the Chagrin River on the present Federated Church lot on Bell Street. In 1884 it was decided that the districts of the Bible Christian Church in the United States would disband and "unite with congenial local congregations."[10] The Bible Christian congregation in Chagrin Falls invited the Congregationalists to move south of the river. One year later, the two congregations undertook an ambitious reconstruction of the Bible Christian Church; William Hutchings designed this reconstruction. Hutchings added vestibules, clock tower, and spire. This brick Victorian Gothic building, anchoring the west end of the current Federated Church complex, served, through a variety of creative adaptations, as the Federated Church sanctuary for the next eighty years until the construction of the current sanctuary in 1965. The 1885 building continues as the iconic structure of the Federated Church and its illuminated tower welcomes everyone who drives down the hill at night from the west into Chagrin Falls.

In 1892, seven years after the Congregationalists moved in with the Bible Christians, the united community began a thirty-seven-year courtship of the Disciples of Christ. This was consummated in 1929 as the Federated Church. One year before federation, a large, three-story educational building was dedicated at the rear of the old sanctuary. In 1957 this building was gutted and rebuilt by Ward and Conrad in four stories with classrooms, offices, a parlor, two kitchens, and a general-purpose room.

At last, after the failure of added balconies and additional services to accommodate the congregation, a major extension of the complex was built toward the east in 1965. Brick arches forming an entrance arcade continue to the east around large, recessed Palladian windows that illuminate the new sanctuary. The lightness of the exterior construction reflects the simple white woodwork of the Wren-Gibbs balconied interior. Because of its lightness, this addition, four times the size of the original church, complements but does not overwhelm the nineteenth-century building. In the end, however, despite farther, and expensive, tinkering with the lower entrance into the large parish hall underneath the new sanctuary by Pieter van Dyke in 1999, the Bell Street site could no longer accommodate the congregation. In 2000 Braun and Steidl completed a Family Life Center on Chillicothe Road on the outskirts of Chagrin Falls. This new post and beam building sits in the middle of a campus ten times the area available in downtown Chagrin Falls. The new building reintroduces the gym that had been eliminated when the educational complex at the back of the original church was reorganized in 1957. It also includes a commercial kitchen, more classrooms and a large, multipurpose room suitable for worship during the summer.

152. St. Christopher's-by-the-River
(1853 and 1928)
Architects: Holsey Gates (1853) and
Frank Walker (1928)
Builders: Holsey Gates (1853) and
Frank Walker (1928)[11]
Location: 7601 Old Mill Road, Gates
Mills

In 1826 Holsey Gates purchased 130
acres along the Chagrin River. Six weeks
later, he and his brothers had built a cabin, damned the river, dug a millrace, and
constructed a sawmill. As years passed,
Gates continued to develop his settle-
ment, adding two more mills, several houses for members of his extended family, a tavern, a school and, in 1853, a church. The earliest evidence of religious
activity in Gates Mills is an 1845 Methodist class book. Methodist circuit riders
tended to the religious needs of the little settlement for seventy-five years.

One can still see what survives of Gates's church from the street—the vestibule, tower, and main body of the sanctuary with three windows on each side.
A comparison of this structure with such small country churches of the period
as that of Hale Farm and that of the early village in Chesterland, shows that this
was a good-sized religious building for its time, testifying to the midcentury
prosperity of Gates Mills. The size makes it surprising that the church never enjoyed a full-time pastor during its first seventy-five years. Similar small country
Greek Revival churches in northern Ohio include St. James's Episcopal Church
in Boardman (1829), St. Peter's Episcopal Church in Ashtabula (1829), Christ
Episcopal Church in Windsor Mills (1832), South Ridge Baptist Church south
of Conneaut (1832), St. Mark's Episcopal Church in Wadsworth (1840), Brecksville Congregational Church (1844), the Universalist Church in North Olmsted
(1847), the Congregational Church in Twinsburg (1848), and the Streetsboro
Methodist Church (1851).[12] What distinguishes St. Christopher's from its Western Reserve contemporaries is not its style but the remarkable conservation of
its structure and, particularly, its surroundings. This resulted from the unusual
character of its parishioners and its immediate community.

Gates Mills did not prosper during the second half of the nineteenth century. By the turn of the century, it had become a largely abandoned, rather
tumbled-down affair. Today's community was the result of the Maple Leaf
Land Company and its Cleveland and Eastern Railway. In 1905 the railway
introduced a "Banker's special"—Gates Mills to Public Square in seventy minutes. The Maple Leaf Land Company had acquired two thousand acres on
both sides of the Chagrin River, including most of Gates Mills. Its speculation
was a response to the nostalgic American historicism of the early twentieth

century that would culminate in 1927 in Williamsburg. Before John D. Rockefeller Jr. in tidewater Virginia, there was Frank Walker in eastern Cuyahoga County. Under Walker's leadership, a general cleanup of Gates Mills and a change in its character took place. Dilapidated mills were torn down. The disreputable Maple Leaf Inn was reborn as the Chagrin Valley Hunt Club. Small, nineteenth-century houses were greatly enlarged with inconspicuous additions. Walker himself designed not so inconspicuous homes for his friends— Walter White (Hawken School), Frank Ginn, A. C. Ernst, and Francis Drury (Gilmour Academy).

Could the small village church be far behind? In 1906, Episcopalians began Sunday vesper services in the church during the summer. By 1926, 34 percent of the population of Gates Mills was Episcopal (23 percent Methodist, 20 percent other, and 24 percent unchurched). The Methodist trustees and their district superintendent met with the dean, archdeacon, and two bishops of the Episcopal Diocese and, with the agreement of the Gates family, the little church was reborn as the Episcopal St. Christopher's-by-the-River.

In his capacity as a principal partner of Walker and Weeks, Frank Walker had been responsible for much of the important religious building about Cleveland—First Baptist (see p. 337), Second Baptist, St. Paul's (see p. 329), and St. Ann (see p. 321). Not surprising, Walker happened to have plans to double the size of Holsey Gates's church and make it liturgically and socially consistent with its new neighborhood. (Almost a hundred years after its conversion, red-coated members of the Hunt Club continue to ride their horses onto the lawn in front of the church for the annual blessing of the hunt, complete with the Lone Ranger's song from the *William Tell Overture* and "How Much Is That Doggie in the Window?" played on the church's carillon.) The original church consisted of only one room with vestibule and balcony. Walker added a chapel and an arched chancel for the altar, the pulpit, the lectionary, the bishop's chair, and the seating for clergy and acolytes. Behind the original church he added education and social space. All of this, with modern heating, required that the church be moved fifteen feet south to accommodate the building to the site (i.e., to prevent it from falling into the river).

An eight-bell peal of bells was hung in the tower in 1927. It replaced a bell that had been given to the Mayfield United Methodist Church. Their bell had been destroyed when their church burned down in 1945. Fifteen additional bells were added to the carillon in 1964. In 2000 a magnificent eighteen-rank Hradetzky tracker organ was installed in the choir loft (originally the balcony).

153. St. Paschal Baylon Parish
(1971)
Architect: Richard Fleischman
Builder: John O'Brien
Location: 5384 Wilson Mills
Road, Highland Heights

St. Paschal Baylon, a sixteenth-century Spanish Franciscan cele-brated for his devotion to the Eu-charist, is the patron of Eucharistic organizations. His life was a logical precedent for St. Peter Eymard when St. Peter established the Congregation of Priests of the Most Blessed Sacrament in Paris in 1857 as an order of priests devoted to promotion of the Eucharist. Although the congregation is now involved in a variety of activities to promote adoration of the Eucharist throughout the Roman Catholic Church, its efforts were originally directed toward priests. The congregation established the Priests Eucharistic League, whose members spend at least an hour a week in devotion before the Eu-charist. The congregation of about one thousand priests is active throughout the world from a Center Eucharistica in Rome. In the United States, the congregation began publishing *Emmanuel Magazine* in 1894. The third-oldest Roman Catholic periodical in this country, at one time it reached one-half of American priests.

The order in North America originally had a distinctly French flavor, be-ing particularly strong in Canada. Its headquarters in the United States was at St. Jean Baptiste in New York. There it became closely associated with the veneration of St. Ann. In Cleveland, the order was established in 1931 as a community of perpetual adoration at a chapel on Euclid Avenue on the Far East Side.[13] In 1953 Bishop Hoban asked the order to establish a parish of St. Paschal Baylon in then rural Highland Heights. Two priests and an old truck, loaded with church and household furniture, made their way from St. Jean Baptiste to Cleveland and moved into a 125-year-old farmhouse. Their loca-tion proved to be a wonderful site for a parish. Schools, monasteries, convents, shrines, and churches rapidly followed each other, continuing through Fleis-chman's landmark "Darth Vader" church in 1971. In 1964 the seminary and novitiate down on Euclid Avenue moved to Highland Heights, and in 1978 the headquarters of the American province of St. Ann moved there from New York together with the staff of *Emanuel Magazine*. The seminarians now study with the Jesuits in Chicago, and the novitiate has moved to Wisconsin. The Highland Heights community, in addition to its activities in the United States, is active in the drought-ridden Cabo Delgado area of northern Mozambique.

The St. Paschal Baylon campus sprawls along a major thoroughfare in an entirely residential area. Its famous church is sited more than a block back from the street so as not to distract drivers. Fleischman's work has repeat-edly involved great sheets of glass. At St. Paschal Baylon, he constructed a giant modern space, the front of which is a perpendicular four-story glass wall. Fleischman divided his monumental four-story cone into eight segments; six angled segments are tiled and two are the awe-inspiring perpendicular glass walls. Thin pillars around a circumferential, transparent glass wall support this great cone.[14] Six years after the dedication of Fleischman's church—unfortunately or fortunately—the movie *Star Wars* swept the country. The principal villain, a character named Darth Vader, wears a space helmet with a remarkable resemblance to the St. Paschal Baylon church. The resemblance is obvious to almost every American familiar with the *Star Wars* films.

Inside the cone, its opaque parts are lined with tongue-in-groove wood paneling. The segments of the cone do not come to a point but are truncated at a circumferential glass clerestory. Wooden semicircular pews seat one thousand. Aside from some plaster and a little brick, it has no other decoration. The great flanks of the cone are powerful enough in themselves to decorate the interior of this church. In the thirty-five years since dedication, there have been some minor changes, but Fleischman's space and massing are so great that the changes are little noticed. The tile sides on the exterior of the cone collect ice and snow that threaten parishioners during the winter. Protective roofs over the principal entrances have had to be constructed to protect them. Inside, supporting the order's mission, St. Paschal Baylon has a glass-enclosed "Chapel of Exposure" for adoration of the Eucharist. The transparency of this chapel (all the glass in this church is clear and unglazed) does not detract from the majesty of the central space.

154. St. Gregory of Narek Armenian Church (1964)
Architect: David Andonian
Builder: Nersess Jebejian
Location: 678 Richmond Road, Richmond Heights

Armenians, one of the smallest ethnic communities in Cleveland, worship in what almost everyone considers one of the most charming sacred landmarks in northeast Ohio.[15] The entire Armenian community, approximately two thousand men, women, and children, would fit into any one of this area's larger religious buildings. As in many areas of American social, economic, and intellectual life, the Armenian minority occupies a much more influential role than its numbers would suggest.

About fifty Armenians came to Cleveland in 1906 from Worcester, Massachusetts, when the American Steel and Wire Company, where they worked, opened a branch here and offered its employees a 33 percent raise if they would move to the Midwest. They would help get Cleveland started on a path that would make it, in the first half of the twentieth century, the wire center of the world. Doubling in number in seven years, the Armenians began to leave the mills to work as merchants and craftsmen. Armenians are independent, and, although they gathered at a coffeehouse on the corner of East 71st Street at Broadway Avenue long enough before the First World War to develop two political parties, they never settled into an Armenian neighborhood. The community was not big enough nor prosperous enough to think of establishing a church until it reached about 1,500 after the Second World War. By then it was divided by its political parties. The Dashnaks (the Armenian Revolutionary Federation) are the largest political party in diaspora Armenia.[16] The most liberal and nationalistic of the Armenian political parties (there are a lot of them), the Dashnaks organized the Armenian Community Center and Holy Cross Church now on Wallings Road in North Royalton. Despite their American and international numbers, the Dashnak's Holy Cross Church has never been as economically successful as St. Gregory of Narek. The more conservative Ramgavars (the Armenian Democratic Liberal Party) established St. Gregory by buying a seven-acre lot in 1958. It included the frame house that is now the church office. Both Armenian communities draw members from all over northeast Ohio. Neighborhood geography was not a consideration in establishing either church.

St. Gregory of Narek was a tenth-century monk and poet whose *Book of Lamentations,* or *Book of Narek,* is a key document in the development of the Armenian language and of Armenian Christian spirituality.[17] His church in Cleveland was dedicated in 1964. A companion education building behind the church was dedicated in 1972.

In a tragedy paralleled only by the Jews, Armenian identity was shaped in the twentieth century by an Old World catastrophe. Between 1915 and 1916, the Turks killed at least a quarter and perhaps half of the people in Armenia. The world seethed in outrage (but did not do anything about it).[18] After the First World War, Woodrow Wilson attempted to carve out of Turkey a generous "Wilsonian Armenia," but that did not materialize. Neither did a proposed League of Nations' American mandate to protect Armenia. Perhaps as a result of this tragedy, Cleveland Armenia maintains much closer ties with its homeland than any other nationality group, and the Cleveland community continues to benefit from infusions of immigrants from the Middle East. The Armenian church plays a major role in the Armenian diaspora because of the importance of church membership in Armenian identify.[19]

Part of the charm of this church is its surroundings. Although it is located along busy Richmond Road and across the street from the giant commercial buildings and parking lots of Richmond Town Square, St. Gregory of Narek is cleverly sited in the middle of what appears to be seven acres of grass. That it shares its lot with the original frame rectory, a substantial education building, and several parking lots does not detract from the focus of the grassy campus on the church. This siting, unique in Cleveland, makes St. Gregory of Narek a Pisan *Campo dei Miracoli* in miniature. Siting may be the reason why this church is held in such high esteem.

St. Gregory of Narek Church, like the Shiva Vishnu Temple in Parma (see p. 302), is an interesting essay in how American religious institutions adapt foreign traditions to the demands, expectations, and resources of their twentieth-century membership. The massing of St. Gregory of Narek, its general plan and elevation, is Armenian. The execution is American. Christianity has been in Armenia for a long time; its churches have been there for just about as long. Churches in Armenia are generally masonry, with narrow, unglazed windows, and with little church furniture or interior decoration.[20] Plumbing, heating, lighting, and parking lots are recent and rudimentary. St. Gregory of Narek, in contrast, is a brick building with large, glazed windows. Brick, in Armenia, would be associated with the Russians. Above the central-plan brick church is a stucco tower, punctured with windows in the drum, under a plain cone roof. Stone trim is limited, except for a delightful little stone arcade at the rear of the building beside the entrance. Across from the entrance and located at the back of the lot stands the complementary educational and social building.

Entering from the west, one finds a large narthex, without decoration except for one crystal chandelier. Traditional narthexes in Armenia are large to accommodate the complexities of the liturgy. This is another church that appears smaller on the inside than on the outside. The two-hundred-seat sanctuary is a plain, wide rectangle with little decoration. Levels are important in the Armenian liturgy and three steps lead up to a large, stained, light-wood altar in the apse with a painting of *Mother and Child*.[21] There are no frescoes, mosaics, or iconostasis—although there is a runner for a curtain that is pulled across the apse during part of the liturgy. St. Gregory has no balcony. Organ, pulpit, two large stained-glass windows of the *Nativity* and the *Resurrection,* glazed windows of religious figures in the drum of the tower, and pews are American innovations. Traditional Armenian congregations stand during the Liturgy; they consider sitting a mark of disrespect. Walls are plain. Four large crystal chandeliers hang in the nave, elegant but not ostentatious, and a smaller chandelier hangs in the apse. One finds a few movable paintings and a few examples of the Armenian blooming cross, the "Cross of Resurrection." Flanking the entrance to the nave from the narthex, two thin pilasters are topped by small, simple, and exquisite capitals with Armenian decoration. On an altar to the right of the chancel, under a large portrait of this *St. Gregory,* rests a copy of his *Book of Lamentations.*

Notes

Preface

1. See their acknowledgments, xi–xii, *A Guide to Cleveland's Sacred Landmarks*.

2. While it is easy to be critical of the eclectic use of medieval styles by nineteenth- and early twentieth-century midwest architects, we need to be wary of ascribing too much "purity" to the European architecture which began to be built in the eighth century. Roger Stalley reminds us, "From time to time modern writers have questioned whether the notion of the 'Romanesque style' has any validity. So much variation exists between different regions in planning, structure, and sculptural embellishment, that it is easy to despair of finding any consistency. It is obvious, however, that architects in widely differing areas employed similar techniques to give expression to their buildings. Rather than insisting on Romanesque as a unified style, it is more useful to think of it in terms of a language, utilized by local masons according to their own traditions and aesthetic choices" (*Early Medieval Architecture*, 211).

3. For starters, Old Stone is oriented toward the north, Saint Peter south, Trinity Cathedral south, Zion Lutheran west, First Methodist south, St. Paul Shrine south, St. Timothy north, and Calvary Presbyterian south.

4. The careful reader of this guide will identify one institution that is questionably in Cuyahoga County.

5. Stalley, *Early Medieval Architecture*, 38.

Acknowledgments

1. Although the *Encyclopedia* is available on the Internet, and some of its articles are updated, most articles concerning churches and religious and ethnic communities have not been revised. Citations in this guide are to the first printed edition. The editors of the *Encyclopedia* invite contributions as the printed *Encyclopedia* is now more than twenty years old.

2. Johannesen, *Cleveland Architecture*.

3. Kaczynski, *People of Faith*.

4. At least one other denomination, in fact, has. See Moore, *Tapestry of Faith*.

5. Kent, Ohio: Kent State University Press, 2008.

6. Kent, Ohio: Kent State University Press, 1999.

7. Cleveland Heights, Ohio: St. Paul's, 1967.

8. Cleveland Heights, Ohio: St. Ann Parish, 1990.

9. *Gamut*, Special Issue, 1990, 45–69.

10. Cleveland: St. Patrick, 1998.

11. Cleveland: Temple Tifereth Israel, 1999.

12. Sacred Landmarks Monograph Series, Ed. Susan Petrone. (Cleveland: Cleveland State Univ., 2000).

13. Virginia Beach, Virginia: Donning, 1994.

14. Cleveland: Church of the Covenant, 1995.

15. Cleveland: Euclid Avenue Congregational Church, 1997.

16. See Davis, *Second Chance,* his story about St. Philip's Christian Church.

17. Mt. Pleasant, South Carolina, 2009, 2010, and 2011.

18. Cleveland: Landmark's Press, 2010.

Introduction

1. Uniformity of style continues in Cleveland among the "Georgian Revival" churches. See the almost identical Archwood UCC and West Park UCC (pp. 226 and 270). See also their similarity with Christ Episcopal (p. 340), St. Dominic (p. 338), Plymouth (p. 335), and First Unitarian (p. 342).

2. There are some important exceptions to this generalization. The signature spire, cladding, and massing of Mormon churches, Kirtland Temple aside, have a remarkable uniformity. The Islamic Center of Cleveland, the Shiva Vishnu Temple, and many of the Eastern Catholic and Orthodox churches certainly have the "look" of their denomination.

3. There are a few defiant holdouts.

4. St. Charles Borromeo Parish in Parma with 12,000 members (more than twice as many as Parkside, Cleveland's largest mega church) has eight masses every weekend.

5. Until relatively recently (see Parkside Church, p. 362) Cleveland clergy, with the exception of Abba Hillel Silver whose congregation expanded into Severance Hall during High Holy Days, did not draw the crowds that some princes of the platform and pulpit attracted in other cities. With the exception of 2,900-seat St. Colman (see p. 254), Cleveland built nothing to compare with Charles Grandison Finney's three thousand-seat Broadway Tabernacle, Henry Ward Beecher's two-thousand-seat Plymouth Church in Brooklyn, and similar gigantic auditorium churches. See Loveland and Wheeler, *From Meetinghouse to Megachurch,* and Kilde, *When Church Became Theatre.* A smaller—and modified—version of the Broadway Tabernacle was built for Finney, by then professor of theology at Oberlin, as the 1844 Oberlin Meetinghouse.

6. St. Christopher was removed from the Roman calendar in 1969, and July 25 is now usually celebrated as the Feast of St. James the Apostle.

7. With one exception, they all have them now.

8. Bishop Rappe's successors continued the struggle to control the growth of their diocese with mixed results.

9. Parkside Church, p. 362, is on the border of Cuyahoga and Geauga Counties.

10. It used to be that Roman Catholic St. Paul was easily distinguished from Episcopal St. Paul's by the possessive. No longer.

1. Sacred Landmarks in the Dual Hub Corridor

1. Van Tassel and Grabowski, *Encyclopedia of Cleveland History,* 998.

2. Rebecca and Lorenzo Carter, in their log cabin, were the only residents of Cleveland in the eighteenth century. Rebecca organized Old Stone Church; her husband organized the first tavern.

3. For Old Stone Church, see Tuve, *Old Stone Church;* Armstrong, *Guide,* 9–11; Johannesen, *Cleveland Architecture,* 5 and 18–19; and Van Tassel and Grabowski, *Encyclopedia of Cleveland History,* 403–4, 14–15, 494, 496–97, 789–90, and 874.

4. The establishment did include a handful of Episcopalians.

5. See Robinson, *Gilead* and also *Home.* For a lucid discussion of the complex interrelationships between the Presbyterians and Congregationalists, see the early chapters of Applegate's *The Most Famous Man in America.* Although the members of Old Stone always considered themselves Presbyterians, all their clergy who served before 1835 were Congregational. Denominational affiliation in the early nineteenth century was complicated by an extremely fluid relationship among Protestants. A couple representing the American Sunday School Union arrived in Cleveland and revitalized Old Stone's Sunday school and then did the same for the Episcopalians, the Baptists, and the Methodists. David Long, the first physician in Cleveland and one of the founders of what became Trinity Episcopal Cathedral (see p. 21), was also a trustee of Old Stone and a member of its Sunday school; he rented pews in both churches.

6. Although it became a department of Western Reserve College, the medical school never moved to Hudson. Moving instead to East Ninth Street at St. Clair Avenue, it was an autonomous institution, frequently at odds with its university for fifty years, until falling under the supervision of the Western Reserve trustees in 1893. Hiram Collins Haydn, Old Stone's third pastor and also president of Western Reserve College from 1887 to 1889, was the person most responsible for moving the struggling institution, which had originally been established for the education of Presbyterian clergy, to Cleveland from Hudson.

7. The same honor was accorded James Garfield in 1881 and William McKinley in 1901. More people viewed Garfield than had viewed Lincoln.

8. William Miller, founder of Millerism, declared that he anticipated the Second Coming to occur between April 14, 1843, and April 14, 1844.

9. Perfectionism is the theory that sanctification is possible in this life and that we are competent witnesses of this. This theory was particularly associated with Oberlin College, an institution with which Old Stone had a close relationship.

10. The Judicial Committee of the Cuyahoga Sabbath Society, of which Old Stone was a member, tried several cases of persons accused of having dishonored their Christian profession by investing in railroads that ran on Sundays.

11. Van Tassel and Grabowski, *Encyclopedia of Cleveland History,* 665.

12. Since 1920, the Goodrich-Gannett Center has received increasing support from the Community Chest.

13. See Tuve, "The Turbulent Decades," *Old Stone Church,* 23–35.

14. Johannesen, *Cleveland Architecture,* 5.

15. Tuve, *Old Stone Church,* 32. Falling steeples are a staple of Cleveland religious history, but most consider this incident the most spectacular.

16. The 1943 death of Amasa Stone's niece Elder Emma Stone Raymond, who had lived in her 3826 Euclid Avenue mansion all her life, finally severed the connection of Old Stone with Millionaire's Row.

17. Everett built the largest house in Cleveland so he could entertain Andrew Carnegie, J. P. Morgan, Ulysses Grant, Rutherford Hayes, William McKinley, and William Howard Taft.

18. For the cathedral, see Lyons and Jurgens, *Life and Times;* Wiatrowski, *Ca-*

thedral of Saint John the Evangelist; Armstrong, *Guide,* 12–13; Hynes, *Parishes,* 9–36; Johannesen, *Cleveland Architecture,* 200–201; Kaczynski, *People of Faith,* x–xviii and 15–18; and Van Tassel and Grabowski, *Encyclopedia of Cleveland History,* 856, 162–64, 513, 821, and 860–61.

19. After its parishioners departed for the cathedral, St. Mary-on-the-Flats became a temporary home for new nationality parishes: Historic Saint Peter (German; 1853–54; see p. 18); St. Mary's of the Assumption (German; 1854–65; demolished 1968); St. Malachi (Irish; 1865–68; see p. 183); St. Procop (Czech; 1872; see p. 238); St. Stanislaus (Polish; 1873–79; see p. 172); and Annunciation (French; 1879; demolished 1924). St. Mary-on-the-Flats was demolished in 1888.

20. For a discussion of attempts to move the cathedral, see Wiatrowski, *Cathedral of Saint John the Evangelist,* 10–14.

21. The oldest parish in Cleveland was St. Mary-on-the-Flats, established in 1835. St. Mary-on-the-Flats church was built in 1840 and demolished in 1888. The oldest existing Roman Catholic place of worship in Cleveland is the Cathedral of St. John the Evangelist, established in 1847, built in 1852, and drastically reconstructed in 1948. For Historic Saint Peter, see Armstrong, *Guide,* 14–15; Hynes, *Parishes,* 164–66; Kaczynski, *People of Faith,* 331–33; Van Tassel and Grabowski, *Encyclopedia of Cleveland History,* 447–40 and 862; and First, *Founded in Faith,* 16–23.

22. German Jesuits fleeing Bismarck were asked, in 1880, to establish a college in Cleveland; they were assigned St. Mary's of the Assumption. In 1935, their higher-education activities were moved to John Carroll University in University Heights. Their church suffered several disastrous mishaps (fire in 1893 and lightning in 1925); it was finally demolished in 1968 and replaced with a science center for St. Ignatius High School.

23. St. Joseph, rebuilt after a dynamiting the night of the controversial execution of the anarchists Ferdinando Sacco and Bartolomeo Vanzetti in August 1927, could not survive urban renewal and freeway construction. Abandoned, the ruins were demolished after being gutted by a fire in 1993.

24. Cleveland weather has not proved congenial to the maintenance of steeples. Tornadoes swept away the landmark steeples of St. Malachi, and, most disastrously, both of those of St. Stanislaus, a 1909 catastrophe which resulted in the death of a small child.

25. A picture of the school appears in Armstrong, *Guide,* 14–15.

26. *Hallenkirchen,* in which the side aisles rise to the height of the central nave, became popular in thirteenth-century Germany. The side aisles brace the central vault and obviate the necessity of the flying buttresses associated with Gothic churches in France. Hallenkirchen are better lighted than French Gothic cathedrals, and the interior space is more unified and free-flowing (less narrow and divided). St. Elizabeth, Marburg (1233–83), is the most famous example.

27. Subsequent "firsts" were First Presbyterian (Old Stone Church; 1820), St. Mary-on-the-Flats (1826), First Methodist (1827), St. John A.M.E. (1830), First Baptist (1833), Schifflein Christi (Lutheran; 1834) and the Israelitic Society of Cleveland (Anshe Chesed-Fairmount Temple; 1839). The first church established in Cuyahoga County was the First Presbyterian Church of East Cleveland (1807). For Trinity, see Armstrong, *Guide,* 16–19; Johannesen, *Cleveland Architecture,* 78 and 88–89; and Van Tassel and Grabowski, *Encyclopedia of Cleveland History,* 981–82, 375–77, 601, 625–26, and 874.

28. This is now Ohio City. In the very early nineteenth century, the village of Brooklyn extended northward along the west side of the Cuyahoga River.

29. Johannesen, *Walker and Weeks,* 111.

30. The first was Ralph Adams Cram's and Bertram Goodhue's 1894 All Saints Episcopal Church in Boston.

31. The Episcopal Cathedral seats about half as many worshipers as a typical Roman Catholic parish church.

32. Johannesen, *Cleveland Architecture,* 88.

33. The cathedral's original organist, Edwin Arthur Kraft (ninety-three others competed for the job), served for fifty-three years. He is remembered by two large windows on either side of the narthex. His specialty was "The Ride of the Valkyries," at the climax of which a special trombone stop spoke through a grate from the crypt. Kraft died following a performance of the "Ride" at the Fairmount Presbyterian Church (see p. 327). Van Tassel and Grabowski, *Encyclopedia of Cleveland History,* 601.

34. William Willet (1869–1921), in partnership with his wife, designed "Early School" (Gothic Revival) glass in protest to Tiffany's opalescent glass. Charles Connick (1875–1945) was, according to *The New York Times,* "the world's greatest artisan on stained windows." Clement Heaton (1861–1940) was a principal in an English firm with a window in Westminster Abbey. Hardman & Co. made the glass for the new Houses of Parliament (1850s). Wilbur H. Burnham was a Boston designer associated with Connick in the early twentieth century.

Michael Tevesz et al. have discussed the Burnham glass in detail, and their *Stained Glass Windows of Trinity Cathedral, Cleveland, Ohio* should be consulted.

35. For Zion Lutheran, see Armstrong, *Guide,* 20–21, and Van Tassel and Grabowski, *Encyclopedia of Cleveland History,* 1080, 645–46, and 1023.

36. For Schifflein Christi, see Van Tassel and Grabowski, *Encyclopedia of Cleveland History,* 872; and Greater Friendship Baptist Church (originally First Evangelical and Reformed Church; p. 101). After many transformations, Schifflein Christi became part of Fellowship United Church of Christ in Wickliffe in 1969.

37. For First Church, see Armstrong, *Guide,* 22–23; Johannesen, *Cleveland Architecture,* 80–81; Moore, *Tapestry of Faith,* 61–64; and Van Tassel and Grabowski, *Encyclopedia of Cleveland History,* 404, 352, and 678–79.

38. Johannesen, *Cleveland Architecture,* 80–81. First Church was completed in 1905. Trinity was planned and built from 1895 to 1907.

39. Ibid., 45. For Johannesen's description of Dyer's work, see 43–45, 75, 79–83, 99, and 193–94.

40. Ibid., 193.

41. An alternative story is that no one would pay the $0.25 due on the recorder's fee on the deed.

42. "Methodists," 678.

43. See this church; University Circle United Methodist Church (originally Epworth-Euclid Methodist Church; p. 47); Cory United Methodist Church (p. 97); St. John A.M.E. Church (p. 126); Lane Metropolitan C.M.E. Church (p. 127); St. James A.M.E. Church (p. 136); Broadway United Methodist Church (p. 168); Shaffer United Methodist Church (p. 177); Brooklyn Memorial United Methodist Church (p. 227); Christ United Methodist Church (p. 263); Lakewood United Methodist Church (p. 282); Pleasant Hills United Methodist Church (p. 301);

Quinn Chapel A.M.E. Church (p. 160); Church of the Saviour (p. 325); and Windermere United Methodist Church (p. 103). See also Moore, *Tapestry of Faith.*

44. For St. Paul Shrine, see Wilson, *Famous Old Euclid Avenue of Cleveland,* 152–59; Cigliano, *Showplace of America,* 263–64; and Jarvis, *St. Paul's,* 1–33. For more recent history, see Armstrong, *Guide,* 24–25; Hynes, *Parishes,* 162–64; Johannesen, *Cleveland Architecture,* 17–18; Kaczynski, *People of Faith,* 40–42, 475–77, and 494; and Van Tassel and Grabowski, *Encyclopedia of Cleveland History,* 862.

45. Jarvis, *St. Paul's,* 41

46. Ibid., 20.

47. Johannesen, *Cleveland Architecture,* 17. Others describe the tower as "unusual," see *A Tour of St. Paul's Episcopal Church.*

48. This altar is now in the St. Martin Chapel of St. Paul's Cleveland Heights (see p. 329). The "high church" ultimately triumphed at St. Paul's Cleveland when it sold itself to the Roman Catholic Diocese.

49. Jarvis, *St. Paul's,* 1.

50. For St. Timothy, see Armstrong, *Guide,* 26–27; and *68th Church Anniversary and Homecoming—St. Timothy.*

51. R. J. Landgraf, conversation with the author, January 21, 2009.

52. For Calvary, see Armstrong, *Guide,* 30–31; Johannesen, *Cleveland Architecture,* 18–19; and Van Tassel and Grabowski, *Encyclopedia of Cleveland History,* 151, 494, and 874.

53. If this sounds familiar, see Temple Tifereth Israel (the Temple), p. 44, and Temple Tifereth Israel East, p. 344, and the Park Synagogue, p. 315, and Park Synagogue East, p. 345.

54. Johannesen, *Cleveland Architecture,* 18.

55. For Liberty Hill, see Armstrong, *Guide,* 32–33 and Van Tassel and Grabowski, *Encyclopedia of Cleveland History,* 36–37, 123, 287, 586, 839, and 1059–60.

56. For Transfiguration, see Armstrong, *Guide,* 34–35 and Van Tassel and Grabowski, *Encyclopedia of Cleveland History,* 375.

57. He wrote a famous essay about it, now in *Ornament and Crime: Selected Essays.* Riverside, California: Ariadne, 1997.

58. There does not seem to be a close correlation between the relative completeness of decoration, once it has gotten substantially started, and the relative completeness of a Gothic or Romanesque Revival structure. Many Cleveland revival buildings appear complete even though they are not completely decorated. After the Stone sisters completed the structure of their Amasa Stone Chapel, for example, see p. 51, Clara Stone Hay gave its magnificent south window in memory of her sister, anticipating that other donors in time would glaze all of the building. This has not happened, but the Stone Chapel with its rich furnishings presents itself as a complete ensemble. Emmanuel-Transfiguration, in contrast, almost undecorated, presents a sadly unfinished appearance.

59. Although cyclonic winds have taken a historic toll of steeples in Cleveland, particularly among Roman Catholic churches, they have spared towers, or towers have been rebuilt. It is not unknown, of course, for towers to be built the old-fashioned medieval way, several centuries at a time. Cram's 1919 St. Mark's Pro-Cathedral in Hastings, Nebraska, was without its Ellis tower until 2000.

60. Euclid Avenue Congregational is blessed with a superb congregational history by the prize-winning Carol Poh Miller. See Miller, *This Far by Faith;* see also

Armstrong, *Guide*, 36–37; and Van Tassel and Grabowski, *Encyclopedia of Cleveland History*, 380–81, 103, 293–94, and 414.

61. Attorney H. Clark Ford's success in obtaining clear title to this property became the basis of the endowment that ensured Euclid Avenue Congregational's survival in the second half of the twentieth century.

62. This is not to be confused with the 1807 First Presbyterian Church of East Cleveland, located in 1810 at 16200 Euclid Avenue in East Cleveland and until 2009, the oldest religious organization in Cuyahoga County.

63. Miller, *This Far by Faith*, 16.

64. Johannesen, *Cleveland Architecture*, 9.

65. Their long-since demolished 1881 Blackstone Building is important in the history of modern architecture. John Edelman, who grew up in Cleveland and worked on the Blackstone Building in the Coburn and Barnum office, went on to become foreman of William LeBaron Jenney's drafting room in Chicago and later office foreman for Dankmar Adler. Louis Sullivan "referred to Edelman as his mentor and credited him with inspiring the concept of 'form follows function'" (Johannesen, *Cleveland Architecture*, 9).

66. At the end of the nineteenth century, the Congregationalists appeared a good deal more militant than today. There is a similar drill room in the 1893 Pilgrim Congregational Church in Tremont (see p. 201).

67. Louise Woodward, "strumming her guitar" (Miller, *This Far by Faith*, 28), would assemble an audience, and then Giuseppe Zottarelli, the Italian-speaking Oberlin theological student recruited by Euclid Congregational, would conduct the devotions.

68. On High Holy Days, Euclid Congregational opened its doors to the overflow from Euclid Avenue Temple.

69. Miller, *This Far by Faith*, 35–93.

70. Ibid., 88.

71. Ibid., 87.

72. For an excellent discussion of Islam in Cleveland, see Mbaye Lo's *Muslims in America*. Despite its title, this book is primarily concerned with Cleveland. For the Uqbah Mosque Foundation, see Lo, *Muslims*, 100–102.

73. The Islamic Center of Cleveland (see p. 300) had begun at CWRU about twenty years before. By 1968 they had moved to a duplex over on Detroit Avenue.

74. NAIT has an interest in one out of four mosques in North America—three hundred properties. NAIT does not administer these institutions but supports, advises, and extends interest-free loans in conformity with Sharia.

75. See Lo, *Muslims*, for an excellent discussion of the evolution of Islam in Cleveland's African American community.

76. Private First Class Frank Petrarca of the Thirty-Seventh Infantry Division was posthumously awarded the first Ohio Congressional Medal of Honor during the Second World War.

77. For the Pentecostal Church of Christ, see Armstrong, *Guide*, 40–41.

78. The Sixth Church was formed on the west side in 1922 from members of the third and fifth. There was also a seventh and an eighth.

79. Chris Krosel, director of archival research for the Catholic Diocese of Cleveland, emphasized (2008 interview) that Pentecostalism, stylistically, is "a very

large tent" with a great deal of parochial freedom in liturgy, practice, and decoration. Pentecostals, she said, frequently retain as much as possible of the decoration of the churches they acquire, including such decoration as stations of the cross that we may closely associate with the Roman Catholic Church.

80. The history of congregation Tifereth Israel is divided to reflect what happened in each of its landmark buildings. For 1850–1924, see Friendship Baptist Church, p. 130; and Dancyger, *Temple-Tifereth Israel,* 1–15. Tifereth Israel's history from 1924 to 1970 is in chapter 1; see also Dancyger, *Temple-Tifereth Israel,* 16–77. For 1970 to the present, see the Temple Tifereth Israel East, p. 344, and Dancyger, *Temple-Tifereth Israel,* 78–157. See also Armstrong, *Guide,* 42–43; Johannesen, *Cleveland Architecture,* 150–60; and Van Tassel and Grabowski, *Encyclopedia of Cleveland History,* 960–61.

81. See Van Tassel and Grabowski, *Encyclopedia of Cleveland History,* 892.

82. Ibid.

83. Silver, *Temple Year Book.*

84. Dancyger, *Temple-Tifereth Israel,* 26.

85. Armstrong, *Guide,* 43.

86. Quoted by Dancyger, *Temple-Tifereth Israel,* 55.

87. The oil can, once ubiquitous in American households, farms, and shops, is now obsolete. Only one company still makes them and it gave several hundred of its last production run to University Circle Methodist, which hands them out to new members.

88. For University Circle Methodist, see Armstrong, *Guide,* 44–45; Johannesen, *Cleveland Architecture,* 160–61 (and 52–53); Moore, *Tapestry of Faith,* 52 (and 56–58); and Van Tassel and Grabowski, *Encyclopedia of Cleveland History,* 377, 378, and 802.

89. The four blue lancet windows, one hundred feet above the floor, are actually nine feet tall.

90. Johannesen, *Cleveland Architecture,* 160–61.

91. Goodhue was, in fact, born in Pomfret, Connecticut.

92. Johannesen, *Cleveland Architecture,* 170.

93. Whitaker, *Bertram Grosvenor Goodhue,* 27, quoted by Johannesen, *Cleveland Architecture,* 161.

94. See McCready, "The Nebraska State Capitol."

95. Goodhue's most famous students were Raymond Hood, designer of the Tribune Tower in Chicago, and Wallace Harrison, designer of the United Nations Headquarters in New York and the Metropolitan Opera House at Lincoln Center in New York. Although Epworth Euclid is always given to Goodhue, it was his last commission and he completed only preliminary sketches before his unexpected death in 1924. Presentation and working drawings were by Walker and Weeks, and they supervised construction from 1926 to 1928.

96. Mont St. Michel had no gym; however, when it was used as a prison, it did have a hoisting treadmill to entertain the prisoners.

97. For a more detailed history of these churches, see Moore, *Tapestry of Faith,* 56–60.

98. Charles and John Wesley were born at Epworth Rectory in Lincolnshire.

99. Johannesen, *Cleveland Architecture,* 52

100. Moore, *Tapestry of Faith,* 57.

101. Another congregation, the Wade Park Methodist Episcopal Church, was established in 1889 as an overflow from the Euclid Avenue church. Wade Park Methodist built a substantial Gothic Revival building at East 86th Street and Wade Park Avenue. Merging with Epworth-Euclid in 1962, the building was sold to the St. Matthew United Methodist Church.

102. Although the chapel was given jointly by Mrs. Mather and her sister, Clara Stone Hay, Flora Stone Mather appears to have taken the lead in this project, as she did in so many other projects in Cleveland.

103. Walter Leedy wrote in detail about the circumstances of this commission. See Leedy, "Henry Vaughan's Cleveland Commission." This was based on Leedy's paper "Hail, Holy Light: The Amasa Stone Memorial Chapel." See also Armstrong, *Guide,* 46–47; Johannesen, *Cleveland Architecture,* 99; and Van Tassel and Grabowski, *Encyclopedia of Cleveland History,* 22, 493–94, 665–66, and 926–27.

104. Magdalen Tower was also the model for that of Windermere United Methodist Church, see p. 103.

105. Wilder, papers of Old Stone Church.

106. For beautiful pictures and helpful descriptions of the Church of the Covenant, see Horstman, *The Covenant Proclaims.* For her usual compelling narrative of this congregation's history, see Miller, *Church with a Conscience.* Miller's book won the 1996 Robert Lee Stowe Award of the national Presbyterian Historical Society. See also Armstrong, *Guide,* 48–49; Johannesen, *Cleveland Architecture,* 100; and Van Tassel and Grabowski, *Encyclopedia of Cleveland History,* 183–85 and 98.

107. Third Presbyterian evolved into Miles Park Presbyterian.

108. This is according to Hiram Haydn, pastor of Old Stone. See Miller, *Church with a Conscience,* 5.

109. T. Sterling Beckwith established a fund to finance Presbyterian Churches. Beckwith funds also financed St. John's Beckwith Memorial Church, a Presbyterian institution in Little Italy at the corner of Murray Hill Road at Paul Avenue. Beckwith's 1863 Euclid Avenue home was formerly the University Club.

110. The third pastor was James Williamson of Beckwith Memorial, part of the third generation of a remarkable legal and entrepreneurial family that had prospered in Cleveland since its beginning. James Williamson's older and reigning brother died unexpectedly in 1903 as the family was completing the eighteen-story Williamson Building on Public Square, the tallest building in Cleveland at that time. James Williamson withdrew from the active ministry to manage his family's interests but continued at the Church of the Covenant as president of its Society (Corporation). Cram's Williamson Chancel is named for James. The Williamson Building was spectacularly demolished in 1982 for construction of the Sohio Building.

111. *The Euclid Avenue Presbyterian Church,* n.p. The "apostle of Gothicism," often described as a "prolific writer," said elsewhere, "So far as the art expression of religion is concerned, nothing has happened since the fall of Constantinople in which we need display any particular interest." Quote by Miller, *Church with a Conscience,* 15.

112. Tittle, 233. Tittle discusses Florence Harkness Severance on 227–33. For Harkness Chapel, see Armstrong, *Guide,* 50–51; Johannesen, *Cleveland Architecture,* 59–61; and Van Tassel and Grabowski, *Encyclopedia of Cleveland History,* 487–88.

113. Johannesen, *Cleveland Architecture,* 60. The Stone Chapel (see p. 51) is a later, more archaeologically exact, development of this style.

114. For Mt. Zion Congregational, see Armstrong, *Guide,* 52–53 and Van Tassel and Grabowski, *Encyclopedia of Cleveland History,* 697.

115. Zion Congregational has been plagued, during its more than a century and a half of existence, with clergy who were ailing, moving, or being promoted. Richard Andrews, who built the present building, served for twenty-one years, the longest tenured pastor in the church's history.

116. "Membership in Mt. Zion has traditionally included many of the city's black leaders and professionals," and it is "known for serving an upper-class leadership elite in the black community" (Van Tassel and Grabowski, *Encyclopedia of Cleveland History,* 697, 294).

117. For Holy Rosary, see Armstrong, *Guide,* 54–55; Hynes, *Parishes,* 51–53; Kaczynski, *People of Faith,* 63–65, 415–16, and 479–80; and Van Tassel and Grabowski, *Encyclopedia of Cleveland History,* 516–17, 559–61, and 638.

118. It is attended, according to Cleveland State University's Neighborhood Link, www.nhlink.net, by "crowds of up to 100,000 in a single night."

119. Parochialism, from the historic disinterest of inhabitants of the Italian peninsula in anything out of earshot of the bells of their church's *campanile:* "Cleveland's Italians lacked any sense of national identity. Italy for them was the village from which they came. What the Italians brought to Cleveland were the traditions, values, patron saints, and dialects from the villages they represented. Their affinities and affiliations were largely with their *paesani* (fellow villagers) . . . Each group of *paesani* feared being absorbed by Cleveland's greater Italian community" (Van Tassel and Grabowski, *Encyclopedia of Cleveland History,* 559, 560). To understand early Italian-American history, see Martin Scorsese's 2007 film *The Golden Door.* An Italian consciousness became widespread in the 1930s, and, by the end of the Second World War the inhabitants of Little Italy were Americans of Italian descent.

120. City Architecture's eight awards for reconstruction of this building include the Cleveland Restoration Society's Adaptive Reuse of a Sacred Landmark Award, the Cleveland chapter of the American Institute of Architects' Preservation Recognition Award, the Northern Ohio Live Award of Achievement, and the Ohio Historic Preservation Office's Award of Merit for Historic Preservation. Another example of the splendid restoration of a religious building for a nonreligious purpose is the Ratner School, formerly B'rith Emeth Temple and then Park Synagogue East, see p. 347. For this building, see Armstrong, *Guide,* 56–57; Johannesen, *Cleveland Architecture,* 201 and 161–63; Van Tassel and Grabowski, *Encyclopedia of Cleveland History,* 183; Fisher, "Ideas Made Here"; and Lewis, "Wizards of Wal-Mart," 34.

121. City Architects, Renovation and Restoration, Nottingham Spirk

122. There is no relationship. Both John Nottingham and John Spirk are from Pittsburgh.

123. Johannesen, *Walker and Weeks,* 99–101.

124. Ibid., 101.

125. For the circumstances of Garfield's death, see Ackerman, *Dark Horse.*

126. Garfield was the progenitor of a large and distinguished Cleveland family: Abram Garfield was founder of the architecture firm that became Westlake, Reed, Leskosky; Henry Augustus Garfield served as fuel administrator (akin to the secretary

of energy) during World War I and later president of Williams College; and James Rudolph Garfield was secretary of the interior under Theodore Roosevelt.

127. For the Garfield Memorial, see Armstrong, *Guide*, 58–59, and Johannesen, *Cleveland Architecture*, 63–64.

128. Johannesen, *Cleveland Architecture*, 63–64.

129. Ibid., 63.

130. For the Wade Chapel, see Armstrong, *Guide*, 60–61; Johannesen, *Cleveland Architecture*, 66–67; and Van Tassel and Grabowski, *Encyclopedia of Cleveland History*, 1021.

131. Including those of Laura Spelman Rockefeller, who waited in the Wade Chapel crypt for the resolution of a tax dispute between the locals and her husband.

132. The immensely wealthy Wade lived across Euclid Avenue from St. Paul Shrine (see p. 28). Although there are several versions of the story, all agree that Jeptha Wade gave the bells for the church on the understanding they would never be rung to disturb his Sunday morning while he was alive.

133. Johannesen, *Cleveland Architecture*, 66–67.

2. North Central Cleveland

1. Van Tassel and Grabowski, *Encyclopedia of Cleveland History*, 525–26.

2. The second Croatian Byzantine Catholic Church was Sts. Peter and Paul, established in Chicago in 1901. Sts. Peter and Paul closed in 1981. For Cleveland's St. Nicholas, see Armstrong, *Guide*, 67.

3. The building can also be entered through a handsome, functional entrance from the small church parking lot behind the building.

4. For North Presbyterian, see Armstrong, *Guide*, 68–69, and Van Tassel and Grabowski, *Encyclopedia of Cleveland History*, 723.

5. In the nineteenth century Protestants frequently used "Sunday school" as a euphemism for a congregation without full-time clergy.

6. North Presbyterian is said to have been named for the Old North Church in Boston. This is certainly curious as Old North Church, the oldest active church building in Boston, was and remains Anglican/Episcopal.

7. See Fidelity Baptist Church (p. 83), Pilgrim Congregational Church (p. 201), Lakewood United Methodist Church (p. 282), and St. John A.M.E. Church (p. 126).

8. For St. Paul's Croatian, see Armstrong, *Guide*, 70–71; Hynes, *Parishes*, 159–60; Kaczynski, *People of Faith*, 328–29 and Van Tassel and Grabowski, *Encyclopedia of Cleveland History*, 861–62 and 307–8.

9. Van Tassel and Grabowski, *Encyclopedia of Cleveland History*, 307.

10. The usual Roman Catholic practice in Cleveland was that a new parish—almost immediately—built a building to serve initially as both church and school. Next, the parish built a separate school building and then a church, at which point the original building became a gym/community center.

11. See also St. Nicholas Parish (Croatian), six blocks down Superior, p. 73.

12. For Immaculate Conception, see Armstrong, *Guide*, 72–73; Hynes, *Parishes*, 55–56; and Kaczynski, *People of Faith*, 76–77.

13. A "chapel of ease," a term used by Roman Catholics and Anglicans, is a church building other than the main church. Examples include St. Nicholas's Chapel in Hertfordshire, All Saints in West Sussex, and Our Lady of the Rosary and St. Albert the Great in Palo Alto.

14. For St. James Episcopal, see Armstrong, *Guide,* 76–77.

15. Most Episcopalians belong to the Episcopal Church—also known as the Protestant Episcopal Church in the United States—established by the remnant of the Church of England that survived the American Revolution. Cleveland Episcopal churches are part of the Diocese of Ohio, and that diocese's bishop has his seat at Trinity Cathedral (see p. 21). American primacy rests with the presiding bishop whose offices are in New York. The Episcopal Church is a province of the Anglican Communion, headed by the archbishop of Canterbury. The 1978 St. Louis division in the Episcopal Church is not related to more recent departures concerning the sexual orientation of clergy.

16. Jarvis, *St. Paul's,* 1.

17. For Fellowship Baptist, see Armstrong, *Guide,* 78–79.

18. The Phillis Wheatley Association was established in 1911 to offer residential, social service, and recreational opportunities to young women in the Cedar neighborhood. Their impressive building, now used as an apartment house, was built in 1927.

19. The thrifty Germans took their frame building apart and gave the pieces to a like-minded Lutheran parish in Elyria.

20. For Fidelity Baptist, see Armstrong, *Guide,* 80–81, and Van Tassel and Grabowski, *Encyclopedia of Cleveland History,* 65.

21. Compare this relatively modest building with the other Badgley churches in this book: St. Timothy Baptist (originally First United Presbyterian; 1891), p. 31; St. George Orthodox (originally Lincoln Park Methodist; 1892), p. 204; Pilgrim (1893), p. 201; St. John A.M.E. (1908), p. 126; and Lakewood Methodist (1913–14), p. 282.

22. Armstrong, *Guide,* 81.

23. Bobby's conclusion is part of a letter to Michael Tevesz of April 17, 2008.

24. Badgley liked to orient his main worship space, on entering, on an angle to the left. Pilgrim is oriented to the southwest and St. John to the northeast, reflecting, respectively, their entrances from the east and from the west.

25. For St. Vitus, see Boznar, *St. Vitus Church;* Armstrong, *Guide,* 82–83; Hynes, *Parishes,* 185–86; Kaczynski, *People of Faith,* 373–75; and Van Tassel and Grabowski, *Encyclopedia of Cleveland History,* 864 and 896–99.

26. Kaczynski, *People of Faith,* 373–74.

27. A substantial Slovene community remained in the Newburgh area and, eight years later, would organize St. Lawrence Church (see p. 170).

28. See Boznar, *St. Vitus Church,* 34–35.

29. The community eventually divided over support of the two rival groups resisting the German occupation of Slovenia: the Partisans, controlled by the Communists under Josip Broz Tito, versus the Catholic anti-Communists. Some of the recent iconography of the church illustrates St. Vitus's position, particularly the left-hand mural in the Marian shrine on the west side of the nave that highlights a large brutish Communist in uniform stabbing a helpless Slovene in the back.

30. See Robertson, *Greatest Thing.*

31. Roman Catholic churches, with their requirement that parishioners expeditiously make their way to the altar in the front of the church, usually have only a small balcony at the rear for organ and choir. Wraparound Wren-Gibbs balconies are usually found in Protestant churches. See http://ech.cwru.edu/ech-cgi/article.pl?id=EOGCEAF.

32. The shrine to Bernadette of Lourdes and the Infant Jesus of Prague may be coincidental additions or may be thank-yous for the long-ago help of Stefan Furdek and his Czech parish of Our Lady of Lourdes.

33. For the exciting details of St. Casimir's tempestuous history, see Armstrong, *Guide,* 84–85; Hynes, *Parishes,* 97–98; Kaczynski, *People of Faith,* 176–78; Van Tassel and Grabowski, *Encyclopedia of Cleveland History,* 772–75; Herman, *Cleveland's Vanishing Sacred Architecture,* 101–10; and First, *Founded in Faith,* 62–67.

34. Kaczynski, *People of Faith,* 178.

35. For the Hitchcock Center, see Armstrong, *Guide,* 86–87; Kaczynski, *People of Faith,* 508–9; and Van Tassel and Grabowski, *Encyclopedia of Cleveland History,* 860.

3. Northeast Cleveland

1. Van Tassel and Grabowski, *Encyclopedia of Cleveland History,* 453.

2. It is rendered both as "Forest Hill" and "Forest Hills." After the death of Laura Spelman Rockefeller in 1915, her family visited Forest Hill infrequently. John D. Rockefeller Jr. broke up the estate in the 1920s. New York architect Andrew J. Thomas designed eighty-one French Norman-style houses that were built in 1925 as part of a projected six-hundred-home development known as Forest Hills Park.

3. For Cory, see Armstrong, *Guide,* 96–97; Johannesen, *Cleveland Architecture,* 159; Moore, *Tapestry of Faith,* 44–46; Park Synagogue, "That Was Then," 1–2; and Van Tassel and Grabowski, *Encyclopedia of Cleveland History,* 300, 37, and 456–57.

4. All quotes are from the Park Synagogue, "That Was Then," except for "The schul with the pool," which was the generic description of Cory on the bus during Nate Arnold's 2008 Jewish Community Center "Jewish Cleveland Tour."

5. See Shiloh Baptist Church (p. 132), New Spirit Revival Center (p. 318), and B'nai Jeshurun Congregation (p. 349).

6. Park Synagogue, "That Was Then," 2.

7. For St. Aloysius (officially the parish of St. Aloysius/St. Agatha), see Armstrong, *Guide,* 98–99; Hynes, *Parishes,* 82–83, 134–36, 167–68; and Kaczynski, *People of Faith,* 140–41, 399–401, 411–12, and 339–40.

8. For Greater Friendship Baptist, see Armstrong, *Guide,* 100–101; and Van Tassel and Grabowski, *Encyclopedia of Cleveland History,* 872.

9. Charles E. Bolton was the father-in-law of Francis Payne Bolton.

10. Windermere ("Vinandr's Lake"), 10.5 miles long, is the largest lake in England.

11. For Windermere United Methodist, see Moore, *Tapestry of Faith,* 123–24, and Austin, *East of Cleveland.*

12. The name of Saul's uncle and Abner's father, Ner, was so obscure a biblical name that Stroup's 1900 yearbook at Drew Seminary misspelled it.

13. Austin, *East of Cleveland,*142.

14. Wyoming Territory gave women the territorial right to vote in 1869.

15. The Austin family continues to be an important patron of this church, greatly assisting—together with the Berea Children's Home—in the ambitious re-

cent rehabilitation of the building.

16. What is now the Berea Children's Home and Family Services began in 1864 as the German Methodist Orphan Asylum for Civil War orphans.

17. For Antioch Christian Fellowship, see "From Storefront to Stonefront," 24–25.

18. The irascible Chase was the first Episcopal bishop of Ohio and the first Episcopal bishop outside the original thirteen colonies. He founded Kenyon College and the Episcopal seminary, Bexley Hall. Although now on the track which leads to the equivalent of canonization in the Episcopal Church, Chase is not without his detractors. He left Ohio in a huff to become ultimately the bishop of Illinois and later the presiding bishop of the national Episcopal Church.

19. For First Presbyterian, see Ule-Grohol, *Spiritual Pioneers* and Van Tassel and Grabowski, *Encyclopedia of Cleveland History,* 404.

20. This church was established thirteen years before the First Presbyterian Church of Cleveland (the Old Stone Church; see p. 12) and nine years before Trinity Episcopal Church (subsequently Cathedral; see p. 21), the oldest religious institution in the city of Cleveland. "Old First" must be distinguished from the similarly named First Presbyterian Church of East Cleveland, begun as a Sunday school in 1828 at Doan's Corners by Sally Cozad Mather Hale, which evolved into the Euclid Avenue Congregational Church (see p. 38).

21. Ule-Grohol, *Spiritual Pioneers,* 31.

22. Ibid., 11.

23. Ibid., 17.

24. Ibid., 17.

25. Ibid., 20–21.

26. Ibid., 26.

27. Ibid., 28–29.

28. For St. Jerome, see Armstrong, *Guide,* 102–3; Hynes, *Parishes,* 128–29; and Kaczynski, *People of Faith,* 236–38.

29. See Michael Tevesz et al., *Stained Glass Windows of Trinity Cathedral.*

30. Unlike Jews and Protestants, who take off their coats when they enter a place of worship and, therefore, require coat racks or a coatroom at the back of the sanctuary, Roman Catholics traditionally leave their coats on or fold them up and put the bundle beside them in the pew. The result is that the traditional Roman Catholic narthex is just large enough so that the nave does not open directly on the street.

31. Missouri Synod Lutheran churches frequently have "Evangelical" in their name although they proudly maintain their separation from the ECLA. The full name of this church, for example, is St. John Evangelical Lutheran Church.

32. For St. John Nottingham, see Armstrong, *Guide,* 106–7.

33. Kudokas, like many in the congregation, was a Lithuanian professional in exile and unlicensed in Ohio. Kudokas designed the church and supervised the construction; Boccia signed the plans. The construction of Our Lady of Perpetual Help tried to be an all-Lithuanian affair. During construction, Father Angelaitis reportedly spent much of his time keeping construction unions at bay to allow the nonunion work (much of it volunteer) of members of his congregation; see Gaidziunas, *Our Lady of Perpetual Help,* 75.

34. For Our Lady of Perpetual Help, see Armstrong, *Guide,* 108; Hynes, *Parishes,* 76–78; Kaczynski, *People of Faith,* 110–11; Van Tassel and Grabowski, *Encyclopedia*

of Cleveland History, 637–38; and Gaidziunas, *Our Lady of Perpetual Help;* Ibid., *A Pilgrim Nation;* and Ibid., *Lietuvos Madonu Sventove.*

35. Gaidziunas, *Our Lady of Perpetual Help,* 70.

36. Lithuania, the largest country in Europe in the fourteenth century, was the last European country to be Christianized.

37. The figure of the *Pensive Christ* is particularly associated with folk art in Lithuania. The forecourt proved more exciting than originally anticipated. In 1982 an automobile, maneuvering in the forecourt, leveled the shrine and it had to be rebuilt.

38. The painting is in the Redemptorist Generalate in the nineteenth-century church of Sant' Alfonso, which is usually known as the church of Santa Maria di Perpetuo Soccorso because of its famous icon.

39. There are approximately fifty thousand crosses of various sizes and configurations on this self-constructed monument to martyrs of independence located north of Siauliai in Lithuania. During its occupation of Lithuania, the Soviet government bulldozed the hill three times in unsuccessful attempts to destroy the monument. The Russians considered, in desperation, building a dam to flood the area.

4. South Central Cleveland

1. For St. Joseph Franciscan, see Armstrong, *Guide,* 114–15; Hynes, *Parishes,* 133–34; Johannesen, *Cleveland Architecture,* 21; and Kaczynski, *People of Faith,* 412–14.

2. For St. Maron's, see Hynes, *Parishes,* 144–45 and 87–91; Kaczynski, *People of Faith,* 403–5; and Van Tassel and Grabowski, *Encyclopedia of Cleveland History,* 860, 853, 38–40, and 559–61.

3. Other churches with ties to the Indians include Lakewood United Methodist (p. 282) and St. Christopher's-by-the-River (p. 366) where, respectively, Richard Jacobs and Bob Feller were members, and St. Patrick–Bridge with its window dedicated to Paddy Livingston, perhaps the major league player with the fewest strikeouts.

4. The Maronite community in the United States is relatively small, ranking behind that of Brazil, Argentina, Mexico, Australia, and Canada.

5. There is disagreement about where Turner Hall, the building the parish bought from a German society, stood. It may have been on Central Avenue.

6. St. Sharbel was a nineteenth-century solitary canonized in 1977. The Masabky brothers were martyred in the turmoil chronically investing the Levant.

7. For St. Philip's, see Armstrong, *Guide,* 116–17 and, in particular, Davis, *Second Chance.*

8. Modern architecture is not easy to find in this guide. Exceptions include: Masjid Al-Islam/Al-Ihsan School of Excellence (Riverside Community Church; 1946), p. 273; West Shore Unitarian Universalist Church (1952), p. 289; Fairmount Temple (1957), p. 350; Church of the Good Shepherd (1958), p. 353; St. Mary Romanian Orthodox Cathedral (1960), p. 265; The Lillian and Betty Ratner School (B'rith Emeth; 1967), p. 347; The Temple East (1970), p. 344; St. Paschal Baylon Parish (1971), p. 368; St. Nicholas Parish (Croation; 1972), p. 73; St. Andrew Abbey (1986), p. 154; St. Alban Episcopal Church (1992), p. 320; Church of the Resurrection (2004), p. 360; Park Synagogue East (2005), p. 345; Temple Emanu El (2009), p. 358; and, of course, Eric Mendelsohn's Park Synagogue (1950), p. 315, the most famous religious building in the Cleveland area.

9. Davis, *Second Chance,* 16.

10. Ibid., 57.

11. St. Philip's is not the only religious institution attempting to deal with the problems of West Central. Many others in this neighborhood in less distinguished buildings as well as many institutions outside West Central have programs to help West Central's inhabitants. Other religious institutions in West Central in this book, all of which have social programs that severely strain their resources, include Triedstone Baptist, p. 124, St. John A.M.E., p. 126, Lane Metropolitan C.M.E., p. 127, and St. Andrew's Episcopal, p. 129.

12. Also known for his Burke Lakefront Airport Terminal and Tower (1963–70), Clarke Tower dorm at CWRU (1968), Beck Center (1978), and Lausche State Office Building (1979).

13. Davis, *Second Chance,* caption facing 96.

14. Harry Liebowitz, the first rabbi, was appointed in 1906.

15. Armstrong, *Guide,* 118. For Triedstone, see also Van Tassel and Grabowski, *Encyclopedia of Cleveland History,* 734–35.

16. For St. John African Methodist Episcopal Church, see Armstrong, *Guide,* 120–21; Van Tassel and Grabowski, *Encyclopedia of Cleveland History,* 857; and *127th Session, North Ohio Annual Conference.*

17. The African Methodist Episcopal Church was established in Philadelphia in 1793. Quinn would go on to become the fourth A.M.E. bishop and then the senior A.M.E. bishop from 1849 to 1873.

18. St. John's A.M.E. became St. John African Methodist Episcopal Church in 1982.

19. Madison designed Lee Chapel A.M.E. and Quinn Chapel A.M.E. Church (see p. 160).

20. For Lane Metropolitan C.M.E., see Armstrong, *Guide,* 122–23 and Van Tassel and Grabowski, *Encyclopedia of Cleveland History,* 183.

21. Medieval and Renaissance architects considered the Pantheon a miracle because they believed all arches and domes required a corner stone. They could not understand how the Pantheon's dome could remain in place since it had an oculus where its cornerstone should be.

22. See True Holiness Temple (Second Church of Christ, Scientist, 1916); Pentecostal Church of Christ (Fourth Church of Christ, Scientist, 1918), p. 43; Nottingham Spirk Design Associates (First Church of Christ, Scientist, 1930), p. 62; and, to a less obvious extent, Fifth Church of Christ, Scientist (1928).

23. The Methodists had merged with Epworth Memorial to form Epworth-Euclid Methodist Church, now the University Circle United Methodist Church, see p. 47.

24. This is an intersection the Christian Scientists now share with the True Sisters Child Care Center (a Jewish philanthropy), Beaumont School for Girls (a Catholic high school), and the convent of Carmel of the Holy Family.

25. For St. Andrew's, see Armstrong, *Guide,* 124–25, and Van Tassel and Grabowski, *Encyclopedia of Cleveland History,* 852–53.

26. In addition to his other civic responsibilities, Cooper served as president of the Cleveland NAACP chapter.

27. For almost a century, St. Andrew's has had a special relationship with its neighboring elementary school, now torn down and being rebuilt. St. Andrew's

staff and members volunteer at the school. The school is a major client of the church's food and clothing distribution programs. Graduations from the school are held in St. Andrew's sanctuary.

28. For Friendship Baptist, in addition to Dancyger, *Temple-Tifereth Israel,* see Armstrong, *Guide,* 126–27; and Van Tassel and Grabowski, *Encyclopedia of Cleveland History,* 960–61, 586, 476, and 660.

29. See also St. Timothy Missionary Baptist Church, p. 31; Mt. Zion Congregational Church, p. 58; and Olivet Institutional Baptist Church, p. 140.

30. The history of the congregation Tifereth Israel is here divided to reflect its history in each of its landmark buildings. For 1850–1924, see here and Dancyger, *Temple-Tifereth Israel,* 1–15. For 1924–70, see Temple Tifereth Israel, p. 44, and Dancyger, *Temple-Tifereth Israel,* 16–77. For 1970 to the present, see Temple Tifereth Israel East, p. 344; and Dancyger, *Temple-Tifereth Israel,* 78–157.

31. Dancyger, *Temple-Tifereth Israel,* 15. Reform congregations originally tended to be much less enthusiastic about Zionism than more traditional congregations. Rabbi Abba Hillel Silver's Zionism was considered an anomaly in his Reform congregation and was not shared by the majority of his congregation during the period when Silver was most active in the Zionist movement.

32. Gries, *Jewish Community of Cleveland,* unpaginated.

33. Urann, *Centennial History of Cleveland,* 109–10.

34. Shiloh is an alternative to Cleveland's famous "Roman row" along I-90 with St. Michael (p. 231) and St. Ignatius of Antioch (p. 244) on the south and St. Stephen's (p. 256) and St. Coleman's (p. 254) on the north. Less conspicuous is the complex of religious organizations at Shaker and I-271 on the Far East Side (pp. 344, 345, 347, 349, and 350), said to be one of the largest concentrations of Jewish institutions in the world. For Shiloh, see Armstrong, *Guide,* 128–29, and Van Tassel and Grabowski, *Encyclopedia of Cleveland History,* 889–90.

35. St. John African Methodist Episcopal Church, one of the oldest churches of any denomination in Cleveland, was established in 1830 (see p. 126).

36. The House of Wills, a famous African American funeral home since 1904, purchased the former Cleveland Hebrew Schools building in 1941. Twenty years before, the schools had purchased the 1900 building from the Cleveland Gesang Verein (the German Singing Society).

37. This was recognized in 2006 by the Cleveland chapter of the American Institute of Architects and by the Cleveland Restoration Society.

38. For St. Adalbert/Our Lady of the Blessed Sacrament, see Armstrong, *Guide,* 132–33; Hynes, *Parishes,* 62–63 and 79–80; Johannesen, *Cleveland Architecture,* 128; Kaczynski, *People of Faith,* 394–96 and 132–33; Van Tassel and Grabowski, *Encyclopedia of Cleveland History,* 478; Herman, *Cleveland's Vanishing Sacred Architecture,* 29–38; and First, *Founded in Faith,* 38–44.

39. A valiant Czech community remained behind on Kingsbury Run, erecting a substantial neo-Gothic masonry permanent church in 1892. By the 1920s the community was so reduced that it contemplated a move to Maple Heights. A resolute few continued on into the 1960s, when St. Wenceslas and its community were finally stamped out by the I-77/I-490/Broadway "interchange to nowhere."

40. For St. James A.M.E., see Armstrong, *Guide,* 123–35, and Van Tassel and Grabowski, *Encyclopedia of Cleveland History,* 855.

41. The church had been built seventeen years earlier for $55,000.

42. See Matthew 28:16–20.

43. For Antioch, see Armstrong, *Guide,* 56; Johannesen, *Cleveland Architecture,* 201–2; Van Tassel and Grabowski, *Encyclopedia of Cleveland History,* 37–38 and 562; and Evans, *Church History.*

44. From East 55th to East 29th to East 24th, until settling at East 89th Street and Cedar Avenue.

45. Rockefeller did not like to give people money for a project without their active participation. He most commonly supported projects by requiring matching funds.

46. For Olivet, see Armstrong, *Guide,* 138–39.

47. St. Elizabeth's precedence can be debated, see Karpi, *For God and Country,* 14–16. For St. Elizabeth's, see also Armstrong, *Guide,* 140–41; Hynes, *Parishes,* 115; Johannesen, *Cleveland Architecture,* 128–29; Kaczynski, *People of Faith,* 201–3; Van Tassel and Grabowski, *Encyclopedia of Cleveland History,* 852, 110, 532–34; Pál and Szendrey, *St. Elizabeth of Hungary 100th Jubilee;* and Tibor, *St. Elizabeth of Hungary Church 110th Jubilee.*

48. Roger Gries's letter to Andras Antal in Tibor, *St. Elizabeth of Hungary Church 110th Jubilee,* 5.

49. See Karpi, *For God and Country;* Pál and Szendrey, *St. Elizabeth of Hungary 100th Jubilee;* Sabol, *Buckeye Neighborhood,* 10, 14–15, 29–30, 34, 67–69, 71–72, 75, 85–86, 88, 100–101, 107, and 122; and Tibor, *St. Elizabeth of Hungary Church 110th Jubilee.*

50. Johannesen, *Cleveland Architecture,* 128.

51. Hannibal, *Guide to Stones.*

5. Southeast Cleveland

1. Robert Madison also has been active in the renovation of Sidney Badgley's 1908 St. John African Methodist Episcopal Church.

2. Most of the refugees welcomed to Cleveland could not afford to settle in the then prosperous Hungarian community along Buckeye Road and, thus, had to establish themselves elsewhere.

3. For First Hungarian Lutheran, see Armstrong, *Guide,* 152–53; Sabol, *Buckeye Neighborhood,* 13, 16–17, 51–52, 69, and 75; and Van Tassel and Grabowski, *Encyclopedia of Cleveland History,* 402.

4. As their daughters and sons move to the suburbs, there seems to be a gathering together of Hungarians in Cleveland, to whom a common language and secular culture become more important than sectarian difference. (The first history of Cleveland Hungarians was written by H. A. Liebowitz, a founder of the Orthodox Oheb Zedek Hungarian Jewish congregation in Glenville.) The community, which included Greek Catholic, Reformed, Presbyterian, and Baptist Hungarians in addition to Hungarian Roman Catholics, Lutherans, and Jews (there were three Jewish Hungarian synagogues), gathered defensively around St. Elizabeth's on Buckeye Road at the bottom of the hill in 2009 when the bishop closed the other two Hungarian Roman Catholic churches in the Cleveland area.

5. About 3 percent of Hungarians are Greek Catholic. The Hungarian Greek Catholic Church is a Byzantine Rite church that uses Hungarian in its liturgy and is in full union with the Roman Catholic Church. In the absence of a Hungarian

Greek hierarchy in the United States, it is governed through the Byzantine Catholic Metropolia of Pittsburgh.

6. Hungary entered the Second World War with the Axis. Its 1943 attempt to make a separate peace with the Allies resulted in German occupation of the country for the remainder of the war.

7. For Full Gospel Evangelistic Center, see Armstrong, *Guide,* 154; Johannesen, *Cleveland Architecture,* 94; Van Tassel and Grabowski, *Encyclopedia of Cleveland History,* 402–3; and Sabol, *Buckeye Neighborhood,* 12, 28, 46, 49–50, 87, and 89.

8. Full Gospel's large corner lot with its large church complex, extensive gardens, and huge parking area is completely surrounded, on the large block southwest of Buckeye at MLK, by St. Andrew Abbey (see p. 154) and the Benedictine High School along with the campus of its former church, now the Cathedral of God in Christ (see p. 156). North, across Buckeye, is the First Hungarian Lutheran Church (see p. 151).

9. The West Siders, now the West Side Hungarian Reformed Church, continue to thrive at 15300 Puritas.

10. This church has somewhat imaginatively been described as Romanesque Revival.

11. For St. Andrew Abbey, see Armstrong, *Guide,* 156–57; Hynes, *Parishes,* 88–85 and 93–94; Kaczynski, *People of Faith,* 142–44, 405–6, and 489–90; Sabol, *Buckeye Neighborhood,* 38, 40–43, 124, and 127; Van Tassel and Grabowski, *Encyclopedia of Cleveland History,* 852 and 895–96.

12. For the Cathedral of God in Christ, see Armstrong, *Guide,* 158–59; Hynes, *Parishes,* 93–95; Kaczynski, *People of Faith,* 405–6; and Sabol, *Buckeye Neighborhood,* 47–48, 76–78, and 103.

13. Kaczynski, *People of Faith,* 406.

14. Responding to seventeenth-century clergy who thought Michelangelo's central plan smacked of paganism, Carlo Maderno also added a three-bay nave to St. Peter. This alteration of Michelangelo's adaptation of Bramante's concept is universally condemned by students of the resulting building.

15. For Our Lady of Peace, see Hynes, *Parishes,* 75–76; Kaczynski, *People of Faith,* 109–10; and Sabol, *Buckeye Neighborhood,* 98–99.

16. Luna Park was within the triangle bordered by Woodland Avenue and Woodhill and Mt. Carmel Roads.

17. Hynes, *Parishes,* 76. The organ did not survive the move into the current building.

18. For a similar ending, see Thomas Hanrahan and St. Ignatius of Antioch Church, p. 244.

19. Trinity College, across the street from the Catholic University of America in Washington, D.C., was known as a women's liberal arts college. It became Trinity Washington University in 2004.

20. Sixty-four percent of Mt. Pleasant is devoted to housing. The Cleveland average is 34 percent.

21. For St. Cecilia, see Armstrong, *Guide,* 170–71; Hynes, *Parishes,* 100–101; Kaczynski, *People of Faith,* 181–83; *St. Cecilia Catholic Church;* and First, *Founded in Faith,* 114–18.

22. Hynes, *Parishes,* 100.

23. The Tiffany-style window came to St. Cecelia with a story. It was privately purchased when St. Agnes was demolished. The window was installed as a bathroom door in a residence. Its elderly owner came to believe the window was talking to her and asking to be taken home. Since it was impossible to take the window back to the demolished St. Agnes, it was given to St. Cecelia.

24. For this building, see Armstrong, *Guide,* 172–73; Hynes, *Parishes,* 45–46; and Kaczynski, *People of Faith,* 391–92.

25. Kaczynski, *People of Faith,* 391.

26. Hynes, *Parishes,* 45.

27. For another example of Wright's Prairie style in Cleveland, see Carl Droppers's 1946 Masjid Al-Islam/Ihsan School of Excellence (formerly the Riverside Community Church), p. 273.

28. Hynes, *Parishes,* 45.

29. The cupola is illustrated in Armstrong, *Guide,* the interfold between pages 172 and 173; and Kaczynski, *People of Faith,* 391.

6. The Broadway Corridor

1. For Our Lady of Lourdes, see Armstrong, *Guide,* 182–83; Hynes, *Parishes,* 70–71; Johannesen, *Cleveland Architecture,* 93; Kaczynski, *People of Faith,* 100–102; and Van Tassel and Grabowski, *Encyclopedia of Cleveland History,* 326–27 and 426–27.

2. Prague, Vienna, and Chicago had larger Czech communities.

3. For similar form, see the Baptist, Episcopal, and Methodist pill hill churches, pp. 325, 329, and 337, and the Church of the Covenant and Amasa Stone Chapel in University Circle, pp. 51 and 52. For the different history, see Armstrong, *Guide,* 184–85; Moore, *Tapestry of Faith,* 30–31; and Hart et al., *Broadway United Methodist.*

4. Hart, *Broadway United Methodist,* n.p.

5. Covenant UMC was a victim of the Interstate System. Originally known as Ebenezer Church, this German Methodist congregation built two frame churches before dedicating a substantial brick neo-Gothic building in 1917 on West 65th Street. Forced out of their third church by the Interstate System, the community settled into five acres on Pleasant Valley Road in Parma as the Covenant United Methodist Church only to find, after the merger of the Evangelical United Brethren and the Methodist Church, that they shared their new neighborhood with three other strong Methodist churches.

6. The original commission for the Broadway Methodist copy was to Vittorio Guandalini, who died before he could begin painting. Before his death, Guandalini put up a scaffold in Santa Maria della Grazie in Milan and made color studies and drawings of Leonardo's painting. For this reason, the most recent 1978–99 restorers of Leonardo's painting examined the Guandalini-Vandelli copy at Broadway Methodist. The Cleveland copy antedates the 1924 Silvestri cleaning of the original in Milan, its 1951–53 Pellicuioli restoration, and the August 15, 1943, explosion from the Allied bomb that destroyed the Refectory of Santa Maria della Grazie and whose vibration may have affected Leonardo's sandbagged masterpiece.

7. For St. Lawrence, see Armstrong, *Guide,* 186–87; Hynes, *Parishes,* 138–39;

Kaczynski, *People of Faith,* 270–71; Rebol, *85 Years of Ministry; St. Lawrence Celebrates 100 Years;* and First, *Founded on Faith,* 68–74.

8. Anthony Pilla in Rebol, *85 Years of Ministry,* n.p.

9. For St. Stanislaus, see Armstrong, *Guide,* 188–89; Hynes, *Parishes,* 175–77; Johannesen, *Cleveland Architecture,* 26–27; Kaczynski, *People of Faith,* 354–56, 495–96, and 496–97; Stefanski, *Slavic Village;* and note 10.

10. For the more exciting details of the tumultuous religious history of the Polish people in Cleveland, see Van Tassel and Grabowski, *Encyclopedia of Cleveland History,* 772–74 (Poles), 863 (St. Stanislaus Church), 598 (Kolaszewski, Anton Francis), and 540 (Immaculate Heart of Mary Parish). See also Kaczynski, *People of Faith,* for the Warsawa neighborhood: 354–56 (St. Stanislaus), 82–84 (Immaculate Heart of Mary), and 120–22 (Sacred Heart of Jesus); in the Pozan neighborhood: 176–78 (St. Casimir); in the Kantowa neighborhood of Tremont: 244–46 (St. John Cantius); in the Barbarowa neighborhood: 163–64 (St. Barbara); in the Josaphatowa neighborhood: 249–51 (St. Josaphat); and in the Corlett area: 420–21 (St. Mary of Czestochowa). For parallel parish descriptions, fifty years earlier, see Hynes, *Parishes,* 175–77, 57–58, 78–79, 97–98, 129–30, 92–93, and 132–33.

11. This association will end in July 2012 when the Franciscans withdraw to Chicago.

12. Barack Obama worked from 1985 to 1988 as a community organizer for eight Roman Catholic parishes on Chicago's South Side.

13. Johannesen, *Cleveland Architecture,* 26.

14. "The richness of the total impression bespeaks a love of craftsmanship and ornamental effect that is unknown to later generations." Johannesen, *Cleveland Architecture,* 27.

15. A Pennsylvania Jones established the Jones and Laughlin Steel Corporation south of Pittsburgh that eventually bought Cleveland's Otis Iron and Steel Co. This became LTV Steel after a 1984 merger with Republic Steel Corp. and is now absorbed by ArcelorMittal—the largest steel company in the world, based in Luxemburg.

David and John Jones joined J. W. Jones to found Jones & Co. In turn, Jones & Co. became Chisholm, Jones & Co., then Stone, Chisholm & Jones, then the Cleveland Rolling Mill Co., which became part of the American Steel and Wire Co. trust eventually absorbed by United States Steel in 1901.

For Jones Road Church, see Armstrong, *Guide,* 192–93, and Van Tassel and Grabowski, *Encyclopedia of Cleveland History,* 581 and 579.

16. Omitted from this list are Reverend T. Henry Jones, pastor 1895–98, Reverend W. O. Jones, pastor 1900–1908, and Dr. J. Vincent Jones, who was pastor when the church annex was constructed in 1913.

17. A *Gymanfa Ganu* is a hymn festival sung in four-part harmony by a congregation separated into the four sections and usually directed by a guest choral director. Dry throats are restored by the subsequent *Te Bach,* celebrated in the church parlor.

18. Other CCCC churches in northern Ohio are located in Parkman, Wellington, and Vermillion.

19. For Holy Name, see Armstrong, *Guide,* 194–95; Hynes, *Parishes,* 47–49; Kaczynski, *People of Faith,* 50–61; and Dalton, *Holy Name Parish.*

20. The assistant at the cathedral responsible for the Newburgh Community—the dynamic O'Callaghan—would go on to organize the church around Youngstown

as pastor of St. Columba (Hynes, *History of the Diocese of Cleveland,* 67), build St. Patrick (see p. 189), and establish St. Coleman (see p. 254). In between these efforts, he would, as leader of "the Twelve Apostles," force the resignation of his bishop and be suspended himself—only once and briefly—for an unrelated matter. For the tumultuous early years of the diocese, see Lyons and Jurgens, *Life and Times.*

21. See "Henry Chisholm" and "Cleveland Rolling Mill Strikes," Van Tassel and Grabowski, *Encyclopedia of Cleveland History,* 182 and 270.

22. The new name evolved from the success of the parish's Holy Name Society. A Holy Name Society is a men's group dedicated to cutting down swearing.

23. For Shaffer UMC, see Armstrong, *Guide,* 200–201, and Moore, *Tapestry of Faith,* 107–8.

7. The Near West Side

1. For St. Malachi, see Armstrong, *Guide,* 206–7; Hynes, *Parishes,* 140–41; Kaczynski, *People of Faith,* 276–78; and Van Tassel and Grabowski, *Encyclopedia of Cleveland History,* 35.

2. Van Tassel and Grabowski, *The Encyclopedia of Cleveland History,* 35, continues: "Closely knit, and resentful of outsiders, as an Irish parish ghetto, the Angle was a virtually 'closed' community. Second and third generations of its sons and daughters married each other and endeavored to remain in the parish by building additions onto the rear of their parents' homes, or buying homes vacated by the deaths of older parishioners."

3. The first Old Stone Church (see p. 12), also built in 1836, was taken down and replaced, through the urging of Samuel Aiken in 1853, with the current Old Stone building designed by Charles Heard and Simeon Porter. For St. John's, see Armstrong, *Guide,* 208–9, and Van Tassel and Grabowski, *Encyclopedia of Cleveland History,* 857.

4. The oldest Gothic Revival church in the United States is Ithiel Town's 1816 Trinity Episcopal Church in New Haven, Connecticut. Trinity Church in Boston, built in 1829 and burned in 1872, is considered to be the second oldest. Trinity Church Boston's Gothic Revival building was replaced by Phillips Brooks's, and H. H. Richardson's Romanesque Revival church in 1876.

5. Ironmonger, lawyer, then priest—Hopkins, as presiding bishop (1865–68; the Episcopal primate), would reunite the Episcopal Church after the Civil War. He is better known for being the father of John Henry Hopkins Jr., who wrote and composed "We Three Kings of Orient Are."

6. Brooklyn Township was established on the west side of the Cuyahoga River in 1818. Its northern part became the City of Ohio in 1836, annexed by Cleveland in 1854.

7. The first church established in Cuyahoga County was the First Presbyterian Church of East Cleveland (1807).

8. See also St. Stephen's (p. 256) and St. Colman's (p. 254).

9. The enclosure is similar to the enclosures for the audiovisual technicians at the rear of Antioch Baptist (see p. 138) and Parkside Church (see p. 162).

10. For Franklin Circle Christian Church, see Armstrong, *Guide,* 210–11; Johannesen, *Cleveland Architecture,* 22; and Van Tassel and Grabowski, *Encyclopedia of Cleveland History,* 420 and 431.

11. Johannesen, *Cleveland Architecture,* 21–23.

12. Franklin Circle Christian was spared the ruin at St. Stephen's, where the tornado largely destroyed its first-generation Mayer windows (see p. 256). This tornado also damaged St. Colman's (see p. 254) and removed the roof, apse, and chancel from St. John's Episcopal (see p. 184).

13. This would be disputed by St. Patrick–West Park, which began monthly services out in the country in 1848. The West Park St. Patrick became part of Cleveland in 1923. For St. Patrick–Bridge, see Armstrong, *Guide,* 112–13; Hynes, *Parishes,* 155–57; Kaczynski, *People of Faith,* 320–21; Van Tassel and Grabowski, *Encyclopedia of Cleveland History,* 861 and 556–57; and *A Light in the City.*

14. The most famous recent graduate of St. Patrick's school is former U.S. Congresswoman and Arab American Mary Rose Oakar.

15. Van Tassel and Grabowski, *Encyclopedia of Cleveland History,* 556–57. The communicants of St. Patrick's were relatively open-minded and genteel compared to the notoriously rowdy and chauvinistic "Angle Irish" whom the St. Patrick's community had set apart around St. Malachi.

16. The exterior of the 1874 First Methodist Church that once stood at East Ninth Street and Euclid Avenue was also of Sandusky limestone. The use of this stone was rare in Cleveland because of the proximity of the sandstone quarries in Berea.

17. Livingston's record of the fewest strikeouts for those batting more than five hundred times is questioned by some because of the limited records of his era.

18. For Trinity Lutheran, see Armstrong, *Guide,* 214–15.

19. Bremer, "Restoration Society Lights 130-Year-Old Steeple."

20. Famously described by Schofield, *Landmark Architecture of Cleveland,* 27, as "a lovely version of a Gothic meeting house."

21. The other prototype for American colonial churches, Giacomo da Vignola and Giacomo della Porta's 1568 Gesu in Rome, so often copied in South America, is seen in Cleveland only in La Sagrada Familia (see p. 248).

22. It also unfortunately dominates the church budget.

23. The Trinity Lutheran organ was Beckerath's first important sale outside Germany. In a tracker organ there is a direct mechanical link between the organist's finger and the opening of the organ pipe. In contrast, in an electrical-pneumatic organ such as a Holtkamp, depression of a key sends an electrical signal that opens the pipe. Organists spend a good deal of time arguing about the advantages of tracker organs. Proponents of the trackers make several arguments. First, this is the action on which Bach played and for which he wrote. Second, trackers are said to provide a faster and more nuanced response (electrical-pneumatic partisans say this is in the imagination of the tracker enthusiasts). Third, tracker actions can be repaired and maintained for more than five hundred years, which cannot be said of any electrical device. Detractors point out that trackers are not only harder to play, but also that they have to be smaller and require the organist to be immediately adjacent to the pipes. Trinity Lutheran's tracker uses a one horsepower motor to blow air through the pipes. No one has suggested that it dragoon some of the surrounding schoolboys, as Bach did, to pump the air by hand.

24. For Donald Rosenberg's review of Mustric's five-CD recording on the Beckerath, with stops pulled by Rebecca Fischer Knab, see "Florence Mustric: Organist Goes on the Record," *The Plain Dealer,* June 23, 2008.

25. For St. Emeric Church, see Armstrong, *Guide,* 216–17; Hynes, *Parishes,* 115–16; Kaczynski, *People of Faith,* 214–15 and 390–91; Peller, *Szent Imre;* Herman, *Cleveland's Vanishing Sacred Architecture,* 39–52; and First, *Founded in Faith,* 86–91.

26. France is the only country in Europe that did not send a substantial number of immigrants to the United States during the waves of immigration in the nineteenth and early twentieth centuries.

27. Peller, *Szent Imre,* 48.

28. For Annunciation, see Armstrong, *Guide,* 218–19 and Van Tassel and Grabowski, *Encyclopedia of Cleveland History,* 36 and 472–74.

29. For Holy Ghost Byzantine Catholic Church, see Armstrong, *Guide,* 220–21.

30. 145–46.

31. *Not* Russian. Linguists differ, with obvious political implications, on whether Rusyn is a separate East Slavic language or a dialect of Ukrainian.

32. Razed for the Innerbelt in 1961, St. John the Baptist moved to Parma as the seat of the Eparchy of Parma.

33. The tension between Roman- and Greek-style painting, naturalism versus symbolism, and the controversy it has aroused, is common not only in Byzantine Catholic rite congregations but also in Orthodox communities. Roman-style iconography was commonly introduced in the 1920s and 1930s, but many congregations now wish to replace it with Greek iconography.

34. For St. Augustine, see Armstrong, *Guide,* 222–23; Hynes, *Parishes,* 91–92; and Kaczynski, *People of Faith,* 161–63.

35. See, among others: St. Emeric Church, p. 194; St. Wendelin Church; Annunciation Greek Orthodox Church, p. 196; St. Andrew Kim Korean Catholic Church; Holy Ghost Byzantine Catholic Church, p. 198; St. Augustine Church, Iglesia El Calvario; Pilgrim Congregational Church, p. 201; St. George Orthodox Church, p. 204; Zion United Church of Christ; Our Lady of Mercy Church, p. 207; Iglesia Hispana Asambleas de Dios; Iglesia de Dios Pentecostal; St. John Cantius Church, p. 209; Saints Peter and Paul Ukrainian Catholic Church, p. 210; St. Theodosius Orthodox Cathedral, p. 231; St. Michael Church, p. 231; Scranton Road Baptist Church; and Immanuel Evangelical Lutheran Church, p. 234. A map (such as that available at www.nhlink.net/neighborhoodtour/tremont) should be consulted to see the degree to which the Tremont neighborhood was destroyed by the interstates.

36. Kaczynski, *People of Faith,* 162.

37. Kilde, drawing her account from Pilgrim Church histories, describes the difficulty that the original Protestant congregation had at St. Augustine with an eighteenth-century axial church plan before moving to a semicircular church plan down the street at their new church (see p. 201). At St. Augustine there had been unremitting tension between those with the best seats up front and those in the back pews who could not hear nor see the person preaching. Kilde, *When Church Became Theatre,* 115.

38. When Anshe Chesed left Euclid Avenue Temple for their high-modern Fairmount Temple, they left much Tiffany glass behind. St. Paul Episcopal took its Tiffany glass with it when it left St. Paul Shrine. However, they stored it for decades next to the furnace and it disintegrated.

39. Active in Canada and the United States at the turn of the nineteenth to the twentieth century, Sidney Badgley built six churches described in this book

in addition to his 1896 Washington Place (formerly the Baricelli Inn), so loved by Cleveland gourmands. Badgley designed the 1891 Fidelity Baptist Church (see p. 83), the 1891 St. Timothy Missionary Baptist Church (see p. 31), the 1892 St. George Orthodox Church across the street (see p. 204), this 1894 church, the 1904 Lakewood United Methodist Church (see p. 282), and the 1908 St. John A.M.E. Church (see p. 126).

40. For Pilgrim, *inter alia*, see Armstrong, *Guide*, 226–27, and Johannesen, *Cleveland Architecture*, 51–52.

41. Despite the seeming inability of anyone to discuss Pilgrim without making reference to it as Cleveland's or the United States' most famous example of an Akron Plan church, it is only one of several variants. The basic plan, which all Akron Plan churches share, is a large space, sometimes called the "assembly area," surrounded by smaller classrooms that are separated from the central space by movable walls. This Akron Plan was developed by Sunday school superintendent Lewis Miller and first built in 1868 as part of Akron's First Methodist Church. This Akron building was destroyed by fire in 1872.

Miller's idea responded to the Uniform Lesson System, widely popular among Protestants in the latter half of the nineteenth century, which directed that all children, irrespective of age, should learn the same weekly lesson (so that everyone in the family was on the same page), but that it needed to be tailored to their age level. The Akron Plan combined the physical arrangement of the rural one-room schoolhouse with the graded separate classrooms of large city schools. Exercises began with everyone going to their classrooms with the walls separating them from the central room open. The superintendent, speaking from a lectern in the central room, began with a prayer and a reading from the day's scripture. The walls were closed while students received age-appropriate instruction and drill. The walls were then reopened and the students recited the day's scripture en masse, concluding their study with a prayer.

Architects and congregations used this concept in at least three different ways. In the most common Cleveland variant in this book, which Badgley claimed to have invented and used here and in his 1891 Fidelity Baptist, 1908 St. John A.M.E., and 1913 Lakewood Methodist Churches, the "Akron Plan" complex was built separate from the sanctuary but shares a common retractable wall so that the spaces could be combined to greatly increase congregational seating on a temporary basis. Another variant, as in the 1893 First Presbyterian Church of East Cleveland (see p. 107), separates the Akron Plan complex completely from the sanctuary, and it functions as an independent unit. Less affluent congregations—for example, the 1887 North Presbyterian Church (see p. 74)—used the permanent sanctuary as the "assembly area" and surrounded it with classrooms with retractable walls. This last variant was popular among small-town Protestant congregations.

42. Johannesen points out that forty-three separate rooms at Pilgrim, "two-thirds of the original structure was devoted to educational, social, and community work." "In 1899 complete photographic views and models of the building were sent to the Paris Exposition, where it was praised," for its integration of sanctuary, kitchen, library, art museum, kindergarten, and gymnasium, "as the finest example of an institutional church." Johannesen, *Cleveland Architecture*, 51.

43. The Humiston Institute was a private coeducational secondary school that

took over the abandoned Cleveland University building in 1859 and was, in turn, replaced there by a homeopathic medical school in 1868.

44. This first building has been St. Augustine Roman Catholic Church since 1895 (see p. 200). In 2008 the City of Cleveland renamed the West 14th at Howard corner to honor Sister Corita Ambro and Father Joe McNulty, who have fed the poor of Tremont from the St. Augustine basement for more than thirty years.

45. Kilde notes that "Pilgrim was somewhat unusual in that when the congregation decided to build a new church in the early 1890s, they did not follow the national trend of leaving their neighborhood into which industry and immigrants were moving but chose a site just a few blocks away from the original church." She then describes in detail the difficult and understandable tension at Pilgrim, which most religious institutions chose to avoid by moving, between ministry to the neighborhood and ministry to member families. Kilde, *When Church Became Theatre,* 190–96.

46. Expanding into five locations by 1880, this program evolved into the Friendly Inn Social Settlement, managed, until 1926, by the Woman's Christian Temperance Union (WCTU) and, since then, by the Women's Philanthropic Union. The Friendly Inns came to provide a wide range of social services in addition to temperance, and this was what induced the women to change their name in 1926.

47. The other two are Iglesia El Calvario (formerly the Cleveland Baptist Temple and originally the Emmanuel Evangelical United Brethren Church) and St. George Orthodox Church (originally the Lincoln Park Methodist Episcopal Church; see p. 204). The Tremont neighborhood is said to have the largest concentration of religious buildings per capita of any neighborhood in the United States. See n. 35, p. 396.

48. Kilde notes that such marquis lighting "was relatively common in religious buildings during the period . . . Just as religious groups eagerly embraced the Internet in the late twentieth century, their ancestors embraced new technologies a century earlier, harnessing their power for the evangelical project." Kilde, *When Church Became Theatre,* 129.

49. At St. John A.M.E. the orientation is toward the northeast corner; Fidelity Baptist is oriented toward the southeast.

50. F. Christian Holtkamp is the fourth generation of his family to build organs in Cleveland. Becoming president of his company in 1995, he was preceded by his father, Walter Jr., his grandfather, Walter Sr., and his great-grandfather, Henry, who began building organs in Cleveland in 1903. Under Walter Sr., the company led the "organ reform movement" in the first half of the twentieth century. Holtkamp organs were designed to play Bach, Buxtehude, Couperin, and Frescobaldi and replaced previous instruments designed to play imitations of orchestral music. The Holtkamp Company has been located on Meyer Avenue on the Near West Side of Cleveland since 1922. Its twenty employees build four to six organs a year.

51. David Maitland Armstrong was an important turn-of-the-century opalescent glass artist. His associates included John La Farge, Charles McKim, Augustus Saint-Gaudens, Louis Tiffany, and Stanford White. He is best known for windows at the Appellate Court Building and Church of the Ascension in New York and G. W. Vanderbilt II's All Souls Church in Asheville. Identification of these windows with Maitland Armstrong is "probable, but not certain," according to Michael Tevesz,

director of the Center for Sacred Landmarks of the Maxine Goodman Levin College of Urban Affairs of Cleveland State University, personal communication.

52. This is according to a 2000 survey by the Arab American Institute, quoted by Lo, *Muslims in America,* 90.

53. Christian divisions in the Middle East are much more complicated.

54. For St. George Orthodox Church, see Armstrong, *Guide,* 228–29; Moore, *Tapestry of Faith,* 96–97; and Van Tassel and Grabowski, *Encyclopedia of Cleveland History,* 854.

55. As their American communities matured, the Vatican removed Eastern Catholic parishes from the initial supervision of their Roman dioceses. They have been joined into independent eparchies subordinate to primates outside of the United States. These primates, in turn, are generally members of the College of Cardinals in Rome.

56. The Cleveland Grays was a social club thinly masquerading as a military organization. Organized as the Cleveland City Guard in 1837, the Grays members played soldier, drank, and socialized in their monumental Richardsonian Armory that hosted the touring Metropolitan Opera, the first Cleveland auto show, and early performances of the Cleveland Orchestra. Incorporated into the army during the Civil, Spanish-American, and First World Wars, the army passed on the Grays as a unit in subsequent conflicts.

57. The destroyed fourth story of the tower had rested on the surviving corbelling at the top of the present third story. When the Orthodox congregation rebuilt their church, they added small onion domes beside the reconstructed spire on Badgley's truncated north tower.

58. For Our Lady of Mercy, see Armstrong, *Guide,* 232–33; Hynes, *Parishes,* 71–73; Kaczynski, *People of Faith,* 102–3; Van Tassel and Grabowski, *Encyclopedia of Cleveland History,* 747–48; Herman, *Cleveland's Vanishing Sacred Architecture,* 119–27; "History of Our Lady of Mercy Church 1922–1997" in *75th Anniversary;* and First, *Founded in Faith,* 126.

59. The Polish National Catholic Church was established by a Roman Catholic priest in Scranton, Pennsylvania, in 1897 because of a perceived bias against Poles among the Irish and German hierarchy of the American Roman Catholic Church. In many ways it functions like the Episcopal Church except that property belongs to the congregation—Mass is celebrated in the vernacular (first in Polish, now in English), clergy are married, and allegiance is to bishops independent of Rome. Although separate, it closely associates with both the Episcopal Church and the Roman Catholic Church. Merger talks have been ongoing for generations. There are four Polish National Catholic Church parishes in northeast Ohio—Sacred Heart of Jesus (Walton Hills), St. Mary's (Parma), Holy Cross (Warren), and Sacred Heart of Jesus (Youngstown).

60. *75th Anniversary,* n.p.

61. St. John was born in Kanty, a small town near Oswiecim (Auschwitz) in south central Poland. He taught sacred scripture at the University of Cracow and is venerated for his good works. He lived simply; he slept on the floor, ate no meat, and, when he went to Rome, he walked.

62. For St. John Cantius, see Armstrong, *Guide,* 234–35; Hynes, *Parishes,* 129–30; Kaczynski, *People of Faith,* 244–46; and *Sto Lat,* 9–104.

63. *Sto Lat,* 29.

64. For Kocinski's tumultuous pastorate, see *Sto Lat,* 30–35. Among Father Kocinski's multiple problems was Our Lady of Mercy (see p. 207), two blocks away, which veered off to join the Polish National Catholic Church from 1915 to 1921.

65. "When they go out on sick calls at night, the two assistant priests . . . go together and each of them carries a gun. 'Can you imagine,' they said, 'having to take a gun along with you when you are taking the Blessed Sacrament to a sick bed?'" *Sto Lat,* 43.

66. Ibid., 52–58.

67. For more than a decade, Lolita's, the most famous restaurant in Cleveland, has stood a block away, on the other side of the Polish Veterans Alliance.

68. Potter's presentation drawing, reprinted in *Sto Lat,* 13, shows only one tower.

69. Ukrainians may, for some purposes, identify themselves as Ruthenian but generally distinguish themselves from the Rutheniains. For the Ruthenians, see Holy Ghost Byzantine Catholic Church, p. 198; St. Mary Byzantine Catholic Church, p. 221; and the Cathedral of St. John the Baptist, p. 310. For the Ukrainians, see also St. Josaphat Ukrainian Catholic Cathedral, p. 308, and St. Vladimir's Ukrainian Orthodox Cathedral, p. 306.

70. For Saints Peter and Paul, see Armstrong, *Guide,* 236–37.

71. The seat of the metropolitan archbishop, the Ukrainian primate in the United States, has become the Archeparchy of Philadelphia.

72. Van Tassel and Grabowski, *Encyclopedia of Cleveland History,* 833.

73. Merrick House, a program of Catholic Charities, was established in 1919 on the corner of West 10th Street at Starkweather Avenue. Expanding over Cleveland, it maintains a Tremont presence on West 11th Street.

74. St. Vladimir's Ukrainian Orthodox Church (now the Spanish Assembly of God) was located a few blocks west up the hill on West 11th Street before also moving to Parma. See St. Vladimir's Ukrainian Orthodox Cathedral, p. 306.

75. The parish believes there is a Civil War-era military tunnel running north and south, parallel to West Seventh, under the church.

76. The Very Reverend John Nakonachny, pastor of St. Vladimir's Ukrainian Orthodox Cathedral, September 2, 2009.

77. For St. Theodosius, see Armstrong, *Guide,* 238–39; Johannesen, *Cleveland Architecture,* 119; Van Tassel and Grabowski, *Encyclopedia of Cleveland History,* 863, 586–87, and 848–49; and Kappanadze, *We Are Thankful.*

78. St. Theodosius is the site of the Cleveland Deanery of the Orthodox Church of America (OCA). The Cleveland Deanery is responsible for the fourteen OCA parishes in Ohio. The Cleveland Deanery is part of the Diocese of the Midwest in Chicago, which, in turn, is part of the Archdiocese of Washington, an autocephalic branch of the Russian Orthodox Church in Moscow.

79. In Tremont—Holy Ghost Byzantine Catholic Church, see p. 198, or Saints Peter and Paul Ukrainian Greek Catholic Church, see p. 210.

80. In Tremont—St. Theodosius or St. Vladimir's Ukrainian Orthodox Church (now the Spanish Assembly of God). See p. 306 for St. Vladimir's Ukrainian Orthodox Cathedral in Parma.

81. Theodosius Uglitsky (ca. 1630–96) was Archbishop of Chernigov, a Cossack center in the northern Ukraine that sometimes rivaled Kiev. St. Theodosius is celebrated for his support of Orthodoxy and opposition to Roman Catholicism.

82. Letter from Eileen Sotak, chair of the Tremont History Project, to Will Underwood, Kent State University Press, July 10, 2007.

83. The Sisters of St. Joseph would become Cleveland's largest teaching order. In 1950 they were teaching 13,260 students in twenty-six schools. For their role in the "Holy City" along Rocky River Drive, see Our Lady of Angels Church, p. 268.

84. The convent was eventually demolished to be replaced with a parking lot. It is described as "huge" in Kappanadze, *Saint Theodosius*, n.p., 13.

85. For an East Side parallel, see John Mary Powers' Meadowbrook Land Company around St. Ann Church, p. 321.

86. Wonderful legends surround Kappanadze's and his family's journey out of Russia after the revolution. It is agreed that they escaped with the help of the America Committee for Relief in the Near East and made the six-week voyage back to the United States on a small cattle boat. At issue is whether they traveled on passports arranged by a high-ranking Communist official who had been a classmate of one of Kappanadze's sons or whether the passports were arranged by a more high-ranking Georgian-seminary classmate of Kappanadze: Josef Stalin.

8. The West Side South

1. Van Tassel and Grabowski, *Encyclopedia of Cleveland History,* 835.

2. For St. Mary, see Armstrong, *Guide,* 246–47.

3. For Our Lady of Good Counsel, see Armstrong, *Guide,* 248–49; Hynes, *Parishes,* 65–67; Kaczynski, *People of Faith,* 95–97 and 505; and Armbruster, *Our Lady of Good Counsel.*

4. Armbruster, *Our Lady of Good Counsel,* 8–11.

5. See St. Ann, Cleveland Heights p. 321, which was designed a decade earlier and built two decades later.

6. For St. Luke's, see Armstrong, *Guide,* 250–52; Historical Committee, *The First Hundred Years;* and Kregenow, *St. Luke's.*

7. Broadview at Schaaf is seven blocks across the interstate north of Parma.

8. The modern deaconess movement began in 1836 when Theodor Fliedner and his wife, Friedericke Munster, opened the first deaconess motherhouse in Kaiserswerth to train women in nursing and hospital administration. Within fifty years there were 5,000 deaconesses in Europe. They were associated with many Protestant denominations. In the United States, the Evangelischer Diakonissen-Verein was established in St. Louis in 1889 after an Evangelical pastor discovered that Roman Catholic nuns were the only source of nursing care for the poor. The Evangelical Deaconess Society came to Cleveland in 1914 as a training institution for deaconesses. It opened its first twenty-two-bed hospital across the street from St. Luke's in 1923.

9. For Archwood, see Armstrong, *Guide,* 252–53; Van Tassel and Grabowski, *Encyclopedia of Cleveland History,* 49; and *185th Anniversary Book,* n.p.

10. See its Archwood neighbor, Brooklyn Memorial United Methodist Church, p. 227.

11. Brooklyn was annexed by the City of Cleveland in 1894.

12. *185th Anniversary Book.*

13. Warner served from 1909 to 1913. The cornerstone was laid in 1911. Next,

due to lack of funds, came what Ludwig Mies van der Rohe called "a creative pause." Building resumed in 1913, and Smith dedicated the church in 1914.

14. For Brooklyn Memorial, see Armstrong, *Guide,* 254–55; Moore, *Tapestry of Faith,* 33–34; and Van Tassel and Grabowski, *Encyclopedia of Cleveland History,* 130. See also successive *Brooklyn Memorial Anniversary Program*s, in particular: *Twenty-fifth* (years after construction of this building); *145th* (years after establishing the congregation); and *175th.*

15. See Brooklyn Memorial's neighbor across the street, the Archwood United Church of Christ, p. 226.

16. Brooklyn Memorial church histories usually ignore this building; thus, they consider their present building their fourth church.

17. See his 1891 Fidelity Baptist (p. 83), 1893 Pilgrim Congregational (p. 201), and 1908 St. John African Methodist Episcopal (p. 126).

18. For Trinity UCC, see Armstrong, *Guide,* 256–57 and a file prepared by Norma Dolezal, now being cataloged in the Cleveland State University Library.

19. They never got their money back. They sold the frame church more than ten years later for one hundred dollars.

20. MetroHealth Medical Center is now digesting what residential property the interstate left behind.

21. Armstrong, *Guide,* 257.

22. Most Christian narthexes in Cleveland are cramped and little more than a means of avoiding the draft of a door opening directly into the sanctuary from the street. Synagogues, temples, and mosques, in contrast, typically have a large and interesting space that prepares a visitor for the main worship area. Exceptionally large Christian narthexes were designed for Lane C.M.E. (p. 127), University Circle UMC (p. 47), and the Church of the Resurrection (p. 360).

23. For St. Michael, see Armstrong, *Guide,* 260–61; Hynes, *Parishes,* 153–55; Johannesen, *Cleveland Architecture,* 26 and 94; Kaczynski, *People of Faith,* 311–13; Van Tassel and Grabowski, *Encyclopedia of Cleveland History,* 600–601; Sheehan, *Story of Saint Michael Church;* and in particular for its pictures, *St. Michael the Archangel.*

24. Johannesen, *Cleveland Architecture,* 94, and figure. The school's "sculptured, ornamented mass and open lantern tower make it one of the most lavish and European-looking of the eclectic Gothic buildings in Cleveland."

25. For Immanuel, see Armstrong, *Guide,* 262–63; *Immanuel Evangelical Lutheran Church;* and Hoyer, *Immanuel.*

26. Hoyer, *Immanuel,* 15.

27. Immanuel has come a long way from 1952 when its congregation voted to protest the appointment of an American ambassador to the Vatican.

28. Immanuel School was established as a mission of Trinity in 1872. Henry Weseloh was assigned responsibility for the mission in 1876. The church was built in 1879. The congregation was organized in 1880.

29. Immanuel is located on the farthest northeastern corner of old Brooklyn. The original Cleveland city limit was immediately east, on the other side of Scranton, and immediately north, on the other side of Seymour.

30. Immanuel is extremely unusual in Cleveland for the tenure of its pastors. As of 2012, it had had only three pastors in 130 years: Weseloh, 1880–1925 (he started organizing the parish in 1876); A. W. Hinz, 1926–56; and Horst Hoyer,

1957–. Compare this with another Brooklyn German parish, what is now St. Luke UCC, which had nine pastors in its first eleven years. In his forty-five years, Wesloh baptized 4,471, married 2,580, and buried 1,799.

31. This was the same storm that brought down the great towers of St. Stanislaus and almost completely destroyed that building (see p. 173).

32. See also Trinity, p. 191, and Zion Evangelical Lutheran p. 24.

33. For St. Rocco's, see Armstrong *Guide*, 264–65; Hynes, *Parishes*, 172–73; Kaczynski, *People of Faith*, 351–52 and 500–502; and Van Tassel and Grabowski, *Encyclopedia of Cleveland History*, 862 and 559–61. The tumultuous early years of St. Rocco are best described in *Our Lady of Mount Carmel*, 2–11; see also Ripepi, *St. Rocco*, 7–14.

34. It is an irony that the schools at St. Rocco and Mount Carmel are now flourishing when so many other parish schools have failed. The anonymous author of the joint St. Rocco/Our Lady of Mount Carmel parish histories commented that "Father Sante's plan for St. Rocco Church included school for the parishioners' children. Most thought that this idea was, at best, ludicrous. No other Italian parish in the Diocese of Cleveland had a school, and it was the general perception of most that Italian families would never send their children to Catholic school." *Our Lady of Mount Carmel*, 8–9.

35. Crosby won an Academy Award for his role as a priest in the 1944 film *Going My Way;* the following year he and Bergman were nominated for Academy Awards for their roles as priest and nun in the sequel, *The Bells of St. Mary's*, the forty-fourth all-time highest-grossing film.

36. This is not to be confused with the much bigger (population 8,000) Nicotera overlooking the Mediterranean on the west side of the peninsula.

37. Usually identified as St. Procopius, this abbot is a patron of the Czech Republic and the former Czechoslovakia. St. Procop parish is particularly proud of being the first nationality church in Cleveland to take in Slovaks. St. Procopius was also the patron of craftsmen and farmers for reportedly having harnessed the devil to a plow.

38. For St. Procop, see Armstrong, *Guide*, 266–67; Hynes, *Parishes*, 170–72; Kaczynski, *People of Faith*, 343–44; Herman, *Cleveland's Vanishing Sacred Architecture*, 77–90; and First, *Founded in Faith*, 24–31. See also the preface to this guide, xiii.

39. For Stephen Furdek's protean, and otherwise highly successful efforts to organize central-European nationality parishes in Cleveland, see Our Lady of Lourdes, p. 167; St. Elizabeth's, p. 142; and St. Vitus, p. 85. Joseph Koudelka would return to establish mighty St. Michael, see p. 231, and then reign, from there, as the first assistant bishop of the Diocese of Cleveland until going back to Wisconsin as a bishop in 1913.

40. Hynes, *Parishes*, 171.

41. G. F. Votteler began making organs in Cleveland in 1885. Herman Heinrich Holtkamp took over the firm in 1903, so the St. Procop instrument should really be called a Holtkamp.

9. West Central Cleveland

1. For St. Ignatius of Antioch, see Armstrong, *Guide*, 272–73; Hynes, *Parishes*, 125–26; Kaczynski, *People of Faith*, 234–35; *St. Ignatius;* and Barrett, *St. Ignatius*.

2. Barrett, *St. Ignatius*, n.p.

3. For St. Rose of Lima Church, see Armstrong, *Guide,* 274–75; Hynes, *Parishes,* 173–75; Kaczynski, *People of Faith,* 352–53; Herman, *Cleveland's Vanishing Sacred Architecture,* 53–66; and *St. Rose.*

4. *St. Rose,* 9 and 10.

5. Ibid., 13.

6. For La Sagrada Familia, see Kaczynski, *People of Faith,* 129–30, and Van Tassel and Grabowski, *Encyclopedia of Cleveland History,* 866–67 and 508–10.

7. The Altenheim Home was organized in 1875 by the West Side Deutscher Frauen Verein; see Johannesen, *Cleveland Architecture,* 56.

8. Our Lady of Divine Providence is the patroness of Puerto Rico, the capital of which is named for St. John the Baptist. Our Lady of Divine Providence, most frequently visualized as a variation of the painting by Scipione Pulzone, is particularly appropriate for a congregation devoted to the Sacred Family. As her name suggests, she is also associated, in Europe and the Americas, with generous divine intervention in circumstances of economic want.

9. For Our Lady of Mount Carmel, see Armstrong, *Guide,* 278–79; Hynes, *Parishes,* 74–75; Kaczynski, *People of Faith,* 105–6, 471–72, and 500–502; and *Our Lady of Mount Carmel.*

10. Desperately searching for someone to establish his school, Gattuso found an Italian community of the Sisters of the Most Holy Trinity in Bristol, Pennsylvania (where Levittown now is, twenty miles north of Philadelphia), in 1927 and persuaded a contingent to come to Cleveland.

11. The Royal, Celestial, and Military Order of Our Lady of Mercy and the Redemption of the Captives was founded in 1218 to ransom common people, "the poor of Christ," from the Muslims. It is one of the oldest active orders. Getting rid of the knights in the fourteenth century, the order has not ransomed any Muslim captives since the early sixteenth century; instead, it has transformed itself into an order concerned with helping those, in addition to prisoners, enchained in a metaphorical sense: victims of substance abuse, mental illness, and poverty. In Cleveland, in addition to their pastoral responsibilities, the brothers minister to those in the county jail, halfway houses, and hospitals. Members' famous "fourth vow," to exchange themselves for anyone in danger of losing their faith, brought them to minister to the struggling Italian immigrant population in Ohio.

12. Kaczynski, *People of Faith,* 501.

13. Ibid., 471.

14. *Our Lady of Mount Carmel,* 7.

15. Ibid.

16. Other nationalities and denominations were extremely helpful in establishing the West Side Italian parishes. German St. Michael Church played a critically important role in organizing the first money raiser to begin St. Rocco church and school.

17. For St. Helena's, see Armstrong, *Guide,* 280–81; Hynes, *Parishes,* 122–23; Van Tassel and Grabowski, *Encyclopedia of Cleveland History,* 855; and "*St. Helena.*"

18. Compare Bishop Hoban's unfortunate clothing of the Cathedral of St. John the Evangelist with Tennessee Orchard Stone in 1948.

19. Like St. Mary Romanian Orthodox Cathedral, St. Helena's is a twentieth-century interpretation of a Maramures-style church. St. Helena's is more traditionalist, and St. Mary is more modernist. See n6, p. 405.

20. For St. Colman's, see Armstrong, *Guide,* 284–85; Hynes, *Parishes,* 106–8; Johannesen, *Cleveland Architecture,* 128–29; and Kaczynski, *People of Faith,* 193–94.

21. For St. Stephen, see Armstrong, *Guide,* 286–87; Hynes, *Parishes,* 177–79; Johannesen, *Cleveland Architecture,* 21–22; and Kaczynski, *People of Faith,* 357–58.

22. Johannesen, *Cleveland Architecture,* 21.

10. West Park

1. For Christ UMC, see Armstrong, *Guide,* 294–95; Moore, *Tapestry of Faith,* 37–38 and 171; and *We Are Family.*

2. John Wesley (1703–91) and his brother Charles Wesley (1707–88) founded the Methodist movement.

3. This is not to be confused with the much larger *Der Vereinigten Brüder in Christo* that merged with the Methodist Church in 1968. The United Brethren in Christ at one time had ten churches in Greater Cleveland.

4. For St. Mary Romanian Orthodox Cathedral, see Armstrong, *Guide,* 120, and Van Tassel and Grabowski, *Encyclopedia of Cleveland History,* 861. In particular, see Grama, *St. Mary,* and Grama and Hategan, *100 Years of Romanian Orthodoxy.*

5. Bucovina is the Carpathian Mountain region shared by Romania and Ukraine located to the east of Transylvania.

6. Maramures is a historical, cultural, and geographic area in the eastern Carpathian Mountains on the northern border of Romania along the Tisza River. The Muramures Depression is surrounded by mountains. The Muramures churches, many of which are listed by the United Nations Educational, Scientific and Cultural Organization (UNESCO) as World Heritage Sites, were built of wood in the seventeenth and eighteenth centuries following prohibition of the construction of masonry Orthodox churches. There are eight types of Maramures churches, but all are characterized by a tall tower above the entrance and a massive roof that dwarfs the body of the church. Maramures churches, because of their isolation and independence, have a particular resonance in the Romanian consciousness.

7. Between 1954 and 1960, the St. Mary Romanian Orthodox parish worshiped in a meeting hall next to their current location. This building, located about fifty feet away from the current complex, was destroyed by fire in 1973.

8. Grama and Hategan, *100 Years of Roman Orthodoxy,* 10.

9. Ms. Stan is best known for having convinced Eleanor Roosevelt to wear a Romanian costume to the 1935 White House Christmas party.

10. The iconography is described and beautifully illustrated in Grama's *St. Mary Romanian Orthodox Cathedral.*

11. For Our Lady of Angels, see Armstrong, *Guide,* 300–301; Hynes, *Parishes,* 61–62; Kaczynski, *People of Faith,* 93–95 and 496–97; and Van Tassel and Grabowski, *Encyclopedia of Cleveland History,* 419–20.

12. This order is "very similar to, but different from," the Poor Clares of Perpetual Adoration at St. Paul Shrine, see p. 28 (conversation between the author and John Cregan, Pastor of Holy Angels, December 3, 2008). The Rocky River Drive religious have been in Cleveland since 1877, first living in a series of convents downtown. The Colettines have flourished in Cleveland and established other

communities in Chicago (1893); Rockford, Illinois (1916); Oakland, California (1923); Capina Grande, Brazil (1950); and Newport News, Virginia (1956).

13. The Sisters of St. Joseph belong to a very large teaching order. In 1950 they were teaching 13,260 students in twenty-six schools in Cleveland. Starting out in Painesville in 1872, they moved to Tremont in 1880, where they built a large stone structure on Starkweather in 1890 for themselves and their St. Joseph Academy. Expanding out of the building, they sold it and its surroundings to St. Theodosius (see p. 212). In 1898 they "purchased 52 acres . . . in the 'wilderness' of Rockport . . . on a mud road called Riverside" (Kaczynski, *People of Faith,* 463). With its many distinguished graduates, St. Joseph Academy is best known for its college-type "block scheduling" (each course is completed in one term by students taking only four 85-minute courses per day).

14. See also Our Lady of Mount Carmel's Nolasco Housing Corporation, Villa Mercede, and St. Peter's by the Lake, p. 249.

15. *The Plan of Union.*

16. For West Park UCC, see Armstrong, *Guide,* 302–3.

17. This later became the site of a nineteenth-century plant to bottle the mineral water. Before the fire—a traditional termination to such enterprises in northern Ohio—the springs developed into a lively amusement park, nationally known for its Cyclone roller coaster.

18. Flora Stone Mather named the settlement house she established in 1897 for Goodrich, now the newly rebuilt Goodrich-Gannet Neighborhood Center on East 55th Street.

19. *History of West Park United Church of Christ,* n.p.

20. Established in Orrville in 1873, the Schantz Organ Company is the oldest pipe-organ builder still operated by its original family. Schantz was a national competitor of the Votteler Company which was taken over by Herman Heinrich Holtkamp in 1903.

21. The most obvious and important difference between the buildings is their proportions: the second story of Archwood is more prominent and its tower and spire are thinner and taller. Nevertheless, it is difficult to tell them apart without comparable pictures in hand.

22. The oldest Roman Catholic parish in Cleveland was St. Mary-on-the-Flats, established in 1835 and taken down in 1888.

23. For St. Patrick's–West Park, see Armstrong, *Guide,* 304–5; Hynes, *Parishes,* 157–58; and Kaczynski, *People of Faith,* 321–24. St. Patrick's was blessed with a particularly good parish history written by its last pastor: Hagedorn, *St. Patrick.*

24. Producing a confusing cacophony in the school between the brogues of the children and the heavily accented English of the German nuns. Hagedorn, *St. Patrick,* 8.

25. St. Angela Merici, Fairview Park; St. Christopher, Rocky River (see p. 288); Our Lady of Angels (see p. 268), St. Vincent de Paul and Annunciation, West Park; and St. Clement and St. Luke, Lakewood.

26. Nawash left four years before the ICC inaugurated its mosque in Parma.

27. For a discussion of the building, see Armstrong, *Guide,* 306–7.

28. Other examples are the 1920 Hope Academy Chapelside, see p. 162, and St. Vincent de Paul Church, on the corner of Lorain and Berea Road, see p. 259.

29. Although Wright's 1893 William Winslow house in River Forest has some Prairie-style elements, his first Prairie-style house is usually considered to be his Frank Thomas House in Oak Park in 1901. These homes were called "Prairie style" after a plan Wright published in the 1901 *Ladies Home Journal,* titled "A Home in a Prairie Town."

11. Lakewood—Rocky River—Westlake—Bay Village—North Olmsted

1. For Transfiguration, see Hynes, *Parishes,* 109–10, and Kaczynski, *People of Faith,* 381–83.

2. Lakewood Avenue should not be confused with Lake Avenue in Lakewood, which runs east and west, just south of the lake.

3. The design seems to have been drafted by Cincik and executed by John W. Winterich and Associates. Unresolved controversy, however, concerns attribution of the artwork in this church. The apse painting and some of the other decoration was by Romeo Celleghin. How much of "the other" was by Cincik and how much by Celleghin has not been determined. See Whitelaw, *The Art of Romeo Celleghin,* 17–18.

4. For Lakewood Presbyterian, see Ritter, *100th Anniversary,* and Reed, *The Windows of the Sanctuary.*

5. Holtz, *Lakewood United Methodist Church,* 6. For Lakewood Methodist, see also Conly et al., *A Living Centennial,* and Moore, *Tapestry of Faith,* 75–76.

6. For Akron Plan churches, and Sidney Badgley's important national role in their construction, see Pilgrim Congregational Church, p. 397, n. 41.

7. For St. James Lakewood, see Hynes, *Parishes,* 127–28; Kaczynski, *People of Faith,* 235–36; Hannibal, *Guide to Stones;* First, *Founded in Faith,* 104–9; Herman, *Cleveland's Vanishing Sacred Architecture,* 9–28; and a parish guide of May 2008, which may eventually be found in the Diocese Archives.

8. Hannibal, *Guide to Stones.*

9. See description in ibid. Hannibal points out that the use of marble in St. James is similar to that in St. Ignatius of Antioch (see p. 244), also designed by E. T. P. Graham.

10. See description in Hannibal, *Guide to Stones.*

11. John Wing was an architect from Fort Wayne, Indiana, who prepared preliminary drawings for St. Peter's in 1923 that closely resembled his St. Paul's Church in La Porte, Indiana. St. Paul's was Daniel Goodwin's previous parish. Later, Wing's drawings underwent a "complete and drastic revision in the interest of . . . lower cost" at the hands of Lakewood architect James Chrisford, who was the supervising architect of the church (parish record, quoted by Wise, *St. Peter's,* 18–19).

12. For St. Peter's, see Wise, *St. Peter's,* and Simon and Simon, *St. Peter's.*

13. Wise, *St. Peter's,* 12.

14. Ibid.

15. Simon and Simon, *St. Peter's,* 3.

16. The Von Gerichten Art Glass Company was established in Columbus in 1894. In 1914, Gerichten opened a second studio in Munich that was destroyed in 1945.

17. St. Peter's glass is particularly well illustrated, in pictures and in text. See Simon and Simon, *St. Peter's.*

18. See 411n14.

19. For St. Christopher Parish, see Hynes, *Parishes,* 103–4; Kaczynski, *People of Faith,* 186–88; and *St. Christopher.*

20. For West Shore Unitarian, see Walther, *A History,* 8. See also Black, *West Shore; A Century of Unitarianism,* 17–19, and Brinnon, "Unitarian-Universalism," Van Tassel and Grabowski, *Encyclopedia of Cleveland History,* 991. For a discussion of Unitarian-Universalism in the United States and Cleveland, see "First Unitarian Church of Cleveland," p. 342.

21. Arnason and Rolenz, *Worship That Works.*

22. For Bay Presbyterian, see Pascarella, *Christ Is Alive and with Us.*

23. For John Knox Presbyterian, see *"Together We Build";* Packard, *John Knox Church; Growing to Serve; Thirty-Fifth Anniversary;* and Gaede, *Churches,* 10, 32, and 39–40.

24. In the Introduction to his *Churches,* Gaede wrote movingly of the frequently unappreciated dynamism of suburban religious architecture. As congregations grow, mature, and associate with a variety of different architects, their churches evolve until, sometimes, the original building is almost unrecognizable.

25. These were Visnapu and Gaede (1956–74), Robert Gaede (1975–84), Gaede Serne Zofcin (1985–91), and Gaede Serne (1992–2006).

12. Brooklyn—Parma—Middleburg Heights

1. The archbishop of Newton has his seat at Our Lady of the Annunciation in the Roslindale neighborhood of Boston. Richard Cardinal Cushing paid for half of Lawrence Cuneo's spectacular 1966 cathedral.

2. For St. Elias, see Hynes, *Parishes,* 112–13, and Van Tassel and Grabowski, *Encyclopedia of Cleveland History,* 854.

3. The Basilian Salvatorian Order, which follows the rule of St. Basil and whose motherhouse is the Holy Saviour Monastery in Lebanon, is one of the two orders of the Melkite Catholic Church. Members of the order have historically been prominent in the hierarchy of the church. Both the current Canadian and the current American Melkite primates are Basilian Salvatorian priests, as have been most of the pastors of St. Elias.

4. The tesserae cannot be counted on to adhere safely to an upside-down surface.

5. For the Islamic Center of Cleveland, see Van Tassel and Grabowski, *Encyclopedia of Cleveland History,* 558.

6. For Pleasant Hills, see Moore, *Tapestry of Faith,* 95–96.

7. For a discussion of the Indian community in Cleveland, particularly on the East Side, and its India Community Center on Cedar Road, see Van Tassel and Grabowski, *Encyclopedia of Cleveland History,* 546–47.

8. See Stapathi, "Temple Architecture."

9. "In its developed forms, this architecture depends for its visual structure, its expression and meaning, on the combination and interrelations of images and shrines." Hardy, *Indian Temple Architecture,* 18, quoted by Branfoot, "Imperial Frontiers," 178 and n. 31.

10. For St. Charles Borromeo, see Hynes, *Parishes,* 101–2; Kaczynski, *People of Faith,* 183–84; and *St. Charles Borromeo Parish.*

11. The Very Reverend John Nakonachny, pastor of St. Vladimir's, refuses to identify one person responsible for building the cathedral and identifies "the clergy and laity."

12. The only religious building, however, actually on the corner of State and Snow is the mammoth St. Francis de Sales Roman Catholic Church. For Ukrainians, see Van Tassel and Grabowski, *Encyclopedia of Cleveland History,* 987–89.

13. Kievan Rus' was a medieval Viking state on the Dnieper River which flourished from the ninth to the fourteenth centuries. It is considered a predecessor of the modern states of Ukraine, Russia, and Belarus. Vladimir the Great (980–1015), Grand Prince of Kiev, converted to Christianity in 988.

14. Cleveland Memory, St. Vladimir's Ukrainian Orthodox Cathedral, see photographs number 17 (of the Cathedral with its original offending ball turrets) and 20 (of the current Ukrainian turrets under construction).

15. This statement may be disputed by St. Colman's Church (p. 254), St. Demetrios Greek Orthodox Church (p. 291), St. Mary Romanian Orthodox Cathedral (p. 265), St. Rocco's Church (p. 236), St. Stephen's Church (p. 256), and Trinity Episcopal Cathedral (p. 21).

16. The comparison is to Ravenna in Italy, which has the world's greatest collection of mosaics, not the arsenal in Portage County, Ohio, where military tanks were made.

17. See Piero della Francesca's portrait of Federico da Montefeltro in his mid-1470s *Madonna and Child with Saints* in Milan and Jan van Eyck's portrait of Nicolas Rolin in his 1435 *Madonna with Chancellor Nicolas Rolin* in the Louvre. Lyn Rodley reminds us, "It is clear from all the above examples that the chief patrons of a church were usually acknowledged in the decoration of the sanctuary bay," *Byzantine Art and Architecture: An Introduction,* 85.

18. Santa Sofia a Via Boccea in Rome was built in 1967 as the mother church for Ukrainian Greek Catholics, when their base in Ukraine, St. George's Cathedral in Lviv, was controlled by the Russian Orthodox Church.

19. Pyrohy is the Canadian Ukrainian variant of the Polish-American pierogi, the Slavic version of the filled and boiled dumpling known in other culinary traditions as ravioli or the wonton.

20. For Ruthenians, see "Carpatho-Russians," Van Tassel and Grabowski, *Encyclopedia of Cleveland History,* 154–55. See also, the Ruthenian Eparchy of Parma at the Cathedral of St. John the Baptist, four long blocks to the southeast (p. 310), Holy Ghost Byzantine Catholic Church in Tremont (p. 198), and St. Mary Byzantine Catholic Church in Old Brooklyn (p. 221).

21. For Ruthenians, see n. 20.

13. Cleveland Heights

1. Cleveland Heights is blessed with a new book by Morton in the Images of America series, *Cleveland Heights Congregations,* which should be consulted and enjoyed concerning the institutions in chapter 13.

2. For Saints Constantine and Helen, see Morton, *Congregations,* 79, 97, and 98.

3. "Leonard Ratner, chairman of the building committee, was unquestionably the chief decision-maker throughout the entire design and construction stage; he also led the fund-raising effort." Leedy, "Park Synagogue," 54.

4. For Park, see Leedy, "Park Synagogue"; Park Synagogue's website, http://www.parksyn.org; Johannesen, *Cleveland Architecture,* 205–7; Morton, *Congregations,* 47 and 54–56; and Van Tassel and Grabowski, *Encyclopedia of Cleveland History,* 37 and 751. For Mendelsohn, see Whittick, *Eric Mendelsohn,* and Von Eckardt, *Masters of World Architecture.*

5. Mendelsohn's first move in Cleveland, after moving into the rabbi's house, was to rearrange the rabbi's furniture.

6. The Akron Plan church was devised by Akron Sunday school superintendent Lewis Miller in the 1860s. It separated a sanctuary from surrounding Sunday school rooms using movable walls that could be opened for exceptional services. It became the plan for most Protestant churches in the later nineteenth and early twentieth centuries. The first Akron Plan church was the First Methodist Episcopal Church of Akron, which no longer exists. The oldest existing Akron Plan church in Akron is the First Congregational Church at 292 East Market Street. One of the most famous Akron Plan churches in the United States is Pilgrim Congregational Church, p. 201.

7. "Eric Mendelsohn," *The Architectural Forum,* 73–77.

8. Johannesen, *Cleveland Architecture,* 207.

9. Leedy, "Park Synagogue," 56.

10. For the New Spirit Revival Center, see their website at http://www.nsrcministries.org; and Morton, *Congregations,* 103, 112, and 121. For a history of the "Civic," see Boyle, *From Ark to Art.* For the history of B'nai Jeshurun prior to its move to Cleveland Heights, see Shiloh Baptist Church p. 132; for its history in Pepper Pike, see p. 349. A continuous history of the congregation is available at http://www.bnaijeshurun.org/history.htm. See also Van Tassel and Grabowski, *Encyclopedia of Cleveland History,* 108, 456–57, and 844, and Morton, *Congregations,* 47, 50–54, and 113.

11. For St. Alban, see Morton, *Congregations,* 25–28, 44, 103, and 119.

12. For a good summary of how Cleveland Heights developed around St. Alban's, see O'Donnell "Cleveland's Park Allotment." See also Barrow, "The Euclid Heights Allotment."

13. For this exciting episode, see Jarvis, *St. Paul's.*

14. The partnership of Frank R. Walker and Harry E. Weeks originally submitted plans for St. Ann's Church in 1927. Weeks died in 1935. Walker died in 1949. Howard F. Horn and Frank E. Rhinehart, who had both been with Walker since 1919, continued the firm as Walker and Weeks until 1953 when it became Horn and Rhinehart. See Johannesen, *A Cleveland Legacy.*

15. See Bellamy's outstanding parish history, *Angels on the Heights.* For a fictional account of St. Ann under John Mary Powers, see Father X (Robert Hilkert)'s *Everybody Calls Me Father.* For more restrained accounts, see Hynes, *Parishes,* 86–87; Kaczynski, *People of Faith,* 148–50; and Morton, *Congregations,* 7, 25, 35–38, 82, 103, 105.

16. See Johannesen, *Cleveland Architecture,* 259n29. St. Agnes would ultimately be pulled down in 1975, leaving only its tower as a funeral monument on Euclid Avenue.

17. Bellamy, *Angels,* 31.

18. Letter from Joseph Schrembs to John Powers, April 24, 1929; Archives, Diocese of Cleveland. Quoted by Bellamy, *Angels,* 46.

19. For a view emphasizing this, see Johannesen, *Walker and Weeks,* 133.

20. These were Ralph Adams Cram, Bertram Goodhue, and Henry Vaughan. For Grace Lutheran, see Morton, *Congregations,* 25 and 40. For the history of Grace Lutheran before its move to Cleveland Heights, see Fellowship Baptist Church (p. 82).

21. Rogers, Richardson, and Rowe, *Church of the Saviour,* 8. For the Church of the Saviour, see also Moore, *Tapestry of Faith,* 40–41; Van Tassel and Grabowski, *Encyclopedia of Cleveland History,* 184; and Morton, *Congregations,* 9, 14, 25, 41, 42, 103, and 124.

22. "Heathen Heights"—a geographical designation much beloved by religious settlers in Cleveland Heights and Shaker Heights—was used to describe whatever was there before they arrived. It is a fluid enough geographical term to allow it to be applied to almost any neighborhood bordering on the East Side of Cleveland.

23. See Hannibal, *Guide to Stones.*

24. Ibid.

25. Bayless quotes a (Presbyterian) church extension committee's ominous report concerning "agitation for the organization of a Federated or Union Church in this community." Bayless, *Jubilee,* 10.

For Fairmount Presbyterian, see Van Tassel and Grabowski, *Encyclopedia of Cleveland History,* 388, and Morton, *Congregations,* 25, 30–32, 44, 103, and 108.

26. Their concern with doctrinal peace only embraced white Anglo-Saxon Protestants. Everybody else was excluded in a series of carefully drafted restrictive covenants.

27. This sorrowful statistic may indicate a higher than usual percentage of officers.

28. Bayless, *Jubilee,* 23 and 27.

29. Ibid., 23.

30. For St. Paul's, see Jarvis, *St. Paul's;* Johannesen, *Cleveland Architecture,* 169–70; Van Tassel and Grabowski, *Encyclopedia of Cleveland History,* 862; and Morton, *Congregations,* 25, 27, 28, 34, 44–46, 103, 104, and 108.

31. Breed's ambitions can only remind us of Cram and Ferguson's 1913–29 Cathedral Church of Bryn Athyn in Bryn Athyn, Pennsylvania, outside of Philadelphia.

32. The Baptists, who did not mess around once their plans were made, started building after St. Paul's and had their building up by June 1929.

33. In 2008, after a joint service downtown with the Roman Catholic community of St. Paul's Shrine commemorating the two-thousandth birthday of St. Paul, an Episcopalian was heard to mutter, "Why would anyone exchange this for that?"

14. Shaker Heights–Beachwood–Pepper Pike–Lyndhurst

1. For Plymouth, see Peck, *History of Plymouth Congregational Church;* Bickel, *History of Plymouth Church;* and Johannesen, *Cleveland Architecture,* 169.

2. Both sides of the transaction agree that the price was $29,000. They disagree concerning who got the better deal. The Congregationalists say they put only $25,000 into the building and profited by $4,000. The Baptists claim the Congregationalists put $40,000 into the building so that it was a Baptist bargain.

3. For First Baptist, see Johannesen, *Cleveland Architecture,* 169–70, and Van Tassel and Grabowski, *Encyclopedia of Cleveland History,* 75–76, 401–2, 845, 946, and 1058.

4. Euclid Avenue Baptist, on the corner of East 18th Street at Euclid Avenue, was the Rockefeller church (after 1868, the Rockefellers lived on the corner of East 40th Street at Euclid). John D. joined Euclid Avenue Baptist when he was a teenager, taught Sunday school, and was superintendent of the Sunday school from 1872 until 1905. (Mrs. Rockefeller maintained her side of the family's association with Plymouth [Congregational] Church [see p. 335].) The Rockefellers, father and son, ultimately contributed $600,000 to Walker and Weeks's ill-fated 1927 Euclid Avenue church; in addition, John Jr. purchased the old Euclid Avenue Church for $600,000. The new building had an auditorium seating 2,200 people. This church could not survive the economic and social dislocations of the 1930s and 40s and suspended services in 1956. The building was demolished in 1961, and the property is now a parking lot. There is a good drawing of this building in Johannesen, *Walker and Weeks,* 106.

5. The Episcopalians down the street at St. Paul's (see p. 329) were not so fortunate. They began building in 1927 while the Baptists were still getting organized. Stymied by the Great Depression, the Episcopalians completed their redesigned and reduced sanctuary in 1951.

6. Another, even more dramatic, exception would be New York's Rockefeller-built Riverside Baptist Church; its tower was two feet more than three times higher than First Baptist's in Cleveland.

7. Johannesen comments, "As with most revivalist work of the period the ultimate aim was not to create a historical replica but to provide sufficient style reference to convey a convincing sense of the meaning of the building. . . . They . . . built in a period when historical style was understood as an expression of content. . . . A permanent expressive value had been embodied in the styles and forms of certain ages. . . . Certain forms had been discovered that were good for all time, and certain intrinsic values and meanings were attached to those forms. . . . These buildings were created with the explicit purpose of . . . adhering to established standards and having lasting value. That purpose has been borne out by time; there . . . buildings look as permanent and as right seventy years after they were erected as they did when new. Furthermore, they do it better than many younger buildings avowedly designed to be 'relevant' to their times. Although clearly of the date when they were built, these buildings have not become 'dated.'" Johannesen, *Walker and Weeks,* 111.

8. Ibid.

9. For St. Dominic, see Kaczynski, *People of Faith* 197–98.

10. Boulevard, Ludlow, Onaway, Fernway, Mercer, Woodbury, and the high school.

11. City Hall, the fire station, and the main library.

12. Plymouth, Heights Christian, and First Unitarian.

13. See Jarvis, *St. Paul's,* 12.

14. Christ Church still uses handmade prayer desks and a lectern made for this church together with two hand-turned oak alms basins inscribed around the rim in German: "The Lord Loves a Cheerful Giver" and "It Is More Blessed to Give than to Receive."

15. See Jarvis, *St. Paul's,* 40.

16. The organ has been replaced with a splendid large tracker instrument.

17. For First Unitarian, see *A Century of Unitarianism,* and Lillian Brinnon, "Unitarian-Universalism," Van Tassel and Grabowski, *Encyclopedia of Cleveland History,* 991.

18. This building was taken down to make room ironically for the Church Square Shopping Center.

19. See Ledebur and Whitelaw, *Village Landmark Churches,* 28.

20. The history of congregation Tifereth Israel is divided to reflect what happened in each of its landmark buildings. For 1848 to 1924, see Friendship Baptist Church (p. 130) and Dancyger, *Temple-Tifereth Israel,* 1–15. For 1924 to 1970, see Temple Tifereth Israel (the Temple), p. 44; see also Dancyger, *Temple-Tifereth Israel* 16–77. For 1970 to the present, see here and ibid., 78–157. When Daniel Silver died in 1989, the Silvers, father and son, had led the Temple for seventy-two consecutive years. For "Silver's" Temple, see also Van Tassel and Grabowski, *Encyclopedia of Cleveland History,* 892 and 960–61.

21. For Montessori Schools, see Van Tassel and Grabowski, *Encyclopedia of Cleveland History,* 687–88.

22. Boyle, *From Ark to Art.* For B'nai Jeshurun, see also Van Tassel and Grabowski, *Encyclopedia of Cleveland History,* 108 and 844.

23. See Van Tassel and Grabowski, *Encyclopedia of Cleveland History,* 36–37 and 123.

24. The Eagle Street Synagogue was approximately where third base is now in the 1994 Cleveland baseball stadium. To build the stadium, Eagle Street, which now runs east and west beside the northern wall of the stadium, had been moved several hundred feet north.

25. Wise, "America's Most Prolific Synagogue Architect."

26. This painter is not to be confused with the Forest City Ratner family, who spell their name with one *t* only.

15. Orange—Solon—Chagrin Falls—Gates Mills—Highland Heights—Richmond Heights

1. For Temple Emanu El, see Litt, "Temple Emanu El."

2. Private communication with the author, April 21, 2009.

3. Steven Denker, the current rabbi, points out that *synagogue* (as in *synod*) is a Greek word meaning "house of assembly."

4. Litt, "Temple Emanu El."

5. For Resurrection, see Kaczynski, *People of Faith,* 115–16, and *Church of the Resurrection.*

6. Kaczynski, *People of Faith,* 116.

7. This sentence ignores not only the extremely powerful (and extremely private) role of nuns in parish administration but also the even more powerful role of the greater body of women in the church.

8. For the Federated Church, see *A History of the Federated Church; Congregational-Disciple Heritage of the Federated Church;* and *Manual—First Congregational Church.*

9. See St. Philip's Christian Church (p. 122) and Franklin Circle Christian Church (p. 187).

10. *A History of the Federated Church,* 15.

11. As far as is known, clergy were not responsible for either of the building campaigns at St. Christopher's. Holsey Gates designed, financed, and had the church built on his property, presumably to enhance his property's value. Frank Walker moved the church and designed and had the 1928 addition built in his capacity as majordomo of the Maple Leaf Land Company.

12. See Ledebur and Whitelaw, *Village Landmark Churches.*

13. For St. Paschal Baylon, see Kaczynski, *People of Faith,* 318–19 and 491–93.

14. It is like Park Synagogue (see p. 315) only bigger. It is unknown whether Fleischman intended this as a tribute to his great modern predecessor.

15. For St. Gregory of Narek, see *St. Gregory of Narek Armenian Church,* and Van Tassel and Grabowski, *Encyclopedia of Cleveland History,* 49–50.

16. Although all numbers are hotly debated, there may be about eleven million Armenians. Three million live in Armenia and 1.5 million live in the United States.

17. St. Gregory of Narek is to be distinguished from the much earlier St. Gregory the Illuminator (ca. 257–ca. 331), the founder of the Armenia Church and the national patron.

18. Some readers will remember being threatened as children, when they had not cleaned their plates, with an admonition to "remember the starving Armenians."

19. Almost all Armenians are Christians, and 93 percent of Armenian Christians belong to the Armenian Apostolic Church. Although Armenia has been surrounded for about the last 1,500 years by Muslims, Armenia was the first Christian country: its church was established in 301. (Constantine allowed Christianity to flourish in the Roman Empire by the 313 Edict of Milan.)

20. An exception is the Cathedral of Ejmiatsin, the headquarters of the Armenian Church. (Ejmiatsin is now officially known as Vagharshapat.) The cathedral, built in 480, has been greatly modified over the last 1,500 years, including the addition of frescoes in the seventeenth century.

21. Like Armenians themselves, Armenian painting is heterogeneous and difficult to categorize. It has incorporated, at various times, influences from Rome, Byzantium, Islam, and China. Traditional Armenian painting, like Coptic traditional painting, appears to combine Roman naturalism and Greek abstraction, as in the work of the Armenian medieval illuminator T'oros Roslin (1210–70), thought to have been so important an influence on Western European medieval Romanesque painting. A more recent Armenian influence on the west was Vostanik Manoog Adoyan (self-styled Arshile Gorky; 1904–48) an early pivotal figure in New York School abstract impressionism.

Bibliographic Note

Religious bricks and stones are falling down all over Cleveland. Religious buildings, the most tangible evidence of spiritual enthusiasm, are not the only things that are disappearing. Memories fade and die out. The papers that supported the memories vanish or are misplaced. "Dust you are and to dust you will return" (Gen 3:19).

Future students of the landmarks described in this book will be unable to find much of the documentation on which it is based. In collecting the information printed here, fading memories were too often reinforced by tear-stained copies of poorly mimeographed documents hurriedly pressed on a rare passerby who was interested.

Church archives, almost always maintained by aging volunteers like the author or by distracted secretaries, are notoriously disorganized. The Archive of the Roman Catholic Diocese of Cleveland, directed by Chris Krosel until her untimely death in 2010 and now by Philip Haas, is the only up-to-date professionally maintained religious archive in northern Ohio. This archive, however, only maintains the records of the diocesan chancery and of closed parishes. It is dependent, obviously, on whatever material unhappy closed parishes bundle up and send in. Furthermore, the records of parishes that have appealed their closure to the Vatican are in limbo.

Other professionally maintained archives such as the Western Reserve Historical Society and the Special Collections of the Cleveland State University Library are slowly making their expensive way through a large backlog. The Cleveland State Library has inherited the extensive records of Cleveland State's Maxine Goodman Levin College of Urban Affairs's Center for Sacred Landmarks. It will also inherit the author's files when this book is published. The Historical Society maintains archives for many important Cleveland religious institutions. The resources for these institutions are limited and their priorities for cataloging extend over a broad range of subjects other than the religious.

Thus, much of the material on which this book is based will disappear. The author has already irretrievably lost a pamphlet congregational history from an important but recently closed Protestant church.

Bibliography

68th Church Anniversary and Homecoming—St. Timothy Missionary Baptist Church. Cleveland: St. Timothy, 2008.

75th Anniversary. Cleveland: Our Lady of Mercy, 1997.

127th Session, North Ohio Annual Conference, St. John African Methodist Episcopal Church. Cleveland: St. John, 2008.

185th Anniversary Book, 1819–2004. Cleveland: Archwood, 2004.

Ackerman, Kenneth. *Dark Horse.* New York: Perseus, 2003.

Applegate, Debby. *The Most Famous Man in America: The Biography of Henry Ward Beecher.* New York: Doubleday, 2006.

Armbruster, Paul, Laura Burnell, and Helen McClelland. *History of Our Lady of Good Counsel Church Cleveland, Ohio.* Cleveland: Our Lady of Good Counsel, 1973.

Armstrong, Foster, Richard Klein, and Cara Armstrong. *A Guide to Cleveland's Sacred Landmarks.* Kent, Ohio: Kent State Univ. Press, 1992.

Arnason, Wayne, and Kathleen Rolenz. *Worship That Works—Theory and Practice for Unitarian Universalists.* Boston: Skinner, 2007.

Austin, Richard. *East of Cleveland.* Dungannon, Va.: Creekside, 2004.

Barrett, Timothy. *St. Ignatius of Antioch Catholic Church,* edited by Christopher Roach. Church in the City Partnership Project. Sacred Landmarks Assistance Program. Cleveland: Cleveland Restoration Society, 2003.

Barrow, William. "The Euclid Heights Allotment: A Palimpset of the Nineteenth Century Search for Real Estate Value in Cleveland's East Side." Master's thesis, Cleveland State Univ., 1998.

Bayless, Frances. *A Jubilee of Christian Service Past and Future.* Cleveland Heights, Ohio: Fairmount Presbyterian, 1992.

Bellamy, John Stark, II. *Angels on the Heights—A History of St. Ann's Parish, Cleveland Heights, Ohio 1915–1990.* Cleveland Heights, Ohio: St. Ann, 1990.

Bickel, Paul. *History of Plymouth Church of Shaker Heights 1916–1966.* Shaker Heights, Ohio: Plymouth, 1966.

Black, Dottie, ed. *West Shore: The First Fifty Years.* Rocky River, Ohio: West Shore, 1996.

Boyle, John. *From Ark to Art: The 20-Year Journey of the Civic, Cleveland Heights, Ohio from Jewish Temple to Multi-Purpose Community Facility.* Sacred Landmarks Monograph Series, edited by Susan Petrone. Cleveland: Cleveland State Univ., 2000.

Boznar, Joseph, ed. *St. Vitus Church–Cerkev Sv. Vida, 1893–1993.* Cleveland: St. Vitus, 1993.

Branfoot, Crispin. "Imperial Frontiers: Building Sacred Space in Sixteenth-Century South India." *Art Bulletin* 90, no. 2 (June 2008).

Bremer, Deanna. "Restoration Society Lights 130-Year-Old Steeple." http://www.clevelandrestoration.org/sacred_landmarks/steeple_lighting.php (n.d.).

Brooklyn Memorial Twenty-Fifth Anniversary Program. Cleveland: Brooklyn Memorial, 1939.

Brooklyn Memorial 145th Anniversary Program. Cleveland: Brooklyn Memorial, 1963.

Brooklyn Memorial 175th Anniversary Program. Cleveland: Brooklyn Memorial, 1993.

A Century of Unitarianism in Cleveland. Cleveland: Unitarian Universalist Association, 1967.

Church of the Resurrection. Solon, Ohio: Resurrection, 2004.

Cigliano, Jan. *Showplace of America, Cleveland's Euclid Avenue, 1850–1910.* Kent, Ohio: Kent State Univ. Press, 1991.

City Architects. "Renovation and Restoration, Nottingham Spirk." http://www.city arch.com/ (2008).

Cleveland Memory Project. "St. Vladimir's Ukrainian Orthodox Cathedral." http://www.clevelandmemory.org/ (2009).

Congregational-Disciple Heritage of the Federated Church—1835–1960. Chagrin Falls, Ohio: Federated Church, 1960.

Conly, Florence, et al. *A Living Centennial.* Lakewood, Ohio: Lakewood Methodist, 1976.

Dalton, John. *Holy Name Parish.* Cleveland: Holy Name, 1984.

Dancyger, Ruth. *The Temple-Tifereth Israel.* Cleveland: Temple Tifereth Israel, 1999.

Davis, Alan. *Second Chance: White Pastor, Black Church.* Dayton, Ohio: Landfall, 1990.

"Eric Mendelsohn." *The Architectural Forum,* May 1947, 86.

The Euclid Avenue Presbyterian Church—Dedication. Cleveland: Euclid Avenue Presbyterian, 1911.

Evans, Geraldine. *Church History.* Cleveland: Antioch, 2008.

Father X. [Robert Hilkert]. *Everybody Calls Me Father.* New York: Sheed & Ward, 1951.

First, Debra. *Founded in Faith. Cleveland's Lost Catholic Legacy.* Cleveland: Landmarks Press, 2010.

Fisher, Anne. "Ideas Made Here." http://money.cnn.com/magazines/fortune/fortune_archive/2007/06/11/100061499/index.htm.

"From Storefront to Stonefront." *Fellowship Magazine,* July 2005, 24–25.

Gaede, Robert. *Churches 1959–2006.* Beachwood, Ohio: AlphaGraphics, 2008.

Gaidziunas, Balys. *Lietuvos Madonu Sventove.* Cleveland: Our Lady of Perpetual Help, 1988.

———. *Our Lady of Perpetual Help Church.* Translated by Algis Ruksenas. Chicago: Draugas, 1979.

———. *A Pilgrim Nation.* Cleveland: Our Lady of Perpetual Help, 1988.

Grama, Remus. *St. Mary Romanian Orthodox Cathedral.* Cleveland: St. Mary Romanian Orthodox Cathedral, 2003.

Grama, Remus, and Vasile Hategan. *100 Years of Romanian Orthodoxy in Cleveland.* Cleveland: St. Mary Romanian Orthodox, 2004.

Gries, Moses. *The Jewish Community of Cleveland.* Cleveland, n.d. unpaginated.

Growing to Serve. North Olmsted, Ohio: John Knox, 1979.

Hagedorn, Tom. *St. Patrick, West Park, 150th Anniversary.* Cleveland: St. Patrick, 1998.

Hannibal, J. T. *Guide to Stones Used for Houses of Worship in Northeastern Ohio.* Sacred Landmarks Series, the Urban Center, Maxine Goodman Levin College of Urban Affairs. Cleveland: Cleveland State Univ., n.d.

Hardy, Adam. *Indian Temple Architecture: Form and Transformation.* New Delhi: Indira Gandhi National Centre for the Arts, 1995.

Hart, Leroy, et al. *Broadway United Methodist Church Centennial 1872–1972.* Cleveland: Broadway Methodist, 1972.

Herman, Barry, and Walter Grossman. *Cleveland's Vanishing Sacred Architecture.* Mount Pleasant, S.C.: Arcadia, 2010.

Historical Committee. *The First Hundred Years.* Cleveland: St. Luke's, 1953.

"The History of B'nai Jeshurun Congregation." http://www.bnaijeshurun.org/history .htm (2010).

A History of the Federated Church—United Church of Christ, 1835–1985. Chagrin Falls, Ohio: Federated Church, 1985.

History of West Park United Church of Christ. Cleveland: West Park UCC, n.d.

Holtz, Henry. *Lakewood United Methodist Church 1876–2001.* Lakewood, Ohio: Lakewood Methodist Church, 2001.

Horstman, Denise, ed. *The Covenant Proclaims.* Cleveland: Church of the Covenant, 2004.

Hoyer, Horst, ed. *Immanuel Evangelical Lutheran Church—Celebrating 125 Years.* Cleveland: Immanuel, 2005.

Hynes, Michael, ed. *Parishes of the Catholic Church,* Diocese of Cleveland. Cleveland: Cadillac, 1942.

————. *History of the Diocese of Cleveland.* Cleveland: Diocese, 1953.

Immanuel Evangelical Lutheran Church 1880–1980. Cleveland: Immanuel, 1980.

Jarvis, F. Washington. *St. Paul's Cleveland, 1846–1968.* Cleveland Heights, Ohio: St. Paul's, 1967.

Johannesen, Eric. *Cleveland Architecture, 1876–1976.* Cleveland: Western Reserve Historical Society, 1979.

————. *A Cleveland Legacy: The Architecture of Walker and Weeks.* Kent, Ohio: Kent State Univ. Press, 1999.

Kaczynski, Charles, ed. *People of Faith.* Cleveland: Roman Catholic Diocese, 1998.

Kappanadze, Jason, ed. *We Are Thankful . . . Saint Theodosius Orthodox Cathedral.* Cleveland: St. Theodosius, 1996.

Karpi, Francis. *For God and Country—Msgr. Charles Boehm.* Youngstown, Ohio: Catholic Publishing Co., 1986.

Kilde, Jeanne. *When Church Became Theatre.* Oxford: Oxford Univ. Press, 2002.

Kregenow, Janet. *St. Luke's United Church of Christ.* Cleveland: St. Luke's, 2003.

Ledebur, Larry, and Susan Whitelaw. *Village Landmark Churches of Northeast Ohio.* Center for Sacred Landmarks "Portraits of Faith" Series. Cleveland: Cleveland State Univ., 2006.

Leedy, Walter. "Eric Mendelsohn's Park Synagogue." Special issue, *Gamut* 1990, 45–69.

————. "Hail, Holy Light: The Amasa Stone Memorial Chapel." Ninth Annual Western Reserve Studies Symposium. Parameters of Faith: Religion in the Western Reserve. Case Western Reserve Univ., Cleveland, Ohio, Oct. 7–8, 1994.

Levy, Michael. *Revelations—Photographs of Cleveland's African American Churches.* Kent, Ohio: Kent State Univ. Press, 2008.

Lewis, Morgan, Jr. "Wizards of Wal-Mart," *Inside Business,* March 2007, 34–38.

A Light in the City. Cleveland: St. Patrick, 2003.

Litt, Steve. "A Handsome Home in Orange for Members of Temple Emanu El." *Plain Dealer,* August 23, 2008.

Lo, Mbaye. *Muslims in America.* Beltsville, Md.: Amana, 2004.

Loveland, Anne, and Otis Wheeler. *From Meetinghouse to Megachurch.* Columbia, Mo.: Univ. of Missouri Press, 2003.

Lyons, John, and William Jurgens. *The Life and Times of Bishop Louis-Amadeus Rappe.*

Manual—First Congregational Church. Chagrin Falls, Ohio: First Congregational Church, 1889.

McCready, Eric. "The Nebraska State Capitol: Its Design, Background and Influence." *Nebraska History* 55, no. 3 (1974): 325–461.

Miller, Carol Poh. *Church with a Conscience*. Cleveland: Church of the Covenant, 1995.

———. *This Far by Faith—The Story of Cleveland's Euclid Avenue Congregational Church*. Cleveland: Euclid Avenue Congregational Church, 1997.

Moore, Gracelouise Sims, ed. *The Tapestry of Faith, the History of Methodism in the Cleveland District of the East Ohio Conference*. Cleveland: Methodist Union, 2003.

Morton, Marian. *Cleveland Heights Congregations*. Mount Pleasant, S.C.: Arcadia, 2009.

New Spirit Revival Center. http//www.nsrcministries.org (2009).

O'Donnell, Kara Hamley. "Cleveland's Park Allotment: Euclid Heights, Cleveland Heights, Ohio, and Its Designer, Ernest W. Bowditch." Master's thesis, Cornell, 1996.

Our Lady of Mount Carmel Church, 1926–2001. Cleveland: Mount Carmel, 2001.

Packard, John. *John Knox Church*. North Olmsted, Ohio: John Knox, 1969.

Pál, Bolváry, and Thomas Szendrey. *St. Elizabeth of Hungary 100th Jubilee*. Cleveland: St. Elizabeth's, 1992.

Park Synagogue. "That Was Then." http://www.parksyn.org/SubCatMain.asp?SubCat Id=119 (February 22, 2012) (29Shevat5772).

Pascarella, Perry. *Christ Is Alive and with Us*. Bay Village, Ohio: Bay Presbyterian, 2007.

Peck, Mary. *History of Plymouth Congregational Church from 1850 to 1908*. Cleveland: Plymouth, 1908.

Peller, Ildiko, ed. *Szent Imre Római Katolikus Magyar Templom*. Cleveland: St. Emeric, 2004.

The Plan of Union. 1856. Reprint, Bedford, Mass.: Applewood, 2009.

Rebol, Anthony. *85 Years of Ministry—St. Lawrence Church*. Cleveland: St. Lawrence, 1996.

Reed, Mrs. Lawrence, ed. *The Windows of the Sanctuary*. Lakewood, Ohio: Presbyterian Church, 1965.

Ripepi, Anthony, ed. *St. Rocco Catholic Church, 1914–2004*. Cleveland: St. Rocco, 2004.

Ritter, Susan, ed. *100th Anniversary 1905–2005*. Lakewood, Ohio: Presbyterian Church, 1905.

Robertson, Don. *The Greatest Thing since Sliced Bread*. New York: Putnam, 1965; reprint New York: HarperCollins, 2008.

Robinson, Marilynne. *Gilead*. New York: Farrar, Straus, 2004.

———. *Home*. New York: Farrar, Straus, 2008.

Rodley, Lyn. *Byzantine Art and Architecture: An Introduction*. Cambridge, U.K.: University Press, 1994.

Rogers, Robert C., Eleanor W. Richardson, and Gordon D. Rowe. *Church of the Saviour—A Faith-Filled Landmark*. Cleveland Heights, Ohio: Church of the Saviour, 2001.

Rosenberg, Donald. "Florence Mustric: Organist Goes on the Record." *Plain Dealer,* June 23, 2008.

Sabol, John T. *Cleveland's Buckeye Neighborhood*. Mount Pleasant, S.C.: Arcadia, 2011.

St. Cecilia Catholic Church. Galion, Ohio: United Church Directories, 1990.

St. Charles Borromeo Parish. Parma, Ohio: Borromeo, 2005.

St. Christopher—75th Anniversary 1922–1997. Rocky River, Ohio: St. Christopher, 1997.

St. Gregory of Narek Armenian Church. Richmond Heights, Ohio: St. Gregory, 2004.

"St. Helena" Romanian Byzantine Catholic Church. Cleveland: St. Helena's, 2006.

St. Ignatius of Antioch 1903–2003. Cleveland: St. Ignatius, 2003.

St. Lawrence Celebrates 100 Years. Cleveland: St. Lawrence, 2001.

St. Michael the Archangel, Celebrating 125 Years of Ministry. Cleveland: St. Michael, 2008.

St. Rose of Lima—Celebrating One Hundred Years 1899–1999. Cleveland: St. Rose, 1999.

Schofield, Mary-Peale. *Landmark Architecture of Cleveland.* Pittsburgh: Ober Park, 1976.

Sheehan, Thomas. *Story of Saint Michael Church.* Cleveland: Koran, 1975

Silver. *Temple Year Book.* Cleveland: The Temple, 1929–30, unpaginated.

Simon, Tim, and Molly Simon. *St. Peter's Episcopal Church 1907–2007.* Lakewood, Ohio: St. Peter's, 2007.

Stalley, Roger. *Early Medieval Architecture.* Oxford History of Art. Oxford: Oxford Univ. Press, 1999.

Stapathi, Ganapathi. "Temple Architecture: The Living Tradition." http://www.ssvt .org (2009).

Stefanski, Ben. *Slavic Village.* Cleveland: Pulaski Franciscan Community Development Corporation, 2002.

Sto Lat 100 Years. Cleveland: St. John Cantius, 1998.

Tevesz, Michael, Nancy Persell, Michael Wells, and James Whitney. *Stained Glass: Windows of Trinity Cathedral, Cleveland Ohio.* Cleveland: Sacred Landmarks Monograph Series, 1999.

Thirty-Fifth Anniversary—John Knox Presbyterian Church. North Olmsted, Ohio: John Knox, 1994.

Tibor, Bognár. *St. Elizabeth of Hungary Church 110th Jubilee.* Translated by Paul Orban and Maria Janossy. Cleveland: St. Elizabeth's, 2002.

Tittle, Diana. *The Severances—An American Odyssey.* Cleveland: Western Reserve Historical Society, 2010.

"Together We Build." North Olmsted, Ohio: John Knox, 1969.

A Tour of St. Paul's Episcopal Church. Cleveland Heights, Ohio: St. Paul's, 2008.

Tuve, Jeannette. *Old Stone Church.* Virginia Beach, Va.: Donning, 1994.

Ule-Grohol, Melinda. *Spiritual Pioneers.* East Cleveland: First Presbyterian Church, 2001.

Urann, C. A. *Centennial History of Cleveland.* Cleveland: Savage, 1896.

Van Tassel, David, and John Grabowski. *The Encyclopedia of Cleveland History.* Bloomington: Indiana Univ. Press, 1987.

Von Eckardt, Wolf. *Masters of World Architecture: Eric Mendelsohn.* London: Mayflower, 1960.

Walther, Roy. *A History of the West Shore Unitarian Church.* Rocky River, Ohio: West Shore Unitarian, 1965.

We Are Family. Cleveland: Christ UMC, 1995.

Whitaker, Charles, ed. *Bertram Grosvenor Goodhue—Architect and Master of Many Arts.* New York: American Institute of Architects Press, 1925.

Whitelaw, Susan. *The Art of Romeo Celleghin.* Sacred Landmarks Monograph. Maxine Goodman Levin College of Urban Affairs. Cleveland: Cleveland State Univ., 2005.

Whittick, Arnold. *Eric Mendelsohn,* 2nd ed. New York: Dodge, 1956.

Wiatrowski, Ralph. *Cathedral of Saint John the Evangelist.* Cleveland: Cathedral of St. John the Evangelist, 1978.

Wilson, Ella Grant. *Famous Old Euclid Avenue of Cleveland, at One Time Called the Most Beautiful Street in the World.* Cleveland: Evangelical Press, 1937.

Wise, Clare. *St. Peter's Church: The First Fifty Years.* Lakewood: St. Peter's, 1967.

Wise, Michael. "America's Most Prolific Synagogue Architect." *The Forward,* March 9, 2001. Available at http://www.michaelzwise.com/articleDisplay.php?article_id=17 (2012).

Index

Hemry organs, 50, 59, 140
Henderson, Shirley, xix
Herczegh, Joseph, 152
Herman, James, 345
Hickey, James, 29, 253
Highland Sixth Presbyterian, 357–58
Hindu temple and community: 302
Hines, Ward, 301
Hisaka, Don, 334, 349
Hispanic churches and communities, xiii, 166, 231, 234, 248, 404n8. *See also entries beginning with "Iglesia"*
Hitchcock Center for Women (originally St. Mary Seminary), 40, 72, **88–90**
Hladni, Mirko, xvii
Hoban, Edward, 16, 183, 232, 368, 405n18
Hobson, Mark, 360
Hoerstmann, Joseph, 271
Holtkamp organs, 15–16, 17–18, 20, 50, 55–56, 81, 87, 158, 173, 177, 204, 257, 269, 281, 287, 330, 336, **398n50**, 404n41, 406n20
Holy City, 259, 268
Holy Cross Armenian, 370
Holy Cross Lutheran, 260–61
Holy Family, Corlett. *See* **Hope Academy Chapelside**
Holy Family, Parma, 295, 297
Holy Ghost Byzantine, 181–82, **198–99**, 211, 310
Holy Grove Baptist, 146–47
Holy Name, 164–65, 171, **175–77**, 189, 193, 236
Holy Redeemer, 60, 94–95,
Holy Resurrection Russian Orthodox, 243, 266
Holy Rosary, 6, 9, 11, 32, **59–62**, 266
Holy Spire, Church of the, 71
Holy Spirit, Catholic, 166
Holy Spirit, Byzantine, 310
Holy Trinity Baptist, 150
Holy Trinity National Polish Cathedral, 164–65
Holy Trinity-St. Edward, 29, 117, 134,
Hoover, Odie Millard, 140
Hope Academy Chapelside, 148, 150, **162–63**
Hope, Bob, 40, 54
Horn and Rinehart. *See* Walker and Weeks
Horowitz, Philip, 347
Horstmann, Ignatius, 17, 99, 232, 252, 272,
Hough Avenue UCC, 39, 70
House churches, 1
House of Our Redeemer Baptist, 165–66
Hradetzky organ, 367
Hubbell and Benes, 67

Hungarian landmarks and communities, 124, 132, 142, 151, 152, 194, 390n4
Hungarian Lutheran, First, 145–46, **151–52**
Hungarian Reformed, First. *See* **Full Gospel Evangelistic Center**
Hungarian Reformed, West Side, 180, 248, 262
Hungarian Seventh Day Adventist, 277–78
Hungarian, First Baptist, 146
Hutchings, William, 364

Idaka Chapel, 337
Iglesia Adventista del Septimo Dia, 242–43
Iglesia Católica Parroquia San Juan Bautista, 180
Iglesia de Cristo Misionora Sinai, 218, 220
Iglesia de Dios Pentecostal M.I., 179–80, 241–42
Iglesia de Jesucristo "Monte Moriah" Inc., 241–42
Iglesia di Dios Pentecostal, 181–82
Iglesia El Calvario, 181–82
Iglesia Emmanuel, 25, 218, 220, **230–31**
Iglesia Hispana Asambleas de Dios, 181–82, 306
Immaculate Conception, 17, 69–70, **78–79**
Immaculate Heart of Mary, 87, 164–65, 209
Immanuel Assembly of God, 295, 297
Immanuel Evangelical Lutheran, 25, 112, 218, 220, 228, **234–36**
Immanuel Pentecostal, 263
Immanuel Presbyterian, 96
Incarnation Episcopal, 148
Independent Evangelical Lutheran, 179–80, 231
Indian temples and communities: 302, 409n7
Indians, Cleveland, 119, 387n3
Ingham, Howard, 105
Ingraham, George Hunt, 322
Inner City Protestant Parish, 122, 186
Institutional churches, 202, 397n42, 398n45
International Style, 48, 125, 136, 231
Irish churches and communities, 4, 78, 175, 183, 189, 200, 246, 254, 271, 321, 394n2
Islambouli, Ramez Al, 41
Islamic Center of Cleveland, 273–74, 295, 297, **300–301**, 373n2
Islamic communities and landmarks, 41, 273, 300, 378n72, 378n74, 379n75
Islamic Trust, North American (NAIT), 42
Israelitic Society of Cleveland, 126, 350, 375n27
Issenmann, Clarence, 15
Italian churches and communities: 59, 119, 236, 249, 403n34, 405n16
Ivancho, Daniel, 221

Nottingham Spirk Design Associates (originally First Church of Christ, Scientist), xv, 9, 11, **62–65**, 323

Novak, David Alan, xix

O'Brien, John, 368

O'Callaghan, Eugene, 189, 254, 393n20

O'Connell, Patrick, 246

O'Hear, John Legare, 329

O'Leary, James, 254

Oheb Zedek Hungarian Orthodox Synagogue. *See* **Triedstone Baptist**

Ohio Street A.M.E., 126

Oil cans, 379n87

Old Stone Church (First Presbyterian), 6, 7, 8, **12–16**, 26, 27, 32, 33, 40, 52, 53, 54, 74, 107, 126, 140, 226, 270, 280, 335, 375n27, 394n3

Olive Grove Missionary Baptist, 145, 146

Olivet Institutional Baptist, 118, **140–42**

Oman, John Jerome, 170

Open Door Missionary Baptist, 117, 118

Organs, tracker, 395n23

Orientation, church xv, 372n3

Orr, R., 151

Orthodox *Metropolia*, 213

Our Lady of Angels, 199, 259–60, **268–69**, 305

Our Lady of Good Counsel. *See* **Mary Queen of Peace**

Our Lady of Lourdes, 19, 85, 142, 154, 156, 162, 164, 65, **166–68**, 170, 176

Our Lady of Mercy, 181,182, 183, **207–8**, 400n64

Our Lady of Peace, 145, 147, **158–59**, 244, 339

Our Lady of Perpetual Help. *See* **St. Casimir**, Collinwood

Our Redeemer Lutheran, 234

Our Savior's Rocky River Lutheran, 276, 277

Owens, Jesse, 15

Paliwoda, Stephen, 210

Panthéon, Paris, 132

Pantheon, Rome, 127

Panuska, Wenceslaus, 238

Park Congregational, 39

Park Synagogue (Anshe Emeth), xiii, xiv, 48, 61, 97–99, 201, 265, 312, 313, 314, **315–17**, 349, 352, 377n53, 414n14

Park Synagogue East (Anshe Emeth), 315, 332–33, **345–47**, 348, 377n53

Parkside Church of the Nazarene, 277, 278

Parkside, 334, 347, 355, 356, **362–63**, 373n5, 373n9

Parkwood C.M.E., 92

Parma Baptist Church, 295, 297

Parsons, Elizabeth, 204

Paskevich, Tony, 362

Patterson, Richard, 3

Paxton, B. W., 129

Payne, Henry, 65

Pearl Road UMC, 216, 217

Pentecostal Church of Christ (originally Fourth Church of Christ, Scientist), 9, 10, **43–44**, 48

Pentecostal Determine Church of God, 165, 166

People's Hope UMC, 242, 243

Percy, Vincent, 40

Perfectionism, 13, 374n9

Perkins + Will, 46, 332, 344

Perkins, Joseph, 65

Peruvian community, 233

Petit and Fritsen bells, 285

Petralia, Sal, 298

Petrarca, Frank, 10

Pevec, Edward, 86

Philips windows, 55, 56

Phillips, Douglas, 253

Phillips, Harold Cooke, 338

Phillis Wheatley Association, 82, 127, 383n18

Pickard, George, 325

Pilgrim Baptist, 116, 117

Pilgrim Congregational, 32, 50, 75, 84, 181, 182, 193, **201–4**, 200, 283, 293

Pilgrim Lutheran, 275–76

Pilla, Anthony, 253

Pleasant Hills UMC, 205, 295, 297, **301–2**

Plum Street Synagogue, Cincinnati, 130

Plymouth, Shaker Heights, 58, 312, 331, 332, **335–36**, 359, 373n1

Polish communities and landmarks, 87, 97, 113, 172, 209, 223, **392n10**, 399n59

Polish National Catholic Church, 207, **399n59**, 400n64

Ponikvar, Bartholomew, 85

Poor Clare (Colettine) Religious, 259, 260, 268, 406n12

Poor Clares of Perpetual Adoration, 29, 406n12

Porter, Simeon, 12, 18

Potter and Gabele, 209, 279

Potter, J. Ellsworth, 156

Powers, John Mary, 321, 327

Pozan, 87

Prairie School style, 163, 258, 261, 274, 407n28, 407n29

Precious Blood, Brothers of the, 134, 223, 224

Presbyterian churches and communities, xiii, 1, 12, 21, 31, 32, 52, 74, 107, 126, 138, 186, 270, 280, 292, 293, 327

Presbyterian, First Magyar, 153

Presbyterian, Second, 52, 53, 54